The Miracle Braves of 1914

Boston's Original Worst-to-First World Series Champions

Edited by Bill Nowlin
Associate editors Bob Brady, Clem Comly, and Len Levin

Society for American Baseball Research, Inc.
Phoenix, AZ

The Miracle Braves of 1914: Boston's Original Worst-to-First World Series Champions
Edited by Bill Nowlin. Associate editors Bob Brady, Clem Comly, and Len Levin.

Copyright © 2014 Society for American Baseball Research, Inc.

All rights reserved. Reproduction in whole or in part without permission is prohibited.

ISBN 978-1-933599-69-4
(Ebook ISBN 978-1-933599-70-0)

Design and Production: Gilly Rosenthol, Rosenthol Design

Cover photograph: George Grantham Bain Collection/Library of Congress
Back cover images: World Series program courtesy of National Baseball Hall of Fame. World Series badge courtesy of Robert Edward Auctions.
All interior photographs courtesy of the George Grantham Bain Collection/Library of Congress, except as noted.
Page 1 - Underwood and Underwood, photograph of Heritage Auctions.
Pages 29, 51, 69, 157, 188, 209, 260, 276, and 314 - Collection of Dennis Goldstein.
Pages 79, 98, 105, 114, 174, 266, and 275 - National Baseball Hall of Fame.
Page 133 - source unknown, located by Mark Fimoff.
Page 140 - Chicago Daily News, American Memory Collection, Library of Congress.
Pages 298 and 300 - Courtesy of Jonathan Fine.
Page 308 - source unknown.
Pages 311 and 315 - Courtesy of Bob Polio.
Pages 327 and 378 - Boston Public Library.
Page 328 - Courtesy of Bob Brady.

The Society for American Baseball Research, Inc.
4455 E. Camelback Road, Ste. D-140
Phoenix, AZ 85018
Phone: (800) 969-7227 or (612) 343-6455

Web: www.sabr.org
Facebook: Society for American Baseball Research
Twitter: @SABR

Table of Contents

THE 1914 BOSTON BRAVES
FOREWORD: Bob Brady..................1

THE BRAVES
Ted Cather: Jack V. Morris..................3
Gene Cocreham: Thomas Ayers..................10
Wilson Collins: Charlie Weatherby..................13
Joe Connolly: Dennis Auger..................19
Ensign Cottrell: Peter Cottrell..................24
Dick Crutcher: Jerrod Cotosman..................29
George Davis: Rory Costello..................34
Charlie Deal: Charles F. Faber..................40
Josh Devore: Peter Gordon..................43
Oscar Dugey: Charlie Weatherby..................49
Johnny Evers: David Shiner..................59

> **The 1914 Evers-Zimmerman Incident and How the Tale Grew Taller Over the Years:** Bob Brady..................64

> **The Evers Ejection Record:** Mark Sternman..................66

Larry Gilbert: Jack V. Morris..................69
Hank Gowdy: Carol McMains and Frank Ceresi..................76
Tommy Griffith: Chip Greene..................79
Otto Hess: Gary Hess..................84
Tom Hughes: Greg Erion..................89
Bill James: David Jones..................95
Clarence Kraft: Jon Dunkle..................98
Dolf Luque: Peter Bjarkman..................102
Les Mann: Maurice Bouchard..................113
Rabbit Maranville: Dick Leyden..................122
Billy Martin: Bob Joel..................127
Jack Martin: Charles F. Faber..................133
Herbie Moran: Charles F. Faber..................137
Jim Murray: Jim Elfers..................140
Hub Perdue: John Simpson..................144
Dick Rudolph: Dick Leyden..................154
Butch Schmidt: Chip Greene..................157
Red Smith: Charles F. Faber..................162

Paul Strand: Jack V. Morris..................166
Fred Tyler: John Shannahan..................173
Lefty Tyler: Wayne McElreavy..................177
Bert Whaling: Charles F. Faber..................180
George "Possum" Whitted: Craig Hardee..................184

MANAGER
George Stallings: Martin Kohout..................187

COACH
Fred Mitchell: Bill Nowlin..................190

OWNER
Jim Gaffney: Rory Costello..................201

The Braves' A.B.C.: Ring Lardner..................215

1914 Boston Braves Timeline: Mike Lynch..................217

A Stallings Anecdote..................259

1914 World Series: Mark Sternman
  Game One..................260
  Game Two..................263
  Game Three..................270
  Game Four..................274

"I Told You So": O.R.C...................277

The Rest of 1914: Mike Lynch..................278

How An Exhibition Game Contributed To A Miracle: Bob Brady..................284

The National League Pennant Race of 1914: Frank Vaccaro..................286

The Press, The Fans, and the 1914 Boston Braves: Donna L. Halper..................289

Return of the Miracle Braves: Bob Brady..................298

Miracle Teams: A Comparison of the 1914 Miracle Braves and 1969 Miracle Mets: Tom Nahigian..................303

An Unexpected Farewell: The South End Grounds, August 1914: Bob Ruzzo..................307

The Time(s) the Braves Played Home Games at Fenway Park: Bill Nowlin 320

The Kisselkar Sign 328

The Trail Blazers in Indian File: R. E. M. - poems for 1914 Braves, collected: Joanne Hulbert 330

The Story of the 1914 Braves: George Stallings 336

"Mr. Warmth" and "Very Superstitious" – two George Stallings anecdotes: Bob Brady 379

By the Numbers: Dan Fields 380

Creature Feature: Dan Fields 384

Contributors 385

Foreword
A Symbol of Hope for a Hundred Years

by Bob Brady

As the president of the Boston Braves Historical Association, I've taken on the challenging assignment of keeping alive the memory of a team that abandoned the city of its birth more than 60 years ago. Each year I'm aided in this daunting task by the recollection of a never-to-be-forgotten (some might even say miraculous) performance a century ago by the Boston Braves during the second half of the 1914 baseball season. That event not only is an integral part of the history of our national pastime but also a source of eternal optimism for those sports fans of underperforming teams and perennial underdogs.

Once a dominating franchise during baseball's early days, the Braves had been in a serious state of decline for many years prior to 1914. Some of that deterioration could be attributed to the birth of the American League in 1901 and the introduction of the Boston Americans (later the Red Sox) as a neighboring competitor. Weakened by the junior circuit's player raids, frequent changes in ownership, and an obsolete ballpark, the Braves struggled both on the field and at the gate. Even their band of loyal followers, the Royal Rooters, had shifted their allegiance to the Red Sox. The Braves' new owner, James E. Gaffney, a New Yorker with ties to Tammany Hall, sought to reverse the team's fortunes. After residing in the National League's basement for four consecutive seasons, Gaffney's Braves surprisingly ascended to fifth place in 1913, led by the irascible George Stallings in his first year at the Tribe's helm. Gaffney also laid out plans to construct a state-of-the-art concrete and steel ballpark at the site of a former golf club a little over a mile away from Fenway Park to replace the Braves' antiquated South End Grounds. Still, expectations for the following season were modest: a return to the senior circuit's first division — a feat not accomplished since 1902.

1914 Boston Braves - L to R (bottom row): Joe Connolly, Fred Mitchell, Willie Connor, Dick Rudolph, Rabbit Maranville, Dick Crutcher, Jack Martin, Johnny Evers. Middle row: George Whitted, Oscar Dugey, Lefty Tyler, Paul Strand, Josh Devore, Larry Gilbert, J. C. Smith, J. H. Moran. Top row: Bill James, Ted Cather, Charlie Deal, George Davis, Ensign Cottrell, Gene Cocreham, Otto Hess, Les Mann, Hank Gowdy, Butch Schmidt, Bert Whaling. Underwood & Underwood photograph, courtesy of Heritage Auctions.

Mired in the National League cellar in mid-July, the ragtag '14 Braves not only rose from eighth to first place in a little over two months, this legendary team played .781 baseball (50 wins, only 14 losses) from July 1 to season's end and finished atop the National League standings an amazing 10 1/2 games ahead of its nearest rival, John McGraw's New York Giants. Much of the credit belonged to the tough and often profane Stallings, who once described his team as comprising "one .300 hitter, the worst outfield that ever flirted with sudden death, three pitchers, and a good working combination around second base."[1] To capture the pennant in the face of his roster's limitations, Stallings deftly refined the art of platooning to capitalize upon strengths and mitigate weaknesses. The eminent baseball writer, historian, and statistician Bill James regards Stallings' skillful maneuvering in 1914 as having an "almost revolutionary impact" on baseball managers.[2] However, despite such adept leadership and a half-season of heroics, the Braves were given little chance of besting the mighty Philadelphia Athletics in the World Series. Their fall classic sweep of the highly favored Mackmen was the final piece needed to forever brand this team the Miracle Braves.

The Tribe's extraordinary achievement 100 years ago perennially gets dusted off by the media during the dog days of summer whenever a bottom-dwelling ballclub exhibits some signs of life. An unexpected winning streak that ignites a spark of hope among a franchise's heretofore frustrated followers often leads them to ask themselves: If the Miracle Braves could do it, why not us? The front offices are challenged not to throw in the towel and begin rebuilding efforts while the team still retains the glimmer of a chance of replicating the Braves' legendary 1914 climb to the top of the standings.

Divisional play and an expanded playoff structure have enhanced the odds that a 21st century version of the Miracle Braves will emerge and follow in the ancient footsteps of Stallings' warriors. However, Boston will always retain its place as the original "Home of a Miracle" when it was the "Home of the Braves."

Notes

1. John C. Skipper, *A Biographical Dictionary of Major League Baseball Managers* (Jefferson, North Carolina: McFarland, 2003), 298.
2. Bill James, *The Bill James Guide to Baseball Managers from 1870 to Today* (New York: Scribner, 1997), 46.

Ted Cather

By Jack V. Morris

A BASEBALL PLAYER fighting during a game isn't that unusual. A player fighting twice in less than a year is probably a little rarer. Fighting twice in less than a year with your own teammates—during a game—may be unprecedented. But that's exactly what happened to St. Louis Cardinals outfielder Ted Cather. The resulting fallout led to him becoming a Boston Brave and helping the Miracle Braves to the National League pennant in 1914.

To the Cardinals and their future Hall of Fame manager Miller Huggins, one incident may have been an accident but twice was certainly a trend. So when Cather got into a fistfight with pitcher Dan Griner during a game in late June of 1914, Huggins had enough of his streak-hitting player and Cather was traded to the last-place Boston Braves.

Little did Huggins know that the trade would help propel the Braves from last to first as Cather, as a right-handed-hitting platoon player, was one of several pieces that fell into place for the Miracle Braves. In the 50 games the 5-foot-10, 178-pound Cather played for the Braves after the trade, against almost exclusively left-handed pitching, he hit .297 with 27 RBIs. *Sporting Life* took notice after the season in a review of the Braves' incredible run when it wrote that the team "was considerably strengthened by the acquisition."[1]

It was quite a turn of events for Cather who, at the end of the 1913 season wasn't even sure if he would be in the major leagues in 1914, let alone play in and win the World Series.

Theodore Physick Cather, born on May 20, 1889 in Chester, Pennsylvania, was the youngest of three sons born to Samuel and Mary Cather.[2] He was named after his maternal grandfather, Theodore Physick.

His father, Samuel, who was a carpenter, was of Scottish descent and pronounced his last name "Car-ther."[3] Both parents had been born on Maryland's Eastern Shore but had moved to Chester, 15 miles south of Philadelphia on the Delaware River, before Ted's birth.

By the time Ted had turned 11, his father was no longer living with the family in Chester but had moved to Rising Sun, Maryland. Ted lived with his mother, two older brothers, his grandmother, and an uncle. By 1902 he was getting noticed as a pitcher while playing for the Larkin School team.[4] As he got older, he found himself pitching for local semipro teams.[5]

Before he got his break in Organized Baseball, Cather worked many jobs to help his family. He was a plumber, barber, druggist, roller-skating instructor, and an asbestos coverer in a locomotive works.[6]

By 1909 Cather was a pitcher of some note in the Philadelphia semipro community. His break came that year when the Johnstown Johnnies of the Class B Tri-State League came to Chester to play a game. Pitching for the Delaware County All-Stars, Cather shut out the Johnnies. Curtis Weigand, manager of the Johnnies, signed him to a contract soon after the game.[7] He made a big splash right away, pitching a two-hitter against Lancaster on May 4.[8]

Weigand also noted Cather's ability to hit the ball and played him in the outfield on occasion.[9] Cather played with the team until July 3. It's not clear whether he was let go or left the team on his own.

But he must have made an impression because Lancaster manager Marty Hogan signed him in January for the 1910 season.[10] Cather responded with a fine season in which he went 20-9, finishing second in the league in wins.[11] It was a good year for Cather: Immediately after the season he was sold to Toronto of the Eastern League[12] and then he was married on November 1 to Martha Worshaw. At the age of 21, Cather's life seemed to be heading in the right direction.

Cather started the season at Toronto in 1911. The *Harrisburg Patriot* reported early in the season that he was "doing good work on the mound"[13] but by mid-season his record was only 3-4 and Toronto, with a chance to add former major-leaguer Les Backman, demoted Cather to Troy of the Class B New York State League.[14] Cather finished at Troy with a 6-7 record. What was once a promising career seemed to be headed in the wrong direction.

But just as in 1910, another opposing team picked him up. This time it was the Scranton Miners of the Class B New York State League. Instead of just pitching for the Miners, Cather was called on to both pitch and play the outfield. In his first game as a pitcher, he took a no-hitter into the ninth inning and went 4-for-4 at the plate with a triple.[15] He played in 80 games for the Miners, 49 as an outfielder.

Cather ended the season batting .312, a figure that caught the notice of the sixth-place St. Louis Cardinals. Looking to find any kind of hitting, the Cardinals drafted Cather from Scranton at the annual meeting of the National Baseball Commission on September 16.[16] A week later he made his major-league debut in Brooklyn in a 7-2 Cardinals' loss to the Superbas.

Playing in the outfield, Cather was red-hot in the five games he played in, batting .421. The buzz began to grow in the offseason that Cather would become a key player for the Cardinals in the 1913 season.

By the time Cather arrived in Columbus, Georgia, for spring training in 1913, he was already penciled in by the press as an extra outfielder on the big-league roster.[17] Cather played well enough to make the roster though he was still shaky in the field. But his hitting won him a spot going north with the big club.

For years after, Huggins was credited with moving Cather permanently from pitcher to everyday player.[18] And while Huggins didn't pitch him (except for one-third of an inning in 1913 in mop-up relief), he hardly can be given credit for seeing Cather's ability at bat. As far back as his first season in Johnstown, Cather had played some games in the field. His 1912 season proved that he was a better everyday player than a pitcher.

Cather started the season on the bench but soon replaced Jimmy Sheckard in the outfield.[19] But just as soon as Cather was getting accustomed to starting, on June 13 he broke his arm when he crashed into wall making a catch on a Gavvy Cravath fly ball. He held onto the ball but was out for about a month.[20]

He made it back onto the field by mid-July and started the second game of a doubleheader against the New York Giants on July 17. In the third inning the Giants' Larry Doyle hit a short fly ball between Cather and Lee Magee. The papers at the time said that it fell in between the two.[21] Magee remembered it three years later as the two colliding on a ball that Magee had called.[22]

As the two ran in at the end of the inning, they began jawing at each other. According to the papers, Cather swung and hit Magee with a punch.[23] As with almost any baseball fight, chaos ensued. Umpire Malcolm Eason and several Cardinals players moved in to break up the melee. Cardinals first baseman Ed Konetchy was punched breaking up the fight.[24]

Ted Cather

The *New York Times* wrote, "The fight stopped the game for a time and the spectators who tried to jump over the boxes into the field [to get a better view of the fight] were turned back by the police."[25]

When peace was brought to the situation, Eason threw both players out of the game. So the fight wouldn't continue in the locker room, 6-foot-5, 228-pound backup catcher Larry McLean was sent with the two to make sure there was no more bloodshed.[26]

National League President Thomas Lynch fined each player $25. He said that the incident "warranted suspension" but that because St. Louis had so many injuries, he wouldn't punish them more than the fine.[27]

A little over two weeks later, Cather and Magee were pictured on the front page of *The Sporting News*. Both were in uniform with boxing gloves on. The picture was entitled "Battling Magee and Kayo Cather." Both players were smiling as *The Sporting News* made light of their battle.[28]

Despite Cather's problems with his fellow outfielder, the newspapers reported that he was making progress as an outfielder.[29]

A wire service story with the headline "Teddy Cathers [sic] Makes Good" was carried in many papers throughout the country. The story related how the Cardinals were turning many of their players into outfielders in the hopes of bettering the team.[30] And Cather was one of their latest successful projects.

While Cather's fielding was getting better, his hitting was not. He was suffering through a long slump. Then on September 1, he broke his leg sliding into second base. His season was over.

Having batted just .213 for the season, Cather was released, along with catcher Skipper Roberts, to Indianapolis on September 12. Cather was facing what could have been the end of his major-league career. His personal life was in a state of flux as well. After the season, he started divorce proceedings against his wife, Martha, on the grounds of unfaithfulness. At the time of the divorce filing, he didn't even know where she was living.[31] She had taken their 3-year-old son as well, which led to one of the more bizarre events in Cather's life.

While driving through Camden, New Jersey, on December 15, Cather saw his mother-in-law walking his son down the street. He stopped the car, jumped out, and grabbed the boy from the woman. His mother-in-law screamed, then ran to the car and interlocked her arms around the steering wheel.[32]

Cather attempted to drive the car but had trouble without hurting the woman.[33] As a large crowd gathered, he handed his son over to the woman and drove away.[34] The story made national news.

But in 1914, luck changed for Cather. The Indianapolis team had a change of heart, decided it didn't want Cather, and returned him to the Cardinals. With the Federal League making raids on the major leagues, the Cardinals needed Cather to fill in as an extra outfielder.[35]

The Federal League also was interested in Cather. Otto Knabe, manager of the Baltimore Terrapins, talked to Cather about playing for his team.[36] But in the end, Cather went to camp with St. Louis and made the squad as one of only two right-handed-hitting outfielders. The other was Cather's former fighting partner, Lee Magee.[37]

Cather started the season on fire. He was among the league leaders in hitting. Toward the end of May, Cather was hitting .352, tied for third in the National League.

But the events of May 27 signaled the beginning of the end of Cather's tenure with the Cardinals. During a 7-4 home loss to the Boston Braves, Cather fought pitcher Dan Griner after Griner became incensed over a play Cather made in the outfield. The two fought long enough for the 6-foot-1, 200-pound Griner to open up a gash on Cather's chin that required five stitches to close.[38] The teammates were fined $100 apiece by Huggins and left home as the team traveled to Chicago.

A month later, despite his hot bat off the bench, Cather was traded with infielder-outfielder Possum Whitted to the Braves for pitcher Hub Perdue. Perdue was 2-5 with a 5.82 ERA for Boston when he was traded, yet the Cardinals were willing to give up both Cather and Whitted for him.

Four years later Miller Huggins explained, "I needed a pitcher badly." He "discovered that Hub Perdue might be had. I was glad to get him as he always pitched great against my club."[39]

After two fights with his own teammates, it was clear to the press that Cather "could not get along very well with several of the players."[40] *Baseball Magazine* wrote that he was "condemned at St. Louis as too crude" and was just "tossed in as part of a midsummer trade for Hub Perdue."[41]

Whatever the reason for the trade, Cather paid off for Braves manager George Stallings. Playing left field when the Braves opposed a left-handed pitcher, Cather hit .295 in 41 games from July 4 to the end of the season.[42] The team turned around shortly after the trade and played great baseball, rising from last place to win the pennant.

In a retrospective after the season, William A. Phelon in *Baseball Magazine* wrote that the trade "is often spoken of as something which counted heavily in the winning of the flag. It did and it didn't. As far as any change in the playing array was concerned it made little difference."

He went on to note that "Cather was little used" but "Whitted made himself a regular outfielder toward the end of the season." But he did believe the trade was responsible in part for the Braves' turnaround. "Where the trade made the most real difference was in the way it woke up the fellows who still clung to the payroll and made them hustle from that time on until the end," Phelon wrote.[43]

The nationally syndicated columnist "Monty" had a different take: Stallings "takes boobs and turns them into star ball players." That was "9/10 of the reason" why Braves played so well.[44]

Whatever effect the trade had, the Braves turned their season around and won the National League pennant. Their reward was to play the powerful Philadelphia Athletics in the World Series.

The Braves continued their amazing play, sweeping the Athletics in four games. Cather played in one game in the Series, Game Two. Batting third in the lineup against future Hall of Famer Eddie Plank, he was 0-for-5 as the Braves eked out a 1-0 win. Plank was the only left-handed starter the Athletics threw against the Braves.

After the World Series Cather was the toast of his hometown, Chester. October 22 was declared "Cather Day." The day included a parade and banquet. The parade consisted of baseball teams from throughout the area.[45] At night, 250 people attended a banquet at the Masonic Hall.[46] Cather, in a brief speech, "predicted that the Braves would carry off both pennants again in 1915."[47] If the Braves would win the pennant in 1915, it would be without Cather, however.

Spring training was a highlight of Cather's 1915 season. After catching a train with a bunch of his teammates from Chester to Macon, Georgia, Cather found himself being tried out in the infield by Stallings. Stallings needed some depth in the infield and felt that Cather had the "natural grace and intelligence" to be a good utility man.[48]

Stallings worked Cather at both shortstop and third base but mostly at third. Third base had been a question mark for Stallings even in 1914, with five players holding down the position at one time or another during the season. Charlie Deal, who had played the most games at the position in 1914, had jumped to the Federal League. With Red Smith getting the starting nod, it fell to Billy Martin, who was a shortstop in the only game he played in 1914, to be Smith's backup for the coming season. But Martin had been injured early in training camp and Stallings decided to move Cather from the crowded outfield battle to the infield.[49]

None other than Grantland Rice noticed that "Cather is playing fine ball at third, fielding well and batting up with the club average and a few points higher."[50] Cather's hometown paper, the *Chester Times*, went even further about "Lucky Ted," writing that he "may get a regular berth."[51]

But when the season began, Cather again found himself on the bench, starting only in left field against left-handed pitchers. He struggled, batting .206 in 40 games. He did, however, hit the only two home runs of his major-league career. Both, curiously, came off future Hall of Famer Rube Marquard in different games.[52]

But it wasn't enough for Cather to keep his spot on the roster as the Braves floundered. On July 12 he played his last major-league game. With the Braves' record at 32-42 after a doubleheader sweep by the St. Louis Cardinals, Stallings released Cather, along with fellow outfielder Larry Gilbert, to Toronto of the International League.[53]

Though Cather never played in another major-league game, the release was far from the end of his baseball career. For the next ten years he played at the highest level of the minor leagues, just a short jump to the majors.

Cather played for less than a month before Toronto released him. On August 10 he signed with Jersey City, where he finished out the season. His combined average was .284.

Soon after the season was over, the Braves, who still had a string on Cather, traded him, outfielder Herbie Moran, and catcher Bert Whaling to Vernon of the Pacific Coast League for promising outfielder Joe Wilhoit.[54]

While Cather's professional career was in disarray, he had managed to get his personal life under control. After finally being granted a divorce from his wife, he married Ida E. Dodge, a 28-year-old nurse. They moved to Charlestown, Maryland, at the head of Chesapeake Bay, a town he would live in for the rest of his life.[55]

Cather's baseball odyssey continued in April 1916. Vernon sold him to Montreal along with infielder Billy Purtell and Herbie Moran.[56] So Cather headed to Hackettstown, New Jersey, where the Royals had their training camp. The Royals were interested in trying Cather at second base.[57]

All of the changes of teams left Cather in a strange position of being paid by three different clubs in 1916, though Organized Baseball's National Commission had to step in to ensure that he got his full amount.

Cather's release from Jersey City to Vernon was brought about by the Boston Braves, who had entered in an agreement with Vernon by which that club would pay Cather $325 a month and Boston would make up the rest of his salary. But Vernon decided it couldn't pay Cather that much, and sent him to Montreal, which would pay him $250 a month. The National Commission ruled that Vernon had to pay the extra $75 a month.[58]

Cather got into 83 games for Montreal, playing solely in the outfield and batting .274. He returned to Montreal for 1917 and didn't fare much better. He batted only .240 in 87 games. But he did manage to supplement his salary by hitting the Durham Bull, Blackwell Tobacco Company's iconic ad for its popular smokeless tobacco product, which adorned the outfield walls of some of the parks in the International League. If you "hit the bull," it was worth $50. Cather did it three times during the season.[59]

After the season the International League ousted Montreal, Richmond, and Providence in an effort to cut travel costs. Binghamton, Jersey City, and Syracuse were added to the league.[60] As a result, Cather was a free agent. He was snapped up by Rochester manager Arthur Irwin and went to training camp.[61] But there was a dispute over who actually owned the rights to Cather and eventually his contract was awarded to Newark.[62]

For the first time in his career, Cather was a regular and played injury-free. He played in all 127 games for the Bears, batting .278 and playing mostly in the outfield.

In 1919 Cather's batting average dipped to .226 in 105 games. After the season he was looking for a new team. When none came knocking, Cather played in an industrial league in Ohio for the 1920 season.[63] But in

1921, Oakland Oaks owner Cal Ewing signed him to a contract that led to Cather's best playing days.[64]

For the next four-plus years, Cather was a mainstay in the Oaks' lineup. In his first season, 1921, he was mostly used as a utility player, getting into 63 games and batting .217. However, for the next couple of seasons, Cather improved on the previous season's performance, culminating in his best season as a pro in 1923. Playing in 184 games that season, Cather led the Oaks in batting average (.344), hits (269), and doubles (46), and was second on the team in home runs (10) and triples (11).

While 1923 was the high mark professionally for Cather, personally it was a low mark as he filed for divorce from his second wife, saying she had struck him.[65]

The 1924 season was another good one for Cather; he batted .300 in 173 games. But the 35-year-old player was noticeably slowing down. The *Oakland Tribune* wrote that he wasn't a "good ground coverer" in the outfield.[66]

Cather started the 1925 season off poorly with the Oaks. By the end of May, he was hitting only .220.[67] On June 14 the Oaks released him so they could sign Chicago Cubs castoff Hack Miller.[68] Sacramento picked up Cather for some of the remaining season but cut him loose after it.

The next year, 1926, became one of new starts for several reasons for the 37-year-old Cather. First, his third wife, the former Clara "Carrie" Bishop of Wilmington, Delaware,[69] gave birth to his second child, a daughter named Mary Theo Cather.[70]

Second, after turning down an offer to become player-manager of the Logan Collegians of the Utah-Idaho League,[71] Cather returned home to Maryland and joined the Easton Farmers of the Class D Eastern Shore League. Buck Herzog, manager of the Farmers, told the press that Cather was "setting a fine example" and had been given the nickname Old Folks by his teammates.[72] He played in the Eastern Shore League for two seasons. In 1927 he briefly succeeded Herzog as manager of the Farmers. He also spent time with the Cambridge Canners of the ESL. At the age of 38 he retired after the 1927 season, going out with a flourish: He had batted over .300 in both seasons.

By the time Cather retired, he was well established as a businessman in Charlestown. He owned the general store in town and became Charlestown's postmaster.[73] He built and operated 10 rental cabins for summer tourists along Chesapeake Bay.[74] Later he became a member of the town commission. He spent the rest of his life in Charlestown.

On March 3, 1945, Cather went into the hospital for an abdominal abscess that turned out to be appendicitis.[75] While recovering in Union Hospital in Elkton, Maryland, on April 9, Cather died of a coronary thrombosis at the age of 55. He was buried in Charlestown Cemetery.[76]

Notes

1. *Sporting Life*, October 17, 1914
2. Baltimore City Health Department Certificate of Death
3. *Richmond News Leader*, October 31, 1991
4. *Chester Times*, October 8, 1914
5. *Chester Times*, October 8, 1914
6. *Chester Times*, March 26, 1913
7. Undated article in Cather's Hall of Fame file
8. *Williamsport Gazette & Bulletin*, May 7, 1909
9. *Philadelphia Inquirer*, June 6, 1909
10. *Trenton Times*, April 4, 1910
11. Baseball-Reference.com has Cather's record as 8-4. But two contemporary sources, the *Spalding Record* and the *Reading Eagle* (October 4, 1910) list his record as 20-9.
12. *Reading Eagle*, October 4, 1910
13. *Harrisburg Patriot*, April 26, 1911
14. *Sporting Life*, July 1, 1911
15. *Chester Times*, May 13, 1912
16. *Sporting Life*, September 21, 1912
17. *Washington Post*, March 10, 1913
18. *Sporting Life*, October 17, 1914
19. *Chester Times*, February 2, 1914
20. Undated article in Cather's Hall of Fame file
21. *Syracuse Herald*, July 18, 1913

22 *Brooklyn Eagle*, July 23, 1916
23 *Syracuse Herald*, July 18, 1913
24 *New York Times*, July 18, 1913
25 Ibid.
26 Ibid.
27 *Alton* (Illinois) *Evening Telegram*, July 19, 1913
28 *The Sporting News*, August 7, 1913
29 *Duluth News-Tribune*, August 4, 1913
30 *Postville* (Iowa) *Review*, August 22, 1913
31 *Chester Times*, October 26, 1913
32 *Sporting Life*, December 20, 1913
33 *Duluth News-Tribune*, December 21, 1913
34 *Philadelphia Inquirer*, December 16, 1913
35 *Baseball Magazine*, February 1915
36 *Chester Times*, February 2, 1914
37 *Sporting Life*, March 2, 1914
38 *Pittsburgh Press*, May 29, 1914
39 *Fort Wayne News & Sentinel*, April 16, 1918
40 *Chester Times*, October 8, 1914
41 *Baseball Magazine*, December 1914
42 *Baseball Digest*, October 1964
43 *Baseball Magazine*, February 1915
44 *Miami Herald Record*, September 10, 1914
45 *Philadelphia Ledger*, October 22, 1914
46 *Chester Times*, October 17, 1914
47 *Philadelphia Inquirer*, October 23, 1914
48 *Boston Journal*, March 13, 1915
49 *Boston Journal*, March 24, 1915
50 *Washington Post*, March 20, 1915
51 *Chester Times*, March 5, 1915
52 Bob McConnell and David Vincent, *SABR Presents the Home Run Encyclopedia.* (New York: Macmillan, 1996), 364.
53 *Brooklyn Daily Eagle*, July 14, 1915
54 *Ogden* (Utah) *Standard*, November 27, 1915
55 *Chester Times*, September 22, 1915
56 *Binghamton Press*, April 4, 1916
57 *Montreal Daily News*, April 21, 1916
58 *Wilkes-Barre Times*, July 1, 1916
59 *Rochester Democrat & Chronicle*, July 20, 1917
60 William Brown, *Baseball's Fabulous Montreal Royals.* (Montreal: Robert Davies Publishing, 1996), 24.
61 *Wilkes-Barre Times*, April 27, 1918
62 *Rochester Democrat & Chronicle*, May 20, 1918
63 *The Sporting News*, February 17, 1921
64 *San Francisco Chronicle*, February 5, 1921
65 *Oakland Tribune*, February 9, 1923
66 *Oakland Tribune*, April 3, 1924
67 *Oakland Tribune*, May 24, 1925
68 *The Sporting News*, June 18, 1925
69 Undated article in Cather's Hall of Fame file
70 *Richmond News Leader*, October 31, 1991
71 *Ogden Standard*, March 30, 1926
72 Undated article in Cather's Hall of Fame file
73 Undated article in Cather's Hall of Fame file
74 *Richmond News Leader*, October 21, 1991
75 Baltimore City Health Department Certificate of Death
76 Bill Lee, *The Baseball Necrology* (Jefferson, North Carolina: McFarland, 2003), 65.

Eugene Cocreham

By Thomas Ayers

Eugene "Gene" Cocreham, the son of a small-town Texas doctor, pursued a professional baseball career in his early 20s and eventually spent part of three seasons pitching in the big leagues. All but two of his 17 big-league appearances came in 1914 for the World Series champion Boston Braves. After his baseball career ended, Cocreham spent a year coaching college baseball and then retired to a quiet life in Texas as an orchard manager and farmer.

Cocreham was born on November 11, 1884, to Thomas Edward Cocreham and his wife, Lola, in Luling, a small town near Austin, Texas. Thomas and Lola, who were 35 and 22 years old respectively when he was born, had been married for six years and Eugene was their first child. Thomas was a native of Arkansas and his wife had been born and raised in Texas. Eugene's paternal grandparents were from Kentucky and his maternal grandparents were Mississippians. Eugene spent his entire childhood in the same house, as in 1910 it was noted that the Cocrehams had lived in that location for 31 years.[1]

Gene, as he was usually known, was the Cocrehams' only child for five years, then was followed by four brothers and three sisters.

Luling was a town of under 1,500 residents at the turn of the century.[2] Thomas Cocreham was a doctor and the proprietor of the town's drugstore, while Lola does not appear to have worked outside the home; it is likely she spent her time with the demanding challenge of raising Gene and his siblings.[3] In 1910 Gene was working as a salesman at the town's furniture store, while also pursuing a semiprofessional baseball career. His two eldest brothers both worked at the town's general store, Roland as a salesman and Lewis as the store's bookkeeper.[4] Given Thomas's position at the drugstore and these connections to many of the small town's central retail stores, it is probable the Cocrehams were one of the town's most prominent families.

Gene took to baseball and was known as a standout outfielder for the local team in his teens. Despite these accolades, it appears he only began playing semipro baseball in 1909, at the age of 24, which may be connected to other opportunities available to him. In the end, it's unclear why the 6-foot-3, 187-pound Texan did not pursue baseball more seriously earlier in his life.

Gene began playing semipro baseball as a shortstop in nearby Flatonia, Texas. With his tall frame, he was encouraged to begin pitching late during that 1909 season and did so to great success.[5] In 1910 he pitched for a semipro team in Brownsville, a bigger town on the northern bank of the Rio Grande.[6]

Cocreham started his career in Organized Baseball in 1911 with the Beeville Orange Growers of the Class D Southwest Texas League. In nine games for the Orange Growers, the 26-year-old Cocreham allowed 45 hits and 18 walks in 59 innings. The right-hander finished the season in the Class B Texas League for the Galveston Sand Crabs and the San Antonio Bronchos. Cocreham went only 1-8 in his first exposure to the Texas League, surrendering 61 hits and 17 walks in 58 innings. He didn't return to the Texas League again for five years.

In 1912 Cocreham started the season with the Manhattan Elks of the Class D Central Kansas League, finishing 10-5 in 15 games. In the middle of the season he moved within the state to the Topeka Jayhawks of the Class A Western League. There was an impressive collection of talent on the 1912 Jayhawks and eight members of the team, Al Bashang, Josh Billings, George Cochran, Joe McDonald, Ross Reynolds, Joe Rickert, Harley "Cy the Third" Young, and Cocreham, ultimately played in the major leagues. Cocreham hurled 174 innings, allowing 154 hits and 81 bases on balls. He posted a record of 7-13 in 29 games for Topeka and, for Manhattan and Topeka combined, he finished with a 17-18 record.

Cocreham pitched a career-high 305⅓ innings in 1913, 297 of them in the Western League for the Jayhawks. Cocreham was one of the linchpins of the staff, along

Eugene Cocreham

with Reynolds and William Fullerton. All three threw over 250 innings for the Jayhawks and none of the club's other hurlers reached 100. Gene finished with a 3.61 ERA, second lowest on the club behind Reynolds, and led the team by pitching in 44 games.

The Texan was sold to Boston by Topeka on July 5, but it was agreed that he would remain with Topeka until October 1.[7] However, dealing with a potential shortage of pitchers, Boston was insistent that Cocreham join the team before the end of the year and on September 10, 1913, he left Topeka to report for duty with Boston.[8]

The 28-year-old Cocreham made his major-league debut when he started the second game of a doubleheader against the Philadelphia Phillies at the Baker Bowl on September 25. The Braves lost the game 7-6 and Cocreham gave up all seven runs in 8⅓ innings. He surrendered 13 hits and four walks, and hit a batter, while striking out three. It may not have been the debut he was hoping for, but Cocreham had reached the major leagues in less than three years after beginning his career in Organized Baseball. It was his only game with Boston in 1913.

All but two of Cocreham's big-league appearances came in 1914, when he worked primarily out of the bullpen for the Braves while serving as a spot starter in three games, one of which was a complete game. His three starts came on June 2, September 5, and September 9. Like his previous major-league start, his first start in 1914 came in the second game of a doubleheader against the Brooklyn Robins, which the Braves lost, 4-3. The second came on September 5 against the Phillies in the final game of a 22-game road trip that had begun on August 13. The Braves were sitting a half-game out of first place and Cocreham pitched the Braves to a 7-1 victory and a tie for first place with John McGraw's New York Giants. Cocreham was handed a start four days later, but was defeated by the Phillies, 10-3.

Cocreham also made 12 relief appearances, finishing the game in ten of those outings. In his only year as a major-league regular, he posted a 3-4 record with a 4.84 ERA in 44⅔ innings. He allowed 48 hits and 27 walks, while striking out 15. He finished with the sixth most appearances on the Braves. He did not pitch in the World Series.

Cocreham's only major-league appearance in 1915 was his last. It came on April 21, 1915, in an 8-4 loss to Brooklyn with the Braves hosting the Robins at Fenway Park. Cocreham relieved starting pitcher Dick Crutcher and went 1⅔ innings, allowing two runs, one earned, on three hits. On April 29 Boston released Cocreham and Adolfo "Dolf" Luque to the Toronto Maple Leafs of the International League, where Cocreham pitched in 16 games.[9] He was one of only six pitchers used during the season by the Maple Leafs, and finished 2-6 in 16 games, pitching 88 innings, before being released at the end of July.[10]

In 1916 Cocreham played for the Kansas City Blues in the American Association. He hurled 133 innings in 22 games and went 7-11. He began the 1917 season with the Blues, going 1-2 in nine games, but spent most of the season with the San Antonio Bronchos of the Class

B Texas League. In 24 games for the Brochos, Cocreham went 11-12. He posted an impressive 2.23 ERA in 206 innings, the lowest of Bronchos pitcher for whom their season's ERA is known.

Cocreham made 18 starts in the 1918 season, winning seven games and losing nine. He registered for the military draft on September 12, listing himself as a self-employed farmer. Three days after Cocreham registered for the draft, his brother Lewis was severely wounded in action near Villers-sur-Prency, France. (Lewis, a sergeant, was awarded a Silver Star for gallantry. He led a patrol in an attack on two enemy machine guns. The patrol captured one of the machine guns, but Lewis was wounded leading a patrol against the second machine gun after one patrol had already been driven off.)[11]

Cocreham did not pitch professionally in 1919, but he returned to San Antonio, now nicknamed the Bears, in 1920. He finished with a 5-1 record in eight starts. In the offseason he was listed as living with his brother Roland on a farm in Luling.[12]

In 1921 Cocreham spent time in the Texas League with both San Antonio and the Shreveport Gassers. He went 6-8 with a 5.52 ERA in his final season in Organized Baseball.

After ending his playing career, Cocreham spent the 1922 season coaching baseball at the Agricultural and Mechanical College of Texas (now known as Texas A&M University) and led the Aggies to a 9-8 record. He didn't return to coach a second season.[13] Cocreham also managed clubs in Gonzales and Lockhart.[14]

Cocreham studied horticulture at the Agricultural and Mechanical College before returning to Luling to take a position as a manager of McKean Orchards, supervising the planting and budding of fruit trees. Toward the end of his life, he returned to being a farmer and was involved in raising broiler chickens.[15]

Cocreham died on December 27, 1945, in Luling of a coronary occlusion complicated by diabetes. He had been ill for five months and hospitalized for the last three months of his life. He was single at the time of his death and was survived by three of his brothers, Roland, Lewis, and Guy, and three sisters. He is buried at Luling City Cemetery.

Notes

1. US Census Bureau, 1910 US Census.
2. Vivian Elizabeth Smyrl, "Luling, TX," *Handbook of Texas Online* (http://www.tshaonline.org/handbook/online/articles/hjl17), Published by the Texas State Historical Association.
3. US Census Bureau, 1910 US Census and 1920 US Census.
4. US Census Bureau, 1910 US Census.
5. *Sporting Life*, October 17, 1914, 7.
6. Baseball Hall of Fame Library, player file for Eugene Cocreham.
7. *Sporting Life*, July 5, 1913, 27.
8. *Sporting Life*, Sept. 20, 1913, 23.
9. "Braves Release Two Pitchers," *New York Times*, April 29, 1915.
10. *Sporting Life*, July 31, 1915, 6.
11. Military Times, Hall of Valor, Lewis R. Cocreham (militarytimes.com/citations-medals-awards/recipient.php?recipientid=33495).
12. US Census Bureau, 1920 US Census.
13. SABR Encyclopedia, "Texas A&M University" (http://sabrpedia.org/wiki/Texas_A%26M_University).
14. Baseball Hall of Fame Library, player file for Eugene Cocreham. The file lists Cocreham as having coached in Gonzales and Lockhart prior to coaching at Texas A&M, but he played through the conclusion of the 1921 season and coached Texas A&M in 1922, so it's unclear exactly when this occurred.
15. Baseball Hall of Fame Library, player file for Eugene Cocreham.

Wilson Collins

By Charlie Weatherby

ONE OF THE fastest men in the South, Wilson Collins could cover 100 yards in 9.8 seconds. A baseball, football, and track star at Vanderbilt University, he was called major-league baseball's first designated runner (he was a pinch-runner in at least half of his games) by *Baseball Research Journal*.[1] In two seasons with the Boston Braves, the 5-foot-10, 165-pound speedster appeared in 43 games, batting .263 in 38 at-bats. Despite his speed, he never stole a base.

A big-hearted and friendly man, Collins fashioned a reputation as one of the South's most successful high-school football coaches during his remarkable 14-year career at Knoxville (Tennessee) High School, winning three mythical national championships. A Tennessee newspaper said, "Year in and year out, Collins has … the best teams in the US. He goes over the country beating the best teams other sections have to offer."[2]

Cyril Wilson Collins was born on May 7, 1889, in Pulaski, Tennessee. He was the younger of Roy P. and Ella (Loyd) Collins's two sons; his brother Clifford was four years older. His father was described as "for more than fifty years one of the leading school teachers in Giles County."[3] Mrs. Collins, along with her husband, was a devout member of the Methodist Church and was noted for bringing cheer and comfort to those who were experiencing times of trouble, sickness, or sorrow. Brother Clifford owned Loyd's Drug Store.

Cyril Collins was known as Willie. His athletic career began at the Massey School, a private prep institution in Pulaski later known as Massey Military Academy. Massey, behind junior pitcher Willie Collins, won the prep championship of Tennessee and Alabama in 1909, a feat it repeated in 1910 when he was team captain.

After his spectacular career at Massey, Collins enrolled at Vanderbilt University in Nashville. In March 1911, the *Atlanta Constitution* pegged him as one who would likely be the baseball team's starting pitcher. Instead, Collins played some early games in center field. Writing about a 6-4 loss to Michigan on April 15, the *Chicago Tribune* noted, "The game was featured by a brilliant stab by Collins … which cut off two runs in the third inning."[4] The Commodores finished the season with an 8-7 record.

With Collins at right halfback, the Vanderbilt Commodores football team finished 8-1, outscored the opposition 259-9, and won the Southern Intercollegiate Athletic Association championship. The *Atlanta Constitution* declared Vanderbilt's backfield (besides Collins, quarterback Ray Morrison, fullback Ammie Sikes, and left halfback Lewis Hardage) the best in the South[5]

Ty Cobb came to Nashville in November 1911 to perform in a play. Coach McGugin, who practiced law in Detroit during the winter, was Cobb's old friend and invited him to participate in a Vanderbilt football practice. When it was over McGugin set up a race between Cobb and several of his fastest players. According to the *Constitution*, Cobb "made a monkey out of Captain Ray Morrison and Wilson Collins, in a practice sprint, distancing them to the tune of about eight yards in a 50-yard dash."[6] The *Nashville Tennessean* agreed: "Ty had a race with several of the fastest Commodores and put them all to rout."[7]

Later published versions turned the result in Collins's favor. In August 1912 *Sporting Life* reported that Clark Griffith of the Washington Senators was trying to sign Collins to a contract. If Griffith was successful, *Sporting Life* said, "he'll have the fastest man in baseball.… Last Fall Dan McGugin … kidded Ty Cobb into a 100-yard dash against Collins. … At the 50-yard mark Collins was looking over his left shoulder at Ty and at the end of the stretch found him 10 yards to the good."[8] A similar story appeared in *Sporting Life* in February 1914: "It is said that last Fall Collins and Cobb met in a 100-yard race, and at the finish Collins was leading Cobb by ten yards."[9]

Collins family lore says that Wilson ran in his football uniform while Cobb was in street clothes, Collins won the race and Cobb was furious. A second race was run and Coach McGugin suggested to Collins that he allow Cobb to win the second time. This time Cobb won, family legend says.

Whatever the outcome, the perception of Collins being faster than Cobb took on a life of its own. In 1916 Les Mann of the Cubs called himself the fastest man in baseball because he won a challenge race with Collins when they were with the Boston Braves in 1913 or 1914. Mann said, "We started and I finished first, two yards ahead of Collins." Braves' catcher Bert Whaling, who had bet on Mann, "cashed in. It sort of surprised the fellows, I guess, for Collins had beaten Ty Cobb in a foot race, so I'm told."[10]

Collins was on the pitcher's mound from the start of Vanderbilt's 1912 baseball season. With what the *Boston Globe* later called his "armor-piercing speed,"[11] wicked curve, and spitball, he shut out Georgia, 2-0, on April 18, giving up two scratch hits while fanning 11. In May Vanderbilt faced Alabama in a series that would determine the Southern championship. In the first game Collins gave up six hits and struck out six in a 4-3 victory. Vanderbilt (15-3) won the championship as Collins posted a 6-0 record on the hill. The *Montgomery Advertiser* called him "the leading pitcher of the team … [who] is thought by many to be the best college pitcher in the south."[12]

At the end of the baseball season, Collins did outdoor work with the Tennessee Power Company at Murfreesboro.

The *Boston Globe* called Collins "one of the [Vanderbilt] track management's best sprinters." Grantland Rice noted that he "had done 9 4/5s on the track before turning to baseball, and this is about as fast as any big-league ball player ever traveled."[13]

In September 1912 Collins scored five touchdowns in a 105-0 rout of Bethel College in the season opener. Vanderbilt (8-1-1) won the Southern Intercollegiate Athletic Association football championship for the third consecutive year. Collins was named All-Southern second team by the *Constitution*, which called him "the fastest back in the South."[14] Georgia Tech coach John W. Heisman picked Collins for his second-team all-Southern squad.

The *Pittsburgh Press* called Collins "the most sought after college pitcher of the year."[15] In February 1913 the *Atlanta Constitution* reported that he had turned down offers from the Athletics and the Senators so he could stay at Vanderbilt. But the offers continued to come, and by mid-April Collins had signed with the Boston Braves for a salary of $2,500. Manager George Stallings had outbid at least six other teams, including an unspecified New York club that offered a monthly salary of $400. Stallings intended to make Collins an outfielder because of his speed.

Collins made his major-league debut in left field on May 12, 1913, in a 6-4 Braves win over St. Louis. His first hit came in his initial at-bat—he was safe on an infield chopper over third in the first inning off pitcher

Wilson Collins

Slim Sallee. He finished the game 1-for-2. Collins was a ninth-inning pinch-runner the next day. He was defensive replacement in left field in the May 14 Cardinals game.

On July 28, with the Boston trailing Chicago 9-3 with two outs in the top of the ninth, Collins ran for John Titus, who had singled. The next batter, Tex McDonald, slashed the ball to shortstop Red Corriden, who booted the ball behind second and then tried and failed to force Collins, who kept running. Corriden recovered in time to throw to third baseman Art Phelan. Phelan tagged Collins but dropped the ball. Les Mann scored on the play. In the excitement after the play, Phelan tucked the ball under his arm. A few seconds later Collins stepped off third and was tagged by Phelan, ending the game. According to baseball historian Bill Deane, this was the fifth time a major-league game ended on the hidden-ball trick.

Collins's last 1913 at-bat earned him a unique double-whammy. On August 2 Boston trailed St. Louis 4-1 in the top of the seventh with runners on first and second. On a hit-and-run play, Collins rapped a hard liner at shortstop Possum Whitted, who made the grab, stepped on second to double up Bill Sweeney, and fired the ball to first baseman Ed Konetchy, tripling up runner Hap Myers. In the space of five days, Collins had been victimized by the hidden-ball trick and a triple play.

In August Stallings sold Collins to the International League's Buffalo Bisons, hoping he would get some work as an outfielder and pitcher. Collins declined to report and returned to Nashville, where he attended classes at the Vanderbilt Law School. In his three months with the Braves Collins had only three plate appearances in 16 games, being used primarily as a pinch-runner and outfield defensive replacement.

After the season the St. Louis Terriers and the Pittsburgh Rebels of the new Federal League tried to sign Collins but failed, Pittsburgh under threat of an injunction obtained by Stallings. Collins did well in spring training. But once the season began he was limited to 27 appearances and 35 at-bats in 1914, mostly as a pinch-runner or late-inning defensive replacement.

The platoon-loving Stallings gave him nine starts, eight versus left-handers and one against a right-hander. His best game at the plate came on June 3 in a 6-3 loss at Brooklyn when he was 2-for-4 with a run and an error in left field.

Collins played in his last major-league game on July 8 in Chicago, as a late-inning replacement for Les Mann in a 7-4 Braves win. The *Boston Globe* said, "Collins, substitute center fielder, really saved the day for Boston. His catch of Corriden's fly in the eighth was the best bet of the day."[16] In mid-July Collins was optioned to the Binghamton Bingoes of the New York State League. One of his better days was a combined 3-for-6 in a July 26 doubleheader sweep of Syracuse. He doubled home two runs during a three-run seventh in the first game and doubled up a runner at first base after catching a fly ball in the second contest. He played in 16 games for the Bingoes, batting .220 and posting a fielding average of .912. Binghamton returned Collins to Boston on August 29 and the Braves released him in September.

Collins returned to his law studies during the winter of 1914-15, this time at Cumberland University Law School in Lebanon, Tennessee. In April 1915 he announced that he had signed a contract with the International League's Jersey City Skeeters. Manager Hooks Wiltse released him after two weeks of spring workouts.

At the behest of George Stallings, Jesse Burkett, manager of the Worcester Busters in the New England League, picked up Collins in mid-May to bat leadoff and play left field. Collins first appeared in a 6-3 win over Lynn on May 18, getting a hit and scoring two runs. One of his best games came ten days later when he had a triple and two singles and scored a run in a 9-4 victory over Fitchburg. He also starred in a doubleheader victory over Lynn on May 31, getting four hits including a double and scoring three runs.

A few good games were not enough for Burkett to keep Collins. He was released in mid-June and soon found his way to the Fitchburg Burghers of the same circuit. There is little evidence of Collins's brief time in Fitchburg; the *Boston Globe* showed him appearing in games on July 7 and 12 with no offensive output. His statistics with Worcester and Fitchburg show a combined 30 games and a .200 batting average. His .912 fielding percentage placed him near the bottom of New England League outfielders.

Despite his setbacks, Collins was not ready to give up on the 1915 season. On July 16 he signed with the Springfield (Massachusetts) Tips of the Colonial League, a circuit subsidized by the Federal League and not part of Organized Baseball. Collins played in 51 games for Springfield and hit .250. His final appearance in professional baseball came on September 6, when he was 2-for-5 with two runs in a 5-4 win over Pawtucket in the season closer. His career average for 97 minor-league games was .230. Kid Elberfeld of the Southern League's Chattanooga Lookouts gave Collins one last chance in March 1916, but released him after four weeks of spring drills. A few weeks later, Collins received his law degree from Cumberland University.

Collins then turned to professional football, probably in the fall of 1915 and 1916, although it is difficult to determine where. A Collins family member said that he played on the West Coast. The *Pulaski Citizen* of March 24, 1921, said Collins was "a star football player of the National Football League,"[17] although the league didn't exist until 1922.

Collins registered for the World War draft in 1917. His registration listed him as a time keeper for the Louisville Gas and Electric Company in Louisville, Kentucky. Sometime that year he journeyed to Placerville, California, on business. With Collins's background in utility work, it is likely that he was employed in some capacity on a Western States Gas and Electric project to increase the capacity of its power plant on the American River, which runs near Placerville.

With the World War raging in Europe, Collins returned to Pulaski and was sent to Camp Gordon, Georgia, an Army basic training facility near Atlanta, arriving on September 5, 1917. He was appointed battalion sergeant major, then on January 5, 1918, was selected to attend officer training camp. Collins also played for the Camp Gordon football team, which won the Army's Southeastern championship.

On April 15, 1918, Second Lieutenant Collins's 321st Machine Gun Battalion sailed to England, then made its way to LeHavre, France. The battalion never saw combat. After the Armistice was signed, the 321st was sent to Coblenz, Germany, where Collins was the assistant division personnel adjutant. He left Germany on April 1, 1919, and was discharged at Camp Pike, Arkansas, on June 12. He returned home to Pulaski and was appointed football coach at Massey Military Academy. He remained there for seven years, posting a 6-2-1 record in 1923, when the team outscored the opposition 149-24.

On April 17, 1920, Collins married Ruth (Porter) Yokley in Pulaski. She was the widow of Hume Steele Yokley, who was in the Army and died from the flu while on the way to Europe in 1918. Wilson and Ruth had a daughter, Ruth Porter Collins, who was born on September 27, 1922. Two other children did not survive infancy, Jane in February 1921 and an unnamed son in October 1933.

In 1925 Collins spent a year coaching football and basketball and teaching English and history at Alabama Military Institute in Anniston, then he spent a year teaching and coaching at Columbia (Tennessee) Military Institute. In March 1927 Collins became Knoxville High School's athletic director and football, basketball, and baseball coach. His presence paid immediate dividends when the 1927 baseball team won the East Tennessee championship and the 1927-28 basketball team went 19-2 and won the city and East Tennessee championships.

Utilizing Dan McGugin's short-punt-formation offense, Collins led Knoxville's Trojans to the mythical Southern prep championship in 1928 with a 9-0-1 record, outscoring the opposition 310-22. More success followed in 1929 as 9-1-1 Knoxville won a state championship. A perfect 13-0 season in 1930 included state, Southern and mythical national championships. Some called this team Knoxville High's greatest — it demolished the opposition by a cumulative score of 592-12 (including

11 shutouts). Bob "The General" Neyland, the University of Tennessee's coach, recruited eight members of the 1930 team to his Volunteer squad. Of those eight, seven played first team.

The championships kept piling up. Knoxville won three more state championships (1931, 1933, 1934), another Southern championship (1933), and two more mythical national championships (1933, 1937). One constant from 1928 to 1934 was suffocating defense—the Trojans shut out opponents in 75 percent of its games. Collins had only one losing season, going 3-8 in 1939. In his 14 seasons, Collins compiled a record of 122-28-5.

Knoxville High School did not have a home field during Collins's first 12 seasons. This problem was remedied in 1939 when Evans-Collins Field, named in honor of W.E. Evans, the Knoxville High School principal, and Collins, was dedicated.

Collins coached basketball for 12 years and never had a losing season, posting a record of 250-52 from 1927-28 through 1938-39, collecting four district championships and three East Tennessee championships. The 1938-39 Trojans (30-4) won the state championship. The baseball team won the East Tennessee championship in 1927, and East Tennessee and Southern championships in 1928.

Collins's personality helped him achieve coaching success. After his death the *Knoxville News-Sentinel* wrote of him, "His influence over the years had reached many a home. … He had developed not only athletes that won championships but young men that had character. He was none of your hard-boiled coaches that … insist on winning at any price. He was rather a father to his boys. He taught them skill [and that] … they must always play fairly. Such standards yielded his dividends. … He loved his athletes. And it's no wonder they loved him." [18]

Collins was sometimes mentioned as a college coaching candidate—Southwestern of Memphis considered him in 1935, as did Vanderbilt in 1940. Collins stayed in Knoxville, where he was influential in the Tennessee Secondary School Athletic Association. He was one of the organizers of the Big Six, a conference of East Tennessee high schools in 1938. For relaxation, Collins played golf at the Cherokee Country Club, where he occasionally won a match play tournament. He also was a college football official in the 1930s. His highest profile assignment was the 1938 Rose Bowl game between California and Alabama.

On January 8, 1941, the *Kingsport Times* reported that Collins was about to retire from coaching; his physician had advised him to curtail his strenuous activities. He died seven weeks later, on February 28, after a ten-day hospitalization for a heart ailment. He was 51 years old. Collins was survived by his wife, Ruth; his daughter, Ruth; his brother, Clifford; and his father, Ray. He is buried in Pulaski's Maplewood Cemetery. He was later inducted into the Knoxville Sports Hall of Fame. In 2009 the Giles County Bicentennial Committee named Collins as one of its 198 most influential citizens.

Sources

In addition to the newspapers cited in the text, the following sources were used.

Syracuse Herald, 1914

Fitchburg (Massachusetts) *Daily Sentinel*, 1915

Hartford Courant, 1915

New York Times, 1916

New Orleans Times-Picayune, 1916

Mountain Democrat (Placerville, California), 1917

State (Columbia, South Carolina) 1917

Oakland Tribune, 1938

Books:

William D. Hunt. *Knoxville High School, 1910-1951, The Alpha and Omega of the Trojan Dynasty*, 3720 Essary Rd., Knoxville, Tennessee 37918: Self-published, 1988.

Articles:

Clifford Blau. "Leg Men: Career Pinch-Runners in Major League Baseball." *Baseball Research Journal* 38, No. 1 (Summer 2009): 70-81.

Vanderbilt University. "Baseball Review." *Vanderbilt University Quarterly* 12 (1912): 213.

Yolanda Hughey Ezell. "Cyril Wilson Collins: Giles County's Own Version of 'Moonlight' Graham." Unpublished biography, Giles County (Tennessee) Historical Society (No date).

Hugh Wallace. "My Earliest Recollections: Pulaski 1901-1914." Unpublished paper, Giles County (Tennessee) Historical Society (No date).

Websites:

Retrosheet.org

Baseball-reference.com (including minor league database)

Ancestry.com

Familysearch.org

GenealogyBank.com

NewspaperArchive.com

VuCommodores.cstv.com

Books.google.com

Rolltide.com

Ronald R. Allen, Running Plays and Passing Days: The first fifty years of high school football in Knoxville, Tennessee, 1900-1950.

http://www.knology.net/~ronallen/HS%20FOOTBALL.htm

Ronald R. Allen, From Cas Walker's to Downtown Hawkers: Some happenings during more than seventy years in Knoxville, Tennessee 1934-2007 with comments, reminiscences, and observations of an old curmudgeon. 2008.
http://www.knology.net/~ronallen/cas.htm

Acknowledgements:

Thanks to Chambliss "Bliss" Pierce, Knoxville, Tennessee, for providing materials and insights regarding Collins, his grandfather; Robert Roe, Pulaski, Tennessee, a cousin of Wilson Collins's daughter, for acting as a liaison with the Giles County Historical Society and its director, George Newman. Bill Deane shared his hidden-ball trick database.

Notes

1. Clifford Blau, "Leg Men: Career Pinch-Runners in Major League Baseball," *Baseball Research Journal* 38, (Summer 2009): 70.
2. Frank Rule, "What's Your Guess?" *Kingsport Times*, October 2, 1938: 8.
3. "Roy P. Collins, Aged School Teacher, Dies At Home Of Son," *Pulaski Citizen*, October 15, 1941: 1.
4. "Michigan Wins and Loses," *Chicago Tribune*, April 16, 1911: C2.
5. "Vandy Has The South's Greatest Backfield," *Atlanta Constitution*, November 26, 1911: D2.
6. "Ty Cobb Wears Vandy Uniform," *Atlanta Constitution*, November 29, 1911: 10.
7. Spick Hall, "Premier Ball Player Joins With Vanderbilt in Practice," *Tennessean*, quoted by Bill Trauber, "Commodore History Corner" (online), March 26, 2008.
8. *Sporting Life*, August 10, 1912: 13.
9. "To Make Speed Count," *Sporting Life*, February 14, 1914: 11.
10. "Leslie Mann of Cubs Is Considered Fastest Man in Big League Ball," *Piqua* (Ohio) *Leader-Dispatch*, December 5, 1916: 7.
11. "South's Greatest College Ball Player Is Collins," *Boston Globe*, April 22, 1913: 7.
12. "Vandy Will Barnstorm Dixie Land This Summer," *Montgomery Advertiser*, June 9, 1912.
13. Grantland Rice, "The Sportlight," *Los Angeles Times*, August 28, 1931: A10.
14. Innis Brown, "Innis Brown's All-Southern Eleven One of Real Merit," *Atlanta Constitution*, December 1, 1912: C8.
15. "Stallings Gets College Star," *Pittsburgh Press*, April 17, 1913: 17.
16. "Echoes of the Game," *Boston Globe*, July 9, 1914: 7.
17. "Soldier Records: Wilson Collins," *Pulaski Citizen*, March 24, 1921; as quoted in Yolanda Hughey Ezell, "Cyril Wilson Collins: Giles County's Own Version of 'Moonlight Graham,'" Unpublished, undated biography, Giles County (Tennessee) Historical Society.
18. "Wilson Collins," *Pulaski Citizen*, March 5, 1941: reprinted editorial from *Knoxville News-Sentinel*.

Joseph Francis Connolly

By Dennis Auger

WHEN BASEBALL FANS think about the national pastime and Rhode Island during the Deadball Era, Napoleon Lajoie stands out as the premier sports personality from "Little Rhody." However, Joseph Connolly, despite just a four-year major-league career (1913-1916), may have had a greater impact on the social, cultural, and baseball fabric of Rhode Island than any other player, including Lajoie. As for Connolly's athletic abilities, Paul Shannon of the *Boston Sunday Post* wrote that the Rhode Islander "is fairly fast, the possessor of a strong wing and he covers a good extent of territory. Furthermore, he is a dependable hitter".[1] Connolly was the offensive star of the Boston Braves during their most successful period of the Deadball Era (.288 lifetime batting average).

The Blackstone Valley River Canal Corridor extends 45 miles from Worcester, Massachusetts to Providence, Rhode Island. At the turn of the 20th Century, textile mills were located in both urban and rural sites along the Blackstone River. This geographical area was also a hotbed of baseball activity in the amateur, semiprofessional, and professional levels. It was within this context that Connolly lived.

Joseph Francis Connolly was the ninth of 11 children of Thomas Francis and Ellen (Powers) Connolly, emigrants from Ireland who married in Cumberland, Rhode Island during the last year of the Civil War, 1865, and established a family farm in the Sayles Hill section of nearby North Smithfield. Until recently, most baseball chronicles listed Joseph's birthdate as either February 12, 1886 or February 12, 1888. But according to the birth records in the North Smithfield Town Hall, Connolly was born on February 1, 1884, a finding that is corroborated by documents in the Rhode Island State Archives as well as the baptismal record at St. James Church in the village of Manville, where the family worshiped because of its proximity to their home. During this historical period, it was the Roman Catholic tradition to have an infant baptized soon after birth. Even though the church register lists his date of birth as February 2, 1884, Joseph was definitely baptized on February 10, 1884. Despite a one-day discrepancy with respect to the day of his birth, legal documentation is in complete agreement regarding the birth year.

Connolly's sons said that their father never liked to talk about his age.[2] The reason for changing his date of birth may have been to protect and advance his baseball career, which was a common practice at the time. Even the family never knew that 1884 was the year he was born, for to them it had always been February 12, 1886. It was a secret that Connolly took to his grave.

Connolly has also appeared in some reference books as Joseph Aloysius Connolly. According to both state and church documents, his name was Joseph Francis Connolly, Francis being his father's middle name. Given his Roman Catholic background, the most plausible explanation for Aloysius is that Joseph accepted this name when

Joe Connolly (left) seated with Rabbit Maranville (right).

he received the sacrament of Confirmation on September 21, 1902. It was then an accepted practice to take a saint's name during the liturgical rite and to incorporate it into one's identity. Baseball annals for the most part refer to Connolly as Joe. Further, his sons said (and Rhode Island newspapers of the period concur) that Connolly preferred the nickname "Joey".[3]

As a youngster, Joey participated in the family's farming chores. His brothers often played baseball with him either on the farm or in the neighborhood. Joseph also found time to play in Manville, later joining a mill league team and eventually climbing to the semipro level. The right-hander pitched for a number of independent clubs, primarily for the Putnam, Connecticut entry in the New England League during 1906-07. His pitching impressed Frank Rudderham, a former National League umpire from Providence, who recommended Connolly to manager Michael Finn, of Little Rock in the Southern Association. According to the *Pawtucket* (Rhode Island) *Evening Times*, Rudderham said Connolly, "had the best curves he ever saw in his life, even after doing big league service."[4]

In a 1908 spring-training outing for his new team, he lost 4-0 to Christy Mathewson and the New York Giants, having hurled a complete game. The pitcher's persona was quiet and "Joey did not smoke, chew, nor drink,"[5] habits he avoided his entire life. One reason for this lifestyle was that some of his older brothers suffered from alcoholism.[6] After registering a 2-5 record during the first two months of the season at Little Rock, Connolly was sent to Zanesville, Ohio, of the Central League where he achieved an impressive 15-8 slate. He also hit .333 in 78 at-bats—the first hint that his future lay in hitting baseballs instead of pitching them.

In 1909 Connolly pitched at Little Rock for two months, then returned to Zanesville, compiling a combined 9-5 season log. He had some limited outfield play at Zanesville and batted .308. Renewing his Zanesville contract in 1910, Joey won 16 games while losing 17 for a team that finished 16 games below .500. His accomplishments included throwing a no-hitter, a one-hitter, a two-hitter, and four three-hitters. The left-handed batter hit .255 in 169 at-bats. Central Leaguers nicknamed him "Old Hickory Jerkey" because of his unusual delivery.[7] The latter, combined with "a fine assortment of speed and curves, made him a cracker jack hurler."[8] Two factors hindered his progression. First, scouts thought he was too small (he stood only 5 feet 7 1/2 inches and weighed 165 pounds), and second, he was experiencing arm trouble.[9] Various people advised him to return to farming.

Connolly's major-league ambition in jeopardy, he remained in Zanesville for the 1911 campaign and insisted on playing the outfield full-time. This was a dramatic change at the age of 27. Manager Joe Raidy resisted this request and limited Connolly's playing time. The demand for a trade and team financial problems led to his being sent to Central League rival Terre Haute. In his first few games there, Connolly "misjudged flies and booted grounders like a rank amateur."[10] But he never gave up on himself and his fielding, running, and hitting improved as he won the league's batting crown with a .355 average and

Joseph Francis Connolly

Connolly hefting a bat before a game.

stole 27 bases. This proved to be his big break, with five teams bidding for his services. Terre Haute sold Connolly to the Cubs, who in turn traded him to Montreal of the International League. In 1912 at Montreal Connolly hit .316. Having established his credentials, he was drafted by the Washington Senators. Despite having a good spring in 1913, he was sold to the Boston Braves.

Manager George Stallings made Connolly his regular left fielder in 1913, even though he often sat him down against left-handed pitchers throughout his career. Though his first major-league season ended prematurely when he broke his ankle while sliding, the 29-year-old rookie led all Braves regulars with 79 runs scored, 57 RBIs, 11 triples, a .281 batting average, and a .410 slugging average. He also stole 18 bases and tied Les Mann with a team-high 34 extra-base hits. As for Connolly's hitting strategy, it included adapting an at-bat to a pitcher's style. If a hurler threw a spitball, Connolly would chop down on the delivered pitch. In another situation, when Connolly first faced Grover Cleveland Alexander, he was outmatched by Pete's "baffling hooks". Thus, on one occasion, he rushed forward and swung before the ball broke. A furious Alexander yelled, "Listen kid, if this ball isn't coming at you fast enough, just let me know."[11] From that day on Alexander threw him only fastballs, which Connolly preferred. One of his 14 career major-league home runs was off the Hall of Famer.

The 1914 Miracle Braves owed their success to players like Connolly. The sportswriters often referred to him as "slugger" or "star." Boston's only regular to hit .300 (.306), he was also the team leader in doubles, home runs, extra-base hits, total bases, and slugging average (third in the National League at .494). Manager Stallings demonstrated his high regard for Connolly by having him hit third in the lineup and by reportedly betting several suits that he would out-hit Philadelphia's Home Run Baker in the World Series. The manager's prediction did not come to fruition as Connolly was limited to one hit (.111) in the Series while Baker finished at .250. Nevertheless, Stallings' respect was further highlighted by a comment made after Game Three of the World Series. On the occasion of a fielding play, Stallings commented that "Connolly showed a remarkable instance of pure grit when he went head-first into the left-field bleachers in a fruitless attempt to get McInnis' two-bagger."[12]

As a member of the world champions, Connolly was the guest of honor at a number of banquets scheduled throughout Rhode Island. Because of his personality and baseball connections, he had been designated a "native son" by several communities. Joey Connolly Days were celebrated in Putnam and Manville. In recognition of his accomplishments, the Braves outfielder was presented with loving cups at both localities. The Manville reception was the apex of Connolly's victory tour. Rhode Island dignitaries, including Congressman Ambrose Kennedy who gave the testimonial, attended it. Joey was "a hero in his own hometown,"[13] but he was also recognized on the national scene. *Baseball Magazine* described Connolly as "the bearer of universal good cheer, the most pleasant, genial, likable person in baseball today."[14] The article labeled him as "the man who always smiles" and "Stallings' heavy slugger."[15]

The Braves challenged unsuccessfully for the pennant during the 1915 and 1916 seasons. In 1915 Connolly hit .298 but his slugging average dropped nearly 100 points (.397). Despite this downturn in power, he still led all Braves regulars in both categories. The drastic change in offensive statistics by Connolly and his teammates was the result of moving from the South End Grounds to the more spacious new Braves Field. The following year, Connolly's production and playing time decreased dramatically. He hit a meager .227 in just 110 at-bats. Boston's contract offer for the 1917 season slashed his salary in half. When the outfielder refused to sign, he was sold to Indianapolis of the American Association. Realizing that his combined income from farming and playing semipro ball locally would exceed that from his major-league contract, he retired.

Connolly began a new phase in his life. On October 25, 1916, he married Manville resident Mary Delaney at St. James Church in Manville. They had three children, Doris, Joseph, and Edward. Besides farming, Connolly continued to play semipro baseball in the Blackstone Valley until around 1928. He coached and managed at the semipro, college, and sandlot levels. Other endeavors marked his life. He was an active member of his church, dedicating his time to Catholic youth activities. An ardent sportsman, Connolly was the founder and first president of the Sayles Hill Rod & Gun Club. On the political front, even though North Smithfield was a Republican enclave, Connolly, a Democrat, won election to the town council and later was elected as a state representative (1933-34) and as a state senator (1935-36). Beginning in the mid-1930's, Connolly was employed as an investigator by the Rhode Island State Board of Milk Control.

On September 1, 1943, Connolly suddenly became ill and died at home, the cause of death being listed as coronary disease.[16] A local headline read, "Joey Connolly Called Out By Great Umpire." [17] Throngs, including church and state dignitaries attended the funeral. The relationship "Old Joey" had with the local communities was confirmed by the fact that the lifelong Sayles Hill resident died there, his funeral was at St. James in Manville, and he was buried at St. Charles Cemetery in Blackstone, Massachusetts.

Having baseball talent, Connolly nevertheless worked hard to refine his skills. Although he achieved success throughout his life, he always remained humble and unpretentious. He shunned the nightlife but enjoyed socializing. During Connolly's major-league days, Sunday baseball was prohibited in Boston, so his teammates would often join him at his farm. Connolly was also a man of principles. When a situation appeared unfair to him, he acted accordingly. He left the Braves over a salary dispute and he resigned as Providence College baseball coach in 1924 over faculty interference. In the latter situation, the friction was primarily with Father Ambrose Howley, the athletic director. Connolly did not believe his services were needed by the college "since there were enough coaches on the field already."[18]

He helped found the Carney Sandlot Baseball League. Upon his death, the league suspended play several days "in reverence to the memory of Joey Connolly."[19] He had recently attended a game and observed his son, Joseph Jr., lash out three hits. Dedication to his family was always a priority. When the children were going

Connolly posing, and contorted.

through their father's belongings, Joseph Jr. relates that they found about ten of his hunting licenses. "And you know," said a smiling Joseph Jr., "his age on those licenses never changed—he never got older!"[20]

Notes

1. *Woonsocket Evening Call,* October 5, 1914.
2. Taped interview with sons Joseph Connolly Jr., and Edward Connolly, July 21, 2001. Interview tape is available from SABR's Oral History Committee.
3. Ibid.
4. *Pawtucket Evening Times,* February 19, 1908.
5. *Woonsocket Evening Call,* October 7, 1914.
6. Taped interview with family members, July 21, 2001.
7. National Baseball Hall of Fame player file, unidentified newspaper article, November 1914.
8. Ibid.
9. Height and weight as listed in the *Baseball Encyclopedia* (2004); an unidentified November 1914 newspaper article in Connolly's Hall of Fame player file lists Connolly as 5 feet 6 1/2 inches.
10. Hall of Fame player file, unidentified newspaper article, November 1914.
11. *Woonsocket Evening Call,* September 3, 1943.
12. *Woonsocket Evening Call,* October 14, 1914.
13. *Pawtucket Evening Times,* October 30, 1914.
14. Samuel M. Johnston, "Good Natured Joe Connolly, The Man Who Always Smiles," *Baseball Magazine,* February 1915, 25-26.
15. Ibid., 25.
16. Death Certificate; Rhode Island Department of Public Health.
17. *Woonsocket Evening Call,* September 2, 1943.
18. Providence College Archives, undated article.
19. *Woonsocket Evening Call,* September 2, 1943.
20. This is from an additional interview with Joseph Connolly, Jr. on September 1, 2001.

Ensign Cottrell

By Peter Cottrell

Ensign Cottrell was a man who was successful at many things in life, but who never reached the level of achievement in the major leagues that some thought he might have. He was a gifted athlete and a scholar who was successful in college, in the minor leagues, and in his life after baseball. While in the major leagues, however, he received few opportunities to show his ability, and on the rare occasions when he played, did little to give his managers the inclination to give him more chances. Of the five major-league teams he played for, he appeared in a single game for three of them, and just two for a fourth, even though he spent a fair amount of time on their rosters.

Ensign Stover Cottrell was born in the village of Hoosick Falls, New York, not far from Albany. His parents, William and Lottie Worthington Cottrell, had both been born in the town of Hoosick, which includes Hoosick Falls. Although his date of birth is generally given as August 29, 1888, both his death certificate and a Syracuse University alumni questionnaire have him a year older, born on August 29, 1887.

Cottrell, also known as Dick, was a left-handed pitcher who was prone to wildness, often walking as many batters as he struck out. He grew up playing baseball and was a varsity pitcher for Hoosick Falls High School, from which he graduated. In 1907 he entered Syracuse University and continued to show his athletic prowess, playing both basketball and baseball. But he was also a scholar, winning an award for the athlete with the best academic record, finishing with an average of 93.7 for his four years of work and earning a degree in civil engineering.

In his senior year Cottrell was the captain and star pitcher of the baseball team. He was reported to have had a record of eight wins with a single loss (to West Point), with five shutouts and two one-hitters.[1] In his final college game, on June 13, 1911, he threw a no-hitter against Columbia, winning 2-1. Cottrell attracted the attention of multiple major-league teams, including the New York Giants and the Cincinnati Reds, but in a scout's letter to Cincinnati president August Herrmann, Cottrell was said to have "'teed' himself up with the Pittsburg club,"[2] allegedly because they had made a close friend of Cottrell as the Pittsburgh representative.[3]

Cottrell, listed as 5-feet-9 and 173 pounds, reported to the Pittsburgh team on June 17, 1911, and within days made his first and only appearance for the Pirates. On June 21 in Chicago against the Cubs, he entered the game in the bottom of the seventh inning with the Pirates trailing 7-1 and quickly discovered the difference between college and big-league batters. He got Heinie Zimmerman, the first batter he faced, to fly out to right, but after a walk, Cottrell surrendered his first hit and run when Joe Tinker tripled to right. A single, two stolen bases, a sacrifice fly, and two doubles soon followed and the single-inning debut finally ended with four runs scored and the Pirates now down 11-1. In the next inning John Shovlin also made his major-league debut as he pinch-hit for Cottrell and struck out in what would be his only at-bat of the season.

Manager Fred Clarke didn't call on Cottrell after that, and when the team left for an Eastern road trip in early July, Cottrell and three other players were left behind with instructions "to work out daily at Forbes Field and be ready to join the team in the East on short notice."[4]

By the end of August Cottrell found himself released unconditionally by the Pirates and quickly caught on with the Scranton Miners of the Class B New York State League. He made his first appearance with the Miners in a complete-game 2-1 loss to Utica, and manager Monte Cross used him as a starter for the rest of the season. Cottrell finished with a 3-3 record in six games with Scranton, including two complete-game losses in which he gave up only two runs. Scranton finished a disappointing seventh place in the eight-team league but the team appeared to have obtained a solid starter heading into the 1912 season.

Under new manager Buck Freeman, Cottrell soon became established in the starting rotation. On April 26, 1912, he started and lost the Miners' second game of the season, but five days later he came back to pitch a complete-game 6-5 victory against the Binghamton Bingoes for Scranton's first victory after three losses. Scranton rapidly fell into the second division and stayed under .500 the entire season, but Cottrell was a consistent winner for the Miners. On August 3 he lost a 2-1 game to Binghamton and saw his record dip to 9-10, but finished the season strongly from that point on with six wins and two losses.

The first of those two losses came on September 2. A morning-afternoon two-city doubleheader was scheduled for that day with the Wilkes-Barre Barons, winners of their previous 24 games; with that morning's game, it looked as though Cottrell was going to end that winning streak. For most of the game he held the home-team Barons hitless and took a scant 1-0 lead into the bottom of the seventh inning. With two outs, however, Wilkes-Barre got its only hits of the game, a double and two singles, and pushed two runs across the plate. The Barons took the contest for their 25th victory in a row. For the afternoon game, the teams traveled to Scranton, and the Miners reversed the score to pin a 2-1 loss on Wilkes-Barre and end the team's incredible run.

In the next to last game of the season, on September 7, Cottrell pitched well but dropped a 2-1 decision to Utica. Scranton ended the season in fifth place with a 62-69 record. Cottrell finished with 15 wins and 12 losses, but those losses included four complete games in which he allowed only two runs and a 16-inning complete game in which he gave up three.

Cottrell's winning record for a losing team had been drawing attention from scouts throughout the season, and on September 16 the Baltimore Orioles of the International League drafted him in the Rule 5 draft. But the Chicago Cubs, who had reportedly tried to acquire Cottrell early in the season, also drafted him and as a major-league club, had priority in acquiring his services.[5] The Cubs had a pennant-contending team that year, but the New York Giants were better, and by September 27, 1912, the second-place Cubs trailed in the standings by ten games. That afternoon, in the first game of a doubleheader, Cottrell made his Chicago debut in relief of Fred Toney, who was knocked out after allowing six runs to Cincinnati in five innings. Cottrell gave up two runs in each of his first two innings, allowing eight hits, a walk, and a strikeout in four innings of relief as Chicago started a five-game skid with a 10-3 loss to the Reds, ending the season in third place.

That appearance would be the only one Cottrell made for Chicago. Connie Mack of the Philadelphia Athletics had also had his eye on the young left-hander. In November, when Chicago mistakenly included his name on a list of players for whom it was seeking waivers, Mack seized the opportunity and grabbed him — Cottrell would start the 1913 season as an Athletic.

Cottrell's chances of making the club weren't assured, however. After being world champions in 1910 and 1911, the

Ensign Cottrell

Athletics had fallen to third place in 1912, but had still won 90 games and had a deep pitching staff. With two winners of more than 20 games in Jack Coombs and Eddie Plank, as well as 13-game winners Chief Bender and Boardwalk Brown, the starting rotation for the 1913 season was established. However, Cottrell and fellow youngsters Herb Pennock, Joe Bush, and Weldon Wyckoff made a strong showing in spring training, and Mack headed into the regular season with a ten-man pitching staff. But even with the early-season loss of Coombs to typhoid fever, there simply weren't enough shots at game time. Cottrell made his American League debut at home in the season's eighth game, on April 23 against the newly renamed New York Yankees. He relieved fellow rookie Bush in the ninth inning of a 4-0 loss, striking out one batter and yielding two hits, including a run-scoring single by Hal Chase, who played center field that day while manager Frank Chance enjoyed a rare start at first base.

Cottrell didn't see action for another six weeks. On June 5, in the third game of a four-game home series against Detroit, he finally got a chance to make his first start in the big leagues. He helped his own cause with a bases-loaded double to score three runs as the A's jumped to a 9-2 lead. By the end of the game, Cottrell had held on for what became an ugly complete-game 10-6 victory, yielding 13 hits and two walks while striking out two. Sam Crawford got four hits, and Ty Cobb was held hitless in four at-bats. As it turned out, that would be the highlight of this chapter of Cottrell's career.

Mack was always looking for new talent, and after only these two appearances, he sent Cottrell to Jack Dunn's Baltimore Orioles in a deal that would soon see Bob Shawkey make his way to the A's.[6] The second-division Orioles put Cottrell right to work on June 19, but he lasted just a third of an inning in a 13-8 victory over the Montreal Royals. He found his bearings in his next start, seven days later, striking out 11 Buffalo batters and limiting the Bisons to four hits and two runs in a 5-2 victory, which ended with his collapsing from the heat after the game. With Shawkey's departure, Cottrell received steady work as a starter and by the first week of August had racked up ten wins. His workhorse status peaked in a stretch between the 8th and the 25th of August as he started and relieved five times each, but his record suffered for it as he took six losses, four at the hands of Montreal. In September manager Dunn used him at a more measured pace and by season's end Cottrell had appeared in 32 games and had compiled a 14-8 record in helping Baltimore finish with a winning season and a third-place standing in the eight-team International League.

The 1914 season brought many changes to the world of baseball in Baltimore, two of which had significant impact on the Orioles. The Baltimore Terrapins of the new Federal League came to town, and the Orioles signed a young left-hander named George Ruth. Ruth picked up the nickname "Babe" in spring training in Fayetteville, North Carolina, and on March 7 Ensign Cottrell was on second base during an intrasquad game when Ruth hit his first home run as a professional. As the team came north to open the season, the Baltimore fans quickly abandoned the Orioles in favor of the major-league Terrapins. Playing before scant crowds, Cottrell got off to a slow start and had a losing record as May ended with the Orioles in third place. But in June he turned things around, starting with a win on the 3rd when he entered the game with one out in the first inning and shut the door on the Jersey City Skeeters in a come-from-behind 4-3 victory. Wins on the 6th and 9th helped the Orioles surge into first place, and on June 13 Ruth and Cottrell teamed up for complete-game victories as the Birds swept the Newark Indians. Seven days later Cottrell was once again part of a doubleheader sweep, this time pairing with Ernie Shore against the Montreal Royals.

By the end of June the Orioles were playing .670 ball, but the financial woes brought on by a lack of attendance had Dunn listening to offers from major-league teams for his players, as well as considering a proposal from Richmond, Virginia, to move his team. In order to survive, Dunn began selling his players and by July 9 five players, including Ruth, had been sold to major-league teams. Cottrell continued his winning ways with a 12-inning shutout of the Skeeters on July 2, and another shutout of Newark on the 11th in which no

Indian made it as far as third base. Four days later Cottrell bested Carl Mays and the Providence Grays with a three-hit, 2-1 victory for his tenth consecutive win. After a loss to Newark, he tossed a 1-0 masterpiece on July 24 against the Toronto Maple Leafs in what would be his final game for the Orioles. With another round of selloffs by Dunn, on July 29 Cottrell and his 13-7 record were headed to Boston to join the Braves.

In last place on the Fourth of July, Boston had climbed to fourth place when Cottrell joined the team, and had won nine in a row when he made his first appearance for the Braves, on August 7, starting a home game against Pittsburgh. The left-hander gave up two runs on three walks and a hit in just 1⅔ innings, and manager George Stallings wasted little time in replacing Cottrell in an eventual 5-1 loss. His wildness cost him dearly, as the Braves relied on a three-man rotation for much of August, and although he was with the team for the rest of the season, Cottrell didn't see action as a Brave again. He was carried on the World Series roster, but he didn't play in Boston's four-game sweep of Philadelphia, and when the Braves awarded winners' World Series shares of just over $2,700 to themselves, they voted only partial shares of $500 to Cottrell and infielder Bill Martin, "which their fellow players considered ample in view of the fact that neither man did any thing in particular toward bringing the pennant to Boston."[7]

Cottrell headed to spring training with the Braves in 1915, but with a strong staff returning from the championship season and a 21-player limit, there wasn't a spot available for him. In the American League, new Yankees manager Wild Bill Donovan needed a left-hander and had seen Cottrell the previous two seasons while manager of the Providence Grays. A deal was struck and Cottrell was sold to New York in early April. By the time he joined the club, the Yankees had established their starting rotation, so Cottrell was destined for relief duties and to hope for a chance to start. The Yankees' quick start that season would keep him waiting. After 24 games New York sported a 16-8 record, and its starters had hurled 22 complete games, with only two appearances by relievers for a total of three innings. But the team started losing and on May 27, New York's 32nd contest of the season, Cottrell finally made it into a game. He pitched the final inning and two-thirds in an 8-2 loss to Chicago, still only the fifth appearance by a reliever for the Yankees that season. On June 9 Cottrell relieved Marty McHale in the second inning of a game against the White Sox, and gave up 14 hits, two walks, and one hit batter in an ugly 13-0 loss. A month later he pitched one final inning in a loss to Cleveland. New York management, having seen their team fall below the .500 mark, decided that changes were in order and released Cottrell and McHale. Cottrell had made seven appearances for the Yankees, all in relief, and all in losses, giving up 29 hits and seven walks in 21⅓ innings for a 0-1 record and a 3.38 ERA.

Once again Cottrell found a job with Jack Dunn, who had relocated to Richmond when competition from the Federal League drove the Orioles out of Baltimore. After the previous summer's sale of its best players, the franchise, now named the Climbers, was struggling with a losing record, and Cottrell was slotted back into his old starting role.[8] On July 15, six days after his last appearance with New York, he went the distance to beat Buffalo 6-4 before a home crowd. He got steady work for the rest of the season, but was less effective than the previous summer, appearing in 20 games for the Rebels with 15 complete games, and ended up with a record of seven wins and 11 losses, allowing just over four runs and 13 walks and hits per nine innings.

After the season Cottrell's rights were sold back to the Yankees, but he decided to retire in order to establish a new career in the field he had studied. In January 1916 he entered Rensselaer Polytechnic Institute for a semester and while there helped mentor the school's pitching staff. In August 1917 he married Evelyn Taylor of Syracuse, and a year later their first child, Jack, was born. Two daughters would later join the family. Cottrell worked for a civil engineering firm in Syracuse and later established his own practice as a civil engineer and surveyor. In early 1947 Cottrell suffered a cerebral hemorrhage and died several days later, on February 27, in Crouse-Irving Hospital in Syracuse. Cottrell was a member of Theta Alpha fraternity and the Syracuse University Hall of Fame, as well as Victor Lodge 680

(F&A M). He was survived by his wife, his three children, a brother and sister, and two grandchildren.

Sources

Smelser, Marshall, *The Life That Ruth Built* (New York: Quadrangle/The New York Times Book Co., 1975).

Baltimore Sun online archives.

Sporting Life online archives.

baseball-reference.com

retrosheet.org

Ensign Cottrell player file from the National Baseball Hall of Fame.

Notes

1. *Sporting Life* 57, No. 15 (June 17, 1911), 3.
2. Author unknown, letter to August Herrmann, February 4, 1911, Ensign Cottrell player file.
3. Unidentified newspaper clippings, Ensign Cottrell player file.
4. *Sporting Life* 57, No. 19 (July 15, 1911), 6.
5. *Sporting Life* 59, No. 10 (May 11, 1912), 11.
6. *Sporting Life* 63, No. 24 (August 15, 1914), 2.
7. *Sporting Life* 64, No. 8 (October 24, 1914), 5.
8. baseball-reference.com and other sources list the team name as the Climbers, but multiple issues of *Sporting Life* refer to the team as the Rebels.

Dick Crutcher

By Jerrod Cotosman

ON A COLD September day in 1914, Richard Luther Crutcher, Jr. pitched the most significant game of his brief major-league career. The stands of Fenway Park were sparsely populated with a thousand hardy souls for whom the warmth of the pennant race outweighed the discomfort of the November-like weather.[1] The Boston Nationals had been expected to contend that year[2] but had started slowly before plummeting into the cellar and remaining there into July. Then they had caught fire and vaulted past the pack to take a 2 1/2- game lead with three weeks to go.

Crutcher had been drafted from the St. Joseph team of the Western League the previous fall and there had been high hopes for the man the *Boston Globe* had referred to as the "Strikeout King."[3] His nickname, Little Dick, stemmed from both his heritage as Richard Luther Crutcher, Jr. and from the 148 pounds he carried on a 5-foot-9-inch frame.[4] Even Deadball Era managers and scouts preferred large, strapping men who could throw hard, and Dick's slight build was repeatedly noted by commentators.

Crutcher was born in Frankfort, Kentucky, on November 25, 1889, to Richard and Emma Crutcher. The Crutchers were farmers who had moved to the city of Frankfort, where the elder Crutcher was involved in politics and the couple ran a boarding house.[5] Their first-born son, Lewis, would play ball in 1907 with Kansas City in the American Association and then for three more years with Frankfort in the Blue Grass League before retiring after the 1910 season to become a bookkeeper with a local firm.[6]

Like his older brother, Dick Crutcher also began his professional career pitching in the Blue Grass League.[7] In 1908 he pitched briefly for Lexington[8] before spending the next two years with the Frankfort nine. Sometime during that summer, Crutcher experienced the first bout of the arm trouble that would surface occasionally throughout his career.[9] The problem passed and he was well enough to pitch during August and September.[10]

Crutcher's debut season was impressive enough that the local papers referred to the "kid" pitcher as an essential part of the team's plans for 1909.[11] However, after beginning the season with Frankfort, he moved west to Oklahoma and signed first with Muskogee[12] and then with the Sapulpa club of the Western Association in July.[13] During his brief time with the Oilers he pitched a one-hitter against Springfield on August 4.[14] Later that year he signed with Enid[15] and spent parts of the next two seasons there, winning 20 games in 1910.

Crutcher then joined the St. Joseph Drummers of the Western League, with whom he spent the next three-plus years. Although 3-7 during the remainder of 1910, he rebounded to 9-4 in 1911 despite missing time because of illness. In 1912 he established himself as a regular by winning 18 of 31 decisions and pitching more than 300 innings for the second-place team. His success contin-

Dick Crutcher

ued in 1913, when he won 19 games and lost 17 for the third-place Drummers. Crutcher struck out 211 batters in 304 innings but also walked 145, by far the most in the league.

The Braves trained in Macon in the spring of 1914 and there was optimism in camp regarding several new young hurlers. Crutcher was well regarded and rated a mention by Hugh Fullerton. The nationally-known sportswriter said of Crutcher, "His right arm ought to figure strongly in the race." Despite a setback with problems in said right arm, Little Dick was slated for regular use when the championship season began.

Unfortunately for Braves fans, the team started poorly and quickly fell off the pace. Opening Day in Brooklyn was a farce as the home team hit Lefty Tyler early and often en route to an 8-2 win. The only bright spot was the performance of Crutcher, who pitched three innings of hitless relief and also doubled and drove in a run in his only at-bat.

On April 22 manager George Stallings gave Crutcher the opportunity to start against the Phillies and he was a success both on the mound and at the plate. The rookie had a pair of hits and pitched a complete game, striking out four while walking only one batter. However, he also gave up ten hits and was consistently in trouble before the Braves broke through in the ninth to get the tiebreaking run, the tally being scored by Crutcher himself. It was an auspicious beginning but it was not a harbinger of things to come.

The rookie pitched well in his next start but lost a 4-0 decision to the Brooklyn Robins. A bloop double followed by an error led to three runs in the decisive sixth inning. The defending champion Giants and Rube Marquard were next and if any team was to be Little Dick's bête noire, it would be McGraw's men, who tormented him numerous times over his career. On this day the first four batters hit safely and Crutcher was gone by the third inning of the 11-2 defeat.

Stallings matched the rookie against Marquard again on May 7 and the results were only slightly better. As was becoming common, Crutcher was in constant danger but managed to take a two-run lead into the late innings. Three hard hits beginning the bottom of the eighth cut the margin to 5-4 and sent Crutcher to the showers. Dick Rudolph relieved and was victimized by some bad breaks in the eventual 7-6 Giants win.

In his next start Crutcher lasted only five innings before being lifted for a pinch-hitter in a 4-2 loss to the Reds. Four days later, on May 19, he held the Pirates scoreless through three innings before the roof fell in and five runs scored, leading to 7-5 Pittsburgh victory. The rookie's wildness was evident in a hit batter and then a pair of walks that opened the floodgates. Those four innings marked the end of Crutcher's stint as a regular Braves starter.

For the rest of the season, Stallings primarily used the rookie in relief with a few spot starts because of doubleheaders or the need to rest other pitchers. Most of the relief outings occurred in low-leverage situations with Boston trailing. If saves were recorded in those days, Crutcher would have had none, and he completed only five of his 15 starts.

Little Dick was matched against Grover Cleveland Alexander in the second game of the Decoration Day twin bill but was pulled in the sixth because of control problems and did not figure in a 3-2 ten-inning Boston win. In his next start, a month later on June 30, he lasted six innings. Wildness was an issue again and he allowed seven hits and four walks in a game that ended in a 5-4 13-inning defeat. But on July 6 Crutcher turned in his best effort, pitching his only major-league shutout, against the Robins. Crutcher allowed six hits and one walk in the 1-0 decision that left the Braves still 14 games out of first place.

On July 19 Crutcher carried another shutout into the seventh inning against the Reds but was pulled after allowing a pair of runs that broke the scoreless tie. The Braves rallied to score three times in the ninth to win and began to build some momentum. They next steamed into the Smoky City and shut out the Pirates in four of five games. The one exception was when Crutcher again weakened and gave up a 4-2 eighth-inning lead. He left with the bases loaded in a tie game and the next batter unloaded them with a double off George Davis, leading to an 8-4 defeat.

In spite of the loss, the Braves continued on a hot streak that saw their record rise to ten games above .500 after a doubleheader sweep of the Reds on August 17. During the streak Stallings had been working his top starters hard and he decided to throw Crutcher into the breach on the 18th. The result was positive—six innings pitched with only a pair of hits allowed—but although the three Cincinnati runs were unearned, the decisive rally was triggered by a pair of walks. The 3-1 defeat did not stop the Braves' surge but it was three more weeks before Stallings gave Crutcher another start.

That start came on the aforementioned unseasonably cold day (September 11) in Boston with the Braves holding a 2 1/2-game lead over the suddenly struggling Giants. A brutal skein of three doubleheaders in four days left the Braves staff worn thin and gave Crutcher the chance. The Braves got to Eppa Rixey for three early runs. Philadelphia plated a run on a double-play grounder in the fourth and then broke free in the fifth, scoring three runs off Crutcher and relief pitcher Paul Strand to take a one-run lead. Boston ended up winning the game, scoring two runs in the last of the ninth, and maintained its lead over the Giants. Crutcher's performance had been disappointing and although he had walked only one batter it had led to a big inning and he had given up eight hits as well. It was Crutcher's last meaningful impact on the pennant race; he sat on the bench as the Braves pulled away from their rivals. Stallings gave him two more starts after things were all but decided. His final appearance was a 15-2 romp over Brooklyn on the next-to-last day of the regular season. Although active for the World Series, Crutcher never made it into a game as the Braves swept the highly favored Athletics.

Crutcher's final 1914 statistics were not pretty: a 5-7 record with an ERA of 3.46 and 48 strikeouts and 66 walks in 158 innings pitched. The sole highlight was a fielding percentage of .981, which placed him fifth in the league among pitchers.   Yet even after a subpar first year, Stallings saw enough promise in the youngster to re-sign him for 1915. Crutcher appeared very much in the defending champions' plans throughout the spring and started the third game of the season, a solid 5-1 win over the Robins. However, Stallings had brought the hook again in the eighth inning, showing the same lack of patience or confidence as in the prior season. The Robins then hit Dick hard four days later and drove him into the bullpen.

It was more than a month before Crutcher drew another start, and he went the distance in a sloppy 5-5 tie against the Giants that was called on account of darkness. On June 20 the Cardinals drove him from the box by the fifth inning of an 8-2 loss. His last major-league appearance came on the 26th, when he relieved Tom Hughes and poured gasoline on the fire by giving up three hits and a hit batter without recording an out. The next day Crutcher, with a 2-2 record and a 4.43 earned-run average for 1915, was released along with catcher Walt Tragessor to Jersey City in the International League.

Dick Crutcher's major-league career was over at the age of 25 and his 1915 Braves totals were particularly grim: 2-2 with a 4.43 ERA. He gradually slid out of the limelight, his name surfacing only briefly in a series of strange incidents. One of these occurred when indifferent outfield play by the great Olympian Jim Thorpe angered Crutcher enough for the smaller man to threaten to "take a little slap" at his Jersey City teammate. Given the size and physiques of the combatants, it was fortunate the confrontation did not lead to blows.[16] Crutcher ended up 9-9 for a mediocre Skeeters team.

Later that year the Braves' share of the gate receipts for a September game in St. Louis was attached by deputy sheriffs as a result of a disagreement with Kansas City's American Association club. The Blues alleged that they had not received agreed-upon compensation from Boston for a player sale, nor had they received Crutcher and Lawrence Gilbert as agreed.[17] There must have been some merit to the Kansas City case; Crutcher played there for the next three seasons.

Dick was a mainstay of the Blues rotation in 1916, compiling a 16-15 record for a fourth-place club. The following year arm troubles struck again and Crutcher was winless in three decisions, leading to friction with management. A syndicated feature ran in many papers insinuating that he was a lazy malingerer who could be great if he wanted to but instead had been suspended for "failing to condition himself."[18] A contemporary article in the *Kansas City Star* stated that Crutcher was consulting a local dentist who believed the arm trouble was caused by abscesses at the roots of his teeth.[19]

Crutcher's 1918 record was similarly truncated and he spent time with both the Blues and with Joplin of the Western Association before traveling north to Wisconsin.[20] He did war work at the Nash Motor plant in Kenosha and pitched for the company team.[21] He also appeared with the Manitowoc Shipbuilders and was the winning pitcher in the game that decided the Lake Shore League championship.[22] After the war he had an unsuccessful stint with Joplin before returning to Wisconsin.

Crutcher pitched for Manitowoc, Oshkosh, and Waukesha along Wisconsin's Lake Shore and, other than an abortive attempt to rehabilitate his arm at French Lick, Indiana,[23] and rejoin Organized Baseball in 1922, he remained in the area for the rest of the decade.[24] He continued to be employed by Nash, pitching for and managing the Nash Motormen semipro team before returning to Kentucky.[25] Back in Frankfort, he found work as a duplicating equipment operator for the state highway department.[26] He had married Ethel Armstrong of Frankfort before the World War. The couple had no children and were divorced by the early 1950s.[27] On June 18, 1952, Crutcher complained of indigestion and went to bed. He died of a heart attack the next day and was buried in Frankfort Cemetery.[28]

Or maybe not. A few years later, baseball writer Shirley Povich encountered someone claiming to be Dick Crutcher. The reporter used the Encyclopedia of Baseball to test the man and while the stranger got the baseball statistics right, he claimed a date of birth of 1893 instead of the listed 1891 (which was off by two years). While Povich was willing to overlook that discrepancy, he could not help but notice that Crutcher was listed as having died several years before. When confronted with the fact, the visitor became angry and stormed out of the office.[29]

Who was it? The 1900 census showed Crutcher with six siblings but neither of his brothers was born in 1893 or 1891. In fact Dick was the youngest boy by several years, having older brothers Lewis (born 1881 or 1882) and Edward (born 1885).[30] Both were still alive at the time and could be possible suspects but to what purpose or motive?[31] Because Little Dick had been a member of the Miracle Braves, a team with a legend that still resonated a half-century later? Regardless of the impostor's identity, the story was a final, bizarre coda to Crutcher's life.

Sources

All statistics are taken from www.baseball-reference.com unless otherwise noted.

All references to standings for the 1914 season are taken from www.retrosheet.org.

Notes

1. J.C. O'Leary, "Never Quit Braves Win Out in Ninth," *Boston Daily Globe*, September 12, 1914.

2. J.C. O'Leary, "Braves Fourth or Better," *Boston Daily Globe*, April 12, 1914.

3. "Braves Get Two New Players," *Boston Daily Globe*, December 31, 1913.

4. "Question Box," *Oakland Tribune*, March 28, 1915.

5. Both the Franklin County Marriage Register for 1878 and the 1880 US Census, First Magisterial District of Franklin County, show Richard Crutcher, Sr.'s occupation as farmer; "Election Officers," *Frankfort Weekly News and Roundabout*, September 24, 1898, and "Entries in Democratic Primaries," *Frankfort Weekly News and Roundabout*, November 5, 1904, show Richard serving as an election judge and as a nominee for the office of Jailer: 1920 US Census, Bridge Precinct, Magisterial District No. 3, of Frankfort shows Richard as the head of household and Emma as "Manager," "Boarding House."

6. *Lexington Herald*, January 23, 1907; "Pitcher Crutcher is Now Bookkeeper," *Lexington Herald*, November 22, 1910. It appears that Baseball-Reference.com has attributed Richard's stint in Kansas City to Dick and his three years with Frankfort to Edward Crutcher.

However, the above sources refer to Lewis (or Louis) as the Crutcher in question in both instances. See also "Among the Sports," *Oklahoma New-State Tribune*, July 29, 1909, which refers to Dick having a brother who played for Kansas City.

7   Commonwealth of Kentucky Death Certificate.

8   "Lexington Will Play Guetigs in Afternoon," *Lexington Herald*, April 19, 1908.

9   The Fan, "Diamond Dust," *Frankfort Weekly News and Roundabout*, August 22, 1908.

10 "Thoroughbreds Win in Romping Style," *Lexington Herald*, September 7, 1908.

11 "Railway Company to Help Frankfort Team, *Lexington Herald*, March 14, 1909.

12 "Among the Sports," *Oklahoma New-State Tribune*, September 2, 1909.

13 "Pioneer Park Bingles," *Muskogee Times-Democrat*, July 23, 1909.

14 "News Notes," *Sporting Life*, August 21, 1909, 23.

15 "Among the Sports," *Oklahoma New-State Tribune*, September 2, 1909.

16 Chandler D. Richter, "Interesting Sidelights on Baseball," *Sporting Life,* November 27, 1915, 10.

17 "Forcing Braves to Come Across," *Canton* (Ohio) *Evening Repository,* September 18, 1915.

18 "He Might Star If He'd Buckle Down," *San Diego Evening Tribune*, July 24, 1917.

19 "Sore Arm? The Causes," *Kansas City Star*, July 22, 1917.

20 "The Blues' Weird Game," *Kansas City Star*, July 20, 1918.

21 "Ball Players on Government Work," *Rockford* (Illinois) *Register Gazette*, August 13, 1918.

22 "Herzog Wins Flag In Shore League," *Racine* (Wisconsin) *Journal News*, September 30, 1918.

23 "Dick Crutcher Starts Work at French Lick," *Manitowoc Herald News*, April 12, 1922.

24 "Crutcher, Who Hurled for Manitowoc in Old Days, Is Dead at 62," *Manitowoc* (Wisconsin) *Herald Times*, June 20, 1952; "Slump of Sunday Puts Oshkosh Back to Second Place in Valley League," *Daily Northwestern*, Oshkosh, Wisconsin, August 15, 1922; Anonymous, "Crutcher Signs," *Sheboygan Press*, September 3, 1920.

25 "Crutcher Leaves Post With Nash," *Milwaukee Journal*, December 24, 1929.

26 Commonwealth of Kentucky Certificate of Death; AP Obituary, "Crutcher of Famous 1914 Boston Braves Dies at 62," *Williamsport* (Pennsylvania) *Gazette and Bulletin*, June 20, 1952.

27 Crutcher's World War I draft registration card from May 28, 1917, states that he was married with no children. The 1920 US Census shows him as married to Ethel Armstrong with no listed children. The Commonwealth of Kentucky Death Certificate shows Crutcher as divorced. None of the obituaries I found mentioned a surviving spouse or children.

28 AP Obituary, *Williamsport Gazette and Bulletin*, June 20, 1952; http://www.findagrave.com/cgi-bin/fg.cgi?page=gr&GRid=53161521.

29 Ralph Berger, "Shirley Povich," *SABR BioProject*, http://sabr.org/bioproj/person/b0dbc9e9.

30 1900 US Census.

31 The Social Security Death Index on www.ancestry.com shows a date of death of 1977 for Lewis and 1963 for Edward.

George Davis

By Rory Costello

SCHOLAR-ATHLETE GEORGE "IRON" Davis was the secret weapon of the Miracle Braves' pitching staff. Manager George Stallings had used the 24-year-old right-hander just three times during the first five months of the 1914 season, but when he turned Davis loose, the Harvard Law School student responded with his career highlight: a no-hitter, on September 9, 1914. During a barrage of doubleheaders down the stretch, he and other members of the supporting cast gave respite to the hard-pressed frontline starters. The Big Three of Dick Rudolph, Bill James, and Lefty Tyler proceeded to pitch brilliantly in the World Series sweep of the Philadelphia Athletics.

Before going to law school, Davis starred at Williams College, in Williamstown, Massachusetts. Amid his studies, he spent parts of four seasons in the majors from 1912 to 1915. His pro baseball career ended in 1916, and George returned to his hometown, the Buffalo suburb of Lancaster, New York. There, for more than four decades, he pursued a career in the law and enjoyed assorted intellectual interests.

George Allen Davis, Jr. was born on March 9, 1890. In many ways, his life echoed his father's. George A. Davis, Sr. (1858-1920), born in Buffalo to British immigrants, was a lawyer with what the *Albany Law Journal* called "a large and lucrative practice," and also was active in public life. Davis married Lillie Nina Grimes of Lancaster, and was Lancaster town supervisor from 1888 through 1897. He also was a New York state senator, and commander of the 74th Regiment of the New York National Guard.

The Davises had one other surviving child besides George, a daughter named Gladys (another boy apparently died young). Lillie, his mother, died on May 1, 1900, when George, Jr. was 10 years old.

In a 1914 feature article on George, Jr., the sportswriter Hugh Fullerton wrote, "Davis was not a strong youth. He was handicapped by physical unfitness."[1] This was perhaps one reason why he went to St. John's Military Academy in Manlius, New York.

After graduating from St. John's, George went to Williams College. Though he eventually became vice-president of his class, he got off to a rocky start academically. His classbook said, "How George occupied himself his freshman year is more or less a mystery, and the class almost lost him." It turned out that the would-be athlete—who apparently had no experience in baseball before he came to Williams—had devoted himself to exercise.

Prefiguring the Charles Atlas ads, "Iron" transformed himself physically, as Ring Lardner wrote. "His strength was confined to his brains and he had the physique of an Oliver Twist. .... Almost unnoticed, he worked long hours in the gymnasium and worked so hard that in a year his pals could scarcely believe he was the same boy."[2]

Hugh Fullerton wrote, "He never had played a game of baseball, and his knowledge was confined to theory. In the gymnasium he commenced working with a baseball, throwing at a padded surface and studying every ball he threw." Fullerton continued, "The coach discovered that there was a pitcher working in the gym who knew more about pitching than any of the regulars did, and Davis was allowed to join the squad and pitch. There were many things he did not know, but his theories worked out and he became a great college pitcher."[3] The coach was Billy Lauder, who oversaw the Williams nine from 1907 through 1910.

After emerging as a star—and lifting his classroom performance to Phi Beta Kappa level—George became team captain for the 1912 season. His accomplishments led major-league teams to take an interest in him. Even before Williams ended its season, Davis began to receive some offers, but deflected them so he could finish out the college campaign.

On June 27, the day after the school year finished, Davis signed with the New York Highlanders, as they were still known (it was their last season under that name before they became the Yankees). His salary was reported to be $5,000—then the biggest ever for a pitcher coming out of college.[4] "Possessing great speed, curves, and control. . .he has been a sensation in the college baseball world and has helped Williams to defeat practically all of her rivals. He is considered the leading college pitcher, either east or west."[5]

Davis made his debut at Hilltop Park in the second game of a doubleheader on July 16. He pitched well but lost 3-1 to the St. Louis Browns. Two runs scored in the third inning because of Ed Sweeney's error at the plate. George's first victory came on August 27, as New York beat Cleveland 6-4.[6] It was his only win against four losses in 10 games that season. After a rough outing against Philadelphia on September 5, he was sent down to the Jersey City Skeeters. That December, the *New York Sun* sniped, "George Davis is the strongest man in Williams College….but we regret that he didn't put all that stuff on the ball when pitching for the Highlanders last summer."[7]

Several college publications show Davis as a member of the Williams Class of 1913. While other sources say that he graduated in 1912, a 1915 feature in *Baseball* magazine said, "He finished all his required work in the mid-winter semester [of 1913] so he was able to take the early training trip with the Yankees to Bermuda."[8] This included some workouts at Hamilton Cricket Field.[9]

He did not make the big club, though; he was sent to Jersey City once again. Manager Frank Chance "did not like Davis because he quit the training camp to get married."[10] Another article added that "Chance did not like the young man's spirit and said he did not take base ball seriously enough."[11]

Davis's wife was Georgiana Jones. A granddaughter, Suzy Kissee, said, "Georgiana (called 'Kiddo' by everyone) was a practical joker and a suffragette. She was the first in her circle to raise her skirts above the ankle, and to be seen in public smoking, drinking, and driving a car. She was a voice for women's rights early in the century. Since her marriage was considered 'high profile' for the day, this took a lot of courage. He enjoyed it all."[12] George and Kiddo had four children: a son, George A. Davis, III, and three daughters, Delancy, Eunice, and Deborah.

After returning from his honeymoon, George went to the minors, although he wasn't happy about it—he reportedly said that he had enough money not to need the sport. He went 10-16 for Jersey City, striking out 199 men in 208 innings, according to the 1914 *Reach Guide*. He was also quite wild, however, and the Yankees sent him to another International League team, the Rochester Hustlers, who had a working relationship with the Boston Braves.

On August 25, the Braves purchased Davis from Rochester before he even pitched once there. George Stallings, as an opposing manager with Buffalo in 1912, knew of the young pitcher and liked what he had seen. The new recruit appeared twice in relief for Boston, allowing four earned runs over eight innings without a decision.

George Davis

Meanwhile, Davis had decided to enter Harvard Law School, and in 1914 he pitched with the Harvard Law team before joining the Braves. He did not get into a game for Boston until July 1, when he started and lost. Meanwhile, at the encouragement of Stallings, George had been developing a new weapon—the spitball. On August 19, the *Pittsburgh Press* reported, "Fred Mitchell, supervisor of pitchers, has had the chap in hand for about a month now and claims that at the present moment he is about the best spitball pitcher in the National League."[13]

The Braves had a September 9 doubleheader against the Phillies at their occasional home that year, Fenway Park. After Boston lost 10-3 in the opener, Davis—who had appeared just twice more in relief since July 1—started the second half of the twin bill. It turned out to be the only no-hitter pitched in the National League that year. Davis walked five batters, three of them in the fifth inning, but Davis struck out Ed Burns, one of his four K's for the day. He then escaped the jam by getting pinch-hitter Gavvy Cravath to hit into a double play.[14] He also survived two errors by Red Smith at third. George even added three hits of his own, as he was always quick to note.

There are some unusual facts about this feat. Davis had the second fewest career wins (seven) of any man with a no-hitter to his credit in the majors. Only Bobo Holloman, with three, had fewer. The no-hitter was also the first ever at Fenway Park, not to mention the only one there by an NL pitcher as of 2013.

Following another relief appearance two days after the no-hitter, Stallings gave Davis four more starts down the stretch. He had declared confidence in his second string and could afford to use them as the Braves pulled away from the Giants—but it was also a matter of necessity. The team played no fewer than eight doubleheaders from September 23 onward, including four straight days from the 23rd through the 26th. Davis pitched creditably, beating Pittsburgh on September 19 and New York on October 1. He lost to Cincinnati on September 23 and at Brooklyn on October 6, the last day of the regular season.

Shortly after the World Series, Davis was back for his second year at Harvard Law. In early 1915, he showed again where his "Iron" nickname came from by setting a university record in the intercollegiate strength test. In those days, college athletes competed in a series of push-ups, pull-ups, dips, and other exercises, doing as many as they could in half an hour. The goal was to measure speed and endurance as well as pure strength. On February 12, Davis surpassed football star Tack Hardwick's mark of 1,381 points, notching 1,437.6. Then on February 24, he leapfrogged his own record with a score of 1,593.8. It was all done for the entertainment of a few friends, according to Ring Lardner.

Although Stallings had hoped to have Davis in spring training, he permitted the pitcher to remain in Cambridge.[15] Returning to the Braves in June 1915, Davis started nine times in 15 appearances. Again he posted a 3-3 won-lost record, while his ERA was 3.80.

The same held true the next season, as Davis returned his contract unsigned in February 1916. It was "understood that he will be tendered a contract which will permit him finishing his course at the Harvard law school before resuming baseball activities."[16] In late August, the Braves sent George to the Providence Grays on loan. His two outings with the Grays were his only pro action all season. Boston recalled him and infielder Joe Mathes on September 7, but he did not get into a game.[17]

Davis signed with the Braves again in February 1917.[18] However, "he received his law degree at the age of 27 and simultaneously announced his retirement from professional baseball."[19] He then went into the Army, like his father, attaining the rank of captain in the infantry. George, who had taken fencing at Williams, specialized in teaching bayonet fighting.

Once World War I ended, Davis returned to Lancaster and joined his father's law firm. He later formed his own partnership. However, as Buffalo baseball historian Joseph Overfield wrote, "In the Davis scheme of things, the law always seemed to be of secondary importance. In 1929, with egregiously bad timing, he gave up law to join a brokerage firm." The stock-market crash wiped out the bulk of the family's wealth.[20]

Davis served as a councilman-at-large in Buffalo from 1927 to 1933. He ran for mayor of Buffalo in 1933, although he lost in the Republican primary. Having returned to the law, he specialized in real estate. Around this time the Davises' daughter Deborah died as a tot of 3 years old. She came down with a severe strep throat.

In addition to his law degree, Davis did graduate study in philosophy and comparative religion at the University of Buffalo. This spurred a new passion: astronomy. He amassed a library of some 1,500 books on the subject. He founded the Buffalo Astronomical Society in 1930 and later became honorary curator of astronomy at the Buffalo Museum of Science, where he taught classes for 30 years. Davis was an authority on astronomical history and especially on star names, contributing several articles to *Sky and Telescope* magazine.[21] Broad study of foreign languages aided him in this pursuit. "He fluently read and wrote Greek, Hebrew, Latin, and Arabic," Suzy Kissee said, "and he read Sanskrit. He learned these languages to help him in his passion." George picked up Arabic using two dictionaries and no tutor. He also owned volumes in Egyptian hieroglyphics, and his monographs showed familiarity with Chinese.

"Another fun fact about him," Suzy Kissee added, "is that he translated books from Latin to English for the library at Harvard when he attended there to help support himself. There is an old news clipping somewhere in the scrapbook that claims he worked on translations in the dugout during games and had to be told when it was his turn!"[22]

George's deep love of books was also visible in his work for libraries. In 1947, he became a trustee of the Erie County public library system. Seven years later he was instrumental in the merger of Buffalo's public libraries with the county's. He continued to serve on the board and strongly supported the development of the Central Library.

On May 10, 1952, Georgiana "Kiddo" Davis passed away suddenly. Suzy Kissee said, "I deeply believe that my grandfather never recovered from her death. I have a picture of them taken nine days before she died, in which they look like a couple of high school sweeties. She kept him laughing. She was known as a practical joker. My mom told the story of her melting down chocolate Ex-Lax and including it in cookies to serve to guests she thought were arrogant!"[23] George did get married again, to Grace Ogilvie, who shared his interest in astronomy.

Davis taking a cut.

Davis retired from his law firm on New Year's Day 1961. He was 70 years old. "In an interview with the *Buffalo Courier-Express*, he said he planned to concentrate on his magnum opus, a two-volume work on the origins and history of the constellations. 'I'll probably be working on it for the rest of my life,' he told the interviewer."[24] That work would remain incomplete, however—George Davis passed away on June 4, 1961.[25] His obituaries did not mention that he ended his own life by hanging himself.

Joseph Overfield offered insight into his friend's highly complex personality. Davis was "an intensely proud man, almost to the point of arrogance … an impatient man who did not suffer fools lightly …[yet] he often exhibited great patience with young lawyers who came under his wing, and it is told he delighted in playing mentor to neighborhood youngsters." Overfield said that George's only substantial asset was his library, and guessed that "he could not face a future of impecunity."[26]

Davis is buried in the family mausoleum at Lancaster Rural Cemetery, along with his parents, sister, wife Georgiana, and children Deborah and George, III.

One may speculate about what George Davis might have achieved in baseball had he placed the sport over academics. There were certainly many lofty predictions. It's a moot point, though, because Davis himself said, "Reading is my favorite sport…. There is nothing, not even baseball, that I like quite as well."[27] Yet even though his time in the majors was brief, he left a small but lasting mark. His Hall of Fame teammate on the Miracle Braves, Johnny Evers, said it well. "He is a fine fellow, a man who has little to say on the club and is generally popular among the players. I was glad to see him get the great reputation which goes to the pitcher of a no-hit game."[28]

Grateful acknowledgment to Suzan Davis Packer Kissee and Mary Tucci Damiani, granddaughters of George Davis, for their personal memories and for furnishing articles from their grandmother's scrapbook. Thanks also to Alan Brownsten.

Sources

Joseph Overfield's 1989 article for SABR provided some other facts on George Davis' life and career at Williams, in baseball, and afterward.

Background on the Davis family, George A. Davis, Sr., and his wife Lillie:

Derby, George, and James Terry White. *The National Cyclopedia of American Biography*. New York: James T. White & Company, 1906: 496.

Hull, John M. "George A. Davis." *Albany Law Journal*, January 7, 1899: 73.

Murlin, Edgar L. *New York Red Book*. Albany, New York: J.B. Lyon Company, 1910: 83.

Chester, Alden and E. Melvin Williams. *Courts and Lawyers of New York: A History, 1609-1925, Volume 1*. New York, NY: The American Historical Society, Inc., 1925:

Hills, Frederick Simon, editor. *New York State Men: Biographic Studies and Character Portraits, Volume 1*. Albany, New York: The Argus Company, 1910: 172.

Who's Who in New York City and State, Volume 9. New York: W.F. Brainard, 1911: 247.

According to *The Braves Encyclopedia*, George Davis, Sr. was also a judge, but neither his entry in the New York Red Book nor any other source confirms this. Confusion may have arisen either with his father-in-law or because Davis was chairman of the Senate Judiciary Committee.

www.findagrave.com

www.thedeadballera.com

Notes

1. Fullerton, Hugh S. "'No-Hit' Davis Is an Object Lesson to All Young Men and Boys." *Pittsburgh Press*, October 12, 1914: 17.
2. Unidentified, undated clipping from George Davis scrapbook.
3. Fullerton, op. cit.
4. "Yanks' New Pitcher." *The Day* (New London, CT), June 27, 1912: 10.
5. "Highlanders Sign Star Collegian." *Pittsburgh Press*, June 27, 1912: 20.
6. Lanigan, Ernest J. "Davis Failure in American League." *Pittsburgh Press*, September 12, 1914: 9.
7. "May Be Strong—But Did Not Show It When Pitching for the Highlanders." *Sporting Life*, December 21, 1912: 14.
8. "George Davis, the No-Hit Hero of the Braves." *Baseball Magazine*, February 1915: 30.
9. "Hard Work for Yankees." *New York Times*, March 7, 1913: 9.
10. "George Davis Makes Stallings Rejoice by Pitching No-Hit Game."
11. "George A. Davis, Jr." *Sporting Life*, September 19, 1914: 1. This article wrongly stated that George had played his college ball for archrival Amherst—prompting an objection from *The Williams Record* and an erratum in *Sporting Life*'s October 1 issue.
12. E-mail from Suzan Kissee to author, January 26, 2010.
13. "Manager Stallings Has Spitball Star." *Pittsburgh Press*, August 19, 1914: 21.
14. "Davis' No-Hit Twirling Keeps Braves in Lead." *The Day*, September 10, 1914: 11.
15. "Davis to Report Late." *The Pittsburgh Press*, January 31, 1915: 28.
16. "Diamond Dust." *The Day*, February 22, 1916: 12.
17. "Braves' Roster Increased." *Pittsburgh Press*, September 7, 1916: 24.
18. "Sherwood Magee Refuses to Sign." *The Day*, February 21, 1917: 11.
19. "G.A. Davis Jr. Dead; Attorney, Widely Known Astronomer." *Buffalo Evening News*, June 5, 1961.

20 Overfield, op. cit.

21 "George A. Davis, Jr. Dies." *Sky and Telescope*, July 1961: 9.

22 E-mail from Suzan Kissee to author, January 26, 2010.

23 E-mail from Suzan Kissee to author, January 26, 2010.

24 Overfield, op. cit.

25 "George A. Davis Jr. Dies." *New York Times*, June 5, 1961: 31; "G.A. Davis Jr. Dead; Attorney, Widely Known Astronomer"

26 Overfield, op. cit.

27 "George Davis, the No-Hit Hero of the Braves": 30.

28 Ibid.: 31.

Charlie Deal

by Charles F. Faber

Although he played in only 89 games for the Braves (10 in 1913 and 79 in 1914), infielder Charlie Deal played an important role in their 1914 World Series triumph. After a salary dispute, he jumped to the Federal League in 1915. It wasn't the first time Deal and the baseball establishment had clashed over money.

Charles Albert Deal was born in Wilkinsburg, Pennsylvania, part of the Pittsburgh metropolitan complex, on October 30, 1891. He was the fifth of six children of Alice Deal and Joseph Deal, a carpenter. He started playing baseball on the sandlots of Wilkinsburg. "That's where I learned almost all the baseball I know," he said in 1915 … Ever since I was able to throw bricks at a lamppost I have been playing ball."[1]

In 1910 the teenage Deal was working as a fitter for an electric company and playing baseball as a second baseman for semipro clubs in the area. The next season Howard Mitlinger of the Huntington club persuaded him to move to third base. While playing at the hot corner, Deal was spotted by a scout for the Philadelphia Phillies, who signed him for $200 a month. However, when he reported to Philadelphia, he was assigned to Lancaster of the Class B Tri-State League, where he was to receive only one-half the stipulated salary. Charlie protested and carried his case to the National Commission, baseball's governing body at the time, which ruled that any player who signed with a major-league club would be restored to free agent status if the club did not pay him the salary specified in the contract or assign him to a minor-league club with no reduction in salary.

His free agency regained, Charlie joined the Bay City club in the Southern Michigan League. After a month he was sold to the Jackson club of the same league, where he was paid $125 a month. The third sacker hit .370 in 68 games, and was purchased by the Detroit Tigers for a reported $2,500. Deal complained that the Tigers had promised him half of the purchase price, but delivered only $300 of the amount. Once again he thought club owners were treating him unfairly. It was not to be the last time he entertained that opinion.

Deal made his major-league debut with the Tigers on July 19, 1912, at the age of 20. The right-hander was listed as 6 feet tall and weighing 160 pounds. (As he matured, his frame filled out. By 1915, he said he weighed 172 pounds.) He was paid $200 a month by Detroit in 1912 and signed for $1,200 for the 1913 season. After one of his early big-league games, a sportswriter penned these lines: "Charlie Deal was the three star special on the infield. He had eight chances and most of them were tough, particularly a one-handed stab of Wagner's high bounder in the ninth. His throwing was a marvel of speed and accuracy, every ball going right into Onslow's pocket."[2] Despite his fielding exploits, Deal did not hit well enough to stick with the Tigers. On June 2, 1913, they released him to Providence of the International League. In 99 games with the Grays, he hit .312. On September 15 he was acquired by the Boston Braves in the post-season draft.

In 1914 Deal opened the season as the Braves' regular third baseman. However, he did not hit well and was demoted to the bench in favor of Red Smith, whom the Braves had acquired from the Brooklyn Robins on August 10. On the final day of the regular season, Smith broke his leg, and Charlie was pressed into service as the third sacker in the World Series against the Philadelphia Athletics. He got off to a tough start. In the first game, at Philadelphia, he hit into double plays three times in succession. (One of them was on a pop-fly bunt.) Fortunately for the Braves, they scored enough runs to win the game easily, 7-1, despite Deal's lack of productivity.

In the second game of the Series, Charlie did not produce through the first eight innings. Three times with runners on base, he hit into force outs. Eddie Plank, the future Hall of Fame hurler for the Mackmen, was holding the Braves scoreless. Bill James was doing the same against the Athletics for Boston. The game went into the ninth inning tied 0-0. In the top of the ninth, with one out, the weak-hitting Deal came to the plate. To everyone's surprise, he lined a drive over Amos Strunk's head. The center fielder had perhaps been playing too shallow, but the ball was well struck. It might have gone for a triple, but Strunk made a remarkable recovery and throw to hold Charlie to two bases. The next batter, James, fanned for the second out of the inning. The A's catcher, Wally Schang, tried to catch Deal off the base. Schang threw to second base, and Charlie took off for third, beating the relay by shortstop Jack Barry. From third, Deal scored on Les Mann's scratch hit off the glove of second baseman Eddie Collins. James set down Philadelphia in the bottom of the ninth, and the Braves were well on their way to a sweep of the defending world champions. During the Series, Charlie Deal made only two hits in 16 times at bat, but by his daring base running the Braves had scored a decisive tally.

In recalling the 1914 season, Deal said: "We were a misfit bunch. There were a lot of old-timers and kids mixed in, guys other clubs had given up on. [Manager George] Stallings did a wonderful job with us. He was a great manager who suffered with every play. One minute he'd be playing and the next minute cursing. How that man could curse!"

After leaving the Braves in a salary dispute, Charlie was asked about Stallings. "Do you figure Stallings was lucky, had excellent material, or is he really a miracle man?" a reporter queried.

"Yes, I guess you could call him a miracle man." Deal replied. "Why did I leave him? Because he answered my request for more money by reciting that ancient and honorable piece about a promising young man with a bright future, lots of time for more money and valuable experience and the balance of that bunkydoodle guff. I'm in it for business, and that's why I jumped, and that's why I never drink, smoke, or chew. I am married and love my home." [4]

For his part in winning the World Series, Charlie thought he deserved a $500 raise. The club refused to part with the additional money. Once again Deal thought he was being treated unfairly. He jumped to the St. Louis Terriers of the upstart Federal League, signing with the Feds on January 29, 1915. St. Louis gave him far more than the amount of the raise he had requested from the Braves. His salary went from $2,400 to $4,500, plus a $3,500 bonus.

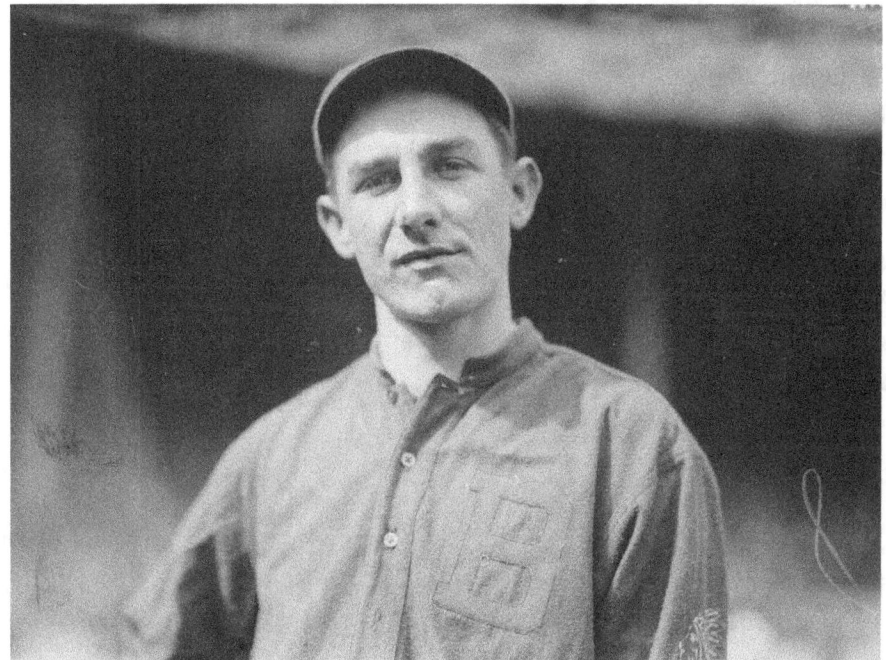

Charlie Deal

During the summer of 1915 Charlie was hospitalized for several weeks with typhoid fever. He was able to play only 65 games for the Terriers, but hit a very respectable .323, his best average ever in the major leagues.

When the Federal League folded, Deal joined the St. Louis Browns of the American League in the spring of 1916. Fully recovered from typhoid, Deal expected to give Jimmy Austin a battle to be the guardian of the hot corner. However, he was unable to hit well, and Austin secured the position. On June 2, the Browns sold Deal to the Chicago Cubs. He spent most of the 1916 season with the Kansas City Blues of the American Association, where he hit .317 in 118 games. In the spring of 1917, Deal beat out Herb Hunter and Rollie Zeider for the third-base position with the Cubs. For the next five seasons he played for the Cubs, emerging as one of the best-fielding third basemen in the league. In 1917 he led the NL in sacrifices. Although he usually hit only around .250, Deal established a reputation for being a hard man to strike out. In his entire big-league career he fanned only 121 times in 851 games. In 1918, he appeared in the World Series again, as the Cubs lost to the Boston Red Sox in six games. He did not repeat his heroics of the 1914 series and went only 3-for-17. After the Series, in response to Secretary of War Newton Baker's work-or-fight order, Deal worked at the Allegheny Steel Company plant in Brackenridge, Pennsylvania. He returned to the Cubs in 1919 for three more seasons. In May 1921 he was hit on the nose by a batted ball and missed several days.

Deal played his final major-league game on October 2, 1921, at the age of 29. In April 1922 he was sent to Los Angeles of the Pacific Coast League to complete a multiplayer deal made the previous December. He played for Los Angeles, Vernon, and Portland in the PCL from 1922 through 1925. In 1926 and 1927 Deal was with the New Orleans Pelicans in the Southern Association. Apparently, minor-league pitching was more to his liking than the major-league variety, for he hit better than .300 in six of his seven seasons in Class A and Double-A ball.

While at Providence in 1913, Deal married a Rhode Island woman named Mary. They had no children. The couple lived in his native Wilkinsburg until about 1920, when they moved to Pasadena, California. After his retirement from baseball, Deal's occupation was listed variously as salesman, realtor, collector, and storeroom keeper. He kept an interest in baseball into his old age. After the major leagues voted to expand to 12 teams each for 1969, Deal wrote to the National Baseball Hall of Fame: "I hope these changes being made are for the betterment of Base Ball, but I have some doubt. Too many clubs and not enough Big League Players. Cut the Pitchers box to 10" high and gloves to size we used in our day." [5]

Charles Albert Deal died in a rest home in Covina, California, on September 16, 1979, at the age of 87. He is interred at the Pasadena Mausoleum.

Sources

Charlie Deal player file at the National Baseball Hall of Fame.

www.ancestry.com

www.baseball-reference.com

www.newspaperarchive.com

Notes

1 *St. Louis Globe-Democrat,* March 20, 1915.

2 *Anaconda Standard,* August 25, 1912.

3 *The Sporting News,* October 6, 1979.

4 *St. Louis Globe-Democrat,* March 20, 1915.

5 Letter from Charles A. Deal to National Baseball Hall of Fame, August 26, 1968.

Josh Devore

By Peter M. Gordon

THE 1914 SEASON was the fourth in a row in which a team with Josh Devore in the outfield went to the World Series. The speedy Devore was a great leadoff man for the Giants championship teams of 1911 and 1912, and played with the pennant winners of 1913 before being traded. He joined the 1914 Braves just before they started their historic surge in July.

Devore had made one of the greatest catches in World Series history to save a game for the Giants in 1912, and as of 2013 still held the regular-season record for the most stolen bases in one inning.

Devore was born in Murray City, Ohio, on November 13, 1887 and was raised on the family farm in the town of New Marshfield, a few miles away. Devore played as much baseball as possible when not doing chores around the family farm and grocery store. Like many boys, he dreamed of a career in professional baseball even though his father actively discouraged it. Nothing his father did, including beatings, could stop Devore from playing ball, at first with local amateur teams, and then with semipro nines.

When Devore reached 17 he moved to Seelyville, Indiana, and clerked in his older brother William's grocery store while starring in the local semipro leagues. William saw an advertisement in a Terre Haute newspaper from a club in Meridian, Mississippi, seeking a left-handed-hitting outfielder. Devore hit left, threw right, and had already reached his full adult size, 5-feet-6 and 160 pounds. Guy Sample, the Meridian manager, thought Devore was too small, but agreed to give him a chance after William put up a $100 cash guarantee that his brother would make good.

Devore later told a reporter that even William's cash investment didn't mean making the Meridian team a sure thing. "It seemed like every aspiring outfielder within two hundred miles of Meridian had hot footed it into town," Devore said.[1] After two weeks of tryouts, Josh made the final three, but he wasn't sure until the season started that he had won the job. Two weeks after that, William got his money back. Josh's swiftness on the bases and in the field earned him the nickname the Seelyville Speed Demon.

Devore hit .242 during his first professional season, and proved the accuracy of his nickname by stealing 33 bases. His 1907 season was a carbon copy of the first, with Devore hitting .241 but stealing 35 bases. The *New York Globe* reported in 1910 that Devore's fence-busting power in the minors brought him to the attention of a scout for the New York Giants.[2] The reporter wrote that the carpenters union in Meridian was very sad about Devore's leaving, since they would lose the extra money they made from repairing the outfield fence. The pleas of the union notwithstanding, the Giants purchased Devore for $750.

There was some dispute about the Giants' obligations to the Meridian Club. The Hall of Fame's files contain letters from Allan Canto, the Meridian club president, to the National Commission complaining that the Giants hadn't fulfilled the terms of the purchase agreement, and Meridian wanted Devore back.

This is just the first of many contradictions in Devore's record that makes it difficult to paint a comprehensive picture of him as a man and a ballplayer. Almost every trait attributed to him is contradicted by another account. For example, reporters talk about Devore's power in the minors, yet he had very little power in the majors. One wonders if Devore's mercurial nature was caused by his drinking. In his *Historical Baseball Abstract* Bill James lists Devore as one of the well-known "drinking men" in baseball during the 1910s. It's possible that these contradictions could be caused by the difference between Devore drunk and sober.

In this case the Giants believed they had purchased Devore, but Meridian disagreed. The dispute ended with Devore the property of the Giants. The Giants' John McGraw sent Devore to the Newark Indians of the Eastern League for most of the 1908 season, and he hit .290, a good average for the era. He led the league with 91 runs scored and stole 48 bases.

Devore's manager at Newark was George Stallings, who would soon move up to manage the Highlanders in New York and later traded for Devore when he was managing the Miracle Braves. The Newark team featured some players besides Devore who would play in the majors like Clyde Engel, Oscar Stanage, and Bud Sharpe, but still finished fifth in the Eastern League.

The Giants called Devore up at the end of the season and paid him $175 per month. Devore got into five games for the Giants in 1908. He batted only .167, and in his first game was sent in to pinch-run and was picked off first. He did score his first major-league run, and garnered his first hit and stolen base. Having proved he could play in the majors, even if he had a lot to learn, Devore was probably looking forward to playing a full season in 1909.

While training with the Giants in the spring of 1909, Devore developed appendicitis and was rushed to the hospital. Although newspaper reports said Devore was recovering well, he played in only 22 games that year and hit .143 with three stolen bases. In addition to his health problems, Devore had a foot problem—it ended up "in the bucket" too many times, especially against good southpaws like Slim Sallee. Devore's front foot would step "in the bucket" rather than straight at the pitcher. In those days before batting helmets, Devore was concerned about getting hit.

As reported by Christy Mathewson, manager McGraw decided Devore needed a special intervention to keep him from shying away from the pitch. One day, after Devore struck out twice against Sallee, McGraw said, "That fellow hasn't got speed enough to bend a pane of glass at home plate. … Go up there next time and get hit and see if he can hurt you. If you don't get hit you're fined $10."

Josh responded to the $10 disincentive by getting hit. He trotted to first base smiling. "What'd I say?" asked McGraw from the coaching box. "Could he hurt you?"

"Say," Josh said, "I'd hire out to let them pitch baseballs at me if none of them could throw harder than that guy."[3] Devore batted with much more confidence after that, so much so that McGraw began playing him against both righties and lefties.

A healthy, speedy Devore returned to the Giants for the 1910 season. He played regularly in the outfield, hitting a career-high .304, with 10 triples, 2 home runs, and 43 stolen bases, fifth in the NL McGraw planned to split the position between Devore and Beals Becker, but Devore played well enough to take the majority of playing time. Devore became the leadoff hitter and main table-setter for the team, which finished second to the Chicago Cubs in 1910 but was about to win three straight pennants. Manager McGraw loved to use the running game during this part of the Deadball Era. Devore was one of several speedsters on the team.

Josh Devore

In his classic *Pitching in a Pinch*, Christy Mathewson wrote about the impact of Devore and the other Giants runners, Fred Snodgrass, Red Murray, Fred Merkle, and Larry Doyle. He said, "Once they get on the bases they were like loose mercury. They couldn't be caught. McGraw stole his way to a pennant with this quintet of runners."[4]

Mathewson writes in more detail about basestealing technique. "If Devore sees Huggins of St. Louis behind the base he slides in front and pulls his body away from the bag so that he leaves the smallest possible area to touch. If he observes the baseman cutting inside to block him off, he goes behind and hooks it with just one toe, again presenting the minimum touching surface."[5] While we can't credit Devore with the invention of the hook slide, because Mathewson thought this technique was worth mentioning, we may be able to credit Devore as one of its earliest and most successful practitioners.

In 1911 Devore, although by some accounts the smallest man in the National League, made a big contribution to the Giants' pennant win. He led off most games, hit .280, scored 96 runs, and led this team of speed demons with 61 steals. The Giants won the pennant by 7 1/2 games over the second-place Cubs. Writing after the 1911 season, Mathewson gave Devore great credit for his success in pressure situations. "Josh Devore is an in-and-out batter, but he is a bulldog in a pinch and is more apt to make a hit in a tight place than when the bases are empty," Mathewson said. "He is the type of ball player who cannot be rattled."[6]

Devore's reported love of gambling may have helped him develop his coolness under pressure. He liked to gamble on the basepaths and in the field, and apparently off the field as well. Several sources said Devore was so fond of gambling that he would have no money left at the end of the season. Yet during his major-league career it was also reported that Devore spent his offseasons in Terre Haute, Indiana, where he owned a boxing club. If he had no money at the end of each season, how did he have money left to buy a business?

Devore may have been cool in the clutch, but off the field he appeared to some to be an overly trusting soul. On the train to the 1911 World Series he was very excited to meet Ty Cobb and talk hitting with him. "Gee," Devore said to one of his teammates when they got off the train, "that fellow Cobb knows a lot about hitting. He told me some things about the American League pitchers just now and he didn't know he was doing it."[7] Cobb gave him a lot of details about Eddie Plank, who was scheduled to start the first game.

Cobb may have targeted Devore because, as is quoted in the book *Busting 'Em and Other Big League Stories*, Cobb said, "Devore was a good money player, able to rise to the occasion." In the event, Plank started the second game, not the first. Based on Cobb's inside information, Devore went confidently to bat four times against Plank and four times struck out. Cobb liked Plank, and deliberately misled Devore. Devore hit only .167 as the Giants lost the Series in six games to Connie Mack's Philadelphia A's. He also went 0-for-3 in stolen-base attempts and struck out eight times. Although disappointing, Devore's Series average was still higher than those of fellow speed merchants Snodgrass, Merkle, and Murray.

The Giants repeated as NL champions in 1912. Devore played both left field and right field, batted 327 times in 106 games, and hit .275 with 66 runs scored and 27 stolen bases. On June 20 he stole four bases in one inning. The Giants defeated the Braves 21-12, and during a long rally in the ninth, Devore singled twice and stole second and third each time. This is still reported as fact by several sources, although it was also disputed by some researchers 50 years after it occurred.

What is certain is that Devore remained a key member of this Giants club that won its second consecutive pennant and this time played a strong Boston Red Sox team. Sportswriters called the 1912 Series a classic as soon as it ended, and it still featured on many lists of the greatest World Series of all time.

Devore led off and scored the first run of the series in the third inning of Game One. He singled, went to third on a single by Doyle, and both of them scored on a single by Red Murray. That put the Giants up 2-0 against Smoky Joe Wood, but the New Yorkers couldn't hold on and lost the game, 4-3. The Series moved to Fenway Park for Game Two, which ended in a tie, called on account of darkness. Devore didn't play in Game Two.

Devore saved Game Three in Fenway for the Giants with what is considered one of the greatest catches in World Series history. Rube Marquard, who had set a record for the most consecutive games won in a season earlier that year, was pitching for the Giants and took a 2-0 lead into the bottom of the ninth. Marquard got Tris Speaker to pop for the first out. Duffy Lewis followed with a grounder in the hole to first baseman Merkle, who flipped to Marquard, covering. Marquard, his attention on the throw, felt for first with his foot but couldn't find it and Lewis was safe with a hit. Gardner doubled Lewis in. Boston manager Jake Stahl, up next, grounded back to the pitcher who got Gardner at third, leaving a runner on first and two down. Stahl pinch-ran for himself with Olaf Henriksen. Merkle booted a grounder by the next batter, Heinie Wagner, which put runners on first and third. More than 34,000 "cranks" in Fenway were screaming as Wagner stole second, putting runners on second and third with two out.

Boston catcher Hick Cady came to the plate and hit a hard liner to deep right. With two outs, Wagner and Henriksen took off at the crack of the bat with the tying and winning runs. Devore started running toward the ball with his back to the plate but he appeared to many observers to have no chance. The Red Sox were already celebrating their win when Devore caught up to the ball. He just barely got his glove on it, tipped the ball in the air, and caught it with his bare hand for the final out. Tris Speaker, writing a column in the *Boston Globe* after Game Three, said, "The catch was as good as any I ever saw."[8] This spectacular play saved the victory and tied the Series.

Devore led off seven of the eight games. His .250 batting average was fifth highest on the team, and his .419 on-base percentage tied Chief Myers for the lead among position players. He led the team in steals with four. During the (infamous for Giant fans) Eighth Game, which the Giants lost in the bottom of the tenth due to errors of commission and omission, Devore went 1-for-3, with two walks, scored the first run, and caught several balls in the outfield. He didn't make any of the key mistakes that lost the game in the bottom of the tenth inning.

Devore started slowly in 1913, hitting .190 in his first 16 games. McGraw had another young outfielder, George Burns, whom he preferred to play. On May 22 McGraw sent Devore, third baseman Heinie Groh, pitcher Red Ames, and $20,000 to the Reds for pitcher Art Fromme. The Giants won their third straight pennant, and Devore hit a respectable .267 with 17 stolen bases for the Reds until August 22, when the Reds sold him to the Phillies. Devore hit .282 in 22 games for the Phils.

Devore had a productive 1913 despite his travels, and started well for the Phils in part-time duty in 1914, hitting .302 in 30 games. Braves manager George Stallings, looking for a speedy left-handed-hitting outfielder to platoon in his current lineup, traded infielder Jack Martin to the Phils for his former Newark Eagles star on July 3. The Braves, in last place at the time, stunned the baseball world by moving from the basement to first before the end of the season.

The acquisition of Devore allowed Stallings to platoon at all outfield positions. Devore hit only .227 during the Miracle Braves' stretch run, but walked enough for a .327 on-base average in his 51 games. Although Devore was known as a good fielder with the Giants, it was said that manager Stallings would turn his back when the ball was hit to him, as if he couldn't stand watching. That led some to think Stallings had no confidence in Devore's fielding, but the real reason was Stallings' superstitious nature. Stallings had turned his back the first time Devore caught a ball, and he kept doing it for the rest of the season as the Braves surged to the pennant.

The pennant chase didn't keep Devore from enjoying himself when the opportunity presented. In *Run, Rabbit, Run*, Rabbit Maranville tells a story about going to a party at a rich man's house in Pittsburgh with Devore and teammates Hank Gowdy, Bill James, Boss Schmidt, and some others. The host offered his guests bourbon, wine, beer, and other liquors. Rabbit and Schmidt tried to stick to beer but succumbed to temptation, while Devore and Gowdy drank nothing but scotch with champagne chasers. The next day, Rabbit and Schmidt were very hung over, but Devore and Gowdy appeared in great shape. They attributed their good health to the combination of scotch and champagne, for which they must have developed quite a tolerance. Maranville, even hung over, hit the home run that won the game.[9]

Devore only got one at-bat during the Braves' upset victory over the A's in the World Series. He struck out, in what was to be his last major-league appearance. The Braves released Devore before the next season.

With the Federal League still active as a third major league, a player with Devore's speed and record with winning teams would have had a good chance to find a major-league job. Instead of trying out for more teams, Devore bought stock in a minor-league team in Chillicothe, Ohio, near his hometown, and became player-manager for the 1915 season. This decision looks very curious from today's perspective, but the difference between the majors and minors wasn't as sharp in 1915 as it is now. A successful minor-league team could make money and pay salaries to some players comparable to those on major-league teams. After playing for four major-league teams in two years, Devore may have wanted the security of knowing he'd stay with the same team for a year. If so, that wasn't how things worked out, since the Chillicothe Babes franchise fell apart in 1915 and Devore ended up playing for other minor-league teams that year and for many years afterward.

Devore's ability to buy into the Chillicothe franchise is another fact that makes one wonder how much he actually gambled during the season. If he gambled away his salary every season, he couldn't have saved enough money to invest in the club. Devore may have been smarter about his wagers than his teammates gave him credit for. All the sources do agree that Devore was an easygoing young man who played hard, made friends easily, enjoyed himself off the field, and made the most out of his speed and baseball ability.

Devore hit .306 his first year back in the minors. He would call Chillicothe home for the rest of his life. In 1916 Phillies manager Pat Moran brought Devore to spring training but he couldn't win a job with the reigning NL champions. Moran sold Devore to Milwaukee in the American Association. Devore hit .244 in 46 games for Milwaukee, and went to Topeka in the Western League, where he hit .301 and stole 19 bases. He moved with the franchise to Joplin in 1917 and hit .280 with 20 stolen bases. Devore played another nine years in the minors, with some time out for military service during World War I.

Devore enlisted in the Army in 1918 and didn't play in Organized Baseball. He jumped back into the American Association in 1919, hitting .310 for Indianapolis, and in 1920 started the first of five consecutive years with Grand Rapids, Michigan. Devore hit for good averages and stole bases even as he approached his late 30s. He hit .344 and .355 in 1920 and '21 while managing the team. In 1924, his last year in Grand Rapids, he hit .278 at the age of 36. In 1925 Devore returned to Chillicothe, where he managed restaurants and lunchrooms and worked as a grocer, the same job he had when he started his baseball career. He lived in Chillicothe for the rest of his life.

Devore and his wife, Catherine, had one daughter, Patricia, who became a national swimming champion. Patricia married William Harkness, who was Yale's lacrosse coach and later athletic director in the 1950s. Devore died in Chillicothe on October 6, 1954, a month before his 67th birthday. He is buried in the New Marshfield Cemetery. His obituary was on the front page of the *Chillicothe Gazette*, which called Devore the greatest ballplayer in the town's history.

Sources

Arnoff, Jason, and Dave Anderson, *Going, Going, Caught: Baseball's Great Outfield Catches* (Jefferson, North Carolina: McFarland & Co., 2009).

Caruso, Gary, *The Braves Encyclopedia* (Philadelphia: Temple University Press, 1995).

Cobb, Ty, *Busting 'Em and Other Big League Stories* (New York: EJ Clode 1914).

Gay, Timothy M., *Tris Speaker: The Rough & Tumble Life of a Baseball Legend* (Lincoln: University of Nebraska Press, 2005).

Honig, Donald, *Baseball America* (New York: Simon and Schuster, 1985).

Hynd, Noel, *The Giants of the Polo Grounds* (New York: Doubleday, 1988).

Maranville, Rabbit, *Run, Rabbit, Run: The Hilarious and Mostly True Tales of Rabbit Maranville* (Phoenix: SABR, 2012).

Mathewson, Christy, *Pitching in a Pinch* (Lincoln: University of Nebraska Press Edition of 1912 book, 1994).

Spalding's official baseball guide, 1910, 1911, 1912, 1913, 1914, 1915.

Vaccaro, Mike, *The First Fall Classic: The Red Sox, the Giants and the Cast of Players, Pugs and Politicos Who Re-Invented the World Series in 1912* (New York: Anchor Books, 2010).

Baseball Magazine

Chillicothe (Ohio) *Gazette*

Rock Hill (South Carolina) *Herald*

Terre Haute (Indiana) *Tribune*

Baseball Hall of Fame Archives, Josh Devore file. Contains several newspaper clippings from various newspapers. The names of the papers are not listed in the file.

Baseball-reference.com

Notes

1. Unattributed article from Devore's Hall of Fame player file; byline, Purves T. Knox.
2. *New York Globe*, October 22, 1910.
3. Christy Mathewson, *Pitching in a Pinch*, 44.
4. Ibid., 256-257.
5. Ibid., 266.
6. Ibid., 69.
7. Donald Honig, *Baseball America*, 68
8. Jason Arnoff and Dave Anderson, *Going, Going, Caught*, 71.
9. Rabbit Maranville, *Run, Rabbit, Run*, 21.

Oscar Dugey

By Charlie Weatherby

Oscar Dugey, a utility player, was called "the luckiest kid in baseball" after playing on two straight pennant winners, in 1914 and 1915. One of the best infielders to come out of the Texas League in the 20th century's first two decades, the 5-foot 8, 160-pound right-hander hit just .194 in 195 games during his six years with the Boston Braves and Philadelphia Phillies. Used primarily as a pinch-hitter and pinch-runner, Dugey played in only 82 games as an infielder/outfielder. *Baseball Magazine* called him a "brainy man.... [who is] only a fair fielder, a weak hitter and has a none-too-strong arm." He was at his best on the basepaths, where *Baseball Magazine's* William Phelon described him as one "who can run like the devil on a wheel." *Sporting Life* said that Dugey "comes up with sensational work when sensational work is needed. [He] can take the hundred to one shots and get away with them. His reckless base running would be the ruin of any other player. ... Jake takes the long chances and wins."

Brainy, quick-witted, and shrewd, Jake Dugey made his mark in the dugout, first as an aide to George Stallings on the 1914 "Miracle Braves," then with Pat Moran's Phillies, and later as a coach with Bill Killefer's Chicago Cubs. The *Boston Herald* said, "Oscar knows baseball as played in the National League as even Pat Moran or John McGraw. You can say no more." The *Wilkes-Barre Times* said Dugey "knows more baseball than lots of veterans nearly twice his age." Renowned as a bench jockey, Dugey was also "one of the craftiest interpreters of signals in either major league," according to the *Fort Worth Star-Telegram*.

The third of six children born to Oscar J. and Mattie Belle (Greene) Dugey, Oscar Joseph Dugey was born on October 25, 1887, in the East Texas town of Palestine. His father was born and raised on a Patterson, Louisiana, sugar plantation owned by his mother and grandfather. He married Mattie, a native of Louisville, Kentucky, in Palestine in July 1879. She was said to be a descendant of Virginia's Robert E. Lee family. A year later he was working as a grocery clerk; by the turn of the century, the elder Dugey, known as O.J., was one of Anderson County's most prominent citizens.

In December 1907, the *Palestine Daily Herald* called O.J. "perhaps the oldest Palestine merchant"; he was the proprietor of the Original Sample Store, a dry goods establishment on Main Street. He was also one of the founders of the Palestine Salt and Coal Company and a powerful member of the Democratic Party in Texas. During the gubernatorial campaign of 1906, O.J. stumped for Thomas M. Campbell, leading the *Daily Herald* to dub Dugey "the most demonstrative Campbell man in Texas." When the governor-elect offered him an appointment in his new administration, O.J. turned it down, saying that he had supported Campbell "from principle and not for office." He continued to be active in local affairs, among others petitioning for new public roads and canvassing businessmen for donations for a new ballpark. Unfortunately, O.J.'s business affairs went awry, causing him to file for bankruptcy shortly before Christmas 1907. A few days later, on January 6, 1908, he died suddenly at his home.

Mattie Dugey didn't live in her husband's shadow and outlived him by nearly 48 years. According to the *Palestine Daily Herald*, she was "a brilliant [play] writer"; her obituary in the *Dallas Morning News* noted that "several of them [are] on file at the Library of Congress in Washington, D.C." In 1906, she traveled to Dallas to try to sell a play entitled *Louisiana Before the War*. Mrs. Dugey moved to Dallas in 1912, a few years after O.J.'s death and after selling the family home at 1211 S. Sycamore. The *Daily Herald* called it "one of the prettiest homes in Palestine." The *Morning News* featured a photo of her in 1924 when there was a reading of *Maelstrom*, a work that "received much favorable attention."

Oscar Dugey learned baseball from his brother Elmo, who was four years older. Elmo was labeled by the *Fort Worth Star-Telegram* as "almost as good as his brother [Oscar]" in 1912 and was reported to have "received a number of very flattering offers to go into the professional ranks, [but] has refused to consider them, and plays only for the sport and the game." Like his brother Oscar, Elmo was a second baseman. He managed the Washer Brothers team in the Fort Worth Commercial League and hit .356 in 1911.

According to the *Palestine Daily Herald*, "(Oscar) Dugey got his preliminary training in the baseball world in this city when he was a member of the Palestine champion team of a few years ago." This might be a reference to the 1905 team, which the paper referred to as "all-professional, with the exception of little Dugey on second, who is as good as any of them." An account of a 1-1 ten-inning tie with Tyler said, "Dugey at second made two fine stops." In 1906, Dugey played second base for the semiprofessional Groesbeck team (31-9) of the Southwest Texas League, earning $30 a month. It was about this time that he acquired the nickname Stump. Dugey split his time in 1907 between the Tulia North Texas League semipro club (earning $50 a month) and the Palestine Elks. After a 1-0 Palestine win over Tyler in July, the *Daily Herald* said, "Broyles, Dugey, Hearne and Bowdon make a fast infield, and very few balls get by this quartette." The *Fort Worth Star-Telegram* mentioned that Oscar was a student at Brantley-Draughon Business College in Fort Worth, probably in 1908, where he played with the student team, soon becoming a star in the local city league.

Oscar broke into Organized Baseball in July 1908 with the Waco Navigators of the Texas League. He played third base in a 3-1 win over San Antonio on July 10, batting 0-for-3. The *Star-Telegram* said "Dugey … played brilliantly at third base" while taking the place of player-manager Bill Yohe, who was sidelined with malaria. One of his best games was three days later, a 2-for-4 performance with a double and a run in a 4-0 victory over San Antonio. Dugey, now called "Kid" by Texas newspapers, didn't continue his brilliant play over the rest of his 27 games, hitting .164 and fielding an unimpressive .880, posting ten errors and finishing 17th of 23 third basemen in the league.

Back with Waco in 1909 for his second of six seasons, Kid Dugey got his first taste of major-league competition in an exhibition game against New York on March 7. The Giants prevailed, 7-1, but Dugey scored the Navigators' only run after hitting a triple in the third inning. The *Daily Herald* said Dugey "was the star attraction of the game, and was given an ovation by the Waco fans and made the Giants take notice of his work."

Meanwhile, other papers were noticing Dugey's work. In late April, the *Galveston Daily News* called him "a gabby but good natured piece of baggage—not excess, either, for he is one of [manager Ben] Shelton's best men." After a 12-5 shellacking of Dallas on May 31, the *Morning News* said, "This Kid Dugey seems to be some 'pumpkins' with the stick. He got hits three trips out of four yesterday and most of his wallops came when men were on the sacks." By the end of the season, Dugey, who had moved from third base to second, had shown marked improvement from his first year, hitting .250 for the last-place Navigators (51-91). His fielding was only marginally better, with an .895 percentage and 51 errors in 106 games, tied for last among the 15 second basemen in the league.

Dugey had to deal with health issues early in 1910, missing part of spring training with the measles and enduring an early May spike wound so serious that a doctor from the grandstand insisted that only a quick transport to the hospital via automobile, not a trolley or horse and buggy, would do. Once he was back in the lineup, Kid hit his stride and was being carefully watched by major-league clubs. In early July, the *Beaumont Enterprise and Journal* noted that "Dugey is playing excellent ball for Waco. It looks as if he is due to be called to a faster team. He is wasting his talents there." His defense was improved, as evidenced by his play in a 6-1 win over Houston on July 16. According to the *Morning News*, "A feature was the playing of Dugey at second, fifteen chances without an error." A week later, in a 7-6 loss to Oklahoma City, Dugey's offensive talents were on display as he went 3-for-3 and stole home.

By early August, last-place Waco was disposing of as many players as possible. Deals for Dugey were at the forefront, and it was reported the he was on his way to either the Chicago White Sox or the Cleveland Naps. Wilson Matthews, a former minor-league manager and then Texas League umpire, told the *Oklahoma City Daily Oklahoman*, "Dugey is the best second baseman in the Texas League. …. He has been hitting well and has been playing grand ball with a tail-end club. … I believe that he has one of the brightest futures of any infielder in the circuit today. Youth, speed, a good batting eye, are all points in his favor." In mid-August, the *Dallas Morning News* announced its Texas League All-Star team, with Dugey as the second baseman. Oscar had hit .237 in 114 games, but the *Star-Telegram* said "[he] is hitting at a .300 clip now and has been steadily improving for a month. … He is in the upper class of base runners."

A deal to send Kid Dugey to the majors never materialized. Instead, he was purchased on August 22 by manager Charley Frank of the Southern Association's first-place New Orleans Pelicans. Early reports said Dugey was setting the Southern Association afire with his hitting. He was 1-for-3 with a run in his debut, a 6-1 win over Nashville on August 28. Three days later, the *Star-Telegram* reported that "New Orleans is so pleased with Dugey that Charley Frank is now after [Waco's] Jack Onslow and Harry Storch."

New Orleans eventually cooled on Dugey as his overall game was not up to Southern Association speed; he was hitless in over half his games, and his wild throw to the plate allowed two runs to score in the first inning of a 4-0 loss to Chattanooga on September 10. When the season ended, the Pelicans (87-53) won the pennant and Kid had hit .138 in 19 games. On December 28, 1910, the Pelicans sent him back to Waco.

Appointed captain of the 1911 Navigators by manager Ellis Hardy, Dugey, now known also as Jake, had a difficult early season. On April 20, he protested an Oklahoma City runner scoring on an overthrow of first base and was ejected and fined. The next day, in a 4-3 loss, he severely broke his ankle sliding into third base and didn't return to action until May 30. Three days later, Dugey's two-run homer in the eighth inning was the winning blow in a 3-1 victory over Dallas. Shortly thereafter, the *Fort Worth Star-Telegram* was reporting that major-league scouts were hovering around Waco watching the work of Dugey and two others. On July 20, the *Star-Telegram* selected him as the second baseman for its midseason All-Star team. Final averages showed that Kid's batting average had slipped to .219 in 110 games for fifth-place Waco. His fielding continued to improve, though, as he recorded a .960 percentage, placing him in the upper echelon of Texas League second basemen.

In mid-November 1911, the *Star-Telegram* reported that "Vic Miller … and Oscar Dugey, the clever little second sacker of the Navigators, have formed a partnership in a pool hall business down in Waco. Rumor has it that the pair are doing a grand business."

On March 17, 1912, Dugey served notice that he was ready for major competition with a 4-for-6 exhibition-game performance against the Chicago White Sox. According to the *Star-Telegram*, "Dugey's hitting was

Dugey with the 1915 Phillies

the feature." His daring and speed on the basepaths was on exhibit on April 14 as he stole three bases in a 6-5 win over Dallas. Two weeks later, he singled in the third and then stole second, third, and home for the Navigators' first run in a 4-1 victory over Austin.

Kid's fielding and hitting had also improved. After a doubleheader split with Dallas on July 4, the *Morning News* reported that "Dugey beat down several fast drives that were labeled hits." After a 3-1 win over Houston on July 22, the *Morning News* said, "Dugey's fielding was sensational." He was equally adept with the bat in July; in a doubleheader split with Galveston on the 18th, Kid was a combined 5-for-9 with five runs, a triple, and a home run. He was 2-for-3 with a run in a 3-0 win over Austin on the 29th. According to the *Morning News*, "The feature of the game was a three-base hit by Dugey, which was but little above the ground the entire distance."

Waco's third-place finish (82-63) was the best of Dugey's tenure with the Navigators. His average improved to .250 in 145 games and he led the league in stolen bases with 54; he was fifth in runs with 85. On defense, he led the league in total chances at second base with 831 and posted a .951 percentage.

In 1913, Dugey's stunning season paved the way for his rise to the majors. In 137 games at leadoff, he hit a personal best .279 (11th in the league), scored 85 runs (second), and stole a league-record 71 bases; his .955 fielding percentage was second among second basemen. Perhaps his finest game was on May 30 in a 3-2 win in 15 innings over Fort Worth. Dugey scored all of Waco's runs, was 5-for-7 with two doubles at the plate, and stole two bases. Another stellar outing came on June 22 in a 5-0 victory against Houston; Dugey was 3-for-4 with a double, three runs scored and four stolen bases. *Sporting Life* said, "Dugey led the attack. ... [his] sensational baserunning was the feature." Other examples were abundant. He had at least three hits in ten other games, invariably coupled with scoring one or more runs, while stroking an extra-base hit and adding a stolen base or two. Sometimes it was just contributing a key blow; on June 2, his home run to deep left in the sixth was all Waco needed in a 2-0 win over Fort Worth.

The first indication that Jake was about to move up to the majors came in mid-June when *Sporting Life* reported that umpire Wilson Matthews had offered the Waco Base Ball Association $2,000 for Dugey, an offer that was neither accepted nor declined. The paper said, "It is rumored that Matthews wants Dugey for the Philadelphia Americans." The answer came on August 13 when Waco sold him to the National League's Boston Braves for $2,000, to be effective at the end of the Texas League season.

In reviewing Dugey's game after the sale, *Sporting Life* said, "Dugey has been the leader of the Waco attack since he first became a member of the squad ... [and] hitting close to a .400 clip for the past few games. No Waco player has ever achieved a greater popularity than 'Stumpy.' [H]e has earned this place. ... His defensive work is on a line with his attack. A large number of the most thrilling catches of Texas League games have been executed by [Dugey]."

Dugey made his major league debut in the first game of a doubleheader in Cincinnati on September 13. Reds manager Joe Tinker and Boston shortstop Rabbit Maranville had a first-inning fistfight and were escorted off the field for the day by the umpires; Dugey took Maranville's place and was 2-for-5 with a run against Reds pitcher Red Ames. Cincinnati won the game 5-4 in 11 innings. Dugey also played third base in the darkness-shortened second game, a 1-0 (5 innings) Boston win, and was hitless in two at-bats. He had ten chances in the field in the two contests and recorded two errors. Two days later, the *Boston Globe* said, "Dugey .... made a good impression." He made three other appearances for the 1913 Braves, two as a pinch-hitter, drawing a walk and striking out. His average for five games was .250.

In December 1913, the *Morning News* reported that Jake Dugey had visited relatives in Dallas and was on his way to Shreveport to visit his sister. A few days later, the *Portland Oregonian* said that Dugey would be spending the winter in Los Angeles, one of 16 major-league players who would vacation in the area.

In February 1914, the *Boston Globe* labeled Dugey "an infielder of considerable promise," but his real on-the-field value was as a substitute for newly-acquired Johnny Evers at second; otherwise, he was a utility outfielder/pinch-hitter/pinch-runner. Given the opportunity, he was capable of making a contribution; Braves manager George Stallings inserted him as a pinch-hitter in the sixth inning of a scoreless game in Pittsburgh on May 12 and Jake came through with an RBI single. The game ended in a 1-1 tie after ten innings because of rain. On July 13 Dugey's two-run homer in the top of the 12th inning, his only four-bagger in the majors, was the winning margin in an 8-7 win in St. Louis. *Sporting Life* called the home run "lucky," saying, "[it] ordinarily would have been a good double, but Dolan fielded it poorly and it rolled to the fence." Another key hit came on September 11 against Philadelphia. With the Braves trailing by a run going into the ninth, manager Stallings sent Dugey to the plate as a pinch-hitter. He singled, moved to second on a wild pitch, advanced to third on Possum Whitted's single, and scored the tying run on Maranville's sacrifice fly. Whitted scored the winning run in the 6-5 victory. The win enabled Boston to stay 2 1/2 games ahead of New York. Dugey hit .193 in 58 games and only twice had more than one hit in a game.

In early August, *Sporting Life* reported that Dugey and Rabbit Maranville had met on July 22, during a Braves series in Pittsburgh, with officials of the Pittsburgh Federal League club, which wanted both to sign contracts and immediately jump to their team. The paper said, "The two players were willing to sign with the Pittsburgh Federal Club for next year, but positively refused to jump at this time."

Jake Dugey's off-the-field work was his biggest contribution to the worst-to-first rise of the Miracle Braves of 1914. According to author David Cataneo, "Stallings obsessively kept the dugout free of pigeons, peanut shells, gum wrappers, and bits of paper. Opposing players threw peanuts to attract pigeons. [Stallings] assigned infielder Oscar Dugey to shoo away the birds, and Dugey claimed his career was shortened by a sore arm caused by heaving pebbles at pigeons." He was also Stallings' "jinx-killer." Dugey once told the *Star-Telegram* that Stallings hated to have strangers staring into the Braves dugout. One of Dugey's duties was to stretch out a tarpaulin to cut off the intruders' view. One stranger got so close that Stallings ordered Jake to "bust his nose, douse him with water, do anything you want, but get him away before he hoodoos us!" Dugey rushed away to get a bucket but returned to find that the stranger had taken the hint and left before Dugey came back.

Dugey didn't play in the 1914 World Series against the Philadelphia Athletics. As the *Saturday Evening Post* told it, "the defeat of the Athletics … in four straight World Series games was accomplished largely by the Boston [bench] jockeys. … Stallings hired three utility infielders, Dugey, Billy Martin, and Eddie Fitzgerald, whose chief value to the team was rattling the smug Athletics. Dugey, who had a dead arm and was never a good hitter, kept a little black book on the temperamental weaknesses of every player." He told the *Dallas Morning News* in 1950, "[We] dug up more dirt on those players than anybody dreamed existed."

Another of Dugey's specialties was flashing and stealing signs. According to Dugey, "The A's were so cocky they didn't even bother to scout us Braves. Chief Bender figured they were about the best sign-stealers in the business. We gave him plenty to work on. The Braves had three or four completely different sets of signals. We'd use one set about two or three innings and then switch. The Athletics nearly went crazy trying to get those signals down. Two or three players were picked off at second when they got too busy watching for signals instead of our pitchers."

After the sweep, it was a busy winter for Jake and the rest of the Braves. Some of the players remained in New England for the fall and played basketball. *Sporting Life* said that "Evers is … a star at the cage game, and Maranville … is also a wonder at this sport. Dugey is reported to be the best basket ball player in New England." Then there was the matter of spending his

World Series winners' share—$2,812; Dugey used his money to buy a farm near his home in Palestine. He also visited friends and family in Dallas during the Christmas holidays. According to the *Morning News*, Dugey "has a host of friends, in fandom and out of it, who are watching his career." An avid hunter, fisherman, and trap shooter, Dugey hosted a deer hunt for several players in Pittsburg, Texas, after the Christmas holidays.

Dugey was on a hunting trip near Shreveport on February 13, 1915, when he received a telegram from Braves president J. E. Gaffney informing him that he been traded to the Philadelphia Phillies three days earlier as part of a December 24 deal that sent Sherry Magee to Boston. Philadelphia also received Possum Whitted on February 14.

A *Star-Telegram* story said Dugey didn't like the idea of leaving a championship club for an also-ran and let Stallings and Phillies manager Pat Moran know it. It was during spring training that Jake asked Whitted why he was sent to Philadelphia; Whitted told him it was because he had recommended Dugey to Moran. Dugey then politely informed Whitted that if Boston won the pennant, he (Dugey) would ship all of his belongings to Whitted's North Carolina home and spend the winter as a guest. "You're on," was Whitted's reply, "but suppose we win the pennant, then what?" "Not a chance," Dugey said, "but if we do, I'll give you $50 to spend for a hunting dog."

After spending spring training laid up with injuries, Jake made his first appearance at second base for Philadelphia on April 28, going hitless in a 3-0 win over Brooklyn. He had another start five days later, in a 3-2 loss to New York, hitting 2-for-4 with a double and a steal of home. For the season, Dugey hit .164 in 42 games, mostly as a pinch-hitter and pinch-runner, appearing in just 14 games as a second baseman when Bert Niehoff needed time off.

According to the *Wilkes-Barre Times*, "Pat Moran made him his field lieutenant and his work on the coaching line was pretty smooth." Former pitcher Al Demaree called Dugey "one of the cleverest in the game at grabbing signs from the pitcher." He was able to recognize the type of pitch from the pitcher's grip. "By a pre-arranged word-sign ... any time Dugey shouted, 'Make it good' to the hitter, he knew a curve ball was coming. If [he] told him to 'crack it,' he was set for a fast ball."

In early June, Dugey visited his mother in Shreveport. According to the *Star-Telegram*, she was "dangerously ill but is recovering." He rejoined the team in St. Louis on June 7. The Phillies had a day off on September 22 during a trip to Chicago and catcher Bill Killefer took Dugey and Eddie Burns to his hometown of Paw Paw, Michigan, for the day.

Oscar Dugey

Philadelphia (90-62-1) won the pennant by seven games over Boston. By September 28, Possum Whitted had a $50 check signed by Oscar Dugey and had ordered his hunting dog.

The Phillies lost the 1915 World Series 4 games to 1 to the Boston Red Sox. Jake Dugey appeared in two games as a pinch-runner; in Game Four, at Boston, Fred Luderus singled and drove in Gavvy Cravath from third with two outs in the eighth. Dugey ran for Luderus and stole second on pitcher Ernie Shore and catcher Hick Cady but was stranded a moment later when Whitted grounded out. Jake again appeared with two outs in the eighth inning of Game Five when Cravath walked and was replaced. Whitted again grounded out to end the inning. Called "one of the luckiest players in baseball" by the *Washington Post* for playing very little for two straight pennant-winners, Dugey pocketed his loser's share of $2,520.17 and headed to Texas for the winter.

Shortly after the end of the season, catcher Bill Killefer and pitcher Grover Cleveland Alexander, then the most famous battery in baseball, joined Dugey to hunt and fish at Ferndale Lake near Leesburg, Texas. After several weeks, Alexander left for his home at St. Paul, Nebraska, with Dugey and Killefer traveling to Dallas to buy supplies, visit with their mothers, and stop by the *Morning News* office to visit old friends. They returned to their camp by mid-December.

By the end of July 1916 Jake Dugey had the best average on the Phillies, .385 in 19 games according to the *Philadelphia Inquirer*, "principally acting as an understudy [to Bert Niehoff], coacher, and morning workout man." On August 20, the *Inquirer* said, "Dugey … is roosting high these days … topping the Nationalmen in hitting with a snug percentage of .333 made in 23 games. …. To be sure [he] has not made many hits, nor has he been at bat very frequently, but his six hits from eighteen trips to the rubber are sufficient to give him the lead." Jake's average fell to .220 in the final weeks of the season as he batted 5-for-32 the rest of the way. His .967 fielding percentage in 12 games was the best of his career.

Jake again spent the winter in Texas, mostly at Leesburg, with Killefer and Alexander joining him on October 17 for several weeks of fishing and hunting.

Dugey wasn't happy with the contract offered by Phillies president William Baker in 1917. According to *Sporting Life*, "O.J. suffered a cut in his contract … but on the evidence of his fellow players and the earnest entreaty of Manager Moran, President Baker added the copeks necessary to satisfy Oscar. The Dugey person appears to be one athlete who has been vastly underestimated by both the home fans and the club managers."

Philadelphia trained at St. Petersburg, Florida, and Dugey had a curious and peculiar way of passing time in the evening, a "sport" he called "flushing chickens." As told by *The Evening Independent*, Dugey, who never married, would wait until about 10 o'clock in the evening, take a soft-drink bottle and stroll down to the private pier on the beach front. Walking along, he would soon spot a couple "spooning" and make a quick flash with the bottle, startling the couple. After walking the length of the pier and flashing his bottle several times, he would yell, "This is a private pier and no trespassing is allowed on it. You have all got to get off." Pair by pair, the couples beat it off the pier and then Oscar would go back to the Edgewater Inn and announce that he had flushed so many chickens. According to the *Independent*, "If Dugey could make as many base hits as he has chased loving couples off the pier this spring he would lead the National League in batting by a big margin."

On April 11, Opening Day, Jake (1-for-4) drove in two runs with a third-inning triple in the Phillies' 6-5 win over Brooklyn. He had an RBI single and scored in an 8-6 victory over Chicago on May 22, enabling Philadelphia to sweep a four-game series and take the National League lead. Sometimes Dugey's defense let the team down. On August 10, the *Philadelphia Inquirer* said second baseman Dugey "was shaky on pretty nearly everything that came his way. He dropped Killefer's good throw on a Jackson steal attempt that ultimately didn't cost anything. In the seventh King of Pittsburgh reached on Dugey's muff and eventually scored [the only run in the contest.]" Dugey hit .194 in 44 games with the 1917 Phillies.

With the end of the season, Grover Alexander visited Dugey and his mother in Dallas; they were photographed buying Liberty Bonds at the City National Bank on October 25. After the short visit, the two went to Shreveport for a hunting trip. Dugey later went hunting in East Texas in December with Hamilton "Ham" Patterson, manager of the Dallas Submarines of the Class B Texas League.

In January, the *Racine Journal-News* reported that Philadelphia would not offer Dugey a contract for 1918. President Baker, who was cash-strapped and had dealt Alexander and Killefer to the Chicago Cubs in December, wasn't in the mood to retain his sore-armed utility player and sold him to the St. Paul Saints of the American Association on April 3. Dugey had worked out with players from the Dallas Texas League squad in mid-March and joined the Saints a month later, seeing action in 15 games during April and May, hitting .137, with just two of his seven hits going for extra bases. He was released shortly thereafter.

Jake Dugey was out of Organized Baseball in 1919. Instead, he was hired as captain of the Maxwell Motor Company semipro team based in New Castle, Indiana. In February 1920, the *Dallas Morning News* announced its All-Time Texas League team and named Jake Dugey as the second team's second baseman.

George Stallings brought Dugey back to the Boston Braves as a coach in 1920. The *Boston Globe* said Stallings "was pretty well pleased. He believes Dugey is one of the best men in this respect that he has ever had." The *Columbus Ledger-Inquirer* described his role as "see[ing] that the men shape into Stallings' system of play." Signed as a player-coach, Dugey appeared in five games as pinch-runner, scoring two runs, for the seventh-place Braves (62-90-1).

Jake made headlines as a coach on April 20, getting into a fistfight with Brooklyn Robins third baseman Hi Myers. According to the *Globe*, Dugey was loudly advising pitcher Joe Oeschger to "dust them off," as Myers had struck out with a chance to drive in a run. The normally mild-mannered Myers responded with "some uncomplimentary epithets" to Dugey and the two were soon exchanging blows, coming to a clinch, and scuffling around on the ground. Neither was damaged but both were ejected from the game. Joe Vila, writing for the *Philadelphia Inquirer*, concluded that "Myers did wrong …. but Dugey …. was primarily to blame. The practice of 'riding' opposing ball players has been characteristic of the Braves ever since Stallings assumed the management. It isn't clean sport and shouldn't be tolerated. Stallings tolerates rowdy conduct, while other big league managers can produce winning teams without it."

Stallings resigned as Boston's manager after the 1920 season, leaving Jake Dugey without a job. In mid-April 1921, he was signed by the Chicago Cubs to assist manager Johnny Evers, thus reuniting him with his close friends Killefer and Alexander. His most noteworthy act was an ejection from a 6-5 loss at New York on July 9 for registering his disgust with ball and strike calls, picking up a glove at first base and hurling it all the way to the plate.

On July 20, Dugey was given his unconditional release by team president William Veeck Sr. Two weeks later, Veeck fired Johnny Evers and named Killefer the new manager. Killefer told Veeck that he wanted Dugey back in the coach's box and was willing to forgo his pay raise in order for Jake to return. The *Chicago Tribune* wrote that Killefer said, "Every player on the team wants Oscar back, and they are willing to chip in to pay his salary." Veeck immediately added Jake to the roster, explaining that he had been let go "under the Evers management." Killefer said he "believes the coach will aid the club materially in restoring the old fighting spirit." The Cubs' (64-89) seventh-place finish suggests that fighting spirit wasn't enough to lift them out of the second division.

The 1922 Cubs (80-74) moved up to fifth place under Killefer and Dugey. Jake was ejected from three contests, once, in the words of the *Tribune*, for "loud talking from the bench" and another "for howling about two decisions on runners at the plate." On August 1, Killefer's mother was killed in a Michigan auto accident. Bill left the team for 12 days to be with his family and Oscar Dugey was left in charge of the club, which was 7-3-1 under his guidance.

Dugey again found himself in charge of the club in March 1923, when the Cubs were training on California's Catalina Island. Killefer was called to Chicago to attend to his seriously ill wife and was again absent for 12 days. In August, the *St. Petersburg Times* said, "Dugey is doing his stuff again. … [S]tories tell of teams that found their signals were in the hands of the enemy when they played Chicago. … [They] had to change their signals several times a game, and yet they seemed to divine every kind of ball that was pitched. Fingers are pointed at Dugey. …. [T]here is nobody apter in 'getting' the stuff of a ball team than Dugey."

Jake had his own bout of illness in September when he was hospitalized for ten days with tonsillitis. The 1923 Cubs (83-71) were Killefer's best club, finishing in fourth place, 12 1/2 games behind the champion Giants.

The 1924 Cubs got off to a good start and were in contention until late June, when Alexander's wrist was fractured by a line drive. Without his pitching, Chicago fell out of the first division over the next two months and found itself ten games behind the Giants. The Cubs (81-72-1) finished fifth, 12 games in back of New York. On November 23, president Veeck announced that Dugey, who was on a player's contract, would be released. According to the *Tribune*, Veeck said, "I like a coach who is more demonstrative in his work. I like to hear them yell on the coaching lines and display a lot of pep and spirit, and Dugey is not that kind of coach." Norman E. Brown, writing in the *New Castle News*, countered by saying that "Dugey wasn't very demonstrative with the Braves back in 1914. He made very little noise while

Left to right: Gowdy, Rudolph, Tyler, Connolly, and Dugey, 1914.

stealing most of the signals that the National League opponents tried to flash around the field." The *News* and the *Tribune* were both of the opinion that other big-league clubs would want him as a coach or that he would wind up managing in the Texas League.

Neither possibility materialized. Jake was next spotted attending the 1925 World Series with Killefer (whose stint as Cubs manager ended that July) in Pittsburgh. Four years passed before he was mentioned in the press again; in July 1929, the *Dallas Morning News* noted that Dugey, who made Dallas his home, was employed as a Texas League scout for Montreal of the International League. A year later, the *Olean Evening News* reported that Oscar was the "constant companion and loudest rooter" for noted alcoholic Pete Alexander, who was attempting an ill-fated comeback at age 43 with the Dallas Steers. "Pete has the stuff," Oscar said, "There is not a minor league batter who can hit him when he keeps himself fit. If Pete keeps in training, he still has plenty of years to play." Alexander's comeback lasted five games, with a 1-2 record, 46 baserunners in 24 innings, and an 8.25 ERA.

Dugey had several jobs after he was out of Organized Baseball. A 1934 *New York Times* retrospective on the 1914 Braves said that he was in the electrical business in Dallas. Dallas city directories from the late 1930s and 1940s show Dugey working for the Ball Motor Company, a business that rebuilt wrecked cars. Perhaps Jake's last connection with baseball was in March 1940, when he worked with former minor-league pitcher Roe Ikard at Harry Wanderling's baseball camps for boys, a month-long series of conditioning, skill-based workouts, and daily practice games.

Jake Dugey spent his later years living at the Ambassador Hotel in Dallas. A March 1965 *Denton Record-Chronicle* article mentioned that he had suffered a stroke in 1962 that left him with impaired vision. A retired painter, he died at Parkland Hospital on January 1, 1966, after he fell and fractured his hip, an injury that was exacerbated by pneumonia and chronic lung disease. He was survived by three sisters, Dimple Whited, Gennevieve Phillips, and Virginia Marshall, and a brother, Frank. Dugey is buried at Oakland Cemetery in Dallas.

Sources

In addition to the newspapers cited in the text, the following sources were used.

Cataneo, David. *Peanuts and Crackerjack: A Treasury of Baseball Legends and Lore* (Nashville: Rutledge Hill Press, 1994), 79-80.

Macht, Norman L. *Connie Mack and the Early Years of Baseball* (Lincoln: University of Nebraska Press, 2007), 634.

Frank, Stanley. "Rough Riders of the Dugouts," *The Saturday Evening Post* Vol. 213, Issue 46 (May 17, 1941), 18, 89.

Phelon, William A. "How I Picked the Loser," *Baseball Magazine* Vol. XVI, No. 2 (December 1915), 116.

Baseball-reference.com (including SABR minor league database)

Retrosheet.org

Ancestry.com

Rootsweb.com

Texashistory.unt.edu

Johnny Evers

by David Shiner

An excellent bunter, accomplished base stealer, and pesky left-handed hitter who usually had the National League's best walk-to-strikeout ratio after his first few seasons in the big leagues, Johnny Evers was considered one of the Deadball Era's smartest and best all-around players. He was just as well known for his fiery disposition. The star second baseman's nickname, "The Human Crab," was originally bestowed on him due to his unorthodox manner of sidling over to ground balls before gobbling them up, but most baseball men considered it better suited to his temperament than his fielding. A 5'9", 125-pound pepper-pot with a protruding jaw that came to be a symbol of the man—for he was always "jawing" about something—Evers developed a reputation as a troublemaker by squabbling regularly with teammates, opponents, and especially umpires. "They claim he is a crab, and perhaps they are right," Cleveland Indians manager Joe Birmingham once observed. "But I would like to have 25 such crabs playing for me. If I did, I would have no doubts over the pennant. They would win hands down."

The older brother of Joe Evers, who appeared as a pinch runner in one game for the New York Giants in 1913, John Joseph Evers was born on July 21, 1881, in Troy, New York. The proper pronunciation of the family's surname has always been a source of confusion, but Johnny clarified the matter during a public appearance in Boston late in his career when he declared, according to a local sportswriter, that "either way was right: that while Ev-ers was the correct pronunciation, everyone in Troy, his home, called him E-vers and always had done so." Johnny tipped the scales at just 100 pounds when he signed with his hometown club in the New York State League early in the 1902 season. When he appeared in a game at nearby Albany the fans reportedly assumed that he was some sort of comic act, but the 20-year-old shortstop proved otherwise when he fielded everything hit his way and won the game with a three-run double.

Later that summer the manager of the Chicago Nationals, Frank Selee, learned that a capable pitcher was toiling for the Troy nine. He arranged an exhibition game between his club and the Trojans, a common practice at the time. The pitching prospect, Alex Hardy, was impressive, so Selee offered the Troy ownership $1,000 for him. Hardy's employers countered by requesting $1,500, claiming that another major-league club was willing to shell out that amount. "I'll tell you what I'll do," Selee responded. "If you throw in that kid who played short today, I'll give you the $1,500." The owners of the Troy team were quick to oblige. Evers was batting .285 and leading the New York State League with 10 home runs (only two less than he hit in his entire 18-year major-league career), but he was regarded as a nuisance because of his short temper and his insistence that the local ballpark be available for practice at all times of

Johnny Evers

Evers waiting for batting practice.

the day. He also committed plenty of errors at short, though he displayed great range in the field.

Making his major-league debut on September 1, 1902, Johnny played his customary position while Selee moved his regular shortstop, fellow rookie Joe Tinker, to third base. Three days later the Chicago skipper rearranged his infield, moving Evers to second and returning Tinker to short, the positions at which they remained for the next decade. Despite occasional flashes of brilliance, Evers' 26-game trial during the final month of that season was unimpressive; he showed promise defensively but batted only .222 without a single extra-base hit, drawing just three walks and stealing a lone base. But regular second-baseman Bobby Lowe suffered a severe knee injury late in 1902. By spring training the following year it still hadn't healed properly, so Evers won the starting job by default. This time he was ready, batting .293, pilfering 25 bases, and contributing solid defense all season long. At the beginning of 1904 Selee sold Lowe to the Pittsburgh Pirates, entrenching Johnny as the club's everyday second sacker.

The scrappy Evers didn't hit his first major-league home run until his 24th birthday, July 21, 1905, when he popped a pitch from future teammate Chick Fraser over the fence in the right-field corner at Boston's South End Grounds. By that point he had already appeared in more than 350 big-league games. But Johnny made up for his lack of power with a mastery of "inside baseball" that became his trademark. In 1906 he stole a career-high 49 bases, and the next season he pilfered 46, both marks placing him in the top five in the National League in those years. Evers also generally increased his proclivity for drawing walks each season, peaking at 108 in 1910, only eight behind league-leader Miller Huggins. That marked his third straight year in the NL's top five in that category. "I am convinced that in my own career I could usually have hit 30 points higher if I had made a specialty of hitting," said the man with a lifetime batting average of .270. "Some lumbering bonehead who does make a specialty of hitting and nothing else may forge well across the .300 line and everybody says, 'What a grand hitter.' The fact is, the bonehead may have been playing rotten baseball when he got that average and someone else who didn't look to be in his class might be the better hitter of the two. Of course there are plenty of times when there is nothing like the old bingle. But there are plenty of other times when the batter at the plate should focus his attention on trying to fool the pitcher. In my own case I have frequently faced the pitcher when I had no desire whatever to hit. I wanted to get a base on balls." And he became a master of that skill.

The mutual antipathy between Evers and his keystone partner, Tinker, was legendary. There was little love lost between them during the Cubs' heyday, and they didn't speak to each other off the field for decades. Some commentators dated their animosity to a highly publicized on-field brawl in 1905, but years later Evers told a different story. "One day early in 1907, he threw me a hard ball; it wasn't any farther than from here to there," Evers claimed, pointing to a lamp about 10 feet from where he sat. "It was a real hard ball, like a catcher throwing to second." The throw bent back one of the fingers on Evers' right hand. "I yelled to him, you so-

and-so. He laughed. That's the last word we had for—well, I just don't know how long." Whatever the reason for their bitterness, Evers and Tinker were an impeccable defensive tandem on the diamond. "Tinker and myself hated each other," Evers admitted, "but we loved the Cubs. We wouldn't fight for each other, but we'd come close to killing people for our team. That was one of the answers to the Cubs' success."[1]

Evers batted an even .300 in 1908, the first of only two times in his career that he reached that exalted level. He also played a crucial role in that year's pennant race, one of the closest and most exciting in baseball history. On September 4 the Cubs were locked in a scoreless duel in Pittsburgh when the Pirates loaded the bases with two outs in the bottom of the ninth. On what appeared to be a game-winning hit to center, the runner at first, Warren Gill, left the field without bothering to touch second base. Evers, standing on second, called for the ball and demanded that umpire Hank O'Day rule the play a forceout, which would nullify the run and send the game into extra innings. Gill's maneuver was customary in those days, and O'Day refused to make the out call. "That night O'Day came to look me up, which was an unusual thing in itself," Evers recalled many years later. "Sitting in a corner in the lobby, he told me that he wanted to discuss the play. O'Day then agreed that my play was legal and that under the circumstances, a runner coming down from first and not touching second on the final base hit was out."[2] Evers' account may not be entirely trustworthy, especially given O'Day's exceptionally reclusive nature and the lengthy period between the event and the retelling, but the incident undoubtedly had a pronounced effect on the umpire, as was demonstrated by subsequent events.

An almost identical situation arose on September 23, this time with the Cubs battling the Giants at the Polo Grounds. When New York's Al Bridwell hit an apparent game-winning single with two outs in the bottom of the ninth, the runner on first, Fred Merkle, headed for the clubhouse without touching second. Evers called for the ball, eventually got one (though probably not the ball Bridwell hit), and held it aloft as he stepped on second base. "I can still see Johnny on second with his hand up in the air," Giants infielder Buck Herzog told reporter Tom Meany some 20 years later. "He looked like the Statue of Liberty."[3]

O'Day was again the umpire, and this time he called the runner out. Given the irregularity of the call, the critical nature of the game, the temperaments of the opposing managers, and the animosity between the Cubs and Giants, O'Day's verdict sparked a firestorm of controversy. Eventually NL president Harry Pulliam ruled the game a tie, to be replayed if it had any impact on the pennant race. It did, as the two teams ended the regular season deadlocked for first place. The Cubs went back to New York for a one-game playoff, winning 4-2 to secure their third consecutive NL pennant. They went on to thrash the Detroit Tigers in the World Series for the second straight year, with Evers batting

Evers with manager George Stallings.

.350 and leading all players on both teams in runs scored. His headiness on the play that became known as "Merkle's Boner" was given due credit for the Cubs' triumph, cementing his reputation as one of the smartest players in baseball.

Evers was as high-strung as he was brainy. One reporter described him as a "keen little umpire-fighting bundle of nerves," and sometimes those nerves got the better of him. In 1911 he played in just 46 games, being out of commission for most of the season by a nervous breakdown which he claimed was due to the loss of his entire accumulated capital in a failed business venture. He bounced back to enjoy the best season of his career in 1912, batting a career-high .341 and leading the NL with a .431 on-base percentage. At the end of that season Frank Chance resigned as manager (or was fired, depending on who you believe), and Cubs owner Charles W. Murphy presented the 31-year-old Evers with a five-year contract as player-manager.

Johnny Evers with Eddie Plank before the 1914 World Series.

The next season started in promising fashion. May 10, 1913 was Johnny Evers Day at the Polo Grounds, and a sizeable number of Troy residents journeyed to New York City to see their favorite son collect a single, a double, and a walk in four trips to the plate. Evers also scored the winning run as his Cubs (often called the "Trojans" in his honor in the newspapers that year) vanquished the Giants, 2-1.[4] But the Cubs failed to improve on the previous year's third-place finish, and after the season Murphy summarily dismissed his manager despite the long-term contract.

The fallout was acrimonious. Murphy initially claimed that Evers had resigned. Johnny angrily disputed that, and the other NL owners unanimously sided with him.

Murphy then tried to trade his ex-manager to the Boston Braves for two players and cash. Evers said he wouldn't report, and his refusal was made more piquant by the fact that the newly-minted Federal League was offering him $30,000 to forsake the NL altogether. Although Evers later claimed that he had no intention of jumping to the new league, that was far from clear at the time. Disgusted by Murphy's tactics and afraid of losing one of their top stars to the upstart league, the NL owners nullified the trade and awarded Evers his release, permitting him to sell his own contract to the Braves for $25,000 plus bonuses and incentives of various sorts. His overall earnings for 1914 made him the highest-paid player in baseball.

The deal was risky for the Braves on several counts. Due to Evers' age (32), slender frame (he spent off-days wolfing down candy bars so he could retain as much weight as possible), hypersensitivity, and proclivity for getting ejected from ballgames, he couldn't be counted on for everyday play. Nevertheless the unorthodox deal benefited a number of people, none more than Evers himself. His new manager, the like-minded George Stallings, quickly appointed him the Braves team captain. Johnny took his duties seriously, running his teammates ragged in practice and taking it as a personal insult when anyone put forth an effort that he regarded as subpar. "He'd make you want to punch him," teammate Rabbit Maranville later recalled, "but you knew Johnny was thinking only of the team."[5] After rocketing from last place to first over the last 10 weeks of the 1914 season, the "Miracle Braves" capped a dream season by sweeping the Philadelphia A's in the World Series. Sensational down the stretch, Evers also was outstanding in the Series, batting .438 with several key hits. To cap off his spectacular season, he won the Chalmers Award as the NL's MVP.

That was Evers' last great year. Injuries and suspensions cost him almost half of the 1915 season. When healthy he performed at his usual impressive level, but his disputes with umpires, never far from the sports headlines even in the calmest of times, became weekly fare. Johnny's nerves were clearly frayed even beyond their usual state. In early August, with the Braves trying to catch the Phillies in the pennant chase, he announced that he needed to leave the team immediately or risk a recurrence of the nervous breakdown he had suffered four years earlier. Evers managed to complete the 1915 campaign, playing in most of his team's games during the Braves' unsuccessful stretch run, but it was his last season as a regular. He had a poor year in 1916, and after batting a meager .193 over the first half of 1917 the Braves placed him on waivers. Evers spent the second half of that season with the Phillies, who played him sparingly and released him at season's end. The following year he earned a spot on the Opening Day roster of the Boston Red Sox but was released before appearing in a single game.

Evers returned to the Cubs as manager in 1921 and skippered the White Sox three years later. He failed to complete either season, and both clubs performed less successfully under his direction than either before or after he took the reins. The White Sox assignment made him the first and so far the only man to manage both Chicago major-league clubs.

During the 1930s Evers ran a sporting-goods store in Albany, New York, which remained in family hands until it closed its doors for good in the 1990s. In 1942 he suffered a stroke that debilitated him for the rest of his life. Johnny Evers died of a cerebral hemorrhage in Albany on March 28, 1947, one year after his induction into the National Baseball Hall of Fame.

Notes

1 Unnamed Troy (NY) newspaper, December 26, 1936. Unattributed quotations in this biography are from undated and unidentified newspaper clippings found in the Johnny Evers file at the National Baseball Hall of Fame.

2 Bill Corum, "Evers to Chance Again," *The Sporting News,* April 9, 1947, 18.

3 Tom Meany, *Baseball's Greatest Teams* (New York: A. S. Barnes & Company, 1949), 109.

4 *Troy Budget*, May 11, 1913, pages unknown.

5 Tom Meany, 170.

The 1914 Evers-Zimmerman Incident and How the Tale Grew Taller Over the Years

By Bob Brady

THE RAPIDLY ASCENDING Braves wrapped up a series at Wrigley Field against the Chicago Cubs on August 26. The Braves lost the well-pitched contest, 1-0, but the game achieved greater notoriety for a near riot that took place in the seventh inning.

Both clubs were scoreless in the seventh until Cubs first baseman Vic Saier sent a Lefty Tyler offering into the right-field bleachers. The next batter for Chicago was Heinie Zimmerman, who manned the hot corner and who possessed a reputation for aggressiveness on the base paths. In particular, Zimmerman had a nasty habit of sliding into a base in a way that threatened injury to the infielder manning the bag. He would slide on his left leg and twist his body, building momentum in his right leg in order to deliver a mighty and potentially wrist-breaking kick to an unfortunately positioned fielder.

The Newspaper Account

As reported in the following day's *Boston Herald*, after Saier's clout, Zimmerman followed with a hit to center that he tried to stretch into a double. Zimmerman didn't have a chance. The Braves' second baseman, Johnny Evers, had the ball in hand by the time Zimmerman was within 15 feet of second base. Zimmerman made a headfirst slide and was easily tagged out. Embarrassed in front of hometown fans, he took a swing at Evers while still on the ground, hitting the Tribe's pugnacious second baseman with a "wicked blow upon the forearm." With his past experience as Cubs manager, Evers was well aware of Zimmerman's reputation of bone-breaking play and proceeded to retag him with an ungentle application of the baseball to his head.

An enraged Zimmerman arose and grabbed for Evers' face. Here, Rabbit Maranville entered the fray. As Zimmerman turned, the diminutive Maranville delivered a straight left that split the six-footer's lip wide open. The third baseman redirected his attention to Maranville but fortunately for Rabbit reinforcements arrived in time to prevent retaliation. 6'2" Butch Schmidt restrained Zimmerman, engaging in a "Teutonic struggle" as other players from both squads milled about. Once matters cooled down, Zimmerman, Evers, Maranville, and Schmidt were banished from the game by umpire Mal Eason. Cubs pitcher Larry Cheney completed his one-hit masterpiece, giving up only Hank Gowdy's sixth-inning single in the process.

Rabbit's Tale

Years later, Rabbit Maranville took the opportunity to spin his version of the "Zimmerman Affair" in his book *Run, Rabbit, Run*. According to Maranville, the offending play was the result of an attempted steal of second by Zimmerman. Aware of the Cub player's damaging sliding reputation, Evers would put his foot up in front of the bag to break the incoming player's momentum. However, Rabbit reported that Evers had forgotten to block Zimmerman and took the catcher's throw with one knee to the ground and caught the runner on the chin with the tag. After the dazed Zimmerman recovered his senses, he grabbed Evers by the neck in a choke hold.

Maranville sought to come to the aid of his teammate, looking for an appropriate angle for an attack. "I finally backed up about five feet and, with a running start and jumping into the air with my fist closed, landed on Heinie's jaw and down he went." He, Evers, and Zimmerman then were bounced from the game.

Maranville recalled walking off the field on one side of Zimmerman, with Evers on the other. The close proximity of the combatants lent itself to a back-and-forth conversation during their exit. Zimmerman expressed the contention that someone from the Braves bench had ran on the field and socked him. Evers was quick to retort, "Rabbit hit you." Zimmerman rejected Evers' confession. "No, he didn't; I know who hit me."

A Historian's View

Harold Kaese was a longtime Boston sportswriter, columnist and a member of the Writers Wing of the National Baseball Hall of Fame. As the unofficial historian of the Boston Braves, he penned the landmark reference, *The Boston Braves: An Informal History*, in 1948 as part of the Putnam series of baseball team histories.

In his *Braves* book, Kaese weighed in with his version of the notorious 1914 incident at Wrigley Field. His account matches Maranville's to the extent that he portrayed the instigating play as an attempted steal gone wrong. Kaese also agreed that Maranville aggressively rose to the defense of Evers. The writer, however, added some additional dialogue to the post-fisticuffs departure of the combatants from the diamond. "'I know who hit me. It was Moose Whaling,' bellowed Zimmerman…." Maranville, in walking the irate Cub from the field, admitted to the blow. "'The hell you did. No midget like you could give me a belt like that. It was Whaling or Butch Schmidt." Zimmerman became so insistent that he challenged Schmidt and a second battle was only averted by three Braves teammates holding back the big Tribe first baseman. Kaese revealed that Zimmerman later learned the true story that he had walked off the field "arm in arm" with the person who had popped him, resulting in the loss "of his fond regard for Maranville."

Reporting Anecdotally

Al Hirshberg was a sportswriter for the *Boston Post* and the *Boston Herald*. He later achieved some notoriety as a book and magazine article author. There are instances among his works where he chose not to let facts interfere with a good story. With the Braves jousting for a pennant in 1948, Hirshberg cranked out *The Braves: The Pick and The Shovel* and filled it with anecdotes that he had acquired during his career. In that work, he presented a version of the August 26 occurrence quite different from all of the others.

Hirshberg portrayed Rabbit Maranville as a "rough and ready ballplayer," but "his quick wit kept him out of trouble." To illustrate his point, the writer seized upon Maranville's encounter with Zimmerman in 1914. By Hirshberg's account, Maranville "once knocked out big Heinie Zimmerman of the Cubs by smashing him over the head with the ball as Zimmerman lumbered into second base."

Hirshberg continued the story noting how Maranville very solicitously helped the dazed and confused Cub off of the field. As the two departed the Wrigley Field diamond, Maranville was said to have shook his head repeatedly, signifying his disbelief on what had just happened. Hirshberg reported that the devious Rabbit remarked to Zimmerman, "Wasn't that a terrible thing for Johnny to do?" According to this writer's version, instead of seeking revenge on the guilty party, "Zimmerman spent the rest of the season trying to get even with Evers."

The Evers Ejection Record

by Mark Sternman

IN A TRANSFORMATIVE season that saw him captain a downtrodden club to glory and win the Chalmers Award as the Most Valuable Player in the National League, Johnny Evers in 1914 was ejected an astounding nine times, a record total that appears all the more incredible given its accumulation over the course of a championship season by the most experienced member of the triumphant team.[1]

Definitively interpreting the reasons for the anger appears impossible a century after the fact, but two factors seem plausible, namely, a deeply personal issue and pennant-race pressures.

In early August, a little more than two months before Boston won the title, Evers lost his daughter, Helen, to scarlet fever.[2] Rumors had spread that Evers would retire or sit out the rest of the season, but manager George Stallings said, "The death of his little girl is a hard blow, but Johnny Evers will bear up under it as he had under all his other trials; you may be sure of that."[3]

Stallings may have had more faith in Evers than the second baseman had in himself. In September, Evers conjectured, "The only member of the Braves likely to crack on the home stretch is myself. I have been in four close finishes for the championship and know what it means."[4]

Regardless of the explanation, Evers hurt his team in the short run while spurring it on to glory over the course of the whole season. Boston won four and lost five of the nine games in which he was ejected. Three of the nine took place during the first halves of doubleheaders, meaning Evers had to miss the second games as well. Boston went 2-1 in those games, leaving the team with a 6-6 record in games missed partly or wholly by Evers due to ejection.

Three of the ejections took place in the seventh inning; Evers also was tossed twice in the third inning and once each in the second, sixth, fifth, and eighth. Since he hit at or near the top of the order, his failure to get thrown out in the first inning seems surprising, especially considering that three of his nine ejections came for arguing balls and strikes. Tag plays also resulted in three ejections, along with two for "talk" (perhaps newspaper-speak for profanity) and one for fighting.

Umpire Mal Eason ("the most sensitive umpire in the business"[5]) threw him out three times; arbiter Cy Rigler got him twice; and Bill Hart, Steamboat Johnson, Bill Klem, and Al Orth[6] got him one time each. The fact that Evers used "the endearing term of 'fathead'"[7] during his first run-in with Rigler gives some sense of the long and tangled history between the two, as Rigler had ejected Evers 13 times before 1914 and would get him twice more in later years.[8]

Umpires may not carry grudges, but Evers sure did. After Orth threw him out after a "called third strike … on a ball … higher than his shoulder and wide of the plate," Evers yelled, "'That was something like one of your reversible decisions such as you made in Pittsburg.'"[9]

Having just completed 12 years at the keystone sack for Chicago, the last of which also saw him manage the Cubs, Evers, perhaps overly excited for facing his former club, was ejected from three games against Chicago; two each against Philadelphia and St. Louis; and one each against Brooklyn and New York.

Six times, Oscar Dugey replaced Evers. Possum Whitted came in twice (once moving over from right field), and Jack Martin made his only second-base appearance of 1914 the remaining time. Boston clearly suffered without Evers on the field,[10] most notably in the three games against the Cubs.

In a 7-5 loss to Chicago in June, Dugey struck out in the ninth inning with a runner at first.

The recap of a win over Chicago in July begins this way: "Evers kicked himself out of the game. … Dugey, who took his place, made a high throw in the seventh inning, which enabled the Cubs to tie the score and the Braves were forced to go 11 innings to trim the West Siders, 7 to 4."[11]

In an August tilt against the Cubs, Boston, down a run in the ninth, allowed hurler Lefty Tyler to hit for himself. He drew a walk but somehow hurt his leg in the process, so Josh Devore pinch-ran for him. (One wonders why Stallings allowed Tyler to hit with Devore in reserve; in a one-run loss later in the season in another game after the ejection of Evers, Stallings did pinch-hit Devore for Tyler.) "Here is where Evers was missed. Dugey flied to center."[12] Chicago won 1-0 on a one-hitter by Larry Cheney.

That shutout featured more fisticuffs by Boston than hits. Two months after the assassination of Archduke Franz Ferdinand of Austria that sparked World War I, a colorful front-page headline read: "FISTS FLY IN BATTLE OF BRAVES AND CUBS; Boston Loses in Pitching Match, But Holds Its Own in Free-For-All; Battleship Zimmerman, Cruiser Evers, Torpedo Boat Maranville and Super-Dreadnought Schmidt Engaged."[13]

Reporter J.C. O'Leary laid the blame entirely on "Swashbuckler Zimmerman"[14] for throwing a punch as Evers tagged him out at second when Zim tried to stretch a single. The National League had a different interpretation of the imbroglio as both Evers and Zimmerman received $100 fines, while Maranville was hit with a $50 penalty.[15]

With an improbable National League pennant and a World Series sweep, Johnny Evers could look back on the 1914 season with a great deal of satisfaction. Although he had his issues in the Series—demonstrably protesting from second base a safe call at first in Game Two and mindlessly holding the ball and allowing an extra run to score in the tenth inning of Game Three—Evers kept his season-long temper mostly in check in the postseason to lead Boston to glory that in the end overshadowed his ire.

Notes

1. Retrosheet has Evers leading the National League in ejections every year from 1910 through 1917 except for 1913 (he played in only two games after 1917). Evers led all NL managers in ejections in 1913 and was the subject of an article entitled "Evers and the Umpires" in the 1914 offseason (*Baseball Magazine*, January 3, 1914, 71-73). Umpires ejected Boston players other than Evers only eight times in 1914, with Schmidt and Tyler both going twice and Connolly, Gilbert, Gowdy, and Maranville once each.

2. Mike Lynch, "Hardly a Miracle," August 12, 2013 (http://seamheads.com/2013/08/12/hardly-a-miracle/).

3. "Evers to Play Tuesday," *Boston Globe*, August 9, 1914, 15.

4. "Echoes of the Game," *Boston Globe*, September 11, 1914, 9.

5. T.H. Murnane, "Rushing Braves Win Two More," *Boston Globe*, September 11, 1914, 1.

6. Evers earned six of Orth's 23 career ejections (four times in 1913, once in 1914, and once in 1915), the highest career percentage of any of the 1914 umpires who threw Evers out more than once.

7. "Obsolete Play Costs Boston a Run," *Boston Globe*, May 27, 1914, 9.

8. The *Cincinnati Times Star* referenced the ill feelings between the two by speculating that they could sue one another: "Rigler vs. Evers, asking damages, for libelous names publicly pronounced on August 11. Defendant sets up counter-claim that names were veracious and fully fitting to plaintiff on said occasion" (" 'Legal' Base Ball," *Sporting Life*, August 22, 1914, 4). Boston's issues with Rigler went beyond just Evers. "Stallings renewed his assertion that Rigler is intentionally making decisions against the Boston team in order to handicap it, and states that Boston has been robbed of every game it has played with Rigler working behind the plate. New York players assert that the pitched ball that caused all the trouble today was low and inside rather than a strike, as the Boston men declare, and McGraw himself scouts the idea that Rigler put Tyler, Evers, and Gilbert out of the game for saying simply 'nothing at all.' [Braves] President [James E.] Gaffney intends to insist, he says, that [National League] President [John K.] Tener assign Rigler to no more games in which the Boston team is engaged." "Doyle Ready to Play," *New York Times*, June 27, 1914.

9. J.C. O'Leary, "Cubs Cut in on Braves' Streak," *Boston Globe*, June 16, 1914, 7.

10. Fielding percentages provide an imperfect record of fielding skill, but note that Evers had a .976 mark at second base in 1914, far superior to Whitted's .933 and Dugey's .891 (Jack Martin had no chances at second). Thanks to Clem Comly for pointing out these figures.

11. "Braves Beat Cubs in 11 Bitter Innings," *Boston Globe*, July 9, 1914, 7.

12. J.C. O'Leary, "Fists Fly in Battle of Braves and Cubs," *Boston Globe*, August 27, 1914, 8.

13. J.C. O'Leary, "Fists Fly in Battle of Braves and Cubs," *Boston Globe*, August 27, 1914, 1. Pugilistic images fit Evers in temperament if not in size, as suggested by this fictitious boxing card that appeared weeks *before* Evers brawled with Zimmerman:

BOXING—BOXING

And Baseball—

Thursday P M., at Biffem Field—

THREE GREAT CONTESTS,

In Three Classes.

Lightweight Championship,
RABBIT MARANVILLE
vs.
HEINIE GROH.

Middleweight Championship,
JOHNNIE EVERS
vs.
BUCK HERZOG.

Heavyweight Championship,
BATTLING SCHMIDT
vs.
TOMMY CLARKE.

REFEREE, CHUCK RIGLER.

Added Attraction: A Nine-Inning Ball Game between the Boston Braves and the Cincinnati Reds.

PRICES: $2.50 Ringside; $2, $1.50, and $1.

Baseball Magazine, August 4, 1914, 40.

14   J.C. O'Leary, "Fists Fly in Battle of Braves and Cubs," *Boston Globe*, August 27, 1914, 1.

15   "Three Players Fined," *Boston Globe*, August 28, 1914, 6. For more on this episode, see "Double-Teaming Zimmerman" in Walter "Rabbit" Maranville, *Run, Rabbit, Run* (Cleveland: Society for American Baseball Research, 1991), 37. Thanks to Bob Brady for suggesting this reference.

Larry Gilbert

By Jack V. Morris

BESIDES HAVING HAD a key pinch-hitting appearance in the 1914 World Series, Larry Gilbert is arguably the greatest minor-league manager of all time. Managing for 25 years solely in the Southern Association, Gilbert's record was 2128-1627, good for an astounding .567 winning percentage. His teams won the pennant nine times, won the Shaughnessy playoffs three other times, and won five of its nine appearances in the Dixie Series, an annual contest between the champions of the Texas League and the Southern Association. So valued was he as a manager that it was reported in 1941 that he was the highest paid manager in the minor or major leagues.[1]

While Gilbert's numbers as a manager are certainly eye-popping, there was much more to the man than that. As a player, he played on a World Series champion and four minor-league pennant winners during his 15-year playing career. His three sons all played in Organized Baseball, and two of them made the major leagues. Beyond his baseball life, Gilbert was a pillar of society in his native New Orleans and later in Nashville.

Lawrence William Gilbert was born on December 3, 1891, in New Orleans, Louisiana, the second of two sons of Rosalie (Norden) and Abraham Edward Gilbert, both native *Louisianans*. Abraham's parents were born in Germany. He was a house painter, and the couple made their home in the Irish Channel section of New Orleans near Athletic Park where the minor-league New Orleans Pelicans played. It would become a second home to Larry.[2]

On a trip out to the country when Larry was a child, his leg became caught in a log wagon, and his right foot was severely injured. Doctors wanted to amputate the foot but Gilbert's mother refused. Instead the doctors sewed the foot back into place with 32 stitches, creating a scar that ringed his ankle for the rest of his life. When the foot healed, his right leg was one inch shorter than his left. It didn't affect his running — in fact, later in life, he was often among the top basestealers in the league. "Curiously enough, this (his shorter leg) doesn't seem to interfere with his work in the field," wrote a reporter while watching Gilbert run in spring training in 1914.[3]

By the age of 14, Gilbert was a regular at Athletic Park as a scoreboard boy and, remarkably, a batting-practice pitcher. He eventually became the soda-water boy and then finally, a mascot for the Pelicans. All the while he was honing his game, playing semipro ball in New Orleans and making a name for himself. Describing his pitching for the semipro team Reliance in 1908, the *New Orleans Daily Picayune* called him "regular shylock on the slab."[4]

In the winter of 1909-10, Gilbert pitched for a semipro baseball team called the Braquets. One of his victories was a 1-0 win over a team that contained some major leaguers, including Philadelphia Athletics pitcher Jimmy Dygert. A teammate of Gilbert's, veteran minor

Larry Gilbert

leaguer Bob Tarleton, who had brought him over to the Braquets, was instrumental in getting him to sign with San Antonio of the Texas League.[5]

For his first minor-league season in 1910, San Antonio sent the 18-year-old to Class D Victoria of the Southwest Texas League. He tore up the league, going 18-7 and leading his team to the pennant.[6]

Before the next season, Gilbert was offered and accepted the job of managing Victoria. But then Jack Burke, Gilbert's former manager at Victoria and the newly-hired manager of the Class C Battle Creek Crickets of the Southern Michigan League, bought Gilbert's contract from Victoria for $200.[7]

At Battle Creek he had another winning season, going 17-15. But during a game on Labor Day, he tore some muscles in his left side. His pitching arm was never the same again. Overuse, since he was Battle Creek's only reliable pitcher, and his use of the curveball were blamed for his injury.[8]

Gilbert started to see some playing time in the outfield, batting .253. In 1912 he made the switch full-time to outfielder. With his pitching career over, Gilbert had to start his baseball career over. Fortunately for him, he was a very popular player in Battle Creek and management was more than happy to bring him back. He rewarded management by batting .302 in 127 games. He remained an outfielder for the rest of his playing career.

Gilbert hoped to play with his hometown New Orleans Pelicans in 1913. Burke, Battle Creek's manager, gave Gilbert his consent to sign with the Pelicans. However, Battle Creek's management then sold Gilbert to Milwaukee of the American Association. After a protracted period that lasted into the beginning of the season (though Gilbert worked out with the Pelicans throughout spring training), Gilbert finally went to Milwaukee.[9]

After Gilbert settled in with the Brewers, he had a fine season, batting .282 and leading the American Association in stolen bases. He helped Milwaukee to the American Association championship and, after the season, was drafted by the Boston Braves. *Sporting Life* wrote that Gilbert "is figured as having a good chance to become the regular centre fielder" for the Braves.[10]

Capping off what was a pretty good year for Gilbert, he wed his hometown sweetheart, Gertrude Wilhelmina Mader, at Sacred Heart Church in New Orleans on October 29, 1913.[11]

As with many baseball players in 1914, rumors swirled that Gilbert would sign with the upstart Federal League. But on January 24, 1914, it was announced that the Boston Braves had received his contract. And on March 10 Gilbert was in Macon, Georgia, with the Braves for spring training. The rookie made a good impression on Braves manager George Stallings, and on Opening Day, April 14, he was in the starting lineup as the center fielder. In the game, Gilbert rapped out his first major-league hit, a single off Brooklyn Dodger Jeff Pfeffer, in an 8-2 loss.[12]

Eight days later Gilbert collided with teammate Joe Connolly as they chased a drive by Philadelphia's Dode Paskert. The result was torn ligaments in Gilbert's ankle, and an infection that severely hampered Gilbert's season. He was out of the lineup until late May. From then on, he was in and out of the lineup. He hit the first of his five major-league home runs during this time, a blast off Cincinnati's Phil Douglas on June 6.[13] In all, he played in 72 games and hit .268.

In August Gilbert was sent home to recuperate in New Orleans because he was "suffering considerably with his leg," according to the *New Orleans Item*. But the pennant-winning Braves felt him healthy enough to keep him on the bench for pinch-hitting duty during the World Series against the Philadelphia Athletics. His only at-bat in the Series came in a pivotal inning. In the bottom of the 12th inning of Game Three, Braves catcher Hank Gowdy led off with a double. Gilbert was sent up to bat for pitcher Bill James and was intentionally walked by pitcher Bullet Joe Bush. Then, on Herbie Moran's bunt, Bush threw wildly to third, allowing pinch-runner Les Mann to score the winning run. It was the Braves' third win and a day later they

Larry Gilbert

closed out the Series, putting an exclamation point on a remarkable season.[14]

Gilbert was the toast of New Orleans. He was the first native of the city to play in a World Series. With his winners' share, he purchased real estate in New Orleans, allowing him and his wife to move out of his parents' home. A Larry Gilbert Day on October 25 included a parade and a doubleheader between semipro teams. Gilbert was slated to play for his old winter-league team, the New Orleans Railway & Light Company club. (In the offseason, Gilbert worked for the company and played on the team.) But after his injury-plagued season, Stallings asked Gilbert not to play winter ball so that his ankle might heal completely for spring training. It was reported that Stallings told Gilbert, "You've had a vacation most of the summer. Now go home and get in good shape for some real play next season."[15]

But rather than sit out and disappoint the 2,500 who came to Larry Gilbert Day, Gilbert played center field and even drove in the winning run of the game. But he did heed Stallings after the game, and sat out some of the winter league season.[16]

The ankle injury bothered Gilbert for the rest of his playing career. He aggravated it again sliding into a base in 1915. By July 12 Gilbert had played in 45 games and was batting only .151. With the Braves in seventh place and seven games out of first place, Stallings sent Gilbert and Ted Cather to Toronto of the International League. Gilbert had played his final major-league game. The *Boston World* wrote, "With the Braves, he has at no time showed anything even approaching the batting prowess he displayed as a Brewer."[17]

Immediately, Gilbert showed that batting prowess in Toronto. By the end of the season, he had batted .325 in 68 games. But the Braves decided they had seen enough of Gilbert, sending him to Kansas City of the American Association.[18]

Gilbert played in 168 games for Kansas City in 1916, batting .275 as the starting center fielder. But the long season wore on Gilbert. He missed his wife and infant son, Lawrence William Jr. So after the season was over, rumors began that Gilbert would retire from baseball and go into private business in New Orleans. "He has business ties here and prefers to stay here," wrote the *New Orleans Item*.[19]

That began a waiting game that lasted into May 1917. Gilbert refused to report to Kansas City; the Blues suspended him, preventing him from playing for any other team in Organized Baseball. When Kansas City finally saw that Gilbert was serious in his insistence that he'd quit baseball before he played any place except New Orleans, the Blues sold Gilbert to the Pelicans for the shockingly steep price of $2,500. But Gilbert was wildly popular in New Orleans and Pelicans president Alexander "A.J." Heinemann was more than willing to pay it.[20]

Gilbert's first game with the Pelicans was May 6, 1917. It marked the start of a long association with the Southern Association that wouldn't end for 46 seasons. He was so popular that when in the first game he tripled to drive in three runs, the hat was passed among the spectators and the $17 collected was given to Gilbert. He was embarrassed by the situation so he donated the money to the Red Cross and wrote an open letter to the New Orleans fans in the *New Orleans Daily Picayune* asking them very politely not to do that again.[21]

Gilbert again hurt his ankle during the season, this time in June, which had him in and out of the lineup for a month. Although he finished second in the league in steals and first among outfielders in fielding percentage, his season was considered "somewhat of a disappointment" when he batted only .269 in 118 games.[22]

As the United States continued its involvement in the World War, Gilbert was called by the draft board for a physical examination on August 16, 1917. But he was soon ruled exempt from service since he was married and had a child and because of his shortened leg. Rumors promptly began to circulate that the still popular Gilbert would be the next manager of the Pelicans. This would happen several times over the next six years. But Gilbert refused to even consider the job unless longtime manager John Dobbs stepped down.[23]

Like most baseball leagues, the Southern Association found 1918 to be a tumultuous year. With the war effort growing for the United States, baseball leagues were feeling the strain to keep able-bodied players. For the Southern Association, it was an abbreviated campaign, ending on June 28. Gilbert's season didn't start off well when he and a few of his teammates had ptomaine poisoning during spring training. By the end of the season, he had rebounded to hit .282; was second in the league in steals with 21 and led the league's outfielders in fielding percentage. With the major leagues having their own man-power shortage, Gilbert was in demand after the Southern Association season but he turned down all the offers.[24]

Instead, Gilbert took a position with the Dantzler Shipbuilding & Dry Docks Company in Moss Point, Mississippi. Dantzler built wooden cargo ships for the United States. Gilbert was also the manager and starting center fielder for the Dantzler baseball team, which played in the competitive Gulf Coast Shipyard League. He put to rest any debate that the professional baseball players who had taken jobs with the shipbuilding companies in 1918 were getting off easy. "They are not showing any partiality to ballplayers," said Gilbert. "If they don't do a certain amount of work, the pay envelope is lighter, and in most instances the fellow who shirks work is discharged."[25]

When the war ended, baseball returned to normal in 1919. Gilbert, for the first time in many seasons, managed to stay healthy and uninjured for much of the season. As a result, it was his best year in baseball. Batting .349, he led the league in batting, basestealing, and fielding. His final batting average might have been even higher but he again hurt his ankle toward the end of the season and slumped through the last month.[26] On top of his excellent season, his second son, Charles Mader Gilbert, was born on July 8.

Having such a season brought the attention of major-league teams again. Gilbert refused offers to join teams in September. He was content to stay in New Orleans and play baseball. In October, to underscore his determination to stay in New Orleans, he paid $12,000 for a gas station across the street from the ballpark. His plan was to build a repair shop on the property and work it in the offseason. His father-in-law would manage the gas station in the summer.[27]

But rumors persisted that Gilbert would be sold to a major-league team. Then in February 1920, *The Sporting News* announced that Gilbert had been sold to Cleveland. He had decided that if he was paid enough, he could leave his family for the season. But even though Gilbert was with the Indians in spring training (which just happened to be in New Orleans), he never signed a contract with the big-league club.[28]

Finally, toward the end of March, Gilbert sat down with Indians owner Jim Dunn. Dunn made his final and best offer. Gilbert turned him down. Dunn then threatened to have Gilbert barred from Organized Baseball. But Indians manager Tris Speaker talked Dunn out of it. Instead, New Orleans refunded the Indians the purchase price of Gilbert.[29]

Gilbert responded with another great season, batting .301. (He hit over .300 for the Pelicans every season from 1919 through 1924, his second-to-last season as a player.)

In October 1920 Gilbert got out of the gas-station business when he leased his property to a New Orleans police detective. His hand was forced when Gilbert's father-in-law became ill and couldn't manage the business. He took a job as a car salesman for Cucullo Motor Company selling Haynes Automobiles.[30]

Finally, after the 1922 season, Gilbert got the chance to manage the Pelicans. John Dobbs had resigned to manage the Memphis Chicks. The New Orleans management worried that he wouldn't hit as well while he was managing. Joe Tinker, Johnny Evers, and Tris Speaker were all mentioned in the press as great ballplayers who became poor hitters when they were managers. But Gilbert produced on the field as well as on the bench and managed the Pelicans until 1939.[31] And in his first year managing, Gilbert led the Pelicans to the pennant. They lost the Dixie Series to Fort Worth of the Texas League in six games.

After the 1925 season Gilbert quit as a player. In 1926 and 1927 the Pelicans won the Southern Association championship but lost both times in the Dixie Series.

On April 4, 1929, Gilbert's third and last son, Harold Joseph "Tookie" Gilbert, was born. Nine months later on January 8, 1930, Gilbert was shocked by the news that his good friend and the president of the New Orleans Pelicans, Alexander Julius "A.J." Heinemann, had committed suicide. Heinemann was distraught over the stock-market crash, which had caused his millions to dwindle to $200,000, and was also upset over financial losses Gilbert suffered after following his advice.[32]

Heinemann's death affected Gilbert not only personally but professionally. Heinemann was involved in most of the player personnel decisions. His co-owner, Charles W. Somers, preferred to let others run the club. So after Heinemann's death, most of his duties were delegated to Gilbert.[33]

In 1932 Gilbert decided that he couldn't handle both the manager and business-manager duties so Jake Atz was hired as manager. The Pelicans finished in sixth place and the following season Gilbert was back as both manager and business manager. He responded by winning the pennant and Dixie Series in 1933.[34]

During the 1934 season, owner Charles Somers died. Fred Baehr, the treasurer for Somers' company, the Somers Coal Company of Cleveland, took over the reins as president. He allowed Gilbert to continue to run the club as he saw fit. For the second year in a row, Gilbert's team won the pennant and Dixie Series.[35]

In 1936 Gilbert's oldest son, Larry Jr., tried out for the Pelicans. He was the first boy in the nation to be signed from the nascent Junior American Legion program. The Pelicans sent him to Des Moines of the Western League but a knee injury caused him to miss the entire season. Larry Jr., a second baseman, eventually played two seasons in Organized Baseball, including the 1938 season for his father. After the 1938 season, doctors discovered that Larry Jr. had a heart ailment and he was forced to retire from baseball.[36]

In April 1937 the Pelicans were sold to new owners. The new ownership, led by Seymour Weiss, kept the front office intact, including Gilbert. But Gilbert would not be working for the new ownership for long.[37]

After the 1938 season, Gilbert shocked New Orleans by announcing that he was leaving the Pelicans. To make matters worse, he was going to Southern Association rival Nashville Volunteers to be their business manager and manager. Gilbert was lured away when Memphis owner Fay Murray offered him half-ownership in the club plus a salary of $10,000.[38]

"You may be sure I thought it over a long time," said Gilbert. "This is my home—the home of my entire family and of 90 percent of my friends. My associations with the new owners of the Pelicans have been perfect—ideal. I could not have hoped for more congenial associates. But the offer from Nashville was one I could not turn down. I owed it to my family to take it. Mr. Weiss and his associates would be foolish to even try to come close to the offer. You may be sure it was an attractive one, since it has prompted me to leave my lifelong connection, transplant myself and keep up two homes." In addition to ownership, Gilbert was guaranteed by Murray to make twice what he was making with New Orleans with a chance to make three times. It was an offer he couldn't refuse.[39]

As if coaching in a new city weren't exciting enough, Gilbert also was coaching his second son, Charlie. Playing center field for the Volunteers, Charlie batted .317 with 14 home runs. The Brooklyn Dodgers purchased his contract after the season for $30,000, $10,000 of which was given to Charlie for a nest egg for his impending wedding. He made the major leagues in 1940, and in all played parts of six seasons in the majors for the Dodgers, Chicago Cubs, and Philadelphia Phillies.

Nashville won the Southern Association pennant and the Dixie Series in 1940. They were only the third team in league history to never relinquish first place during the regular season. *The Sporting News* named Gilbert Minor League Manager of the Year.[40]

But 1941 turned into one of the darkest years of Gilbert's life. On March 4, the 60-year-old Fay Murray died, leaving Gilbert as acting president of the ballclub. Five months later he was dealt a harsher blow when his oldest son, Larry Jr., died of pneumonia brought on by his heart ailment.[41]

Ted Murray, Fay's son, took over as president of the Nashville club, leaving Gilbert to his usual business manager and manager duties. Gilbert responded with pennants and Dixie Series championships in 1941 and 1942. In 1943, with his son Charlie again on the team, he won a fourth straight pennant but, because of World War II, there was no Dixie Series.[42]

Gilbert's youngest son, Tookie, was becoming a fine player in his own right. So in 1946, with several teams bidding for his service, Gilbert capped the bidding at $50,000. The name of any team willing to pay that amount was written on a piece of paper and placed in a hat. Gilbert's wife, Gertrude, pulled the New York Giants slip from the hat. Mel Ott, the Giants' representative, signed Tookie immediately. Tookie eventually played in the major leagues with the Giants in 1950 and 1953.[43]

Charlie Gilbert's playing career was winding down during this time and, in 1948 he asked the Phillies to sell him to Nashville, ostensibly to play one more season with his father and to also start to learn the business of baseball. He had a tremendous year for Nashville in 1948, batting .362 and hitting 42 home runs. But 1948 was his last year as a player. He worked as Larry's assistant from 1949 until 1955. In the 1960s Charlie became a scout for the New York Mets.[44] He died in 1983.

The year 1948 marked the end of Gilbert's managing career. He was 56 years old and ready to relinquish his on-the-field duties. He went out with a bang as the Volunteers won 11 straight games at the end of the season to clinch the pennant.[45]

Gilbert remained as business manager through 1954. That season had been a financial failure with losses estimated in the $40,000-to-50,000 range. Only 89,470 fans came to games in Nashville. So on May 21, 1955, Gilbert sold his share of the team to Ted Murray, ending his association with Organized Baseball at the age of 63.[46]

He retired to New Orleans at his home on the banks of Lake Pontchartrain. Almost immediately, a group of dissatisfied New Orleans baseball club stockholders wanted Gilbert as their business manager. He turned them down; however, he did take a position on their board of directors.[47]

In 1964 Gilbert was named to the Louisiana Sports Hall of Fame and the Greater New Orleans Baseball Hall of Fame. He was also later posthumously named to the Tennessee Sports Hall of Fame.[48]

On January 11, 1965, Gilbert entered New Orleans' Mercy Hospital. He never left. On February 17 Gilbert died of congestive heart failure at the age of 73. He was survived by his wife, Gertrude; his two sons, Charlie and Tookie; six grandchildren; and one great-grandchild. More than 1,000 people visited the funeral parlor to pay their last respects. Gilbert was buried in Greenwood Cemetery in New Orleans.[49]

Three months after his death, the New Orleans baseball field commonly known as "Muny Park" was renamed Larry Gilbert Baseball Stadium. As of 2013 it still stood.

Notes

1 S. Derby Gisclair, "Pelican Briefs" http://www.neworleansbaseball.com/articles/pelicanbriefs/LarryGilbert-ManagerRecord.pdf; Fred Russell, "They're Simply Wild About Larry," *Saturday Evening Post*, March 30, 1942, 11, 38, 40

2 Russell, op. cit., loc. cit.; *The Sporting News,* November 29, 1945.

3 Russell, op. cit., loc. cit.; *The Sporting News*, November 29, 1945; Frank G. Weaver, "You Have To Hustle to Win," in *Association Men*, June 1922, 447, 459-460; *Sheboygan* (Wisconsin) *Press*, March 18, 1914

4 Russell, op. cit.; Gisclair, *Baseball in New Orleans* (Charleston, South Carolina: Arcadia, 2004), 42; *The Sporting News*, November 20, 1924; *Sporting Life*, October 3, 1914; *New Orleans Daily Picayune*, August 5, 1908

5 *The Sporting News*, November 29, 1945; *New Orleans Item*, October 20, 1914, September 7, 1919; *New Orleans Daily Picayune*, December 31, 1909

6 *The Sporting News*, August 20, 1925

7 *New Orleans Daily Picayune*, January 16, 1911; *Galveston* (Texas) *Daily News*, April 6, 1911; *San Antonio Light*, April 4, 1911

8 *Saginaw Daily News*, September 13, 1911; Weaver, op. cit., loc. cit.

9 *New Orleans Daily Picayune*, March 6, 1913, November 22, 1913; *Adrian* (Michigan) *Daily Telegram*, March 14, 1913; *Atlanta Constitution*, April 6, 1913

10 *Sporting Life*, December 20, 1913

11 *New Orleans Daily Picayune*, October 22, 1913

12 *Sporting Life*, January 31, 1914; *New Orleans Times-Picayune*, January 22, 1914; *Brooklyn Daily Eagle*, April 15, 1914

13 *Sporting Life*, May 2, 1914; *New Orleans Item*, April 28, 1914; *Sporting Life*, May 30, 1914; Bob McConnell, *SABR Presents The Home Run Encyclopedia* (New York: Macmillan, 1996), 558

14 *New Orleans Item*, August 25, 1914, October 4, 1914

15 *New Orleans Times-Picayune*, October 14, 16, and 20, 1914; *New Orleans Item*, May 28, 1914; *Lima* (Ohio) *Daily News*, October 14, 1914; *Lowell*(Massachusetts) *Sun*, October 19, 1914; *New Orleans Times-Picayune*, October 20 and 25, 1914; *Sporting Life*, December 12, 1914

16 *New Orleans Item*, October 26, 1914; *New Orleans Times-Picayune*, January 14, 1915

17 Weaver, op. cit., loc. cit.; *Brooklyn Eagle*, July 14, 1915; *Sporting Life*, July 24, 1915

18 *Sporting Life*, September 25, 1915

19 *New Orleans Item*, December 22, 1916, April 5, 1917; Weaver, op. cit., loc. cit.;

20 *New Orleans States*, April 4 and 22, 1917; *New Orleans Times-Picayune*, May 6, 1917

21 *New Orleans Times-Picayune*, May 8, 1917

22 *New Orleans Item*, June 10, 1917, March 14, 1918

23 *New Orleans States*, August 13, September 1 and Setember 17, 1917

24 *New Orleans States*, June 29 and July 2, 1918

25 *New Orleans States*, July 14 and August 31, 1918

26 *New Orleans States*, October 19, 1919

27 *New Orleans States*, August 12 and October 19, 1919; *New Orleans Item*, October 16, 1919

28 *New Orleans Item*, November 14, 1919 and March 5, 1920; *The Sporting News*, February 12, 1920; *New Orleans Times-Picayune*, March 15, 1920

29 *New Orleans Times-Picayune*, March 20 and March 24, 1920

30 *New Orleans States*, October 14 and November 7, 1920

31 *New Orleans Item*, October 2, 1922; *New Orleans Times-Picayune*, January 2, 1923

32 Russell, op. cit., loc. cit.; Gary Higginbotham,, "A.J. Heinemann," http://www.sabrneworleans.com/publications/garyhigginbotham/Heinemann%20(Higginbotham).pdf

33 David L. Porter, *Biographical Dictionary of American Sports: Q-Z* (Westport, Connecticut: Greenwood Press, 2000), 1446

34 *New Orleans Times-Picayune*, December 31, 1931

35 *The Sporting News*, January 31, 1935

36 *The Sporting News,* March 26 and May 7, 1936, February 16, 1939, November 29, 1945.

37 *The Sporting News*, April 22 and October 14, 1937

38 *The Sporting News*, November 9, 1938; Russell, op. cit., loc. cit.

39 Ibid.

40 *The Sporting News*, September 12, 1940, and January 2, 1941

41 *The Sporting News*, January 18 and August 8, 1940, March 13, 1941; *New Orleans Times-Picayune*, August 24, 1941

42 *The Sporting News*, April 3 and November 27, 1941

43 *The Sporting News*, October 23, 1946, and May 27, 1953

44 *The Sporting News*, April 14, 1948

45 *The Sporting News*, September 15, September 29, and December 15, 1948

46 *The Sporting News,* December 14, 1949, September 22, 1954, and June 1, 1955

47 *The Sporting News*, December 29, 1954, June 1, 1955, June 29, 1955, March 7, 1956, February 18, 1965

48 *The Sporting News*, February 22 and November 7, 1964, March 1, 1969

49 *New Orleans Times-Picayune*, January 29, February 19, and February 20, 1965

Hank Gowdy

By Carol McMains and Frank Ceresi

Best known today as the first active major leaguer to enlist for service in World War I, Hank Gowdy was a "fair-haired skyscraper" (he stood 6'2" and weighed 180 pounds) who caught more than 100 games in only three of his 17 seasons in the majors.[1] Gowdy had what we would now call a Zelig-like ability to turn up as a prime actor in some of baseball's most dramatic scenes. He was key to the Boston Braves' amazing 1914 season, starring in their famous World Series victory, but a decade later he was blamed for the loss of another legendary Series. (His misplay is a primary reason why coaches now teach young catchers to hold onto their masks until they know exactly where the ball is, then to toss them well out of the way.) After retiring from baseball, Gowdy returned to the army once again and served his country during World War II.

The son of Horace C. and Carrie (Burhart) Gowdy, Henry Morgan Gowdy was born on August 24, 1889, in Columbus, Ohio. As a youngster Hank sold peanuts at Columbus's Neil Park and played football, basketball, and baseball at Hubbard Elementary School and North High School. After trying out with the Columbus Senators, he began his professional career in 1908 as a first baseman with Lancaster of the Ohio State League, remaining there for two seasons. In 1910 Gowdy enjoyed a breakout year with Dallas, leading the Texas League in doubles (44) and home runs (11) while batting .312 and stealing 29 bases. John McGraw signed him for the New York Giants and gave him a seven-game tryout that September. With 21-year-old Fred Merkle firmly entrenched as the Giants first baseman, McGraw advised Gowdy to take up catching if he hoped to remain in the major leagues.

The following year Gowdy had appeared in only four games when the Giants traded him and Al Bridwell to Boston for Buck Herzog on July 22. Thereafter he became the Doves' semi-regular first baseman, batting .287 in 29 games as a fill-in for player-manager Fred Tenney. Following McGraw's advice, Gowdy made the switch to catcher in 1912 but spent most of the season on the Boston bench, appearing in only 22 games behind the plate as a third-stringer behind new player-manager Johnny Kling and Bill Rariden. To that point he had never played an entire season at catcher, so in 1913 yet another new Braves manager, George Stallings, sent him to Buffalo of the International League to hone his skills. Gowdy batted .317 in 104 games, earning a late-season call-up to Boston. In 1914 the gawky 24-year-old became Boston's regular catcher, appearing in a career-high 128 games, 105 of them at catcher. Later Stallings himself stated flatly that his mild-mannered backstop was his most valuable player during that season's miracle run.

A lifetime .270 hitter who batted just .243 in 1914, Gowdy claimed that he should have hit .300 that year: "I hit just as hard during the season as I did during the Series, except that during the season they were going right at somebody while in the Series they were going safe."[2] In Game One of the World Series he was 3-for-3 with a single, a double, and a triple, and he and first-baseman Butch Schmidt, the two slowest men on the team, executed a successful double steal. In Game Three at Fenway Park, which the Braves had borrowed from the Red Sox for the Series, Boston was down by two runs when Gowdy led off the tenth inning with a blast into the center-field bleachers. It was the only home run of the Series, and it ignited a rally that tied the score. In the 12th Gowdy got his third hit and second

Gowdy on left, with Lefty Tyler and Joe Connolly.

Gowdy came up big with the bat in the 1914 World Series.

double of the game, a bullet to left field. Running for him, Les Mann scored the winning run on a wild throw. In the Game Four finale Gowdy went three-for-four, giving him a .545 average for the Series.

Over the next couple years Hank Gowdy remained a Boston mainstay behind the plate, catching an average of 115 games per season. In 1917 he took the step that, despite his 1914 heroics, assured his lasting fame. The United States entered World War I in April, and on June 1 Gowdy became the first active major leaguer to enlist, joining the Ohio National Guard. (Eddie Grant had enlisted in April, but he had retired as a player.) The big catcher reported for duty six weeks later and was overseas by early 1918. Gowdy served with distinction in the famed Rainbow Division, so-named by General Pershing because it had the uncanny luck of being surrounded by rainbows during the heavy combat it faced. Arriving in the Lorraine region of France in March, Gowdy endured trench warfare in its most brutal sense as the Germans made their fierce last effort to overrun the Allies on the Western Front. He carried the colors for the Fighting 42nd and returned to the United States a genuine hero, as popular in Boston as the mayor himself.

Turning down an offer of $1,500 a week for 30 weeks to tour the country and speak of his heroics, Gowdy returned to the Braves and on May 23, 1919, hit the first big-league pitch he'd seen for almost two years for a single. He went on to catch 74 games and bat .279, a 65-point improvement on his last pre-war season. In 1920 Gowdy was behind the plate for duration of the 26-inning classic in which Boston's Joe Oeschger and Brooklyn's Leon Cadore locked up for a 1-1 tie. In the 17th inning he played a key role — actually two key roles — in what one reporter called "the most remarkable double play ever seen in Boston."[3] With the bases loaded and one out, Brooklyn catcher Rowdy Elliot tapped back to Oeschger, who fired to Gowdy to force Zack Wheat at the plate. But Gowdy's throw to first base was low and Walter Holke bobbled it. Big Ed Konetchy, running from second, tried to score on the fumble. Holke's return throw was off to Gowdy's right. He reached for it, grabbed it, then "threw himself blindly across the plate to meet Konetchy's spikes with bare fist," a vivid snapshot of the Deadball game.[4] That season Gowdy batted just .243, but in each of the next two post-Deadball Era seasons he established new career highs by hitting .299 and .317.

In June 1923, with Stallings long gone, the Braves once again mired in mediocrity, and Gowdy off to a miserable .125 start, McGraw brought the veteran catcher back to the Giants in a four-player deal. Though he never played more than part-time, Hank posted the best offensive statistics of his career in his two-year stint in New York, batting consistently in the .320s and establishing a career high with four home runs in 1924. He also played in two more World Series. In the 12th inning of Game Seven of the 1924 fall classic at Griffith

Stadium, Gowdy literally stepped into the spotlight again — this time as a goat. With one out and no one on, Washington's Muddy Ruel popped up what looked like an easy foul. Gowdy tore off his mask, tossed it to the ground, and promptly stepped in it. "I thought my foot was being held in a bear trap," Gowdy later recalled.[5] He staggered around and couldn't reach the ball, which dropped to the ground. Given new life, Ruel doubled and later became Washington's winning run when Earl McNeely hit a hopper over Freddy Lindstrom's shoulder at third. Sportswriters, calculating the winning team's share, called Gowdy's misfortune "a $50,000 muff."

Partway through the 1925 season the Giants released Gowdy even though he was batting .325. He spent the next three seasons in the high minor leagues before returning to Boston as a coach in 1929-30. Gowdy celebrated his 40th birthday in 1929 but still managed to hit .438 in 16 at-bats for the Braves that season. He went on to coach for the Giants and the Cincinnati Reds during the 1930s, then joined the army as a major in World War II, becoming the chief athletic officer at Fort Benning, Georgia, where the baseball diamond is now called Hank Gowdy Field. Gowdy died at age 76 on August 1, 1966, in his hometown of Columbus.

Though married for many years, he and his wife left no children.

Note: A slightly different version of this biography appeared in Tom Simon, ed., Deadball Stars of the National League *(Washington, D.C.: Brassey's, Inc., 2004).*

Sources

For this biography, the authors used a number of contemporary sources, especially those found in the subject's file at the National Baseball Hall of Fame Library.

Notes

1. The "fair-haired skyscraper" description comes from Harold Kaese, *The Boston Braves, 1871-1953* (Boston: Northeastern University Press, 2004), 150.
2. Charles Einstein, *The New Baseball Reader* (New York: Penguin, 1992), 261.
3. Andrew Paul Mele, ed., *A Brooklyn Dodgers Reader* (Jefferson NC: McFarland, 2005), 30. The article "Brooklyn v. Boston in 26 Innings" is written by Ralph D. Blanpied.
4. Ibid.
5. Harold Kaese, "Gowdy Class in Tough Era," *Boston Globe*, August 7, 1966.

Gowdy seeming to cavort with his catcher's glove.

Tommy Griffith

By Chip Greene

On July 7, 1910, in New Bedford, Massachusetts, the hometown New Bedford Whalers squared off against the Lowell Tigers in a Class B New England League game. On the mound for the Whalers was 20-year-old Tommy Griffith who, in his second professional season, was on his way to winning 19 games for the pennant-winning New Bedford club. That performance, coming a year after his 14-win debut campaign in 1909, made the young right-hander a rising star among the league's pitchers. This showdown at New Bedford was destined to be perhaps his singular mound achievement. After the Whalers scored two runs in the first inning, Lowell tied the game in the second, and there the score remained for the next 16 innings. In each of the 13th, 14th, 15th, and 18th innings, Lowell almost forged ahead, but in each inning they had runners cut down at either third or home. Finally New Bedford pushed a run across in the bottom of the 19th inning and gave Griffith the victory, 3-2. The next day, the press lauded not only the young hurler's ironman effort, but also, in a sign of things to come, his defensive skills.

"Griffith," wrote a reporter for the *Lowell Sun*, "…had a remarkable fielding record, taking part in 20 plays without an error. He had three putouts and 17 assists. He allowed 12 hits, but outside of the second inning, when two came together, he kept them well scattered."[1] Over those 19 innings, Griffith struck out six and walked only three.

Where had the Whalers found such a bright pitching prospect? Little is known about the life of Thomas Herman Griffith before his arrival in New Bedford, or about how he came to join the team. We do know he was born on October 26, 1889, in the small town of Prospect, Ohio, 40 miles north of Columbus. His was the third generation of Griffiths to call the Prospect area home. Griffith's grandfather, also named Thomas, a farmer, had settled there after emigrating from Wales; and the ballplayer's father, David, was a carpenter. Tommy was the youngest of four children born to David and his wife, Mary. Throughout his life he always remained close to the place of his birth.[2]

In four seasons with New Bedford, Griffith won 58 games and lost 45. As he developed as a pitcher, he also proved quite skilled with the bat (in 42 games in 1912 he batted .286 and had a slugging average of .381). In 1913, with the Whalers in desperate need of hitting, Griffith was moved full-time to the outfield. It was a move that ultimately propelled him to a 13-year major-league career.

On July 7, 1913, the *Sun* wrote that "Griffith, the Whalers' right fielder, is developing into a star. He was a great pitcher not long ago and now is doing equally well in the field and at the bat."[3] After 95 games that season, usually batting fourth, the left-handed hitter was batting .346 and had a .474 slugging average. Six weeks later, on August 17, the Boston Braves purchased his

Tommy Griffith

contract for $1,300.⁴ Two days later, in Boston, Griffith made his major-league debut, batting second for the Braves and playing right field against the Cincinnati Reds. The *Lowell Sun* wrote that Griffith "gave a good account of himself in his opener with the Braves yesterday. In the first game [of a doubleheader, he] connected for a brace of singles. The Boston critics think that Griffith will be a fixture in the Braves' lineup."⁵ As it turned out, though, his time with the Braves was short-lived.

While Griffith possessed abundant skills on the baseball diamond, he also displayed another natural talent. One afternoon, after he had had a particularly bad day at the plate, manager George Stallings alluded to the young outfielder's gift when he told Griffith, "Listen here, young feller, you can't sing your way through this league."⁶ In truth, Griffith possessed a very good singing voice; he even led the Braves' quartet. After the 1913 season he and teammate Rabbit Maranville went on the vaudeville circuit and sang songs that Griffith himself had composed. Their partnership lasted about a month before Maranville quit the stage to coach basketball in Springfield, Massachusetts. It's unclear whether Griffith continued as a solo act.

Griffith batted .252 in 37 games for the 1913 Braves. The 24-year-old made the 1914 squad in spring training at Macon, Georgia, but when the season began, he got off to a miserable start. By the middle of May, his average hovered around .100, and he showed no signs of breaking out of a batting funk. James McGill, president of the American Association's Indianapolis Indians, offered to buy Griffith's contract. Manager Stallings gave his consent, but Griffith balked, demanding that McGill raise his salary. McGill offered to match Griffith's Boston salary but not exceed it. When Griffith still refused, the deal was off. Several days later Griffith changed his mind and decided to join Indianapolis after all (leaving his former Boston teammates to win the World Series without him). He played his first game with the Indians on May 23; hit a game-winning home run on the 28th, and finished the season with a .340 batting average for the Indians. The young man seemed too talented to remain in the minor leagues for long. Playing in a period that spanned both the Deadball and lively ball eras, Griffith was a solid if unspectacular hitter (it was once reported that he "never was strong against southpaw twirling"), finishing his career with a .280 batting average and .711 OPS (on-base average plus slugging average). The 5-foot-8-inch, 180-pounder had little home-run power but was a classic line-drive, contact hitter, usually putting the ball in play and rarely striking out—he averaged just 26 whiffs per season in the eight years in which he played over 100 games. Two additional skills made him an extremely valuable commodity: his tremendous defense and outstanding speed.

Throughout his career, the press often highlighted Griffith's play in the field. "Tommy Griffith raced far for and captured a line drive while running at full speed," said a game review in 1914.⁷

"One of the fastest players in the field and getting down to first base," observed another reporter a year later, adding that Griffith "played the angles in right field better than any man the Indians have had in the position in the last two seasons … one of the league's leading outfield assists men."⁸

In 1919, when Griffith was playing for Brooklyn, sportswriters rhapsodized that Griffith was "covering the difficult sun field in the Flatbush stadium in a manner that is far better than his many most ardent admirers have anticipated";⁹ and that "few members of Brooklyn have played right field as well as Tommy. … He plays the ball off the right field wall better than Casey Stengel."¹⁰

Even at the age of 32, while still with the Dodgers, Griffith continued to field his position "like an antelope."¹¹ All in all, as one headline described it, Griffith never failed to deliver "Some Brilliant Defensive Work."¹²

As the 1915 season dawned, Griffith had returned to the National League. During his outstanding 1914 performance in Indianapolis, the outfielder had attracted the interest of the Federal League, which had "tried hard to lure [him] away from the Indianapolis club but without success."¹³ (Griffith must have at least been intrigued by the Federal League overture, because

Tommy Griffith

accounts indicate that they "offered him a salary far in excess of the amount an Association club could pay."\)[14] Not wanting to lose his right fielder without compensation, in January, Indianapolis manager Jack Hendricks sent Griffith to the Cincinnati Reds "in exchange for three players who were regulars on American and National League clubs last season."[15] (The identity of the three players obtained by Indianapolis is unclear.) As he was then living in Radnor, Ohio, 120 miles from Cincinnati, the trade must have undoubtedly pleased Griffith.[16] And as subsequent events unfolded, he had a reason far beyond baseball to celebrate the transaction.

On the field, the 1915 season was arguably Griffith's finest. While leading the league in games played (in addition to their regularly scheduled 154-games schedule, the Reds had six tie games that season, so Griffith played in 160 games), he batted .300 for the first time and set personal highs in seven offensive categories. That season he married Dette Louise Bidenharn, whom he had met when both were rooming at the same Cincinnati boardinghouse. (They were married for 51 years, until Griffith's death in 1967, and had three daughters.)

The Reds were barely more than a mediocre team during Griffith's time there. Then, in February 1919, he was traded to Brooklyn with shortstop Larry Kopf for disgruntled Brooklyn first baseman Jake Daubert. (Kopf refused to report to the Robins and just before the season began, Cincinnati reacquired him.) It was the second time in Griffith's career that he had been traded away from a team that was about to win the pennant and World Series. (The first time was when the Miracle Braves shipped him to Indianapolis.) As Brooklyn struggled through a sub-.500 season in 1919, Cincinnati rose from third place to first, and defeated the Chicago White Sox in the infamous 1919 Black Sox World Series. Whether or not their victory influenced the 29-year old Griffith's decision, after the season the ballplayer said he planned to retire. "Griffith has started the Winter league's string of retirement yarns; he says that he will play baseball no more and will go into business in Columbus, Ohio," a sportwriter proclaimed.[17]

Earlier, Griffith had become a stock salesman. During the just-completed season, in fact, he had sold stocks while traveling with the team and had been doing well, reportedly making enough money to make the venture a "pleasant and profitable pastime."[18] (His decision to retire was also undoubtedly due to lingering resentment over his trade the previous year, as it was reported that "intimate friends say he is peeved because he was traded off the Cincinnati club.")[19] When Brooklyn opened spring training camp in Jacksonville, Florida, in March 1920, Griffith was a no-show. He wasn't going to stay away for long, however. In 1920, after hovering around .500 for most of the first month, the team climbed into pennant contention and stayed there all season long. In May, manager Wilbert Robinson and team owner Charles Ebbets got Griffith's new employer to guarantee that Griffith would not lose his chance for advancement or seniority if the ballplayer returned to the club. Griffith, who'd been playing with a local semipro team to stay in shape, agreed to come back. When he returned on May 27, Brooklyn's record was 16-13. Over the remainder of the season the team played .616 ball (77-48) and finished with a record of 93-61, to win the National League flag. Although they lost to the Cleveland Indians five games to two in the World Series, Griffith finally got to play for a pennant winner (he hit .190 in the seven games, going 4-for-21, with three RBIs). There was no further talk of an early retirement.

The next two seasons were Griffith's best statistically since his breakout year with Cincinnati in 1915, particularly where his power was concerned. However, injuries and age also began to slow him down. During Griffith's "retirement," Robinson had stocked the club with some promising young outfielders, so as Griffith battled to get into shape during the spring, he found himself each year sharing playing time in right field with much younger men. As he got older, it was harder to stay in shape. A sportswriter reported in 1921 from the team's training camp in Hot Springs, Arkansas, that "Tommy is a chubby party and the older he grows the more difficulty he experiences in taking off the extra pounds."[20] Nonetheless, Griffith accepted the challenge presented by the younger prospects and posted the best batting and OPS averages of his career. On August 4, 1922, he suffered his first serious injury when he wrenched his knee while running the bases. At the time he was batting .312. He was out until September 3, and finished the season having played in just 99 games. That October Griffith turned 32 and it was questionable how many effective years he had left.

In 1923, Griffith was healthy again, and spent all of that season in right field, hitting a solid .293 with 66 RBIs. In 1924, his average slipped to .251 but he helped as the Dodgers fought for the pennant all season long, finishing 1 1/2 games behind the league champion New York Giants.[21]

The 1925 season was Griffith's final one as a major leaguer. As the team convened for spring training in Clearwater, Florida, it was apparent that Robinson intended to make a change in right field. During the offseason he had signed from the Pacific Coast League an outfielder named Dick Cox, who in 1924 had hit .356, with a .565 slugging average and 25 home runs for Portland. As camp progressed the press reported that "Cox remains in the outfield while Tommy Griffith is hitting harder for the second team than he ever did before in spring practice."[22] For his part, Griffith had "paid stricter attention to his condition in the winter"[23] in an effort to keep his job. Nonetheless, he couldn't regain his position. He went north with the team as the fourth outfielder, yet after playing just seven games for Brooklyn (two in the outfield), on May 9 Brooklyn traded the veteran to the Chicago Cubs for infielder Bob Barrett. Griffith did well in his final 76 major-league games, batting .285 with a .780 OPS. After the season the Cubs dropped him and he spent 1926 with Little Rock and Atlanta in the Southern Association, then retired from baseball.

Griffith and his family continued to live in Cincinnati. In the 1930 US Census he listed his occupation as a dealer in radio, and on his World War II draft registration, he said he was employed at the Hamilton County Court House. Sometime later, too, he also owned an insurance agency. There is no record that Griffith ever held a baseball position after retiring as a player, but in 1945, it was reported that he was one of a group of former players backing Ohio Supreme Court Justice Charles S. Bell as successor to the late Kenesaw Mountain Landis as commissioner of baseball.[24]

Thomas Herman Griffith died of pneumonia on April 13, 1967, at the Jewish Hospital, in Cincinnati. He was 77 years old. One year later, his wife, Dette, died in a long-term care facility at the age of 78.

Notes

My sincerest appreciation to SABR member Bill Mortell for his invaluable genealogical research.

1   *Lowell Sun,* July 8, 1910
2   Tommy's mother died some time before 1900, when he was about ten years old. In 1901 David married Annie Mass, who was also from the Prospect area. They had three daughters.
3   *Lowell Sun,* July 7, 1913
4   Griffith's player file, National Baseball Hall of Fame
5   *Lowell Sun,* August 20, 1913
6   *Canton Repository,* November 7, 1926

7   *Indianapolis Star,* July 12, 1914
8   *Indianapolis Star,* January 9, 1915
9   *Fort Wayne News and Sentinel,* May 17, 1919
10 *The Sporting News,* December 13, 1923
11 *The Sporting News,* September 14, 1922
12 *Indianapolis Star,* July 12, 1914
13 *Rockford* (Illinois) *Republic,* October 2, 1920
14 *Indianapolis Star,* January 9, 1915
15 Ibid.
16 Griffith listed Radnor as his residence on his World War I registration.
17 *Portland Oregonian,* November 5, 1919
18 *Rockford* (Illinois) *Republic,* October 2, 1920
19 *Waterloo* (Iowa) *Evening Courier,* January 12, 1920
20 *The Sporting News,* February 24, 1921
21 On June 3, 1924, Griffith was the right fielder when the author's grandfather, Nelson Greene, a pitcher, made the only start of his 15-game major-league career.
22 *Adrian* (Michigan) *Daily Telegram,* March 10, 1925
23 *The Sporting News,* February 26, 1925
24 *Zanesville* (Ohio) *Signal,* April 7, 1945

Otto Hess

By Gary Hess

Otto Hess was a "one year wonder" pitching for Cleveland in 1906 whose late-career comeback culminated in a supporting role on the 1914 Miracle Braves. A 6-foot-1,170-pound left-handed pitcher, Hess was born in Berne, Switzerland, on October 10, 1878—the only Swiss-born major leaguer to date—and emigrated with his parents to the United States in 1888.[1] He enlisted in the US Army at the outbreak of the Spanish-American War and was stationed in the Philippines from 1898 to 1900.[2]

Hess's baseball career before he signed with Cleveland in the summer of 1902 is unclear. Newspaper references to his pitching with Columbus in 1901 are not substantiated, and it appears that he was not discharged from the Army until February 1902. In any event, he made his major-league debut with the Cleveland Broncos on August 3, 1902, pitching two innings. Two days later he gained his first major-league victory, "wobbling" to a complete-game, ten-inning 7-6 win over Washington at Cleveland's League Park. The Senators tested Hess by laying down 14 bunts. He booted three for errors, four others were legged out for hits, and seven were sacrifices. Hess pitched in five more games, three as a starter, finishing with a 2-4 record, a 5.98 earned-run average, and a 2.061 WHIP (walks plus hits per inning pitched). Seasoning was called for and Cleveland sent him to Kansas City of the Western League for the 1903 season, where he benefited from having future Hall of Fame pitcher Charles "Kid" Nichols as his manager.[3]

Hess returned to Cleveland, rechristened the Naps, in 1904. In his first full season in the major leagues, he was regarded as a young pitcher of considerable promise. Pitching 151⅓ innings in 21 games for the fourth-place club, he finished with an 8-7 record and a 1.67 ERA. He completed 15 of the 16 games he started, including four shutouts. Early in his career Hess acquired a reputation for suddenly losing his stuff. "Though he was said to be unhittable at times," wrote Russell Schneider, "Hess also had a reputation for being erratic from one inning to the next...."[4] One example occurred at New York on July 14, 1904, when he gave up ten runs in one inning in a 21-3 loss to the Highlanders. At Kansas City Hess had gained a reputation as a hitter with some power, which led Naps manager Bill Armour to have him play 12 games in the outfield. This experiment, however, was disappointing, as Hess batted just .120 for the season.[5]

With Napoleon Lajoie taking over as player-manager in 1905, Cleveland battled for first place until late July, when the team was four games ahead, but injuries precipitated a late-season collapse that led to a fifth-place finish, 19 games behind the pennant-winning Philadelphia Athletics. Hess's season paralleled that of the team. Starting 25 games, he won 10 and lost 15 with a 3.16 ERA, which was well above the league ERA of 2.65. Nonetheless, he pitched four shutouts, all in the early months of the season, including a two-hit, 2-0 win over the Tigers in Detroit on April 27 and a ten-inning, 1-0 win over New York at League Park on May 26, with his single driving in the game's only run. Despite Hess's disappointing hitting the previous season, Lajoie expanded his double-duty role as an outfielder. Hess responded with his best season at the bat. Playing 27 games in left field, he had 44 hits in 175 at-bats for a .251 average. He hit two home runs, just two fewer than the team's co-leaders, Terry Turner and Elmer Flick.[6]

The following season—1906—was the high point of Hess's career. It was also Cleveland's most successful season to that point with an 89-64 record, but despite leading the league in runs scored, base hits, batting average, slugging average, earned run average, and fielding average, the Naps finished in third place, five games behind pennant-winning Chicago and two behind New York. Midseason injuries to three key players, including ace pitcher Addie Joss, ruined the Naps' pennant prospects, as the team, which had been battling for first place, fell off the pace with an 11-14 record in August.

Hess, the only southpaw on the eight-man staff, was its workhorse, pitching in 43 games (third in the American League) and a total of 333 innings (second in the league). The season began auspiciously. Lajoie had Hess start the season opener at St. Louis and he came through with a three-hit 3-1 victory.

After the injury to Joss, Lajoie relied more heavily on Hess, who started seven of the team's 26 games in August. Showing signs of being overworked (he also played six games in the outfield during the season), Hess won only two while losing five of those August starts. One of the victories was a two-hit 4-1 win in Philadelphia. The Naps, bolstered by the return of Joss, made a valiant but ultimately futile comeback in September with Hess pitching some of his strongest games. When the White Sox came to Cleveland for a big series in early September, the Naps swept a Labor Day doubleheader with Hess, in relief, winning the opener, 10-3. That was a personal milestone: Hess's first victory over Chicago in 12 starts against the White Sox over four seasons.

Three weeks later, on September 25, Hess pitched was at his best, a one-hit 5-0 shutout of the Athletics at League Park; he carried a no-hitter into the ninth inning when a pop fly by the opposing pitcher, Jack Coombs, fell between two fielders for the Athletics' only hit of the afternoon. And finally, on October 3, Hess gained his 20th victory, a 4-3 win over Detroit at League Park. That victory gave the Naps a trio of 20-game winners, Joss and Bob "Dusty" Rhoads having already attained that milestone.[7]

Hess finished with a 20-17 record including seven shutouts (fourth most in the American League) and a league-leading three saves. He was also among league leaders with 36 games started (fourth), 33 complete games (third), 167 strikeouts (fourth), and a 1.83 ERA (sixth). He also led the league in hit batsmen with 24. The website thisgreatgame.com ranks Hess as the league's second "most productive" pitcher of 1906 (Al Orth of New York was first), with Rhoads and Joss third and fourth respectively.[8]

Hess's "breakthrough" season was widely praised. One sportswriter saw an end to the days when he was "as erratic as effective and often negated in one inning the efforts of an afternoon."[9] Grantland Rice wrote of Hess's transformation from being "erratic and wilder than an amateur automobilist" to a pitcher who had "with a world of speed and a curve that fairly cracked off at right angles … set in about the middle of the race, mowing his rivals down game after game … [winning] about four-fifths of his battles."[10] Lajoie spoke glowingly: "I don't believe there's a pitcher in either league who has greater natural ability. I've figured all along that the time would come when he would be a world beater. … [He has] terrific speed … the sharpest break to his curveball I've seen anywhere, and now that he has settled down and has picked up fine control, I can't see how anybody can beat him often. I'd rather bat against any other pitcher I know than this fellow. It has taken him quite a while to come around just right, but I believe he's there right now."[11]

But Hess had reached his peak and the next two seasons brought only

Otto Hess

disappointment culminating in his return to the minor leagues.

In 1907 a leg injury sidelined Hess through much of the season. He pitched in only 17 games, finishing with a 6-6 record and a 2.89 ERA. Many anticipated a comeback in 1908 but, bothered by a sore arm, he pitched a total of only seven innings in four games, all in relief, before being sent to Columbus of the American Association, where he managed to win nine games and lose four.[12]

The modest success at Columbus marked the beginning of a comeback that would eventually earn Hess another three years in the major leagues. New Orleans of the Class A Southern Association acquired his contract from Cleveland and over the next three seasons—1909 to 1911—Hess was one of the league's best pitchers, posting records of 18-12, 25-9, and 23-8 and leading the league in wins and winning percentage the last two of those years as the Pelicans captured successive pennants.

At the end of the 1911 season, the Boston Rustlers, soon to be rechristened the Braves, acquired Hess. He joined a "practically unknown" staff,[13] but one sportswriter gave Hess little chance to succeed even surrounded by mediocrity: "The once Cleveland southpaw seems destined for a minor league berth again, thus proving that once a pitcher over 24 years of age leaves the 'big show' it is almost a waste of time trying to get him back."[14] Hess, in fact, became a mainstay, along with Hub Perdue and Lefty Tyler, of the staff, albeit on the National League's worst team, which finished with a 52-101 record. Aside from a one-hitter against Chicago in May, Hess struggled through the first months of the season. Capping his frustration was a 19-inning, 7-6 loss at home to Pittsburgh on July 31. Hess, who went the distance against three Pirates pitchers, yielded three runs in the 19th inning, the final run being driven home by the 38-year-old Honus Wagner. By late August Hess had a 4-17 record, which made that springtime prediction of his comeback being a "waste of time" seem prescient. Then Hess suddenly became the pitcher who had shown such promise a decade earlier. He concluded the year with eight straight wins, capped by a 14-2

Hess getting limber.

victory over Philadelphia. The comeback was "a great record for this veteran on a tail-end team."[15]

Hess finished with a 12-17 record and a 3.76 ERA. He was among the National League leaders in games started—31 (14th), innings pitched—254 (16th), complete games—21 (11th). Overall, Hess's record, considering his dreadfully slow start and the Braves' dismal record, was remarkable and assured his return in 1913.

George Stallings, who replaced Johnny Kling as Boston's manager, set about rebuilding the Braves into a contender. The housecleaning over the next two seasons meant that by 1914 Hess was among only five members of the woeful 1912 team who were still on the roster. In 1913 the Braves moved up to fifth place with a 69-82 record. Hess, however, pitched less effectively. He remained among the team's top four pitchers in games

(29), games started (27), complete games (19), and innings pitched (218), but he again lost 17 games while winning only 7. With Bill James and Dick Rudolph joining Lefty Tyler as a trio of talented young starters, Hess's days as a regular starter were ending.

On the Miracle Braves of 1914, Hess played a secondary role. Yet he did not deserve the disparaging remark of Harold Kaese, who in his history of the Braves in Boston wrote: "The Braves of 1914 had other pitchers besides Rudolph, Tyler, and James, believe it or not, but none of them was very conspicuous." The second-line pitchers won just 25 games, while Rudolph, Tyler and James won 69, "which explains why they were so well remembered while the others are forgotten."[16] Although once again losing more games than he won (5-6), Hess was effective. He pitched in 14 games for a total of 89 innings, starting 11 and completing 7. His two most noteworthy victories came over Chicago. On May 22 he shut out the Cubs, 2-0, to give the Braves their first back-to-back wins of the season. By the time the Miracle had unfolded, Hess pitched the second game of a September 26 doubleheader, which was played at Fenway Park, winning 12-2, for a sweep that increased the Braves' lead to 8 1/2 games. Not a bad performance, overall, for the 35-year-old veteran, who was described by Stallings at season's end as "our old reliable Otto Hess."[17]

Yet Hess's major-league days were numbered. He pitched sparingly (four games and 14 innings) in the first few months of the 1915 season before the Braves released him on June 14. The day before, in his final big-league game, he had pitched five scoreless innings of relief as the Braves lost at Chicago. A newspaper account of his career aptly summed up his comeback with the Braves as a "pretty good record."[18] He concluded his major-league record with 70 wins and 90 losses and an ERA of 2.98.

Military service framed Hess's baseball career. By the time it was ending—pitching stints with Vernon of the Pacific Coast League in 1916 and Atlanta of the Southern Association in 1917—the United States was again at war. And as in 1898, Hess enlisted in the Army. He is one of five major-league players who served in both the Spanish-American War and World War I.[19]

Hess contracted tuberculosis while in France during World War I and eventually succumbed to the disease, dying at the US Veterans' Hospital in Tucson, Arizona, on February 25, 1926. He was buried in Fairview Park Cemetery in Fairview Park, Ohio. He was survived by his second wife, Irene G. Sweet of Cleveland, whom he had married in 1923; his first wife, Grace Fusbaugh, also of Cleveland and whom he married in 1908, died in 1914.[20]

Sources

Most of the statistics are derived from Baseball-Reference.com.

Notes

1. Some sources list November 13, 1878 as Hess's birthdate, but October 10, 1878, is the date indicated on his death certificate in 1926 and most other sources, including Retrosheet. His year of birth is also occasionally indicated to be 1879 or 1880.
2. Ancestry.com/U.S. Federal Census 1900; Ancestry.com/U.S. Army Register of Enlistments, 1798-1914; Ancestry.com/New York Passenger Lists 1820-1957.
3. John Snyder, *Indians Journal; Year by Year and Day by Day with the Cleveland Indians Since 1901* (Cincinnati: Clerisy Press, 2008), 36; Ancestry.com/U.S. Army Register of Enlistments, 1798-1914. Unidentified news clippings of July 1914 and August 1917 (Baseball Hall of Fame/Hess Clippings) make references to Hess pitching minor-league baseball at Columbus in 1901 and "returning to the minors" in 1903; Baseball-Reference.com/Hess does not credit him with minor-league experience before 1903. Nor does it list him on the 1901 Columbus Senators roster.
4. Russell Schneider, *The Cleveland Indians Encyclopedia* (Philadelphia: Temple University Press, 1995), 170.
5. Snyder, *Indians Journal*, 43; Schneider, *Indians Encyclopedia*, 169-70.
6. Snyder, *Indians Journal*, 46-48.
7. Rod Caborn and Dave Larson, "1906 Cleveland Naps, Deadball Era Underachiever," *Baseball Research Journal*, 41: 1 (Spring 2012), 78-85; Snyder, *Indians Journal*, 49-52; http//www.BaseballLibrary.com.
8. thisgreatgame.com/1906.
9. Unidentified newspaper, December 15, 1906, Baseball Hall of Fame/Hess Clippings.
10. Rice, "Cleveland Chat," *Sporting Life*, January 12, 1907, 9.
11. Lajoie, quoted in Rice, "Cleveland Chat," *Sporting Life*, January 12, 1907, 9.

12   Schneider, *Indians Encyclopedia*, 16-17; David S. Neft & Richard M. Cohen, *The Sports Encyclopedia: Baseball* (rev. ed., New York: Grosset & Dunlap, 1981), 37, 40.

13   "Diamond Dots and Dashes," *Baseball Magazine*, September 1911, 45.

14   "Minor League Section," *Baseball Magazine*, July 1912, 63.

15   *Sporting Life*, October 12, 1912, 3; Harold Kaese, *The Boston Braves 1871-1953* (Boston: Northeastern University Press, 2004), 131, 141; BaseballLibrary.com/Otto Hess.

16   Kaese, *Boston Braves*, 151.

17   *Sporting Life*, November 14, 1914, 6; BaseballLibrary.com.

18   Unidentified newspaper clipping, 1915, Baseball Hall of Fame/Hess Clippings.

19   Baseball-reference.com/Spanish-American War Veterans, World War I veterans.

The others whose names appear on both lists are Ben Caffyn, Joe Doyle, John Grimes, and Gabby Street.

20   Arizona State Board of Health: Death Certificate/Otto Hess; *Sporting Life*, October 31, 1908, 9; Ancestry.com/Cuyahoga County Marriage Records and Indexes, 1810-1973; Ancestry.com/1910 U.S. Federal Census; *Sporting Life*, January 17, 1914, 16.

Tom Hughes

By Greg Erion

WHEN ONE EXAMINES the Miracle Braves' performance it is obvious that the bulk of the pitching effort rested with just three men: Dick Rudolph, Bill James, and George Tyler. Starting 107 of the 158 games the team played, they won 68 of the Braves' 94 victories. Yet, when Boston clinched the pennant against the Chicago Cubs, it was neither Rudolph, James, nor Tyler who won the game. It was "Salida Tom" Hughes, recalled from the minors just weeks earlier.[1] Hughes' recognition as Salida Tom is important in that five men named Tom Hughes played in the major leagues. Four were pitchers, including Long Tom Hughes, a contemporary of Salida Tom. Their respective exploits on the mound were then — and still are — confused with each other's.

Although overshadowed by Rudolph, James, and Tyler in 1914, Hughes proved a mainstay of the Braves staff the next two seasons, showing ability as both a starter and reliever. His time with the Braves represented his second stint in the majors; he had pitched for the New York Highlanders from 1906 through 1910 with middling success.

Thomas L. Hughes was born at Coal Creek, Colorado, on January 28, 1884. He was the youngest of five children. His parents, Richard and Kelzia Hughes, had emigrated from Wales. The 1880 US Census listed Richard as a miner, later a locomotive engineer.[2] The family moved frequently, possibly because the father's work on the railroad. In 1900 the Hughes family was living in Trenton City, Missouri, which contained a Rock Island Railroad facility; ten years later they had moved to the railroad town of Salida, Colorado, and it is from there that the pitcher's moniker stemmed.

According to *Baseball Magazine*, young Hughes was working in a railroad repair shop as a blacksmith when he was contacted to play professional baseball. The article indicated that he was living in Salida at the time, but it seems more likely that Hughes resided in Missouri with his parents, because he began play in the Missouri Valley League, which consisted of teams from Missouri and eastern Kansas, considerably distant from Colorado.[3]

During his first season, 1904, Hughes pitched for the Pittsburg Coal Diggers and Topeka Saints, posting a combined 10-26 record.[4] In 1905, with the Topeka White Sox of the Western Association, he improved to 14-18. Sensing potential, the New York Highlanders drafted him and sent him to Atlanta of the Southern Association for seasoning. In 1906 Hughes had a breakout season with the Atlanta Crackers, finishing with a 25-5 record. His performance earned a call-up to New York in September.

Hughes made his major-league debut against the St. Louis Browns on September 18. Eleven days later he earned his first big-league win, a complete-game 5-4 effort over the Boston Americans. Hughes spent most of the next two seasons back in the minor leagues, initially with Montreal and then Newark in the Eastern League, fash-

Tom Hughes

ioning successive 14-17 and 16-9 records. Significantly, as it would turn out later, his manager at Newark was George Stallings. Called up to the Highlanders again at the end of 1907, Hughes appeared in four games, winning twice.

In 1909 Hughes became a member of the Highlanders' starting rotation. Appearing in 26 games, starting 15, he finished with a 7-8 record for the fifth-place New York club. While earned-run averages did not become an official statistic until 1913, subsequent research found that Hughes's ERA for 1909 was 2.65. This seems an impressive figure by today's standards; in truth, it was just average, worse than the league average ERA of 2.47.

The Highlanders vaulted from fifth to second place in 1910. Despite their improvement, not all was well within the organization. Manager Stallings resigned during the closing weeks of the season after first baseman Hal Chase continually second-guessed his managerial decisions—with team owners William Devery and Frank Farrell not backing Stallings. Stallings went on to manage the Buffalo Bisons in the International League for two years while Hughes pitched for the rival Rochester Bronchos (later Hustlers). In 1914 they reunited when Stallings became manager of the Braves, playing a key role in resurrecting Hughes's major-league career.[5]

Hughes's performance in 1910 was mediocre. Finishing at 7-9, he was the least effective of the regular starters. He did, however, show flashes of excellence. On August 30 against the Cleveland Naps, Hughes threw 9⅓ innings of no-hit ball in a scoreless tie before being touched for two hits in the tenth, then surrendered a barrage of hits and runs in the 11th, losing 5-0. Adding insult to injury, several news reports of the game, including that in the *Cleveland Plain Dealer*, identified Hughes as Long Tom Hughes. This was one of several examples where the simultaneous careers and accomplishments of Salida Tom and Long Tom were confused.[6] Although a solid effort, Hughes's performance against the Naps seemed to confirm his reputation as one who weakened in the late innings. That he could not go the distance proved detrimental to his career with the Highlanders after the season ended.[7]

In January 1911 the Highlanders sold Hughes' contract to Rochester of the Eastern League. Press reports noted his reputation as a "hard luck" pitcher who pitched well but would then be "touched up for a few hits in a bunch, and lose his game."[8]

While professional disappointment occurred, personal happiness abounded. On March 11, 1911, Hughes married a neighbor, Esther Lee Wilson; the 1910 census shows the Hughes and Wilson families living on the same block. She had been supporting her widowed mother and sister through employment as a bookkeeper and stenographer at the local Red Cross Hospital. After their marriage, Hughes moved into the Wilson residence.[9]

The wedding took place in Denver; the bride's mother and uncle accompanied her to the ceremony. Hughes was described as "an old Salida boy" and "exceedingly popular locally." The "old Salida Boy" description was something of a stretch; Hughes had lived in Salida something less than ten years. The couple left the day after the ceremony for Anniston, Alabama, where Hughes began spring training. Their marriage lasted 50 years, until Hughes's death in 1961.[10]

For the next four seasons, 1911-1914, Hughes pitched for Rochester. He kept in contact with former teammates from the majors. In 1913, prior to the beginning of spring training, Salida's *Mountain Mail* reported that Russ Ford, a pitcher for the Highlanders, had visited Hughes in Denver, where Hughes served as enrollment clerk for Colorado's House of Representatives.[11] Hughes, apparently an enterprising sort, also owned a "gent's furnishing store" in Salida at about the same time.[12]

The Rochester Bronchos of the Eastern League (later the International League) were at the highest level of minor-league play. Hughes pitched well, averaging 16 wins per year for a team that regularly finished in the first division and won the league championship in 1912. In 1914 he led the league with 182 strikeouts; his solid performance led to his purchase by the Braves on September 5, 1914.[13]

George Stallings was then manager of the Braves. Stallings had witnessed his performance with the Highlanders and with Rochester. And Fred Mitchell, who essentially served as Stallings' pitching coach on the Braves, coached with Stallings on the Highlanders, then played with Hughes at Rochester in 1911. The day Hughes was purchased, the Braves were in a first-place tie with the Giants; they finished winning 27 of 34 games to sweep past New York. Hughes contributed two victories to the late-season run; his first, a complete-game 3-2 effort on September 29 against Chicago, clinched the pennant for the Braves.

It was the Braves' first championship since the old Beaneaters took the title in 1898. Hughes won again on October 5 against Brooklyn as Stallings was clearly resting James, Rudolph, and Tyler for the World Series against the Philadelphia A's. Even though Hughes came to the Braves late in the season, the team's victory brought him acclaim in hometown Salida. Salida's *Mountain Mail* noted, "Mr. Hughes grew up in this city, spends his winters here and has a multitude of friends who take delight in his success and who would like to see him have a chance in the World Series. His friends here have great confidence in him."[14]

Hughes did not appear in the World Series, as the Braves dispatched the A's in four straight games. Joining the team late, he was not eligible to receive $2,812 in World Series winning player shares.[15] His late-season performance, however, gained him a place with the Braves for the next season.

The Braves' efforts to defend their world championship proved unsuccessful in 1915; they finished second to the Philadelphia Phillies. Pitching proved the major culprit in denying a second straight title. Although Rudolph won 22 games, James and Tyler both fell off their pennant-winning efforts, the illness-plagued James especially, as he dropped from 26-7 to 5-4. This created an opportunity for Hughes, who responded with 16 wins. Pitching in a league-leading 50 games, he started 25 and sported a 2.12 ERA, fifth in the senior circuit.

Hughes led the league with nine saves, (a statistic not recorded or recognized at the time). His double-duty performance that year was rare. As of 2012, Hughes was one of only 17 pitchers to have started 20 or more games and finished 20 or more games in relief in a season.[16]

In 1916 Hughes posted a 16-3 record, leading the National League in winning percentage (842.). On June 16 he threw the second no-hitter of his career when he blanked Pittsburgh 2-0. The game ended with a flourish, Hughes recording the final out by fanning Honus Wagner.[17]

With his effort against Cleveland in 1910 recognized as a no-hitter at the time, Hughes became only the second pitcher besides Cy Young to throw a hitless games in both the American and National Leagues. His record-setting efforts did not stop with the no-hitter. A week after his hitless gem, he entered a game in relief against Philadelphia, and held the Phillies hitless for 3⅔ innings before allowing a hit that ended a streak of 15⅔ hitless innings over four games including the no-hitter. At least one newspaper called this a record,[18] but another quickly noted that it had fallen short of a record set in 1904 by Cy Young.[19] Nevertheless, Hughes's pitching was superlative. Misfortune struck later in his season, which ended when a pitch from Phillies pitcher Erskine Mayer struck his wrist and broke it on September 7.

There are different accounts of what happened to Hughes in 1917. *The Sporting News* wrote that he was a holdout during spring training.[20] Hughes must have come to an agreement quickly, because in mid-March he was mentioned by the *Boston Globe* as pitching a practice game, his first appearance since his wrist was broken. "He worked … only three innings, but feels no ill effects from the injury," the *Globe* wrote.[21] But two weeks later he was reported to have a sore arm.[22] Harold Kaese's history of the Boston Braves states that Hughes was out of action because of a sore hand.[23] Based on subsequent events, it was probably a sore arm. Whatever the cause, Hughes was out of action until midseason.

Salida Tom Hughes

When he returned, he appeared in just 11 games, starting eight and fashioning a 5-3 record with a 1.95 ERA.

Hughes was unable to pitch for most of 1918; he appeared in just three games. On April 19 he pitched a complete game against the Phillies, losing in the tenth, 4-3, despite hitting a solo home run in the seventh himself. It was reminiscent of his losing no-hit effort against Cleveland eight years earlier. Eight innings of relief against the Phillies five days later, again in a losing effort, and a single inning in relief against St. Louis on July 17 were his last appearances in the major leagues.

For his major-league career, Hughes showed a 56-39 record with a 2.56 ERA, slightly better than the major-league average during the years he pitched (2.68). A more recently developed tool suggests his effectiveness with the Braves. His WHIP (walks and hits per inning pitched) was 1.022, the best in Braves franchise history for those who pitched 300 innings or more.[24] He was extremely effective at the height of an abbreviated major-league career.

Hughes's days of playing professional baseball were not quite done. In July 1919 the *Los Angeles Times* noted that Johnny Powers, owner of the Los Angeles Angels in the Pacific Coast League, had offered Hughes a tryout, noting that he had the potential to start or relieve. Within days, the tryout apparently successful, Hughes signed a contract. He believed he had overcome "a cold in his arm" which caused his release from the Braves.[25] On July 19 he started against the Vernon Tigers and pitched shutout ball until the fifth inning, when his arm went dead. In dramatic fashion, the *Times's* Harry Williams, reporting on the game wrote, "Two months of faithful preparation, more months of careful nursing of the old wing to bring it back to life went for naught, and the hope of all this was shattered when the arm dropped limp at his side. Tom Hughes had failed to come back.[26]

Soon after, the *New York Times* reported that Hughes had quit for good after "one disastrous trial on the mound."[27] The *Los Angeles Times* subsequently reported that Hughes "whose attempt to come back with the Angels failed," was now a used-car salesman.[28]

But Hughes had seven more years of pitching left. In 1920 he asked Powers for another tryout and was successful. In what was left of the 1920 season, Hughes made an effective comeback, going 7-4 for the Angels. Any doubts that his arm had returned to form were erased in a game against the San Francisco Seals on September 26; he pitched all 15 innings to win a 3-2 decision. Unlike the dark description of his setback the year before, Hughes's effort was described in colorful euphemisms of early 20th century sports reporting: "And above all the hectic disturbance, glimmering like a comet at midnight, shone the name of Tom Hughes, whose rejuvenation as a pitcher is undoubtedly the most phenomenal comeback in the history of the game."[29]

Hughes went on to pitch for the Angeles through 1925. During that time he won 70 and lost 61, serving as a coach and temporary manager on occasion.[30] The old man of the team, he treated his teammates to cigars when his only child, Thomas Jr., was born on April 28, 1925. That season was his last with Los Angeles.

In 1926 Hughes split his time between Little Rock of the Southern Association and Beaumont and San Antonio of the Texas League, compiling a 5-12 record with a 4.60 ERA. By then he was 42 years old and it was time to retire. Hughes had proved that he could come back from the arm ailment that ended his major-league career. After retiring from baseball, Hughes worked in the insurance business, then during World War II in the production of airplanes.[31] His son, Thomas Jr. graduated from the United States Naval Academy and served three years on active duty. After the war, young Hughes established himself as an executive in the insurance industry. In 1955 he died at the age of 29 in an auto accident on the Hollywood Freeway.[32]

Six years later, on November 1, 1961, Salida Tom died, succumbing to the combined effects of pneumonia, emphysema, and tuberculosis, a disease he had contacted 11 years earlier. Burial was at Forest Lawn Memorial Park alongside Thomas Jr.[33] At the time of Hughes' death, he was widely described as one of a few pitchers who had thrown no-hitters in the American and National League,[34] but this was before the retroactive canceling of his effort against the Cleveland Naps.

Researching Hughes's life and career reveals little of his personality. In a day when player interviews were rare, few quotes attributable to Hughes could be found. Thus, he appears through the lens of time as a one-dimensional individual—except for one incident hinting at his strength of character, as described in a short article in his file at the Baseball Hall of Fame.

Dated October 7, no year given, the article tells of a horse-drawn carriage occupied by two young women that went out of control. Hughes, hearing their screams, ran into the street and grabbed the horse's bit strap. The animal reared and dragged Hughes several feet before stopping. The article observed that Hughes "probably saved the young women from serious injuries."[35] At that one instant, Salida Tom proved he could do more than pitch.

As of this writing, the statistics for Salida Tom's post-major-league career have been mistakenly placed in the minor-league record of Long Tom Hughes in baseball-reference.com. Efforts were being made to correct this. In addition, many newspaper articles over the years have confused the two men.[36]

Notes

1. This article is immeasurably better thanks to the assistance of Dr. Arlene Shovald of Salida, Colorado, whose research generated a great deal of information about Hughes. Dr. Shovald provided all notes referring to *The Mountain Mail,* Salida's newspaper. Barbara Erion's knowledge of Ancestry.com yielded knowledge of the Hughes family, especially his wife and son.
2. Data on the Hughes family obtained from Ancestry.com.
3. Ward Mason, "Vote for Hughes," *Baseball Magazine*, November 1916, 40. The article is vague about who the person was who enticed Hughes into professional baseball.
4. All baseball statistics except as described in Note 42 are from baseball-reference.com/players/h/hugheto02.shtml or Retrosheet.
5. Bill James, *The Bill James Guide to Baseball Managers From 1870 to Today* (New York: Scribner, 1997), 45; Ed Fitzgerald, ed., *The American League* (New York: Grosset & Dunlap, 1959), 8.
6. From various Cleveland and New York newspaper clippings in the Tom Hughes file at the Baseball Hall of Fame, September 1910.
7. Under guidelines then governing, Hughes received credit for a no-hitter. It was a feat recognized for more than 80 years until the Major League Committee for Statistical Accuracy redefined a no-hitter in 1991 as one in which "a pitcher (or pitchers) allows no hits during the entire course of a game, which consists of at least nine innings."
8. Three Yankees Sold," *New York Times*, January 4, 1911, 11.
9. 1913-1914 Salida City Directory; email from Dr. Arlene Shovald, February 16, 2013.
10. "Hughes-Wilson Nuptials," *The Mountain Mail*, Salida, Colorado, March 10, 1911; "Former Salidian Esther W. Hughes Dies in California," *The Mountain Mail*, June 26, 1967.
11. "100 Years Ago," *The Mountain Mail*, Salida, Colorado, February 5, 2013, 11.
12. Mason, *Baseball Magazine*, 40.
13. http://www.baseball-reference.com/players/h/hugheto02.shtml
14. "Salida Boy Wins National Baseball Fame," *The Mountain Mail*, Salida, Colorado, October 1914, 11.
15. Mason, *Baseball Magazine*, 40.
16. http://highheatstats.blogspot.com/2011/11/10-gs10-gf-not-for-anyone-2011.html

17 "Tom Hughes Pitches No-Hit, No-Run Game, *Boston Daily Globe*, June 17, 1916, 7.

18 "Tom Hughes Makes New Baseball Record, *Hartford Courant*, June 25, 1916, Z6.

19 "Young in 23 Hitless Innings; Pitching Record for Majors," *Washington Post*, July 16, 1916, S2.

20 "Braves Look in Mirror and See Team to Head Off Giants," *The Sporting News*, March 15, 1917, 1.

21 "Stallings Acts as Drillmaster" *Boston Daily Globe*, March 15, 1917, 7.

22 "Yankees Get Rest," *New York Times*, April 2, 1917.

23 Harold Kaese, *The Boston Braves, 1871-1953* (Boston: Northeastern University Press, 2004), 179.

24 http://en.wikipedia.org/wiki/Tom_L._Hughes.

25 "Baseball Notes," *Los Angeles Times* July 10, 1919, III2; "Morley Signs Up Tom Hughes," *Los Angeles Times*, July 14, 1919, 15.

26 "Tigers Down Angels Again", *Los Angeles Times*, July 20, 1919, 18.

27 "Hughes Leaves Baseball," *New York Times*, August 6, 1919, 16.

28 "Baseball Notes," *Los Angeles Times*, October 16, 1919, III1.

29 "Wonder Where Tom Hughes Got the Goat Glands," *Los Angeles Times*, September 27, 1920, 16.

30 "Seraphs Knuckle to Work," *Los Angeles Times*, March 1, 1923, III2.

31 "Thomas Hughes, former Salidian, Dies in California," *The Mountain Mail*, Salida, Colorado, November 2, 1961.

32 "Ex-Baseball Star's Son Dies in Crash, *Los Angeles Times*, March 10, 1955, 5.

33 "Thomas Hughes, former Salidian, Dies in California," *The Mountain Mail*, Salida, Colorado, February 5, 2013, 11.

34 "Obituary," *The Sporting News*, November 8, 1961, 24.

35 Hughes file, Baseball Hall of Fame.

36 Statistical data for Salida Tom Hughes's performance in the Pacific Coast League is contained in Dennis Snelling, *The Pacific Coast League: A Statistical History, 1903-1956* (Jefferson, North Carolina: McFarland, 1995), 271. Baseball-reference.com/players/h/hugheto02.shtml mistakenly attributes Hughes's PCL statistics to Long Tom Hughes. The latter had been retired from the game by then. Numerous references to Salida Tom Hughes in the *Los Angeles Times* mention prior experience with the Braves, a team Long Tom never played for. An article referring to the birth of Salida Tom's son, Thomas Jr., in the *Los Angeles Times* identifies the birthdate of Tom Jr. as April 28, 1925, the date that is on an application for a headstone signed by Mrs. Thomas Hughes dated April 6, 1955. An email from Bob Hoie to the author on February 9, 2013, contains further detail that Salida Tom pitched for the Angels in the 1920s. Long Tom Hughes did pitch for the Angels, but in 1914 and 1915.

Bill James

By David Jones

AT THE END of the 1914 season, 22-year-old Bill James stood on the cusp of baseball stardom. He had just pitched his Boston Braves to the most improbable pennant in baseball history, and followed up on that performance by beating the mighty Philadelphia Athletics twice in three days during that year's World's Series. He was such a uniquely gifted pitcher that John J. Ward of *Baseball Magazine* predicted, "The further acquisition of experience should [make him] one of the greatest all-round pitchers in history." When he wrote those words, Ward probably never could have imagined that this talented pitcher, who already had 32 major-league wins behind him, had but five more in front of him.

William Lawrence James was born March 12, 1892, in Iowa Hill, California, the third of four children of William and Emma James. Located 30 miles northeast of Sacramento, Iowa Hill was gold-mining country, and that is how James' father supported the family. When Bill was 11 years old, the family moved 50 miles north to Oroville, where the senior James took on work as the manager of a dredge mining company. Bill's parents wanted a similar future for their son and encouraged him to study mining engineering at the University of California, but Bill had other ideas. During his three years at Oroville Union High School, he matured into a 6'3", 195 lb. pitching prodigy blessed with an exceptional fastball. After high school Bill briefly acquiesced to his parents' wishes and attended classes at St. Mary's College in Oakland. But when Seattle of the Northwestern League offered him a contract prior to the 1912 season, he left school for good.

In Seattle James added a spitball and change of pace to his arsenal. The impressive results that followed hastened his development into the most touted prospect in all of baseball. James pitched Seattle to the pennant in 1912, at one point reeling off 16 consecutive victories. At season's end, his 29-7 record and 2.17 ERA landed him a contract with the National League's Boston Braves. It also left him with the nickname "Seattle Bill," a moniker designed mostly to avoid confusion, as the 1912 Cleveland Naps already featured a "Big Bill" James and a William "Lefty" James.

"Seattle Bill" joined a Boston club that had long since cemented its place as the most wretched franchise in all of baseball. Going into 1913, the Braves had not enjoyed a single winning season since 1902 and had not finished within 50 games of first place since 1908. With the arrival of new manager George Stallings, the Braves showed modest improvement during James's rookie season, as the club climbed to fifth in the standings and moved to within 31 games of first place. James performed well in his first season, posting a 2.79 ERA while splitting time between the starting rotation and bullpen.

The Braves' stunning reversal of fortune in 1914 has long since entered baseball annals as the most unlikely championship run in history, but the critical role James played in the Boston uprising has undeservedly faded into obscurity. From July 9 until the end of the season,

Bill James

Lefty James keeping loose.

he went 19-1 with a 1.51 ERA. His only loss came on August 22 in Pittsburgh, when he was beaten 3-2 in 12 innings. Without that setback, James would have ended his season with a record-breaking 20-game winning streak. With it, he still assembled the best season of any pitcher in the National League. James led the NL in winning percentage (.788), and he finished in the top five in wins (26), ERA (1.90), innings pitched (332 1/3), and strikeouts (156).

In Game Two of that year's World's Series, James matched up against Philadelphia's Eddie Plank in a classic pitchers' duel at Shibe Park. Plank pitched brilliantly that afternoon, surrendering seven hits and holding the Braves scoreless until Boston pushed one run across in the ninth inning. But James was better, allowing just two hits, fanning eight, and coaxing a game-ending double play with the tying and winning runs on base to preserve the 1-0 victory. Two days later, James was called into action again when Game Three stretched into extra frames. Pitching on one day's rest, James held the Athletics hitless in the 11th and 12th innings before Boston scored the winning run in the bottom of the 12th on a Joe Bush throwing error. In a span of three days, James had won two games, pitched 11 innings, and allowed just two hits. The Braves completed their sweep of the Athletics the following afternoon.

Despite his success and status as a World's Series hero, James expressed ambivalence about life in the major leagues. "I like the game well enough," he told *Baseball Magazine* after the Series. "But I can't get used to the long jumps from one city to another. It looks nice from the outside to think of traveling around the country, but one sweep of the circuit is enough. After that it becomes hard and disagreeable work." Ironically, he got his chance to see major league baseball from the outside soon enough.

James reported late to camp the following spring after a brief holdout induced the Braves to double his salary, but it soon became apparent that he was a mere shadow of the pitcher who had dominated the league the previous year. From the start of the season James complained of chronic arm fatigue. Initially the press took a dim view of the injury, dismissing his protests as the petulant whining of an overpaid athlete. But by June, reduced velocity and flagging endurance forced James out of the starting rotation. After a poor relief appearance on July 30, he was shelved for the rest of the season.

The Braves hoped that a long winter's rest would restore strength to James' right arm, but it was not to be. In late March 1916, teammate Johnny Evers signaled the end was near when he admitted to reporters: "His arm is gone. Bill knows it and we know it." Shortly thereafter, the 24-year-old pitcher was placed on the voluntary retired list. The press described the injury as a "dead arm," but in all likelihood James suffered from a torn rotator cuff, a condition the medicine of the day was powerless to correct.

Nonetheless, the man who had once bemoaned the transient life of a professional baseball player attempted several comebacks. After undergoing numerous shoulder operations, James tried to return to the Braves in 1918 but the comeback was aborted before the start of the regular season. After serving in the 63rd Infantry

James looking things over.

during World War I, James pitched one game in relief for the Braves in 1919. He spent the next several years bouncing around the Pacific Coast League as a player and coach before concluding his career with Sacramento in 1925.

In retirement Bill James lived in Oroville with his wife, Harriet Newman, whom he had married in 1924. The couple had one daughter, Janet, born in 1926. James worked as a truck driver for an oil company for several years and later as an assessor for Butte County. He died of a stroke on March 10, 1971, two days shy of his 79th birthday, and is buried in Memorial Park Cemetery in Oroville.

Note: A slightly different version of this biography appeared in Tom Simon, ed., Deadball Stars of the National League *(Washington, D.C.: Brassey's, Inc., 2004).*

Sources

For this biography, the author used a number of contemporary sources, especially those found in the subject's file at the National Baseball Hall of Fame Library.

Clarence Kraft

By Jon Dunkle

Over time, Clarence "Big Boy" Kraft was probably the greatest power hitter to play for the 1914 Boston Braves. Looking at the records of the major leagues, one would never know it. Even though he played for one of the most memorable teams in history and would become one of the most prolific power hitters in the game, his time with the 1914 Boston Braves was so fleeting and had such little impact on the Braves' fortunes that it would be easy to overlook his three brief appearances in uniform. However, starting in the months after his stint with the Braves and extending 44 years beyond, Kraft had a significant impact on the sport and on the lives of many people.

Clarence Kraft was born on June 9, 1887, in Evansville, Indiana, on the same farm on which his father was born.[1] The first of John and Anna Kraft's five children, he grew up in Evansville and was deeply involved with athletics, playing baseball, basketball, and ice hockey and running track.[2] He also showed an early interest in automobiles and after a brief time in business college, went to work selling and repairing cars.[3]

On the baseball diamond Kraft was a dominant force, both on the mound and at the plate. It was his success as a pitcher on the local sandlots that initially drew the attention of professional baseball. In 1910, at the age of 22, Kraft made his professional debut with the local Evansville team, a member of the Class B Central League. After one game Evansville sent him to McLeansboro of the Class D Southern Illinois League. McLeansboro overwhelmed the rest of the league, going 20-5. The league folded on July 11 and McLeansboro joined the stronger Kentucky-Illinois-Tennessee (Kitty) League two weeks later.[4] The Class D Kitty League had re-formed in 1910 after being defunct for two years and was enjoying a resurgence in interest through the first 60 games. McLeansboro and Vincennes were added to the league and a second 60-game season began.[5] The McLeansboro team continued its dominance over the opposition in this second season, going 40-18 and being the only team in the league with a winning record. Despite playing just 51 games in the league as a pitcher and outfielder, Kraft tied for the league lead in home runs with four. He made more of a mark on the mound with a 13-2 record, the best winning percentage in the league.

Kraft's success was noted throughout baseball. In January 1911 Toledo of the Class A American Association drafted him from McLeansboro.[6] The Cleveland Naps of the American League were also interested in Kraft, primarily as a pitcher, and they secured his rights from Toledo and took him to spring training. The jump to the big leagues was too much for Kraft and the Indians returned him to Toledo, which then also released him. Kraft caught on with Flint of the Class C Southern Michigan Association.[7]

With Flint Kraft continued to pitch and play the field. Once again he paced his league in home runs, this time

Clarence Kraft

with 19. On the mound he was not as stellar, posting a 6-12 record. He returned to Flint for the 1912 season. In July Kraft clouted eight home runs in nine days, and Cleveland came calling again, purchasing the rights to both Kraft and a teammate, Billy Hunter.[8] Once again the Indians changed their minds. New Orleans of the Class A Southern Association signed Kraft and optioned him to Clarksdale for yet another season in the low minors, this time the Class D Cotton States League.

On the mound Kraft had his ups and downs in 1913, winning seven games and losing seven. He pitched his best game as a professional for Clarksdale, hurling a one-hitter against Meridian.[9] He continued to hit and when the league folded in August, New Orleans reclaimed Kraft. Kraft made a couple of pitching appearances, his final stints on the mound, but made an impression with the bat. He hit a home run that was announced as the longest ever hit at Pelicans Stadium in New Orleans.[10] He finished the season with a .362 batting average, prompting *Sporting Life* to call him the Southern League's "best natural slugger since the days of Joe Jackson."[11]

Entering the 1914 season, life was as much business as baseball for the major leagues and Clarence Kraft. Nashville of the Southern Association purchased his contract from New Orleans for $400.[12] Less than two weeks later, the Brooklyn Superbas of the National League drafted Kraft, paying Nashville $1,500.[13] In April the Superbas released Kraft to the Boston Braves. On May 1 Kraft made his debut in the major leagues, coming in as a replacement for first baseman Butch Schmidt. Batting against future Hall of Famer Rube Marquard, he singled. He pinch-hit twice after that, on May 11 and May 15, and then his career in the major leagues ended.

For someone no longer in the major leagues, Kraft continued to make a splash. Boston released him back to Brooklyn and the Superbas then tried to send him back to Nashville. Kraft opposed the decision and went to the Base Ball Players' Fraternity for help.

The Base Ball Players' Fraternity, an early union formed in 1912 to help protect major-league players, had met with the National Commission, baseball's governing body, after the 1913 season with suggestions for changes. The commission, faced with the threat of a third major league, the Federal League, had worked to appease the Fraternity and implemented many of the suggested changes. One of them, that a player being optioned or released from a major-league team be first offered to Double-A teams before being sent to a lower classification, was the source of Kraft's discontent. The Newark Indians of the Double-A International League had claimed Kraft but the National Commission ruled that Nashville had put in a claim first. Kraft refused to report to Nashville and went to Newark to play.[14]

The conflict continued until the Fraternity threatened to strike over the issue. Faced with the potential of a work stoppage, Superbas owner Charles Ebbets offered Nashville $1,000 to withdraw its claim to Kraft.[15] Nashville agreed, making $2,100 in profit from Kraft without his ever setting foot on the diamond for the club.

Kraft finished out the 1914 season with Newark and began 1915 with the team. The Federal League had relocated its Indianapolis franchise to Newark in 1915, and the presence of a major-league team forced the movement of the Newark International League to Harrisburg in July. For the season, Kraft posted a .307 batting average and led the league with 24 triples.[16]

Kraft continued his team-hopping in 1916, signing with Louisville of the Double-A American Association. In June he was traded with two other players to Milwaukee of the same league but all three refused to report, asserting that they should receive bonuses before signing with Milwaukee. The argument was settled and all three players joined Milwaukee.[17]

Over the course of Kraft's three seasons at the Double-A level, he performed solidly but not spectacularly. He was strictly a first baseman during this time and as he entered his late 20s, his contractual difficulties coupled with his performance did not bode particularly well for his return to the majors. When Wilkes-Barre of the Class B New York State League purchased Kraft for the 1917 season, it seemed as if his career was on a decline. Still, he hit .311, his highest season batting average since 1913, and tied for the league lead in home runs with seven. The Wilkes-Barre team was a powerful one and Kraft once again belonged to a championship squad, his first since McLeansboro.

In 1918, with the US now in the World War, many minor leagues shut down, including the New York State League. Kraft joined the Fort Worth team in the Class B Texas League. He was on his way to another successful season at the plate, hitting .308 in 70 games, but was drafted to serve in the Army in June. As more players joined the war effort, the Texas League was forced to cease operations weeks later.

Kraft used his automotive experience to his benefit and to his country's. He joined the 309th Motor Transport Corps and spent six months serving in France. He returned from the war to his home in Missouri, where he married his girlfriend, Dorothy Goessling. Soon afterward they moved to California to be closer to Kraft's sister but then went to Texas after Fort Worth signed Kraft yet again.

Fort Worth had the best record in the Texas League in 1919 but lost the playoff series to Shreveport. The following season, Fort Worth devastated opponents, topping the standings by 23 games over the second-place Wichita Falls squad, and was crowned champion. During this time, Kraft contributed to the team's success but not in a large way. In 1919 he hit .275 with 11 home runs. In 1920, those numbers dropped to .258 and six. The batting average was the lowest of his career as was his .359 slugging percentage. Before the 1921 season, the Texas League was reclassified as a Class A league. The season that should probably have been the culmination of a mostly lackluster career turned out to be the genesis of a rejuvenation that put Kraft among the greatest minor-league home-run hitters of all time.

Signs that Kraft was a better ballplayer than he had been in recent years appeared early in the 1921 season. On April 23 against Wichita Falls, he went 5-for-5, hitting a single, a double, and three home runs. In one game, Kraft had hit half as many home runs as he had in 151 games the previous season.

Kraft never slowed down and when the season concluded, Fort Worth was once again champion of the Texas League. Kraft set league records in hits (212) and total bases (376). He led the league in runs scored (132) and won the batting title with a .352 average, almost 100 points higher than he had hit the season before.

Fort Worth's stranglehold on the Texas League continued into 1922. Since losing the playoff series to Shreveport in 1919, the Panthers had won both halves of the season in 1920 and 1921, eliminating the need for a playoff to determine the champion. In 1922 they swept the season again. Once again Kraft led the league in runs batted in (131) and home runs (32) while batting .339.

The 1923 season was almost an exact reprise of the season before. Fort Worth took the championship and Kraft led the league in home runs, again with 32. He hit .324 and his slugging percentage of .589 was identical to his percentage in 1922.

Going into the 1924 season, it seemed as if Kraft and the Panthers were unstoppable. A few years before Kraft had appeared to be on his way out of professional baseball. Now he was a top power hitter for one of the best minor-league teams in the country. Then, incredibly, both Fort Worth and Kraft got even better.

In 1924 the Panthers won 109 games while losing only 41. They finished 30 1/2 games ahead of second-place Houston in claiming their fifth straight league championship. In May Kraft went on a tear similar to the one he had gone on in Flint a decade before, clouting eight home runs in nine games. He set league records with 196 runs batted in, 414 total bases, and 55 home runs. (The RBI record was still the standard in the Texas League as of 2013.) Kraft batted .349, slugged an incredible .713 and led the league with 150 runs scored.

Despite being at the top of his game and though Fort Worth offered him a two-year contract at $10,000 a year, Kraft, then 37 years old, decided to retire from baseball at the end of the 1924 season to pursue his automobile business. Fort Worth wasn't the only team interested in keeping Kraft in the game. He rejected an offer to return to the major leagues. The Cincinnati

Reds wrote Kraft to see if he would be willing to join the Reds for the 1925 season. Kraft responded that technically he was still on Fort Worth's reserve list and that after seven years in Fort Worth, he doubted that any team could provide terms that would interest him in leaving.[18]

Although Kraft would not play again, the Cats were eventually able to draw him back to the diamond. Eight years after he last stepped on the playing field, Kraft returned as president of the Fort Worth ballclub.[19] When the club was struggling with financial difficulties, Kraft stepped in and was able to utilize his business acumen to solidify the Cats' financial standing. He returned to his car dealership and worked there until 1942. With World War II causing a scarcity of automobiles, Kraft ran for political office that year and was elected county judge. He was re-elected in 1944 and 1946 and retired from the position in 1948. As a judge, Kraft strove hard to curb juvenile delinquency and established stringent criteria for county probation officers.[20]

In the winter of 1957, Kraft suffered a stroke. He then contracted pneumonia. In March 1958 Kraft suffered a heart attack that claimed his life at the age of 70. He was survived by his wife and three children. Despite being a bit player in the drama of the Miracle Braves, Clarence Kraft went on to have an illustrious career and become a legend in his own right.

Notes

1 *Fort Worth Star Telegram*, March 26, 1958, 1, 4.

2 Church of Jesus Christ of Latter-day Saints, comp., "1900 United States Census and National Index," *FamilySearch* (Online: Intellectual Reserve Inc., 2009), <http://www.familysearch.org/>, accessed {February 2010}.

3 *Fort Worth Star Telegram*, op. cit.

4 Lloyd Johnson and Miles Wolff, eds., *Encyclopedia of Minor League Baseball* (Durham, North Carolina: Baseball America, 1977).

5 J. Foster, ed., *Spalding's Official Baseball Guide* (New York: American Sports Publishing, 1911), 239.

6 *Sporting Life*, January 11, 1911, 12.

7 *Sporting Life*, April 22, 1911, 3.

8 *New York Times*, July 21, 1912, 7.

9 *Sporting Life*, July 5, 1913, 32.

10 *Sporting Life*. August 15, 1913, 23.

11 *Sporting Life*, September 27, 1913, 23.

12 *Nashville Tennessean*, September 6, 1913, 7.

13 *Sporting Life*, November 15, 1913, 6.

14 Scott Longert, "The Players' Fraternity," *Baseball Research Journal*, 30 (Society for American Baseball Research, 2001), 42-43.

15 *New York Times*, July 22, 1914, 11.

16 *Minor League Baseball Stars* (Kansas City: Society for American Baseball Research. 1984), 64.

17 *Sporting Life*. July 1, 1916, 12.

18 Correspondence, Clarence Kraft player file, National Baseball Hall of Fame.

19 Unattributed newspaper clipping dated August 11, 1932, found in Kraft player file at the National Baseball Hall of Fame.

20 *Fort Worth Star Telegram*, op. cit.

Adolfo "Dolf" Luque

by Peter C. Bjarkman

BASEBALL WAS ALREADY a fixture on the Cuban scene by the early 1870s and it had arrived burdened with its own home-grown Cuban apostles and its own full-blown and home-spun creation myths. It is well documented that a pair of Havana-bred brothers named Guilló (often misspelled as Guillot) had returned from Mobile, Alabama's Springhill College as early as 1864 with bats and balls stuffed in their luggage. Nemesio and Ernesto Guilló were soon organizing impromptu pickup matches among former schoolmates in the central Havana barrio of Vedado.

Within a handful of summers (by 1871) the first native Cuban ballplayer—namely one Esteban "Steve" Bellán, who had earlier joined the college nine at Fordham College—had gained a toehold within the North American professional ranks as an infielder with the Troy (New York) Haymakers of the then "major-league" National Association. Although it would be another four decades (1911, to be precise) before any more Cubans followed Bellán into the true "big leagues" of the north, Havana was nonetheless already featuring its own professional circuit before the end of the 1870s, a mere two years after the founding of North America's venerable and still-standing National League.

Yet despite this primitive-era debut of island baseball and the surprisingly early trickle of Cuban players northward, there was but a single Cubano who garnered even moderate attention in the US leagues during pro baseball's initial three-quarters of a century. Racial barriers had almost everything to do with this, of course. The grandest of the early Cuban hurling and slugging phenoms were simply too black in skin pigment ever to penetrate America's exclusively white-toned national sport during the race-driven eras of Adrian "Cap" Anson and Kenesaw Mountain Landis.

Thus just one lonely pioneer—Adolfo Luque (LOO-kay), a fireplug right-hander who debuted with Boston's National Leaguers in 1914 and was already a veteran mound-corps mainstay with the Cincinnati club when the infamous 1919 Black Sox World Series rolled around—was left to carry the Cuban big-league banner throughout the half-century preceding World War II. Perhaps more embarrassing for Cuban baseball than the mere isolation of Luque's big-league career was the persistent flavor of his negative image in Chicago, Boston, New York, St. Louis, and all points north. Unfortunately, this light-skinned if dark-tempered Cuban idol maintained a lasting reputation with big-league fans and ballpark scribes alike that was never quite as "fair and balanced" as most Cuban fans would have wished for back home.

Adolfo Luque today, of course, holds a rare place in Cuban baseball lore—the only Caribbean islander to earn even a modicum of big-league fame during the first half-century of modern major-league history. Between Nap Lajoie and Jackie Robinson, the few

Dolf Luque

dozen Cubans who worked their way north were either brief curiosities in Organized Baseball (journeyman "coffee-tasters" like receiver Miguel Angel "Mike" González with the National League Boston and St. Louis outfits, and erratic outfielder Armando Marsans with Cincinnati) or else passing shadows who barely tasted the proverbial cup of big-league coffee (altogether forgettable names like Rafael Almeida, Angel Aragón, José Acosta, and Oscar Tuero). Numerous others—including some of the most famous and talented back home in Havana (Martin Dihigo, Cristóbal Torriente, and José Méndez head the list)—toured with black barnstorming outfits that rarely, if ever, passed before the eyes of the white baseball press.

By sharp contrast, Luque was something altogether special. His big-league credentials would by career's end nearly approximate the numbers posted by many of his contemporaries destined for Cooperstown enshrinement once the game decided to formalize its history with a sacred hall of immortals. Twice (with the Reds in 1919 and the Giants in 1933) he experienced the pinnacle of World Series victory. As a near-200-game winner, he blazed trails that no other Latin ballplayer would approximate for decades. And back in Cuba he generated a feverish following for the big-league game and in the process carved out as well a lasting loyalty for "our beloved Reds" ("*nuestros queridos rojos*") among baseball-crazy Habaneros. Yet, for all that, his career was destined to be cursed by the fate that eventually became a personal calling card for nearly all early Latin American ballplayers blessed with appropriate talent and skin tone to make their way to the baseball big-time. Among North American fans and writers Dolf Luque would always remain a familiar stereotype—a cartoon figure rather than a genuine baseball hero. At least this was the case at all stops north of Key West or Miami.

One incident above all others seems to have clinched the popular distortions. Perhaps the most spurious of apocryphal tales within the ample catalogue of legends that often substitute for serious baseball history is the one surrounding the fiery-tempered Luque, who eventually pitched a dozen seasons for the Roaring Twenties-era Cincinnati Reds. Legend has it that Luque, after taking a severe riding from the New York Giants bench, stopped in mid-windup, placed the ball and glove gingerly alongside the mound, then charged straight into the New York dugout to thrash flaky Giants outfielder Casey Stengel to within half an inch of his life.

This tale always manages to portray Luque within the strict parameters of a familiar Latin American stereotype—the quick-to-anger, hot-blooded, and somewhat addle-brained Latino who knows little of North American idiom or customs of fair play and can respond to the heat of combat only with flashing temper and flailing fists. The image has, of course, been reinforced over the long summers of baseball's history by the unfortunate (if largely uncharacteristic) real-life baseball events surrounding the most notorious among Latin hurlers. Juan Marichal once brained Dodger catcher Johnny Roseboro with his Louisville Slugger when the Los Angeles receiver returned the ball to his pitcher (with the Giants ace at bat) by firing too close to Marichal's head. The Giants' Rubén Gómez was equally infamous for memorable head-hunting incidents featuring Brooklyn's Carl Furillo and Cincinnati's Frank Robinson. Gómez once plunked heavy-hitting Joe Adcock on the wrist, released a second beanball as the enraged Braves first sacker charged toward the mound, then retreated to the safety of the dugout only to return moments later wielding a lethal unsheathed switchblade knife.

The oft-told story involving Luque's kamikaze mission against the Giants bench seems, in its most popular version, either a distortion or an abstraction of real-time events. Neither the year (it had to be between 1921 and 1923, during Stengel's brief tenure with McGraw's club) nor circumstances are usually mentioned when the legend is related, and specific events are never detailed with any care. The true indiscretion here, of course, is that this story always seems to receive far more press than those devoted to the facts and figures surrounding Luque's otherwise proud and productive 20-year big-league career. This was, after all, a premier pitcher of the early lively-ball era, a winner of nearly 200 major-league contests, the first front-line Latin American big-league ballplayer ever, and the first among his countrymen to pitch in a World Series, win 20 games in a single summer or 100 in a career, or lead a major league in victories, winning percentage, and ERA. Dolf Luque was, indeed, far more than simply the hot-spirited Latino who once, in a fit of temper, silenced the loquacious Charles Dillon Stengel.

For the record, the much ballyhooed incident involving Luque and Stengel does have its basis in raw fact. And like the Marichal-Roseboro affair four decades later, it appears to have contained details infrequently, if ever, properly reported. The setting was actually Cincinnati's Redland Field (later Crosley Field) on the day of a rare packed house in midsummer of 1923. The overflow crowd—allowed to stand along the sidelines, thus forcing players of both teams to take up bench seats outside the normal dugout area –added to the tensions of the afternoon. While the Giants bench, as was their normal practice, spent the early innings of the afternoon disparaging Cincinnati hurler Luque's Latin heritage, these taunts were more audible than usual on this particular day, largely because of the close proximity of the visiting team bench, only yards from the third-base line. Future Hall of Famer Ross Youngs was reportedly at the plate when the Cuban pitcher decided he had heard about enough from offending Giants outfielder Bill Cunningham, a particularly vociferous heckler seated on McGraw's bench. Luque did, in fairness of fact, at this point leave both ball and glove at the center of the playing field while he suddenly charged after Cunningham, unleashing a fierce blow that missed the startled loudmouth and landed squarely on Stengel's jaw instead. The unreported details are that Luque was at least in part a justified aggressor, while Stengel remained a totally accidental and unwitting victim.

The infamous attack, it turns out, was something of a humorous misadventure and more the stuff of comic relief than the product of sinister provocation. While the inevitable free-for-all that ensued quickly led to Luque's banishment from the field of play, the now-enraged Cuban soon returned to the battle scene, again screaming for Cunningham and brandishing an ash bat like an ancient lethal war club. It subsequently took four policemen and assorted teammates to escort Luque from the ballpark a second time. Thus the colorful Cincinnati pitcher had managed to foreshadow both Marichal and Gómez –later club-wielding Latin moundsmen—all within this single span of intemperate high-spirited action.

Unfortunately, what originally passed for comic interlude had dire consequences in this particular instance. Luque had suddenly and predictably played a most unfortunate role in fueling the very stereotype that has since dogged his own career and that of so many of his countrymen. Yet, like Marichal, he was in reality a fierce competitor who almost always manifested his will to win with a blazing fastball and some of the cleverest pitching of his age. He was also a usually quiet and iron-willed man whose huge contributions to the game are unfortunately remembered today only by a diminished handful of his aging Cuban countrymen. So buried by circumstance are Luque's considerable and pioneering pitching achievements that reputable baseball historian Lonnie Wheeler fully reports the infamous Luque-Stengel brawl in his marvelous pictorial history of Cincinnati baseball—*The Cincinnati Game*, with John Baskin—then devotes an entire chapter of the same landmark book to "The Latin Connection" in Reds history without so much as a single mention of Dolf Luque or his unmatchable 1923 National League campaign in Cincinnati.[1]

It is a fact now easily forgotten in view of the near tidal wave invasion of Latin players during the 1980s and 1990s—especially the seeming explosion of talent flooding the majors from the hardscrabble island nation of the Dominican Republic—that before Fidel Castro shut down the supply lines in the early '60s, Cuba had dispatched a steady stream of marginally talented athletes to the big leagues. After Esteban Bellán, an altogether average infielder with the Troy Haymakers and New York Highlanders of the 1870s National Association, the earliest National Leaguers were Armando Marsans and Rafael Almeida, who both toiled briefly with the Cincinnati club beginning in 1911. (Marsans also had brief sojourns in the Federal League and with the American League New York ballclub.) After the color

Another photo of Luque with the Reds.

barrier was dismantled in 1947, the 1950s ushered in quality Cuban players as widely known for their on-field abilities as for their unique pioneering status — Sandy Amoros of the Dodgers; Camilo Pascual, Pete Ramos, Connie Marrero and Julio Bécquer with the Senators; Minnie Miñoso, Mike Fornieles, and Sandy Consuegra of the White Sox; Chico Fernández of the Phillies and Tigers' Roman Mejías with the Pirates; Willie Miranda of the Orioles; and stellar lefty Mike Cuéllar, who launched an illustrious big-league pitching career (highlighted by the first Cy Young Award claimed by a Latin American native) with Cincinnati in 1959.

The best of the early Cubans, beyond the least shadow of a doubt, was Luque, a man who was clearly both fortunate beneficiary and ill-starred victim of racial and ethnic prejudices that ruled major-league baseball during his era. While dark-skinned Cuban legend Martín Dihigo was barred from the majors, the light-skinned Luque was quietly welcomed by management, if not always warmly accepted by the full complement of Southern mountain boys who staffed most big-league rosters.

Yet while Luque labored at times brilliantly in the big leagues during the second, third, and fourth decades of the past century, his achievements were always diminished in part because he pitched the bulk of his career in the hinterlands that were Cincinnati, and in part because his nearly 200 big-league victories were spread thinly over 20 years rather than clustered in a handful of 20-win seasons (he had only one such watershed year). And in the current Revisionist Age of baseball history writing — when Negro Leaguers have at long last received not only their belated rightful due, but a huge nostalgic sympathy vote as well — Martín Dihigo is now widely revered as a blackball icon and even enshrined within Cooperstown's revered portals for his wintertime Cuban League and summertime Mexican League play, while Luque himself lies nearly obscured in the dust and chaff of baseball history.

The memorable pitching career of Dolf Luque might best be capsulated in three distinct stages. Most prominent were the glory years with Cincinnati Reds throughout the full span of the Roaring Twenties, baseball's first flamboyant and explosive decade after the pitching-rich but offense-poor Deadball Era. But first came the formative years of apprentice moundsmanship divided between two distinct baseball-oriented countries. Launching his professional career in Cuba in 1912 as both a pitcher and hard-hitting infielder, Luque displayed considerable talent at third base as well as on the hill. A mere six months after debuting with the Cuban League Fe club (0-4, but with three complete games) the promising youngster was promptly recruited by Dr. Hernández Henríquez, a Cuban entrepreneur residing in New Jersey and operating the Long Branch franchise of the New Jersey-New York State League.

A sterling 22-5 record that first New Jersey summer, along with a strange twist of baseball fate, soon provided the hotshot Cuban pitcher with a quick ticket to big-league fame. This was the epoch when professional baseball was still banned in New York City on Sunday, and thus visiting major-league clubs often supplemented sparse travel money by scheduling exhibition contests with the conveniently located Long Branch team on the available Sunday afternoon open dates. It was this circumstance that allowed Luque to impress Boston Braves manager George Stallings sufficiently to earn a big-league contract early in the 1914 season, the very year in which Boston surprisingly charged from the rear of the pack in late summer to earn a lasting reputation as the Miracle Braves—winners of an unexpected National League flag. In his debut with Boston, Dolf Luque became the first Latin American pitcher to appear in either the American or National League, preceding Emilio Palmero with the Giants by a single season and Oscar Tuero with the Cardinals by a full four campaigns.

Luque's truncated "cup of coffee" in Boston was little beyond a blip on the radar screen of his eventual lengthy big-league sojourn and gave little signal of the personal triumphs and near-legendary moments that would lie ahead for the pioneering Cuban. Nor had he yet raised many eyebrows back on his native island, having at the time logged only three winter-league seasons in which he had appeared in a total of 15 games for the Fe and Habana clubs, posting three complete games and only two victories (both with Havana in the 1913-14 campaign), and boasting an unimpressive 2-8 ledger on the eve of his North American professional debut.

Stallings' slow-starting Braves were still buried in the National League cellar when the 23-year-old Cuban rookie made his big-league debut on May 20 in Pittsburgh; the lackluster Beantowners had won only four of 22 outings at that point in the season. The initial outing was a moderate success to be sure, an eight-inning complete game 4-1 defeat that constituted more than 60 percent of Luque's eventual 13⅔ innings of labor with the Boston club. He would make only one additional big-league appearance that summer (two-thirds of an inning). Of the dozen pitchers who labored for the eventual National League champions during the summer of Boston's late-season "miracle" comeback, only two (Luque and southpaw Ensign Cottrell) failed to register a single victory on a staff paced by a pair of 26-win workhorses (Bill James and Dick Rudolph). By the time the club enjoyed its late-season surge and entered a fall classic showdown with the Philadelphia Athletics, the Cuban rookie was no longer part of the active pitching roster.[2]

Given a second shot with Stallings' newly-crowned world champions in the spring of 1915, Luque again enjoyed a single early-season start alongside a second brief relief appearance; the total ledger consisted of five innings, no decisions, and a 3.60 ERA that stands as rather mediocre during the heart of the Deadball Era. Dropping to second place in the aftermath of their surprise pennant victory, the Braves used 13 different hurlers during the course of the 1915 campaign and Luque and veteran Gene Cocreham were the only pair to show zeros in both the win and loss columns. It would be three full years before the Cuban import (by then approaching his 28th birthday) would again savor a taste of North American big-league action.

Those brief appearances with Boston in 1914 and 1915 provided little immediate success for Luque, who soon found himself toiling with Jersey City and Toronto of the International League and Louisville of the American Association in search of much-needed minor-league seasoning. A fast start (six wins in 12 appearances) in the 1918 campaign brought on "stage two" for Luque—a permanent home in Cincinnati that would span the next dozen seasons. The Cuban fastballer was an immediate success in the Queen City, winning 16 games over the course of the 1918 and 1919 seasons, throwing the first big-league shutout by a Latin pitcher, and playing a major role out of the bullpen as the Reds copped their first-ever National League flag in 1919. Luque himself made history that fall of 1919 as the first Latin American native to appear in World Series play. He tossed five scoreless innings in two Series relief appearances while the underdog Reds outlasted Charlie Comiskey's Chicagoans in the infamous Black Sox Series.

But it was Luque's 1923 campaign that provided his career hallmark and that was, by any measure, one of the finest single campaigns ever enjoyed by a National League hurler during any epoch. Few moundsmen have so thoroughly dominated an entire league for a full campaign. Luque won 27 games while losing but 8, leading the circuit in victories, winning percentage (.771), earned-run average (1.93) and shutouts (6). The six shutouts could well have been ten—he had four complete-game scoreless efforts erased as late as the ninth inning. His 1.93 ERA would also not be matched by another Latin hurler until Luis Tiant registered an almost unapproachable standard of 1.60 in the aberrant 1968 season (the summer known as the Year of the Pitcher, when an entire league checked in with a 2.98 mark and five American Leaguers posted sub-2.00 figures). That same summer of 1923 Luque also became the first pitcher among his Spanish-speaking countrymen to bang out a major-league homer, while himself allowing only two opposition round-trippers in 322 innings, the second stingiest home run allowance ever for a pitcher in the National League and close on the heels of the 1921 standard of one homer in 301 innings pitched recorded by Cincinnati Reds teammate and eventual Hall of Famer Eppa Rixey.

One can best appreciate Luque's 1923 performance merely by reviewing the day-in and day-out consistency of his remarkable summer-long craftsmanship. A game-by-game perusal reveals the Reds ace winning both of his decisions in April, standing 3-1 in May, 5-1 in June, 7-1 in July (including wins in both ends of a twin bill in Boston on July 17), 4-2 for the dog days of August, and 6-3 down the stretch run of September. So consistent was the Cuban's overall performance that he registered 28 complete games (second in the league to Brooklyn's Burleigh Grimes), paced the league with six shutouts, trailed only Grimes again in innings pitched (322 to 327), gave up the league's fewest hits per nine innings pitched (7.8), yielded the lowest opponents' batting average (.235), and outstripped the league's second stingiest hurler by almost a full run per game (that being teammate Eppa Rixey, who owned a 2.80 ERA).

In the terms of John Thorn and Pete Palmer's Total Pitcher Index (which rates a pitcher's effective performance against that of the entire league), Luque's 1923 campaign ranks fourth best in the two decades separating the century's two great wars (1920-1940). Only Bucky Walters in 1939, Lefty Grove in 1931, and Carl Hubbell in 1933 outstripped Luque by the yardstick of the Thorn-Palmer statistical measure. Yet, despite Luque's top-drawer performance (coupled with added 20-victory campaigns by teammates Eppa Rixey and Pete Donohue), Cincinnati nonetheless saw its pennant hopes slip away to John McGraw's powerhouse Giants. It was the front-running New Yorkers who bested Luque in three of his eight losses (the other defeats coming at the hands of Chicago twice and Brooklyn, Philadelphia, and Pittsburgh, each once). Havana's pride and joy was especially devastating on opposing teams in their own home parks, winning a dozen decisions against a mere pair of road-trip setbacks registered in Chicago in late June and Pittsburgh in early September.

The 1923 season was a high-water mark never again to be equaled by the imported hurler today known back home as the Pride of Havana. Next in the evolution of Luque's career came the dozen waning seasons as a fill-in starter, even if he was still a significant contributor with the Reds, Dodgers, and Giants. After losing 23 games with the second-place Reds in 1922 and then pacing the league in victories with the runner-up Cincinnati club of 1923, Dolf Luque would never again enjoy a 20-victory season, though he did come close to the milestone 20 total on both ends of the ledger (wins and losses) with a 16-18 mark (plus a league-leading 2.63 ERA) during the 1925 campaign. He did win consistently in double figures, however, over a ten-year span extending through his first of two brief seasons with Brooklyn at the outset of the 1930s. It is one of the final ironies of Luque's career that while he was not technically the first Latin ballplayer with the Cincinnati Reds (following Marsans and Almeida in that role), he did actually hold this distinction with the Brooklyn Dodgers team which he joined in 1930. And while it was with the Reds that he had made his historic first World Series appearance, it was with the Giants a decade and a half later that he made a truly significant World Series contribution at the very twilight of his career, gaining the crucial Game Five victory in the

1933 Series with a brilliant four-inning relief stint against the then-powerful Washington Senators in the nation's capital.

The third and final dimension of Luque's lengthy career is the one almost totally unknown to North American fans: his brilliant three decades of seasons as both player and manager in the winter-league play of his Caribbean homeland. As a pitcher in Cuba, Luque was nearly legendary in stature, compiling a 93-62 (.600) career mark spread over 22 short seasons of wintertime play, yet ranking as the Cuban League's leading pitcher (9-2) on only a single occasion, in 1928-29. In 1917 he was also the league's leading hitter (.355), and he capped it all by managing league championship teams on eight different occasions (1919-20, 1924-25, 1934-35, 1939-40, 1941-42, 1942-43, 1945-46, and 1946-47).

Luque's reputation in the wintertime Cuban League was arguably in the end most durable as a manager. This claim stands despite the fact that his pitching achievements were considerable, and also despite the fact that Luque was for most of his career a playing manager and not simply a bench-riding skipper. But as a field manager Luque has few rivals anywhere in Cuban League annals, as any mere statistical summary will attest. As a pitcher, by contrast, he was remarkable but hardly unique. His record does not match that of Martín Dihigo, who recorded 106 victories in 19 winters. Yet no one else pitched 22 winter seasons in Cuba, nor were there any other 93-game winners outside of Dihigo. (Cup-of-coffee big leaguer Adrian Zabala also compiled 90 victories over the course of 16 Cuban seasons.) But José Méndez, Adolfo Luján, and Bebé Royer did record higher lifetime winning percentages (as did of course Dihigo) and all logged more seasons as individual league leaders. Luque's victory totals on the mound in Cuba are as much a testament to his longevity as to his year-in and year-out dominance.

But as a manager there is only the venerable Miguel Angel González to rival Luque for years of service and overall winning success. Luque was notably the only manager to log time with each of the "big four" teams in Cuba, serving the bulk of his career at the helm of Almendares (where he first managed in 1920), but also spending three seasons on the bench with Habana (1924, 1955, 1956) and one each with Cienfuegos and Marianao. His one bench assignment with Los Elefantes (1946) gained for Cienfuegos the club's very first pennant in team annals.

Luque posted seven outright titles during his 19 years at the helm of Almendares (where he won 401 overall games), his career winning mark stood at 565 and 471 (.545), and he experienced only seven losing ledgers, five with Los Alacranes (the Almendares Scorpions). Luque's 24 total winters as a Cuban League manager is outpaced only by Miguel Angel González with 38 (all served with Club Habana), and his 565 wins are also outdistanced only by the unapproachable 917 rung up by Miguel Angel. But while Luque was a regular winner with Almendares (finishing first or second in 14 of 19 years with the Blues), González—like the venerable Connie Mack—amassed his victory totals largely through relentless accumulation. Miguel Angel suffered a handful of the most embarrassing Cuban League seasons on record during his own marathon career (including an unimaginable 8-58 ledger in 1938) and yet still posted a career winning percentage of .538 (a fraction behind Luque). González's record 13 league pennants surpass Luque's total by a half-dozen but were earned over a career 37 percent longer. And Luque's managerial record is also augmented by back-to-back Mexican League pennants earned with Nuevo Laredo in the early 1950s.

Perhaps Dolf Luque's most significant contribution to the national pastime (both American and Cuban versions) was his proven talent for developing big-league potential in the players he coached and managed over several decades of winter-league play. One of Luque's brightest and most accomplished students was future New York and Brooklyn star hurler Sal "The Barber" Maglie, who learned his brazen style of "shaving" hitters close to the chin from his tough Cuban mentor. Luque (who had developed his own "shaving" techniques with National League hitters two decades earlier) was Maglie's pitching coach with the Giants during the latter's rookie 1945 season, as well as his manager with

Cienfuegos in the Cuban League that same winter, and at Puebla in the Mexican League in the winter seasons of 1946 and 1947. Maglie often later credited Luque above all others for preparing him for major-league success.[3] And so did Latin America's first big-league batting champion, Roberto "Beto" Avila, who also played for Luque in Puebla during the Mexican League campaigns of 1946 and 1947. Another of Luque's disciples was future Washington and Minnesota ace Camilo Pascual, who first mastered a knee-buckling curveball when Luque coached him with the Cienfuegos Cuban winter-league club. It was this very talent for player development, in the end, that perhaps spoke most eloquently about the onesidedness of Luque's widespread popular image as an emotional, quick-tempered, and untutored ballplayer during his own big-league playing days.

When it comes to selecting a descriptive term to summarize Luque's career, "explosive" has often been the popular choice. For many commentators, this is the proper phrase to describe his reputedly excessive temperamental behavior, his exaggerated on-field outbursts, his infrequent yet widely reported pugilistic endeavors (Luque never shied away from knocking down his share of plate-hugging hitters, of course, but then neither did most successful moundsmen of his era). For still others, it characterizes a career that seemed to burst across the horizon with a single exceptional year, then fade into the obscurity of a forgotten journeyman big leaguer. But both notions are wide-of-the-mark distortions, and most especially the one that sees Luque as a momentary flash upon the baseball scene.

"Durable" would be the far more accurate epitaph. For Dolf Luque was a tireless warrior whose pitching career seemed to stretch on almost without end. His glorious 1923 season was achieved at the already considerable age of 33; he again led the National League in ERA (2.63) two summers later at age 35; he recorded 14 victories and a .636 winning percentage in 1930 while laboring for the Dodgers at the advanced age of 40; his two shutouts that season advanced his career total to 26, a mark unsurpassed among Latin pitchers until the arrival of Marichal, Pascual, Tiant, and Cuéllar in the decade of the '60s. Referred to widely as the rejuvenated "Papá Montero" by 1933, he recorded eight crucial wins that summer and the clinching World Series victory at age 43. His big-league career did not end until he was 45 and had registered 20 full seasons, only one short of the National League longevity standard for hurlers held jointly by Warren Spahn and Eppa Rixey.

Luque's special claim on durability and longevity is even further strengthened when one takes into consideration his remarkable winter-league career played out over an incredible 34 winters in Cuba. Debuting with Club Fe of Havana in 1912 at the age of 22, the indefatigable right-hander registered his final winter-season triumph at age 46 in 1936, then returned a full decade later to pitch several innings of stellar relief work in the 1945-1946 season at the unimaginable age of 55. Luque's combined totals for major-league and winter-league baseball—stretching over almost 35 years—comprise 284 wins, a figure still unrivaled by any of his Latin countrymen save Tiant and Dennis Martínez. And for those critics who would hasten to remind us that longevity alone is not sufficient merit for baseball immortality, it should also be established that Luque's 20-year ERA of 3.24 outstrips such notable enshrined or wannabe Hall of Famers as Bob Feller, Early Wynn, Robin Roberts, Nolan Ryan, and Lew Burdette, to name but a few of baseball's most unforgettable mound stars.

Perhaps the greatest irony surrounding Dolf Luque's big-league career in the end is the misconception that he was merely a cold, laconic, and hot-tempered man, either on the field or off. Upon the occasion of the Cuban hurler's premature and largely unnoticed death at 66 (of a heart attack in Havana on July 3, 1957), legendary sportswriter Frank Graham provided the final word and perhaps the most eloquent tribute to this Pride of Havana who had reigned so stoically as the first certified Hispanic baseball star:

It's hard to believe. Adolfo Luque was much too strong, too tough, too determined to die at this age of sixty-six.... He died of a heart attack. Did he? It sounds absurd. Luque's heart failed him in the clutch? It never did before. How many close ballgames did he pitch? How many did he win ... or lose? When he won, it was sometimes on his heart. When he lost, it was never because his heart missed a beat. Some enemy hitter got lucky or some idiot playing behind Luque fumbled a groundball or dropped a sinking liner or was out of position so that he did not make the catch that should have been so easy for him.[4]

Like many Cuban ballplayers of his era, Adolfo Luque emerged from working-class origins, having been born Adolfo Luque Domingo de Guzman in the low-rent district of Havana on August 4, 1890, and almost nothing is known of his modest childhood years. He joined the newly formed republican army sometime late in the 20th century's first decade, serving as an artilleryman and also building a small local reputation as a hard-slugging third baseman on the infantry baseball club. Early military baseball experience ironically opened the door on an athletic career when the Vedado Tennis Club team—one of the best in the country's thriving amateur league—recruited his services and promptly converted him (as the result of his obviously strong arm) to a pitching assignment. Within a matter of months Luque was signed on by the Fe ballclub of the professional league, where in 1912-1913 he lost all five decisions of his first two pro campaigns.

From his earliest days as a budding professional through his lengthy big-league and winter-league careers, the stocky 5-foot-7 rough-and-tumble ballplayer was best known for his surly personality and quick-fire temper, even among those loyal countrymen who saw him as national hero after his miraculous 1923 big-league season in Cincinnati. It was that rough-around-the-edges personality that earned him the Papá Montero nickname that became his popular handle on his native island. The odd moniker referred to a legendary Afro-Cuban rumba dancer celebrated in song and verse (especially in the popular rumba lyrics composed by Eliseo Grenet) as a high-living pimp and trickster. In the case of the white-skinned Luque, the implied reference was not a racial one but rather a suggestion of the ballplayer's exceptional charisma, assumed sexual prowess, and overly aggressive on-field and off-field behavior.

Much of this off-color reputation was built around not only the Stengel incident, or Luque's penchant for tossing close to batters' heads, but also several widely told if perhaps apocryphal tales involving the use of firearms. Rumor had it that Luque often carried a gun, sometimes even while in uniform, and may well have used it to intimidate his wayward charges on more than one occasion while managing in the Cuban winter league. One account involved Negro league legends Ted "Double Duty" Radcliffe and Rodolfo Fernández. Supposedly an enraged Luque—believing that his imported African American catcher had been dogging it on the field—attempted to fire off a round at Radcliffe in the Tropical Stadium locker room. The frightened Radcliffe was supposedly saved only when Fernández pushed away the manager's arm as he attempted to gun down his goldbricking backstop. A second incident involved black pitcher Terris McDuffie (who pitched for Luque's Marianao club in the early '50s), a heavy drinker and womanizer cut in Luque's own model. This account suggests that McDuffie once told Luque he had a hangover and thus was not up to starting a game, yet then quickly changed his mind once the short-tempered manager returned to the locker room from his adjacent office waving a loaded pistol.[5]

If some of the tales surrounding Luque's outrageous public behavior might well be based more on fancy than fact, it is nonetheless common knowledge that he was indeed prone to expensive tastes and extravagant personal indulgences. He was a flagrant womanizer, a heavy drinker, a brash and often profane public figure, and a reckless gambler (with a passion for the brutal cockfights that were then still legal in Havana). He squandered most of his baseball earnings on his lavish lifestyle and thus died only one step ahead of the poorhouse.

Little more is known of the details of Luque's adult family life away from the public spotlight than of his obscure Havana childhood. He was married to a Mexican woman, Yvonne Resek, a native of Puebla whom he met while managing in that city and who ultimately survived him. His then-still-living widow was the guest of honor at his 1985 posthumous induction into the Mexican Baseball Hall of Fame. On that particular ceremonious occasion in Monterrey, Mrs. Luque uttered the provocative statement that she wasn't in fact the pitcher's widow since she didn't believe that Luque was actually deceased. In support of her bizarre (perhaps tongue-in-cheek) claim, Resek cited an incident from the famed athlete's earlier life when he seemed to reappear from the dead. The story was that Luque and some fellow ballplayers were once on a ship bound from Havana to Miami that was reportedly lost in the Bermuda Triangle. As the tale has it, a day of mourning was proclaimed in Havana to honor the lost athletes, but three days later the ship miraculously landed safely in Miami. That incident gave birth to yet another famed rumba tune entitled *To Cry for Papá Montero*. One other known detail of the pitcher's life is that his only daughter, Olga Luque, was a talented swimmer who competed on several occasions (including the 1938 Central American Games) for the Cuban national aquatic team.

Luque was far more than the man who courted baseball legend by once belting the loud-mouthed Casey Stengel. It would surely be an exaggeration to argue for Luque's enshrinement in Cooperstown solely on the basis of his substantial yet hardly unparalleled big-league numbers, though some have grabbed immortality with far less impressive credentials. It would be equally a failure of historical perspective to dismiss him as a journeyman pitcher of average talent and few remarkable achievements. Few other hurlers have enjoyed such dominance over a short span of a few seasons. Fewer still have proved as durable or maintained their dominance over big-league hitters at so hoary an age. Almost none have contributed to the national pastime (Cuba's and North America's) so richly after the door slammed shut upon an active big-league playing career. Almost no other major-league pitcher did so much with so little fanfare.

The case for depositing Cuba's most renowned hurler of the post-Deadball Era in the hallowed halls of Cooperstown, like all those pleas for reassessment of ballplayers standing squarely on the cusp of greatness, may arguably reflect the narrow prejudices of the advocate as much as the considerable merits of the nominee. It could very well be countered that Luque, like Roger Maris or Brady Anderson, was largely a one-season aberration whose 1923 "year in the sun" far outstripped any of his other achievements. Or one might well take the position, as in the case of Brooklyn's Gil Hodges, that the Cuban right-hander was not even the best player on his own team at the time of his loftiest triumphs. But the numbers amassed across the full decade of the '20s — ten consecutive seasons of double-figure victory totals, three seasons pacing the senior circuit in shutouts, and a pair of ERA crowns — at least work in Luque's case to neutralize if not silence such naysaying. And when it comes to recognizing trailblazing pioneers among Latin ballplayers on the big-league scene before Jackie Robinson, on that front alone Havana's Dolf Luque remains lodged in a class entirely by himself.

This was a pitcher, let it never be forgotten, whose numbers for decades stood unmatched by any of his Hispanic countrymen, one who today still remarkably outstrips all Latino-bred pitchers with perhaps few exceptions of the immortal Marichal, the legendary Tiant, and the more contemporary Dennis Martínez, and possibly now the flamboyant Pedro Martínez. In the oftentimes falsely attributed phrase of the same Casey Stengel who was once an accidental recipient of one of Dolf Luque's most torrid knockout pitches — "You can look it up!"[6]

The author wishes to express his indebtedness to Andy Sturgill, whose peer review and numerous insightful suggestions served to strengthen this biography considerably.

Sources

Bjarkman, Peter C., *A History of Cuban Baseball, 1864–2006* (Jefferson, North Carolina, and London: McFarland & Company Publishers, 2007).

Figueredo, Jorge S., *Who's Who in Cuban Baseball, 1878–1961* (Jefferson, North Carolina, and London: McFarland & Company Publishers, 2003).

González Echevarría, Roberto, *The Pride of Havana: A History of Cuban Baseball* (New York: Oxford University Press, 1999).

Kaese, Harold, *The Boston Braves* (New York: G.P. Putnam's Sons, 1948).

Rathgeber, Bob. "A Latin Temper on the Mound—Adolfo Luque," in *Cincinnati Reds Scrapbook* (Virginia Beach, Virginia: JCP Corporation of Virginia, 1982), 54-55.

Torres, Angel, *La Leyenda del Béisbol Cubano, 1878-1997* (Montello, California: self-published), 1996.

Wheeler, Lonnie, and John Baskin, *The Cincinnati Game* (Wilmington, Ohio: Orange Frazer Press, 1988).

Notes

1   Lonnie Wheeler and John Baskin, *The Cincinnati Game*.

2   Luque's role with the 1914 and 1915 Braves was so insignificant that the Cuban benchwarmer receives no mention whatsoever in the pages devoted to those years by Harold Kaese in his classic 1948 Putnam Series history of the storied ballclub.

3   Maglie's indebtedness to Luque's coaching and its impact on his own eventual big-league successes during the 1950s is mentioned by both Roberto González Echevarría (*The Pride of Havana*, 145, 329) and by Maglie biographer Judith Testa (in her SABR Biography Project essay found on the SABR BioProject website).

4   Frank Graham, Adolfo Luque obituary, *New York Journal American*, July 4, 1957.

5   Both Luque gun-toting incidents—including Rodolfo Fernández's eyewitness report of the Radcliffe saga—are detailed by Roberto González Echevarría (*The Pride of Havana*, 145).

6   A somewhat different version of this biography appeared as Chapter 2 ("Adolfo Luque—The Original 'Pride of Havana'") of my book *A History of Cuban Baseball, 1864-2006*. An even earlier version was published as "First Hispanic Star? Dolf Luque, Of Course" in SABR's *Baseball Research Journal* 19 (1990), 28-32.

Les Mann

by Maurice Bouchard

PHILADELPHIA A'S STAR left-hander and future Hall of Famer Eddie Plank had scattered five hits and had not allowed a run as the Boston Braves batted in the top of the ninth in Game Two of the 1914 World Series. Unfortunately for Plank and his mates, Braves starter Bill James was pitching just as well. After the pesky Rabbit Maranville grounded out to short to start the ninth, Plank could be forgiven if he thought he was going to get out of the ninth without damage. The next batter, substitute third baseman Charlie Deal, 0-for-3 so far, had squandered a couple of earlier opportunities. Now, though, with the bases empty, he doubled over center fielder Amos Strunk's head, then stole third with the pitcher James at the plate. Plank struck out James, and leadoff hitter Les Mann, just three years removed from high-school baseball, came to the plate. Like Deal, the youngster Mann was not an everyday player. He was part of manager George Stallings' platoon of outfielders. Les had not started Game One but had started against the lefty Plank. He hit just .247 during the regular season but had reached Plank for a single in the fifth. With a 2-and-2 count and Deal dancing off third, Mann flicked a Plank offering just out of the reach of second baseman Eddie Collins's outstretched glove. Deal scored easily. The Braves hung on in the home half of the ninth and took a commanding lead in the World Series as they headed north to Boston.

Leslie Mann was born in Lincoln, Nebraska, on November 18, 1892, to Samuel R. Mann, owner of a clothes cleaning business and a dye manufactory, and Minnie L. Schmidt, a first generation German-American.[1] Leslie was the fifth of six children born between 1887 and 1895, the youngest of three sons.

Les, as he was known, went to the Whittier elementary school in Lincoln and showed athletic prowess early in his life. He likely learned sports from his older brothers. Channing and Les played baseball for St. Mark's Sunday school starting in 1906 and the team regularly won city championships. The team formed the core of what would become Girard's Indians, the first semipro uniformed traveling baseball team in Nebraska. After graduating from Whittier in the spring of 1907, Les went to Lincoln High School in the fall. An athletic standout for four years, he was as late as the 1970s considered (and may still be) the greatest athlete in the school's history. He played football (halfback, kicker, and punter), basketball (guard), and baseball (third base); he was the first freshman at the school to play varsity in all three sports. Lincoln High won Missouri Valley championships in basketball and football during Les's tenure at the school. He was very fast and won many individual honors in track, including first place in the 100- and 220-yard dashes in Nebraska state meets and Missouri Valley regional meets. In 1910 Mann placed second in both events in the National Track and Field Meet held in Chicago. A perennial letterman, he made All-State in football, basketball, and baseball in his senior year.

As a 16-year-old (perhaps), Mann played for the Nebraska City Foresters in the six-team, Class D Missouri-Iowa-Nebraska-Kansas (MINK) league in 1910 (as a third baseman) and 1911 (as an outfielder), hitting .292 in 78 games and .327 in 95 games respectively.

From Lincoln High Mann went to the International Young Men's Christian Association Training School (now Springfield College) in Springfield, Massachusetts. He went to Springfield, whose mission was to train Christian lay leaders, on the recommendation of George Pinneo, a Springfield alumnus and the director of the Lincoln Y. Pinneo was Mann's coach at the Y and also at Lincoln High School. He was an early, positive influence on the impressionable Mann. (It is unclear, though, how Mann maintained his college eligibility after having played professional baseball for two summers.)

Mann did not disappoint at Springfield. He made the varsity football team as a freshman, the first to do so, and was also nominated for All-American honors. He starred in many games including a 9-5 upset of Syracuse

Les Mann

on October 28, 1911, in Syracuse in which, although injured earlier in the game, he kicked a field goal and returned a punt 90 yards for a touchdown, "with good interference and splendid sidestepping," reported the *Springfield Republican*. Mann also played an important role in a game on November 23, 1912, in which Springfield hosted the Carlisle Indians with Jim Thorpe. Though the local eleven lost, 30-24, the Maroon made the game much more competitive than expected. It took one of Thorpe's greatest games for Carlisle to prevail. Thorpe scored all 30 of Carlisle's points (four touchdowns, three points after the touchdowns, and one field goal). Mann had two touchdown passes, a field goal, and three points after, accounting for 18 of Springfield's 24 points. He also punted beautifully and returned kicks as well. After the game, Thorpe is said to have told Les, "We did not expect to have such opposition or meet such an athlete as you. We had to change our entire strategy; you changed the whole outcome of our game both offensively and defensively. We were lucky to win."[2] Thorpe, six years Les's senior, and Mann would be teammates on the 1919 Boston Braves.

Mann also excelled in basketball and baseball at Springfield. The Boston Braves could not help but notice the athletic talent in their virtual backyard, and signed him early in 1912. (he had left school in early February) to a contract worth $150 per month. The 5-foot-9, 175-pound Nebraskan was sent to Seattle in the Class B Northwestern League, where he played center field and helped the Giants to a 99-66 record and a championship. Les, a right-handed thrower and batter, hit .300 with 23 homers in 163 games. Based on his performance in Class B, Mann was drafted by the International League's Buffalo (New York) Bisons for the 1913 season.

Mann was back on the gridiron for the Training College in the fall. In addition to the aforementioned Carlisle game, another highlight of the 1912 season occurred on October 26 in Burlington, Vermont. The Maroon beat the University of Vermont 7-0 with Mann running back a punt 60 yards for the only score.

Mann was voted captain of the Springfield football team at the end of the 1912 season even though his teammates knew it was unlikely he would return to play the following season. In fact, he did not play, it appears, because of fear of injury, not due to eligibility concerns. According to the *Springfield Republican* of October 6, 1913, his Braves contract prohibited him from playing football.

Mann, although busy with sports and school, found time to contribute to the local amateur athletic scene during his stay in Springfield. He refereed local high-school and YMCA basketball games. He coached club football and he even coached the Hartford Carpet Company's company rugby team, the Brussels, in nearby Thompsonville, Connecticut.

Again leaving school early, Mann reported to Buffalo as expected but played in only nine games for the Bisons in April 1913. Former Seattle teammates Bill James and Bert Whaling, each now with the Braves, recommended Les to their manager, Gentleman George Stallings. Bill McKechnie, the Braves' incumbent in center field, was waived to the Yankees and Mann was called up to Boston. Interestingly, Stallings, to get his Mann, had to trade his nephew, Art Bues, to the Bisons. Mann made his major-league debut on April 30 at the South End Grounds in Boston against the Philadelphia Phillies. He played center field, batted sixth, went 0-for-4 and did not have a putout. His first major-league hit came two days later, in the ninth game played at brand-new Ebbets Field in Brooklyn. Mann hit a single off Superbas southpaw Frank Allen. In the ninth, with the scored tied 1-1, Mann hit an inside-the-park, three-run home run (on a ball that Brooklyn center fielder Charley — later Casey — Stengel misjudged) to lead Boston to the 4-1 victory. In the game account, the *New York Times* reported noted Mann's "long running catch" as an example of his "high-class fielding."[3]

About 2,000 Springfield fans flocked to the Braves game on July 19 to honor native son Rabbit Maranville but honored their adopted son Mann as well, with a black leather traveling bag. In the eighth, with the score knotted, 4-4, Mann, facing Chicago Cubs starter Larry Cheney, hit a ground-rule double into the overflow crowd of 15,000. He moved to third on a sacrifice and scored the eventual winning run on a squeeze play.[4] Mann finished his rookie season reasonably well for the fifth-place Braves. He played in 120 games, 103 of them in center field. He hit .253 with 24 doubles, 7 triples, 3 homers, and 51 RBIs. His 24 doubles led the team and he was among the team leaders in a few other categories. Mann stole seven bases but was caught 16 times.

Mann went back to Springfield in the fall and although he was precluded from playing football, he helped coach McCurdy by coaching the quarterbacks and the punters. He also continued to referee basketball and coach club teams when asked.

Not much was expected of the 1914 Braves, who had finished 31 1/2 games behind the pennant-winning Giants in 1913. In spring training, manager Stallings would commit to only "select company."[5] After the Braves lost a doubleheader to Brooklyn on the Fourth of July, just matching the previous year's fifth-place finish looked like a challenge, but the Braves were about to embark on one of the greatest extended displays of winning baseball in major-league history. Earning their moniker, the Miracle Braves, Boston won 72 of the next 91 games (including a sweep of the Philadelphia A's in the World Series), a .791 clip. While his team was putting together an amazing season, Mann was not equaling his rookie campaign. Undoubtedly, this was a disappointment for Mann and for Braves management. They likely would have expected their young center fielder to blossom in his sophomore season. He did have a few more triples and one more home run. He walked a bit more and struck out less often. However, his batting average dipped and he was driving in fewer runs. Right-handed pitchers were especially troublesome and eventually Stallings benched Mann against right-handed pitching

Mann played in three of the four games in the World Series, starting Game Two against A's left-handed starter Eddie Plank. In Game Three he ran for catcher Hank Gowdy in the bottom of the 12th and scored the winning run, and came off the bench in the bottom of the sixth in Game Four when A's lefty Herb Pennock entered the game. Mann was the left fielder when the A's Stuffy McInnis made the final out. Les had a tough time getting to the dugout as exuberant fans mobbed him and tore off his uniform.[6] He was 2-for-7 (.286) in the World Series with a big RBI and a critical run scored.

Mann was back in Springfield on October 15 (the Series ended October 13) and attended classes on the 16th. He did not complete the semester, however. He stayed in Springfield long enough to be feted, with Rabbit Maranville, by the Springfield city fathers and by his classmates at the Training College. Mann returned to Lincoln at the end of the month, to a parade, many honors, and celebrations. He planned to return to college in January for the spring semester.

Mann made $2,100 playing for the Braves in 1913 and $2,700 in 1914. He asked for $4,000 for 1915. Further, he asked for a waiver of the release clause, in effect a guaranteed contract. In return, Mann allegedly promised to hit .300. The Braves offered $3,000, an offer Mann declined. His refusal of the Braves' offer reportedly caused much snickering among players who thought he was lucky to get a raise, Stallings having "bolstered up" his outfield. Turkey Mike Donlin, erstwhile Giant and no doubt still smarting from being on the receiving end of last season's Miracle, claimed, "[T]hat bird [i.e., Mann] is the luckiest man I ever saw. He always throws to the wrong base, and yet someone always blunders into his throw and is retired, never thinking for a minute that he will be bone enough to throw to the wrong base with the play right in front of him."[7] An anonymous reporter wrote, "[o]ther players say that (Mann) thinks about as fast as the fellows who steal third with that base occupied." On his return trip to Springfield from Lincoln, Mann met Joe Tinker in Chicago. Tinker managed the local Federal League franchise, the Whales. The ChiFeds offered Mann an "iron clad" two-year deal, likely at $4,000 per season, as well as a $1,000 signing bonus. Les jumped to the upstart league, signing his contract on February 19, 1915, and had a great year.[8] He hit .306 in 135 games and led the league in triples with 19 (interestingly, he only had 12 doubles). He had career highs in many offensive categories while helping to lead the Whales to the Federal League pennant.

The Federal League ceased operations after the 1915 season. As part of its "peace accord" with the National and American Leagues, many of the ChiFed contracts, including Mann's, were assumed by the Cubs. Mann played 373 games for Chicago over the next three seasons, averaging .278 with 20 doubles, 9 triples, 2 homers, and 43 runs driven in. His best year was his last full year, 1918. Although still only 25, Mann was named captain of the team and did not disappoint. He led the team in doubles (27) and extra-base hits (36), and was among the team leaders in batting average, runs scored, triples, RBIs, and stolen bases. He played in 129 of the Cubs' 131 games. More importantly, he led the Cubs from a fifth-place finish in 1917 to a pennant in 1918, their first since 1910.

The 1918 season was unusual due to the World War. Players were subject to the "work or fight" rule, and were either being drafted or were leaving their teams for jobs that were unequivocally essential. (Baseball's status as an essential job was unclear all season.) Mann, for example, left the Cubs on August 29, 1917, to work as a physical education instructor (under the aegis of the YMCA) at Camp Logan, near Houston, Texas. While he was not in the Army, Mann's job was considered essential and he was exempt from the draft. He was reluctant to leave the job for baseball in 1918, fearing his exemption would be lost. Ultimately he was granted a furlough from his YMCA job, allowing him to return to the Cubs in March 1918.[9]

With attendance down substantially and increasing clamor for able-bodied men to be fighting instead of playing, baseball's National Commission decided to end the season after play on September 2. Even before the Series started, some players were irritated with the projected size of the World Series share. Earlier in the season the American and National Leagues changed the formula for how the players' share was calculated. Many owners thought the World Series players were making too much money from the Series. The new formula called for the second-, third-, and fourth-place teams in each league to share in the pool. Further, the formula capped the Series-winning share at $2,000 per player and the losers' share at $1,400. Most players in the 1918 World Series thought those numbers were guaranteed. The owners and the National Commission thought otherwise. Finally, the Cubs players and their American League opponents, the Boston Red Sox, were forced to contribute 10 percent of their World Series share to the war effort. Once the National Commission, ever worried about its image, went public with this plan, there was no way for the players to oppose it. Doubtless many players would have contributed something anyway, but they did not want to be forced.

Attendance for the first four games of the Series, the only four that mattered for the players' pool, was abysmal, just 70 percent of the previous year's total. Players realized before Game Four that their World Series bonuses would be the lowest in history. The 10 percent tariff stung that much more. Mann and Boston's captain, Harry Hooper, were the leaders and spokesmen for the players. They met several times during the first five games of the series, including on the train during the travel day from Chicago. Mann and Hooper helped avoid a work stoppage prior to Game Four, but when the final attendance numbers were announced, the players, including Mann and Hooper, demanded action. They tried to meet with the National Commission but were rebuffed repeatedly. Consequently, the players refused to take the field prior to Game Five in Boston, hoping to get the attention of the commission and to force it to guarantee $1,500 per player for the winners and $1,000 for the losers. It was all in vain. The players had no leverage. The fans and the press were against them and the commission threatened to donate the players' money to charity if they did not play. Reality set in and the players took the field an hour or so past the scheduled time. The Cubs won that game but the Red Sox took Game Six and the championship. Mann appeared in every game and had just five hits in 22 at-bats with two RBIs. He did have a sensational catch of a long fly to left in Game Five when, despite tripping on Duffy's Cliff, the incline in deep left field, caught Hack Miller's effort while seated on the hill.

While the World Series uncertainty was unfolding, Mann's wife of two years, Norfolk, Nebraska, native Jessie Cooper, was ninth months pregnant. She gave birth to their only child, Leslie Jr., on September 17 in Chicago six days after the Series concluded in Boston.

Mann began the 1919 season very poorly, hitting just .095 (2-for-21) in April. Although he raised his average as the weather got warmer, including .277 in July, on August 2 he was traded with infielder Charlie Pick back to his original team, the Boston Braves, for 33-year-old veteran infielder Buck Herzog. Mann's second stint in Boston did not last as long as the first. He played in 40 games for the Braves in 1919 and 115 in 1920 (hitting .283 and .276 respectively). His average was respectable but his power numbers were way down. He was not stealing bases or getting the extra-base hits he had in the past.

The seventh-place Braves needed more production from its left fielder. In November 1920 the Braves sold Mann's contract to the St. Louis Cardinals. Mann's average improved dramatically in St. Louis but his playing time diminished as well. One highlight from the 1921 season came at Sportsman's Park on June 13 at the expense of New York Giants left-hander Art Nehf. Mann hit home runs off Nehf in his first two at-bats. This game may have been in John McGraw's mind when, five years later, he told reporters, "Against a left-hander, I'd rather have Mann up there in the pinch than any other hitter in the National League. He knows he can hit them, and they know he hits them."[10] By 1922, though, Mann was not an everyday player, appearing in just 84 games (the fewest to that point in his career) with 147 at-bats.

In early August 1922, Mann received a curious letter from Giants pitcher Shufflin' Phil Douglas. The Cardinals and Giants had been battling for the pennant all summer, with the Giants holding a half-game lead after play on August 5. Douglas, a teammate of Mann's with the 1918 Cubs, was a very effective pitcher at times (he led the league in ERA in 1922) but was also an alcoholic. After a couple of rough outings and borderline criminal treatment by John McGraw, the big pitcher wrote a letter to Mann offering to quit the Giants if "the goods" were delivered to his house. The implication was that the Giants would be hard-pressed to win the pennant without Douglas, paving the way for the Cardinals to win it. Mann, a Christian, a non-gambler, and by all accounts as upstanding a citizen as could be found in the major leagues, was an unfortunate choice as penpal for Douglas. Shufflin' Phil realized his mistake almost immediately and attempted to call Mann in Boston, where the Cardinals were playing the Braves. It was too late, though. Mann had already shown the letter to manager Branch Rickey, who advised him to inform Commissioner Kenesaw M. Landis. Judge Landis banned Douglas, then 32, from baseball for life.

Mann later wrote, in relation to another matter, that he thought the Douglas letter was a frame-up for him: Unspecified people wanted to "get" Mann and if Mann ignored the letter from Douglas, these people would use the inaction to get Mann banned from baseball. No reason was given for this except that Mann did not approve of gambling in the clubhouse (e.g., card games for money) and this put him at odds with virtually all his teammates and coaches.[11]

Mann, now in his 30s, was strictly a platoon player, yet limited playing time seemed to agree with him. He had another two-homer day on May 11, 1923, at the Baker Bowl in Philadelphia. Mann did not start the game, but when Phillies pitcher Lefty Weinert relieved starter Petie Behan, Mann was called into service. He hit a two-run shot in the sixth and a solo shot in the eighth, part of a 14-run losing effort (the Phillies scored 20). He had ten multihit games although he appeared in just 38 of the Cardinals' 80 games in 1923. Mann, though hitting a gaudy .371 (33-for-89) for the Cardinals, was waived to the Reds in mid-July. In Cincinnati he was the fifth outfielder and played in just eight games, getting only one at-bat over the next three weeks.

Disgusted and homesick, Mann went home to Nebraska and was suspended by the National League. The homesickness did not last, however. Mann latched on with an independent team in Creston, Iowa, for a few games until Judge Landis told him to desist.[12] Reds owner August Herrmann expected to have Mann back with the Reds for the 1924 season but was apparently surprised to learn that his player, for whom he had paid $10,000, was suspended by the league. He was also apparently surprised to learn that Mann wanted to retire and that the Cardinals knew it before they sold him to the Reds. Mann told Herrmann in April that he was going to retire and asked for his release. Hermann could not release Mann until he was reinstated by the league. After a series of arcane bureaucratic maneuvers and a change of heart by Mann, in early June, he was transferred to the Braves for his third incarnation with that team.[13]

Mann played the remainder of the 1924 season with the Braves, all of the next two seasons and 29 games in 1927 before being waived to the Giants on July 18. John McGraw, tired of being on the receiving end of Mann's prowess against lefties, now had a veteran right-handed batter on his bench. Mann, who had an occasional start in the outfield, hit .328 (.352 against southpaws) and slugged .507 in 67 at-bats for the third-place Giants. The Giants competed for the 1928 pennant with the Cardinals all season before finally settling on second place. Mann, in his final major-league season, was McGraw's fourth outfielder, getting into 82 games, his most since 1922. He hit .264 with very little power and 25 RBIs. He played 68 games in the outfield, mostly in right, but played center and left as well. Mann was hitting in the low .300s in early June and was the cleanup batter for several games in June and July. He played his last major-league game on September 30, 1928, at the Polo Grounds. He had a single in two at-bats. Except for a very brief stint with the Buffalo Bisons in 1929, Mann's playing career was over.

Mann played 16 seasons in the big leagues. He played in 1,498 games and hit .282 with 203 doubles, 106 triples, 44 homers, and 503 RBIs. He struck out about 40 percent more often than he walked (464 strikeouts vs. 324 walks). Although very fast, he was not a productive basestealer. His best year was 1918, when he pilfered 21 sacks. It was good for tenth place in the league but not even half of league leader Max Carey's 58. Mann played 1,368 games in the outfield with 173 assists and 97 errors (.966 fielding percentage). He twice led the National League in assists among left fielders but in those same years, 1918 and 1919, he led the league in errors as well. Les had at least six four-hit games. The first came on May 19, 1916, and the last came on July 18, 1925.

Mann may have retired from playing (officially, he was released by the Giants) but he was far from retiring. From his earliest experience in sports at the Whittier School and St. Mark's to the day he died, Mann was a tireless promoter and advocate for amateur sports, especially baseball. Except for managing the Harrisburg (Pennsylvania) Senators in 1934 to an eighth-place finish in the New York-Penn League, he spent the rest of his life working in amateur athletics.

While still an active player, Mann spent the offseason engaging his passion. He was the director of physical education and basketball coach at the Rice Institute (now Rice University) from 1919 through 1922. He was the head basketball and baseball coach at Indiana University in 1923 and 1924. Perhaps as early as 1919 he coached at Amherst College as well. He went back to Springfield in 1925 to assume the head coaching job in basketball and baseball through 1928. He continued as an assistant football coach in 1929. In December 1929 the American and National League owners hired Mann to conduct an educational tour of the country. The audience was baseball coaches working in the amateur ranks. Major-league baseball donated $60,000 per year to improve amateur instruction and Mann was hired to promulgate that message.

Mann organized a baseball school that had Rogers Hornsby, Grover Cleveland Alexander, and George Sisler as instructors. By 1924 Mann had a business called Leslie Mann Coaching System based in Bloomington, Indiana (where Indiana University is located). He was an early adopter of film to enhance baseball and football instruction. His company letterhead promoted the use of "Stereopticon Pictures," an allusion to Mann's invention, the Mannscope (sometimes called the Mannoscope). This device, patent number 1,645,108, was a film projector capable of stopping on an arbitrary frame, allowing the instructor to illustrate the finer details of a skill. The Mannscope, capable of operating in reverse as well, was a precursor to the video systems prevalent today in all levels of sports instruction.

On February 19, 1931, Mann, secretary-treasurer of the Amateur Athletic Federation, announced the formation of the United States Amateur Baseball Association (USABA, later the United States Baseball Congress), whose main purpose was sponsorship of an international tournament. He wanted baseball to become an Olympic sport and the tournament, he hoped, would showcase the sport. The tournament, to be played in the following year in Los Angeles or San Francisco, would include eight teams from the United States and eight from outside the US (Hawaii and seven foreign countries). Mann was named national director of the USABA and the board included well-known college coaches as well as Avery Brundage, president of the American Olympic Association. Les tried but failed to get the US Olympic Committee to include baseball as a demonstration sport in Los Angeles in 1932. (The committee chose football and lacrosse.)

Mann, having taken a team of all-star baseball amateurs, including future major leaguer Jeff Heath, to Japan to play against Tokyo University in October 1935, persuaded the Germans to allow baseball at the 1936 Berlin Games. Though the International Baseball Congress was created at the Games with 21 nations joining, no other country sent a baseball team to Berlin, so Mann staged a single exhibition game before 90,000 (Mann often claimed there were 125,000) mostly confused Germans. Mann split his contingent, college players who could afford the $500 traveling expenses, into two squads who played for seven innings in the poorly-lit Olympic Stadium. Prior to the game, in an effort to please the crowd, the American players stood on the sidelines and gave what the Associated Press called a Nazi salute, a characterization later disputed by at least some of the players.[14] The game itself was hardly artistic, but Mann's boys had shown enough to get a commitment from the International Olympic Committee to make baseball an official sport at the 1940 games in Japan.

Mann led a team of American amateurs to England in August 1938 to play for the John Moores Trophy. In addition to the US and England, Canada, Australia, France, Holland, and Belgium all provided teams. The All-England team bested the Americans four games to one, a result Mann hoped would shock the youth of America into action.[15] After World War II began, Mann, who now had an office in the Orange Bowl in Miami (and would referee the odd football game), moved the John Moores Series (as it was now called) to Havana in 1939 and 1940. The US did not manage a victory in 1939 but was more competitive in 1940 before losing to the Cubans again. The 1940 tournament, with teams from Mexico, Venezuela, Puerto Rico, Hawaii, and Nicaragua as well as Cuba and the United States, was exciting and a huge success with some 100,000 people seeing the games.[16]

It was not the international competition for which he had yearned, but the ever-enthusiastic Mann was not deterred. He immediately made plans for the 1940 Olympic Games in Tokyo. (Mann had high regard for the level of play in Japan.) He started to plan for tournaments in Japan in 1937 and 1939. Neither tournament took place. As late as 1939 Mann hoped to establish Olympic baseball in London in the 1944 Games, but the 1940 and 1944 games were canceled because of the war. It was not all disaster for Mann, though. Through the USABA he was able to get baseball on the Olympic radar at least, where it had not been since 1912, and between 1931 and 1943 the USABA introduced baseball to 27 countries. During World War II, Mann worked for the USO and eventually was its director of athletics, based in Hawaii.

After the war Mann moved his family to San Gabriel, California, where he continued promoting international amateur baseball and baseball education. In 1946 he founded the United States Amateur Football Association (USAFA), the gridiron analog of the USABA.[17] Mann was also secretary of the International Amateur Football Federation. His idea was to make American football an Olympic sport. In December 1948 four teams — the United States, Canada, Hawaii, and Mexico — competed for the Amos Alonzo Stagg trophy at Gilmore Stadium in Hollywood, California. Frank Finch, reporting in the *Los Angeles Times*, wrote, "[f]inancially and artistically, the series was a flop." The four games drew a total of 7,100 fans. Mann and his backers took a financial beating. Although he said at the time that he would continue the series the following year, the A.A. Stagg trophy was retired.[18] Mann continued to promote amateur baseball and football through the 1950s. He apparently (it was planned, but it is not clear that it happened) took an all-star amateur baseball team to South Africa for ten weeks at the end of 1955.

Athletic honors eventually came Mann's way. In 1957 he was the 23rd person inducted into the Nebraska Sports Hall of Fame. When Springfield College decided to create an athletics hall of fame in the early 1970s, the three giants in the inaugural class were basketball inventor James Naismith, football coaching pioneer Amos Alonzo Stagg, and Leslie Mann.

In the early 1960s Mann worked as a sports specialist for the Los Angeles Parks and Recreation department. On January 14, 1962, Mann, reportedly still in excellent physical condition, suffered a fatal heart attack while driving. He was survived by his wife, Jessie, and their son, Leslie, Jr. After a funeral service at Todd Memorial Chapel in Pomona, California, he was cremated.

Sources

Books

Ty Waterman and Mel Springer, *The Year the Red Sox Won the Series* (Boston: Northeastern University Press, 1999)

Allan Wood, *Babe Ruth and the 1918 Red Sox* (San Jose, California: Writers Club Press, 2000)

The Baseball Encyclopedia. 9th ed. (New York: Macmillan, 1993)

Newspapers, magazines

Boston Globe

Chicago Daily Tribune

Christian Science Monitor

Hartford Courant

New York Times

Pittsburgh Sunday Post

Springfield (Massachusetts) *Republican*

The Sporting News

Times Record, Troy, NewYork

Pete Cava, "Baseball in the Olympics." *Citius, Altius, Fortius* 1 no. 1 (1992): 7-15, http://www.la84foundation.org/SportsLibrary/JOH/JOHvIn1/JOHvIn1e.pdf.

Mike Lynch, "Phil Douglas." *SABR BioProject*. http://sabr.org/bioproj/person/3db5329e. Accessed January 1, 2013

Channing Mann, compiler. *Portrait of a Champion: A Tribute to Les Mann, November 18, 1893- January 14, 1962*. (Springfield, Massachusetts: Springfield College, 1972)

Joseph L. Reichler, ed. *The World Series* (New York: Simon and Schuster, 1978)

M.E. Travaglini, "Olympic Baseball 1936: Was es Das?" In *National Pastime*, Winter 1985, 46-55

Websites

ancestry.com

baseball-reference.com

retrosheet.org

sabr.org

Notes

1. Sources vary as to the date of Mann's birth. Macmillan Baseball Encyclopedia, 9th ed,, the 1900 US census, and Mann's death certificate have 1893. The Spalding Guide (1915) has 1891 while his World War I draft card, completed and signed by Mann, has 1892.

2. "Springfield College—1911-1914," Portrait of a Champion, 20.

3. "Stengel Misjudges Mann's Long Hit," *New York Times,* May 3, 1913, 12.

4. "Braves Do Their Part by Winning," *Boston Globe,* July 20, 1913, 9.

5. "Braves Fourth of 'Better,'" *Boston Globe,* April 12, 1914, 16.

6. Charles E. Parker, "Frenzied Fans Swarm Diamond," *Boston Post,* October 14, 1914.

7. "Mann Hold-out Proves His Nerve," [unknown newspaper], March 16, 1915.

8. "Mann in Line," [unknown newspaper], February 20, 1915.

9. "Mitchell May Lose Services of Les Mann," [unknown paper], March 9, 1918.

10. Frederick G. Lieb, "Les Mann, 'Miracle Braves' Outfielder, Succumbs at 68," *The Sporting News,* January 24, 1962.

11. Mike Lynch, "Phil Douglas," SABR Bio Project, http://sabr.org/bioproj/person/3db5329e. Accessed January 1, 2013.

12. Leslie Mann to Auggust [sic] Herrman, May 13, 1924. Leslie Mann clippings file, Giamatti Research Center, National Baseball Hall of Fame and Museum.

13. Leslie Mann to A G Hermann [sic], April 22, 1924, and August Herrman to Leslie Mann, May 14, 1924. Leslie Mann clippings file, Giamatti Research Center, National Baseball Hall of Fame and Museum.

14. "Teams Give Nazi Salute," *New York Times,* August 13, 1936, 14.

15. "Mann is Rapidly Nearing Olympic Baseball Goal," *Christian Science Monitor*, October 13, 1938, 10.

16. Ed Rumill, "In the Dugout: Baseball Congress Moves Forward," *Christian Science Monitor,* January 8, 1941, 15.

17. Al Wolf, "Local Men Performed With Braves in 1914," *Los Angeles Times*, September 29, 1948, C2.

18. Frank Finch, "U.S. All-Stars Sink Hawaii," *Los Angeles Times,* December 27, 1948, C1.

Rabbit Maranville

By Dick Leyden

Standing only 5′5″ and weighing a good deal less during the Deadball Era than his listed playing weight of 155 lbs., Rabbit Maranville compiled a lifetime batting average of just .258 and is known as much for his zany escapades and funny stories as for anything he accomplished on the diamond, but his outstanding glove work kept him in the big leagues for 23 seasons and eventually earned him a plaque in Cooperstown. "Maranville is the greatest player to enter baseball since Ty Cobb arrived," said Boston Braves manager George Stallings. "I've seen 'em all since 1891 in every league around the south, north, east, and west. He came into the league under a handicap—his build. He was too small to be a big leaguer in the opinion of critics. I told him he was just what I wanted: a small fellow for short. All he had to do was to run to his left or right, or come in, and size never handicapped speed in going after the ball."[1]

The third of five children, Walter James Vincent Maranville was born on November 11, 1891, in Springfield, Massachusetts. His mother was Irish but his father and the Maranville name were French. Walter (then known as "Stumpy" or "Bunty") attended the Charles Street and Chestnut Street grammar schools and played catcher during his one year at Technical High. His father, a police officer, allowed him to leave school if he apprenticed for a trade, so at age 15 he quit to become a pipe fitter and tinsmith. To his father's dismay, Walter devoted less attention to his apprenticeship than he did to baseball. He was playing shortstop for a semipro team in 1911 when Tommy Dowd, manager of the New Bedford Whalers of the New England League, signed him to a contract for $125 per month. The 19-year-old shortstop batted .227 and committed 61 errors in 117 games.

It was at New Bedford in 1912 that Maranville acquired his distinctive nickname. Some sources say that it came from his protruding ears, but he told a different story: "I was very friendly with a family by the name of Harrington. One night I was down to their house having dinner with them when Margaret, the second oldest daughter, asked me if I could get two passes for the next day's game, as she wanted to take her seven-year-old sister to see me play. I said, 'Sure, I'll leave them in your name at the Press Gate.' She said, 'And come down to dinner after the game.' I left the two passes as I promised and after the game I went down to their house for dinner. I rang the door bell and Margaret came and opened the door and said, 'Hello Rabbit.' I said, 'Where do you get that Rabbit stuff?' She said, 'My little seven-year-old sister (Skeeter) named you that because you hop and bound around like one.'"[2]

Maranville improved his batting average to .283 during his second year at New Bedford, and the Boston Nationals purchased his contract for $1,000. Reporting to the club on September 4, Rabbit got into 26 games and made 11

Rabbit Maranville

errors while batting .209. "The fall of 1912 my fielding was above the average, but my hitting was not so good," he recalled. "However, I was the talk of the town because of my peculiar way of catching a fly ball. They later named it the Vest-Pocket Catch. Boston wasn't drawing any too good, but it seemed like everyone that came out to the park came to see me make my peculiar catch or get hit on the head."[3] Maranville settled himself under pop-ups with what seemed to be total unconcern, arms at his side; as the ball plummeted towards earth, apparently ignored, he suddenly brought his hands together at waist level and let the ball fall into the pocket of his glove. "Many of the players passed different remarks about my catch which wouldn't go in print," Rabbit said. "I do, however, remember what Jimmy Sheckard said: 'I'll bet you he don't drop three balls in his career, no matter how long or short he may be in the game. Notice the kid is perfectly still, directly under the ball, and in no way is there any vibration to make the ball bounce out of his glove.'"[4]

At training camp in the spring of 1913, new manager George Stallings scheduled two-a-day practices, one in the morning and one in the afternoon. "The players would dress after the first workout and return to the hotel where they'd loaf for an hour or so," Rabbit recalled. "Seizing the opportunity that was before me, I got a dozen kids to pitch to me before the next session, sometimes to the point that I was groggy."[5] Despite his hard work, Maranville still couldn't crack the starting lineup. "Coming from the park after our afternoon session, I was walking with a big first baseman by the name of Gus Metz. He said, 'Rabbit, did you see where they have the ballclub picked?' I said, 'No, who have they decided on for shortstop?' He said, 'Art Bues, Stallings' nephew.' I said, 'If I couldn't play ball better than that guy I'd quit.' Walking behind us was Stallings, and he overheard what I said unbeknown to us. That evening after dinner I was loafing around the lobby of the hotel when Stallings came along and said, 'I want to talk to you.' We went over to a sofa and sat down. Stallings said, 'You don't like my selection of Bues for shortstop over you.' I said, 'No, I don't.' 'Well,' Mr. Stallings said, 'you have a lot to learn and I'm running this club and I'll make my own selections no matter what you or anybody else thinks.' I said, 'That's okay with me; I'm not trying to run your ballclub, but if I'm not a better ballplayer than that relative of yours, I'll quit.' He said, 'No, you will not; I'll keep you until we get back to Boston, then use you in a trade if I have the opportunity.'"[6]

Maranville sat the bench during the 1913 exhibition season until the Braves arrived in Atlanta on Easter Sunday. After going to church that morning, he put on his uniform in his hotel room and boarded the team bus. "Going up Peach Tree Boulevard on our way to the park, a player who I don't remember right off hand told me I was to play shortstop that afternoon as Bues came down with a sore throat," Rabbit recalled. "We left Bues in Atlanta as he was a very sick boy and came into New York to open the season with the Giants. Game time came along and Stallings yelled down the bench at me, 'Rabbit, you're playing shortstop today.' I

Maranville taking a cut.

said, 'Yes, and you will never get me out of there.'"[7] Maranville picked up three hits against Christy Mathewson on Opening Day as the Braves won, 8-3. He went on to hit .247 in 143 games that season and remained the regular shortstop for Stallings' entire tenure in Boston.

Maranville appeared in all 156 games during the miracle season of 1914, driving in 78 runs out of the cleanup spot even though he batted only .246. He came up with many big hits during the Braves' pennant drive, but none was more important than the game-winning home run he belted in the tenth inning on August 6 — even though he was suffering from a severe hangover from drinking too much champagne at a dinner party the night before. "In the clubhouse while I was undressing Stallings came over to me and said, 'You go back to choking up; you are no home-run hitter,'" Rabbit remembered. "Truthfully, I never did see the ball I hit, and years later Babe Adams, who was the pitcher that day, asked me if it was a curve or a fastball I hit over the fence. I told him I never saw it and he said, 'I know darn well you never did.'"[8]

Maranville's greatest contributions, of course, came with the glove. Boston had purchased second baseman Johnny Evers from the Chicago Cubs during the previous winter, and he and Rabbit gave the Braves the best middle infield in baseball. Though no sportswriter ever penned a poem about Maranville-to-Evers-to-Schmidt, that combination turned far more double plays in 1914 than Tinker, Evers, and Chance ever did in any one season. "It was just Death Valley, whoever hit a ball down our way," Rabbit recalled. "Evers with his brains taught me more baseball than I ever dreamed about. He was psychic. He could sense where a player was going to hit if the pitcher threw the ball where he was supposed to."[9]

Evers' omniscience paid off in a big way during Game Two of the World Series. Heading into the bottom of the ninth, the Braves led, 1-0, but the Athletics had men on first and second and only one out. The batter was Eddie Murphy, a fast left-handed hitter who Maranville claimed hadn't hit into a double play all season. Rabbit was already playing only 10 feet from second base, but Evers looked over and told him to move closer. The young shortstop followed orders, moving only five feet from the bag. Bill James was about to deliver his pitch when Evers called time and instructed Rabbit to move even closer. Maranville moved within one yard of second base. On James' first pitch, Murphy hit a rifle shot between the pitcher's legs. Rabbit was practically standing on second when he fielded the grounder and fired the ball to first to complete a game-ending double play. "If it hadn't been for Evers insisting I play closer to second base, I would never have made the play, which seemed almost impossible to make from the spectators' point of view," he said.[10]

Evers and Maranville finished one-two in the 1914 Chalmers Award voting, and that off-season they were approached by Bill Fleming, a scout for the Federal League's Chicago Whales. "We met him and he laid down $100,000 in front of Evers and

The Rabbit poses, pretending to field a grounder.

$50,000 in front of me as a bonus with a three-year contract to play for the Chicago Feds," Rabbit recalled. "Evers refused and so did I."[11] Maranville remained a fixture in the Braves infield for another six years, though he missed nearly all of 1918 when he enlisted in the Navy and served as a gunner aboard the USS *Pennsylvania*. On November 10, 1918, Rabbit told his shipmates that they would get big news the next day. "Everyone kept asking me what the big news was going to be," he remembered. "I said, 'Wait until tomorrow; I will tell you then.' At 6:30 the next morning we got word that the armistice had been signed. That afternoon I was called in to the captain's quarters. The captain said to me, 'How is it you knew the armistice was going to be signed today? Who gave you that information?' I said, 'I didn't know anything about the armistice being signed. The reason I said the big day is tomorrow and they would hear great news is that today is my birthday.'"[12]

In January 1921 the Braves traded Maranville to the Pittsburgh Pirates for Billy Southworth, Fred Nicholson, Walter Barbare, and a sum of money said to be $15,000. Rabbit remained with the Pirates through the 1924 season, giving them their first reliable shortstop since the retirement of Honus Wagner. He then spent one season with the Chicago Cubs, serving as player-manager for a short time, and another with the Brooklyn Dodgers, drawing his release in August 1926. A drunk by his own admission, Maranville was considered washed up as a big leaguer, but he swore off alcohol at Rochester in 1927 and returned to the NL in 1928 as the starting shortstop for the St. Louis Cardinals, appearing in the World Series and batting .308, the same average he had posted in the 1914 World Series. Over the caption "Rab's Top Fan," the New York *Journal-American* ran a photograph of Rabbit's father with his arm around his son, wearing a look of genuine pride on his face.

Maranville returned to Boston in 1929 for a second stint with the Braves, playing regularly at shortstop for three years and second base for two. Legendary sportswriter Grantland Rice thought of Rabbit at that point in his career "as the link between the old days and the new in baseball. He broke in with the hard-bitten crew in Boston and wasn't exactly a sissy, reveling in the atmosphere in which he found himself. For years he was a turbulent figure on the field, fighting enemy ball players and umpires — and even the players on his own team when he found it necessary."[13] Then in his early 40s, Maranville still played with the same old hustle, and it ultimately caused the end of his major-league career. In a 1934 spring exhibition against the Yankees, with Boston down by a run, Rabbit attempted to score even though the catcher was blocking the plate. When the dust finally cleared, Maranville lay in agony, a bone jutting out of his ankle. "Out!" roared the umpire. Rabbit reportedly pointed to his limp foot resting on the edge of the plate and said, "You see where that foot is, don't you?"[14] He then passed out.

After missing the entire 1934 season, Maranville tried to come back in 1935 but played only 23 games before giving up. "For a quarter of a century I've been playing baseball for pay," he wrote in 1936. "It has been pretty good pay, most of the time. The work has been hard, but what of it? It's been risky. I've broken both my legs. I've sprained everything I've got between my ankles and my disposition. I've dislocated my joints and fractured my pride. I've spent more time in hospitals than some fellows ever spend in church. I've ridden on railroad trains until a steam shovel couldn't lift the cinders I've combed out of my hair. I've eaten lousy food and slept on lousy beds. I've been socked with fists and pop bottles and insults. I've been awakened out of bed in the middle of the night by fat-headed bums who only wanted to know what Pop Anson's all-time batting average was. I've lost a lot of teeth and square yards of hide. But I've never lost my self-respect, and I've kept what I find in few men of my age — my enthusiasm."[15]

Maranville managed at Elmira in 1936, Montreal in 1937, Albany in 1939, and back home in Springfield in 1941. When he finally left Organized Baseball for good, he worked for youth baseball programs in Rochester, Detroit, and finally New York City. As director of the New York *Journal-American* sandlot baseball school after World War II, Rabbit taught thousands of kids how to play the game in clinics at Yankee Stadium and the Polo Grounds. Among his pupils were future big leaguers Whitey Ford, Bob Grim, and Billy Loes.

Rabbit Maranville died at age 63 of coronary sclerosis on January 5, 1954, just a few weeks before his election to the National Baseball Hall of Fame. He is buried in St. Michael's Cemetery in his hometown of Springfield.

Note: A slightly different version of this biography appeared in Tom Simon, ed., Deadball Stars of the National League *(Washington, D.C.: Brassey's, Inc., 2004).*

Sources

For this biography, the author used a number of contemporary sources, especially those found in the subject's file at the National Baseball Hall of Fame Library.

Notes

1 "Maranville Best Shortstop," September 1914 newspaper interview with George Stallings.

2 "Springfield's Rabbit," *Springfield Republican*, August 5, 1979.

3 Citation from unknown source, in Maranville's player file at the National Baseball Hall of Fame.

4 Walter "Rabbit" Maranville, *Run Rabbit Run* (Phoenix, AZ: Society for American Baseball Research, 2011), 13.

5 "The Credo of Maranville," St. Louis newspaper (newspaper unknown), August 3, 1933. Located in Maranville's player file at the National Baseball Hall of Fame.

6 Maranville, *Run Rabbit Run*, 14.

7 Maranville, *Run Rabbit Run*, 15.

8 Maranville, *Run Rabbit Run*, 22.

9 Maranville, *Run Rabbit Run*, 16.

10 Citation from unknown source, in Maranville's player file at the National Baseball Hall of Fame.

11 "Springfield's Rabbit," *Springfield Republican*, August 5, 1979.

12 Maranville, *Run Rabbit Run*, 41.

13 Grantland Rice, unattributed newspaper column, January 1937.

14 "Maranville Mourned As Hustler and Scrapper," January 6, 1954. Located in Maranville's player file at the National Baseball Hall of Fame.

15 Rabbit Maranville, "Hot Stove Stuff," *American Legion Monthly*, No. 11, January 1926.

Billy Martin

By Robert W. Joel

ON OCTOBER 6, 1914, in the second game of a doubleheader, 20-year-old Bill Martin made his major-league debut against the Robins in Brooklyn. His performance was utterly unremarkable: He went hitless in three at-bats and committed an error at shortstop. No one at the time would have expected that this single game would constitute the entire major-league career of Bill Martin.

Bill Martin was one of the greatest all-around athletes ever to come out of the Washington, D.C., area, as he was a three-sport star, later inducted into Georgetown University's Hall of Fame. Numerous major-league teams competed for his services and expectations for his career were sky-high. Martin's career in the major leagues might not have turned out as anticipated, but his life was anything but ordinary as he went from starring on the collegiate playing fields to hobnobbing with the political elite in Washington.

Born on February 13, 1894, in Washington, William G. Martin was the only son born to William S. and Mary E.S. Martin. He had an older sister, Lucile, and three younger sisters—Loretta, Rosemary, and Julia. William S. Martin drove a soda-water truck as his occupation, yet the family lived a privileged lifestyle. Young Billy attended the elite and prestigious Georgetown Prep, where he starred in both baseball and football. William A. Martin, Jr., the great-grandson of William S., speculated that "maybe there was something other than soda in that Schweppes truck that my great-grandfather used to drive around Washington!"[1] This would not be the last reference to "bootlegging" within the Martin family.

Martin entered Georgetown University in 1909. A right-handed thrower and batter, at 5-feet-8 and 170 pounds he was muscular and built like a fireplug. The young Irishman had a fiery disposition and seemingly boundless amounts of energy. He immediately made a name for himself playing on the hardwood court, the gridiron, and the baseball diamond as a freshman. By 1912, Martin was an established local star attracting much attention from area teams desiring his services. He played baseball for the Potomac Electric and Power Company ("Pepco") nine and led the team to the district amateur championship.[2] The first of many injuries occurred that fall as he broke his leg during a Georgetown football game.[3] He missed the remainder of the football season as well as the basketball season. The injury was merely a prelude to what was to lie ahead for the young athlete.

By April 1913 Martin was offered a contract to play for the Erie Sailors of the Class B Interstate League. The *Pittsburgh Press* reported that he would sign the contract and report to Erie "at the close of the college year, in June."[4] For reasons that are unclear, Martin did not report to Erie. And then the injury bug struck once again. He broke his nose, according to the *Washington Post*, while playing end for Georgetown against Virginia Medical College in a football game on October 18, 1913.[5]

For the Georgetown star, 1914 proved to be a momentous year, filled with great highs and equally devastating lows. After closing out his fine basketball career for the Blue and Gray, Martin was enjoying his final season for the varsity baseball squad. It was widely known that he was being scouted by several major-league teams, including Cleveland, Cincinnati, and the Boston Red Sox. Cleveland was rumored to have signed him to a contract, allowing him to report at the close of the college season. On June 6 the Georgetown team arrived by train in Princeton, New Jersey, to take on the Princeton squad. When the train carrying the Georgetown team pulled into the station in Princeton, the train car carrying their equipment did not arrive. The players scrambled around and borrowed whatever uniforms, gloves, and gear they could from their opponents. Martin borrowed a pair of shoes that were more than a size too large for him and broke his ankle late in the game when "in rounding one of the sacks he caught his foot in the bearings and met with the unfortunate accident."[6]

While Martin was recovering in the hospital, the Cleveland Naps surrendered their claim to his services. Cincinnati and the Boston Braves put in claims for the injured player. The conflicting claims went before the National Commission, which awarded his rights to the Braves. Boston manager George Stallings signed him to a contract in July after consulting with a physician and with team owner James E. Gaffney. Martin was sent home to recuperate and was told to report on August 1.[7]

With his leg sufficiently healed, Martin joined the Braves as scheduled. Stallings told the *Washington Post* "that in Martin he thought he had a most promising youngster."[8] By the time Martin joined the team, the Braves had battled their way out of the cellar to reach .500 and were now in fourth place, eight games behind the first-place New York Giants.

Though Martin had experience at other positions around the infield, he was a shortstop and therefore played behind future Hall of Famer Rabbit Maranville, regarded as the finest shortstop in the National League.

Martin and Oscar Dugey were the utility infielders and did not figure to receive much playing time as the Braves drove their way up the standings.

The Braves clinched the pennant on September 29. Stallings had no intention of easing up; he wanted to bury the Giants and maintain the fighting spirit of his team. He did, however, intend to play his substitutes. Stallings told the *Washington Post* that "Martin will most likely be played in the coming series with Brooklyn."[9]

The Braves were closing their amazing season with back-to-back doubleheaders in Brooklyn. They swept the first doubleheader and lost the first game of the second set. (Hard-hitting third baseman Red Smith slid awkwardly into second base and broke his ankle in the game.) Stallings sent out a lineup of mostly substitutes, including Martin, making his major-league debut at shortstop.

Martin's debut went all but unnoticed by the press given the sportswriters' attention to Smith's injury. Martin

Billy Martin

went hitless in three at-bats, facing the Robins' starter, Nap Rucker, one of the toughest left-handed pitchers in the league, and a young right-hander, Johnny Enzmann, who relieved Rucker in the sixth inning. Martin booted a ball during one of his two chances at shortstop. The Braves won, 7-3, to close out the regular season. Martin certainly could not have known as he left the field that he would never again play in a regular-season major-league game.

The Braves' surprising victory over the Athletics produced a couple of disappointing events for Martin. At the end of the final game, unruly fans stole many souvenirs from the players, including Martin's prized Mackinaw sweater. He was so upset to lose his prized possession that he offered a sizable reward for its return. More disappointing was the decision by a committee of veteran players to not award Martin a full World Series share of $2,708.86. Martin, pitcher Ensign Cottrell, who joined the team in July, and several other members of the Braves organization received just $500. Stallings displayed his feelings for Martin by handing him a personal check for $500.[10] The veterans were probably justified in their decision to cut out the young players as neither had played much down the stretch, nor participated in the World Series. Yet Stallings valued their attitude and spirit, which made them ballplayers in his eye.

The Braves entered the 1915 season with great promise and hope, as the championship team returned largely intact and made some key additions. Younger ballplayers like Martin expected to play a much more prominent role. While the young superstar Maranville was a lock at shortstop, the great second baseman Johnny Evers was now 34 years old and entering his 17th major-league season. At third base, Red Smith's future was still in question after his severe leg injury. As the team headed south to Macon, Georgia, for spring training, all indications were that Martin was progressing well and continuing to impress his manager. But Martin's energy and perhaps overzealousness got the best of him on March 11.

The team played a scrimmage game against Mercer College in Macon and Martin entered the game in the eighth inning to take over for Maranville. The *Boston Daily Globe* reported that "In his one time at bat, he failed to get on base, and it is figured by Stallings that Martin, who is exceptionally ambitious to make good, decided to finish his day's work by practicing with the college team."[11] After the Braves' 11-2 victory, the players headed back to their hotel for the evening, but Martin joined the Mercer squad's practice session. It was nearly dark when Martin broke his ankle once again during sliding drills.

According to the *Globe*, the injury was identical to the one he had suffered the previous June in Princeton.[12] Stallings, informed of the accident by the Mercer coach, went to the hospital to check on Martin and was informed that he would have to remain in the hospital for a week and would be out of action, "under the best of circumstances," for at least a month. "The Boston Manager was very much upset over the occurrence, as he valued the young player highly and figured on him as a very promising asset to the club," the *Globe* reported. (According to the *Washington Post*, Stallings looked upon Martin as "another Johnny Evers.")[13]

On March 17 the *Globe* reported better news: "The latest report on Martin's condition is decidedly cheering, as it had been discovered by the doctors in their final examination that the break is not as serious as was first thought." The paper speculated that he should be able to report by the middle of May and return to action by the end of June.[15] Meanwhile Stallings began to evaluate potential replacements. (Several other players were injured, as well.) A utility infielder, Ed Fitzpatrick, had already been working out with the team and the team acquired a veteran middle infielder, Dick Egan, from Brooklyn in late April.

July began on a positive note for Martin; he married Martha Millar, a native of Ireland, on July 6 in Ellicott City, Maryland. But the *Globe's* prognosis proved overly optimistic. Martin couldn't return to the Braves until late July. He remained with the club for a month, but saw no action. The end came on August 21, when he was unconditionally released. "With Egan and Fitzpatrick as utility infielders, there was no chance to use Martin," the *Globe* wrote, adding, "An effort was made to place him with a minor league club, but it failed: hence his unconditional release."[14]

Martin's career with the Braves was over, but his professional sports career was not. There are no records that indicate he signed anywhere for the remainder of the 1915 season; perhaps he allowed his leg to continue healing. John McGraw invited him to spring training with the Giants the following year.

Martin joined the Giants at their spring-training camp in Marlin, Texas, and by all accounts had an impressive spring. He "played short for the Rookies at Marlin and managed the team on the way north."[15] It looked as if he might benefit from injuries to other players. Hans Lobert, the Giants' starting third baseman, and his backup, Herbert Hunter, had both been injured in the spring. McGraw started the season on April 12 with another young third-sacker, Fred Brainard, who played poorly enough that a mere two games into the season, the Giants manager brought in two new players, Bill McKechnie and Bill Martin.[16] McKechnie was a veteran who had been with several teams and was a serviceable player. (He later became a Hall of Fame manager, spending 25 years, winning four pennants and two World Series.)

This time around, the press was not complimentary toward Martin: "The trouble with Martin is that he cannot hit. He has a good arm, is a fine fielder, but is useless at the plate."[17] McGraw must have come to a similar conclusion; Martin never appeared in a game for the Giants. In July J.C. Kofoed of *Baseball Magazine* sang his praises, writing, "A few like [Joe] Schepner and Martin seem likely to make good in a few years. The latter has a marvelous faculty for judging ground balls, and a pair of hands like Milton Stock."[18] Kofoed was wrong about both players.

Though the exact date is unclear, Martin was released by the Giants and signed with the Syracuse Stars of the New York State League. He batted a respectable .256 and led the league in fielding percentage at short-stop. The Stars, whose best pitcher was Howard Ehmke (31-7) won the league championship. From this point forward, details of Martin's career are difficult to come by. He was sold to Bridgeport of the Eastern League in March 1917. In late August, the *New London Day* reported that Martin had been thrown out of a game after fighting with the opposing pitcher.[19] On November 29, 1917, the Martins' first child, a daughter, Patricia, was born.

After the United States entered the Great War in 1917, the federal government promulgated a "work or fight" order requiring able-bodied men of draft age to either join the military or work in war-related industries. In the spring of 1918, the Martins moved to Wilmington, Delaware, where Bill went to work for the Bethlehem Shipbuilding Company and played for the Harlan semipro team, which Bethlehem sponsored. He worked on ships at the docks for five days and played ball on the weekends. Harlan actually fielded two teams, and Martin's had seven players with major-league experience. "The teams are composed of the greatest array of baseball talent that has ever represented this city in any league," said a Wilmington newspaper, the *Delmarva Star*.[20] Harlan's team won "the shipworkers' baseball championship of the Atlantic Coast," defeating the Standard Team of New York, 4 to 0."[21] After the baseball season, Martin helped assemble and coach a Harlan football team, and continued coaching and playing for the team in 1919. He also took on coaching another local team, the Brownson eleven.

With the dawning of the '20s, Martin again felt the itch to return to professional baseball and signed with the Petersburg Goobers of the Virginia League on August 9, 1920. He played in the Virginia League for a few seasons, though detailed records are poor. The league had numerous difficulties as Martin's team, Petersburg, went bankrupt in 1921 and was taken over by the Tarboro (North Carolina) Tarbabies. Martin also played in 1921 for the Wilson (North Carolina) Bugs, who had a claim to first place until a controversy regarding salary limits knocked them out of contention.[22] Sometime during 1921 he was a manager, but for which team and for how long is unknown. What is known is that Martin played at both shortstop and second base, while hitting a respectable .270 for the 1921 season.

The Martins had a second child on October 22, 1922, a son named William A. Martin. After bouncing around the Virginia League for a few years, Bill decided to move back to his hometown. He ended his baseball career in 1924 on the roster of the Eastern League's Bridgeport Bears. Details of this period are sketchy at best, but we do know that Bill went back to coaching football and was again successful. He coached the Georgetown Knickerbocker eleven to the district championship of 1924. The strength of the team was described by the *Washington Post*: "Under the guidance of Billy Martin the club has been scored on but once this season — that by the Navy Yard Marines in the opening game."[23]

By 1930 Martin listed his occupation as "Real Estate Sales."[24] The Martins lived in a large house on a hill in the Washington suburb of Arlington, Virginia. Despite being a minor-league baseball player and semiprofessional football coach, the family lived an upper-class lifestyle — this during the early years of the Great Depression. As his father before him, despite a modest career, Bill was able to afford the luxuries of life including sending his son to his alma mater, the venerable Georgetown Prep. According to Billy A. Martin, Jr., Bill's grandson, "In all of the pictures that I saw of my father during his early years, he was always dressed in the finest clothing while the other kids essentially were wearing hand-me-downs or rags. After all, it was the Great Depression."[25] Martin's grandson mentioned a possible explanation for the surprising wealth: "I have heard the story several times of my grandfather driving his convoy of 'bootlegging trucks' down a dark country road where they were intercepted by another group who forced them all out of their trucks at gunpoint and lined them up. They pointed to my grandfather and told him to move to the side and proceeded to gun down the rest of his men with their tommyguns. Why they spared his life, I do not know."[26]

After Prohibition ended in 1933, Billy Martin and his father opened Martin's Tavern in the Georgetown section of Washington. Since its opening, every president from Harry S. Truman to Barack Obama has stopped at the D.C. landmark. John F. Kennedy not only preferred a regular booth there as a young senator, but also proposed to Jacqueline Bouvier in booth number 3, while Richard Nixon favored booth number 2.[27] Billy Martin preferred to hold court in a back room aptly named the Dugout, where cards, politics, and gin flowed liberally every night. Many ballplayers were said to have stopped in regularly to see the gregarious Martin and swap old stories. The fourth-generation Billy Martin, Jr., who began working in the tavern in 1982, relayed this story of his grandfather's hefty political clout: "My grandfather was sitting in the Dugout with his good friend [Speaker of the House] Sam Rayburn and a young congressman from Texas named Lyndon B. Johnson. Johnson kept waxing on about D.C. politics when Rayburn finally told him to 'shut up and listen to Billy Martin if you actually want to learn something about this town!'"[28]

Bill Martin's son, William A. Martin, followed in his father's footsteps and was also a star athlete at Georgetown Prep and Georgetown University. He was a Golden Gloves boxing champion at Georgetown with a career record of 44-0, saw action with the Navy off Okinawa during World War II, and played golf on the Pro-Am tour during the 1950s. The son retired to Florida after turning over the tavern to Billy Jr. in 2001 and died in 2004. As of 2013 Bill's daughter Patricia Martin Simpson was living in Stuart, Florida.

As for William G. "Bill" Martin, he lived life to the fullest and could always be found at his beloved tavern, where he was the life of every party. His health began to decline while he was still a relatively young man and he suffered a fatal stroke following complications from diabetes on September 14, 1949. He was buried in Cedar Hill Cemetery in Suitland, Maryland.

Grateful acknowledgment to William A. "Billy" Martin, Jr. for sharing his personal memories and knowledge of his family history.

Notes

1. Telephone conversations with William A. Martin, Jr., and exchange of e-mails on several dates between February 22, 2010 through April 6, 2010.
2. "Bill Martin To Sign With The Erie Team," *Pittsburgh Press*, April 10, 1913, 1.
3. "National League Notes," *Sporting Life*, August 22, 1914, 7.
4. "Bill Martin To Sign With The Erie Team."
5. "Long Run Wins for G.U. Over Virginia Medics," *Washington Post*, October 19, 1913, Sports, 7.
6. "Billy Martin Is Made Brave By Accident Which Breaks Leg," *Washington Post*, October 4, 1914, Sports, 4.
7. "National League Notes." *Sporting Life*, August 22, 1914, 7.
8. "Braves An Impressive Bunch, With Hustle Their Big Asset." *Washington Post*, October 1, 1914, Sports, 10.
9. Ibid.
10. "Braves Given Banquet; Get World's Series Coin," *Washington Post*, October 15, 1914, Sports, 10.
11. "As In 1914, Ankle Fracture Robs Champs of Too-Ambitious Martin," *Boston Daily Globe*, March 12, 1915, 8.
12. Ibid.
13. "Billy Martin Breaks Ankle At Braves Camp In Macon, Ga," *Washington Post*, March 12, 1915, 8.
14. "Billy Martin Breaks Ankle."
15. "Fred Snodgrass, Late Of Giants, Signed By Boston." *Boston Daily Globe*, August 22, 1915, 9.
16. "New York Has One Big Need," *Pittsburgh Press*, April 14, 1916, 40. Some sources render Brainard's surname as Brainerd.
17. Ibid.
18. "The Youngsters Of 1916." *Baseball Magazine*, July 1916, 48.
19. "Lively Fist Fight In Savin Rock Park," *New London Day*, August 30, 1917, 10.
20. Former Professional Big League Stars In Action With Harlan Baseball Teams," *Delmarva Star* (Wilmington. Delaware), May 26, 1918, 13.
21. "Harlan Nine Gains Title," *New York Times*, September 15, 1918.
22. "Virginia League," *Spalding's Official Base Ball Guide*, 1922, 219-221.
23. "Knicks Slight Favorite To Beat Mercury Team," *Washington Post*, December 13, 1924, 19.
24. Fifteenth Census of the United States, 1930.
25. Conversation with William A. Martin, Jr.
26. Ibid.
27. "Restaurant Review: Martin's Tavern," *Washington Post*, March 30, 2006, Online Edition.
28. Conversation with William A. Martin, Jr.

Jack Martin

By Charles F. Faber

Jack Martin, a slick-fielding but light-hitting shortstop, began the 1914 season with the Boston Braves but was traded away just before the last-place team began its drive for the National League pennant. He spent only two years in the major leagues but was a longtime minor-league player and manager.

John Christopher Martin was born in Plainfield, New Jersey in the central part of the state, on April 19, 1887. The son of Adeline and James B. Martin, a trolley conductor, Jack played baseball at Plainfield High School and for the town's amateur clubs. By 1909 he had attracted considerable attention as a slick fielding shortstop for the New Brunswick Brunswicks, one of the top semipro teams in the area. Owned by the Brunswick Amusement Company, the club not only played other semipro teams but took on professional team,s including major-league teams. A brilliant fielder who owed his spot on the team to his glove work, Jack was not much of a hitter. He rarely hit a home run, but thought he had clouted one in a 1909 game. He hit a fly ball, which the outfielder misplayed so badly that Jack rounded the bases, and put in a claim for a pair of new shoes which a local merchant was offering to any Brunswick who hit a home run. The scorer refused to award him a pair of $5 shoes, saying the hit was not a legitimate home run.

The sports columns of the *New Brunswick Times* were filled with praise of Jack's fielding prowess. Typical comments were: "Jack Martin fielded a phenomenal game and the fans applauded him to the echo repeatedly. … Jack Martin's stop and put out on Hemphill's near hit over second was about as clean an exhibition of quick fielding as we have seen. …"[1]

In August 1909 Martin got a trial with the Worcester Busters of the New England League, managed by future Hall of Famer Jesse Burkett. The *Worcester Star* reported as follows: "Manager Burkett had a young fellow practicing at short yesterday, who showed up great. He is an amateur named Martin, from Plainfield, N.J., who is visiting ex-Councilman Jeremiah W. Mara, brother-in-law of W.E. Bransfield, of the Philadelphia National League team. Mr. Mara is a close friend of Burkett's and knowing the youngster could play ball, sent him to Burkett. The latter had Martin out with the rest of the players yesterday, and the spectators commented freely on the great work the youngster showed. Burkett will take him on the trip today."[2] (W.E. Bransfield was Kitty Bransfield, the longtime first baseman for the Pittsburgh Pirates and Philadelphia Phillies.)

The *Times* quoted another paper as saying: "The manager and players are in great glee at prospects of another base ball find. Young Martin, the New Jersey lad, who practiced before the games at Boulevard Park last week, was signed by Burkett and accompanied the club on its trip. He didn't get into any game, but he was out practicing regularly until yesterday when he went to

Jack Martin

New Jersey to play a couple of games. He will be back in Worcester tomorrow. Burkett and the players say he's a wizard at picking up grounders and acts well in the practice setting. They think they see in him another base ball star."[3] Martin's own take on the situation was that he would get good money as a bench warmer and would probably be given a chance to make good in some of the games. As it turned out, he did not get into any games in 1909. Upon his return to New Jersey, the New Brunswick newspaper reported, "Wake up and rejoice. Jack Martin, the great and only lightning short stop, will, in all probability, be with the Brunswicks again this season, as Jesse Burkett has not as yet sent him a contract for the Worcester club in the New England League."[4] Jack indeed started the 1910 season with the Brunswicks. However, Burkett had signed him to a contract at the end of the 1909 season and ordered him to report to Worcester on April 17.

Martin's experience in Worcester was not a happy one. What happened is a matter of dispute. The *New Brunswick Times* said that he wanted a pay raise but Burkett would not give it to him and tried to farm him out to Newport. Martin refused to be demoted and caught the next train back to Plainfield. This report suggested that as the player had jumped his contract, he would be blacklisted by Organized Baseball.[5] A few days later the newspaper said that in spite of rumors to the contrary, Martin would not be charged with breaking his contract with the Worcester club. He had not hit well enough to please Burkett and was due to be released if he had not quit.[6] Burkett's feeling about Martin's hitting may have been justified. In 29 games for Worcester, the young man hit .208 with no home runs and only three extra-base hits.

Martin's 1910 adventures continued. He played for the Brunswicks for a month or so. In late July local newspapers reported that he had joined the Bridgeport club of the Connecticut League, but there is no evidence that he ever played for the Orators. In August he considered joining an independent club in Paterson, New Jersey, but the National Baseball Commission issued an order forbidding players in Organized Baseball to play for or against Paterson, because that club was using the blacklisted Andy Coakley. Martin returned to New Brunswick and scored the first run for the Brunswicks on September 25 as they took an early lead over the Brooklyn Superbas in an exhibition game before succumbing to the National League club, 5-2.

During the offseason, Martin was signed by the New York Highlanders (later called the Yankees) and assigned to Richmond of the Virginia League. In 1911, for the first time in his career, he played the entire season with one team, appearing in every one of the Colts' 118 games. He also improved at the plate, hitting .318 for the season, an average he did not reach again until the 1920s. After the Virginia League season ended, Martin was ordered to report to New York. Although he expected to play in a few American League games, it did not happen. By October he was playing for his hometown Plainfield independent club, which won the championship of the Central New Jersey Baseball League. Gambling was rife at baseball games in those days, and large sums of money exchanged hands as Plainfield defeated Somerville in the decisive game by a score of 2-1. Both clubs were stocked with professional players, including at least three major leaguers (Cy Seymour, Andy Coakley, and Red Kleinow.) Martin spent the winter teaching finer points of the game to members of the Plainfield High School baseball team.

Martin started the 1912 season with the Rochester Hustlers of the International League. While there he caught the eye of the Boston Braves, who offered $4,000 for him, but he was already the property of the Highlanders. The big-league club immediately called him up and he made his major-league debut on April 25, a few days after his 25th birthday. The right-hander stood 5-feet-9 and weighed 159 pounds during his inaugural season in "The Show." During most of the 1912 season, Martin was the Highlanders' regular shortstop, but he failed to hit well enough to remain with the club (.225) and in August he was traded along with Jack Quinn to Rochester for shortstop Tommy McMillan, and finished the season with Rochester. This trade turned out to be one of the most lopsided deals in the history of baseball, as McMillan never played a game in the majors after 1912 and Quinn went on to win over 200 big-league games from 1913 to 1933. Martin remained with the Hustlers in 1913, hitting .294. In September he was drafted by the Boston Braves.

The Braves had the amazingly agile Rabbit Maranville at shortstop, so they decided to use Martin as a backup for Charlie Deal at third base. Martin and Deal competed for duties at the hot corner during the first half of the season. By midseason it was apparent that the light-hitting Martin was not going to win the competition, so he was traded to Philadelphia for outfielder Josh Devore on July 3. At that time the Braves were in last place in the National League, so Martin had no part in their drive for the pennant. Martin is barely mentioned in Harold Kaese's definitive history of the Boston Braves.

Martin finished the 1914 season with the Phillies, playing his final major-league game on October 6. Although he signed with the Phillies for 1915, he did not get into any games for them that season. On May 4 he was optioned to St. Paul of the American Association. In two consecutive years he had started the season with the eventual National League champion, but was long gone before World Series time.

After one year in St. Paul (where, as usual, he hit poorly but fielded brilliantly), Martin was sold to Milwaukee of the same league. A Milwaukee sportswriter welcomed him: "Martin, who was a Saint last year under a Philadelphia option, was one of the keenest players in the A.A. last season. His work … fairly sparkled. … Martin is only 22 [sic] years old and looks like one of the most promising youngsters in the game. He is a wonderfully clever fielder, has a great whip and covers an ocean of ground."[7] Jack played for the Brewers from 1916 through 1918. He managed the club from July through September in 1916.

In 1919 the San Antonio club of the Texas League purchased Martin from Milwaukee for $500. He was named captain of the Aces and thrilled San Antonio fans with his brilliant fielding. One sportswriter penned the following tribute: "Capt. Jack Martin pulled one of the most sensational one-handed spears that has ever been seen on the local lot. Robertson was at the bat. He ripped off a burner directly at second base. The ball took a high bound. Martin went after it, grabbed it with his bare mitt, touching the bag, forcing Patterson at second, and threw out Robertson at first. While we are on the subject of Jack Martin it should be said that the doughty little infielder is playing the greatest game of his career and recently he has taken almost entire control of the team. He directs the play and when a pitcher is going bad, he does the yanking. … Since Martin has taken more active control the playing of the Aces has improved materially."[8]

But Martin spent only half of the season in San Antonio, then he was on the move again. He finished 1919 in St. Paul; he played for Atlanta of the Southern Association in 1920; and in 1921 and 1922 he managed the Daytona Beach Islanders of the Class C Florida State League. Late in 1922 he was back in St. Paul for his third stint with the Saints. He played a few games for Seattle of the Pacific Coast League in 1923. In 1924 he was with St. Petersburg of the Florida Sate League until that circuit disbanded on August 6. He finished the season with Newark of the International League.

Martin was out of Organized Baseball as a player for four years, then returned to the playing field for the Springfield Senators of the Three-I League in 1929 and 1930. He played his last game for the Senators at the age of 43. During his 20 years in professional ball, he had played for 12 minor-league and three major-league clubs. His best years at the plate were the two seasons with Daytona, when he hit .313 in 1921 and .336 in 1922. Wherever he played, he drew praise for his fielding. He often said that he was a mediocre player, never a star, yet he was proud of what he accomplished. He was especially proud of the fact that among the past and future major leaguers he managed at Milwaukee was Jim Thorpe, hero of the 1912 Olympics and (according to the Associated Press) the greatest American athlete of the first half of the 20th century.

Martin married Myra Hinkle in 1912. They had two daughters, Dorothy and Norma. Throughout his lifetime he maintained his residence in New Jersey. From 1954 he resided in Brick Township and was active in civic

Jack Martin

affairs. In 1978 he was honored by the Brick Township Council for having been an inspiration to the youth of the community. He continued his interest in baseball. In his later years he spent his winters in Florida and was an annual visitor to the Yankees' spring training games. When the Yankee Alumni Association was founded in 1977, investigation revealed that Martin was the oldest living ex-Yankee. "I never lost my enthusiasm for baseball," he said. "It was a tremendous thrill when Mr. (George) Steinbrenner started the Yankee Alumni Association. When they sent me the alumni pen it was one of the highlights of my life."[9]

Until he was in his 90s he attended old-timer games, where he enjoyed being introduced as the oldest living former New York Yankee. After having been introduced to a crowd at Yankee Stadium on June 21, 1977, he suffered a heart attack. He was taken to Montefiore Hospital in the Bronx and was never able to leave. While in the hospital he gave out autographed pictures of himself to the doctors and nurses. On the Fourth of July 1980, the last living member of the Miracle Braves died. Jack Martin was 93. He was buried in Laurelton Cemetery, near his Brick Township home.

Sources

Jack Martin player file at the National Baseball Hall of Fame

www.ancestry.com

www.baseball-reference.com

www.newspaperarchive.com

Notes

1. *New Brunswick Times*, October 13, 1909.
2. As reported in the *New Brunswick Times*, August 10, 1909.
3. Ibid.
4. *New Brunswick Times*, March 17, 1910.
5. *New Brunswick Times*, June 7, 1910.
6. *New Brunswick Times*, June 11, 1910.
7. Lester B. March, January 8, 1916; clipping in National Baseball Hall of Fame file.
8. *San Antonio Evening News*, June 7, 1919.
9. 1977 Yankee Scorebook in files at National Baseball Hall of Fame.

Herbie Moran

By Charles F. Faber

Herbie Moran, a late-season acquisition in the Boston Braves' pennant drive in 1914, acquired for his speed and outfield defense, was one of the heroes of the Braves' unexpected Series sweep: The winning run in Game Three scored when his bunt with runners on first and second in the 12th inning was fumbled by Philadelphia Athletics pitcher Bullet Joe Bush. It was the first walk-off victory in a World Series game.

John Herbert "Herbie" Moran was born in Costello, Potter County, Pennsylvania, in the north-central part of the state, not far from the New York state line, on February 16, 1884. He was the eldest son of Mary Bailey and James "Jimmy" Moran, both offspring of immigrants from Northern Ireland. A day laborer, Jimmy moved his family to the county seat at Coudersport, which Herbie came to regard as his hometown. By 1910 Jimmy had become a polisher at a machine shop in Coudersport, and Herbie lived next door with his wife, the former Scena Haskins, whom he had married on February 27, 1906, and their two sons, Vincent and James. A third son, William, was born in 1914. Scena died in October 1918, perhaps as a result of the influenza epidemic that took so many lives in the United States and around the world in 1918 and 1919.

Called Little Herbie because of his diminutive stature (5-feet-5, 150 pounds), Moran batted left-handed and threw right-handed. He played baseball at the Peddie Institute, a private boarding school in Hightstown, New Jersey, before starting his professional career in 1905 with the hometown Coudersport Giants in the Class D Interstate League. In 1906 he played for the DuBois Miners in the same league. In 1907 he moved to Trenton of the Class B Tri-State League and began to attract the attention of major-league scouts for his superb fielding and fine baserunning. He was reputed to be a ballhawk with a rifle arm and a ferocious competitive spirit. It was rumored that Fielder Jones recommended Moran to the Chicago White Sox, but he signed with the Philadelphia Athletics and made his major-league debut on April 16, 1908. However, he barely hit his weight in Philadelphia (.153 in 19 games), and he was soon sent back to Trenton, where he hit .295, his career high, and smacked his only minor-league home run. (He hit two homers in the majors, one for Brooklyn in 1912 and one for Cincinnati in 1914.)

The Boston Doves purchased Moran's contract from Trenton on September 12, 1908, and he enjoyed a second stint in the majors. This time he hit for a .276 average, though in only eight games. Moran went back and forth between the majors and the minors over the next few seasons. In 1909 he was at Providence for 154 games, where he hit a respectable .268, stole 58 bases, and led the Eastern League with 92 runs scored, earning another brief shot at the big leagues. He started the 1910 season in Boston, but collected only eight hits in 67 times at bat, for an atrocious .119 average. On May 12 he was released to the Kansas City Blues of the American Association; less than one month later he was with Rochester in the Eastern League. He hit .291 for the Bronchos in the remainder of the season. In September he was drafted by the Brooklyn Superbas, but he spent all of 1911 in Rochester, getting into 152 games and batting .289.

Moran spent the next four seasons in the major leagues. In 1912 he hit .276 in 130 games for the Superbas, and in 1913 he hit .266 in 132 games. In January 1914 Brooklyn placed him on waivers and he was acquired by the Cincinnati Reds; in 107 games for the Reds he batted .235. On August 23 Moran was sold to the Braves, who wanted him to help in their remarkable run to the pennant. In the last game he played for the Reds, Moran hit a game-winning ninth-inning double to send the New York Giants down to a 3-2 defeat and into a tie with the surging Braves. For the Braves he hit .266 in 41 games, driving in only four runs but scoring 24.

Much has been written about manager George Stallings acquiring Moran in order to be able to platoon his outfielders. The advantage of having a left-handed batter face a right-handed pitcher and vice versa had been recognized long before 1914, but Stallings was said to be the first to play the percentages wholesale.[1] Actually, Stallings did not platoon Moran much during the drive. Herbie played in 41 of the 46 games the Braves played after his acquisition. Bill James, who presented a lengthy history of platooning in one of his early books,[2] concluded that 1914 was the first time a National League manager had platooned in a World Series, and quite possibly the first time a National League manager had ever platooned. Stallings certainly did some platooning, but he was not dead-set on it. Moran started all three World Series games against right-handed pitchers and sat out the game started by a lefty. However, when a left-handed reliever entered the fray in Game Four, Stallings left Moran in the game.

In the 1914 Series, Herbie got only one hit, but he played a large part in the Boston sweep. Game Three went into extra innings at Fenway Park, the Braves' home field for the World Series. Philadelphia took the lead by scoring two in the top of the tenth, but the Braves came back in the bottom of the frame. Hank Gowdy opened the home half by hitting a home run. Moran worked Joe Bush for a walk and sped to third on a single by Johnny Evers. Joe Connolly hit a sacrifice fly and Little Herbie scampered home to tie the game. Neither team scored in the 11th or the top of the 12th.

A *New York Times* reporter described the scene in the last of the 12th: "The purple haze of eventide was gathering over Fenway Park and the 35,520 persons who had sat for more than three hours were restless and fatigued as they looked down, from all sides of the solid banks of humanity, at the figures which moved about phantomlike in the twilight."[3] Gowdy led off with a double. Leslie Mann came in to run for him. Larry Gilbert was walked intentionally. With two on and nobody out, the situation called for a sacrifice bunt by Moran. Herbie's bunt went straight to the mound. Bush picked up the ball and fired to third, trying to force Mann at the bag. The throw was wild, and Mann dashed home with the winning tally. Moran had won the World Series for the Braves on a sacrifice bunt that led to the first walk-off error in World Series history. The *Times* scribe reported: "The crowd went wild. All the feeling and enthusiasm which had been bottled up as the game seesawed one way and then the other, burst forth with unrestrained fury. The mob jammed down to the field and smothered the Boston players in a demonstration of fanatical joy which has rarely been seen at a baseball game."

Moran played one more year in Boston, hitting exactly .200 in 1915. He played his last major-league game on October 7, the closing day of the season. On the 13th he was traded, along with catcher Bert Whaling to Venice club of the Pacific Coast League for outfielder Joe Wilhoit. Herbie never played in the PCL. Instead, he went to the International League, where he toiled for Montreal in 1916 and 1917. He had two decent years with the Royals, hitting .271 and .284. In 1918 he played for the Little Rock Travelers, hitting .263 in the war-shortened Southern Association season. In compliance with Secretary of War Newton Baker's work-or-fight order, Moran took a job in September at the Du Pont de Nemours munitions plant in Hopewell,

Herbie Moran

Virginia. In 1919 he was the playing manager of the Sioux City Indians of the Western League.

In the early 1920s Moran played for and managed semipro teams in Pennsylvania and New York. The *Olean* (New York) *Evening Herald* reported on a game between the Olean All-Stars and a team from Dansville, managed by Moran, who also played center field and was the leadoff hitter. "A feature of the game was the base running of Herb Moran, 'the old timer,'" the paper wrote. "Herb burned his way over the paths with a speed that would rival the fastest of younger ball players."[4] The "old timer" was 38 years old.

Moran served as a scout later in the 1920s, for Montreal and perhaps other clubs. In 1932 he was named manager of Williamsport of the Class B New York-Penn League, but lasted only one season as the Grays finished in seventh place. Five years later, in 1937, he gave Organized Ball one more try, managing New Waterford (Nova Scotia) in the Cape Breton Colliery League. He had no more success in Canada than he had in the United States as the team finished in the league cellar. After that, Herbie dropped out of the news. Moran worked as a guard at Bausch and Lomb from 1940 until his retirement in 1953.

He married a second wife, Mildred Labbe, who bore him a son, Nicholas. Herbert Moran died of hypertensive cardiovascular disease at his home in Clarkson, New York, on September 21, 1954. His funeral was held in Brockport, New York, and he was buried in Coudersport. He was 70 years old and was survived by Mildred and his four sons.

Sources

In addition to the references in the text, the writer utilized Herbie Moran's player file at the National Baseball Hall of Fame and the following sources:

Peter Filichia. *Professional Baseball Franchises.* New York: Facts on File, 1993.

Lloyd Johnson and Miles Wolff, eds. *Encyclopedia of Minor League Baseball.* Durham, North Carolina: Baseball America, Inc., 1993.

www.ancestry.com.

www.baseballanalysts.com.

www.baseball-reference.com.

www.newspaperarchive.com.

Notes

1 Tom Meany. *Baseball's Greatest Teams* (New York: A.S. Barnes, 1949), 167.

2 *Bill James Historical Baseball Abstract* (New York: Villard Books, 1988), 112-23.

3 *New York Times*, October 13, 1914.

4 *Olean Evening Herald,* June 15, 1922.

Jim Murray

by James E. Elfers

THE BEST DESCRIPTION of Jim Murray would be marginal major leaguer. Talented enough to make a splash at various levels of the minor leagues, he never possessed the talent to earn much more than a cup of coffee with three major-league teams. Standing 5-feet-10 and weighing 180 pounds, he was a rather unimportant cog in the 1914 Braves' miraculous season. He was gone from the club on July 10. His biggest contribution to the Braves was his salary dispute, which dragged into the next season.

James Oscar Murray was born on January 16, 1878, and raised in Galveston, Texas. The son of Richard Murray, a Canadian immigrant and Mary Murray, who, like her son, called the Texas coastal town home her entire life. The only time Jim was away from Galveston, he was in the majors. In fact his sojourn in professional baseball began in his own backyard. At the age of 19 in 1897 he broke in with the Galveston Sandcrabs of the Texas League. As a left-handed thrower and a right-handed batter he presented a rare combination in baseball. How good a player Murray was may never be known, because no statistics can be found for his first few years of professional baseball. What is clear is that he made steady progress up baseball's ladder.

In 1900 Murray set the Virginia League on fire, leading it with eight home runs and driving in a respectable 38 runs. At the same time Christy Mathewson was leading the same league in wins, strikeouts, and winning percentage. In the minor leagues Murray generally hit in the high .200s; he reached the .300 plateau just four times in a career that spanned more than two decades (1897-1920). Murray first really made his mark in the Texas League, playing for San Antonio and Houston in 1899, and then in Virginia for Portsmouth and Newport News in 1900 and 1901, hitting around .300 in those three years By 1902 Murray had worked his way up to the Class C New England League. A solid .289 season with Manchester earned him the opportunity to play with the Chicago Cubs. He debuted on September 2, 1902, and a 12-game stint with the Cubs indicated that he was not yet up to snuff for the majors. He batted just .170 with eight hits, three runs and one RBI. Even for the offense-impaired Deadball Era those were not good numbers.

In 1903 Murray played in the Eastern League for Toronto and in the New England League again with Manchester. In 1905 he played for three teams, Harrisburg, Buffalo, and Toronto. The years he spent in the high minor leagues were the closest he ever became to being a star.

While the date of the specific game is lost to time, a Galveston sportswriter almost 40 years later described what was no doubt Murray's greatest day on the diamond: "It was after Jim Murray contributed a home run, a triple, and two singles to knock home eight runs in a game for the Buffalo Bisons with the Baltimore Orioles at Buffalo that the sports editor on the Buffalo

Jim Murray

paper saw fit to write his headline this way—OH: YOU JIM WOW!"[1]

It was flashes of brilliance such as those that piqued the interest of major-league clubs. Time after time, however, the majors decided that Murray was not what they were really looking for. After his dozen games with the Cubs, nearly a decade passed before he was again called up by a big-league club. Not even with the pathetic, perpetual sad-sack St. Louis Browns could Murray make a go of it. He joined the Browns for the 1911 season and lasted just 31 games before he was sent back to Buffalo. St. Louis finished in last place at 47-107, according to Retrosheet. (Other sources have it 45-107.) Murray produced a grand total of eight runs and his batting average of .186 was only incrementally higher than it had been in 1902 with the Cubs, The only surprise was some power. During his stint with the Browns he hit his only three big-league homers; all were solo home runs. Murray spent the next three years back in Buffalo, and while a bit long in the tooth at the age of 33, he put it all together and had three straight seasons of batting .300 or better in 1911-13. After 1913, his contract was purchased by the Boston Braves with an eye toward 1914, and at 36, Murray was given his third chance for a roster spot in the majors. He joined the Braves on April 22, 1914. It was a turbulent time. The Federal League in its first year was wreaking havoc with the major leagues. Salaries were being inflated everywhere. The crosstown Red Sox, in order to keep Tris Speaker out of the clutches of the Brooklyn Feds, paid a salary of $16,000 a year for three years with a $5,000 signing bonus. This was a nearly incomprehensible amount of money for a professional athlete of the time. One statistician was so struck with the amount that he went to the trouble of figuring out Speaker's hourly remuneration. He concluded, "Speaker will get $58.44 an hour or $116.88 a game."[2]

In a similar vein, the Braves sent cash and a player to pull Johnny Evers away from the Cubs. To keep him from the Federal League, Evers received $25,000. It was a bold step for the usually bargain-basement Braves. For major-league players of every stripe, and especially for stars, money seemed to be growing on trees as long as the Feds were in operation. Manager George Stallings, after the Braves' 1913 season, their most successful in decades, saw something in his 1914 team. It took a while for his vision to come to fruition.

Stallings was familiar with Murray, having managed him in Buffalo in 1905-06 and 1911-12, and was initially enthusiastic about him. As *Sporting Life* described the situation, "The Braves got such a bad start and the players were hitting so poorly that Manager Stallings started out to quietly strengthen his team. Stallings wants to fight in boosting up his club and the players know that they must deliver the goods if they want to stay with him. His outfield was particularly weak at the bat so he scurried around to make a deal with the Buffalo club for the services of Jim Murray, the outfielder. Murray is not a particularly fast runner but he can hit the pill and that is what Stallings needs just now."[3]

Murray had hit an even .300 with the 1913 Bisons. With the Braves, at the higher level of play, his batting average fell to .232—respectable for the Deadball Era, but not what Stallings had been hoping for. Of Murray's 34 hits, 28 were singles; he had four doubles and two triples. His fielding percentage of .941 needed improvement as well. At 36, Jim was too old to learn new tricks. After Murray went 0-for-2 on July 10, Stallings decided that enough was enough, and on July 11, Murray was sold to the St. Paul Apostles of the American Association. Stallings had not seen much of a future for Murray, and indeed Murray spent the next four years working his way back down the ladder of Organized Baseball.

Murray left the Braves under a cloud. Apparently Stallings had held on to him for a month longer than he would have liked in order to find a minor-league club with which the player would be content. After that, things get murky. Murray placed a claim with the National Commission at the close of the 1914 season. He said Stallings had assured him that the Braves would pay Murray's salary while with the Apostles. When the American Association season ended on September 27 and the Braves season ended on October 7, Murray claimed that he was owed $180.70 by the Braves. While the commission did find a telegram from Stallings informing St. Paul that Murray's salary was $400 a month, both Stallings and the president of the Apostles claimed that there was no provision to pay him after the American Association season ended. The National Commission agreed with this version of events and turned down Murray's appeal.[4]

The rest of the 1914 season must have been galling to Murray. Upon his dismissal and that of Wilson Collins (whom Stallings thought much more of), the Braves became positively incandescent, reeling off eight straight wins as part of a 34-10 stretch that put them within hailing distance of John McGraw's tired New York Giants. The Giants-White Sox world tour of 1913-1914 may have left the New Yorkers vulnerable to the Braves. For whatever reason, the Giants withered under the Miracle Braves' assault. Meanwhile, Murray was marking time in Minnesota, playing just adequate baseball for a last-place team.

Although he was aging, Murray was game to play anywhere. By 1916 he was bouncing between Class B and Class D ball. He even tried his hand as player-manager for the Oklahoma City Senators of the Western Association in 1917. Coming in as a midseason replacement, Murray could do no better than drive his team to a fifth-place finish in an eight-team league. In his last hurrah, he came out of retirement in 1920 to embarrass himself with his hometown Galveston Pirates. Now 42 and mired in Class B, even he had to admit that baseball was over for him.

Nearly a lifelong bachelor, Murray was employed as the night clerk at the Malloy and Son Funeral Home in Galveston. Always willing to share stories of his baseball adventures, he proudly displayed the scrapbook he kept from his playing years. There was not much family to share it with; Jim had two sisters, one unmarried. Jim had briefly married but was divorced by the time of his death at the age of 67 from a heart attack on April 25, 1945. His employer provided the service and the Galveston Episcopal Cemetery provided a place for his final repose.

Perhaps Murray's most fitting epitaph was a poem about himself that he displayed in his scrapbook. In a style now long gone from the sports pages, a local advertising agent named Henri Parmalee channeled Grantland Rice and waxed rhapsodic about Murray's long forgotten minor-league career. Evidence suggests that the poem was published in 1909 in St. Paul when Murray was putting up less than respectable numbers for the Saints and Parmalee was also residing in that city.

The bags were filled when up came Chick,
His willow in his hands,
He taps it lightly on the plate
And cheers ring from the stands

But Chicken fanned the humid breeze,
From the bleachers came a sigh
Jimmie Murray then took Leslie's place
Once more our hopes beat high

The first ball pitched he let go by
The second was a foul
The third he hit full, hard and square –
The bleachers raised a howl

Far out to right the horsehide flew,
Above the fielder's head
It reached the fence and bounded back
So fielder Hayden said

Before the ball could be relayed
The bags were empty, quiet
Four runs were chalked up by the Saints
It was a goodly sight

And when we prate about the days
The days that now are not
We'll tell them the story
Of Murray's mighty swat.

Sources

In addition to the sources cited, the author used Retrosheet and Baseball-Reference.com. Thanks to Daniel O'Brien and Bill Nowlin for research and contributions to this biography.

Notes

1 Orland Dodson, "Baseball was Tops When Jim Murray Was a Star," *Galveston Daily News*, April 26, 1945, 10.
2 James E. Elfers, *The Tour to End All Tours: The Story of Major League Baseball's 1913-1914 World Tour* (Lincoln, Nebraska: University of Nebraska Press, 2003), 240.
3 *Sporting Life*, May 2, 1914, 7.
4 *Base Ball Magazine*, January 1915, 92.

Hub Perdue

by John A. Simpson

ALTHOUGH HE ANSWERED to a variety of nicknames—Rub-Dub-Hub, Hurling Hub, the Tennessee Cyclone, the Untamed Son of Sumner County, the Gallatin Squash—his family, friends, and baseball fans simply called him Hub. Herbert Rodney Perdue was one of the most personable and exciting pitching prospects to emerge from the hills of Middle Tennessee in the first decade of the 20th century. Perdue exhibited a light-hearted personality on and off the baseball field that concerned contemporary critics. Yet, his time in baseball overlapped the entire Deadball Era (1900-1923), and he set one professional pitching record that has stood for practically a century.[1]

Hub was born the fifth of six children to Marion Blair and Zoritha E. Perdue in the Sumner County, Tennessee, hamlet of Bethpage on June 7, 1882. The locale, little more than a post office, bank, general store, and several smaller buildings, was surrounded by fine farmland. The rural area 14 miles northeast of the city of Gallatin remained Hub's residence for the rest of his life.

Not much is known about Perdue's childhood. As an adolescent he earned spending money by hunting squirrels and selling them to a local market for a dime apiece. Not owning a rifle, Hub killed his prey with a most primitive weapon—rocks. He later quipped that throwing rocks at these small and fleet targets strengthened his arm, eyesight, and throwing technique. On December 29, 1900, only three months after graduating from high school, Hub married Mable Polk of Oaktown, Indiana. The young couple had two children, Marion Polk (born 1902) and Kathryn Ashby (1909). Hub and Mable remained together for the rest of their lives—almost 60 years.[2]

Hub honed his hard-throwing pitching skills in local "cow pasture games." Then, in the summer of 1901, P.L. "Butch" Anderson recruited an amateur nine in Gallatin and scheduled weekend contests from late May to mid-September.[3] Perdue's stature as a raw talent with a blazing "smoke ball" had already earned him considerable notoriety in unorganized baseball contests throughout the county, and he joined the Butchers in 1902. The team developed into a regional town-versus-town powerhouse within two years.

In 1905 the Butchers' player-manager, Willy Guild, placed Perdue with the Paducah Indians in the Kentucky-Illinois-Tennessee (Kitty) League with a contract for $75 a month. "It is said by experts," reported the *Paducah Sun*, "that [Perdue] pitches the best drop ball in the South."[4] Hub was released without explanation prior to Opening Day, so he donned the uniform of South Kentucky College in Hopkinsville and tossed a one-hitter and struck out 21 batters. "The magnificent pitcher" caught the attention of the owner of the Hopkinsville Browns, the local entrant in the Kitty League, who promptly signed him.[5] It took less than a month for Perdue to establish his reputation as "a phenom" with a "tantalizing up-shoot" and "baffling spit ball."[6] When the franchise suddenly folded on July 20, Perdue possessed a solid 11-5 record, and both league leaders (Paducah and Vincennes) vied for his services.

Perdue chose Vincennes, which was only a few miles from his in-laws' farm, and he was sensational with the Alices over the final month, when he faced Paducah six times. In a scheduled 13-game postseason championship series against the Indians, Hub went 2-1, including the deciding seventh victory, to cop the crown for Vincennes. A ninth game was played the next day to increase revenues, and modern record-keepers have erroneously identified that meaningless contest as the deciding game for the league crown.[7] Perdue had had a satisfying rookie season in Hopkinsville (11-5) and Vincennes (8-4) where he logged 253 innings pitched. As a reward, he was invited to a tryout in Nashville, but first-year manager Mike Finn deemed Perdue not quite ready for "fast company."

In 1906 Perdue picked up exactly where he had left off. By mid-July he had amassed an eye-popping 16-4 record, and opponents bestowed his first nickname,

"Rub, Dub, Hub."[8] Several interesting idiosyncrasies came to light in his sophomore season. For instance, he swung a heavy 42-inch cudgel which contributed to his poor batting; he wore a heavy red overcoat and later a red long-sleeve flannel undershirt regardless of team colors; he manipulated managers to pitch on or near his birthday; he enjoyed umpire-baiting and coaching third base; and, above all, he displayed clownish antics on and off the field. Perdue finished with a second consecutive league title and improved pitching statistics: a 25-8 record in 321 innings pitched and 260 strikeouts. His WHIP (walks and hits per inning pitched), a remarkable 0.75, owed to less than one walk per 12 innings pitched, and one one-hitter, two two-hitters, seven three-hitters, and one four-hitter. Several major-league teams took notice, and Chicago Cubs manager Frank Chance purchased his contract for $800.[9]

In March 1907 Hub arrived in West Baden, Indiana, a resort community and home to the Cubs' spring-training facility. The players "enjoyed taking the waters" between workouts, and Perdue struck up an immediate friendship with Mordecai "Three Finger" Brown, who showed the wide-eyed rookie his mangled right hand, the result of a farm-machinery accident as a youth. Perdue admired Brown's physical courage as well as his openness in sharing secrets about the craft of pitching in the big leagues.[10] Perdue struggled against major-league hitters, however, so Chance turned him over to Johnny Dobbs, the rookie skipper of Nashville. Dobbs was ecstatic to receive the castoff, who reportedly had mastered the spitball from three different release points—overhand, underhand, and side-arm.

Dobbs' roster was a tenuous mixture of grizzled veterans, career minor leaguers, and a sprinkling of young rookies. Perdue justified his lack of immediate success in the Southern Association, claiming that he was "a warm-weather pitcher," an excuse he resorted to frequently throughout his career.[11] A case of mumps sidelined him, but Perdue pitched well enough to keep his team out of the cellar. But he cavorted with bad attitudes on the club and known gamblers in the grandstands; and he demonstrated a worrisome inconsistency by neither winning nor losing more than two games in a row. He

Hub Perdue

finished at 11-15, and sportswriter Grantland Rice wondered whether he'd return.

In 1908 Perdue improved markedly under new manager Bill Bernhard, a former major-league hurler with strong connections to Cleveland. Perdue attributed his new-found success to giving up cigarettes and listening to Bernhard's advice on pitching mechanics. "A fellow that wouldn't work for Bernhard wouldn't be willing to work for anybody," confided Perdue.[12] After requesting more slab work, he twirled almost every series opener in the second half. His most memorable performance took place on July 9 when he locked in a pitchers' duel with Mobile's Lucien "Clarence" Torrey. Both hurlers gained strength as the contest entered extra innings. The umpire ended the three-hour marathon after 17 frames without a single run crossing the plate. The Perdue-Torrey nondecision went down as the second longest game in Volunteer history and the longest scoreless contest ever in the Southern Association.[13] Then arm fatigue limited Perdue's appearances for several weeks. Upon his timely return, he led the Vols during their crucial September pennant run with a 4-1 record. "Hurling Hub" drew great personal satisfaction in completing his fourth professional season with a third league title, but he was deeply disappointed in not being drafted by a major-league team despite posting a 16-12 record.

"Sumner's Son of the Smoke and the Spit" was poised for a breakout year in 1909, and Perdue shattered his self-perceived notion as a slow starter with six straight lopsided victories to begin the new campaign. He lost only three times in July and August, and despite his overpowering domination of the entire circuit with 23 victories, Perdue went undrafted for a second straight year. He was devastated and the next season he reported to Nashville woefully overweight at 200 pounds, and his 5-foot-10-inch frame was shaped like a Hubbard squash, said Rice. Also, he complained of a lingering sore shoulder so the club ordered an x-ray that proved inconclusive. Things improved in July when Purdue won five straight, but then he dropped 11 of his last 13 decisions to finish at 12-17. Despite these wretched results, Charlie Ebbets surprised the baseball establishment and drafted Perdue, but less than a month later the Brooklyn mogul mysteriously waived him and a National League rival picked him up: the lowly Boston Rustlers, soon to be the Braves.

Hub was the first player to return a signed contract to Boston. In his National League debut he pitched one inning of relief against his idol, Grover Cleveland Alexander of the Philadelphia Phillies. But elbow soreness caused management to authorize "electric treatments." Perdue did not respond favorably to the therapy so they ordered an x-ray, which revealed a chipped bone that was causing inflammation. Surgery was performed to remove the irritating splinter and Perdue rehabbed for more than a month.[14]

The crowning moment in Perdue's rookie season did not take place on the field but rather on the bench. In mid-August the team had acquired the aging Cy Young in an effort to boost ticket sales. Toward the end of his final season in baseball, the legendary hurler gifted Perdue his red flannel undershirt. Hub had the treasured garment altered and he wore it beneath his game jersey for good luck, hoping that some of Cy's success would rub off on him.[15]

By the end of his first season in the majors, Perdue produced a 6-10 record, an inflated 4.98 ERA, and a 1.61 WHIP. When healthy, Perdue was prone to falling behind early or else he failed to hold onto late-inning leads. He was also susceptible to the long ball, ranking sixth in the National League in home runs given up despite only 19 starts.

In 1912 Johnny Kling was promoted to manage the worst team in professional baseball (44-107 in 1911). A catcher by trade, Kling knew all of Perdue's strengths and weaknesses. The two were destined for a rocky relationship. Hub started the home opener on April 11 and despite some wildness he bested Alexander and the Phils. Then, four days later, he shut out the visiting world champion Giants and Mathewson. Perdue quickly returned to his streak pattern by winning four straight and then dropping five in a row. He failed to win a game in May and only temporarily broke the slump on June 11. During this downturn, Hub was involved in two highly publicized flare-ups with Boston management. First team president John Montgomery Ward attempted, without success, to offer hitting and pitching tips to his beleaguered hurler. Then Kling criticized Perdue in front of the entire team for "quitting" in a heartbreaking loss to Rube Marquard, who had just notched his 16th consecutive victory at the expense of Hub's seventh loss in nine tries.

The stage was set for a colossal meltdown. In the clubhouse Hub lashed out at everyone; he called Kling "a fathead" for allegedly pandering to high-paid hurlers who loafed on the bench; he criticized the owners who agreed to trade a talented young outfielder for an over-the-hill veteran; he even targeted teammates, asserting that the anemic Braves offense required four base hits in order to tally a single run. To punctuate his anger, Hub shredded his uniform, packed his bag, said farewell to the players, and informed reporters that he would never play for Boston again. Then he stormed out. The rhubarb received considerable attention in Boston newspapers, and Kling suspended Perdue indefinitely without pay.[16] Quietly, the manager opened negotiations with several other teams to trade his quarrelsome ace.

Perdue's status remained in limbo as the Braves left for a Western road trip. Shortly after the Fourth of July, Perdue and president Ward made their peace, and he rejoined the club in St. Louis. In spite of these confrontations, Ward tendered Perdue a new three-year contract one month later. Why? "With a winning team," claimed *Sporting Life*, "Hub Perdue would soon be touted as one of the wonders of the big leagues. He is a cool fellow and works best when in trouble."[17] Thus, Perdue had emerged as the ace in the Boston stable. In one of his often-overlooked contributions to baseball, Hub was elected by teammates to represent them on the board of directors of the newly formed Fraternity of Professional Baseball Players of America.

Perdue had noticeably improved in several important categories in 1912 despite missing more than 20 days for disciplinary and injury reasons. He led the pitching staff with 13 wins and ranked third in innings pitched (249) and games started (30). The season also witnessed the birth of his newest nickname from the pen of Grantland Rice, the enduring "Gallatin Squash."[18] On the forgettable side, Perdue led the National League in home runs allowed and was fourth in total base hits and earned runs. His batting woes continued and he did not register a single RBI.

In 1913 Hub welcomed the selection of fellow Southerner George Stallings as the newest skipper in Boston. But Stallings was a no-nonsense individual, and he was fated for numerous run-ins with the affable Tennessean. On Opening Day Hub toed the slab in the Polo Grounds in front of 20,000 raucous fans who anticipated a one-sided slaughter. But Hub outdueled Jeff Tesreau and limited the Giants to two hits in a stunning shutout. By June the press was touting Perdue as a "Giants Killer,"[19] and his growing notoriety allowed Stallings, who desperately sought to add an outfielder, to dangle his hurler as trade bait to the Reds and Superbas.

A pivotal series in Pittsburgh in mid-July sealed Perdue's future with the Braves. As Hub prepared to take his first at-bat against Babe Adams on July 14, Stallings pulled him aside with special instructions to take his batting more seriously and "mix 'em up." In his first plate appearance, Hub struck out batting right-handed. On his second trip, he switched to the left side and likewise struck out. In his third attempt, the jester took called strikes from each side of the dish to record his third "K." Stallings fumed over Perdue's cavalier attitude in the batter's box. "When I got back to the bench," Hub later recalled, "George demanded to know what in the h___ I thought I was doing." "Obeying instructions," Hub replied, "but I don't believe George sees the joke yet."[20] Perdue had fallen out of favor with Stallings.

The Boston Braves climbed to fifth place in 1913 and Perdue claimed several personal bests. He established his first winning record in the majors (16-13), shared most team wins with Lefty Tyler and whittled down his ERA to 3.26—an improvement of 0.54 from the previous year. His WHIP dipped to 1.13 and he appeared in more than 200 innings for the second consecutive year. Perhaps most impressive, however, was his complete domination over the Giants (3-0 and two nondecisions that resulted in Boston victories). In fact, so impressed was McGraw that he invited Perdue to accompany his postseason barnstorming world tour.[21] Perhaps the mogul hoped to obtain the secret behind Hub's mastery over his beloved Giants. Perdue revealed that he owed his success with the spitball to a special brand of chewing tobacco, the Pat Burnley twist; its spittle gave his fingers just the right amount of lubrication to make the ball behave in unexpected ways. Supposedly, McGraw ordered all of his pitchers to use Perdue's brand. Incidentally, the Tennessean declined McGraw's offer to join the overseas excursion.

Prior to the start of spring training in 1914, Stallings directed Perdue and team captain Bill Sweeney to report early to Hot Springs, Arkansas, in order to "boil out." Then, less than a week later, Stallings announced a blockbuster trade: Perdue and Sweeney were shipped to Chicago for temperamental infielder Johnny Evers and cash considerations. The deal flabbergasted the two Bostonians, and Evers refused to report until all of the financial details had been hammered out. Sportswriters William A. Phelon and F.C. Lane called the proposed swap of Perdue-Sweeney for Evers the trade of the decade.[22] Eventually, President John K. Tener of the National League interceded in the controversy and ordered Sweeney to Chicago and Evers to Boston, and returned Perdue to Stallings.

As the trade brouhaha simmered, however, Perdue was approached in Hot Springs by an unidentified agent who offered him a substantial salary increase to jump to the Federal League. And when Henry "Doc" Gessler, the new skipper of the Pittsburgh Stogies of the Federal League, had checked into the Braves hotel in Macon, Georgia, he invited Hub to his room "for a social call."[23] Stallings was tipped off to the clandestine meeting and, armed with a court injunction and a deputy sheriff, the Boston mogul stormed into the room while Perdue hid in the bathroom. Once Gessler was informed that he had violated Georgia state law regarding legal contracts, he left town immediately. Perdue pleaded his innocence, but Stallings was not convinced. Gentleman George had big plans for Boston in 1914 and they did not include the Gallatin Squash.

Hub was winless in the first month of the new season and his ERA ballooned to over 5.00. When umpire Bill Klem confiscated eight baseballs allegedly "tampered" by Perdue (and sent them to President Tener for inspection), Stallings acted. On June 24 Perdue appeared in his final game for Boston. Four days later the Boston manager shipped Perdue and his abysmal 2-5 record to St. Louis for versatile utilityman George "Possum" Whitted and infielder Ted Cather. There would be no miracle finish for Perdue in 1914. "Stallings doesn't like any fooling around," the Tennessean recalled, "and I always like to have a little fun."[24] Said Fred Russell, the sports editor of the *Nashville Banner* and later a Perdue confidant, Hub had joked his way right off the Boston roster.[25]

On the surface, the trade favored Perdue. The Cardinals, usually a lower-rung team, were currently ahead of the Braves by five games. Also, Hub was joining a pitching crew full of promise — Bill Doak, Slim Sallee, and Pol Perritt. He also teamed with another colorful baseball comedian, outfielder Steve Evans. But most important, Perdue really liked manager Miller Huggins and the warm weather in St. Louis.

Perdue's folksy charm quickly endeared him to local fans, who believed he was the missing link to lead the Cardinals out of the second division and into contention for the NL pennant. his first mound victory came against Boston. But old tendencies quickly returned when he could not string together more than two consecutive wins or losses. Moreover, the Braves were ascending just as the Cardinals were descending, and when the former swept the latter an early-September series, the Redbirds were done. They settled for third place as the Braves miraculously copped the NL pennant and upset the favored Philadelphia A's in the World Series. At first Perdue felt no regret in his trade to St. Louis. "It is worth the [lost] money to be out of the reach of Stallings' sharp tongue," said the Gallatin Squash.[26]

Perdue's overall record with the Braves and Cardinals (10-13) was nothing special, but not so with his surprising drop in ERA — from 5.82 in Boston to 2.82 in St. Louis. He topped 200 innings pitched for the third consecutive season. Hub appeared twice in the City Championship Series against the St. Louis Browns, when an unfounded rumor spread that manager Fielder Jones of the St. Louis Terriers was expressing serious interest in obtaining him.

Perdue shocked everyone when he reported to spring training in 1915 more than 30 pounds lighter, but the trimmed-down version did not look as good on the mound. Indeed, something was drastically wrong. Huggins began to use Perdue sparingly and against weaker lineups. Eventually Hug relegated Hub to middle-relief assignments out of the bullpen, but his decreased productivity even revealed itself there. A blown save against the Cubs on June 24 (13-10) illustrated his advanced level of deterioration in the box and the local sports media had seen enough.

Perdue experienced one last moment of high drama before his anticipated exit from the big stage. On August

23 he tossed three innings of relief against the Giants in game one of a doubleheader in the Polo Grounds to earn a win. In the third inning of the second game, Huggins called on him to battle Mathewson. Perdue not only shut down the Giants for six frames but he swatted a single and scored the winning run for his second victory of the afternoon. But the end was near. Hub's final major-league start took place on September 1 in Pittsburgh, and he registered only four outs while allowing four runs on six hits and a wild pitch. Hub toed a big-league rubber (in relief) for the final time on September 30.

In Perdue's final season in the majors, his record dropped (6-12) while his ERA rose (4.26). He relieved in more games (18) than he started (13), and he led the National League in relief losses (5). In 115 innings pitched, Perdue's lowest in the majors or minors, he surrendered 141 hits, including seven home runs. In the offseason the Cardinals attempted to release Perdue to San Francisco but he refused to travel west.

Big-league dreams die hard, however. Although he had previously voiced strong objections on returning to the minors, Hub no longer had any control over the situation. In March 1916 the Louisville Colonels of the American Association were gathering in Columbia, Tennessee, for spring training, and Perdue paid them a visit. "Derby Bill" Clymer, the manager, offered him a limited tryout and when the Colonels broke camp they had Perdue in tow. Satisfied with three limited outings against Nashville, Frankfort, and the Chicago Cubs, Clymer welcomed Perdue onto the roster but it must have been a close call because he was absent from the Opening Day team photograph.[27]

Perdue was a popular choice with Louisville boosters owing to his happy-go-lucky personality, entertaining antics in the third-base coach's box, and quick start on the mound. A fierce competition soon developed between four teams—Louisville, Minneapolis, Indianapolis, and Kansas City—and Perdue made modest contributions to the club's successes before his old injury reappeared. After yet another x-ray, Clymer sent Hub home to rest for two weeks; he was gone for over a month. When he returned to action, his on-and-off pattern caused added concern. Then, in late August, at the height of the tight pennant race, Perdue's team boarded a northbound train for an important road trip while he jumped on a southbound "rattler" bound for Nashville to begin an unauthorized 12-day absence only to return after Labor Day.

The Colonels won 101 games and the American Association championship with the help of Perdue's 14 mound victories. He tossed 222 innings (second on the staff), produced a respectable 1.10 WHIP (third) and dropped four of nine games by only one run. But he missed six weeks of the season due to injury and unexcused absence. After only three appearances in 1917, Clymer released him.

Perdue's second tour in the Southern Association (1917-1921) started less than a week after his dismissal from Louisville when he signed with Kid Elberfeld's Chattanooga Lookouts. Surprisingly, there were no public outbursts between the volatile Tabasco Kid and the jocular Gallatin Squash. From the outset, Elberfeld gave Perdue the ball every fifth day throughout the season and he missed only one start. The Kid was determined to squeeze every ounce of baseball out of Perdue before he expired, and the results were quite impressive—15 wins (second on staff), 217 innings pitched (fourth), 1.95 ERA (first), and 1.07 WHIP (second). For once, Perdue had finished a season strongly in winning his final seven of eight games. Had Perdue reinvented himself?

As the country's involvement in the Great War escalated in 1918, Perdue signed with the New Orleans Pelicans, who reportedly made him the highest paid pitcher in the Southern circuit. Reunited with manager Johnny Dobbs, Hub responded positively to the high expectations placed upon him. When the league shut down on June 28 owing to the government's "work or fight" policy, Perdue led the league with 12 mound victories and secured his sixth team championship. Equally impressive were his WHIP (1.08) and innings pitched (122). He briefly transferred allegiances to the

Minneapolis Millers for a month before the American Association shut down, too.

The 1919 season had a storybook ending for Perdue but it started inauspiciously when he slipped on a muddy mound during an exhibition in Beaumont, wrenched his back, and sat out until mid-May. Upon his return, he strung together two four-game win steaks, but an opposing club accused him of throwing an emery ball while another charged him with "paraffining" the baseball.[28] Certainly no one argued with Hub's staggering home record (12-0) before he succumbed to defeat on August 9. However, the Pelicans could not take advantage of Hub's magical twirling to overtake Atlanta. Then, on September 11, Perdue was spiked during a collision while covering home plate and he complained about a sore back. Dobbs removed his ailing hurler from the game and the injury ended his season. But Hub had ample reason to celebrate. In 1919 he won 17 games along with three other milestones—260 innings pitched (the most since Vincennes), and a staggering WHIP (0.904) and ERA (1.56); the latter is a league record that still stood in 2013.[29]

Perdue still suffered from back spasms when the next season began. By Memorial Day he was 1-4 in eight starts, and Dobbs had no choice but to release him. Right away, Hub signed with Nashville. The Vols were struggling and in desperate need of a fresh start. In his four-hit debut, "The Gallatin Gunner looked like Walter Johnson and Christy Mathewson all rolled into one," observed the *Nashville Tennessean*.[30] But then he dropped four in a row, and quarreled incessantly with umpires who accused him of throwing the outlawed spitball. By the end of July, Perdue's record had plummeted to 4-9, and manager Roy Ellam shut him down. Hub's combined stats with the Pelicans and Vols—5-13 in 147 innings pitched—were the worst and lowest full-season figures of his entire career. Ellam reassigned him to scout for young prospects for the remainder of the season. There is little doubt that Hub faced retirement; but there is also no denying that, during his last active stretch during the late Deadball Era (between August 10, 1917, and July 16, 1919), Perdue was the most dominant pitcher in the Southern Association at 34-9.

New opportunities sometimes present themselves at unexpected moments in life, and such was the case for Perdue. On October 6, 1920, president J.A.G. Sloan fired Ellam, reasoning that he'd been too lenient in his handling of the players. Exactly who would succeed Ellam filled Nashville's sports pages, but Sloan ended the speculation several days later. "We have decided to give Mr. Perdue a trial as manager," the club's director announced.[31] Hardly a glowing endorsement.

Perdue faced an uphill rebuilding task in 1921. Only three position players and three mediocre pitchers returned; all other players had either been released, drafted, or signed elsewhere. Hub attended baseball's annual winter meeting in Chicago where Evers offered him a promising southpaw, Wallace "Cy" Warmoth. When training camp officially opened, Perdue greeted over 40 prospects, but he was forced, out of necessity, to settle on aging veterans at key positions like shortstop, catcher, and first base.

Nashville boosters were hopeful that Perdue would restore the franchise to its glory days, but less than a month into the season he struggled to put forth a consistent lineup owing to absenteeism, injury, family bereavement, and "dissipation." Furthermore, the Vols suffered from a porous defense and a weak offense despite boasting several of the league's current top hitters. Dissatisfied players bickered among themselves, fought with fans in the stands, and blamed others for their misfortune. President Sloan publicly called out Perdue to restore order and lead by example. He begged Perdue to take the mound himself. "You are in a warm climate now," he challenged the Gallatin Squash. "What is your alibi?"[32]

Perdue shocked his detractors several weeks later when he beat the first-place Crackers at Atlanta. He even swatted a single and double, and some claimed his two-bagger would have been an easy triple for anyone else; the rotund Perdue had to walk between first base and second base. Then, just as the Vols were flirting with the .500 mark, they began a precipitous descent. Three straight double-digit losses threw fans and owner into a funk. Seven straight losses during a nine-game homestand, including four to in-state rival Memphis (one of best minor-league teams of all time) were a harbinger.

After one debacle, Perdue called a closed-door meeting and told his players to renew their efforts and not be so easily discouraged. Then the Vols boarded a train for Birmingham. Hub must have been suspicious when Sloan accompanied the team on the trip, a rare occurrence. Sensing his job was on the line, Perdue opened the series on the hill. A mistake! Barons batters jumped on him for four runs on four hits in the first four outs of the game. The rout was Hub's farewell appearance in the Southern Association.

The Vols went through the motions in Mobile, New Orleans, and Atlanta, and Nashville sportswriters questioned their efforts with box-score headlines like "Ho, Hum!" and "SAME OLD TALE."[33] By the time the Vols limped home on June 25, they had dropped 19 of 25 games. The next morning Hub opened the sports page of the *Nashville Banner* to a shocking headline: "New Manager Coming to Vols."[34] The board of directors had voted to dismiss Perdue while the team was in transit from Atlanta, and someone had leaked the decision to the press before anyone had notified him.

Perdue was in a state of disbelief. Once he verified with Sloan that the report was true (the team president brashly requested that Hub manage the afternoon game), Hub announced: "I am done with ball forever."[35] Once his temper had cooled, Hub reflected on his former team: "That team of mine couldn't beat an egg."[36] In reality, Perdue was the first managerial casualty in the Southern Association caused by the demise of the Deadball Era.[37]

After his release, Hub lobbied without success to fill several managerial vacancies in the Southern, Kitty, and Sally Leagues. When fellow Tennessean and former Atlanta manager Billy Smith offered him a player's contract with Shreveport in the Texas League, Hub jumped at the opportunity. The Gassers were perennial losers, but Smith thought he might be able to tap Hub's expertise as a tutor for his young pitching corps. Perdue debuted against Jake Atz and his powerful Fort Worth Panthers, and he baffled his opponent with a six-hit shutout to earn the Gassers' first victory. But the Gasmen quickly descended into the league's cellar. Many of the losses were one-sided double-digit affairs, and disgruntled patrons called for a managerial change. Perhaps Smith thought that Perdue was angling for his job. No matter. Hub was traded to Wichita Falls before the position became available. As it turned out, the change of scenery worked out well for Perdue because Walter Salm's Spudders were contenders. He usually worked only once a week and mostly on the road. Yanked 12 times from starting roles, Perdue was eventually limited to middle-relief roles since his erratic tendencies increased. His biggest thrill in the circuit came when he started the first Texas League game ever broadcast live over radio. Perdue won ten games, but he was a mere shadow of his former self and Wichita Falls released him shortly after the season.

It is hard to image what possessed Perdue to sign with Charlotte in 1923. It is even harder to speculate on what was running though the mind of Hornets player-manager Dick Hoblitzell. Hobby had assembled a powerful roster that included second baseman Chick Knaupp, Hub's managerial nemesis in Nashville. Perdue's highlight consisted of four innings of relief in both games of a doubleheader against Augusta that earned him two victories on the same afternoon — the fifth and final time he accomplished such a feat in 19 years. The Hornets cruised toward a championship, Hub's seventh, but he would not be aboard at the end. Instead of appearing on the mound for his 41st birthday, Hub was released. The Gallatin Squash was washed up.

In retirement Perdue operated the family farm but he itched for a job in the limelight. So he decided to run for Sumner County clerk on the Democratic ticket during the Great Depression. Asked why he filed for public office, Perdue replied in typical down-home humor: "I want to build me a new tobacco barn."[38] On August 2, 1934, Hub defeated Harvey L. Brown and one month later he was sworn into office. Re-elected twice, Perdue oversaw three significant projects during his tenure in office — a WPA project to rebuild the 100-year-old county courthouse on Public Square; the construction of several TVA power plants; and the extensive use of Sumner County by the Army in its preparations for the Normandy invasion. Losing his bid for a fourth term to an Army veteran in 1946, Hub retreated to his back porch and brooded for weeks, filling a brass kettle with an endless trail of cigarette butts.

At the age of 64, Perdue retired for good from public life but he never completely separated from baseball. He was a familiar fixture at Nashville's Old Timers Baseball Association banquets beginning in the 1940s. At the same time he attempted without success to secure a salaried position as a scout for the Reds, Dodgers, Giants, Cardinals, and Pirates. Instead, he worked freelance throughout Middle Tennessee, and actually signed two pitching prospects.

It had been a long time since the early days of Rub, Dub, Hub, and Perdue's health began to deteriorate in the early 1960s, possibly the result of his lifelong habits of smoking, drinking, and chewing tobacco in conjunction with the never-ending battle with his waistline. Yet he loved to reminisce about his playing days in the Deadball Era, and three specific memories stood out to him as his greatest baseball accomplishments: his back-to-back victories over future Hall of Famers Alexander and Mathewson to open the 1912 season, his 17-inning, no-decision game in Mobile (1908), and his miraculous 1.56 ERA mark in the Southern Association (1919). He also reveled in his unique nickname the Gallatin Squash, and a later moniker bestowed by Nashville newspaperman and confidante Elmer Hinton, who once called Perdue a "clown prince of the diamond."[39] On his deathbed Perdue proclaimed that he never threw a spitter because he did not know how to control it. A joker to the very end.

Herbert Rodney Perdue, the ex-ballplayer with "a million-dollar arm and a two-cent head,"[40] died on October 31, 1968, on a date set aside for frolic. He is buried in the Perdue section of Lower Bethpage Cemetery, only yards away from his childhood stamping grounds.

Notes

1. For a full-length biography of Perdue, see John A. Simpson, *Hub Perdue; Clown Prince of the Mound* (Jefferson, North Carolina: McFarland Press, 2013).

2. Sumner County, Tennessee, Marriage Records, County Clerk's Office, 1899-1900; *Gallatin Examiner and Sumner County Tennessean*, May 26, 1960; *Sumner County News*, May 26, 1960. Also see John David Collier, "Herbert Rodney 'Hub' Perdue," *Precious Memories* (n.p.: 1999), 41.

3. The concept of "cow pasture games" appears in Elmer Hinton, "Gallatin Squash," *Nashville Tennessean Magazine*, October 7, 1945. Also see Collier, "Herbert Rodney 'Hub' Perdue," *Precious Memories*: 41; John Bibb, "It's All in the Juice," *Nashville Tennessean Magazine*, August 9, 1959.

4. *Paducah Sun*, January 6 and 30, 1905.

5. *Paducah Evening Sun*, May 9, 1905. It is not known whether Hub was enrolled in South Kentucky College as a student.

6. *Gallatin News*, May 6 and 27, June 10, 1905.

7. Lloyd Johnson and Miles Wolff, eds., *The Encyclopedia of Minor League Baseball*, 1st ed. (Durham, North Carolina: Baseball America, Inc. 1993), 110.

8. *Paducah Evening Sun*, July 13, 1906.

9. *Paducah Evening Sun*, August 24, 1906; *Vincennes Daily Sun*, August 25, 1906; *Vincennes Capital*, August 21, 1906; *Vincennes Morning Commercial*, August 25, 30, 1906. Notice to the reader: all of Perdue's season-ending statistics found in the narrative from this point forward are gleaned from two websites: baseball-reference.com and Retrosheet.org.

10. *Chicago Daily Tribune*, March 6, 1907. Also see Cindy Thomson, *Three Finger Brown: The Mordecai Brown Story* (New York: Bison Books, 2009), 100.

11. *Nashville Banner*, May 11, 1907.

12. *Nashville Tennessean*, July 3, 1908.

13. Fred Russell and George Leonard, *Vols Feats: Records, History, and Tales of the Nashville Baseball Club in the Southern Association, 1901-1950* (Nashville: Banner Press, 1950), 40; John A. Simpson, "The Greatest Game Ever Played in Dixie," *The Nashville Vols, Their 1908 Season, and the Championship Game* (Jefferson, North Carolina: McFarland Press, 2007), 88, 112.

14. *Boston Daily Globe*, May 20, 1911.

15. *Boston Daily Globe*, July 28, 1912.

16. *Boston Daily Globe*, June 26-28, 1912; *Sporting Life*, July 6, 1912. Also see *Nashville Tennessean*, January 20, 1913.

17. *Sporting Life*, September 7, 1912. Also see Harold Kaese, *The Boston Braves, 1871-1953* (Boston: Northeastern University Press, 2004), 131.

18. *Boston Daily Globe*, January 13, 1913.

19 *Boston Daily Globe,* April 11, June 26, 1913; *New York Times,* April 11, 1913. Harry Coveleski is generally considered the first "Giant-killer" after defeating New York three times in five days in 1908.

20 The story first appeared in the *St. Louis Daily Globe-Democrat,* September 12, 1914. Also see *Baseball Magazine,* August 1945, 308; Simpson, *"The Greatest Game Ever Played in Dixie,"* 220-21.

21 *Sporting Life,* February 7, 1914. The tour visited 27 American cities before heading overseas to visit 13 countries in 34 days. See James E. Elfers, *The Tour to End All Tours: The Story of Major League Baseball's 1913-1914 World Tour* (Lincoln: University of Nebraska Press, 2003); *Boston Daily Globe,* September 30, 1913.

22 See caption in Photographs, *Baseball Magazine,* May 1914, frontmatter.

23 For a complete account of the Gessler affair, see *Boston Daily Globe,* March 19, 21, 22, 1914; *Atlanta Constitution,* March 21, 1914.

24 *St. Louis Daily Globe-Democrat,* September 12, 1914.

25 Russell, *Vols Feats,* 32; Russell, *Bury Me in an Old Press Box* (New York: A.S. Barnes and Company, 1957), 100.

26 *St. Louis Daily Globe-Democrat,* September 25, 1914.

27 *Louisville Courier-Journal,* April 1, 2, 17, 18, 1916; *New York Tribune,* March 26, 1916.

28 *New Orleans Times-Picayune,* July 25, 28, 1919.

29 Marshall D. Wright, *The Southern Association in Baseball* (Jefferson, North Carolina: McFarland & Co., 2002), 199. Wright entitles his chapter on the 1919 season "Hub Perdue." Also see Johnson and Wolff, eds., *The Encyclopedia of Minor League Baseball,* first edition, 149.

30 *Nashville Tennessean,* June 6, 1920.

31 *Nashville Tennessean,* October 10, 1920. *The Sporting News* announced the hiring with a headline: "THIS IS NO JOKE WITH SQUASH." See *The Sporting News,* November 11, 1920.

32 *Nashville Banner,* May 16, 1921; *Nashville Tennessean,* May 16, 1921.

33 *Nashville Banner,* June 24, 25, 1921; *Nashville Tennessean,* June 24, 25 1921.

34 *Nashville Banner,* June 26, 1921. The evening newspaper contained a similar headline: "Hub Perdue Relieved As Skipper of the Vols." See *Nashville Tennessean,* June 26, 1921.

35 *Nashville Tennessean,* June 27, 1921. Sloan picked second baseman Chick Knaupp to run the team for the second half of the season.

36 *Nashville Tennessean,* June 30, 1920.

37 For a detailed analysis of this hypothesis, see Simpson, *Hub Perdue; Clown Prince of the Mound.*

38 Collier, *Precious Memories,* 42.

39 Hinton, "The Gallatin Squash," *Nashville Tennessean Magazine,* October 7, 1945.

40 The quote is attributed to Hub's grandson. See Jimmy Perdue, "Gallatin from Kerosene to Nukes," (unpublished paper),1; in Jimmy Perdue Family Collection, Gallatin, Tennessee.

Dick Rudolph

By Dick Leyden

Though he stood only 5' 9.5" and weighed just 160 lbs., Dick Rudolph was a large component of George Stallings' "Big Three" that helped lead the 1914 Boston Braves to their miraculous pennant and World Series sweep. "He was the bellwether of the pitching staff," said Braves coach Fred Mitchell, "and being a little fellow, I believe his success had much to do with big Bill James and George Tyler putting out that little extra effort to keep pace with the cocky kid from the Bronx."[1] Unlike the hard-throwing James and Tyler, Rudolph was a "pitching cutie" who relied on his great curveball and spectacular control. He also threw a spitball, but "about the best you could say for it was that it was wet," recalled his catcher Hank Gowdy.[2]

Richard Rudolph was born in New York City on August 25, 1887. All he ever wanted to do was pitch in the big leagues. Late in the summer of 1905 he mailed the following letter to Garry Herrmann, owner of the Cincinnati Reds:

> Dear Sir,
> According to the league schedule your team will be in New York and Brooklyn the latter part of this month. I would like to have a chance to pitch against the Brooklyn team for your club to show my ability, as I would like to be with your team next year. Or if preferable against the New York National League team. It don't make any difference to me. All I want is a chance to show what I can do. And I think that now is as good a time as any, as I am sure you will not regret the favor.
> Hoping that you can see your way clear to grant my wish, I beg to remain,
>
> Yours truly,
> Richard Rudolph[3]

Ignored by Herrmann, young Rudolph enrolled that fall at Fordham University and played baseball there the following spring. When he learned that the "outlaw" Northern League had sent collegians like Ed Reulbach and Jack Coombs to the majors, he headed to Vermont to pitch for the Rutland team that also included Eddie Collins. When that team folded, Rudolph joined New Haven of the Connecticut State League for the rest of the summer. He did well enough that he decided not to return to Fordham, but to devote all of his energy to pursuing his dream of pitching in the major leagues.

Ed Barrow signed Rudolph to a 1907 Eastern League contract with Toronto. "Baldy" was a fine minor-league pitcher, posting 13, 18, 23, and 23 wins in 1907-10. Back in New York, his brother, who worked at the old New York *Press*, kept his name in the local papers by planting stories of the "It's a crime that Rudolph doesn't get called up" type. At the close of the 1910 season the New York Giants gave him a shot, probably at the behest of Toronto manager Joe Kelley, John McGraw's old Baltimore Orioles teammate. "He has terrific speed, good control, is a quick thinker and mixes up his 'assortment' as well as any twirler in the big leagues,"

Dick Rudolph

Kelley said. "I look for him in a few years to be even or as great as Mathewson."[4]

As it turned out, Matty had no immediate worries. Rudolph mopped up in two Giant wins, and then got the starting assignment of which he had dreamed. It was a nightmare. The Phillies pounded him for 15 hits and the Giants lost, 8-2. The *Press* was forced to change its tune: "Dick Rudolph, from the wilds of the Bronx, found his path strewn with base hits when he made his first local appearance [in a major-league uniform]."[5] Rudolph was again hit hard in an April 1911 appearance, and that was enough for McGraw. Back in Toronto Dick posted 18- and 25-win seasons, good enough to lead the International League in victories and winning percentage in the latter season. It has been said that Rudolph's size and prematurely thinning hair (making his real age appear suspicious) contributed to McGraw's decision not to bring him up again, despite his great success in Toronto.

Convinced that he had to get back to the majors soon if he was ever to get back at all, the 25-year-old Rudolph returned to his old strategy of self-promotion. He found a sympathetic ear in Fred Mitchell, third-base of the Boston Braves. "I was going south in 1913 to join the Braves, who were training at Macon, Georgia, that season," Mitchell recalled. "A young fellow got on the train in New York. Apparently he knew me, but I didn't know him. After a while he came over to my seat and asked me if I was a ballplayer. I told him I was a coach for the Braves. He told me he was Dick Rudolph of the Toronto club, but was thinking about quitting if he wasn't sold to the major leagues. 'I know I can pitch better than some of those fellows in the Big League,' said Rudolph, 'if I only get the chance. But if I don't, I'm quitting anyway.' Well I had a talk with him, and found he had a good record in Toronto, but that John McGraw had not given him much of a look. I told him not to be too hasty about quitting. I advised him to get in shape and maybe [the Braves] would be interested in his services. He did as he was instructed. After he was beaten by the Newark club 1-0 in his opening game, he turned in his uniform and said he was through. He then got in touch with me again. I got in touch with Jim McCaffrey, the owner of the Toronto club, and asked what he wanted for Rudolph. Jim (for whom I had previously played) said, 'Oh, he'll be back in a couple of days.' I told him he wouldn't, and he better sell him to the Braves. Well after a couple of days when Rudolph failed to return, McCaffrey got in touch with us and agreed to let us have him for $5,000 and a pitcher named Brown. That was one of the greatest bargains that [Braves owner] James Gaffney ever got in his life."[6]

Rudolph became an immediate success in Boston, posting a 14-13 record and 2.92 ERA in 1913. Mitchell attributed the rookie's solid performance to his brains and cunning. "He was one of the smartest pitchers who ever toed the rubber," said the Braves coach and future manager. "He wasn't fast but had a good curve ball, which he mixed with a spitball, and he could almost

Rudolph playing catch.

Rudolph was 26-10 for the Braves in 1914, and 2-0 in the World Series.

read the batter's mind. I've often sat on the bench with him and heard him tell whether a batter would take or hit. He made a real study of the profession."[7] During the miracle season of 1914 Rudolph won a total of 26 games, including 12 consecutive victories. On Labor Day he beat Mathewson, 5-4, in the first game of a morning-afternoon doubleheader to move the Braves into first place, which they locked up for good after a loss in the afternoon game with a win the next day. In the World Series Rudoph beat Chief Bender, 7-1, in Game One, and Bob Shawkey, 3-1, in Game Four.

Over the three-year period 1914-16, Rudolph was one of baseball's best and most durable pitchers, hurling over 300 innings each season. His performance in 1916 may have been even better than 1914; though he won seven fewer games, he lowered his ERA from 2.35 to a career-best 2.16 and led the NL with 8.9 base runners allowed per nine innings. Dick developed arm trouble in 1918, when he pitched just 154 innings. Though he bounced back with one more workhorse season in 1919, he pitched in only 25 games over the next eight years, when he was more of a coach than a pitcher. Rudolph left the Braves after the 1927 season, retiring with a career record of 121-108 and a 2.66 ERA.

The following year Rudolph and the Braves' traveling secretary bought the Waterbury, Connecticut, club in the Eastern League. They lasted but one losing season. Dick then joined his brother in a Nyack, New York, undertaking business for a few years. Eventually he returned to baseball, this time as the supervisor for Stevens Brothers Concessionaires at Yankee Stadium and the Polo Grounds. Closing the circle of his baseball career, he returned to Fordham as a volunteer freshman baseball coach. Dick Rudolph died of a heart attack in the Bronx on October 20, 1949, at the age of 62, and is buried in Woodlawn Cemetery.

Note: A slightly different version of this biography appeared in Tom Simon, ed., Deadball Stars of the National League *(Washington, D.C.: Brassey's, Inc., 2004).*

Sources

For this biography, the author used a number of contemporary sources, especially those found in the subject's file at the National Baseball Hall of Fame Library.

Notes

1   John Drohan, *The Sporting News*, November 2, 1949: 14.
2   Undated clipping in Rudolph's player file at the National Baseball Hall of Fame.
3   Letter of August 16, 1905 in Rudolph's player file at the National Baseball Hall of Fame.
4   1910 *Who's Who in Sport*, author unknown, in Rudolph's player file at the National Baseball Hall of Fame.
5   *The Sporting News*, November 2, 1949: 14.
6   Ibid.
7   Ibid.

Butch Schmidt

By Chip Greene

On March 1, 2012, a businessman named Andrew W. Schmidt, III died in Baltimore, Maryland, the city of his birth. He was 80 years old. For 38 years, until the company closed in 1991, Schmidt had operated A.W. Schmidt and Son, a wholesale meatpacking house on Harford Road in Baltimore. The company had been in that general location, and in the Schmidt family, since it was founded in 1880 by Schmidt's grandfather, Andrew W. Schmidt, Sr.

At first glance there would seem to be little connection between the owner of a Baltimore meatpacking plant and one of the most surprising World Series triumphs in history. There was no mention of such a link in Andrew Schmidt's obituary. Yet, almost 60 years before Andrew died in Baltimore, his uncle, Charles John Schmidt, also died in the city. In addition to operating the same family business, Charles had once played first base for the World Series champion Boston Braves. Throughout his life, everyone knew *that* Schmidt as Butch.

Butch's father, Andrew Sr., arrived in the United States from his native Germany in 1870, when he was 18 years old. Ten years later he opened his butcher business on Harford Road, and the following year he married Baltimore resident Margaret Demling. They had five children. Butch, born on July 19, 1886, was the third, and the first of two sons. (Andrew Jr., Andrew III's father, was born in 1899.)

Little is known about Charles Schmidt's formative years. From an early age, however, he learned the ropes in the business that eventually provided his livelihood. In 1916 he told *Baseball Magazine:* "I have worked in a market ever since I was thirteen years old," laboring side-by-side with his father at the family meat market.[1] During those years he also developed skills on the baseball diamond. Playing on semipro teams around Baltimore, in a circuit known as the B&O Railway League (the February 5, 1916, edition of *Sporting Life* said that Schmidt got his start with the Evergreen Lawn club), the young man won "some local reputation," although he "never took the game seriously at that time" as he was "busy learning the ins and outs of selling beef and mutton." (Schmidt also tried another sport during those years, if only briefly. "I played one game [of football] when I was sixteen," he later related. "Our club was made up of boys from the market and we played a crowd of clerks from uptown. Neither side knew much about football, but what we lacked in science we made up in strength." As it happened, Schmidt's team "grew kind of concerned lest some of those clerks should get hurt, and, well, I never played football after that.")

It's likely that by 16 Schmidt was already a physically imposing young man. (By that time, too, he also may have gained the nickname Butcher Boy by which he came to be known as a major leaguer.) Years later, in his prime, it was written of the Braves' first baseman that he was "quite a giant of a man." At 6-feet-2 and 215 pounds, he was "a man of huge strength who is popularly supposed to be the most powerful player

Butch Schmidt

physically on the diamond." He possessed a "Cy Young build" and "great strength," and, it was predicted, "should emulate Eddie Plank as an indestructible athlete."[2] No doubt years of lugging sides of beef had helped hone Schmidt's solid physique.

Like much of the baseball talent spawned in Baltimore in those days, Schmidt was discovered by Baltimore Orioles owner Jack Dunn, who signed the 21-year-old after watching him play on the sandlots. Whether Schmidt's signing took place in 1907 or '08 is unclear, but he first took the field for the Eastern League's Orioles in 1908. Initially, Schmidt was a pitcher, a left-hander. He spent the first ten days of the 1908 season on the bench; at that point Dunn determined that the raw rookie needed seasoning, so he sent Schmidt to the Holyoke (Massachusetts) Papermakers in the Class B Connecticut State League. There, Schmidt won 10 games before Dunn recalled him in August to help with the Orioles' drive toward the pennant. Schmidt did just that. In 11 appearances, seven as a starter, he won five games as Baltimore took the flag.

Schmidt's work for the Orioles in 1908 gained him notice from other organizations. The man who became his greatest baseball benefactor, George Stallings, managed Newark, a Baltimore rival in the Eastern League, and was impressed with the left-hander's performance against his club. That fall Stallings became the manager of the American League's New York Highlanders, and he drafted Schmidt.

When Schmidt arrived at spring training in 1909, he was a newlywed. During the fall, he had wed Amelia Shuppner at her Baltimore home at 48 Harford Road. Presumably the two had been childhood friends, as the 1900 census listed the Schmidt family's address as 78 Harford Road. Throughout their marriage of almost 44 years (they had two children, Helen and Charles John), Butch and Amelia lived on Harford Road. On his World War II draft registration Schmidt listed his address as 3014 Harford Road, the same as his business. Except for his baseball career, he was a butcher the whole time.

Schmidt appeared in only one game for the Highlanders, pitching in relief against the Tigers on May 11 and giving up eight runs. Sometime after July 4 Stallings returned the 23-year-old to Baltimore. This time things were different. In addition to his pitching prowess, Schmidt had also proved a good hitter. One day, Dunn started Schmidt at first base and the left-hander produced a 4-for-4 afternoon. That marked the end of his pitching career. Rather than keep him on the bench between starts, Dunn, as he would do several years later with another left-handed pitcher, George Herman Ruth, moved Schmidt into the lineup full time. From then on, he was a first baseman. That relief appearance against the Tigers was his only one as a pitcher in the major leagues.

Schmidt spent the next three seasons with his hometown team. As the Orioles moved from Class A to Double-A in the International League, he posted solid offensive numbers, twice topping .290. However, he seems never to have won over the hometown fans. *Sporting Life* later wrote that "Schmidt's career in Baltimore was not a bed of roses, and he decided a change would prove beneficial."[3] Thus, after the 1912 season he was traded to league rival Rochester. That move eventually returned him to the major leagues.

Despite the Miracle Braves achievements, Schmidt considered 1913 at Rochester his finest season. Three years later, when he had retired from the game, he told *Baseball Magazine*, "Of course there is much more honor in playing on a major league team, particularly on a world's championship team. But … I believe the season of 1913 was my best. I hit well all through the year, while in 1914, though I finished strong, I was not a consistent player."[4] Indeed, in 123 games with Rochester Schmidt batted .321, slugged .410, and "developed into a more consistent fielder than he had ever seemed before."[5] George Stallings, then managing the Braves, who "had never lost faith in the bulky first baseman"[6] purchased Schmidt's contract from Rochester in August 1913. The big first baseman played in 22 games for Boston at the end of the season and repaid Stallings' trust, finishing with averages of .308 batting, .423 slugging, and .983 fielding. With just 23 major-league games under his belt, the 27-year-old was just a year away from achieving the pinnacle of his sport. (The transaction that brought Schmidt to Boston is unclear. While several websites indicate that the Braves purchased his contract outright, an article in the April 3, 1915, issue of *Sporting Life* indicated that the Braves had sent third baseman Joe Schultz to Rochester in the deal.)

The offseasons for Schmidt were never a time of rest. Each year he returned to Baltimore to work at the family business, and the fall of 1913 was no exception. Working 16-hour days at the meat market added bulk to his frame, so when 1914 spring training arrived, his challenge was to shed some weight, reduce the flab that had gathered over the winter, and get lighter on his feet. It was never an easy chore. (In February 1915, *Baseball Magazine* wrote that "Schmidt had an awful time getting down to weight this season."[7]) In the Braves' "miracle" year of 1914 Schmidt's development mirrored the team's. "During April and May," *Baseball Magazine* wrote, while Boston played ineptly and floundered in last place, Schmidt "seemed clumsy, heavy-gaited, and his thickness of body made him seem thick-headed, too." To make way for Schmidt at first base, the Braves had sold Hap Myers, 1913's regular at that position, to Rochester, and Schmidt's slow start caused some to question why "Stallings had displaced lean, agile, fast-stealing Myers with Schmidt."[8] As the season progressed, Schmidt began losing weight in the summer heat and his play came around. So "by the time the club was well advanced in its upward rush," forging from last place on July 1 to win the National League pennant, "Schmidt had become a crackerjack." Over the closing weeks, as the Braves raced for the flag, "he batted .350 and fielded like a wizard," becoming in the process one of the league's best first basemen.

Perhaps most impressive was Schmidt's defense. While his batting surge at season's end lifted Schmidt's final batting mark to .285 (he finished second in the league in singles and third in hit by pitches), it was his glove that arguably proved most invaluable to the club. With a .990 fielding average, fourth best in the league, Schmidt finished second in assists and third in putouts, and led the league's first basemen in double plays, teaming with future Hall of Famers Rabbit Maranville and Johnny Evers. So good had he become defensively that Schmidt drew comparisons with the man recognized at the time as the best in the business, the Philadelphia Athletics' Stuffy McInnis.

"'Butch' Schmidt of the Braves," wrote the *Boston Daily Globe*, "is the best first baseman in the game until you see 'Stuffy' McInnis, and 'Stuffy's the best till you see 'Butch.' Both are good enough to get by."[9]

Schmidt prepared to hit.

Never was that comparison more apparent than during the 1914 World Series. With one play, Schmidt opened many eyes and made his reputation. One scribe wrote that during practice before Game One "McInnis … made his bulky rival look foolish by his greater agility and accuracy."[10] Moreover, they also disparaged him as "a clumsy old cow," and with the lumbering Schmidt on first base, there was little doubt that the A's would have "unlimited fun running the bases." But as it turned out, those notions were dispelled by the "first thrilling play of the first inning of the first game."[11]

Baseball Magazine called it the play that "stunned [the A's], gave them a wallop on the jaw, and benumbed their faculties."[12] In the bottom of the first inning, with runners on first and second and one out, cleanup hitter Frank "Home Run" Baker lifted a foul popup to the edge of the bleachers in short right field. At full speed Schmidt ran to the stands, reached in and caught the ball, then wheeled and fired across the diamond to put out the A's leadoff man, Eddie Murphy, who was trying to advance to third base. That double play ended the threat and "then and there, something snapped in the heartstrings of Mack's men. They never recovered."[13] Many years later, Schmidt's obituary in the *Baltimore Sun* said that "Connie Mack often credited Schmidt with the play that sparked the Braves to a four straight upset."[14] In any event, it was the highlight of Schmidt's career. He hit .294 in the World Series, batting behind cleanup hitter Possum Whitted.

That career lasted just one more year, however. In 1915, as the Braves failed to repeat their magical season, Schmidt, who was laid up for several weeks after being spiked, played in 127 games and batted hit .251. In January 1916 he wrote to Braves owner Jim Gaffney and manager Stallings advising them that he was retiring from baseball to devote his time to his family's business. He was 29 years old.

With two years remaining on his contract, Schmidt denied that his decision had anything to do with money. *Sporting Life* printed a statement from him that said:

"It is with great reluctance that I am retiring from base ball, but I must take care of my business and look out for the future. There are no personal differences between the Boston club and myself, and probably the most pleasant days of my career on the diamond have been spent under George Stallings. I consider that I have several more years of major league ball before me, and at the expiration of my contract, I probably would have to stand a reduction in salary, which I would not accept. So, in order to guard against the future I think the time is ripe now for me to give up the sport. I am perfectly satisfied with my contract with Boston, but I consider at the end of possibly five years I will make just as much money out of my business as I would get by playing ball for two or three more years. If I play ball, my business is bound to suffer, and I don't want that to happen. So, looking the situation straight in the face, I think I am taking a step in the right direction."[15]

There appeared to be little reason to doubt his sincerity. Andrew Sr., his father, died in 1917, so it's likely that if he was too ill in 1916 to continue in the business, Butch may have felt obligated to assume the responsibility of carrying on. He told *Sporting Life*, "So pressing is my business, I will be unable to play even Saturday ball with any team in Baltimore. I won't play on Sunday. Perhaps I may be able to slip away once in a while to play a game during the week."[16] But there is no record that he ever did.

For a brief time there were hints that Schmidt might come back. In January 1917 *Sporting Life* wrote, "It is reported that first baseman 'Butch' Schmidt is to return to the Braves and that [Ed] Konetchy is to be shifted to the outfield";[17] and the next month the paper said that " 'Butch' Schmidt … is becoming restless. He wants to return to his old berth and threatens to join the Braves at their training camp in March."[18] But he never did.

Schmidt ran the family business for the rest of his life. Just after retiring, he was interviewed by *Baseball Magazine* in his merchant's stall at Baltimore's Richmond Public Marketplace, where, it was reported, "a continual line of customers … stepped briskly … to drop a word with the tall butcher-ball player."[19]

"I have a good trade here," Schmidt said. "People know they can rely on my judgment of meat and upon my word and they trust me to see that they are satisfied. … Occasionally a woman will stop and inquire about how we kill the animals which furnish us with meat. … (M)ention of killing … make[s] them shudder. They don't like to think of depriving dumb creatures of life, but they have no objections to eating meat. And they know someone must kill in order that others may eat."[20]

It was a world far removed from the thrills of the World Series.

Schmidt's final appearance in Boston came a little over a year before his death. In June 1951 he returned to take part in the Braves' salute to the '14 champs during the National League's Diamond Jubilee commemoration. He died in Baltimore on September 4, 1952, after collapsing while inspecting cattle at the Union Stockyards. He weighed more than 240 pounds and for the previous five or six years he had been having trouble with his heart. Schmidt was 66 years old. Ownership of the family business passed to Schmidt's son, Charles, who died in 1981.

Butch Schmidt was buried at the Druid Ridge Cemetery, in Pikesville, Maryland.

In 1981 Schmidt was elected to the Maryland State Athletic Hall of Fame. That day, a reporter from the *Baltimore Sun* interviewed Tommy Thomas, a Maryland baseball legend who had been a teammate of Schmidt's on the Orioles. Thomas remembered Schmidt as "just a damn fine player. Not sensational, but when the game was over, you always realized he had done something to help the team win." And of Schmidt's giving up the sport to devote his life to the meat market, Thomas said, "He just decided there was a better future for him there than in baseball."[21]

Indeed, for Schmidt it seems to have been the right decision.

Sources

My sincerest appreciation to SABR member Bill Mortell for his diligent genealogical research.

In addition to the sources cited, the author also consulted citypaper.com/news/story.asp?id=13918 (*Baltimore City Paper*, August 1, 2007)

Baseball-Reference.com

Retrosheet.org

Notes

1. John J. Ward: "'Butch' Schmidt, the Player-Worker," *Baseball Magazine*, March 1916.
2. Ibid.
3. *Sporting Life*, February 5, 1916.
4. John J. Ward: "'Butch' Schmidt, the Player-Worker."
5. Ibid.
6. Ibid.
7. Wm. A. Phelon, "Sidelights on the New World's Champions," *Baseball Magazine*, February 1915. All subsequent quotes in the paragraph are from the article.
8. Myers never played for Rochester. Instead, he jumped to the Federal League's Brooklyn team.
9. *Boston Daily Globe*, May 5, 1915.
10. Wm. A Phelon, "Sidelights on the New World's Champions."
11. Ibid.
12. Ibid.
13. Ibid.
14. *Baltimore Sun*, September 5, 1952.
15. *Sporting Life*, February 5, 1916.
16. Ibid.
17. *Sporting Life*, January 6, 1917.
18. *Sporting Life*, February 3, 1917.
19. John J. Ward: "'Butch' Schmidt, the Player-Worker."
20. Ibid.
21. *Baltimore Sun*, January 19, 1981.

Red Smith

By Charles F. Faber

A MEDIOCRE FIELDER at third base, Red Smith was a good enough hitter to hold down third base for the Brooklyn Robins, until he clashed with his new manager, Wilbert Robinson. Robbie regarded Smith as a troublemaker, and Smith was summarily shipped to the Boston Braves—in time to make an important contribution as the Braves won the National League pennant, and then spend five more years with the team.

James Carlisle Smith was born on April 6, 1890, in Greenville, South Carolina, the second of four children of Ellen Bramlett and James Benjamin Smith, a railway postal clerk. His family moved to Atlanta when he was a child, and he called the Georgia capital home for the rest of his life. Outside of baseball he was known as Carlisle, but his baseball teammates and fans called him Red in homage to the color of his hair.

A hard hitter in college, Smith almost forsook baseball for a career in engineering. He attended a military prep school and played baseball and football at Alabama Polytechnic Institute (now Auburn University) in 1908 and 1909. The latter year was a very busy one for the young man. In the spring he was a hard-hitting outfielder for the Alabama Polytechnic baseball team. During the early part of the summer he played for the Georgia Railway and Electric Company semipro team. Later he made his professional debut as a 19-year-old third baseman for the Anderson Electricians in the Class D Carolina Association, appearing in 48 games and hitting for a .238 average. In 1910 he hit .237 but showed some power at the plate, clouting four home runs and compiling a .353 slugging average. After two seasons with Anderson, he joined the Nashville Volunteers of the Southern Association in 1911. At Nashville his hitting improved greatly, as he posted a .316 batting average and a slugging percentage of .424. However, toward the end of July he announced that he would retire from baseball at the end of the season. He had continued his engineering studies at Alabama Polytechnic during the offseasons and would graduate in 1912. He was engaged to an Atlanta heiress, Rosalie Eubanks, whose parents had died the previous winter. They planned to marry in the fall. Smith had secured an important position with the Atlanta Traction Company and planned to put his engineering skills to work.

However, events interceded to change his mind. Smith nearly won the Southern Association batting championship in 1911. He and Del Pratt of Montgomery both hit .316, but when the statistic was carried out to four decimal places, Pratt edged the redhead by a margin of .0006. Red's hitting attracted the attention of Brooklyn scout Larry Sutton, and the Dodgers, or Superbas, as they were usually called (the nickname Robins came later), purchased his contract. Smith made his major-league debut on September 5, 1911. In 28 games he hit .261 and won the favor of Brooklyn fans and manager Bill Dahlen. As planned, he married his Rosalie. However, for the next 18 years his career was in baseball, not engineering. From 1911 to August 1914, he played third base for Brooklyn. In 1912 he was the club's regular third baseman and hit .286. He had perhaps his best year in 1913, when he led the league in doubles and finished in the top ten in hits, total bases, extra-base hits, sacrifice hits, runs batted in, slugging average, and on-base percentage plus slugging average (OPS). Although sportswriter Tom Meany described the right-handed third sacker as a "squatty slugger," he was listed as 5-feet-11 and 165 pounds.

In November 1913 Dahlen was let go as Brooklyn manager. Many fans advocated popular first baseman Jake Daubert becoming his replacement. Hughie Jennings and Roger Bresnahan also were rumored to be in the running. However, owner Charles Ebbets selected Wilbert Robinson. Although Smith got off to a good start in 1914, he soon clashed with Robinson. He also fell out of favor with the fans, who had supported him so warmly in his early days in Brooklyn. The redhead had threatened to jump to the Federal League and had met with representatives of the league. He also was considered one of a clique of players who were striving to have Robinson replaced as manager by Daubert. Robbie regarded Smith as a troublemaker, and resolved to get rid of him. His chance came when Brooklyn signed third baseman Joe Schultz from the Rochester club The Robins sold Smith to the Boston Braves on August 10, 1914. Unfortunately for Brooklyn, Schultz never played a single game in the major leagues that season, and the club was stuck with weak-hitting Gus Getz at the hot corner.

According to sportswriter Harold Kaese as Smith was leaving the owner's office after signing his contract, he said, "I'll see you tomorrow afternoon." Braves president J. E. Gaffney responded, "You mean tomorrow morning." "What do you mean? Does this club still have morning practice?"

"Yes, sir. Every day except Sunday," Gaffney replied. Smith showed his disdain for Brooklyn's practices, laughing, "Why, we quit having morning practice a month ago at Brooklyn." Kaese wrote that Smith reported in uniform bright and early the next morning.[1]

Smith was an important contributor for Boston down the stretch, hitting .314 with an on-base percentage of .401 for the Braves as they continued their dramatic drive to the pennant. When the Braves acquired Smith, they had already started their climb up the standings and were now in fourth place. Aware of Red's reputation as a malcontent, Boston manager George Stallings lavished praise on the third sacker, securing him a raise in salary and assuring him that he was just the man to win the championship for the team. The psychology paid off as Smith compiled the highest batting average of any of the Miracle Braves over the course of the 60 games in which he played. His hitting more than compensated for the fact that he had the lowest fielding average on the club during that interval. After all, guardians of the hot corner frequently have the lowest fielding percentage on their clubs.

Unfortunately, a serious mishap befell Smith on the last day of the season. It happened in the ninth inning of the first game of a doubleheader against his former team at Ebbets Field. On that occasion Smith was wearing a new pair of shoes with spikes longer than those he was accustomed to. He hit a long drive that bounced off the right-center-field wall. Red rounded first and headed for second, trying to stretch the hit into a double. As he neared second base he began a hook slide. Meanwhile, Brooklyn's George Cutshaw received the throw from the outfield and lunged toward the runner. Smith's right shin struck Cutshaw's left leg and the long spikes dug into the dirt and threw the whole weight of his body on the ankle joint. His body was thrown several feet past the bag. He was taken by automobile to St. Mary's Hospital in Brooklyn. The attending physicians reported that Smith had suffered an anterior dislocation of the ankle joint of his right leg, a fracture of the fibula three inches above the joint, a fracture of the tibia, and ruptures of the ligaments of the ankle joint. The doctors were uncertain whether Smith would ever regain full use of the badly damaged ankle. Unable to compete in the World Series, he was temporarily replaced at the hot corner by Charlie Deal.

Red Smith

As the Braves never again won a pennant while Smith was with them, the accident deprived him of the only chance he had to play in a World Series.

Red was a good, solid hitter throughout his major-league career. He recovered fully from his broken ankle and played five more years for the Braves. In 1915 he slugged the first grand slam hit at the new Braves Field. He had solid years at the plate for the Braves from 1915 through 1918, hitting .295 in 1917 and a major-league career-high .298 in 1918. Because of a low fielding percentage, Red was sometimes considered a poor fielder. He led the National League in errors three times. However, he had good range in the field, leading the circuit in putouts three times and in assists four times. On June 12, 1919, the Braves secured third baseman Tony Boeckel from Pittsburgh. Manager Stallings moved Smith to the outfield, where he finished his major-league career. In February 1920 he was sent on waivers to the New York Yankees, and a few days later the Yankees sold him to the Washington Senators. He wound up playing for the Vernon Tigers of the Pacific Coast League, and played in the minors until 1928. In his nine seasons in the majors he had played in 1,117 games, hit .278 with an on-base percentage of .353. Among his 1,087 hits were 208 doubles, 49 triples, and 27 home runs. He scored 477 runs and batted in 514.

From 1920 through 1923 Smith was with Vernon and then Los Angeles in the PCL, hitting over .300 in three of the four years. In 1924 and 1925, he was with Atlanta in the Southern Association, leading the league with a .385 average in 1924 and hitting .344 the following year. He split the 1926 season between Atlanta and the Jacksonville Tars of the Southeastern League. The 1927 season was divided between Peoria of the Three-I League and Nashville. His .370 average for Peoria was best in the circuit. He closed out his baseball career in the Class B Three-I League in 1928 with Springfield and Peoria. During his 12 seasons in the minors (including 1909-1911) he played in 1,610 games and collected 1,907 hits, including 339 doubles, 69 triples, and 58 home runs. He averaged .327 and posted a .431 slugging percentage. For his total career—majors and minors combined—he fell short by only six hits of reaching the 3,000 mark.

Smith also garnered some minor-league managerial experience. In 1921 he piloted the Columbia Mules of the Class D Alabama-Tennessee League for a few games. He managed the Jacksonville Tars of the Class B Southeastern League for part of the 1926 season. In 1928 he was skipper of the Springfield Senators of the Three-I League for a partial season. In none of his three managerial experiences did he manage for an entire season.

In 1930 Smith worked as an insurance agent, living in Atlanta with his wife, Rosalie; daughter Margaret; and son James Carlisle, Jr. Later he served as a tax investigator for the city of Atlanta for 27 years before retiring. In his last years he lived in Marietta, a suburb of Atlanta. He was overjoyed when the Milwaukee Braves moved to Atlanta in 1966. His daughter, Margaret, then Mrs. Leo Sudderth, Jr., said her father was the "most enthusiastic booster the Braves had when they moved to Atlanta. …Daddy maintained his interest in baseball through the years. But he was really excited when his Braves came here."[2]

Unfortunately, Smith had only one season in which to cheer the Braves in his hometown. He died at the age of 76 in Atlanta's Piedmont Hospital on October 11, 1966. The cause of death was listed as aortic insufficiency brought on by congestive heart failure. He is buried in Westview Cemetery in Atlanta.

Sources

Red Smith player file in the National Baseball Hall of Fame.

www.ancestry.com.

www.baseball-reference.com

www.newspaperacrchive.com

Frank Graham. *The Brooklyn Dodgers: An Informal History*. New York: G. P. Putnam's Sons, 1945.

Jack Kavanagh and Norman Macht. *Uncle Robbie*. Cleveland: Society for American Baseball Research, 1999.

Harold Kaese. *The Boston Braves, 1871-1953*. Boston: Northeastern University Press, 2004.

Tom Meany. *Baseball's Greatest Teams.* New York: A.S. Barnes and Co., 1949.

Notes

1. Kaese, p. 147
2. United Press International dispatch from Atlanta, carried in the *Lima News*, October 12, 1966.

Paul Strand

By Jack V. Morris

Paul Strand had a dream season in 1923. Playing for the Salt Lake City Bees in the Pacific Coast League, Strand won the Triple Crown, and, in so doing, set the PCL record for home runs in a season with 43 and the Organized Baseball record for hits in a season with 325. A former pitcher with the 1914 Miracle Braves, now nine years later turned into a power-hitting outfielder, he was called another Babe Ruth.

However, 1924 turned into a nightmare season. After Connie Mack paid $35,000 and sent three players to Salt Lake City, the much-hyped Strand played only 47 games for the Philadelphia Athletics, batting .228 before Mack traded him in disgust to Toledo of the American Association. Worse yet, his name would become synonymous with the word "flop" in the nation's sports pages for years to come.

Strand's is a remarkable story. Well before his incredible 1923 season, he was signed by the Boston Red Sox after pitching in only four games in his minor-league career. He was reputed to have been the youngest player in the major leagues for two straight seasons, 1913 and 1914. And he pitched a perfect game in the minor leagues. Yet it was for his failure to produce in his brief time during the 1924 major-league season that he was best known.

Paul Edward Strand was born on December 19, 1893, in Carbonado, Washington, a coal-mining town southeast of Tacoma, to parents Gustav and Hannah (Wickman) Strand. He was the second of five children. Gustav and Hannah were born in Sweden and had immigrated to Washington in the 1880s. Gustav was a coal miner when he first came to the United States but by 1930 worked as a laborer in a lumber mill.[1]

When Paul was 3, his family moved to South Prairie, a few miles from Carbonado, where he grew up. He attended Buckley High School, playing football and baseball. In the summer when he wasn't working as a clerk in a grocery store, he played for a number of town teams including South Prairie and neighboring Wilkeson.[2]

While pitching for the Buckley town team in 1910 the 16-year-old Strand was spotted by Spokane Indians owner Joe Cohn. Fifty years later, Strand told the *Salt Lake Tribune* that he had gone to Spokane, a team in the Class B Northwestern League, and asked for a tryout but all contemporary stories claim that Cohn discovered Strand.[3]

Whatever the story, Strand was in spring training with Spokane in 1911. Standing an even 6 feet tall and weighing 190 pounds, the broad-shouldered Strand was an imposing left-handed power pitcher. In his first game in spring training, he defeated the Gonzaga College team to rave reviews. "Strand's speed was terrific," wrote the *Oregonian*.[4]

When the regular season began, Strand continued to blow away the competition. He won his first three games easily, striking out 30 in 25 innings of work. The newspapers loved the big blond local boy. The *Tacoma Times* ran a headline after his first minor-league win that read, "Kid Strand Real Thing." The *Seattle Times*, after his third win, called him the "most-talked-of young ball player in three leagues." Even *The Sporting News* got into the act, writing that Strand was "said to be a Walter Johnson and a Vean Gregg combined" and that he "appears to be a real find."[5]

Cohn, a wheeler and dealer with players, jumped at the chance to peddle Strand. He started contacting major-league teams offering them Strand. Brooklyn passed on the 17-year-old but, on May 11, Boston Red Sox owner John I. Taylor, sight unseen, offered Cohn $5,000 for the rights to Strand with the understanding that he would finish out the season with Spokane and be Red Sox property in 1912. So incredible was the offer, "the largest price ever paid for a Northwestern League ballplayer" according to Cohn, that many local papers though it was a publicity stunt.[6]

However, things started to go downhill for Strand. He lost a game right before he was sold to the Red Sox. Then from May 14 to June 27, he went 2-3 and was quite unimpressive. After a relief appearance on June 30, he was sent home and shut down for three weeks. When he returned in late July, he lost one game and then left his next game in the second inning with a sore arm. He didn't pitch another game the rest of the season.[7]

In the meantime, the Red Sox sent superscout Ted Sullivan to get a look at Strand. But with Strand injured, Cohn put Sullivan off. Sullivan later claimed that Cohn hid Strand from him. Cohn finally sent Strand home for good in late August, ending his 1911 season.[8]

It's unclear what transpired next. One story said that the Red Sox paid $2,500 and were to pay the rest upon delivery after the 1912 season. Strand was to play for Spokane again during that time. However, Cohn dealt Strand to the San Francisco Seals of the Pacific Coast League before spring training. Things didn't go well for Strand. His arm still bothered him. Strand "pitches like he has a kink in his arm," wrote the *Oregonian*. Then in a practice game, he gave up nine runs in one inning. On April 3 he was on his way back to Spokane.[9]

While Strand claimed his arm was fine, telling the *Seattle Times*, "My arm is in great condition and I am fit as a fiddle," he didn't pitch well in spring training. As a result, Cohn sent him to Walla Walla in the Class D Western Tri-State League. Strand responded by "burning up the bushes" and made it back to Spokane by July 14.[10]

He continued to pitch well for Spokane. By season's end, he accumulated an 8-7 record for the Indians, which included a one-hitter against Vancouver. Somewhere, along the line, the Red Sox dropped their claim on Strand. *Sporting Life* wrote, "For some reason, the deal was never completed. Perhaps the change in ownership of the club [Taylor had sold a half-interest in the team to James McAleer] caused Strand to be lost in the shuffle." So, on September 16, the Boston Braves drafted the unprotected Strand at the National Base Ball Commission meeting in Cincinnati. It cost the Braves $1,200, a bargain compared to what the Red Sox had offered the year before. Strand wasn't the only player from the Northwestern League drafted by the Braves. Boston manager George Stallings took eight players in all from the league.[11]

Strand was still attending high school when he had to leave in March 1913 to travel to the Braves' spring-training camp in Athens, Georgia. Stallings tutored the young pitcher on the finer points of the game. "This rookie is coming along nicely and shows unusual aptitude in getting sense of instructions given him and following them," wrote Al E. Watts of the *Boston Herald & Traveler*. Strand also began to try new pitches. Watts wrote that he had the best "hook" of any of the rookie pitchers. He also threw what was called a "typical Matty fadeaway," a reference to the screwball Christy Mathewson threw. In addition, Bill James taught Strand the spitball, though press reports claimed it to be a "dry spitball" pitch.[12]

Despite all the pitches he was cultivating, Strand saw very little action in 1913. He pitched in seven games with no wins or losses and an ERA of 2.12. He was wild,

Paul Strand

walking 12 in 17 innings. His future was uncertain with the Braves when he went back to high school in October. There were questions about Strand's maturity and commitment. Bill James, a rookie pitcher himself with the Braves in 1913, told the *Seattle Times*, "If Paul Strand only had a little "pep" and "ambish" he would be a sensation in the National League. … But he's just an overgrown kid and does not seem to take much interest in the game." In December Stallings decided to give Strand another chance and invited him to spring training in Macon, Georgia, in 1914.[13]

On March 3 Strand arrived in camp eager to prove to Stallings he belonged on the team. He was, for the most part, sharp and the *Boston Journal* noted that he "looks better than a year ago." Strand made the team as a reliever and spot starter. He pitched in only 16 games but when he got into a game, he pitched well, with a 6-2 record and a 2.44 ERA. He walked 23 and struck out 33 in 55 innings. Fred Mitchell, who was listed on the Braves roster as a catcher but was the team's de facto pitching coach, helped Strand with his control.[14]

Perhaps Strand's best game was on June 25, against the New York Giants. He pitched six innings in relief, getting the 7-6 win and driving in the winning run with a double. The victory lifted the Braves momentarily out of the cellar of the National League, but a doubleheader sweep by the Giants the next day put the Braves back in last place. However, it wasn't long before the Braves made their incredible trip to the top of the standings and a World Series win. Despite his season, Strand did not get into a game during the astonishing four-game sweep of the Philadelphia Athletics. Nonetheless, like all the Braves, Strand was awarded a full share of the winners' money and a gold medal with a "monster diamond" and the words "World's Champion, 1914" engraved on it.[15]

Going into spring training in 1915, with Strand finally finishing high school, expectations were high. Stallings told the press that he "will be a wonder this year." When Strand wasn't pitching, Stallings was trying him out in the outfield, "where he is showing great," wrote the *Boston Journal*, which added, "He is very fast and covers ground like a shadow. If Paul does not become a great pitcher—and that is what he gives promise of—a first class outfielder might be made of him." But first and foremost to Stallings, he was a pitcher. "Paul Strand impresses me as the best young left-handed pitcher I have ever had," said Stallings toward the end of spring training.[16]

Stallings was counting heavily on Strand when the season began. But by May, he had developed a sore arm. It was an injury that Strand pointed to years later as the beginning of the end of his pitching career. The Braves kept him on the roster, however. He was used as a pinch-hitter in 16 games and as an outfielder in five. By July 13, with the Braves struggling, Stallings decided to shake things up. He sent outfielders Ted Cather and Larry Gilbert to the minor leagues and suspended Strand for "failure to get in condition." The press said it was his "rheumatic shoulder" that caused the suspension. On July 26 Stallings lifted the suspension when Strand claimed his arm was feeling better. But Strand pitched only sparingly. For the season he pitched in six games, a total of 22 innings, with a 1-1 record and 2.38 ERA. It wasn't exactly the season Stallings had hoped for from Strand.[17]

Still, Stallings was willing to give Strand another chance in 1916. He arrived in camp in Miami early knowing that, as the *Boston Journal* wrote, it was "practically (his) last chance to hang on." While Strand pitched fine in camp, Roger Bresnahan, manager of the American Association's Toledo Iron Men, made it clear he wanted Strand for his team. Strand made the Braves out of training camp, but six games into the season, before he had had a chance to pitch for the Braves, he was shipped to Bresnahan's club with the caveat that he could be recalled by the Braves. The Braves never called.[18]

Strand had trouble with his control in Toledo. He finished the season pitching in 24 games with an 8-5 record. But because of injuries, he also saw some significant time in the outfield. He got into 37 games as a nonpitcher. *Sporting Life* wrote that Strand "has the earmarks of a future pasturer when he tires of pitching."

That day was coming sooner rather than later. Strand gave it one more season before he moved to becoming an everyday player.[19]

Toledo reserved Strand for the 1917 season but in February Bresnahan cleaned house, releasing five pitchers including Strand. The press reported that Strand was headed to Memphis of the Class A Southern Association but when spring training camp began, he was with Seattle Giants of the Class B Northwestern League.[20]

With Seattle Strand started having success he hadn't had as pitcher since 1912. On May 13 he pitched a perfect game against Spokane, striking out five and so thoroughly dominating Spokane that "not a single play in the field by the Giants could be called sensational." He finished the season with a 9-7 mark in 19 games. Again, because of injuries to his teammates, he played a number of games in the outfield, and hit .285.[21]

In 1918, with the United States fully involved in the World War, Strand joined the Navy and was stationed at the Bremerton (Washington) Navy Yard as a radio operator first class. In his spare time, he played baseball for the Navy Yard. As was typical during the war years, Bremerton had an excellent baseball team, headed by Strand and Bill Cunningham, a minor leaguer who eventually made it to the major leagues with the New York Giants and Boston Braves. The Navy Yard team was so good that it defeated Strand's old team, the Seattle Giants, 6-3, in April.[22]

That year in the Navy, Strand moved from pitcher to full-time outfielder. He played so well that he was picked for an all-service team for the Northwestern US. So when the war ended, Strand decided he'd start all over again and try to work his way back as an outfielder.[23] In 1919 he started with Peoria of the Class B Illinois-Indiana-Iowa League and then moved to Joplin of the Class A Western League. He was back on the West Coast in 1920, first playing with the Yakima Indians of the Class B Pacific Coast International League, where he led the league in hitting at .339, then finished up with Seattle in the Double-A Pacific Coast League. He started 1921 with Seattle but on April 30 he was sold along with pitcher Monroe Swartz to Salt Lake City. It was there that Strand really made a name for himself.[24] Strand finished 1921 batting .314 but he was just warming up. The next two years were, arguably, the greatest two hitting years in minor-league history. In 1922 Strand won the PCL Triple Crown, pounding out 289 hits in 178 games, setting Organized Baseball's record for the most hits in a season (and was widely claimed as the "world's record" for hits). He batted .384 for the season with 28 home runs. He had a hitting streak of 33 games during the season. The longest he went hitless was a four-game streak toward the end of the season. By late July Strand was hitting over .400, propelled to that level by an astounding .481 in 37 games in the month. He especially liked hitting at home, batting .436. Yet despite these gaudy numbers, Bees manager Duffy Lewis had trouble finding a major-league buyer for Strand. So when 1923 rolled around, Strand was still with Salt Lake City.[25]

The press suggested several reasons for the snub. One was that he had already had his shot in the majors. Another blamed his poor fielding. A third reason given was his awkward batting style (though he threw left-handed he batted right-handed) which was "devoid of anything approximating form or grace." Whatever the reason, Strand took out his frustrations in 1923 on the Pacific Coast League pitchers.[26]

Incredibly, Strand had a better season in 1923 than in 1922. On April 28, in a 5-3 game with two outs in the ninth, Oakland pitcher Harry Krause intentionally walked Strand with the bases loaded, though it brought the tying run to third base. The strategy paid off as Krause got the next out to win the game. On May 13 against Vernon, Strand and teammate Oscar Vitt hit two home runs each in the same inning, the 12-run third. By July, major-league clubs finally took notice of Strand. The White Sox sent scout Danny Long to take a look at him. But it was Connie Mack who showed the greatest interest. By August the Athletics were looking for some power in their outfield so they sent Harry Davis to scout Strand. Davis liked what he saw, offering cash for Strand. Bees owner H. William Lane insisted on players instead of cash, so Strand continued to play for Salt Lake City.[27]

On August 25 he tied the PCL record for home runs in a season with 33 and set a new record the next day. In late August Mack took matters into his own hands and traveled out to Salt Lake City to talk to Lane. It was speculated in the press that Mack had offered anywhere from $50,000 to $100,000 for Strand but Lane turned him down.[28]

On September 15 Strand broke his year-old "world's record" for hits in a season. Six days later he broke his PCL home-run record when he drove a ball through a hole in the left-field fence in Los Angeles. At the end of the season, he won the PCL Triple Crown. He batted .394 with 43 home runs and 187 RBIs. In the process he also set league records for runs scored in a season (180) and total bases (546). He even set marks in the field: the most chances (612) and the most caught flies (599). He was the most talked-about minor leaguer in the land.[29]

Finally, on December 12, 1923, at a baseball meeting in Chicago, Lane sold Strand to Connie Mack for an estimated $35,000 and three players: infielder Clarke "Pinky" Pittenger and pitchers Hank Hulvey, and Harry O'Neill. Some papers claimed the price was as high as $150,000. It wasn't Mack's only high-profile purchase that winter. He also bought Al Simmons from Milwaukee of the American Association and Max Bishop from Baltimore of the International League. After the purchase of Strand, Mack told the press, "I don't expect Strand to do wonders, but I do believe he will give us the needed punch."[30]

In the offseason, when talk came around to the Athletics, it almost always centered on Strand. Expectations for him and the A's were high going into spring training. But Strand couldn't have gotten off to a worse start. He initially held out for more money from Mack, and was one of the last players to report to camp. Then Mack and the Athletics coaching staff started tinkering with his batting stance and swing.[31]

Yet when the season started, it appeared that Strand was fine. Though he didn't show any power, he was getting his share of hits for the first week or so. But from April 24 to May 14, Strand went 7-for-52, and his average dropped to .197. He also showed no power—five doubles and one triple to that point. He was benched for almost two weeks in the middle of May. When he got back into the lineup, Strand started to hit a little. He eventually raised his batting average to .256 on June 7 but then went into another extended slump. By the end of June, rumors started that Mack was looking to trade Strand.[32]

On June 28, just 47 games into his career with the A's, Mack traded Strand and pitcher Rollie Naylor to Toledo of the American Association for outfielder Bill Lamar. While it was no secret that Strand was struggling, it still came as a shock when Mack unloaded him. *The Sporting News* wrote that "his release came as a big surprise to many fans." Strand never made it back to the major leagues.[33]

While there were many conjectures on why Strand failed, probably the most widely held was that he was under enormous pressure to produce. Strand himself told the press, "I was pressing, trying too hard." Fellow rookie and future Hall of Famer Al Simmons agreed. "Many a newcomer into the league has failed because of an overdose of publicity," Simmons told *The Sporting News* years later. "And that was the fate of Paul. He tried too hard to live up to the expectations of the fans."[34]

Of course, when Strand got to Toledo, he tore up the American Association pitching. Playing with Toledo for the rest of 1924 and all of 1925, he batted .323 and .300 respectively. But by then no major-league team would touch the "flop."

Before the 1925 season, Strand married Esther Elizabeth Carbis of Salt Lake City on January 16. Now that he made his home in Salt Lake City, he pushed to get back to the Pacific Coast League. Not only was it home but he had his most success as a player playing on the West Coast.[35]

During Strand's season and a half with Toledo, there were many rumors that he was headed back to the PCL and more specifically Portland. But Toledo wanted too much money and it wasn't until the 1926 season that Strand finally returned to the Coast League.[36] But first he was traded by Toledo to the league rival Columbus Senators for catcher Luke Urban. He played 47 games with Columbus before Portland finally purchased him on June 8. Strand had "been homesick for the West Coast" wrote the *New York Evening World-Herald*.[37]

Strand was relieved to be back in the PCL. "I have been thinking about nothing much else for two years than returning to the Coast league," he said. He finished 1926 batting .326. In 1927 he had another excellent season, batting .355 for Portland. That season also marked his last mound appearance in Organized Baseball when he pitched for one inning. But by 1928, with no major-league teams interested in him, Strand was sold to the Atlanta Crackers of the Southern Association. He again struggled away from the West Coast. He was benched on June 12 and Atlanta traded him to Little Rock. He finished the 1928 season batting just .273. After 16 seasons in Organized Baseball, Strand retired at the age of 34.[38]

After his baseball career, Strand took a job with his father-in-law's company, K&K Plumbing & Heating Company. He worked there for the rest of his life and eventually became the owner.[39]

For several decades after Strand's "flop" in 1924, the press pointed out the problems with counting on players who excelled in the minor leagues. When the Yankees signed Joe DiMaggio after his tremendous 1935 season in the PCL, *The Sporting News* warned that what happened to Strand could happen to DiMaggio.[40]

Strand's wife, Esther, died on August 20, 1946. Two years later, he married elementary school teacher Loraine McCormick. In 1970, he was elected to the Utah Hall of Fame. Four years later, on July 2, 1974, at his home in Salt Lake City, Strand died of natural causes at the age of 80. He was buried at Salt Lake City Cemetery. He was survived by Loraine. He had no children with either wife.[41]

In 1999, the *Salt Lake Tribune* ranked Strand as 43rd of Utah's 50 greatest athletes of the 20th century—a tribute to those spectacular seasons he had in 1922 and 1923.[42]

Notes

1   Strand wrote his full name as Paul Oscar Edward Strand on his World War registration card. Otherwise, all other sources list him just as Paul Edward Strand.

2   *Seattle Times*, May 1, 1911, July 31, 1921; *Hobart* (Washington) *Republican*, May 17, 1911.

3   *Tacoma Times*, April 3 and May 4, 1911; *Salt Lake Tribune Home Magazine*, October 28, 1962.

4   *The Oregonian, Portland*, March 27, 1911.

5   *Tacoma Times*, April 22, 1911; *Seattle Times*, May 1, 1911; *The Sporting News*, May 18, 1911.

6   *Seattle Times*, May 5, 1911, May 12, 1911; *Denver Post*, May 12, 1911; *The Oregonian*, May 14, 1911.

7   *The Oregonian*, July 23, 1911; *Tacoma Times*, July 31, 1911.

8   *The Oregonian*, August 17, 1911; *Seattle Times*, August 24, 1911, September 18, 1911.

9   *Seattle Times*, January 22, 1912; *Oregonian*, February 3, March 12, and April 4, 1912; *Watertown (NY) Daily Times*, May 4, 1912 .

10   *Seattle Times*, April 10, April 18, and July 15, 1912; *Oregonian*, July 5, 1912.

11   *Boston Journal*, September 17, 1912; *Sporting Life*, September 21, October 5, November 16, and November 23 1912; *Trenton (New Jersey) Times*, December 4, 1912. The other seven players were Win Noyes, Bill James, Cecil Thompson, Lucien "Lefty" Gervais, Bert Whaling, Rex Devogt, and Hap Myers. Incredibly, all but Thompson played for the Braves in 1913.

12   *Sporting Life*, January 4 and March 22, 1913; *Boston Journal*, March 6, 1913; *Springfield* (Massachusetts) *Daily News*, March 18, 1913; *Trenton Times*, May 12, 1913; *Salt Lake Tribune*, August 18, 1960.

13   *Seattle Times*, December 30, 1913, and January 1, 1914; *Sporting Life*, December 20, 1913.

14   *Tampa Morning Tribune*, March 4, 1914; *Boston Journal*, April 6, 1914; *Sporting Life*, August 29, 1914; *Anaconda* (Montana) *Standard*, January 7, 1917.

15   *Boston Journal*, June 26, 1914; *The Oregonian*, January 8, 1915.

16   *The Oregonian*, January 8, 1915; *Seattle Times*, February 4, 1915; *Boston Globe*, March 6, March 9, and April 14, 1915; *Macon* (Georgia) *Telegraph*, March 6, 1915.

17   *Boston Globe*, May 30 and July 27, 1915; Gerry Hern, "Strand's Story of Record Flop," *Baseball Digest*, September 1951, 83-85; *The Oregonian*, June 27 and July 14, 1915; *Springfield Daily News*, July 14, 1915;

18 *Richmond Times-Dispatch*, October 1, 1915; *Miami Herald Record*, March 6, 1916; *Boston Journal*, March 11 and April 22, 1916; *Denver Post*, April 22, 1916; *Boston Globe*, April 23, 1916.

19 *The Oregonian*, August 15, 1916; *Sporting Life*, July 8, 1916.

20 *Sporting Life*, November 4, 1916, April 14, 1917; *Duluth* (Minnesota) *News-Tribune*, February 19, 1917; *Oregonian*, April 1, 1917.

21 *Seattle Times*, May 14 and July 12, 1917.

22 *The Oregonian*, January 17, 1918; *Canton* (Ohio) *Repository*, June 6, 1924; *Bellingham* (Washington) *Herald*, April 6, 1918; Lawrence Perry, *Our Navy in the War* (New York: C. Scribner & Sons, 1996), 256; *Seattle Times*, April 21, 1918.

23 *Seattle Times*, July 26, 1918.

24 *Wilkes-Barre Times*, May 15, 1919; *Rockford* (Illinois) *Register-Gazette*, August 25, 1919; *Seattle Times*, May 19, September 11, September 21, 1920, and February 9 and March 6 1921; *Salt Lake Telegram*, April 30, 1921.

25 *The Sporting News*, December 21, 1922, January 25, 1964; *Seattle Times*, October 14, 1922; *Salt Lake Telegram*, July 21 and July 23, 1922; uncredited chart in Strand's Hall of Fame file; Louisville's Jay Kirke had set the previous record of 282 hits in 1920.

26 *San Jose* (California) *Evening News*, December 30, 1922; *Seattle Times*, April 8, 1923.

27 *Oakland Tribune*, April 29, 1923; *Salt Lake Telegram*, May 14, 1923; *Cleveland Plain Dealer*, July 22, 1923; *New York Evening World-Herald*, August 16, 1923; *The Sporting News*, August 9, 1923.

28 *San Diego Union*, August 26, 1923; *The Oregonian*, August 27, 1923; *The Sporting News*, August 30, 1923; *Seattle Times*, September 3, 1923.

29 *San Diego Union*, September 22, 1923; *Canton* (Ohio) *Repository*, January 20, 1924.

30 *Riverside* (California) *Daily Press*, December 12, 1923; *Springfield Republican*, December 16, 1923; *The Sporting News*, December 20, 1923. The amount Mack paid for Strand was disputed in the press. Strand years later told the press he didn't know how much Mack paid for him but had heard up to $150,000. Mack, 25 years after the fact, claimed he paid $40,000. Retrosheet (www.retrosheet.org) lists the price at $35,000.

31 *Tampa Morning Tribune*, March 5, 1924; Gerry Hern, "Strand's Story of Record Flop," *Baseball Digest*, September 1951, 83-85; *Salt Lake Tribune*, March 25, 1962.

32 *The Oregonian*, June 23, 1924, *Oakland Tribune*, July 5, 1924.

33 *The Sporting News*, July 3, 1924.

34 Gerry Hern, "Strand's Story of Record Flop," *Baseball Digest*, September 1951, 83-85; *The Sporting News*, November 5, 1942.

35 *Ogden* (Utah) *Standard-Examiner*, January 15, 1925.

36 *The Oregonian*, January 22 and February 17, 1925; *The Sporting News*, January 22, 1926.

37 *Cleveland Plain Dealer*, February 24, 1926; *New York Evening World-Herald*, June 8, 1926.

38 *Dallas Morning News*, December 9, 1927; *New Orleans Times-Picayune*, June 13, 1928.

39 *Salt Lake Tribune*, August 21, 1946, July 3, 1974.

40 *The Sporting News*, December 26, 1935.

41 *Salt Lake Tribune*, August 21, 1946, July 3, 1974.

42 *Salt Lake Tribune*, December 26, 1999.

Fred Tyler

By John Shannahan

It was a small story in a national publication, and it suggested the possibility of a baseball first.

Under the headline "Brothers Constitute a Battery," the May 28, 1914, issue of *Leslie's Illustrated Weekly* wrote, "The Boston Nationals have a battery this season composed of brothers, George and Fred Tyler. It is said that this is the first time in the history of modern baseball that such a combination has been seen in fast company. George Tyler, the pitcher, is a great left-handed twirler, but catchers who have worked with him declare his delivery is one of the hardest to handle. Manager Stallings, seeking for a means to remedy this condition, asked George with what backstop he worked best. 'My brother Fred catches me better than anyone I ever had' was the reply. Immediately the absent brother was summoned to camp, and though lacking experience, he is being whipped into shape to take his place behind the plate when his brother goes on the mound."

It was a wonderful story about a family with New England baseball roots, but by the time the story was published, Fred had been optioned out by the Braves, and the anticipated brother-battery never occurred at the major-league level. George "Lefty" Tyler would enjoy a 12-year major-league career, winning 127 games and pitching in the 1914 and 1918 World Series. But other than for a brief four-day period, Fred Tyler's professional career would be primarily characterized by the gritty old mill towns of New England in which he played.

Fred "Clancy" Tyler knew something about old mill towns. He was born in Derry, New Hampshire, on December 16, 1891, the third son of John F. and Martha McCannon Tyler. John, like his father, worked in the shoe industry, an industry that dominated Derry life in the latter half of the 19th century and well into the new century.

A prime source of local civic pride and entertainment at the time was the Derry Athletic Association, which was founded in 1904. The club's baseball team was a southern New Hampshire powerhouse, and in time included a number of players answering to the last name Tyler.[1]

Fred debuted with the association's team on the Fourth of July 1907 in the second game of a doubleheader against the Newburyport Athletic Club. Brother George had taken the mound in the morning game, losing 6-1, with oldest brother Arthur playing first base and contributing a 1-for-4 performance at the plate while scoring Derry's lone run. In the afternoon encounter, Fred caught and got one single in four at-bats as Derry won, 4-3. Interestingly, the umpire for the afternoon game was also named Tyler.[2]

Fred dropped out of school after the eighth grade, and while working at a local shoe factory, became a mainstay of the Derry squad.[3] Brother George departed for Lowell of the New England League in 1909, and was purchased in 1910 by the Boston Doves, with whom he finished the season. In 1911, while Fred was having a trial with Lynn and semipro ball, George became a regular in the Boston pitching rotation (the team known as the Rustlers for 1911 was re-christened the Braves in 1912), but returned in October 1913 to Derry for the Athletic Association's last game of the season, against the Manchester All-Stars. Now more commonly known as Lefty Tyler, he dominated the overmatched All-Stars, 16-4, a game that included brothers Arthur, Fred, and William.[4]

The Braves had finished 31 1/2 games (yet still in fifth place) behind the National League champion New York Giants in 1913, and with the 1914 season approaching, the *Boston Globe* reported on February 22 that the team would begin spring training on March 3. The *Globe* added, "The New England contingent of Braves [are] scheduled to leave for training camp in Macon, Georgia, on February 28, on the midnight train to New York. The Boston party [includes] Walter Maranville, Tom Griffith, Leslie Mann, George Tyler, and Fred F. Tyler, George's brother, who is to be tried as a catcher."[5]

Later that week, the *Globe* reported, "The catching department will have Bert Whaling who is at present at Hot Springs taking the baths, and Harry Gowdy for the regular men to start the spring training, and there are also three youngsters who are eager to make good as backstops, Dick Lewis, Walter Kenefick, and Fred Tyler."[6]

With spring training set to begin, the *Globe*'s J.C. O'Leary wrote, "The rookies are all husky young fellows. Fred Tyler, a brother of George, whom manager Stallings is going to give a trial behind the bat, is a fine physical specimen, being a heavier man than his brother and having the physique of an ideal catcher."[7] For Tyler, who stood 5-feet-10 1/2 and weighed 180 pounds, the future looked bright.

The weather was good that spring, the players losing only two full days during their five-week Southern stay. "Manager Stallings is well satisfied with the way the men have come along. He has hardened them gradually and has been careful not to over work them," reported the *Globe*.[8]

The paper added, "Fred Tyler the young catcher, a brother of George, is being carried along, which would make it appear that Stallings thinks there are some possibilities in him. He is getting some valuable experience and is a willing worker. The coaching he is receiving, together with his natural aptitude, should make a ball player of him, and the longer he stays with Stallings the better it will be for him. ... Stallings has a lot of work cut out for the boys when they reach home, early in May, after the opening series with the other Eastern clubs. Then he will further develop team work, and get his team playing what he describes as "organized ball." He says he will have a very different team the latter part of May, so far as efficiency goes, from what he has now, and it certainly is no weakling at the present time."

With the season set to begin, an April 12 *Globe* story headlined "New Faces With Braves" failed to mention Tyler, and on May 6, as the team prepared to leave on a four-week road trip, it was announced that catcher Fred Tyler, having yet to play in any games, would be left behind.

Fred Tyler

Tyler spent the summer of 1914 with the Jersey City Skeeters of the Double-A International League. Playing in 74 games, he batted .251 with one home run. Meanwhile, the Braves, having endured a horrible start that had them mired in the National League cellar on July 4, staged a miraculous finish, assuming first place on September 8 and clinching the National League pennant on September 30.

Having clinched the pennant, the Braves still had eight National League games to play in the last week before they would face Connie Mack's Philadelphia Athletics in the World Series. As the season wound down into its final days, it was apparent that the Braves' regular catching duo of Gowdy and Whaling were in need of some rest. While acknowledging that Whaling missed much of the season on account of injuries, the *Globe* said that "Gowdy and Whaling are two good catchers; the former has developed into a star, and has become so good behind the bat, and is so strong as a batsman that he has been doing the bulk of the work this season, although he probably would not have been worked so hard, except for the injuries Whaling has suffered. Whaling is a fine backstop and a good sticker."[9]

After the Braves' 7-6 victory over the New York Giants on October 1, under a subheadline titled "Gowdy Somewhat Crippled," the *Globe* had reported that " 'Hank' Gowdy is somewhat "bunged up." His throwing this afternoon was off the mark and gave the Giants some of their runs. He undoubtedly will be all right for the big series. His injuries have all been caused by foul tips."[10]

The Braves lost 11-5 to the Giants on the 2nd, and with three doubleheaders remaining to close out the season, a new yet familiar name was about to appear in the lineup. On the 3rd Fred Tyler made his major-league debut. He had finished his season with Jersey City (batting .251) and planned to return to Derry and play out the year with the Derry Athletic Association, when the call from Boston was received. He caught both games of the October 3 doubleheader, batting eighth, going 0-for-4 in a 4-1 victory, and then 0-for-3 against the Giants' future Hall of Fame pitcher Rube Marquard in a 1-0 loss.

The Braves then moved to Brooklyn for a pair of doubleheaders against the Dodgers. On October 5 Tyler knocked his first major-league base hit, going 1-for-4 in the day's first game, a 15-2 Braves victory. He added a second hit with a 1-for-3 second game, a 9-5 win. The season ended the next day with the teams splitting a doubleheader, Tyler going a combined 0-for-5 but throwing out future Hall of Famer Zack Wheat on an attempted steal. Tyler threw out five of ten attempted basestealers during his brief stay. He had caught three consecutive season-ending doubleheaders and collected two hits in 19 at-bats for a .105 batting average.

The World Series began in Philadelphia on October 9. With Hank Gowdy back behind the plate, the Braves swept the Athletics, the winning game being played at Fenway Park on October 13. George Tyler pitched ten innings with no decision in Game Three. Brother Fred did not appear in the Series.

The battery of brothers George and Fred Tyler finally appeared together in 1914, after they traveled back to Derry in late October to join brothers Bill and Arthur in a 3-2 Derry Athletic Association victory over the All-Stars of the Manchester Manufacturers League.

Before the start of the new season, Fred and George visited Braves President James Gaffney in late January 1915. The visit was to "show how life on a farm agrees with ball players," reported the *Globe*, adding, "Fred will go south with the Braves and work out with the catchers, as he is a fair catcher."[11]

Fair catcher or not, the major-league career of Fred Tyler was over. He was sold on February 27 to Rochester of the International League and then released to Newark, before landing with the Syracuse Stars of the Class B New York State League, where he batted .301. In April 1916 he was sold to the Worcester Busters of the newly formed Eastern League. A headline in the *Worcester Telegram* blared, "Hamilton Buys Tyler From Syracuse Club—Worcester Manager Makes Deal For Hard Hitting Catcher and Brother of Boston Braves' Crack Southpaw Twirler."[12] The Worcester manager was future Hall of Famer Sliding Billy Hamilton, for whom Tyler toiled in the first of his four modest seasons for the Busters. Tyler batted .237 in 1916 and .271 in 1917, before serving in the US Army during World War I as a sergeant in the 151st Depot Brigade. He returned to Worcester to bat .316 in 1919 and .229 in 1920, by which time he had married a woman more than five years his elder. He followed with seasons of .268 and .291 for the Eastern League's Waterbury Brasscos. He later played for Lawrence before retiring as a player.

After retiring, Fred returned to Derry, and worked for the rest of his life in the shoe industry, returning to the occupation that long before baseball had been the means by which his family had subsisted. He died at the age of 53 on October 14, 1945, of complications caused by a perforated stomach ulcer. He was survived by his wife, Marion Corson Tyler. They had no children. He is buried at Forest Hill Cemetery in East Derry, New Hampshire.

Sources

In addition to the sources in the endnotes, the author also consulted Ancestry.com, Baseball-Reference.com, and Baseball-almanac.com

Photo courtesy of Rick Holmes, The Derry Museum.

Notes

1. Richard Holmes, *The Road to Derry: A Brief History* (Charleston, South Carolina: The History Press, 2009).
2. *Derry News*, July 12, 1907
3. Notes of Rick Holmes, The Derry Museum.
4. *Derry News*, October 17, 1913
5. *Boston Globe*, February 22, 1914
6. *Boston Globe*, March 2, 1914
7. *Boston Globe*, April 6, 1914
8. Ibid.
9. *Boston Globe*, October 4, 1914
10. *Boston Globe*, October 2, 1914
11. *Boston Globe*, January 25, 1915
12. *Worcester Telegram*, April 6, 1916

Lefty Tyler

By Wayne McElreavy

Lefty Tyler was the third of the Miracle Braves' Big Three, and the only one who didn't win a 1914 World Series game (though the Braves won his only start). During the astonishing run from last to first, Tyler was, according to sportswriter Tom Meany, "untouchable when he had to be, which was most of the time." He was especially known for his grit in low-scoring games—30 of his 127 major-league victories were shutouts, ten of them 1-0 squeakers. Also known for his great "slowball" (changeup), Tyler employed an overhand crossfire delivery (until 1940 pitchers weren't required to make their first step within the width of the pitcher's plate). His unorthodox style allowed him to hide the ball longer, making his fastball more effective and aiding his sweeping curve.

The second of John F. and Martha Jane (McCannon) Tyler's four sons, George Albert Tyler was born on December 14, 1889, in Derry, New Hampshire. His father worked in the local shoe shops. All four Tyler boys starred for the local town team, the Derry Athletic Association. Arthur (1887-1932) was in the insurance business and was the only one who didn't play professionally. Fred (1891-1945) was a longtime minor leaguer who joined Lefty on the Braves for the final days of the 1914 season. Bill (1895-1967) followed Lefty as the ace of the Derry Athletic Association and pitched in the low minors.

Lefty Tyler became prominent in local circles by 1906 by pitching for various sandlot teams as well as St. Anselm College in nearby Goffstown, New Hampshire. The following year, Lefty, Arthur, and Fred joined the Derry Athletic Association with Lefty pitching nearly every game, Fred as his batterymate, and Arthur manning third base.

In 1909 Tyler ran off a string of 34 consecutive shutout innings for the Derry Athletic Association, including a 17-strikeout game. Those feats attracted the attention of former major-league pitcher Alexander Ferson, who recommended him to Lowell of the New England League. Tyler made his professional debut with Lowell on July 2, 1909, leaving in the fifth inning with a deficit but escaping with a no-decision. He went on to post a 5-5 record, splitting his time between starting and relieving.

A 19-16 record with fourth-place Lowell in 1910 earned Tyler a late-season look with the cellar-dwelling Boston Nationals, who purchased his contract on August 26, though Tyler initially held out. It was his understanding that Bill Cunningham of the New Bedford club had received part of his sale price to the Washington Senators. Upon hearing of his sale to Boston, Tyler approached Lowell club manager James Gray for a similar deal. Satisfied that Lowell would square up with him, Tyler reported to Boston and made two relief appearances without a decision.

After being named Boston manager for 1911, Fred Tenney learned of Tyler's dissatisfaction (he had received none of the sale money from Lowell). Tenney contacted Lowell on Tyler's behalf. Gray offered $100, while Tyler wanted $200. (His monthly salary had been $125.) When Tyler offered to split the difference, the Lowell club directors met and decided to rescind their offer, claiming that Cunningham had not received any purchase money from New Bedford.

Despite his dissatisfaction over the Lowell matter, Tyler pitched well enough to break spring-training camp with Boston. He was originally slated to be sent to the Southern League for seasoning, but the pitching staff was too thin for him to be farmed out. With Rube Waddell toiling in the minors, Tyler was the only big-league pitcher using the overhand crossfire delivery.

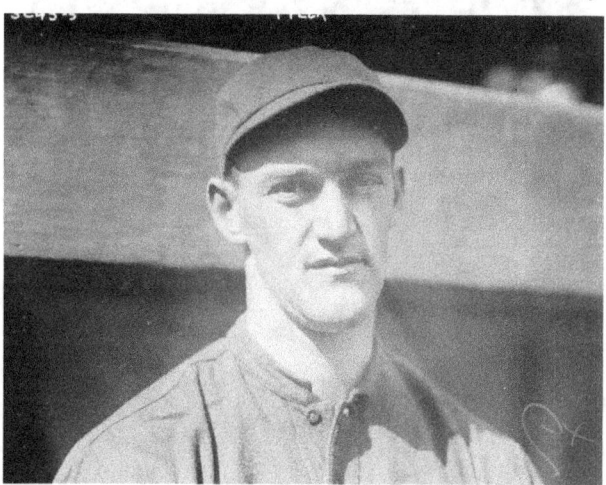

Lefty Tyler

With last-place clubs behind him, Tyler went 7-10 with a 5.06 earned-run average in 1911 and 12-22 with a 4.18 ERA in 1912, leading the majors in losses during the latter season.

Things started to change for Tyler in 1913. Off the field, he married Lillian McCarthy of Lowell on January 29. He also made Lowell his permanent residence and would reside there for the remaining 40 years of his life. On the field, he led the National League with 28 complete games while lowering his ERA to 2.79 and posting a 16-17 record for new Braves manager George Stallings.

Tyler went 16-13 with a 2.69 ERA during the great 1914 season, putting together a string of 23 consecutive shutout innings during the second-half stretch run. In the final week, his brother Fred was recalled from Jersey City. Many sources erroneously include the Tylers on lists of major-league brother batteries; Lefty's final regular-season appearance came on October 2, but Fred didn't make his major-league debut until the following day. To rest catchers Hank Gowdy and Bert Whaling for the World Series, Stallings had Fred Tyler catch both games of three consecutive season-ending doubleheaders, the full extent of his major-league career. Lefty started Game Three of the World Series sweep. He was lifted in the bottom of the tenth inning for a pinch-hitter with his team down 4-3. The Braves tied the game and later won it in the 12th.

Tyler's fine 1916 season of 17-9 with a 2.02 ERA and twice as many strikeouts as walks was sandwiched by seasons of finishing just over .500 with near equal walk/strikeout ratios and ERAs at or above the league average. In 1916 he ended the Giants' record winning streak at 26 when he beat them, 8-3, on September 30.

On January 4, 1918, former Braves coach Fred Mitchell, then managing the Chicago Cubs, acquired Tyler in exchange for second baseman Larry Doyle, catcher Art Wilson, and $15,000. It was a steep price to pay, but Lefty made the trade worthwhile by posting the best season of his career, going 19-8 with a 2.00 ERA. On July 17 he tied the existing National League record by pitching 21 innings to beat the Phillies, 2-1. The war-shortened season likely cost Tyler his only 20-win year, but the Cubs took the pennant.

In the 1918 World Series, Mitchell started only left-handed pitchers (Tyler and Hippo Vaughn each started three games) to keep Babe Ruth out of the Red Sox lineup when he wasn't pitching. Tyler won Game Two, 3-1, on a complete-game six-hitter, helping himself with a two-run single. He left Game Four for a pinch-hitter with the Cubs down 2-0 in the eighth inning. Chicago tied the game but Boston scored in the bottom of the inning and held on for a win. With the Cubs down three games to two, Tyler lost a 2-1 heartbreaker in the deciding sixth game. Both Boston runs were unearned.

Tyler noticed soreness in his shoulder during spring training in 1919. He insisted on pitching through the pain and took a no-hitter into the seventh inning against St. Louis in his first start before finishing with a complete-game, four-hit win. In his next start, on May 2, he beat Pittsburgh, 4-2, but pain forced him from the game. Current rules would not have allowed him to receive the win as he left the game after 4⅓ innings. After this game, Tyler admitted that his arm had not improved. Mitchell rested him until May 16, when he tossed a complete-game five-hitter in a losing cause against the Giants. He appeared four days later in relief but couldn't complete the inning. After a month's rest, Tyler allowed six hits and three walks in a complete-game 2-0 loss

Tyler won 16 games for the 1914 Braves.

to Cincinnati on June 24. He started on June 28, but left the game after allowing a hit and a walk. It was his last appearance of the 1919 season.

Tyler was diagnosed with neuritis and it was believed he was finished as a pitcher. Hopeful that his career could be saved, the Cubs sent the 29-year-old to the Mayo Clinic in Rochester, Minnesota, for a thorough examination. He was declared to be in perfect health except for very bad teeth. All but three teeth were extracted, and Tyler rested up for the 1920 season.

Returning to the Cubs in 1920, Tyler posted an 11-12 record and was released the next season after going 3-2 in ten games. He finished the 1921 season pitching eight games with Rochester of the International League, going 4-1 but with a 5.01 ERA. The Braves signed Tyler in February 1922, but he never pitched again in the majors. He played for various semipro clubs before becoming player-manager of Lawrence of the New England League in 1926; he was 3-3 in eight games as a pitcher and batted .280 in 72 games as a first baseman as Lawrence finished in fifth place in the eight-team league.

After his playing days, Tyler umpired from 1928 to 1930 in the New England League and in 1931 and '32 in the Eastern League. He worked for the New England Power Company for a time, then as a shoe cutter in the mills around Lowell.

Tyler was greatly affected the remainder of his life by the death of older brother Arthur, whose body was found the morning of December 2, 1932. Arthur had driven his vehicle onto the Derry Athletic Association ball field during the night and shot himself. Tyler suffered another setback when he received notice in October 1943 that his son, George A. Tyler, Jr., a Flying Fortress pilot, was shot down and imprisoned in a German POW camp. This incident had a happy ending when the younger Tyler was released after several months in captivity.

Tyler died suddenly at his home of a heart attack on September 29, 1953—exactly 39 years from the day that the Miracle Braves clinched the pennant. He left two children, George Jr. and his daughter, Jean. He is buried in Lowell's St. Patrick Cemetery.

Note: A previous version of this biography appeared in Tom Simon, ed., Deadball Stars of the National League *(Washington, D.C.: Brassey's, Inc., 2004).*

Sources

For this biography, the author used a number of contemporary sources, especially those found in the subject's player file at the National Baseball Hall of Fame Library. Among the sources consulted were:

Derry News, various articles 1906-33

Lowell Sun, various articles 1943-53

Manchester Union-Leader, various articles 1910-21

Derry Public Library—baseball folder in vertical file

Notes from the Tom Shea collection, courtesy of Dick Thompson.

John Frisbee, director of the New Hampshire Historical Society, Concord, New Hampshire, 1990.

George A. Tyler (grandnephew of Lefty Tyler), telephone conversation, 2003

Bert Whaling

By Charles F. Faber

Bert Whaling, a slick-fielding catcher, began the 1914 season as the Boston Braves' number one catcher, but lost the job to Hank Gowdy because of his weak hitting. Relegated to second-string status, Whaling still led the league in throwing out would-be base stealers.

Albert James Whaling was born in Los Angeles on June 22, 1888, the youngest of nine children born to Canadian immigrants Charles and Catherine (McCarthy) Whaling. Charles worked variously as a farmer, laborer, night watchman, and as a Los Angeles city policeman and special officer.

As a teenager, young Whaling starred on the Los Angeles area sandlots. He started his professional career with Portland of the Pacific Coast League in 1908. The 20-year-old catcher hit only .145 in 71 games for the Beavers and was unable to stick with the club. He started the 1909 season with the Salt Lake Mormons of the Inter-Mountain League. In mid-July the team relocated to Livingston, Montana, but the league soon disbanded, and hitting and fielding statistics are not available. After the demise of the Inter-Mountain League Whaling caught on with the Seattle Turks of Class B Northwestern League and played in 11 games, again hitting well below .200 at .158. At the end of the season he returned to Los Angeles and played for the Maier's club in the semipro California Winter League, where one of his teammates was his brother Bob, the first baseman. Bob and Bert were teammates at least once more in the winter league, playing for Vernon in 1911. Altogether Bert played in that circuit in at least seven seasons between 1908 and 1925.

Whaling apparently was out of Organized Baseball in 1910 and the early part of 1911, but he played somewhere in Montana, probably for semipro teams in Hamilton and Anaconda or Butte. A dispatch from Hamilton to the *Anaconda Standard* dated August 12, 1911, stated: "Mr. and Mrs. Bert Whaling left here Saturday morning for Seattle where Mr. Whaling will play with the Seattle club in the Northwestern League."[1] On March 31, 1912, the same newspaper carried an article about Bob Whaling reporting to the Butte club: "Whaling, the first base aspirant, is a brother of Bert Whaling, who played with the Hamilton club last year, later getting to go to the Cleveland Americans via Seattle. If he can live up to the name with club as the catching gentleman used to do, he will be good news to many a game."[2]

Whaling did not get into any games with Cleveland, and was sent to Seattle, where he appeared in 29 games and hit .265 toward the end of the 1911 season. In March 1912 he went to the Naps' training camp in Mobile, but was released in April. He returned to Seattle and started the season as the regular catcher for the Giants, as the former Turks were now called. He played in 138 games, the most he ever played in one season, and hit a respectable .264. On June 24, 1912, Whaling's contract was purchased by the Boston Braves, but he finished the season with Seattle.

Whaling made his major-league debut on April 22, 1913, as the Braves were losing a home game to the Brooklyn Dodgers, 5-3.

Bert Whaling

During the game he relieved starting catcher Bill Rariden and went hitless in one time at bat against Cliff Curtis. Whaling was used sparingly early in the season and did not collect his first hit until May 1, when he singled off Eddie Stack in a 4-2 loss at Brooklyn. For the remainder of the season he split catching duties with Rariden. Whaling appeared in 79 games, 77 of them as catcher, fielded .990, and became the first rookie catcher in major-league history to lead his league in fielding percentage. At 6 feet and 185 pounds, the 25-year-old backstop was rather stockily built and slow afoot, but he excelled at throwing out baserunners with his strong right arm.

In 1914 Whaling inherited the starting role because Rariden had jumped to the Federal League. However, he failed to hit well enough to keep the job, and Hank Gowdy, back up from the Buffalo Bisons of the International League, was promoted to the starting position. Whaling hit only .209 in 60 games as the second-string catcher. Despite leading the league in throwing out would-be base stealers, he spent more and more time on the bench as the season progressed. Unfortunately for him, he never got into a single game in the World Series as the Miracle Braves swept the Philadelphia Athletics.

Although Whaling's size would be barely average, if that, among modern players, he was hefty enough to earn the nickname Moose during his playing career. Among all the position players on the Braves 1914 roster, only Clarence "Big Boy" Kraft, who appeared in a mere three games in his entire major-league career, and burly first baseman Butch Schmidt packed more weight than Whaling. His powerful build earned him some notoriety in 1914, as evidenced by this account by Tom Meany: "Rabbit Maranville, the midget with the arms and shoulders of a weight-lifter, flattened Heinie Zimmerman during a ruckus with the Cubs but for years afterward der Zim refused to believe that the Rab had cooled him off. He always insisted that the coup de grace had been administered by one of the larger Braves, Butch Schmidt or Moose Whaling, a reserve catcher. He just couldn't see himself kayoed by the little tyke."[3]

In 1915 Whaling was again the backup to Gowdy, playing in 72 games. He made his final major-league appearance on October 7, going 1-for-3 in a 15-8 loss to the New York Giants on the last day of the season. During his three years in the majors Whaling had played in 211 games, hitting for an average of .225, with an on-base percentage of .283 and a .276 slugging average. He hit no home runs. He partly compensated for his deficiencies at the plate by twice leading the league in a fielding category, but fielding prowess was not enough to keep him in the majors. A week after his final big-league game, Whaling was traded, along with outfielder Herbie Moran, to the Vernon Tigers of the Pacific Coast League for outfielder Joe Wilhoit. Not wanting to return to the minors, Whaling considered joining the Federal League, before reluctantly agreeing to play for the Tigers. That was a wise decision, as the Federal League went out of business before the start of the 1916 season.

In December 1915 a bizarre incident almost cost Whaling his life. He had gone with some friends to China Rock, just south of Redondo Beach, and he'd tried to pry an abalone off the rocks with his bare hands. When the waves receded, he found his hand had been stuck and held fast, pinned to the rock. The others were out of hearing, but finally found him. A newspaper account said, "Whaling had to be resuscitated with stimulants, as the waves had beaten him until his strength was gone."[4]

Whaling hit only .200 for Vernon in 70 games in 1916, and dropped out of Organized Baseball for three years. When he registered for the draft in Bisbee, Arizona, on June 5, 1917, after the US entered the World War, he reported his occupation as copper miner for the Phelps Dodge Corporation. (He may not have actually done much mining, but probably was on the company's payroll so he could play for its semipro baseball club.) He joined the Navy, attaining the rating of steamfitter second-class. In August 1918 a Service League was formed in the Los Angeles area, and Whaling was appointed manager of the Submarine Base club. After his return to civilian life, he traveled around the minor leagues, playing for six teams in seven years in such

In 1914, Whaling appeared in 60 games for the Braves.

places as Regina, Beaumont, Edmonton, Denver, Des Moines, and Salt Lake City.

In 1926 Whaling started the season as a catcher and acting manager of the Salt Lake City club of the Utah-Idaho League. He was expected to manage only until Billy Orr could get his root-beer business in Peoria straightened out, but the manager decided he could not leave Illinois and resigned on May 20. Salt Lake owner George O. Relft removed the term "acting" from Whaling's title. The Bees did not fare well under Whaling's leadership, and he was replaced as manager of the last place club in midseason by Chet Chadbourne. Whaling could have continued as a catcher, but chose to end his playing career in an encounter with Ogden on July 2, 1926. At the age of 38, he made his final game as a player in Organized Baseball a memorable one, collecting three hits and throwing out the only two men who attempted to steal second base. In the 37 games he played for Salt Lake City in 1926, Whaling hit .333, the only time in his professional career that he topped the .300 mark. Previously his highest batting average had been .272, attained in 1923 in the Western League with Denver and Des Moines.

Whaling was more successful in his other managerial experience, as he piloted the Phoenix Senators to the Arizona State League pennant in 1928. The contrast between conditions under which the Senators played and the conditions enjoyed by the present-day Arizona Diamondbacks is striking. The Senators played in Riverside Park, which had a wood frame grandstand and an infield of gravel and sand. Ticket prices were usually 25 cents for general admission and 50 cents for box seats. On Fridays women were admitted free. All games were played during the day, of course, under the blazing Arizona sun, with temperatures frequently soaring well over 100 degrees. Pitchers sometimes changed their flannel uniforms after every inning, hanging one jersey up to dry while wearing another. Travel to road games was by automobile over Arizona's main roads, which were graded and oiled. Baseball gear was strapped to the sides of the cars.

When his baseball career was over, Whaling and his wife, Pansy, returned to the Los Angeles area. Their last known address was in Burbank. They had no children. For some time Bert worked in the motion-picture industry as a sound man. Albert James Whaling died at the Sawtelle Veterans Hospital in Los Angeles County on January 21, 1965, at the age of 76. The cause of death was listed as metastatic adenocarcinoma. He was buried in the Los Angeles National Cemetery.

Sources

Charles F. Faber, *Major League Careers Cut Short* (Jefferson, North Carolina: McFarland, 2011)

Filichia, Peter. *Professional Baseball Franchises* (New York: Facts on File, 1993)

www.ancestry.com.

www.baseball-almanac.com.

www.baseball-reference.com.

www.newspaperarchives.com.

www.sabr.org.

www.usfamily.net.

Notes

1 *Anaconda Standard*, August 13, 1911

2 *Anaconda Standard*, March 31, 1912

3 Tom Meany. *Baseball's Greatest Teams* (New York: A.S. Barnes, 1949), 173

4 *Los Angeles Times* , December 10, 1915. China Rock had been named after two Chinese men who lost their lives while pinned to the rocks by abalones.

George "Possum" Whitted

By Craig Hardee

MANY PLAYERS SPEND their entire playing careers hoping for the opportunity to play in a World Series. Some players get to play in one World Series, while even fewer get to play in two World Series.

But Possum Whitted not only played in two World Series, he did it in consecutive years for different teams. In 1914 he was traded in midseason from the St. Louis Cardinals to the Boston Braves, becoming a part of the Miracle team that went from last place on July 4 to first place in early September and then swept the Philadelphia Athletics in four games in the World Series.

Traded again during the offseason to the Philadelphia Phillies, he again played for a pennant-winning club, but the Phillies lost the 1915 World Series to Boston Red Sox in five games.

George Bostic "Possum" Whitted,[1] one of only five major leaguers to have played at least 40 games at every position except pitcher and catcher, was born on February 4, 1890, in Durham, North Carolina, to Julius Monroe Whitted and Ella Frances Howerton Whitted. The 1900 census shows Whitted as one of eight children, while the 1910 census shows him as one of ten children, with six children living. The elder Whitted worked in successive decades as a teller, a bookkeeper, and a public accountant.[2] Whitted's mother apparently never worked outside the home.

There seems to be a difference of opinion on how Whitted got the nickname Possum. One source reported that he picked it up as a boy.[3] Another said he got the nickname because of his tales of possum hunting in the woods around Durham.[4] Either way, it was a nickname that stuck with Whitted throughout his major-league career. (Possum is the colloquial name for opossum, a marsupial found in abundance in the Carolinas.) Whitted also had the nickname Poffin Belly.

He had an interesting childhood, evidenced by a clip from his Hall of Fame Library player file. "He is said to have fallen out of a second story window at the age of six months without injury. He was kicked by a mule and the mule broke his own leg. He did not want to go to school and the school burned down."[5]

Whitted attended Trinity Prep School (now Duke University) for a time, but joined the ranks of professional baseball in 1910, playing first base for the semipro Wadesboro Independents. As he told sportswriter J.C. Kofoed for an article in *Baseball Magazine*, "I had a very successful season with that club in 1910. ... But I wanted a bigger game. When our season ended I traveled down to Savannah and induced the manager of the South Atlantic team there to give me a try-out. Eight games in the outfield was the extent of my apprenticeship with Savannah. Because I failed to hit hard from the start I was released, but Jacksonville signed me up — probably because of my first base record with Wadesboro. About a dozen men had tried to play the near corner for the Jacks, but I was lucky enough to win the post, and finished the season there."[6]

Between the two South Atlantic League Class C teams, he batted .189 in 21 games, but Jacksonville saw enough talent in him to bring him back in 1911. Whitted told Kofoed, "In 1911 I automatically became the regular incumbent of that position (first base), but I shared in the financial and artistic failure of the league. I batted only .229!"[7]

Jacksonville brought him back in 1912, and Whitted had the breakthrough year that would send him to the majors. He said, "The following season was a reverse in every way. I was shifted from first to third base, and my hitting immediately began to improve."[8]

Whitted batted .307 in 1912 for Jacksonville, which finished first in the league and defeated Columbus in the playoffs. About his year, he said, "I finished the season third in hitting and run getting, first in base running and fielding. The upshot of it was that the St. Louis Nationals bought me, and I received my first taste of big league ball."[9]

In his first taste of major-league experience, at the end of the 1912 season, Whitted batted .261 in 12 games. With three doubles and seven RBIs in that limited playing time, it's easy to assume that the Cardinals expected great things from Whitted in the future. But it would not happen with the Cardinals. In 1913, Whitted batted only .220 in 123 games, and at the start of 1914 his hitting dipped to .129 in 20 games.

Asked whether the change from Class C to the majors was great, Whitted said, "Great? I should say so. The Cardinals were demoralized, and I was shifted from one position to another, playing third base, shortstop and the outfield. My hitting was not what it should be, and at the beginning of 1914, though it improved, it did not suit Miller Huggins, and he traded Teddy Cather and I to the Braves."[10] The trade to the Boston Braves came on July 4, 1914, a day pinpointed as the time the Braves began to lay claim to the nickname Miracle Braves by beginning their improbable rise from last place to winning the National League pennant going away.

Whitted's hitting did improve with the Braves; he batted .261 with 31 RBIs and his first two major-league home runs in 66 games. His versatility in the field was also very useful to the Braves. Sportswriter Harold Kaese wrote, "Whenever Evers was hurt and unable to play, either Oscar Dugey … or Whitted substituted for him at second base."[11] Whitted played every position for the 1914 Braves except pitcher and catcher.

One of the factors in the Braves' turnaround was manager George Stallings' platooning of his outfielders depending on whether the Braves pitcher was left-handed or right-handed. This was not the first time platooning was employed, but it was still a rather novel concept in 1914. Whitted alternated with left-hander Larry Gilbert in center field.

Whitted played in every inning of the Braves' World Series sweep, batting fourth throughout the Series even though the Athletics started three right-handed pitchers. He was just 3-for-14, but one of his hits was a two-run triple in Game One.

After playing a key role in the Braves' run to winning the World Series, Whitted may have assumed that he would be with the Braves for years to come. But in December the Braves traded Whitted, infielder Oscar Dugey, and cash to the Philadelphia Phillies for infielder-outfielder Sherry Magee. (Whitted and Dugey went to the Phillies in February 1914.) Manager Stallings was happy to get Magee, a good hitter, but parted with Whitted reluctantly. "… (H)e hated to see Whitted go," Kaese wrote. "He regarded Whitted as a key player on the 1914 Braves, because he could fill in acceptably for Evers at second base, aside from playing a good game in center field."[12]

Whitted's new team won the pennant in 1915, finishing seven games ahead of the Braves. Whitted contributed a steady .281 average in 128 games, mostly playing the outfield with a few games at first base. In the World Series he was just 1-for-15 with one RBI as the Phillies fell to the Boston Red Sox in five games.

Whitted was remarkably consistent with the Phillies, batting .281, .281, and .280 in 1915, 1916, and 1917. Writer F.C. Lane, in a 1919 article, commented, "… (G)ive the first prize of all consistent batting to George Whitted with his batting mark of .281 in 1915, .281 in 1916 and .280 in 1917. We will cheerfully buy a ticket to the bleacher for any big league sticksmith who betters that mark."[13]

Whitted played in 24 games for the Phillies in 1918 before going into the Army. Back from military service in 1919, he rejoined the Phillies and was batting .249 in early August when he was traded to the Pittsburgh Pirates for outfielder Casey Stengel. Whitted enjoyed one of the best stretches of his career with the Pirates, batting .389 in 35 games in the final seven weeks of the season. He played two more seasons with the Pirates, batting .261 in 1920 and .283 in 1921. He played third base almost full-time in 1920 and was back in the outfield in 1921.

In 1921, the Pirates came close to winning the pennant, but faded in the stretch. Pirates owner Barney Dreyfuss blamed the loss of the pennant on too much "horseplay," with Whitted being one of the pranksters along with

Possum Whitted

Charlie Grimm, former Brave Rabbit Maranville, and Cotton Tierney joining in. According to sportswriter Fred Lieb, the four formed a singing quartet, with Whitted singing baritone."[14]

Whitted ended his major-league career with one fruitless at-bat for the Brooklyn Robins in 1922 after the Pirates sold him to the Robins in March 1922.

Fred Lieb and Stan Baumgartner, in their history of the Phillies, said of Whitted, "He did not have the natural ability of some of the other stars of the club, but he was fast and how he hustled! In his own way, he was a National League version of Ty Cobb. George would kill you for a run, or dive into a stone wall to make a catch. He hustled from the moment he got on the ball field until he left."[15]

Whitted remained active in baseball until 1937, playing and managing with several minor-league teams, including a stint of six years with his hometown Durham team of the Class C Piedmont League. In 1929 he led Durham team to a first-place finish, but lost in the playoffs. In 1930 Durham finished second but won the playoffs.

Whitted's obituary in *The Sporting News* said he was involved in baseball until 1941, but apparently he was not serving as a player or manager during that time, since there are no records of it.

During World War II, Whitted was the athletic director for the shipyards in Wilmington, North Carolina. After the war, he worked for Wilmington street department, then in the parks and recreation department until he retired. Whitted died on October 15, 1962, of complications after hip surgery. He was 72 and was one of the last surviving members of the Miracle Braves of 1914.

Sources

In addition to the sources noted in this biography, the author also accessed the following sources:

Whitted's player file from the Giamatti Library, National Baseball Hall of Fame.

Retrosheet.org.

Baseball-Reference.com.

BaseballLibrary.com.

BaseballHistorian.com.

Ancestry.com.

Notes

1   See baseball-reference.com.
2   See the 1900, 1910, and 1920 United States census.
3   Possum Whitted entry at www.Baseballlibrary.com.
4   Possum Whitted entry at www.Baseballhistorian.com.
5   Unattributed clipping from Whitted's player file at the National Baseball Hall of Fame Library.
6   J.C. Kofoed, "The Most Improved Player In The Game," *Baseball Magazine*, September 1915, 45.
7   Ibid.
8   Ibid.
9   Ibid.
10 Ibid.
11 Harold Kaese, *The Boston Braves 1871-1953* (Boston: Northeastern University Press, 2004), 151.
12 Kaese, 168.
13 F.C. Lane, "Odd Types of Consistent Batting," *Baseball Magazine*, August 1919, 213.
14 Frederick Lieb, *The Pittsburgh Pirates* (New York: Putnam, 1948), 191.
15 Frederick Lieb and Stan Baumgartner, *The Philadelphia Phillies* (Kent, Ohio: Kent State University Press, 2009), 113.

George Stallings

By Martin Kohout

A DIGNIFIED, FASTIDIOUS Southerner who managed in street clothes and nervously slid up and down the bench so much that he frequently wore out his trousers, George Stallings compiled an 879-898 record and won only one pennant in 13 seasons as a major-league manager, yet that single gonfalon was enough to ensure his undying fame as "The Miracle Man." Indeed, the amazing ascension of his Boston Braves to the 1914 National League flag, followed by their sweep of Connie Mack's heavily favored Philadelphia Athletics in the World Series, still may be the most unlikely triumph in baseball history. The captain of those 1914 Braves, Johnny Evers, wrote that Stallings "will crab and rave on the bench with any of them," yet he also wrote that "Mr. Stallings knows more base ball than any man with whom I have ever come in contact during my connection with the game." He was, wrote Harvey T. Woodruff in the *Chicago Tribune*, "a pitiless and abusive critic while the game is on. When the game is over, he is mingling with his players, among whom he is immensely popular, laughing and jollying them in preparation for the morrow."[1]

The son of William Henry and Elizabeth Virginia (Atwell) Stallings, George Tweedy Stallings was born in Augusta, Georgia, on November 17, 1867 (not on November 10, 1869, as his tombstone says). William Stallings was rather prosperous; the 1870 shows him with real estate valued at the time of $12,000. He served as county treasurer for Richmond County at the time. Ten years later, he was listed as a contractor. He and his wife had five children – all boys – and a servant (a butler) named Sam Jones.

George, the fourth-born of the five Stallings sons, attended Richmond Academy, and it is often reported that he graduated from the Virginia Military Institute in 1886 and attended the College of Physicians and Surgeons in Baltimore. His name doesn't appear on VMI alumni rolls, however, and it is also doubtful that he actually attended medical school. Stallings married Bell White on April 2, 1889, in Jones County, Georgia.

They had two sons before Bell divorced him in 1906. Stallings later married Bertha Thorp Sharpe, the widow of major leaguer Bud Sharpe, with whom he had one son.

If Stallings' reputation depended solely on his playing career, no one would remember him. He made his big-league debut with the NL champion Brooklyn Bridegrooms in 1890, appearing in four games and going hitless in 11 at-bats before receiving his release. Stallings also appeared in three games while managing the Phillies in 1897 and 1898. His entire major-league playing career consisted of two hits in 20 at-bats. Stallings had more success in the minors - an 1897 publication claimed that he "was probably a member of more champion clubs than any other player of the present day." The Phillies discovered him in 1886 while he was catching for an amateur team in Jacksonville, Florida. In need of seasoning, Stallings spent the next four years bouncing around the minors. After his short stint with Brooklyn, he switched to the outfield in 1891 "to give the [San Jose] team the benefit of his speed in the game every day," and in fact he led the California League in stolen bases that year.[2]

Stallings' managerial career began in 1893 when he managed his hometown team, Augusta of the Southern League. During the off-season he also served as the first baseball coach at Mercer College in Macon,

George Stallings

Boston Mayor John "Honey Fitz" Fitzgerald, Lefty Tyler, Bill James, Dick Rudolph, George Stallings before Game Three of the 1914 World Series at Fenway Park.

Georgia, where he was succeeded in 1897 by Cy Young. In 1894 Stallings split the season between Kansas City of the Western League and Nashville, and the following year he managed Nashville to a Southern League pennant. After guiding Detroit of the Western League to fourth place in 1896, he was tapped to take over the Phillies. Stallings' first tenure as a major-league manager gave no hint of future success. The Phillies lurched to a 55-77 record in 1897, finishing tenth in the 12-team NL. In 1898 they got off to an even poorer start (19-27), and Stallings was fired in mid-June.

George returned to the helm in Detroit in 1899 and was still managing there in 1901, after the Western League had renamed itself the American League and declared itself a major league. The Tigers finished that first big-league season third, with a 74-61 record, but Stallings ran afoul of AL president Ban Johnson, who claimed that the manager had tried to sabotage the new circuit by selling the Tigers to NL interests. Stallings later insisted that he couldn't have sold the Tigers even if he'd wanted to, because Johnson himself owned 51 percent of the club's stock. Nevertheless, he didn't return to Detroit. Stallings managed Buffalo of the International League from 1902 through 1906, and Newark in 1908. (He was out of baseball in 1907, tending to the peach crops and cattle he raised on his plantation, the Meadows, in Haddock, Georgia, just outside Macon.)

In 1909 Frank Farrell asked Stallings to take over his troubled New York Highlanders, who had staggered home dead last during a dissension-torn 1908 season. Under Stallings the Highlanders improved to 74-77 in 1909. They were playing even better in September 1910 when Highlanders star Hal Chase, with an assist from Ban Johnson, convinced Farrell to fire Stallings and install Chase as manager. The club was 78-59 (.569) at the time. The Highlanders won ten of their last 14 games under Chase to finish second, but they fell back to sixth in 1911 and Chase was relieved of command.

Stallings spent 1911 and 1912 back in Buffalo before James Gaffney summoned him to replace Johnny Kling as skipper in Boston. George took over the bedraggled Braves after the team had posted four straight last-place finishes. His first glimpse of his new charges wasn't encouraging: "I have never seen any club in the big leagues look quite so bad," he later recalled. Managing the 1913 Braves, which led the NL with 273 errors, must have been a trying experience for a man who "could fly into a schizophrenic rage at the drop of a pop fly," yet the team won 17 more games than it had in 1912 and rose to fifth place.[3]

No one expected the Braves to finish in the first division in 1914. Sure enough, Boston was in last place on July 15, though only 11 1/2 games behind the league-leading Giants. From that point on, however, the Braves proceeded to win 52 of their last 66 games and finished the season with a 94-59 record, 10 1/2 games ahead of New York. Stallings was profoundly superstitious - if his team mounted a rally he would freeze in position until the rally ended - and it's fun to imagine what his antics must have been like during the Braves' incredible run. Once, or so the story goes, he happened to be leaning over to pick up a pebble when the Braves started a rally; after it was over, he was so stiff he had to be helped off the field. Stallings also abhorred peanut shells and pieces of paper on the field, much to the delight of mischievous opponents.

Certainly the stalwart pitching of Bill James, Dick Rudolph, and Lefty Tyler, and the solid play of the veteran Evers and young Rabbit Maranville, had more to do with accomplishing the "miracle" than the 46-year-old manager's silly superstitions, but many of his players freely attributed their success to his guidance. Stallings is credited with pioneering the use of platoons to maximize the Braves' feeble offense (only one regular topped .300, and no Boston outfielder accumulated even 400 at-bats), but his ability to persuade his players that they were winners was probably more important than his strategic decisions.

Following the remarkable 1914 season, Stallings managed the Braves to second place in 1915 and third in 1916. Beginning in 1917, however, the team finished in sixth or seventh for each of the next four seasons, and their record got worse each year. Stallings resigned after the 1920 season. He guided Rochester of the International League from 1921 until he resigned in July 1927.

Stallings signed on to manage the Montreal Royals in 1928 but spent much of the year hospitalized for heart disease in Macon and Atlanta. When a doctor asked him if he knew why his heart was so bad, he supposedly replied, "Bases on balls, you son of a bitch, bases on balls."[4] George Stallings died at home in Haddock, Georgia, on May 13, 1929, and is buried in Macon's Riverside Cemetery.

Note: A previous version of this biography appeared in Tom Simon, ed., Deadball Stars of the National League *(Washington, D.C.: Brassey's, Inc., 2004).*

Thanks to David Fleitz.

Sources

Alexander, Charles C. *John McGraw* (New York: Viking, 1988).

Brandt, William E. "The Breaks." *Saturday Evening Post,* July 19, 1930.

Evans, Billy. "The Baseball Hero of 1915?" *Harper's Weekly,* March 6, 1915.

Evans, Billy. "The Braves in War Paint." *Harper's Weekly,* September 5, 1914.

Frommer, Harvey. *Baseball's Greatest Managers* (New York: Franklin Watts, 1985).

James, Bill. *The Bill James Historical Baseball Abstract* (New York: Villard, 1986).

Kohout, Martin. *Hal Chase: The Defiant Life and Turbulent Times of Baseball's Biggest Crook* (Jefferson NC: McFarland and Co., 2001).

Lieb, Fred. *Baseball As I Have Known It* (New York: Coward, McCann and Geoghan, 1977).

Lieb, Frederick G. *Connie Mack: Grand Old Man of Baseball* (New York: G. P. Putnam's Sons, 1945).

Maranville, Walter "Rabbit". *Run, Rabbit, Run: The Hilarious and Mostly True Tales of Rabbit Maranville.* (Society for American Baseball Research, 1991). Reprinted 2012.

Ritter, Lawrence S. *The Glory of Their Times: The Story of the Early Days of Baseball Told by the Men Who Played It* (New York: Vintage, 1985).

Schoor, Gene. *The History of the World Series: The Complete Chronology of America's Greatest Sports Tradition* (New York: William Morrow, 1960).

Stallings, George T. "The Miracle Man's Own Story." *Collier's.* November 28, 1914.

Notes

1. *Chicago Tribune,* September 6, 1914.
2. *Chicago Tribune,* September 6, 1914.
3. Tom Meany, "The Miracle Man," *Baseball Digest,* July 1949, 71. This article was an excerpt from Meany's book, *Baseball's Greatest Teams* (New York: A.S. Barnes, 1949).
4. Jonathan Weeks, *Baseball's Most Notorious Personalities: A Gallery of Rogues* (Lanham, MD: Scarecrow Press, 2013), 113.

Fred Mitchell

By Bill Nowlin

A LIFE IN baseball is how one might best describe the life of Fred Mitchell. He pitched in the very first game ever played by the Boston Red Sox franchise (an exhibition game in Charlottesville, Virginia), and 18 years later managed the Chicago Cubs against the Red Sox in the 1918 World Series. His major-league playing career ran from 1901 to 1913; he appeared as a pitcher in 97 games and recorded a 31-49 record with a 4.10 earned run average. At the plate, he was a .210 hitter in 572 at-bats spread across 201 games. At one time or another, he played every infield position, the outfield, and even caught 62 games for the New York Highlanders in 1910. He was one of the few who played for the Red Sox, the Boston Braves, and the Yankees (albeit while the teams were known as the Americans, Braves, and Highlanders.)

Mitchell managed the Cubs for four years (1917-1920) and the Braves for the three succeeding years (1921-1923), then resumed work as baseball coach at Harvard, for which he worked until he retired in 1939. He was the manager of Harvard's team from 1926-1938.

He was born in Cambridge, Massachusetts, as Frederick Francis Yapp. Fred's granddaughter Lisa Mitchell says her great-grandmother Elizabeth's maiden name was Mitchell and Fred used the name professionally simply to make life easier. "The family tombstone in Stow (Massachusetts) is still under Yapp."[1] It's understandable that one might prefer to dodge the sort of catcalls that might come one's way with the surname Yapp—with "yap" being a slang word for mouth, we can imagine all the taunts and ribbing: "Shut your big yap" and the like. An article in the *Chicago Daily Tribune* said it was Boston Americans manager Jimmy Collins who urged Mitchell to change his name because he feared that the ribbing of the fans could drive him out of baseball.[2] His birth date is listed in the baseball record books as June 5, 1878.

Fred changed both his first and last names legally on August 20, 1943—from Frederick to Fred and from Yapp to Mitchell. The same document his daughter Dorothy still has also changed the surname for her mother Mabel, and that of her brother Fred and herself. The third child in the family was already married and had assumed her husband's name, so she was not included.[3]

Fred's parents were Charles Yapp, listed in the 1880 Census as a groom in Cambridge, aged 28, having been born in England and becoming a U.S. citizen in 1871. His wife, Elizabeth, 25, was "keeping house," with three young children: William, who was 4 years old at the time, Emma (age 2), and Frederick (age 7 months). All three children are listed as born in Massachusetts. Regarding the child named Emma that is listed in the census record, the family is convinced that there was no daughter named Emma. Fred's daughter has the family Bible and a number of family records, and there is no indication, nor does she recall any mention of anyone named Emma. There was a later daughter named Mabel, who was born in October 1880. It must be noted that census information is notably unreliable; but showing Fred as seven months old could fit with his reported June 5, 1878, birthdate, if the census takers began collecting information in early 1879. The 1900 Census had Fred as born in 1887, clearly wrong—or he would have made his major-league debut at the age of 13.

Elizabeth had been born in Ireland (according to the 1880 Census) or England (as was stated in the 1900 Census). She became a naturalized American citizen in 1872. Fred was the middle of three children, his daughter Dorothy says, born between William and a sister named Mabel. Furthermore, she adds, "I'm pretty sure my grandmother and grandfather (Yapp) were not citizens of the U.S., though the census may have said so. I remember in World War II some kind of official documents had to be obtained for anybody who was not a citizen, and Grandma had to obtain one. (Grandpa was dead.)"[4]

The 1879 Cambridge city directory showed Charles Yapp as a "hostler" at the Massachusetts stables at 90 Washington, two half-blocks from this author's current residence. In 1880, the family lived at 137 North Harvard Street.

Twenty years later, when Fred was just a year away from becoming a professional baseball player for the Boston Americans, the 1900 Census had Charles Yapp working as a horse shoer and residing at 9 Appian Way in the Allston section of Boston, on the other side of the Charles River from Cambridge. His two sons were in the same trade, William working as a horse trainer, and Fred as an assistant horse shoer. Charles Yapp was apparently active in competitive horse racing in the Greater Boston area; his name turns up as a driver in trotter racing results from the early 1880s into the mid-1890s, traveling as far as Saratoga, New York, and the state of Maine. One race reported in the *Boston Globe* as late as September 1910 featured two Yapps, perhaps Charley Yapp and his son William. A feature story in the April 21, 1889, *Globe* described Charley as "a thickly-set man, standing about 5 feet 9 inches and weighs about 160 pounds in the sulky. He has the reputation of going through a field as coolly as any man who ever drove a horse and he is not particular as to the chances he takes. He drives to win and has put as many horses to the front in proportion to the number he has handled as any one." Though a profession of some danger, he had never suffered an injury of any kind. Some eight years later, however, Charles seems to have borne financial misfortune, declared insolvent as a racing track lessee and manager.[5]

The family also lived in Lawrence, Massachusetts, for a while. Fred played second base at school there, and a bit of semipro ball. In 1896, Fred's father leased a half-mile racetrack in Concord, New Hampshire, and the Yapps moved there for two years. The lease included a 30-room hotel, complete with bar, and Fred became the "all-round man clerk and bartender." He also played some semipro ball, both in Lawrence (both the *Boston Globe* and the *Harvard Crimson* say that Mitchell played for the 1897 Lawrence club in the New England League as a pitcher) and in Concord, where he pitched for a local man named Al Larsson. Unfortunately, when Charles Yapp staged a race meet at the track, the weather was bad and he "went broke"—he had to forfeit the lease and the family moved back to Boston—to Allston. Fred stayed on to play baseball, but at the end of the month, he wrote his daughter in a 1968 letter, "Larsson jumped town owing the players a month's salary. I was dead broke and hungry." Most of the players went back to their hometowns, but Mitchell met up with the manager of the Plymouth (New Hampshire) Fair, who came to Concord looking for the Larsson team to come play a couple of games at the fair. He had $500 to spend. Mitchell assembled a team from players around Concord, including a high-school catcher and a pitcher named Honey

Fred Mitchell

Annon, to whom he paid $20. "Our uniforms were of all colors, and we were a sight to look at," the letter said. The ragtag bunch was put up at the fair's expense, but they wore their spikes into the hotel and cut up the carpet and scratched the highly-polished floors, almost getting themselves thrown out.[6]

Honey Annon won the first game, and Mitchell won the second. When Fred was paid, the skeptical promoter asked if the mismatched aggregation really was the Larsson team. "There were a few fill-ins," Mitchell admitted. "Well, they looked funny, but they sure could play ball," the man replied. Fred Mitchell's first job as a manager had been a success. More than 20 years later, while Mitchell was managing the Cubs, John McGraw beckoned him into the bar at New York's Imperial Hotel and introduced him to his friend Al Larsson. "I think I've met Mr. Larsson before," Fred said. "He left me stranded in Concord, New Hampshire, and he owes me $150." "That's nothing," McGraw replied. "He left me stranded in Cuba." Larsson blamed the Concord matter on his brother.[7]

After the fair—Mitchell says Annon was the only player he paid—he joined the rest of the family in Allston. His father still had no work, but after a while Fred began to work for Austin's Livery Stable in Melrose, for $15 a week. He slept in the hayloft on a cot, taking care of 16 horses, and washed their buggies and harnesses each night. "I delivered three doctors' horses and buggies before eight o'clock each morning and hitched them to posts in front of each doctor's home." This was another day and time. After three months, Fred quit and moved back home, where his father had borrowed some money and bought a blacksmith shop on Beach Street in Brookline, next to Boston. Fred worked there for a while and played a few semipro games around town to pick up a few dollars from time to time.

As for Fred and baseball, he seems to first turn up in the *Boston Globe* (as Yapp), pitching and hitting cleanup for the Cambridge Athletic Association in a July 1, 1899, game won, 13-10, by the Brighton YMCA. He tripled and homered in the game, but his pitching (dubbed "a heady game," in which he struck out eight and walked one) was undercut by 10 Cambridge errors, six by shortstop Murphy.

There was a younger child in the family by the time of the 1900 Census—Mabel, born in October 1880 and working as an assistant bookkeeper; it appears that William had married a Scotswoman named Agnes and the two of them had a young daughter, Mary, born in 1898.

The book *Red Sox Century,* by Glenn Stout and Dick Johnson, has a photograph said to be of Mitchell with the 1900 Boston Nationals on page 7. But he never played for them that year, and his first appearance in professional baseball was as a member of the Boston Americans in 1901. It was only in 1906 that he had his first taste of minor-league ball, and it was in another country, playing for the Toronto Maple Leafs. Author Johnson surmised that the photograph was probably taken in spring training when Mitchell might have been a candidate for the team, but he didn't make the

Another view of "Mitch".

final cut.[8] Mitchell's daughter and grand-daughter both are firm that the man in the photograph is not Fred Mitchell.

Fred told his daughter how he came to become a member of the very first Boston Americans team. An "old catcher" named Harry Pope caught Fred in Allston, and he'd spent a few summers catching for a team called the Roses in St. John, New Brunswick. In the summer of 1900, he talked Fred into traveling there with him and they took the boat from Boston. "I won most of the games I pitched for the Roses, and attracted the attention of John Graham, the track coach at Harvard, who spent his summer vacation in St. John. He recommended me to Hughie Duffy when we returned to Boston." Hall of Famer Duffy was looking for players to sign up for the new American League team to be founded in Boston, and Duffy's brother-in-law, Mike Moore, signed Mitchell early in 1901 for a $50 advance against a contract of $300 per month. Another player for the Roses, Larry McLean, also signed with the new team, and both were given tickets to Charlottesville, Virginia, for the first spring training.

Charles Yapp had moved his family to the countryside by the 1910 Census. He's listed as a farmer in Stow, Massachusetts. Elizabeth was now, oddly, six years younger than her husband, rather than the three years younger she had been in 1880, and she was now listed as neither from England nor Ireland, but of Scot English heritage (the 1920 Census gives her birthplace as Scotland). Fred, age 32, is listed in 1910 as a "ball player." No others were shown in the home. Mitchell purchased the 93-acre farm in Stow for his parents in 1906, according to a July 8, 1983, article in the *Stow Villager*.

The *Chicago Tribune* article from December 19, 1916, noted that Mitch was playing for the Eastern League's Lawrence team in 1900 when the Americans purchased his contract; there's a problem with this, however: There was no Lawrence team in the Eastern League (or in organized baseball) in 1900. There had been a team in Lawrence in 1899, managed by Tim Murnane. Mitchell probably played for Lawrence in 1899 and then St. John in 1900.

The first practice of the new American League Boston franchise was held on April 1, 1901, on the grounds of the Charlottesville YMCA, the very afternoon of the day when Collins and Chick Stahl arrived in town. There were 12 players in all, Cy Young being given permission to get into shape at home. Games were planned for the weekend against the University of Virginia and other colleges in the area. By his own assessment, Mitchell wrote, "I was a little wild, but fast, and had a good curve ball. One of the older players started to rave about me to Mgr. Collins. 'Jimmy,' he said, 'this kid has got it!' Collins picked up a bat and came up to the plate. I blew a few fast ones past him and he called me over to him and said, 'Young fellow, you can work with the older pitchers from now on, and if you want a rubdown, you go up to the trainer of the University of Virginia and he'll take care of you.' I was a pretty happy kid that night. I knew I had made the Club!"[9]

The first exhibition game the Boston Americans ever played took place on the road, on April 5, 1901. The *Washington Post*'s account of the game said that all four of the Virginia team's hits were made off Kane, and that both Mitchell and Connor held them hitless, though Mitchell walked one and hit another batter. "Mitchell showed the most speed," said the *Globe*. He also showed some speed as the experienced horseman he was. Several of the players rented horses on a Sunday to ride up to visit Thomas Jefferson's home, near Charlottesville. "I thought I'd have a little fun. I put my horse into a fast trot, then a gallop, and the other horses started to follow me. You never saw such bouncing in your life. They were hanging on for dear life and hollering at me to pull up. I pulled up after a bit and most of the boys got off the horses and walked back leading their horses. Some of them couldn't walk naturally for two or three days."[10]

On April 26, it was Win Kellum who had the honor of pitching the first regular-season game for the franchise. Win lost, 10-6, to Baltimore—the franchise that moved to New York in 1903 and eventually became the Yankees. The next day, Mitchell saw some duty. Cy Young started the game, but was both wild and hittable. Boston was down 11-3 after six innings, and Collins called in Mitchell to finish the game. Baltimore manager John McGraw was coaching on the sidelines and tried to rattle Mitchell by calling out the names of each of the great hitters as they came to bat. It didn't work; he allowed just two hits and one run, and collected a hit himself in his first major-league at-bat. He struck out his second time up. The final score was 12-6.[11]

Mitchell's first start was in Chicago on June 1, and the White Sox scored five runs in the bottom of the first, the biggest blow a bases-clearing triple that followed a single, a walk, a hit batsman, and two errors. From that point on, Mitchell shut them down, allowing just one hit in the eighth and one in the ninth, while Boston rang up 10 runs in all. He later recounted that first day to the *Chicago Tribune*: "I was scared stiff and the first inning was awful. I was shaking with stage fright and walked two or three guys and then someone swatted one. Freddie Parent chose that time to kick a couple of grounders." Down 5-0, Mitchell was pleased to be picked up by a teammate. "There was one fellow on the club at that time who was my friend, and that was Buck Freeman. He came in from right field after the inning and I remember just what he said to Jimmy Collins. 'You're not going to take the kid out, are you, Jim?' 'Not on your life,' answered Jim. I went back and had my head with me from then on and stopped the White Sox." Mitchell went on to describe the two-run homer Freeman hit in the fourth inning and the three-run homer he hit in the eighth.[12] Mitchell (and Buck and the Boston bats) won the game, 10-5.

Mitchell won his second start as well, 7-4, in Milwaukee. His first start at the team's home field, the Huntington Avenue Grounds on June 17, saw him win the first game of a doubleheader from the White Sox, 11-1 (allowing five hits, with his "slow curves" noted in the papers) while Cy Young won the afternoon game, 10-4. The one run was unearned, due to an error by Buck Freeman.

It wasn't all good; Mitchell was pounded by Cleveland on the 24th, defeated 7-1. He was ineffective in a relief stint in July, though he'd handily beaten Baltimore on Independence Day. A couple of times he was banged out of the box early, leaving in the first inning on July 27. As the year wore on, there seemed to be more times he faltered; he wound up his first year with a 6-6 record and a 3.81 earned run average, the fourth pitcher on the team behind Cy Young (33-10, 1.62 ERA), George Winter (16-12, 2.80), and Ted Lewis (16-17, 3.53). His batting average was .159 (7-for-44, with two triples). In a postseason benefit game in Boston against the White Sox, Mitchell gamely played second base, but committed five errors. The following day, he pitched and lost in Lynn against a picked team but it was no hard-fought game; Cy Young played in right field with the aid of a bicycle. Mitchell played right field in another exhibition game, against Greenfield, and pitched and lost a 4-3 game against players from Franklin and Marlboro on October 5. (All these teams were from Massachusetts.)

Fred Mitchell was back with Boston in 1902, but he was admittedly "green" and the team had quite a few seasoned pitchers. It wasn't clear how much work he would get. He appeared in just one game before he was sent to the Philadelphia Athletics. He'd been used only in spring training and exhibition games (losing to Hoboken, 6-3, on May 11 due to costly errors). His one game for Boston was in the May 30 doubleheader against Detroit, in relief of Pep Deininger, pitching the final four innings and seeing a 5-5 tie become a 10-5 loss. The *Boston Globe* termed the pitching of both men "far below the standard of the suburban league." On June 2, as the team headed out on a road trip, Mitchell was "loaned to Connie Mack of Philadelphia."[13] As Mitchell explained it to his daughter, "Connie Mack had some trouble — losing players over in Philadelphia — and Jimmy Collins, our manager, came to me and said, 'How would you like to go to Philadelphia, over to Connie Mack?' 'Well,' I said, 'If I could get regular work, I'd like to go.'" Mack secured Rube Waddell from the Giants, and picked up some other people. "We got together and won the pennant!"[14] Waddell and Mitchell roomed together.

Had there been a World Series in 1902, Mitchell might have played in it, though Rube Waddell, Eddie Plank, and Bert Husting would have been the starters. The Athletics won the AL pennant (Boston finished third), and Mitchell was 5-7, with a 3.59 ERA. As with Boston, he walked far more men than he struck out. Despite winning the pennant, there was no one to play—it was only in 1903 that the first World Series was played—and in 1903, Mitchell was playing for the Philadelphia Phillies. Retrosheet says that before the season began he "jumped from the Philadelphia Athletics to the Philadelphia Phillies." That's the same word Mitchell used in his 1968 interview. He said he'd gone to Mack's office at the start of 1903 and asked for a raise. Mack turned him down flat. (Mitchell had been 5-8 with a 3.59 ERA; there were at least four A's pitchers much better than he.) Mitchell told Mack that since he didn't have a contract, "I'm going to shift for myself. … I'm going to jump."[15] The two Philadelphia teams met in the preseason spring series and Mitchell shut down the Athletics in the first game (1-0 against Eddie Plank) and the fourth (2-0 against Waddell.)

He won his first two starts in the regular season—against the Boston Nationals (Beaneaters) on Patriots Day, and shutting out the Brooklyn Superbas on April 24. It was a year in which he won 11 games for the seventh-place Phils, but he lost 17 games. Nonetheless, Mitchell took advantage of the time, he told his daughter: "I commenced to learn something about pitching." No Phillies starter won more than 13. He hurt his arm in 1904 and his 4-7 showing wasn't impressive enough to warrant keeping him, so a deal was made to send him to Brooklyn later in the year, where he won two and lost five. His arm was still bad, and in 1905, Mitchell was 3-7 for Brooklyn. Thus ended his major-league pitching career. Fred had filled in as a position player in 12 games in 1904—nine of them at first base. He played a smattering of games in the infield in '05, too, before being cut loose in late August. In his obituary, the *Boston Herald* cited a "chronic arm ailment" as ending his 1905 season. He next turned up in the major leagues as a catcher, for the New York Highlanders in 1910.

The 5-foot-10, 185-pound right-hander was signed by manager Ed Barrow of the Eastern League (Class A) Toronto Maple Leafs, and pitched three seasons there, from 1906 through 1908. Earned run averages weren't computed in the league at the time, but existing stats do show his most active season of all (239 innings) in 1906, under Barrow, and an 11-15 record for a last-place team. He was one of four Toronto pitchers to record 11 or more wins. In 1907, he was 6-3 in an even 100 innings of work. He was able to get in more work in 1908, throwing 166 innings with a 6-10 mark, including a no-hitter against Montreal. In the three years, his WHIP (walks and hits per inning pitched) was a very respectable 1.152. If all the runs he allowed were earned runs, which they surely were not, he'd have posted an ERA of around 3.50. The actual figure would have been substantially lower.

In 1909, none of the major-league clubs had picked Mitchell up and even though his arm seemed to be better, he still couldn't snap off an effective curveball. He decided he'd become a catcher, and told the Toronto manager, Joe Kelley, "I'm going to be a catcher or else I'm going home."[16] He was talked into sticking around, and when two of the Toronto catchers got hurt, Mitchell moved from throwing to receiving. He appeared in 109 games for the Maple Leafs as the team's first-string catcher. He came through at the plate as well, batting .295. He'd earned himself a promotion back into the American League, and caught for New York in 1910, signed in January and joining the team for spring training in Athens, Georgia, under manager George Stallings. He appeared in 68 games, almost precisely splitting playing time with Jeff Sweeney, who had 19 more at-bats. Mitchell's .230 was better than Sweeney's .200 but it was Sweeney who stuck with the Highlanders and Mitchell whose playing career was finished (save for four plate appearances with the Boston Braves in 1913—in which he singled once, executed a sacrifice, and struck out twice.) A third catcher on the 1910 New York team was Mitchell's former teammate with Boston in 1901 and 1902, Lou Criger.

Mitchell played in the postseason for the Highlanders as they fell in a city series against the Giants, Mitchell catching right to the very last game of the year. On January 3, 1911, the Highlanders sold Mitchell to Rochester in the Eastern League. He was one of three players sent to Rochester, apparently as — in effect — players to be named later in a deal that allowed New York to bring up catcher Walter Blair late in 1910. There's a story behind the sale. Mitch and Lou Criger had become suspicious that Hal Chase was throwing games ("he was a little on the crooked side"). Stallings said he wouldn't manage the team as long as Chase was on it. New York owner Farrell fired Stallings and made Chase manager! Chase heard that Mitchell had accused him in a meeting with Farrell and sold him and Jimmy Austin, and fired Criger.

Stallings had been fired in mid-September 1910, and spent 1911 and 1912 managing in Buffalo. Mitchell rejoined Stallings in Buffalo after the 1911 season (he'd hit .292 for the Rochester Bronchos in 1911.) It's a little difficult to pin down some of Mitchell's moves, but a March 19, 1912, item in the *Hartford Courant* reports that he has "been in charge of the Buffalo teams in the absence of Manager Stallings." Mitchell hit .232 for the Double-A Bisons. Stallings became manager of the Boston Braves in 1913 and acquired Mitchell ("the stocky Buffalo catcher") from Buffalo, planning to use him "as instructor and trainer of his young catchers and pitchers."[17] Mitchell even appeared in those four games for the Braves. In 1911, Fred had married Mabel Dorothy Goulding, and she came to stay at the farm on Walcott Street in Stow. In 1915, the couple had their first child, also naming her Mabel.. Her second daughter she then named Dorothy. When the third child turned out to be a boy, he was appropriately named Frederick F. III.

In early 1914, Mitchell — though "of the George Stallings aggregation" — worked coaching the baseball team at the Georgia Military College of Milledgeville.[18] Mitchell was on the Braves roster as a catcher but, the *Washington Post* reported, "he never plays, his duty being to warm up and instruct the young pitchers."[19] In effect, he was the team's pitching coach, in an era which had less formal nomenclature for coaches. These were the "Miracle Braves" of 1914, who had a losing record as late as July 31 (44-45, nine games out of first place) but went on to win the pennant by winning 27 of their last 33 games.

Looking ahead to the World Series, Stallings closed his remarks to newsmen by declaring as one of his most valuable men, "Fred Mitchell, my right eye." A Stallings-bylined article in the *Boston Globe* added, "The fans do not appreciate the work Mitchell is called upon to do. ... He is the hardest worker on the team." He detailed some of Mitchell's instructional work with Paul Strand and George Davis. The three Braves aces (Bill James, 26-7; Dick Rudolph, 26-10; and Lefty Tyler, 16-13), Stallings wrote, "Mitchell, almost single-handed, is responsible for their remarkable showing this year. Mitchell has worked with the catchers with equal care and has made [Hank] Gowdy, once turned back by McGraw, one of the best backstops in the league."[20] Stallings also praised Mitchell's work coaching runners and batters during games. Braves swept the World Series from the purportedly unbeatable Philadelphia Athletics in four games. Sportswriter Frederick Lieb heaped praised on Mitchell, declaring that their success "would not have been possible with the battery coach, Fred Mitchell ... one of the few men who ever played in the majors on both ends of the battery." Lieb agreed with Stallings as to the three Braves pitchers, but quoted Stallings as giving Mitchell credit for George Davis's no-hitter: "The kid never could have done it without 'Mitch' having told him how to pitch to each batter."[21]

That December, Mitchell worked training ballplayers at St. Mark's School, in Southborough, Massachusetts. He also worked as a scout for the Braves, and in mid-February was reported at Dartmouth trying to sign shortstop Fletcher Low. Later in the month, he headed for Macon for spring training, where he took on Braves coaching duties once more and carried through the full 1915 season, even added to the reserve list at the end of the year — though there were some hoops he had to jump through. When rosters had to be cut to 21 men, he had been put on waivers and was dropped from the active roster, working as a "scout" once more. When rosters expanded, he was signed again as a player and resumed coaching at third base. He actually had done some scouting, with Art Nehf perhaps his best signing.

On December 1, 1915, the *Harvard Crimson* reported that Mitchell had been appointed coach of Harvard's baseball team, but would work for the Braves as well, simply turning up later than usual for the Braves. On the 7th, the Braves officially gave him his unconditional release, allowing him to take the position with Harvard.

Working with the Harvard nine saw one early success: On April 10, 1916, the varsity team took on the Boston Red Sox, world champions both in 1915 and again in 1916, in an exhibition game at Fenway Park. Harvard shut out the Red Sox, 1-0, both teams collecting five hits. Eddie Mahan pitched for Harvard. The Crimson posted a 21-3-1 season. Because of the World War, Harvard did not field a team in 1917. When baseball resumed, Mitchell's replacement as Harvard head coach was old friend Hugh Duffy.

Mitchell became acting manager of the Braves in early August, when Stallings was suspended for three days "for words addressed to Umpire Rigler" after the August 2 game. The Braves apparently decided to better lock Mitchell in, and signed him in September to a three-year contract that prevented him from continuing as head coach of the Harvard team, but he took charge of each fall's practice season for the university team. It was a "dual job" that required a little give-and-take from both sides regarding scheduling. Just two months later, word began to circulate that the Chicago Cubs were considering Mitchell as manager to take over from Joe Tinker, assuming that the Braves would let him out of their contract. Stallings said that, despite having worked with him for 10 years, "I would not stand in his way if there is an opportunity for him to better himself, but I will not give him away. He is too valuable a man, and besides, I had to pay the Buffalo club for him when I took over the management of the Braves."[22]

The Cubs may have actually wanted Stallings, but taken Mitchell instead. They traded for him, sending outfielder Joe Kelly and some cash to acquire Mitchell from the Braves, and Cubs owner Charles Weeghman signed him to a two-year contract on December 14, 1916. The next day's *Chicago Tribune* wrote that Weeghman had traveled to New York determined to secure John McGraw, George Stallings, or Fred Mitchell. "If Mitchell is good enough for the Braves, he's good enough for the Cubs," the owner declared (and saved himself a fair amount of money in the process, as Mitchell's salary going into negotiations was reportedly $5,000 compared with $20,000 for either of the other more experienced men. "I know Chicago needs rebuilding," he told the *Tribune*.

That seemed like an understatement at the time. The *Tribune* pointed out that most of the bigger-name players on the team had passed their prime, and that there were only "about half a dozen men of undisputed major league ability."[23] *The Sporting News* correspondent from Boston declared, "Good old Mitchell was handed over to the tender mercies of the bunch of restaurateurs, meat packers, chewing gum makers, and others who own the Cubs. … Mitchell knows what he is up against, but he is reconciled and even hopeful."[24] Within two years, the Cubs won the pennant.

Mitchell got the team off to a strong start in 1917. By May 17, they were 22-9 and Grantland Rice's column in the May 19 *Boston Globe* recalled how instrumental Mitchell had been with the Miracle Braves of 1914. Taking over the Cubs, Rice wrote, "the general dope was that he had tail-end material and faced a famine. He was given a ball club composed in the main of athletes cast adrift, and many of these were injured or dismantled or out of gear." Why were they playing so well? "Mitchell is the type of manager capable of lifting the best from each player's system." The Cubs finished in fifth place, not much different from the year before, but there was a sense that things were getting better rather than the foreboding sense under Tinker that they were sure to get worse.

Weeghman spent some money in the offseason, acquiring Grover Cleveland Alexander and Bill Killefer, and was hunting for a couple of other players as well. As William Wrigley purchased increasingly larger shares of the Cubs, and replaced Weeghman as principal owner, there was more reason for hope.

In 1918, while managing the Cubs, Mitchell may have been the first to employ what is today known as the Williams shift. When first implemented by Cleveland manager Lou Boudreau to defend against left-handed slugger Ted Williams, it was initially known as the Boudreau shift—but giving it Williams's name may have inadvertently harkened back to Mitchell's innovative stacking up of fielders on the right side of the diamond against left-handed hitter Cy Williams in 1918, his first year with the Phillies. Cy had been with the Cubs for the prior six seasons, and Mitchell would have seen him hit all year long in 1917.

The Cubs breezed through the abbreviated 1918 season, finishing up a full 10 1/2 games ahead of the second-place New York Giants. Veteran southpaw Hippo Vaughn had another excellent year, his 22-10 record leading the league in wins. His 1.74 ERA also led the league. Claude Hendrix was another 20-game winner (20-7, 2.78 ERA) and Lefty Tyler was every bit as good (19-8, 2.00). The pitching staff's ERA as a whole was a miserly 2.18, though the Red Sox staff ERA was just 2.31. The Cubs were odds-on favorites going into the September 5 start of the World Series; their team batting average also gave them an edge—.265 to Boston's .249.

Babe Ruth just barely beat Vaughn, 1-0, in the first game, but beat him Ruth did. Tyler gave the Cubs a 3-1 win in Game Two, and the battle was joined. The Red Sox won it in six games, despite Cubs pitchers collectively registering a stupendous 1.04 earned-run average across all six games, holding the Red Sox to a team batting average of .186, and despite outscoring Boston 10-9. It was almost as close a low-scoring season as one could have, and many sportswriters simply ascribed the difference to more of the breaks going Boston's way. Talking privately with his daughter, Mitchell was asked how the Red Sox had been able to beat the Cubs. He said, simply enough, "They had pretty good pitching and they had a little better hitting ballclub than mine, but the games were very close. They could have been turned either way."

Had Grover Cleveland Alexander not been taken off to war early in the 1918 season, he might well have made all the difference. Alexander had won 30 or more games three years in a row for the Phillies. He was traded to the Cubs in December 1917, but pitched in only three games before he was drafted. Mitchell told his daughter that he'd tried hard to buy Rogers Hornsby, too, and secured Wrigley's authority to offer as much as $125,000, but Branch Rickey of the Cardinals somewhat reluctantly turned him down: "We can't make that deal. We'd love to make it, but if we sold Hornsby we might as well toss in the franchise," Rickey said.[25] Mitchell had been the man who spotted shortstop Charlie Hollocher, playing for Portland in the Pacific Coast League. He spotted him through his careful reading of *The Sporting News*, and decided to wire the Portland president to ask how much it would take. "$5,000 and a pitcher" was the reply. Mitchell closed the deal, and Hollocher reported to the Cubs in the spring of 1918, hitting .316 in his first season in big-league baseball.

Mitchell added the position of president of the Cubs to his portfolio in December 1918, and soon hired the man who became his successor: Bill Veeck Sr., whom Mitchell plucked from a position as a sportswriter for the *Chicago American* and installed as business manager of the ballclub, offering more than double the salary the paper had provided. It was, he said, a mistake. He complained to his daughter that when Philip Wrigley promised to split any dividends from the club with both Mitchell and Veeck, the new business manager stopped spending money: "Instead of buying ballplayers, he was standing pat, and my ballclub was getting old." Mitchell asked Veeck one day where the scouting reports were, why he hadn't been seeing them. Veeck had them in his desk drawer. Veeck wasn't involved in baseball operations but had decided on his own that the players being scouted weren't worth investing in. Veeck apparently bad-mouthed Mitchell and worked the board of directors sufficiently against him that Mitchell was out after the 1920 season and Veeck was installed as the new president. In Mitchell's four years at the helm, the Cubs had won 308 games and lost 269, with the one pennant.

As soon as word got out, Mitchell received wires from the Braves, the Yankees, and one from Harry Frazee of the Red Sox. The Yanks wanted him as a coach; no, thanks. He waited on Frazee for two or three days, but the Sox owner was under the weather, and so he took up the offer from owner George Grant of the Braves, joining as field manager from 1921 to 1923, then as business manager after the Braves brought in Dave Bancroft as field manager. Mitchell's tenure was disappointing in terms of results: 168-274. The Braves finished fourth in 1921, with a marginal winning record, but lost an even 100 games in both 1922 and 1923, dead last in '22 and only a step out of the cellar in '23. Right-hander Joe Oeschger was a 20-game winner the first year, but collapsed to become a 21-game loser the second and posted a poor 5-15 record the third. His ERA had plunged, but few on the team performed as well.

After being relieved of his post on the field, Mitchell remained as business manager of the Braves and continued to work as a scout. In the meantime, he was able to work things out with Harvard in January 1924 that he could coach the Harvard batterymen—the pitchers and catchers. On taking an initial three-year position with the college team, he told the *Harvard Crimson*, "I shall be able to put in every afternoon until the middle of April," said Mitchell. "I want all the pitchers and catchers in college—both Freshman and Varsity—to report at the Locker Building this Wednesday. The routine work will begin Thursday."[26] He worked for the Braves in the mornings, and the afternoons at the university.

Mitchell finally resigned from both positions in 1938 to retire to his home in Newton Centre, outside Boston. There were times when the positions conflicted, such as in March 1925, when the Braves called him urgently to their St. Petersburg spring training camp; Mitchell promised Harvard he'd put in more time to make up for the lost time.[27] Harvard was sufficiently satisfied with his work ethic and results, and that December the college appointed him head coach of the team on a three-year contract. He was taking the place of the resigning E.W. Mahan—whom Mitch had coached as a Harvard student back in the spring of 1916.[28] One of his assistants beginning in 1926 was Fred Parent, a teammate from the 1901 and 1902 Boston Americans.

Another former Red Sox player, albeit from the time after Mitchell had left the team and it had adopted the name, was Harold Janvrin, who joined as a coach in 1930. One of the better products of Harvard at the time was Charlie Devens (Class of 1932), who pitched for a while for the Yankees. He told the *Crimson*, "Coach Mitchell's coaching, together with that of Herb Pennock and Cy Perkins of the New York Yankees, have been the chief factor in whatever pitching success I have enjoyed thus far."[29]

Prompting Mitchell's 1938 decision to resign was some of the politics within the athletics department at Harvard. For a while, the college experimented with a "noncoaching system" meant to empower the players more, with Mitchell and the other coaches more in the background. Some felt this placed too much of a burden on the team captain, who was—after all—a student. Among those who feared losing Mitchell was captain Ulysses Lupien of the Class of 1939. Lupien wrote a letter to the *Crimson* in March 1938, reading in part, "We are especially privileged to have a man of Fred Mitchell's character and ability as our coach. We wish to express publicly our respect and confidence in him." Mitchell did resign. Lupien debuted with the Red Sox in September 1940. At Harvard, reports *The Second H Book of Harvard Athletics*, Mitchell oversaw teams compiling a record of 216-134 (with a few ties); Fred Mitchell was inducted into Harvard's Hall of Fame in 1958.

Mitchell continued to live in Greater Boston, and was feted at a number of events and anniversaries over the years. In May 1951, he was among many former players celebrating the 50th anniversary of the Boston Americans. He noted how concerned they had been as to whether the new team would catch on. "We could see both parks from the train," he recalled, as well as how pleased they were that the Americans had outdrawn the Nationals by a huge margin. Remembering some of the deceptions they'd used in the early days, he added, "I yearn for the days when we'd warm up a right-hander in front of the grandstand and then bring out a lefty who had been warming up under the grandstand. That would foul up a batting order."[30] The very next month, Mitchell was back for another ceremony, this one at Braves Field celebrating the 75th anniversary of the National League.

Fred's obituary says he left his two daughters, Mabel L. Bassett of Los Angeles and Dorothy Patti of Needham, and son Fred Mitchell Jr. of Needham. Fred Jr. passed away from cancer in 1998 at age 71, but as of late 2009, Mabel was 94 and Dorothy was 85.

Sources

The sources used for this article are identified within the text. This biography was greatly enriched by the assistance of Fred's granddaughter Lisa Mitchell. The author also consulted Retrosheet.org and Baseball-Reference.com, and Mitchell's player file from the National Baseball Hall of Fame.

Notes

1. E-mail communication July 7, 2009.
2. *Chicago Tribune*, December 15, 1916.
3. E-mail communication from Dorothy Patti, October 27, 2009.
4. E-mail communication from Dorothy Patti, October 26, 2009. Dorothy explains the listing of England as Elizabeth's place of birth as perhaps a minor fib: "The Irish were looked down on in Massachusetts and she didn't want anyone to think she was an Irish Catholic. Her older sister, my Aunt Mary Mitchell, told us this behind Grandma's back. She probably also fibbed about being six years younger than her husband, instead of three."
5. *Boston Globe*, September 10, 1897.
6. There are references in the *Chicago Tribune* of December 15, 1916, and the *Washington Post* of December 19, 1916. A considerable amount of material on Mitchell's early years comes from a letter he wrote his daughter Mabel Mitchell Bassett in 1968, following a lengthy interview she did with him on July 13, 1968.
7. Fred Mitchell 1968 letter to Mabel Mitchell Bassett.
8. Communication from Richard A. Johnson, September 14, 2009.
9. Letter to Mabel Mitchell Bassett, 1968.
10. Letter to Mabel Mitchell Bassett, 1968.
11. Mabel Mitchell Bassett interview with Fred Mitchell, July 13, 1968.
12. *Chicago Tribune*, January 9, 1917.
13. *Boston Globe*, June 3, 1902.
14. Mabel Mitchell Bassett interview with Fred Mitchell, July 13, 1968.
15. Mabel Mitchell Bassett interview with Fred Mitchell, July 13, 1968.
16. Mabel Mitchell Bassett interview with Fred Mitchell, July 13, 1968.
17. *Christian Science Monitor*, February 27, 1913.
18. *Atlanta Constitution*, March 6, 1914.
19. *Washington Post*, August 30, 1914.
20. *Boston Globe*, October 8, 1914.
21. *The Sporting News*, October 6, 1948.
22. *Los Angeles Times*, December 6, 1916.
23. *Chicago Tribune*, December 17, 1916.
24. *The Sporting News*, December 21, 1916.
25. Mabel Mitchell Bassett interview with Fred Mitchell, July 13, 1968.
26. *Harvard Crimson*, January 7, 1924.
27. *Harvard Crimson*, March 6, 1925.
28. *Harvard Crimson*, December 7, 1925.
29. *Harvard Crimson*, November 18, 1933.
30. *The Sporting News*, May 23, 1951.

Jim Gaffney

by Rory Costello

DESPITE FREQUENT CITATIONS over the years, it is not common knowledge that the Braves got their nickname and first Indian-head logo under James E. Gaffney. Then again, nearly a century and two franchise moves have gone by since the owner of yesteryear (December 1911 to January 1916) rechristened his team. The change celebrated his ties to New York City's political machine, Tammany Hall. "The Big Wigwam" provided not only the Native American imagery but also Gaffney's fortune—the fruits of "honest graft," as Tammany colleague George Washington Plunkitt called his own insider dealing.

Whatever one may think of how this man got ahead in life, Gaffney was a good owner in the most important ways. He bankrolled talent, upgraded his ballpark, and hired a winning manager in George Stallings. He also had the sense to give Stallings autonomy with the team—as well as a stock incentive. It all paid off. As William Phelon wrote after the Miracle Braves won their 1914 title, "Fortune was surely kind to Jim Gaffney in his baseball ventures."[1]

"Who was Gaffney? He was the policeman who turned to politics who to turned to contracting to become several times a millionaire."

In his history of the Boston Braves, notable Boston sportswriter Harold Kaese described Gaffney deftly in the space of a page, asking and answering this question several times for effect. Kaese set out the guideposts by which we may explore this operator's life and career in depth. Plunkitt's credo could just as easily have been Gaffney's: "I seen my opportunities, and I took 'em."

Gaffney's name is now on the periphery of history. Even contemporary stories gave just a superficial view of his personality—but one of his descendants has shed some more light on this area. Doreen Mannion's great-grandmother Annie was Jim Gaffney's sister. Her family still owns and resides in the house at Cedarhurst, Long Island, that Jim built on speculation. He "graciously" allowed Annie to live there and his sister Mary to live in another house that he built next door, also on spec.

"I've been on a lifelong quest to learn as much as I can about Gaffney," Mannion said. It started with stories from her grandfather, Charlie Mannion. "My grandfather always referred to him as 'Uncle Moneybags.' There was a huge portrait of him hanging above a desk at the family house in Cedarhurst that fascinated me. His tie clip was a question mark. Years later I learned that this was the infamous 'missing portrait' that authorities searched for high and low. Little did they know it was tucked away out in the pastures of Long Island!" This portrait is among Mannion's most prized possessions.

Doreen likened "Big Jim" to another brash, fast-talking Braves owner of more recent times: Ted Turner. "I find the parallels between him and Turner fascinating. Both were scoundrels. Turner loved yacht racing; Gaffney fancied himself a horseman. The size of both men's egos: tremendous. The most prominent feature of the monument that Gaffney put up at his parents' grave is the size of his own name, and he is not even buried with them!

"If Gaffney lived in a later time, I have no doubt he would be as well-known as Turner. It is incredible to me that someone who is the reason that the governor

Jim Gaffney

of New York state was impeached for the only time in history, who was behind the building of the first baseball stadium where public transportation brought fans right into the park, who owned the team with the most miraculous comeback of all time, has been forgotten by history."[2]

"Who was Gaffney? He was an East Side boy, reared in the gashouse district where kids grew up to be burglars, cops or firemen."

The Gashouse District lay on the East River. Its other bounds were 14th Street to the south, 27th Street to the north, and Park Avenue South to the west. The nickname arose in 1842 when a gas plant was constructed on East 21st Street. The foul odor and health hazard from this and other leaky plants meant that the poorest immigrants—chiefly the Irish at first—lived there. The original Gashouse Gang, which inspired the nickname of the 1934 St. Louis Cardinals, roamed the neighborhood.

James Edward Gaffney was born on March 7, 1868, in Manhattan. His parents were Patrick Gaffney and Anne Gaffney (née Masterson). Both were born in Ireland, Patrick in 1840 and his wife in 1845. It is not certain when they arrived in America, but the Irish famine of 1845 to 1849 triggered an ongoing wave of emigrants. The Irish-born population of New York City was approximately 70,000 in 1845, but it tripled to 204,000 by 1860.[3]

Patrick Gaffney, a brickmason and policeman, died in February 1881. He left his wife and five daughters (along with Anne and Mary, there were Margaret, Elizabeth, and Agnes)—plus the man of the house, 12-year-old Jim.

"Gaffney became a cop for a little while, then turned to politics and was soon elected district captain."

Kaese was perhaps drawing from Gaffney's funeral service notice in the *New York Times*. It said, "He began his career as a policeman and, after a brief period, left the force and was next heard from again as an election district captain in the district ruled by Billy Murphy, an older brother of Charles F. Murphy."[4] Gaffney's association with the hugely influential Charlie Murphy and his brothers was central to his career.

While the Mannion family could document that Patrick Gaffney was on the police force, their visit to the NYPD archives found no such record for James. Perhaps the seed of the *Times* information came from the sketch of Gaffney on the front page of *Sporting Life* on May 4, 1912, for it is not readily apparent in earlier press coverage.

In 1890, Gaffney married Essa "Essie" Smith.[5] The couple had one daughter, named Irene (which was Essie's middle name). Essie was the subject of a fulsome 1904 article in the *New York Times* magazine, which depicted the pretty redhead as a woman ahead of her time: a savvy political player with strong business sense.[6]

"He served on the Board of Aldermen. He became a partner of Charles F. Murphy, a Tammany chieftain."

Several articles describe Gaffney as Charlie Murphy's brother-in-law, but actually Essie was a dear friend of Margaret Graham, the widow whom Murphy married in 1902.[7] "Silent Charlie" was not just any Tammany sachem; he became the last supreme leader of the organization. Murphy was the basis for the character of political boss Jim Gettys in the movie *Citizen Kane*.[8] Gustavus Myers, who chronicled the history of Tammany Hall, devoted several chapters of his book to the former shipyard worker and saloonkeeper.

Murphy grew up in the Gashouse District ten years ahead of Gaffney. He and his seven siblings all "obtained at least the rudiments of a public school education," but the streets provided their true schooling.[9] Without confirmation, it is fair to guess in view of his father's early death that the same was true of Gaffney.

Tammany made Murphy leader of the Gashouse District in 1892. "Every night, when a district leader, Mr. Murphy could be found, from 7 to 10 o'clock, leaning against a lamp post at the northwest corner of Twentieth Street and Second Avenue."[10]

Billy Murphy, alderman of Manhattan's Twelfth District, passed away in January 1894.[11] Another brother, John

John Francis "Honey Fitz" Fitzgerald, mayor of Boston, full-length portrait, standing, facing front, Hank Gowdy, Mr. Gaffney, and others, on opening day of the World Series, Boston.

J. "Jack" Murphy, filled out the term.[12] This provided the opening for Gaffney—who had worked with Jack as a bartender for Charlie—to serve the Gashouse District.[13] Starting in 1897, he represented the Board of Aldermen's Eighteenth District through the end of 1905.[14] "Under the tutelage of Little Tim Sullivan he became prominent in that body."[15]

Charlie Murphy became dock commissioner of New York City in 1897, during the administration of Mayor Robert Van Wyck, who was widely regarded as a pawn of Tammany. It was the only salaried municipal post Murphy ever held, and during his time in office through 1901, his fortune somehow grew from $400,000 (accumulated in 18 years of running saloons) to at least $1 million.[16] Gaffney also had a finger in this pie.

In the summer of 1903, the New York District Attorney's office launched an investigation into the Dock Board under Van Wyck. The probe concerned "methods of the board in granting leases and conducting their business generally."[17] Gaffney and John Murphy were arrested in early July, and "Big Jim" was indicted later that month, "charged with violating Section 1,033 of the New York City charter, which provides that no member of the Board of Aldermen or other city official shall become interested, directly or indirectly, in the lease of any property belonging to the city."[18]

That September, the New York State Supreme Court dismissed Gaffney from custody on technical grounds. Previously, his contracting company—wife Essie was the secretary—had disregarded an order by the grand jury to produce its books![19] In February 1904 District Attorney William T. Jerome dismissed the indictment against Gaffney.[20]

"The New York Construction Company, of which Gaffney was president, excavated for both Pennsylvania Station and Grand Central Terminal."

Gustavus Myers described how—while Murphy was still in office as dock commissioner—his brother Jack,

Gaffney, and another political lieutenant named Richard Crouch formed the New-York Contracting & Trucking Company.[21] This company succeeded Jim's own enterprise, James Gaffney & Co.[22] It was speculated, but could never be proved, that the three were front men for Charlie.

In 1902 Murphy succeeded Richard Croker as boss of Tammany Hall. The following November George B. McClellan, Jr. (son of the Civil War general) ran for mayor of New York against reformer Seth Low, former Columbia University President. Ahead of the election, the City Club of New York, an anti-Tammany reform organization, issued a statement on the candidates for municipal offices. The pamphlet had stinging words for Gaffney and his politico-business methods: "Gaffney is not popular in his district, being considered too much of a hog. His firm is exceptionally aggressive in seizing upon every private privilege accessible, and it employs the cheapest of labor."

It provided other interesting color on the company's activities, though, including how Gaffney had once been a truck driver himself. From its modest start, filling in the back of city bulkheads and dumping at 20 cents a load, the New-York Contracting & Trucking Company grew to a force employing 500 draft horses (in the process, muscling out many of the district's small carters).[23] Jim and Jack made money coming and going. After obtaining contracts for work on West Side subway lines, they were able to use their piers and dumping privileges to get rid of their own rubble and be paid for it.

When McClellan defeated Low, it set the stage for a vivid appearance by Gaffney. Author Jill Jonnes described it in her book about the construction of Penn Station and its tunnels, *Conquering Gotham*.

"About a week later in Philadelphia at the Broad Street Station offices, William Patton [assistant to Alexander Cassatt, president of the Pennsylvania Railroad] was surprised by the unexpected appearance of Mr. James E. Gaffney, a rather rough-looking, large and fleshy fellow wearing a loud suit and derby. Patton readily recognized him as Manhattan's Eighteenth District Alderman, and one of Tammany's ringleaders in the fight to prevent Cassatt's winning the franchise.

"Here in the PRR's home offices, Gaffney was the soul of shameless affability. He had traveled down, he confided proudly to Patton, as the emissary of Mr. Charles F. Murphy. 'Mr. Murphy would be very glad,' he suggested, 'if Mr. Cassatt would give careful consideration to the bid made by the New York Contracting & Trucking Co., of which Mr. John J. Murphy — brother of Chief Murphy — was president.… Mr. Murphy is very anxious to see these people get the contract if their prices are anywhere near right.'"[24]

Jonnes noted how the low bidder mysteriously bowed out days after Cassatt informed Murphy of the contract award (a process that Myers detailed at length). "Exulted the shameless Alderman Gaffney, 'You can bet all the money in New York that it is true and that we have got that contract.' Giddy with victory and feeling garrulous, Gaffney regaled a reporter with the immensity of it all.… The key to it all: Murphy and Gaffney hoped to have thousands of jobs to bestow upon the faithful followers of the [Tammany] Tiger."[25]

Myers wrote, "By 1905 it was estimated that the New York Contracting and Trucking Company or its offshoots had received contracts aggregating $15,000,000 — all contracts from corporations and interests benefiting from the city government or depending upon favors from it. Yet two years previously this very company was a nonentity as far as securing large contracts were concerned, and none of its heads had any experience in the contracting business. Now in a certain well-understood field, it was virtually free from competition.… Under Murphy's leadership the obvious methods used were those of 'honest graft.'"[26] Tammany's methods of dissuading other bidders included throwing up obstacles such as indefinite labor slowdowns.

Gaffney really had the luck o' the Irish. In March 1905 he and Essie were dining with friends. Jim wanted to order chops — but his companions insisted that he order oysters, and he bit into a large pearl.[27]

It does not appear that "Big Jim" was involved in the Grand Central Terminal project.[28] Perhaps Kaese meant to refer to the bids that another Gaffney venture submitted to build subway lines on the East Side in 1908-09. On July 20, 1909, a *Wall Street Journal* editorial said, "The more the Bradley-Gaffney-Steers combination is looked into the less it will stand the light of day."[29]

"He was Tammany's Man of Mystery."

When Charles Murphy took the Tiger's reins in 1902, the *New York Sun* described John Murphy and Gaffney as his "constant attendants and advisers. They are near him when he is at Tammany Hall, and they are never far away when he is at the Anawanda Club."[30] The Anawanda Club was the Democratic (i.e., Tammany) headquarters of the Gashouse District. It was located at 345 Second Avenue, at 20th Street—Murphy's lamppost stood on the same corner. Jim and Essie lived in an apartment above the club for a time before moving to grander quarters.[31]

It is interesting to note that the introduction to the minor classic *Plunkitt of Tammany Hall* describes George W. Plunkitt too as "one of the closest friends and most valued advisers of Charles F. Murphy."

"He was a big, red-faced, healthy-looking specimen—modest, quiet and retiring."

Though existing photographs of the ruddy Irishman are in black and white, we do have the large portrait of him that Doreen Mannion owns; it was done in 1912.[32] As for his size, he stood 6 feet tall and weighed 185 pounds as of 1911. At that time, he was described as "always in condition, being a very active golfer."[33] The "quiet and retiring" part is at odds with other descriptions, though.

"Who was Gaffney? The New York Herald *said: 'Jim Gaffney is the most picturesque figure that the recent turbulent times have brought to the surface. As a power under cover, his position has been unprecedented.'"*

U.S. Senator James Aloysius O'Gorman put it more bluntly in 1913: "Don't you know that Gaffney is Murphy's chief bagman?"

"John Montgomery Ward, New York lawyer, wanted the [Boston Braves] club. His angel, he thought, was James E. Gaffney."

William Hepburn Russell, who had purchased the Boston National League franchise in 1910, died on November 21, 1911. As *McClure's* magazine wrote in 1912, "Ward …had an option on the team, so the tale is told, but had no money of consequence. There were various bidders, and there seemed little chance of Ward's getting a backer. Almost on the expiration of the option, he got on the track of Gaffney, who had been a great 'fan' for years." The article then presented a comical imagining of the deal, but, turning serious again, added that the franchise's value had declined sharply since its heyday in the 1890s. "What Gaffney will do with it is a speculation for the 'fans,' but those who know the Gaffney business methods predict great things."[34]

The deal, which *Sporting Life* detailed more fully, came together on December 12, 1911. Ward became president of the club and Gaffney the treasurer. *Sporting Life* reported that the amount paid for Russell's stock (945 of the 1,000 shares outstanding) was $174,000.[35]

Rebranding was among the new ownership's first steps. The Braves name had served as an occasional alternate for Beaneaters in the past, as seen in 1904 and 1905.[36] At least one account in December 1911 said that Ward suggested the Braves concept, associated with Tammany and its followers since the society's beginnings. Gaffney liked it.[37] Thus the Rustlers name, which had been in effect only for 1911, was discarded. Another key reason was to change the team's luck and sell more tickets.[38]

Shortly thereafter, Ward felt compelled to dismiss the rumors that Charlie Murphy was a silent partner. " 'Absolute rot' was the way Mr. Ward put it."[39] It is worth noting, though, that Murphy was a longtime fan who had organized a club called the Senators in the Gashouse District back in the 1870s.[40]

There was irony in the transaction. William Hepburn Russell, who like Ward was an attorney in New York, had Tammany connections—but severed them. He served as the city's commissioner of accounts under

Mayor Low. Russell had charged that Murphy, as dock commissioner, had leased piers to another Tammany figure named Daniel McMahon at below-market rates.[41] Eventually the city's Finance Department determined that this was not the case.[42]

"Gaffney was a fan, a close friend of Clark Griffith, and an avowed rival of Frank J. Farrell, owner of the New York Highlanders. One reason why Gaffney bought the Braves, it was said, was his desire to have a winning team before Farrell, in which he was successful, since Farrell never had a winner."

According to *Sporting Life*, Gaffney was "a very intimate friend of Clark Griffith and the latter got him interested in base ball."[43] The two men almost certainly met when Griffith was player-manager for the Highlanders from 1903 to June 1908. There was also a rumor that Gaffney put up $200,000 for Griffith to buy the Washington Senators.[44] Ward denied this, saying, "Whatever interest Griffith has in the Washingtons, he bought himself with money received from the sale of his ranch.[45] The *McClure's* story fell somewhere in the middle, stating that Griffith bought $25,000 in Senators stock with Gaffney's backing.[46] The club's principal owner then was Thomas Noyes, proprietor of the *Washington Star*; Noyes sold controlling interest to Griffith in 1919.

During the 1914 World Series, "in the official program at Fenway Park there was a picture of Griffith and Jim Gaffney taken together. Underneath the caption read, 'Clark Griffith, the man who induced James Gaffney to enter base ball.'"[47] *Sporting Life* alleged, "He [Gaffney] tried to buy the Boston Club two years ago."[48] The weekly had reported in November 1910 that Gaffney "had recently shown a disposition to enter the national game," but that his offers for the Cardinals and Reds had been turned down.[49]

Frank Farrell was a notorious gambling kingpin in New York who ran a string of poolrooms. Big Bill Devery co-owned the Highlanders with Farrell from 1903 to 1915. He was a picturesque former beat cop "who boasted that he had carried his father's dinner-pail when the elder Devery was laying the bricks of Tammany Hall." Devery became chief of police under Mayor Van Wyck.[50] He was also Richard Croker's right-hand man, and he took a Tammany approach to police work. "His philosophy was simple. He saw nothing wrong with his code. The police ...should get their share of whatever was going round."[51]

At one time Gaffney and Farrell worked together, controlling the National Sporting Club, a Tammany-dominated outfit founded in 1907.[52] This club, whose membership was exclusive, mainly promoted boxing. Boston sportswriter Tim Murnane described the men as "warm friends."[53] Farrell hired Griffith and also named a prize racehorse that he owned "Jim Gaffney."[54] As *New York Sun* sportswriter Joe Vila wrote after Gaffney's death, however, "a quarrel of a trivial nature split Gaffney and Farrell wide apart."[55]

"Ward was elected president, Gaffney treasurer of the new syndicate. But if Ward held the scepter, Gaffney wielded the power."

Naturally, money equaled power. The new owners also had to assume a land mortgage of $210,000, and they decided to revamp their ballpark, South End Grounds. They renovated the field, reconfigured its dimensions, and expanded seating capacity. *Sporting Life* columnist W.S. Farnsworth said, "Altogether it will take three quarters of a million or more to get the property on a proper working basis. The outlay on new talent is not included in this estimate."[56]

On July 31, 1912, only seven months after he acquired his interest in the Braves, Ward sold out to Gaffney and resigned as president of the club. *Sporting Life* reported, "It is understood that Ward and Gaffney didn't agree on matters of business policy and that for some time it was probable that one would buy out the other." Gaffney also bought out the other owner, John Carroll—another Tammany crony—and took over as president.[57]

Sporting Life columnist A.H.C. Mitchell wrote, "Until I can learn just what the trouble was between Ward and Gaffney, it will be better not to make any comment in these columns." At least publicly, Gaffney backed Ward when the latter made the Braves players carry their own bags, as he had done in his playing days, and pay for their own taxis.[58] One reason may have been that Gaffney liked Mike Donlin, who was "thoroughly disgusted" when Ward made Johnny Kling manager for the 1912 season. The Braves then dealt Turkey Mike to Pittsburgh.[59] Gaffney also signed Rabbit Maranville for the team, taking New Bedford manager Frank Connaughton's word over Ward's.[60]

Only a few weeks before, Gaffney had strongly denied the notion that Ward would leave. He said, "President Ward has been elected to serve three years as president of the Boston club, and he will serve out that term. Make that as strong as you will. If he does retire, if he gets out of base ball, I get out, too."[61]

That article went on to support the previous report that Gaffney had been interested back in 1910. "I could have purchased this club before Mr. Russell did, but I wasn't ready then, because Mr. Ward [then feuding with American League President Ban Johnson] wasn't ready." On a final note, he added a baseball truism, "Young blood and more speed are what we require, and what we are after."

Gaffney did not wait long to take action. In August 1912 *Sporting Life* reported that he had come to terms with George Stallings to manage the Braves in 1913. "He and Gaffney are very warm friends. Gaffney learned to admire him when Stallings was manager of the New York Americans, succeeding Clark Griffith." According to Joe Vila's 1932 recollection, it was the taunts of Frank Farrell and his friends over the Braves' poor showing that also prompted Gaffney to hire the Highlanders' discard.[62] Stallings, who was then managing Buffalo in the International League, denied that he was going anywhere.[63] Gaffney confirmed the signing officially, however, that October.

In November Gaffney said, "I have left the playing end of the club entirely in the hands of Stallings. He is a base ball man and I am not. He can buy or trade whatever players he chooses. I won't interfere with him. I did not interfere with Kling—reports to the contrary notwithstanding." Big Jim had opened up his checkbook to field a winner. He may have underrated his own eye for talent, though, since he was "particularly sweet" on pitcher Bill James, whom he purchased from Seattle in the Pacific Coast League. He said, "James to me looks like a wonder. I have been told he looks like a second Mathewson."[64]

Gaffney provided an extra carrot for Stallings—he made him a stockholder. "President Gaffney said he thought a manager who was also part owner would be able to exercise better control over the players than one who was merely an employe [sic] of the club."[65]

The Braves did improve measurably in 1913, climbing out of the cellar (52-101 in 1912) to fifth place (69-82). Gaffney was critically ill with intestinal trouble in the early part of the season and underwent an operation in April. He lost 40 pounds. After getting out of the hospital, he saw his team play for the first time that year on May 1, against Brooklyn; Casey Stengel's two home runs won the game for the Dodgers. Big Jim recuperated at his home in Cedarhurst (the Gaffneys also had a Manhattan townhouse at 72nd and Broadway.) He needed a second operation in June, and it took him until August before he was close to full recovery.[66]

In early August Gaffney showed a progressive approach, visiting the Long Branch club in the New York–New Jersey League and purchasing the release of several Cuban players. The most prominent was Adolfo "Dolf" Luque, who would make his big-league debut with the Braves in 1914. Boston already controlled catcher Miguel Ángel "Mike" González, who had played one game with the Braves in 1912 and later became famous for his classic summation, "Good field, no hit."[67] The deal led to a clash with Frank Farrell, who said that he had a prior claim, though it was a verbal contract.[68]

Among other things, in late August Gaffney also sent an open telegram to National League President Thomas Lynch exhorting him to review the league's umpires. The broadside came after ump Cy Rigler suspended second baseman Bill Sweeney (acting manager while Stallings was absent) for a protest during a game with Pittsburgh. The point of interest was that Gaffney had helped keep the president in office by casting the tie-breaking ballot in 1912 during a movement to depose

Lynch.⁶⁹ After the season, however, he threw his support behind Lynch's successor, John Tener.

"Even while owner of the Braves, he was the subject of an inquiry into the awarding of contracts in New York."

This was the biggest issue surrounding Gaffney in 1913. It made the headlines from March of that year into early 1914. New York Governor William Sulzer had appointed John A. Hennessy to investigate graft in state government. In October 1913 Manhattan District Attorney Charles Whitman then instituted "John Doe" proceedings (essentially an inquest during which a judge determines if a crime has been committed and by whom) to investigate Hennessy's charges. It was during this time that James A. O'Gorman—who became Senator only after a group led by Franklin Delano Roosevelt blocked Charles Murphy's ally—made his "bagman" remark about Gaffney.

To summarize the relevant section of Gustavus Myers' history, Sulzer—a longtime Tammany loyalist who had served nine terms in the U.S. Congress—was elected governor in 1912. According to Sulzer, Charlie Murphy expected him to remain "pliable and docile" concerning the Tiger's interests. Among other things, the governor alleged that Murphy said, "If I wished a new state superintendent of highways, 'Jim' Gaffney was the best all-around man for the job."⁷⁰

Sulzer declined to appoint Gaffney, whose name had arisen in various conflicted deals related to contracts for roadbuilding, the Catskill Aqueduct, and barge canals. In response Murphy announced, "Well, it's Gaffney or war." Sulzer held his ground after O'Gorman's impassioned plea not to give in—which featured some more choice words for Gaffney. Murphy then brought his power in the state legislature to bear, and Sulzer was impeached. He was removed from office that October.

Murphy disavowed the "Gaffney or war" quotation and the threats to wreck Sulzer's administration. Gaffney, George W. Plunkitt, and another Tammany figure, J. Sergeant Cram, also denied the charges made by Hennessy and Sulzer.⁷¹ One of the more sensational aspects of the John Doe inquiry came in February 1914, when D.A. Whitman sought older pictures and movie footage of Gaffney—as well as his portrait—because his appearance had changed following his illness and operations.⁷² This came after state contractor James C. Stewart, who had alleged that Gaffney sought kickbacks from him, testified that he could not identify Gaffney positively—effectively blunting the inquiry.⁷³

New York City's chief magistrate, William McAdoo, dismissed the John Doe proceedings in April 1914. Though some minor indictments resulted, the overall outcome was mixed. "The testimony which District Attorney Whitman succeeded in bringing out shed light on some interesting political practices … [but his] attempt to convict 'the man higher up' by tracing money secured in this way to the coffers of Charles F. Murphy and James E. Gaffney was unsuccessful."⁷⁴

It does not appear that this entanglement discomfited Jim Gaffney much. When he appeared before the Supreme Court Grand Jury in March 1914, he "was smiling when he went into the Grand Jury room, and he had the same broad smile when he emerged."⁷⁵ At any rate, the conclusion of this inquiry came just in time for the great season that lay ahead: the ascent of the Miracle Braves.

Actually, to start that season Gaffney promptly went back into court, but this time he prompted the proceedings. The Baltimore club in the upstart Federal League had induced pitcher Jack Quinn (4-3 in eight games for the 1913 Braves) to jump ship. Gaffney brought suit for $25,000, saying, "I don't want the money, but my lawyers declare I have a dead open and shut case, and I want to teach the Federal Leaguers a lesson." The *Sporting Life* account added, "Quinn offered to jump the Feds if the Boston Club returned the $3,500 advanced to him by the Baltimore Feds, but Gaffney turned down the offer promptly."⁷⁶

Early in the season, while the Braves were stuck in last place, Gaffney continued his beefing against umpire Cy Rigler (who eventually worked in ten World Series). His faith in the team was also shaken at times. He later recalled that after a drubbing in both ends of a doubleheader, "That team looked to me like the worst combination of ball players ever gathered together.... the Dodgers simply wiped up the lot with my team.... I had enough. I got out of my seat and jumped for the nearest exit. On the way I met [club secretary] Herman Nickerson. 'Say, when you see Stallings, tell him to take that ball club and dump it into the ocean,' I said."[77]

Gaffney's memory may have folded together the sweep that the Braves suffered versus the Giants on June 26 and Brooklyn's sweep on July 4. Independence Day was the low ebb, though—after that, the Braves began their surge. Perhaps superstition helped a bit. During the World Series celebration, "Gaffney showed the crowd the little purple aster in his buttonhole. That's the Braves' lucky flower, for ever since the Braves started to win the Boston owner has worn a fresh one on his coat every day. No matter where the team was on the road, the purple aster came to the hotel every day."[78]

Near the end of the regular season, there was a distracting rumor: On October 1, the newspapers reported that Gaffney was in negotiations with Frank Farrell and Bill Devery to buy the Yankees. Supposedly Stallings was going to come with him.[79] Nothing came of this, though: Farrell and Devery sold to Colonels Jacob Ruppert and Tillinghast L'Hommedieu Huston in 1915.

After the 1914 World Series Pittsburgh's owner, Barney Dreyfuss, commented on Gaffney as a sportsman. "I venture the assertion that throughout that series, Mr. Gaffney never thought how much money he would get out of it. I believe he never thought of anything except victory for his team."[80]

Dreyfuss wasn't exactly right, but he was close. Before the fourth and final game of the Series started, Gaffney reportedly said, "Boys, I want you to go out and win this series in four straight. I beg of you to win today. I know that it would make a difference of $50,000 to me to have the series go two more games, but, boys, I implore you to bring the series to an end today. Let us set a record they will never beat."[81]

Gaffney also offered another notable remark after the Series. While disclosing that his club had made no

Gaffney showing newly opened Braves Field to Federal League executives C.B Comstock, George Ward, Harry Sinclair, and James Gilmore.

money, he said, "The Braves have won the world championship and that is enough. They have vindicated George Stallings and Johnny Evers and have given me a chance to laugh at my old friend Farrell."[82]

In November 1914 Gaffney prepared to drop his suit against the BaltFeds, "with a view to showing the utter contempt in which [Jack] Quinn and the Federal League are held by the Boston owner."[83] Gaffney went on to make public comments in this vein. "I said then and I repeat now that every player who quit me will remain out of the major league if I have my way. I didn't lose anybody worth worrying about, it is true. But that is not the point. A player who would jump a contract would throw a ballgame, in my opinion."[84]

It was rich to hear pronouncements on the sanctity of contracts coming from Gaffney. The soundness of his judgment was mixed, too. Although outfielder Guy Zinn never returned to the majors, Jack Quinn got 181 of his 247 wins after he returned from the Federal League. On the other hand, the notoriously crooked Hal Chase was a prominent jumper. Allegations of game fixing also clung to Benny Kauff, "The Ty Cobb of the Feds," although it remains debatable whether he was truly involved with the Black Sox scandal of 1919. Gaffney's feeling against the "outlaw" Kauff ran so high that he refused to let the Braves take the field against the Giants on April 29, 1915. The game was going to be forfeited until John Tener ruled that it should proceed with Kauff on the bench.[85]

The Braves slipped to second place in 1915, the last season that Gaffney would own the club. The year's most notable event—leaving aside the owner's near-drowning on a quail hunt at George Stallings' Georgia estate that January!—was the opening of Braves Field in August. It wasn't the first ballpark Gaffney had worked on. His company had built the stands for the Polo Grounds at Coogan's Bluff.[86]

The *SABR Research Journal* of 1978 and the Boston Braves Historical Association newsletter of Spring 2009 both described Braves Field and its history. Gaffney started by purchasing the former Allston Golf Club. (As Harold Kaese noted, he put the park on the back of the property and "was able to sell the frontage at a handsome profit.") He also oversaw the construction, making the playing field vast on purpose because he liked seeing inside-the-park homers. Gaffney promised that the park would be "a model baseball plant—in fact, the last word in such plants." In many ways, though, Braves Field proved to be an albatross, notably in its dimensions with the advent of the lively ball.

Boston Mayor James Curley approved the vote of the city's street commissioners to name the broad thoroughfare along the park's eastern edge Gaffney Street.[87] The owner added his own sentimental touch, inviting old friend Clark Griffith to throw out the first pitch on August 18, with George Stallings catching. According to Gaffney, the pitch was to count officially as a ball or strike.[88] The Old Fox did indeed get it over the plate, but as the box scores showed, the delivery remained ceremonial.[89]

During the 1915 World Series, Gaffney helped bring peace between the Federal League and the majors, brokering a settlement.[90] After the season, he sent a letter to all members of the Braves team about rowdyism, which *Baseball* magazine printed in full the following February.[91] It was one of his last acts as owner. In January 1916 Gaffney and club director Robert H. Davis sold the franchise to a group headed by Harvard football coach Percy Haughton. Coming off the World Series win, he had said it would take $1,500,000 to buy his club.[92] He wound up accepting $500,000.

The deal came as a surprise. *Baseball* magazine wrote, "Why should a mighty magnate, master of a great ball club and of a splendid stadium, sell out his prize?" The article speculated that Gaffney was interested in the New York Giants; his partner was said to be oil magnate Harry Sinclair.[93] Other stories in the press indicated that Gaffney's business interests in New York were claiming more of his attention. Big Jim's own statement said, "When I discovered that I could secure a price upon the stock that would net me a handsome profit, I could not as a business man turn down the proposition."[94]

As Father Gerald Beirne of the Boston Braves Historical Association said in 2011, "Gaffney came across to me as much less flamboyant than Ted Turner. Gaffney's reputation at NL owners' meetings was one of quiet distinction, he knew how to get things done. And he was most instrumental in settling the Federal League problem, over Ban Johnson's truculence. For one of lowly, humble, uneducated beginnings, Gaffney seemed above the petty squabbling of the other so-called moguls, whose bickering got them nowhere. Being probably the only Catholic in the group in that era had to be a disadvantage, and yet he seemed to gain their respect. *The Sporting News* regretted his leaving baseball, saying 'the National League will miss him.'"[95]

Gaffney continued to own Braves Field, but he never re-entered baseball, although he was "still deeply interested" and "still a big power behind the throne."[96] As Gerald Beirne wrote in 2010, "(T)he cozy Boston-New York businessman's relationship quietly persisted, through some of the team's New York-based directors. Gaffney's connections were Robert Davis, Frederick Killeen, and attorney John Toole, all of New York." Beirne pointed to a pattern of numerous trades between the Braves and Giants in subsequent years, noting a line from *New York Times* sportswriter John F. Kieran—"it came across as 'two organizations with one set of books.'"[97]

Joe Vila said that health was an issue; "(T)hough Gaffney loved the game he did not care again to stand the wear and tear."[98] Even so, rumors continued to surface over the next couple of years. In October 1916 he expressed a desire to buy the Dodgers from Charles Ebbets if the price was right. Ebbets wanted $750,000.[99] That December Barney Dreyfuss reportedly had his Pittsburgh club up for sale, but here too the sides were not able to agree on a price.[100] In October 1917 there was talk that Gaffney would take the Braves back off Percy Haughton's hands and install Johnny Evers, whom he had acquired for the Miracle Braves, as manager.[101] Then in December 1918, the *New York Times* reported that Gaffney was looking to buy the Boston Red Sox and move them from Fenway Park to Braves Field.[102] If that deal had gone through, it might have been another grudge for Red Sox fans to nurse against Harry Frazee—but then again, would Gaffney have sold Babe Ruth?

In 1923 the *Palm Beach Daily News* ran a most intriguing interview with Gaffney, who was wintering in Florida with Essie for a month at the Breakers Hotel. He was going to every game between the African-American squads of the Breakers and a rival hotel, the Royal Poinciana. Gaffney called John McGraw "the greatest baseball club manager of all time" and "the greatest man in either league." He also named Johnny Evers as "the world's greatest baseball player."[103]

Even more interesting were Gaffney's remarks on the business of baseball—it would have been fascinating to see him in the free-agent era, competing with the likes of George Steinbrenner. "The enormous differences in the cost of running a baseball club and hiring ballplayers of the National Pastime of today, and a few years ago, is *[sic]* a fine thing for the game, and will prove beneficial in the end in spite of the criticisms that baseball clubs are spending too much money for players and for operating baseball clubs, or, in other words, 'buying a pennant.'" He added, "It brings the game to a higher standard."[104]

As late as 1925, Gaffney was mentioned as a possible buyer for the Dodgers, following the deaths of Charles Ebbets and Edward J. McKeever.[105] By this time, however, his primary pursuit was horseracing. Like many Irishmen, Gaffney loved "the sport of kings"—he had owned horses since the early 1900s (not to mention a donkey on his Cedarhurst property). Perhaps this influenced the dimensions of Braves Field. On another note, he had faced another graft allegation in 1908, denying before the Legislative Investigating Committee that he had received $125,000 from turf interests to buy the votes of four Tammany members of the Legislature to defeat the Hart-Agnew Anti-Race-Track Gambling bills.[106]

In May 1931 Gaffney's horse Irene's Bob (named for his daughter's son) won the Juvenile Stakes at Belmont Park. The *New York Times* called him "former owner of the Boston Braves and more widely known twenty years ago than at present."[107] Indeed, when he passed away a little more than a year later at age 64, the obituaries were not lengthy.

Gaffney and Essie were spending the summer of 1932 in East Hampton, Long Island. On Sunday, August 12, he suffered a cerebral hemorrhage, and he died on August 17 with his wife and daughter at his side. The *New York Times* said that he would be buried in Calvary Cemetery in Queens. Gaffney is interred, however, at Gate of Heaven Cemetery in Westchester County.

The Commonwealth Realty Trust, acting as trustees on behalf of the Gaffney estate, continued to own Braves Field through early 1949. Essie Gaffney, who lived until 1955, was still one of the stockholders. After owner Lou Perini and his associates moved the Braves to Milwaukee, they sold the facility to Boston University, which renamed it Boston University Field and then Nickerson Field. On November 11, 1995, Gaffney Street was renamed Harry Agganis Way to honor the Red Sox star who died at age 25 in 1955.[108]

James E. Gaffney's tenure in baseball was short—just four seasons. Had he stayed on the scene longer, various alternate histories might have unfolded and he could be better remembered today. Maybe the Braves would not have taken a back seat to the Red Sox when Boston was a two-team town. Maybe the Brooklyn Trust

Company would not have held the Ebbets estate's half of the Dodgers ... and then Walter O'Malley would not have gotten involved with that franchise. However, Robert Fuchs, son of Judge Emil Fuchs, who owned the Braves from 1922 to 1935, summed it up succinctly: "Gaffney knew when to buy and when to sell."[109]

Thanks to Doreen Mannion, great-great-niece of Jim Gaffney, Eric Costello, and Father Gerald Beirne for their assistance.

Sources

Harold Kaese. *The Boston Braves, 1871-1953*. Boston: Northeastern University Press, 2004 edition (originally published 1948, 1954): 128-129.

Gaffney family names:

RootsWeb's WorldConnect Project: http://worldconnect.rootsweb.com/

FamilySearch Database: http://www.familysearch.org/Eng/Search/frameset_search.asp

Gaffney's middle name:

"Post and Paddock Entries." *Daily Racing Form*, June 11, 1931: 15.

www.ancestry.com (1870 and 1880 census information).

Encyclopedia of New York.

www.findagrave.com

Notes

1. William A. Phelon. "Sidelights on the New World's Champions." *Baseball*, February 1915: 43.
2. Boston Braves expert Bob Brady says of Braves Field, "A special spur off of the Commonwealth Avenue line was specifically constructed that connected Babcock Street and Gaffney Street through tracks that ran through stadium property with an exclusive ballpark stop. Travelers were dropped off and picked up within the confines of the ballpark's footprint during game days. I believe that this was a first among the concrete and brick stadia. Whether any of the precursor old wooden ballparks had a similar feature is not within my field of knowledge." E-mail from Bob Brady to Bill Nowlin and Rory Costello, September 3, 2011. For further detail, see "A Streetcar Named Braves Field." Boston Braves Historical Association newsletter, Spring 2010.
3. Ira Rosenwaike. *Population History of New York City*. Syracuse, New York: Syracuse University Press, 1972: 41.
4. "J.E. Gaffney Services to Be Held Tomorrow." *New York Times*, August 18, 1932: 19.
5. "J.E. Gaffney Dies at East Hampton." *New York Times*, August 17, 1932: 17.
6. "Mrs. Gaffney." *New York Times*, June 26, 1904: Magazine-2.
7. Ibid.; Nancy Joan Weiss. *Charles Francis Murphy, 1958-1924*. Northampton, Massachusetts, Smith College, 1968: 36.
8. Pauline Kael (1985). *The Citizen Kane Book*. Boston: Little, Brown, 1971.
9. Gustavus Myers. *The History of Tammany Hall*. New York: Boni & Liveright, 1917: 299.
10. Ibid.: 303.
11. "Funeral of Alderman W.H. Murphy." *New York Times*, January 11, 1894: 2.
12. "Tammany's New Boss." *New York Sun*, November 10, 1902.
13. "Yielding to Graft." *Boston Evening Transcript*, April 29, 1904: 2.
14. "For Aldermen." *New York Times*, October 12, 1905: 2.
15. "J.E. Gaffney Services to Be Held Tomorrow."
16. "Tammany's New Boss"; Myers, op. cit.: 301.
17. "Alderman Figures in Dock Inquiry." *New York Times*, June 26, 1903: 5.
18. "Alderman Indicted in Pier Lease Case." *New York Times*, July 22, 1903: 14.
19. "Putting Up Strong Men." *Boston Evening Transcript*, September 22, 1903: 9.
20. "Gaffney Charges Dropped." *New York Times*, February 17, 1904: 5.
21. Myers, op. cit.: 302.
22. "Alderman Gaffney Indicted." *New-York Tribune*, July 22, 1903: 1.
23. *Statement by the City Club of New York as to Candidates for Municipal Offices*. October 30, 1903: 11.
24. Jill Jonnes. *Conquering Gotham: a Gilded Age Epic*. New York: Viking, 2007: 157-158.
25. Ibid.: 161.
26. Myers, op. cit.: 318-319.
27. "Priceless Pearl Found." *New York Times*, March 22, 1905: 9; "The 'Bone' in the Oyster." *Hartford Courant*, March 23, 1905: 8.
28. This immensely complex feat of engineering began in August 1903, and the original excavation contractor was O'Rourke Engineering and Construction, which suffered heavy losses and dropped out in 1907. The New York Central Railroad then finished the job over the next six years with its own labor force. Kurt Schlichting. *Grand Central Terminal: Railroads, Engineering, and Architecture in New York City*. Baltimore: The Johns Hopkins University Press, 2001: 69.
29. "McAdoo Version is Popular." *Public Service*, September 1909: 74.
30. "Tammany's New Boss."
31. "Mrs. Gaffney"
32. "Seeks Old Picture of 'Jim' Gaffney." *New York Times*, February 1, 1914: 14.
33. "Boston Bosses." *Sporting Life*, December 23, 1911: 7.

34 Edward Mott Woolley. "The Business of Baseball." *McClure's*, Volume 39, May to October 1912: 249-50.

35 "Boston Bosses." The total purchase price was later reported as $187,000. See also W.S. Farnsworth. "Ward's Opportunity." *Sporting Life*, January 6, 1912: 12.

36 "Brooklyns the First to Score." *The World*, April 21, 1904: 2; "St. Louis Squad Scalped by the Boston Braves." *Los Angeles Herald*, June 22, 1905: 4.

37 "The Name's All Right." *Milwaukee Journal*, December 20, 1911: 25.

38 Jeffrey P. Powers-Beck. *The American Indian Integration of Baseball*. Lincoln, Nebraska: University of Nebraska Press, 2004: 172.

39 "No Syndicate Ball." *Sporting Life*, December 30, 1911: 7.

40 "Tammany's New Boss."

41 "Tammany's New Boss."

42 "Justifies Pier Leases." *New York Times*, August 5, 1903: 14; "Pier Report Favors Gaffney." *Boston Evening Transcript*, August 5, 1903: 3.

43 "Boston Bosses."

44 "Tammany Leader Said to Be Real Owner of Boston." *Pittsburgh Press*, December 22, 1911.

45 "No Syndicate Ball."

46 Woolley, op. cit.: 255.

47 J. C. Isaminger. "Griffith 'Disloyal." *Sporting Life*, October 24, 1914: 16.

48 "Boston Bosses."

49 *Sporting Life*, November 26, 1910: 17.

50 Lothrop Stoddard. *Master of Manhattan: The Life of Richard Croker*. New York Longmans, Green and Co., 1931: 207; " 'Big Bill' Devery Dies of Apoplexy." *New York Times*, June 21, 1919: 1.

51 Ibid.: 206.

52 Donald Spivey. *Sport in America: New Historical Perspectives*. Westport, Connecticut: Greenwood Press, 1985: 109.

53 Tim Murnane. "New Boston Magnates." *Sporting Life*, December 30, 1911: 13.

54 "Jim Gaffney Wins Albany Handicap." *New York Times*, August 22, 1907: 8.

55 Joe Vila. "Gaffney Death Recalls Ending of Federal War." *New York Sun*, August 25, 1932.

56 "Ward's Opportunity."

57 "Ward Steps Out." *Sporting Life*, August 10, 1912: 4.

58 "Ward's Winning Way." *Sporting Life*, May 11, 1912: 1.

59 Tim Murnane. "The Donlin Transfer." *Sporting Life*, February 24, 1912: 3.

60 Robert S. Fuchs and Wayne Soini. *Judge Fuchs and the Boston Braves, 1923-1935*. Jefferson, North Carolina: McFarland & Co., 1998: 73.

61 "Ward's Tenure." *Sporting Life*, July 13, 1912: 1.

62 Vila, op. cit.

63 "Braves' Boss." *Sporting Life*, August 24, 1912: 4.

64 "Boston Budget." *Sporting Life*, November 16, 1912: 17.

65 "Boston Braves Ready for the Business of the Next Campaign." *Sporting Life*, December 14, 1912: 14.

66 *Sporting Life*, April 12, 1913: 6; "Stengel's Hitting Lands Close Game," *New York Times*, May 2, 1913: 9; *Sporting Life*, May 3, 1913: 1; *Sporting Life*, May 17, 1913: 23; *Sporting Life*, June 14, 1913: 15; *Sporting Life*, August 2, 1913: 6.

67 "Cubans for the Boston Club." *Sporting Life*, August 16, 1913: 10.

68 "Magnates Clash." *Sporting Life*, August 16, 913: 1.

69 "Boston Magnate's Break." *Sporting Life*, August 30, 1913: 6.

70 Myers, op. cit.: 361-362.

71 "Murphy And M'call Are Still Silent." *New York Times*, October 25, 1913: 2.

72 "Seeks Old Picture of 'Jim' Gaffney."

73 "Met by Stewart, Gaffney Balks." *New York Times*, January 31, 1914: 1.

74 Alice M. Holden. "The Graft Investigations of a Year." *National Municipal Review*, Volume III, 1914: 530.

75 "Got None Of $41,250 Graft, Says Gaffney." New York Times, March 21, 1914: 1.

76 A.H.C. Mitchell. "Boston Braves." *Sporting Life*, April 18, 1914: 7.

77 Frank Menke. "Sport Dope." *St. Petersburg* (Florida) *Evening Independent*, October 29, 1914: 6.

78 "Braves Capture World's Series In Four Straight." New York Times, October 14, 1914: 9.

79 "Owner of Braves Reported to Have Bought Yankees." *Pittsburgh Press*, October 1, 1914: 24; "Owner of Braves Sells Club to Buy Yankees." *Chicago Tribune*, October 3, 1914: 17.

80 Ralph S. Davis. "Boston's Triumph Pleases the Fans." *Pittsburgh Press*, October 14, 1914: Sports-4.

81 Ibid.

82 Vila, op. cit.

83 W.J. McBeth. "Tired of Lawing." *Sporting Life*, November 7, 1914: 6.

84 W.J. McBeth. "Some Gaffney News." *Sporting Life*, November 21, 1914: 2.

85 "Trouble at Giants' Game." *Reading Eagle*, April 30, 1915: 16.

86 Francis C. Richter. "Senior League." *Sporting Life*, December 23, 1911: 10.

87 "Clipped Tips." *The Day* (New London, Connecticut), August 18, 1915: 12.

88 "Griffith to Twirl for Braves Tomorrow." *Lewiston* (Maine) *Daily Sun*, August 17, 1915.

89 "Braves Open New Park and Win." *Reading* (Pennsylvania) *Eagle*, August 19, 1915: 10.

90 Vila, op. cit.

91 "Clean Baseball." *Baseball*, February 1916: 83.

92 McBeth, "Some Gaffney News."

93 William A. Phelon. "Baseball History in the Making." *Baseball*, March 1916: 18; "Percy Haughton Owner of Braves." *The Day*, January 10, 1916: 12.

94 "Braves Sold to Haughton." *Pittsburgh Press*, January 9, 1916.

95 E-mail from Gerald Beirne to Rory Costello, September 7, 2011.

96 "One Hit for the Cardinals." *New York Times*, April 14, 1916: 10; "Nicknames Given Major Leaguers." *The Day*, July 19, 1917: 10.

97 Beirne, Fr. Gerald. "Were the Boston Braves Really Controlled by the Giants and Tammany Hall?" *Outside the Lines*, newsletter of SABR's Business of Baseball Committee, Fall 2010. E-mail from Gerald Beirne to Rory Costello, September 7, 2011.

98 Vila, op. cit.

99 "James Gaffney Willing to Buy Brooklyn Club." *Hartford Courant*, October 12, 1916: 16.

100 "To Increase Price of Bleacher Seats." *New York Times*, December 16, 1916: 10.

101 "Gaffney May take Boston Club Again." *Pittsburgh Press*, October 14, 1917.

102 "Gaffney Is Possible New Owner of Red Sox." *New York Times*, December 23, 1918: 12.

103 "Cost Increase of Running Ball Clubs Is Beneficial." *Palm Beach Daily News*, February 5, 1923: 1.

104 Ibid.: 4.

105 "Death Takes Second Owner of the Robins." *New York Times*, April 30, 1925: 1.

106 "Gaffney Denies Having Graft Fund." *New York Times*, October 23, 1910: 16.

107 Bryan Field. "Irene's Bob First in Juvenile Stakes." *New York Times*, May 27, 1931: 39.

108 "Getting His Way." *Boston Globe*, November 12, 1995:

109 Fuchs and Soini, op. cit: 26.

The Braves' A. B. C.

A is for August, a month that is hot.
   And some people like it, while others do not.
   The Braves seemed to like it in spite of its heat,
   For during its progress they couldn't get beat.

B is for Brown, and he catches the pill
   When Gowdy and Whaling are both of them ill.
   They say he's descended from old Mr. Brown
   And was born on a farm or perhaps in some town.

C is for Catcher and also for Crutcher;
   The former's not much and the latter's not mucher.
   It's for Collins, Cottrell and for Cocreham, too,
   Whom I never heard of and neither did you.

D is for Dugey and Deal and Devore,
   And also one other—a total of four;
   The other is Davis, whom I never say,
   But he once went to school with my brother-in-law.

E is for Evers, whom we've not forgotten.
   He used to play ball for the Cubs, but was rotten.
   He was canned from the beautiful job that's now Hank's,
   And ever since then he's been murmuring "Thanks."

F is for Fred—Freddie Mitchell's his name.
   He seldom infrequently gets in the game.
   He once was a catcher, but now he is through;
   He merely tells others what they ought to do.

G is for Gilbert, and also for Gowdy.
   The latter I know well enough to say "Howdy."
   The dope on young Gilbert is not to be had,
   But possibly old Billy Gilbert's his dad.

H is for Hess; old, antique Otto Hess,
   Who's seventy-seven years old, more or less.
   He pitches left handed and hits the ball well
   And hopes the French army will finish in disgrace.

I is for me, who am writing this thing,
   I followed the Braves down to Georgia one spring.
   But those whom I followed have all got the can,
   With one lone exception—George Tyler's the man.

J is for James, whom his teammates call Bill,
   He pitches and puts lots of stuff on the pill.
   A lucky young pitcher is William Bill James,
   For he pitches but one out of every three games.

K is for Kick, which is part of the pastime
   And often prevents its completion in fast time.
   It's also for Kale, which the Braves will all get
   If they win this here race, which is not over yet.

L is for Lose, which I'm now telling you
   Is something the Braves have forgot how to do.
   It's also for Last, which is where they were at
   Before they went crazy as any old hat.

M is for Mann and Moran and Maranville,
   Not one of whom comes from Decatur or Danville.
   And neither Moran nor Maranville now can
   When size is considered, be classed as a man.

N is for Nickerson, Brave secretary.
   He once was a capable, clever, and very
   Efficient and breezy baseball writing cuss,
   And look at him now! There is still hope for us.

O is for Ouch! Which is frequently spoken
   By persons whose knee-caps and knuckles are broken
   By Boston men's wallops, both liners and grounders,
   In the game of baseball, which is glorified rounders.

P is for Pitcher Perdue, known as Hub,
   Who was recently swapped to the St. Louis club,
   And if the Braves cop, I do hope they'll be fair
   And cut in poor Hub for a full (loser's) share.

Q is for Quinn, now a Federal hurler,
   And quite a consid'rable sort of a twirler.
   A job as a Boston Brave pitcher was his,
   So he's pulling for Boston to win (Yes he is!).

R is for Rudolph, once canned by the Giants,
   And now he's one-third of the triple alliance,
   Consisting of Tyler, himself, and Bill James,
   Whose purpose in life is to pitcher all the games.

S is for Strand, Smith, and Schmidt and I guess
   That Stallings' last name is begun with an S.
   He's boss of the Braves, and as such he's a star,
   For look what he's got! And then see where they are!

T is for Tyler, left handed but sane.
   He works like a horse, but he doesn't complain.
   He's awfully chesty, so I have hear tell,
   Because he's a friend of R. W. L.

U is for Unies, and I will admit
   That the Braves' Uniforms don't look pretty nor fit,
   But as long as they're winning their games, I suppose
   We would love 'em if they didn't wear any clo'es.

V is for Verses, things written in rhyme,
   I write clever verses when I have the time.
   This verse I'm now writing might be very clever,
   But I can't be working on one verse forever.

W stands for both Whitted and Whaling.
   The latter's first catcher when Gowdy is ailing.
   And when Mr. Stallings wants some one to hit it,
   He sometimes most gen'rallly leaves it to Whitted.

X will now stand for X-cuse me, which I
   Am anxious to say to young Connolly. Why?
   Because I forgot him when I was at C,
   And I don't want him to be angry with me.

Y is for You, you brave Boston brigade!
   You're made of the stuff of which champions are made!
   If you win the title, you ought to feel great,
   (Until the Athletics have trimmed you four straight.)

Z is for Zowie! and Zowie's the noise
   That is made by the bats of the Connie Mack boys,
   When the bats meet the ball, as they usually do,
   (James, Rudolph, and Tyler, I'm sorry for you.)

      Ring W. Lardner
      Chicago Daily Tribune, September 4 and 5, 1914

1914 Boston Braves Timeline

By Michael T. Lynch, Jr.

1914—January

January 1—According to the *Boston Globe*, the Braves would be taking some of the tallest men in major-league baseball to spring training, including 6-foot-3 1/2-inch pitcher Gene Cocreham, as well as one of the smallest in 5-foot-5 shortstop Rabbit Maranville.

January 2—The *Globe* reported that the Braves were high on pitchers Gene Cocreham and George "Iron" Davis, and that Cocreham "showed up well" in 1913 and "gave the Boston manager the impression that he had a good prospect," even though Cocreham started just one game in 1913 and allowed seven earned runs in 8⅓ innings of work.

Meanwhile minority owner Joseph J. Lannin sold his shares of Braves stock to the team's vice president, C. James Connolly, while Lannin's son, Paul, sold his shares to C. Frank Curley, so his father could purchase a controlling interest in the Boston Red Sox.

January 6—Braves secretary Herman Nickerson released this statement pertaining to the Federal League's raid of players from National and American League rosters: "With all the attendant newspaper excitement over the Federal League's attempt to raid major league ball clubs for players, the Boston National League club feels safe, insofar as it has had no indication of any member of the squad being in the least dissatisfied with treatment in the past.

"President James E. Gaffney has not sent out any contracts to his players, and will not do so until after the commission has passed upon the Players' Fraternity demands. He feels that these demands are in every particular reasonable, and if the Boston club had a vote in the matter it would certainly grant the requests.

"All talk of players jumping from the Boston club to the Federal League is regarded by the Braves' officials as being without foundation, for they feel the players realize the possibilities that lie in the club's success in 1914 and are content to remain with a major league."

January 7—At the request of Braves president James Gaffney, left fielder Joe Connolly had his right leg X-rayed in New York to ensure that it had healed properly after Connolly broke it while sliding in September 1913. The X-ray showed that Connolly's leg had healed "perfectly" and would be "good as ever" heading into spring training.

It was also reported that the Braves had agreed to terms with three Cuban players, two of whom were misidentified as Angel Luque and Adolph Villazon, their first names having been switched. Luque, of course, was Adolfo Luque, who enjoyed a successful 20-year major-league career mostly with Cincinnati. In 1913 "The Pride of Havana" went 22-5 for Long Branch of the Class D New York-New Jersey League and batted .281, prompting Braves manager George Stallings to call Luque a "considerable pitcher" and a "man who can hit."

January 10—Former Braves first baseman Ralph Edward "Hap" Myers jumped to the rival Federal League after anchoring the initial station for the Braves in 1913. He had been sold to Rochester on October 8, 1913, and it was reported that he would be playing for Buffalo in 1914, but he spent the 1914 and 1915 seasons with the Brooklyn Tip-Tops in the Federal League.

January 12—The Braves acquired pitcher Willard Meikle after he went 13-9 for the Seattle Giants of the Class B Northwestern League in 1913.

The *Boston Globe* also reported that shortstop Walter "Rabbit" Maranville had no intention of jumping to the Federal League and "would rather play with Boston than any other club in the country." He made an appearance at the Braves offices and told secretary Nickerson, "I'll be out there in short field [in 1914] and show you something."

January 13—President Gaffney announced that pitcher Dick Rudolph had signed his contract for the 1914 season. The 26-year-old went 14-13 with a 2.92 ERA in 1913, his rookie season, while splitting time between the rotation and the bullpen.

January 14—Catcher Hank Gowdy signed his contract and completed the Braves' battery. It's also reported that the Braves had signed infielders J.C. Martin and Bill Sweeney, pitcher Hub Perdue, and Octavio Gonzalez, who played for Habana of the Cuban National League.

January 21—The Braves announced two more signings, of outfielder Tom Griffith and pitcher Paul Strand, giving the team 18 players either under contract or having agreed to terms. Among those in the fold, Charlie Deal was expected to make the competition at third base stiff after he batted .312 for Providence of the International League in 1913 and proved he had "intimate knowledge of the position" in a brief trial with the Braves.

January 24—The Braves secured the services of 22-year-old outfielder Larry Gilbert, who had paced the Double-A Milwaukee Brewers in home runs with 10 in 1913. In fact, Gilbert finished third in the American Association in homers, behind only Joe Riggert (12) and Jap Barbeau (11).

January 25—"Boston Nationals After New Grounds" trumpeted the *New York Times* in its January 26 edition. According to the article, President Gaffney had secured an option on a tract of land in Somerville, a city three miles northwest of Boston, for the purpose of building a new stadium. Although many changes were being made to the Braves' home ballpark, the South End Grounds, Gaffney admitted that the park's limited seating capacity and expensive location were no longer ideal. The team was also looking at a tract of land at the Forest Hills terminus of the elevated railway system.

January 28—The Braves received the signed contracts of third-base prospect Charlie Deal and pitchers Angel Villazon and Frank Schmitt. Villazon was a teammate of Octavio Gonzalez on the Habana Cuban National League team and Schmitt apparently got into the Braves' good graces again despite refusing to sign with them in 1913, which earned him a place on the ineligible list. Schmitt pitched well for a team in Dunkirk, New York, and president Gaffney recommended his reinstatement without being fined by the National Commission.

The Braves also secured the services of Walter Kenefick, a Springfield, Massachusetts, native discovered by Rabbit Maranville, and made a "very liberal" salary offer to hurler George "Lefty" Tyler that the team expected to be accepted.

January 31—Catcher Bill Rariden, a native of Bedford, Indiana, jumped to the Federal League for a reported three-year contract worth $6,000 per annum. Rariden had played for the Braves since 1909 but couldn't resist the chance to play for the Indianapolis Hoosiers, who played only 76 miles from his home town.

February

February 3—Only days after losing Rariden to the Feds, Braves fans woke up to news that another of their backstops, Bert Whaling, was considering a jump to the Federal League as well. According to the *Los Angeles Times*, Kansas City Packers manager and starting first baseman George Stovall made Whaling a "splendid offer" and the catcher was said to be "considering the offer very seriously."

February 4—The signed contracts of Oscar Dugey, "an infielder of considerable promise," and utilityman Joe Schultz arrived at the Braves' offices, giving them 24 men who'd either signed their contract or accepted terms.

February 9—Contracts were sent to pitchers Bill James and Dolf Luque after terms of their deals were finalized.

Exhibition games and travel plans were also finalized. President James Gaffney, manager George Stallings, and secretary Herman Nickerson met at the Waldorf-Astoria Hotel and settled on exhibition games to be played for charity in Macon, Georgia, on March 19;

Bridgeport, Connecticut, on April 12; and Far Rockaway in New York on May 10.

Travel to spring training in Macon will include a party of New Englanders composed of players Joe Connolly, Tom Griffith, Rabbit Maranville, Leslie Mann, Dick Rudolph, Lefty Tyler, Walter Kenefick, and James Neary; photographer Jack Williams; secretary Nickerson; and reporters from Boston newspapers that would leave by train on February 28. Dick Lewis, a catching prospect, was to remain in New York to attend his brother's wedding; Sweeney and Perdue were to spend three weeks in Hot Springs, Arkansas, to get in shape before moving on to Macon; and Stallings was to head to his plantation in Haddock, Georgia, before going to Macon to meet his players.

February 10—The National Commission convened in New York to decide the fate of Cubs second baseman and manager Johnny Evers, who had been fired as manager by Cubs owner Charles Murphy after the skipper led the team to a third-place finish in 1913. The commission asked Evers to produce his contracts so they could determine whether or not he was a free agent, something Evers insisted he was. "Evers claimed the contracts were interlocking," reported the *Boston Globe*, "so that when he was dropped as manager the Chicago club automatically dispensed of his playing services. He declared this left him a free agent to sign where he wished." President Gaffney announced he was ready and willing to pay $25,000 for Evers' release.

February 11—The Braves' schedule was released and had them starting the season on the road with a four-game series in Brooklyn April 14-17. They would then travel to Philadelphia for another four-game set before opening at home against the Robins on April 23.

But the big news was the trade of Johnny Evers to the Braves for Bill Sweeney and Hub Perdue, a transaction that was convoluted to say the least. According to the National Commission, Evers was not legally released as Cubs manager before owner Charles Murphy hired a new manager, Henry O'Day. Murphy finally admitted that he'd failed to give Evers his ten-day notice of release before signing O'Day as his new manager, so the commission assumed "all rights and responsibilities" for Evers' contract, "thus helping Murphy out of an embarrassing position" and making Evers a free agent.

Evers refused to accept the proposed trade unless he received acceptable terms, and threatened to sign a three-year contract from the Federal League that called for $40,000 with $15,000 coming upon delivery of a finalized deal. According to Evers it wasn't about the money as much as it was about Murphy's acquisition of two valuable players, something that Evers "was determined Murphy shall not do" because he'd be profiting from the deal. The Braves were happy to assume both of Evers' contracts, the first of which paid him $6,000 per year as a player, and the second of which paid him an additional $4,000 a year as manager, but Evers stood firm.

Federal League President James Gilmore had dispatched Evers' former teammate and double-play partner, Joe Tinker, to try to persuade Evers to join the Federals, an odd choice considering that Tinker and Evers despised each other. Gilmore vowed to spend as much money as necessary to fight the trade in court.

National League magnates tried to persuade Evers to accept the trade, and Gaffney had a long talk with Evers following the NL's meeting, but the second baseman refused and insisted he wanted to hear from the Cincinnati and Brooklyn National League clubs before making a decision. Gaffney told Evers he'd offer as much money as any club, but the Reds and Robins promised the same. Meanwhile Charles Weeghman, owner of the Chicago Chi-Feds, vowed to outbid other suitors by $5,000.

Negotiations ended when Evers left for a theater engagement with his wife.

February 13—According to T.H. Murnane of the *Boston Globe*, second baseman Johnny Evers finally agreed to a four-year deal with the Braves that called for $10,000 a year and a signing bonus of $15,000. Evers refused to comment about the exact dollar amount but told Murnane that he was "treated handsomely."

Even better for the Braves was that they were able to retain Sweeney and Perdue, although it was expected that Cubs owner Charles Murphy would eventually receive some sort of compensation. According to the final agreement, Evers was to receive a $2,000 bonus if the Braves won the pennant, $1,500 if they finished second, and $1,000 if they finished third. His signing bonus was also reported to be as high as $20,000.

February 14—A day after it was reported that Johnny Evers received a $20,000 bonus from the Braves, president Gaffney denied the report, calling it "groundless." He did, however, praise National League President John K. Tener for his "diplomacy and fairness" in his handling of the Evers case, while also complimenting Evers for the "honorable way in which he acted."

Evers responded by expressing appreciation for the generous contract he received, but also admitted he would have liked another chance at managing the Cubs. "I might have made a better showing than in 1913, might even have led the team to the top of the National League," Evers said from his home in Troy, New York.

Word out of New York City, where Tener, Gaffney, and National Commission Chairman August Herrmann held court at the Waldorf Astoria Hotel, had the Braves retaining Bill Sweeney and Hub Perdue after the National League agreed to a financial settlement with Charles Murphy. Gaffney announced plans to keep Sweeney, but was already in the process of trying to trade Perdue, giving the New York Giants the first chance to acquire the 32-year-old right-hander.

February 17—In an article in the *Boston Globe*, Mel Webb, Jr. waxed poetic about Johnny Evers, who earned the sobriquets "The Human Crab" or just plain "Crab" because he resembled one when he fielded grounders and was said to have the temperament of a crab.

"A crab in baseball is a chap who cannot find any fun in having things break for the other fellow," wrote Webb. "He's a fighter, a player who works hand and heart for every point; an aggressive, fearless competitor who thinks only baseball while in the game and who tolerates no mistakes either in himself or in his mates. He's the sort of chap who would rather go without a meal than lose a game of ball—and his ill-temper and churlishness need never appear far beyond the limits of the diamond."

While Evers was being celebrated, Hub Perdue was expressing regret over signing a three-year deal with the Braves in 1913, admitting that though he liked James Gaffney and the Braves organization, he wished he had an opportunity to sign with a Federal League team after the 1914 season.

February 18—Johnny Evers arrived in Boston from Troy and was met by Gaffney, Stallings, and Nickerson for a large lunch that included speeches by Gaffney, Stallings, and Evers. Evers announced he'd play wherever Stallings told him to and that he hadn't felt so well in years; Stallings predicted that the team would finish better than fifth and announced that Sweeney would retain his captaincy; Gaffney said his job was to bring in the best players he could, and that the day Stallings quit the Braves was the day he'd sell his stock in the team.

February 19—The Braves announced the hiring of former Boston Beaneaters great Tommy McCarthy as a scout. McCarthy, who had once stolen 93 and 83 bases in a season for the St. Louis Browns of the American Association, was said to be enthusiastic, and T.H. Murnane of the *Boston Globe* speculated that McCarthy and Evers would provide the Braves with "a lot of good inside stuff."

In other news, president Gaffney vowed to fight to keep Bill Sweeney in Boston after Charles Murphy threatened to take his case to court even though an agreement had already been made between Murphy and Tener. Sweeney was scheduled to leave for Hot Springs, Arkansas, the following morning, "feeling sure that he was to remain with the Braves another season."

Catcher Bert Whaling was expected to report to Hot Springs for a "course of baths" before heading to Macon for spring training, while Lefty Tyler's younger brother, Fred, a catcher, was to be given a tryout with the team.

February 22— Braves players were expected to arrive in Macon, Georgia, on March 2 with training to begin on March 3 and the first exhibition game to be played against Macon on March 19. George Stallings also agreed to a second game against Fred Lake's Fitchburg New England League squad on April 25 in Fitchburg, Massachusetts. "Lake's popularity in New England, particularly in Fitchburg, and the interest in the Braves' recruits will furnish an interest that means big attendance at this game," wrote the *Boston Globe*.

February 24—Johnny Evers arrived in Chicago to pack for his trip to Boston, then on to Macon. In Chicago he told reporters that he doubted he'd receive the $20,000 bonus promised him because it was contingent on both Bill Sweeney and Hub Perdue reporting to the Cubs, and he was afraid one of them would fail to report.

February 26—As if the Evers deal weren't convoluted enough, it became even more so when Sweeney suffered the first "accident" of the training season while bunting in a batting drill in Hot Springs, Arkansas, where a handful of players began practicing prior to their trip to Macon. According to reports, Sweeney squared around to bunt against Yankees hurler Ray Keating and was hit in the mouth with the pitch after he missed it with his bat. He suffered bloody and swollen lips, couldn't eat or talk, and was forced to use his hands to communicate.

This on the same day it was reported that National League officials would urge the Braves to turn Sweeney and Perdue over to the Cubs as compensation for Evers.

February 27—Pitcher Jack Quinn, who was very good in eight appearances for the Braves in 1913, signed a contract with the Baltimore Terrapins of the Federal League, much to the lament of George Stallings, who had expected Quinn to be the ace of his staff.

February 28—Six members of the Braves—Rabbit Maranville, Tommy Griffith, Les Mann, George and Fred Tyler, and Walter Kenefick—boarded a train for New York en route to their final destination of Macon, Georgia. Joe Connolly boarded at Providence, Rhode Island, for a trip that was expected to end on March 2 at 6:15 P.M.

March

March 1—Pitcher Dick Rudolph and infielder Jack Martin boarded the train to Georgia in New York, increasing the party to nine. According to the *Boston Globe*'s James O'Leary, who was traveling with the team, Fred Tyler was a "fine physical specimen" who had the "physique of an ideal catcher," Kenefick was a "likely-looking youngster" who Maranville insisted was "good enough to stick," and the rest of the Braves all looked well after their winter's rest.

He also reported that club secretary Herman Nickerson was confused by reports that Quinn had signed with Baltimore, mostly due to the fact that Quinn had sent in measurements for his uniform and hadn't returned an advance the team sent him to cover the cost of transportation.

March 4—The Braves practiced for an hour and a half in the morning, then another two hours in the afternoon in sessions that were described as "much harder and faster" than the previous day's workouts. Evers, Angel Villazon, Paul Strand, Octavio Gonzales, and Dolf Luque joined the squad for the first time, but neither Luque nor Gonzales had a uniform and couldn't participate in practice. Pitcher Bradley Hogg arrived later that night.

Evers took up his familiar spot at second base and immediately clicked with Maranville. "The way that he and Maranville worked together gave an inkling of how these two will make things hum later in the season," wrote O'Leary in the *Globe*. Evers was even more impressed with Maranville as a teammate than he was as an opponent. Others who stood out early on were Villazon, who impressed catcher Hank Gowdy with his "stuff," Strand, and Fred Herche, a pitcher who "worked so hard that he will not have to tackle the race track in order to reduce his weight. He worked every minute, either in the field or in the box, and is a pretty lively proposition."

March 5—Rain washed out the Braves' practice, so after a 30-minute meeting with Stallings the players either hung around their hotel, went to the movies, or went to court to watch trials. "Altogether it was a pretty dull day," O'Leary reported. Stallings telegraphed Sweeney at Hot Springs and told him, Perdue, and Bert Whaling to report to Macon by March 9. First baseman Butch Schmidt arrived from Baltimore later in the evening.

March 6—The recent arrivals of Hogg and Schmidt, and debuts by Gonzales and Luque, gave the Braves 28 men on a soggy field for a two-hour practice, most of which was spent hitting. Other arrivals included infielder Oscar Dugey and pitcher Arthur Duchesnil, neither of whom arrived in time to practice. Sweeney, Perdue, and Whaling were expected to arrive in time to participate in a five-inning practice game between split squads.

"Stallings has a lot of material that looks good, and he has a faculty of making wise selections," wrote O'Leary in the *Globe*. "He will have to do some experimenting with catchers, but developing catchers from raw material has been one of his specialties, and it is safe to say that he will have one or two to help out Whaling and Gowdy."

March 7—Despite a day that was described as "cold and raw" and that kept Les Mann from practicing for the second straight day so as not to exacerbate his cold, the Braves got two practices in with 32 men in attendance. The new men were schooled in Stallings' signals and O'Leary opined that Larry Gilbert had an outfield spot "just about cinched" and had the "makings of a star." He called Joe Schultz, Oscar Dugey, Jack Martin, and Octavio Gonzalez "classy fielders," and added that Schultz was also a "nifty" hitter.

March 8—After spending a few weeks in Hot Springs, Bill Sweeney, Hub Perdue, and Bert Whaling arrived in Macon to rave reviews. "All three looked fine and were apparently benefited by the baths and the work they did at the Springs," reported O'Leary. He described Perdue as "being lighter now than he ever has been at this time of the year since he has been in the big league." About the other two he wrote, "Whaling says that all the rheumatism has been boiled out of him and that he is in fine trim. Bill Sweeney never looked better."

Neither Sweeney nor Perdue would comment about their status with the Braves, a decision that still hadn't been made by National League President John Tener. Word out of New York was that a proposed sale of the Cubs was being held up by the confusion over compensation for the loss of Evers. One rumored deal had the Phillies and Giants involved in a four-way trade that would have sent shortstop Mickey Doolin from Philadelphia to New York for a Giants pitcher who, along with another Phillies player, would have been sent to the Braves for Sweeney.

What the Cubs would have received wasn't made clear, but when Doolin signed with Baltimore of the Federal League, the deal fell through.

March 9—In a six-inning game that pitted the Braves against each other, coach Fred Mitchell's team beat catcher Hank Gowdy's squad by a score of 3-1. The winners rapped out only two hits, both by Bill Sweeney, but plated two unearned runs in the third after Paul Strand issued free passes to Mitchell and Lefty Tyler, who advanced to second and third on a bunt by Maranville, then came home on a throwing error by first baseman Butch Schmidt.

Strand allowed only one hit in three innings for the losing squad, as did Angel Villazon; Tyler allowed five hits in three innings and Dolf Luque followed with three innings of three-hit ball.

That same day it was reported that catcher Bill Rariden, who'd played for the Braves since 1909, had signed a contract with the Indianapolis Hoosiers of the Federal League.

March 10—The Gowdys exacted revenge on their opponents with a 3-1 victory in another six-inning game, this time against the Whalings, led by catcher Bert Whaling. Whaling's squad boasted the first-string infield of Bill Sweeney at first, Johnny Evers at second, Charlie Deal at third, and Rabbit Maranville at short, but Gowdy's team was said to have the better pitching.

It was on display as Gene Cocreham and Willard Meikle combined to allow only four hits. Cocreham fanned Evers twice, no small feat considering Evers had struck out only 14 times in 1913, and both hurlers were deemed "promising" by James O'Leary in thr *Globe*. Fred Herche fanned five for the Whalings.

March 11—The *Chicago Tribune's* Harvey Woodruff reported from Tampa, Florida, that Bill Sweeney would be reporting to the Cubs as compensation for the Evers deal. "Manager [Hank] O'Day received a telegram today from Secretary C.H. Thomas at Macon, Ga., the training grounds of the Boston Braves, stating that Sweeney had signed a Cub contract for three years and would leave Macon tonight," wrote Woodruff. He also reported that the telegram made no mention of Hub Perdue, but that he was not "badly needed" by the Cubs.

Walt Dickson, a 35-year-old hurler who pitched for the Braves in 1912 and 1913, signed with the Pittsburgh Rebels of the Federal League.

March 12—With Perdue's status apparently cleared up, the hurler shook hands with George Stallings and promised he'd "work his head off" for the Braves. His mound work, however, was delayed by rain and field conditions that were fit only for light batting and sliding practice. In fact, the veteran pitchers were told not to bother showing up for workouts.

March 13—With the weather cleared, the Braves were able to get two practice sessions in, one of which resulted in another win for the Gowdys over the Whalings, this time by a 5-3 score. The game was knotted at 3-3 before the Gowdys plated two in the seventh inning to settle the affair. Gene Cocreham was impressive again, allowing only an infield single in his four innings of work. Team president James Gaffney was said to be pleased by his team's workout and was of the opinion that he had a first-division club.

March 14— An article written for the *Boston Globe* by Philadelphia Athletics second baseman Eddie Collins described George Stallings as a skipper who "gets very excited or wrought up over a game, especially if things are breaking bad for his team." Collins explained that a member of the Braves told him no one liked sitting next to Stallings on the bench if they were losing. " 'Move down' was the byword on the Boston bench," Collins wrote.

Meanwhile, on the field the Gowdys and Mitchells played to a 3-3 tie. Strand and Meikle did the pitching for the Gowdys, Dick Rudolph and Fred Herche for the Mitchells. Strand allowed only one hit, a run-scoring double by Maranville, and Herche came on in the fifth with no outs and the bases loaded and got out of the inning without allowing a run. Afterward, Stallings, Gaffney, Evers, Maranville, Boston newspapermen, and other guests left for Stallings' plantation in Haddock, Georgia, for a night of entertainment that included singing, dancing, and games.

March 15—The *Globe's* James O'Leary reported that Stallings greeted his guests at his plantation, "The Meadows," with a barbecued pig, and later there was "a 'frolic' by the plantation workers, men, women, and children." The party broke up and the players returned to Macon to prepare for games against the Cleveland Bearcats of the American Association.

March 16—An exhibition game against the Cleveland American Association squad in Americus, Georgia, resulted in an 8-6 loss for the Braves. The Braves scored first, plating one in the bottom of the first inning, but pitcher Bradley Hogg ran into trouble in the third and allowed five runs on two singles, three doubles, and a triple to give the Bearcats a 5-1 lead. The Braves eventually tied the score at 5-5 in the seventh, and each team scored a run in the ninth before Paul Strand surrendered two in the tenth on five hits.

Johnny Evers managed the team in George Stallings' absence, leading O'Leary to believe that Evers was to be named team captain. "Evers kept the men hustling in the field," reported O'Leary, "… and between him and Stallings there is likely to be some infield work developed this season that has not been apparent in the Boston team for years."

March 17—The Braves' veterans rebounded on St. Patrick's Day and pummeled the Cleveland Bearcats,

12-4, on the strength of three hits by third baseman Charlie Deal and two doubles by right fielder Tommy Griffith. Among the regulars only Butch Schmidt failed to record a hit.

Cocreham held the Bearcats to only one hit until the fifth inning, when he allowed three runs on two doubles, two singles, and two walks, the defining blow being a two-bagger belted over the right-field fence by former Brooklyn Superbas and Chicago Cubs star Jimmy Sheckard. But the Braves had already plated ten runs by then, including seven in the top of the fifth.

To honor the holiday, Johnny Evers, Rabbit Maranville, Joe Connolly, and Tommy Griffith wore green sashes and shamrock badges on their uniforms.

In a separate game, the Braves' youngsters took on Mercer College and defeated them 13-2, thanks mostly to the fantastic performance of Dolf Luque, who fanned 10 of the 12 batters he faced in four innings of work. Fred Herche also turned in a fine performance, marred only by two unearned runs scored thanks to errors by second baseman Wilson Collins.

March 18—The Braves were victorious on and off the field, pounding the Macon Peaches of the South Atlantic League, 20-3, while also securing an injunction against the Federal League in an effort to protect their players against "any agent or agents … from attempting to do business with any player under contract to the Boston club."

The injunction issued by Judge Mathews of the Superior Court of Georgia against the Federal League was thought to be more than enough to keep agents away from the Braves. "The state of Georgia is about the worst place in the United States that the Federals could pick out for any flirtation with ball players under contract," wrote James O'Leary. "It has very stringent laws regarding labor contracts and makes people live up to their agreements."

In the game, Macon took a 3-0 lead into the top of the fourth but the Braves put on a hitting clinic and plated 11 runs to effectively put the game on ice. Prior to the onslaught, the Braves' only hit was a Maranville double, but in the fourth almost everyone got a hit, and some had two. Les Mann rapped out a single and a triple and went 4-for-5 in the contest, and Butch Schmidt singled and doubled, and scored two runs. Boston scored two more in the fifth, five in the sixth, and two in the seventh, and every member of the starting lineup scored at least once, with outfielder Larry Gilbert leading the parade with four tallies.

March 19—A day after drubbing Macon, the Braves beat a much tougher opponent, the Newark Indians, champion of the International League in 1913, by a score of 3-2. Rabbit Maranville was the star, collecting two hits and two runs and fielding 11 chances without an error. Dick Rudolph tossed four scoreless innings, allowed only three hits, and kept the Indians from advancing past second base. Gene Cocreham allowed a run to Newark in the seventh and Lefty Tyler surrendered the second run in the bottom of the ninth, but secured the win.

March 20—It didn't take long for a Federal League agent to suffer George Stallings' wrath. Doc Gessler, a former major-league outfielder who was hired to manage the Pittsburgh Rebels, was thought to be in his hotel room talking to Hub Perdue and Wilson Collins. Gessler was handed a writ by Deputy Sheriff Robert Barnes who had accompanied Stallings to Gessler's room. Neither Barnes nor Stallings actually saw Perdue and Wilson with Gessler, but the Braves skipper was aware that Perdue had been invited to Gessler's room. Perdue took Wilson along as a witness just in case Gessler made him a contract offer.

According to James O'Leary's report in the *Globe*, Gessler hid Perdue and Wilson in his bathroom when Barnes knocked on his door. After Gessler was served papers, he accompanied Barnes and Stallings down to the hotel lobby. "I know those two men are up in your room right now," Stallings said to Gessler. "You have been enjoined, as you know, from talking to my men, or even being in their company or in the same building with them. If I know of your talking with them or being even in their presence, I will have you put in jail."

Gessler later denied knowing about an injunction and insisted he never would have come to Georgia had he been aware of it. In fact, his plan was to continue on to Augusta to try to enlist other players, but he decided to head to Lynchburg, Virginia, instead. "I know when I am beaten," he told reporters. "I do not propose to take any chances of getting into trouble over this matter."

Earlier that day, the Braves defeated Newark again, this time by a count of 5-3, in a game in which one of the Newark players collapsed and was believed to be dead. With Maranville at bat in the bottom of the first, Newark's first baseman, identified as "G. Smith," was seen to "crumple up and lurch heavily to the ground." When trainers from both teams reached him, he was unconscious and had no pulse. After several minutes of "working over him in an effort to produce heart action," Smith regained consciousness and was to be taken to the hospital.

Apparently he improved so much during the drive that he was taken back to the team's hotel and attended to by a physician who told Smith his heart was too weak for him to be a ballplayer. G. Smith was alleged to have been the son of former major-league shortstop Germany Smith, and was in his first professional season.

Perdue pitched the first four innings and allowed only one hit, but it was enough to plate a run. Arthur Duchesnil tossed the final three frames of the seven-inning affair and allowed the two other runs, one of which scored when Duchesnil failed to back up third, forcing Bert Whaling to corral Joe Connolly's wild toss from left field and leaving home plate uncovered.

"Something will probably be said by Manager Stallings at the daily meeting tomorrow about the importance of backing up," wrote O'Leary. Connolly and Whaling paced the team with two hits each, and Gilbert and Whaling scored four of the team's five runs.

March 21—Hub Perdue told James O'Leary that Doc Gessler had treated him well when he first came up to the big leagues, and Deputy Sheriff Barnes and Stallings had merely interrupted a social call when they served Gessler with a writ. Stallings wasn't buying it, however, and declared that he would seek an injunction "to enjoin any interference with his players anywhere in the United States."

The weather was too cold and wet to practice so Stallings took another contingent to his plantation that included Herman Nickerson, Dick Rudolph, George Tyler, Tom Griffith, Joe Connolly, Wilson Collins, and Johnny Evers.

March 22—The *Boston Globe* reported that Johnny Evers used part of his bonus to purchase a house in his hometown of Troy, New York. For $11,000 Evers was able to buy a home described as "being one of the newest and most attractive in the community … a handsome structure, situated in a most attractive locality with plenty of breathing space."

After three weeks of watching the action, the Globe's O'Leary predicted that the Braves' regular season starting lineup would feature Butch Schmidt at first base, Evers at second, Charlie Deal at third, Maranville at shortstop, and an outfield of Joe Connolly, Larry Gilbert, and Tommy Griffith. He wasn't real high on the group of catchers, but reported that Fred Tyler "was in fine shape and coming along good," and said Stallings would need a third backstop just in case Gowdy and Whaling got hurt. He also liked Jack Martin and Oscar Dugey as spare infielders and Leslie Mann as a "handy" backup for all three outfield positions. About Gilbert he wrote, "(H)e looks as if he would become a star, even among the big league artists."

March 23—The Braves defeated Georgia Military College in a game that was much closer than the final 9-2 score. Going into the eighth inning Boston held a slim 2-1 advantage, much to the delight of the coeds from the Georgia Normal and Industrial College, but the Braves poured across five runs in the eighth on six hits, including a bases-clearing double by Hank Gowdy. The Braves tacked on two more in the ninth on five walks.

The Cuban duo of Angel Villazon and Dolf Luque allowed only four hits and two runs, each surrendering two hits and a run. Both runs were unearned, though, the first coming on an error by Evers in the second and the other coming in the ninth on a wild pitch. Connolly, Griffith, and Gowdy recorded two hits each, and Schmidt led the way with two runs scored.

Prior to the game a serious accident that could have cost the Braves dearly was avoided when Mrs. Bud Sharpe regained control of her car after it hit a rut and was "shot into the narrow bank beside the road on the further side of which there was a sheer drop of about 20 feet." Mrs. Sharpe had been ferrying passengers to the game from Stallings' plantation, including Dick Rudolph, Wilson Collins, and Johnny Evers' wife and son when the near-accident occurred. According to Stallings, who was driving directly behind, Mrs. Sharpe's car jumped several feet off the ground when it struck the embankment, but she was able to steer the automobile back onto the road. Collins's leg was "jammed" by one of the car's doors, but no one else was hurt.

March 24—Another game against the American Association's Cleveland Bearcats resulted in a 6-0 loss thanks to the pitching of Lefty George and a hurler identified only as "Benn," each of whom allowed only three hits in the eight-inning contest. "Seattle Bill" James started for the Braves and surrendered four runs in three innings. Gene Cocreham tossed three innings of shutout ball in relief; Paul Strand allowed a run in his inning of work and Dolf Luque pitched the ninth, putting men on second and third courtesy of a walk, a single, and a wild pitch, before the game was called on account of darkness. None of the Braves' hitters stood out.

March 25—For the second straight time and third time in four meetings, the Cleveland Bearcats beat the Boston Braves, this time thanks to heroics by Ray Bates and Billy Southworth. The latter made a spectacular catch in the bottom of the seventh inning to rob Gowdy of what would have been a three-run homer, prompting James O'Leary to write in the *Globe*, "A finer catch has seldom, if ever, been made on a ball field." According to O'Leary, Southworth "climbed up the bank near the fence [in left field], and by a wonderful one-handed catch, after a jump, nipped the ball just as it was about to clear the fence and drop into the race track outside."

Two innings later Bates, Cleveland's third baseman, belted a three-run homer in the ninth inning off Hub Perdue to give the Bearcats a 3-2 victory. The blast ruined what was a fine performance by Dick Rudolph, who held Cleveland to three hits and no runs in five innings. Perdue surrendered five hits in four innings, including the game-winning blow, but drove in both Boston runs with a bloop single in the bottom of the eighth. Butch Schmidt and Hank Gowdy recorded the only other Boston hits as "Frost" and "Deshner" combined on a three-hitter.

March 26—To the surprise of no one, Johnny Evers was named team captain by manager George Stallings. Then the Braves got down to business and spent two hours on their hitting and an hour and a half on fielding. "It was a perfect Spring day," according to O'Leary, "and nearly everyone cut loose for all he was worth." Stallings also made a roster move, sending 25-year-old pitcher Bradley Hogg to Mobile of the Class A Southern Association.

March 27—A split squad that included only three men who played their regular positions was beaten by Macon, 4-0, thanks mostly to a three-run seventh-inning rally against Angel Villazon. A recruit named "Vaughan" held the Braves to only six hits, and no Boston runner advanced past second base in a nine-inning contest that was played to benefit the Macon Drum and Bugle Corps.

The Braves regulars were scheduled to play the Southern Association's Atlanta Crackers, but the game was rained out. Boston was still able to work out between showers, to the benefit of themselves and Rochester manager John Ganzel, who expected to land some of the Braves' castoffs.

March 28—Lefty Tyler became the first Braves hurler to go the distance when he tossed nine innings against Atlanta in a 7-4 victory. Boston plated four in the first off a pitcher named Efird on three singles, a walk, and a fielder's choice. The Crackers responded with three runs in the second on three singles, including one by former Red Sox second baseman Amby McConnell, and a double off the bat of Nealon Lynch, who poled out three hits in the game.

The Braves scored another in the fourth, but Atlanta stayed close by tallying again in the sixth before Boston put the game away with two runs in the top of the ninth. Rabbit Maranville led the 12-hit attack with three safeties, and Larry Gilbert, Tommy Griffith, and Hank Gowdy recorded two hits apiece. Gowdy and Gilbert both rapped out triples, and Gowdy's was almost a home run but he was tossed out at the plate.

"The Braves showed more aggressiveness at bat than they have at any time this season," wrote James O'Leary. "All in all, the Boston team looked better in today's game than it has all Spring."

March 29—According to O'Leary, the Braves pitchers would be going nine innings for the remaining spring games, "if they can stand the route." George Stallings was confident his hurlers could handle the load after being brought along "slowly and carefully."

During workouts, Maranville and Evers worked on a play they were expected to employ with runners on first and third, in which one of them would intercept the throw from the catcher during a double steal and quickly fire to home to nab the lead runner. "It is a beauty to watch," O'Leary opined. "They are not yet perfect in it, but will soon have it down so fine that a runner will have to go some to score from third on a throw to second, if the catcher does his part in the play perfectly. ..."

March 30—The *Boston Globe* printed the Braves' spring stats and Rabbit Maranville was the clear star to that point, batting .417 with three doubles and four steals, while fielding flawlessly and recording 30 assists. His double-play partner, Johnny Evers, was struggling, though, hitting only .222 and leading the team in errors with three.

"In the infield, Maranville's phenomenal work on the batting side is one of the big surprises of the year," wrote the *Globe*. "The confidence he has gained by his one year in the majors has apparently made him a hitter who will be tagged dangerous, although it is hardly expected that he can maintain the pace that will keep him anywhere near his present mark of .417."

About Evers the newspaper wrote, "Evers ranks lowest of the infielders, but there is little doubt that he will pick up as the season advances."

Bozeman Bulger reported in the *New York World*, "There is more genuine enthusiasm around this camp that I have seen since starting this exploration of the brush. From early morning until knocking off time in the afternoon here things go with a bang and a rush." According to Bulger, Stallings was convinced his team had a legitimate chance at a pennant and insisted that Larry Gilbert was the second coming of Red Sox star and future Hall of Famer Tris Speaker.

On the field, Dick Rudolph followed Lefty Tyler's complete game with nine exceptional innings of his own, in which he allowed no runs and only four hits, all singles. Only one Atlanta Cracker made it to second base in the 1-0 victory. Atlanta pitchers Frank Browning and Parson Perryman were in constant trouble, stranding men in scoring position in the first, third, sixth, and seventh innings, and allowing a run on consecutive doubles by Charlie Deal and Hank Gowdy in the fourth.

Maranville and Evers combined for four hits in eight at-bats and earned plaudits for a nice play that resulted in a force at second in the sixth. The game also featured a near fistfight between home plate umpire Augie Moran and Crackers manager Bill Smith, who took exception to Moran's ball and strike calls and threatened to punch him in the face. Moran pointed at his jaw and told Smith to "shoot." Smith declined the invitation and walked back to his bench, but catcher Joe Dunn continued to squawk and was ejected from the game. When Smith explained that Dunn was his only catcher, Moran allowed him to continue playing.

Before the game some of the Braves competed in a series of 100-yard sprints. Dick Lewis, a former hurdler at Exeter and Harvard, gave Fred "Dumpling" Herche a five-yard head start but still beat him. Hank Gowdy narrowly defeated Butch Schmidt and Bert Whaling;

and Les Mann won the third heat, beating Wilson Collins, Oscar Dugey, and Octavio Gonzalez by two yards.

In sadder news, pitcher Arthur Duchesnil received a letter notifying him of the death of his sister in Montreal, and Herche received a telegram letting him know that his sister was seriously ill with diphtheria.

April

April 2—A day after beating Macon, 6-1, the Braves destroyed them by a count of 13-0 on the strength of home runs by Rabbit Maranville and Bert Whaling, and a triple and two doubles off the bat of Tommy Griffith. Bill James and Willard Meikle combined to hold the Peaches to no runs on only six hits. Cuban recruits Angel Villazon and Octavio Gonzalez were released to Macon as Stallings began trimming his roster prior to the regular season.

April 4—Despite outhitting the Atlanta Crackers of the Southern Association, the Braves fell, 4-3, mostly because of sloppy fielding that resulted in three errors. The battery consisted of Dick Rudolph, Paul Strand, and Hank Gowdy.

April 10—With the Braves in town to play the Washington Senators, Stanley T. Milliken wrote a glowing review of Stallings' squad in the *Washington Post*, calling Rabbit Maranville "one of the greatest fielding shortstops in the game today," and writing that Joe Connolly was "fast on his feet, a good fielder and a dangerous hitter." According to Milliken, many experts believed the Braves to be a contender with "an outside chance at the bunting [pennant]."

Unfortunately the team then went out and lost to Washington, 7-4. They had the difficult task of facing Walter Johnson, who was in prime form, surrendering only four hits in seven innings while fanning seven. The Braves were able to touch Johnson for two runs, the second one coming on a Hank Gowdy two-out fifth-inning double followed by a Dick Rudolph single. Rudolph wasn't as good on the hill as he was at the plate, however, allowing five runs on eight hits in only four innings before being replaced by Hub Perdue.

Joe Engel relieved Johnson and allowed only one hit in two innings, but walked five batters, leading to the Braves' final two runs in the eighth. Connolly lived up to his billing and paced the Braves with two hits. Johnny Evers continued to struggle, going hitless in four at-bats and committing another error. He also earned the enmity of Washington fans thanks to an eighth-inning altercation with Nats catcher Eddie Ainsmith who, while officiating behind the plate, called Connolly out on strikes. Evers was coaching at third and took exception to the call, spewing out expletives "the exact wording of which would hardly look well in print," wrote Milliken, finishing his outburst by calling Ainsmith a "yellow slob."

Players intervened and separated the two, but plans were made to "have it out" after the game, which is precisely what happened. Ainsmith followed Evers into the clubhouse after the game and demanded an apology. Instead the 125-pound Evers shouted, "We'd have it out if I were half as big as you are!" Ainsmith offered to take on the Braves' biggest man and Butch Schmidt, who outweighed Ainsmith by at least 20 pounds, accepted the challenge, "throwing in a few uncomplimentary remarks as emphasis."

Ainsmith grabbed Schmidt by the throat and punched him in the jaw. Despite being surrounded by Boston players, Ainsmith escaped injury when Washington manager Clark Griffith intervened. "The players were separated, but shot a volley of profanity back and forth as they were forced to their respective dressing rooms," Milliken reported.

April 11—For the second straight day the Braves fell to the Nationals in a game that was not as close as the score would indicate. Washington hurler Joe Boehling stymied Boston's bats for seven innings, allowing only a wind-blown single that dropped behind the mound untouched before the Braves rallied for four eighth-inning runs off relievers Harry Harper and Bert Gallia, who barely held on for the 5-4 victory. The Braves might have had a chance to tie or win the game at a later stage, but it was called so the players could catch a train to Providence, Rhode Island.

Lefty Tyler allowed all five runs in seven innings of work. The Braves managed only two hits, but were issued nine walks and left eight men on.

April 14—BRAVES OFF TO A FEEBLE START, screamed the *Boston Globe* on April 15. "Boston Team Plays Ragged Ball in Opener at Ebbets Field," read the subhead. The Braves opened the regular season in Brooklyn and easily fell to the Robins, 8-2, in front of a crowd of 12,000 who braved the cold weather to see the opener. After National League President John Tener threw out the ceremonial first pitch, it was all downhill from there as the Robins scored in four of the first five innings to take an eight-run lead against Lefty Tyler.

Former Cubs star Ed Reulbach held the Braves scoreless until the seventh inning, when they plated both of their runs on an error, a Bert Whaling single, and a double by pitcher Dick Crutcher, who had replaced Tyler in the sixth. As bad as Tyler was on the mound, he led the team with two hits. And, in addition to his two-RBI double, Crutcher pitched three hitless innings in relief.

Off the field, James Gaffney filed a lawsuit against the Baltimore Terrapins of the Federal League, Federal League President James Gilmore, and pitcher John Picus "Jack" Quinn in the United States District Court in Baltimore for alleged conspiracy brought about when Quinn signed a contract to play for Baltimore after having already agreed in writing to contract terms with the Boston Braves.

The suit was for $25,000 for the loss of Quinn, who allegedly agreed to a deal several weeks prior to signing with Baltimore and whose contract with the Braves had already been approved by David Fultz, president of the Baseball Players' Fraternity. The suit also alleged that Terrapins director Edward Hanlon and manager Otto Knabe had signed Quinn to a contract and gave him a check for $3,500 even though they were well aware that Quinn had agreed to terms with Boston. And apparently Gilmore went back on his promise not to sign Quinn until the case had been reviewed by a "joint conference."

Baltimore's attorney, L. Edwin Goldman, called the suit an "obvious bluff and a confession that [the Braves'] contract is not good in equity."

April 15—While rain was putting a halt to the Braves' second game against the Robins, manager George Stallings made no excuses about his team's loss on Opening Day. At least not at first. "I have no alibis for defeat," he told reporters. "When a team is beaten the way we were beaten, and the way the Giants were beaten in Philadelphia, what's the use of talking?" He then proceeded to offer alibis about plays that were made by the Robins that weren't made by his team, and the age of his squad. "It was a kid team that started the game for us yesterday, for, barring [Johnny] Evers, not a player was more than 25."

April 17—The second game of the Braves' regular season went much like the first, prompting the *Boston Globe* to report, "COULD NOT HIT, FIELD, THROW. Outside of These Trifling Weaknesses, Braves Were All Right." Against rookie southpaw Raleigh Aitchison, the Braves mustered only five hits, two by Hank Gowdy, in a 5-0 loss. Meanwhile Braves hurler Dick Rudolph held the Robins to only one run through seven innings before Brooklyn plated four in the eighth. Regardless, the *Globe* opined that "the pitching of Mr. Rudolph of the Bronx was weak at critical stages of the conflict. ... [T]here was always the depressing possibility of impending disaster. ... [T]he impending calamity hung over the Boston team all through the game, like the cleaver of Damocles."

The Robins threatened in almost every inning but the Braves' slick glove work kept them from scoring for the most part. Rabbit Maranville saved a run in the first with a "wonderful stop" and "good throw" to end the inning, and Tommy Griffith made an excellent play in the second to keep Red Smith from scoring Brooklyn's second run on a hit by Dick Egan. But Brooklyn finally broke through in the eighth and secured its second straight win over Boston.

April 18—Boston moved on to Philadelphia and continued to disappoint, losing 5-3 thanks to a three-run sixth inning that broke a 2-2 tie. Hub Perdue got the start for the Braves but fell behind immediately when he served up a solo homer in the first inning to Phillies center fielder Dode Paskert, a leadoff blast into the left-field bleachers. Even though the Braves "connected with [Cy] Marshall's delivery hard and often enough," they recorded only five hits because most of their drives were hit right at a Phillies defender. The Braves took a 2-1 lead in the second inning on a two-run triple by Perdue, but it was mostly downhill from there.

Philadelphia plated three in the sixth, then Paskert snuffed out a Braves rally in the top of the seventh when he snared a bases-loaded drive off the bat of Johnny Evers in deep center field to end the inning and keep the Braves off the scoreboard. Boston scored a run in the eighth to make things interesting, but fell to 0-3 when the Phillies closed out the game.

April 19—The Braves continued their losing ways, except this time they fell to the minor-league Baltimore Orioles in an exhibition game. A young left-handed recruit named George Herman "Babe" Ruth tossed the first three innings for the Orioles in the 3-2 victory which featured an inside-the-park home run by Braves right fielder Les Mann, who barely beat the throw home by Claud Derrick to give Boston a 1-0 lead in the second inning. But Baltimore scored three of the game's final four runs for the win.

April 21—Boston finally recorded a win in a 4-3 victory over the Phillies that was sloppy to say the least. Braves hurler Dick Crutcher worked his way out of several jams to earn the win, displaying a "[Christy] Mathewson style of effectiveness—that of being able to retire batters when men were on the runways and when a hit threatened disaster." Among the ten hits Crutcher allowed were doubles by Dode Paskert, Dummy Murphy, and Gavvy Cravath, a triple by Fred Luderus, and a home run by Sherry Magee, but a late rally was snuffed out in the ninth on nifty work by Larry Gilbert, who played Beals Becker's hit perfectly and threw him out at second when he tried to stretch it into a double. With a runner on third and two outs, Crutcher fanned Milt Reed to end the contest.

The Braves rapped out 12 hits against Phillies hurler Joe Oeschger, 11 of them singles, and only Gilbert failed to hit safely. Still, their runs mostly came courtesy of three Philly miscues. Hank Gowdy continued his hot start, going 3-for-3 with a walk, and raised his average to .667 for the young season.

April 22—The Braves' success was short-lived as they fell to the Phillies, 3-1, behind the "clever" pitching of Grover Cleveland Alexander, who buckled down with men on base and escaped a handful of jams to earn the win. Braves right fielder and cleanup hitter Tommy Griffith had two chances to put the Braves on the board, but grounded into a bases-loaded double play in the third, then struck out in the eighth with two men on and two outs. Not surprisingly, Boston's lone run came on a long home run by Hank Gowdy. He would have had another if not for a fantastic play by Dode Paskert that kept his seventh-inning drive from going into the center-field seats.

Dick Rudolph surrendered only six hits to the Phillies, but one was a solo homer by Gavvy Cravath, and the others knocked in enough runs to provide the margin of victory. In addition to losing the game, George Stallings also lost Gilbert in the fourth inning when he suffered a spike wound to his right leg after colliding with Joe Connolly while chasing a long fly ball. Later in the same inning Jack Martin had to leave the game after Gowdy accidentally gouged the back of the third baseman's hand while both went after a slow roller down the third-base line. In the fifth Griffith collided with Butch Schmidt while both chased a foul pop fly, but neither was injured and Schmidt held on to the ball for the out.

April 23—Boston opened at the South End Grounds and made the most of the home cooking, beating the Robins 9-1 in front of 6,000 patrons who sat through 33-degree temperatures to watch the ceremonies, which included the presentation of a diamond pin and gold belt buckle from the players to manager George Stallings. Brooklyn took an early 1-0 lead with a run in the first off Lefty Tyler, but it was all Braves from there. Tyler was far from masterful as he issued 11 walks and seven hits in eight innings, but he somehow stranded 16 runners on base, and received plenty of support from his teammates, especially Rabbit Maranville who had a chance at a triple play in the third inning but had to settle for a double play instead.

All but Les Mann recorded a hit for the Braves, including a three-bagger by Connolly, and Maranville, Johnny Evers, and Butch Schmidt scored two runs apiece. Evers' shoddy fielding from spring training carried over into the regular season and he committed two more errors, giving him three in his first six games. He injured his foot on a double in the third, but stayed in the game much to Stallings' relief. Prior to the game it was reported that Larry Gilbert sprained his ankle during his collision with Connolly the day before and that the wound on his leg was infected.

April 24—A week after being whitewashed by Brooklyn's Raleigh Aitchison, the Braves went 8⅔ innings against the 26-year-old portsider before finally scoring off him in the bottom of the ninth. They managed only a single run in an 8-1 loss that dropped them to 2-5 and a four-game deficit behind the first-place Pittsburgh Pirates. Aitchison wasn't exactly dominant, allowing nine hits and six walks, but the Braves continued to struggle with men on base and ran into some bad luck when Zack Wheat turned a Hank Gowdy potential three-run drive in the seventh into a double play. Despite being robbed of extra bases and runs batted in for the second time in three days, Gowdy extended his hitting streak to six with a hit in four at-bats.

Evers led the Braves' attack with three hits and knocked in their only run, but it went for naught as Hub Perdue was battered for five runs in four innings of work. Gene Cocreham wasn't much better in relief, issuing seven walks in five innings, but he held the Robins to three runs, two of which came on a Wheat two-run homer in the seventh.

April 25—The Braves' struggles continued as they were dominated by Ed Reulbach, who had recovered from a bout of bronchitis just in time to hold Boston to three singles in a 4-0 shutout that dropped the Braves to 2-6. Only Evers, Connolly, and Gowdy hit safely, the latter extending his hitting streak to seven games. Boston hurler Dick Crutcher wasn't exactly effective, allowing four runs on 11 hits and three walks, but he was also the victim of a Maranville error in the sixth that should have been a double play but scooted through the shortstop's legs for a two-run miscue and was followed by a Casey Stengel single that plated Brooklyn's third run of the inning.

April 27—With no games to report on due to inclement weather and poor ground conditions, the *Boston Globe* opined about the sad state of the Braves instead. "The team has not been hitting at all well," wrote the paper, "and to date the pitchers have not shown the expected form. At the same time the team's defense has been fairly good, but without the hits there has not been a chance to win the games, in several of which the Braves' opponents have had a very easy time of it." The *Globe* also reported that only Hank Gowdy, Johnny Evers, and Charlie Deal had batting averages over .300, while the outfield as a whole had been mostly awful, hitting .238 (Joe Connolly), .200 (Larry Gilbert), .118 (Les Mann), and .065 (Tommy Griffith). Rabbit Maranville was hitting only .160 and Butch Schmidt was at an even .200.

Gowdy was hitting a robust .417 and would have showed even better had he not been robbed by great plays by Dode Paskert and Zack Wheat. Evers was batting .310 and Deal was at .308 but in only 13 at-bats. Interestingly, the pitchers were hitting the stuffing out of the ball—Dick Crutcher (.375), Hub Perdue (.333), Dick Rudolph (.333), and Lefty Tyler (.500) were hitting a combined .391—but pitching substandard ball, at least as a whole. Crutcher (1-1 with a 1.57 ERA) and Tyler (1-1, 2.57) were holding their own, and Rudolph (0-2, 3.38) wasn't as bad as his record, but Perdue at 0-2 with an ERA of 8.10 had been a disaster so far.

April 28—James O'Leary reported in the *Boston Globe* that Stallings had settled on a new lineup and batting order prior to a series against the New York Giants, sending Tommy Griffith to the bench, moving Joe

Connolly from left to right field and inserting 36-year-old minor-league journeyman Jim Murray in left. Though Larry Gilbert was thought to be close to returning, Stallings wasn't taking any chances. He also shook up his batting order, moving Rabbit Maranville from his usual leadoff spot to third in the order because, according to O'Leary, Maranville "has been 'waiting them out' too much," and was being placed in a spot where "he will have more of a chance to hit them out."

Connolly was to be moved to the top of the order, followed by Evers, Maranville, Murray, Schmidt, Deal, Gowdy, Mann, and the pitcher. Unfortunately the new lineup produced the same results as the old as the Braves dropped the first game of the series against the Giants, 3-1. Giants hurler Al Demaree scattered four singles over nine innings and the Braves would have been shut out were it not for two errors in the fourth that gave them a gift run. Dick Rudolph pitched well enough for Boston, giving up three runs on eight hits and a walk, but received no offensive support. Evers had two hits, Maranville took advantage of his new place in the order and rapped out a hit, but Gowdy went hitless and ended his streak at seven.

April 30—After two straight days of rain that washed out the Braves' tilts against the Giants, Stallings trotted his team onto the marshy field for some much-needed practice after the skies cleared long enough to get some work in. The Braves' skipper wasn't messing around, either, having his men bat for an hour, then pitting them against each other in a 14-inning contest eventually won by the regulars, 5-2.

May

May 1—The Braves would have been better off had it continued to rain as the Giants jumped all over pitchers Dick Crutcher and Lefty Tyler for 11 runs on 16 hits in a convincing 11-2 drubbing. Crutcher allowed four hits to the first four Giants he faced, including two doubles, and it was all downhill from there. He lasted only two innings before giving way to Lefty Tyler, who didn't fare much better, although it wasn't until the top of the ninth that he finally melted down and allowed six runs.

The only real highlights for the Braves were the hitting of Johnny Evers, who went 3-for-5 with a double, and a defensive play by Les Mann that the *Globe*'s James O'Leary called "one of the greatest jumping one-handed catches ever seen on the grounds." Giants center fielder Bob Bescher drove a ball to deep center field in the second inning that looked like it would surely go for extra bases and plate at least two runs. "No one thought he had a chance to touch the ball," wrote O'Leary of Mann. "He got away fast on his sprint, however, and as the ball was apparently about to sail over his head, he shot up into the air, shoving his hand up to full reach." Mann failed to secure the ball on his initial stab, but gathered it in before his feet hit the ground.

May 2—Boston dropped its ninth game in 11 tries after the Phillies rudely welcomed Hub Perdue with two first-inning singles followed by back-to-back homers by Hans Lobert and Sherry Magee that plated three runs. The damage would have been much greater had Dode Paskert not gotten hit by Beals Becker's single as he was moving from first to second. Paskert was called out, but it mattered little when Lobert smacked one over the right-field wall and Magee followed with a drive into the center-field bleachers.

That was all Phillies hurler Rube Marshall would need as the Braves could muster only two runs off the 23-year-old in nine innings of effort. Fred Luderus added an unnecessary insurance run in the fourth when he slammed a Perdue offering into the wire netting atop the upper corner of the center-field bleachers for a solo homer, then the Phils tacked on two more in the eighth off "Seattle Bill" James for good measure. Butch Schmidt and Bert Whaling combined for five of the Braves' seven hits but the rest of the lineup went just 2-for-25.

May 4—Batting records released by the *Boston Globe* showed one reason why the Braves had gone only 2-9 in their first 11 games: Only Johnny Evers and Hank Gowdy were contributing to the offense, the former hitting .341 with three doubles and two sacrifices, the latter hitting .323 with a triple and homer among his ten hits. The next highest averages belonged to Butch Schmidt and Charlie Deal, both of whom were batting .250. On the other hand, pitchers Dick Crutcher and Lefty Tyler were a combined 6-for-16, a .375 average.

Stallings' men must have read the paper because later that day they rapped out 15 hits in a 10-7 victory over the Phillies. Dick Rudolph wasn't exactly masterful as he fell behind 5-0 in the first inning on three walks, two singles, two doubles, and an error, but he buckled down and held the Phils to only two more runs the rest of the way. The offense was led by Joe Connolly, who had three hits, including a homer, and Schmidt and Deal, who combined for six hits, three of which were doubles.

May 6—After consecutive rainouts that erased two contests against the Phillies, the Braves embarked on a road trip that was to keep them from Boston until the first week of June and pit them against every other NL team. Their first stop was New York, where they'd be playing a three-game series against the Giants. Pitcher Dolf Luque was left behind but was to report to the team when they reached Cincinnati, and outfielder Larry Gilbert didn't accompany the team, either, as he continued to recuperate from a sprained ankle.

May 7—The Braves held a 6-3 lead against the Giants going into the eighth inning before New York plated four in the bottom of the frame for a come-from-behind 7-6 victory. Despite allowing 13 hits, five walks, and six of the Giants' seven runs in seven innings, Dick Crutcher walked away with a no-decision while Rudolph took the loss after Les Mann misplayed an Art Fletcher line drive to center, which pushed across the winning run.

May 8—After another rainout, Braves skipper George Stallings vented to the press about his team's poor play, blaming it on the weather. "This is aggravating, yet it cannot last much longer," he said. "It is bound to change, and so is the playing of the Braves bound to change for the better. . . . Therefore, under the conditions, there is nothing for us to do but wait for good weather and a turn of the tide."

May 9—In addition to lousy weather, Stallings and the Braves also had to battle the umpires in their uphill climb out of the cellar. In this case it was home plate umpire Cy Rigler, who called an apparent third strike from Lefty Tyler a ball in a crucial seventh-inning at-bat by Giants backstop Chief Meyers, who socked the next pitch for two bases and plated the only two runs of the game in a 2-0 whitewash won by Christy Mathewson.

May 11—Fresh batting statistics showed that Charlie Deal and Butch Schmidt had joined Evers and Gowdy in the .300 club. Beginning on May 1, Deal fashioned a modest six-game hitting streak to raise his average to .333 and he led the team with four doubles. Schmidt didn't have a streak, but from May 2 to May 11 he went 10-for-20 and lifted his average to .304.

Unfortunately the Braves fell to the Giants again, this time by a count of 8-6. With the score 4-1 in New York's favor, Schmidt tied the game with a three-run homer in the sixth inning, but Hub Perdue surrendered four more runs in the bottom of the inning and the Braves could only pull to within two before falling to defeat for the 12th time in 15 games.

May 12—The *Boston Globe* reported that George Stallings had filed a protest with National League President John Tener on the grounds that Cy Rigler made a handful of calls that went against the Braves in their 2-0 loss to the Giants on May 9. In addition to the missed third strike during the Meyers at-bat, Rigler was also alleged to have called Bert Whaling out on a fly ball that was trapped by Fred Snodgrass, and allowed a double play in which interference on Giants second baseman Larry Doyle should have been called but wasn't.

The charges against Rigler went even deeper, though, as Stallings accused the arbiter of being bitter after the Braves manager refused to sign a prospect recommended by Rigler—"He's been throwing the hooks into my club ever since," Stallings insisted. According to Stallings, the game should have been replayed.

On the field the Braves played the Pittsburgh Pirates to a 1-1 tie that was called after ten innings due to darkness and an electrical storm. Dick Rudolph would have single-handedly beaten the Pirates had Les Mann not made a baserunning blunder in the sixth that cost the Braves a run. Rudolph went the distance and surrendered only three hits, two of which came in the sixth inning when the Pirates knotted the game at 1-1. Prior to that, Rudolph rapped out a hit and scored what should have been the Braves' second run were it not for Mann's gaffe. On the other hand, a great catch of a popup down the left-field line by Rabbit Maranville kept Pittsburgh from breaking the tie and earning a victory.

May 13—As if things couldn't get any worse for the hard-luck Braves, "Seattle Bill" James allowed only two hits and a walk but lost 1-0 to the Cincinnati Reds to drop the team to a pathetic 3-13 on the same day that Stallings' protest was denied. James walked leadoff hitter Herbie Moran in the bottom of the first, and Mann came around to score on a double by Buck Herzog. From there James surrendered only a single to catcher Tommy Clarke and kept the Reds off the bases in his final five innings. As usual, the Braves could muster no offense despite putting ten men on base.

As for the protest, President Heydler ruled that it would be denied based on the fact that protests could only be filed by team presidents and not by managers; that it wasn't based on a rule interpretation but rather a judgment call; and that if Rigler had recommended a player to the Braves it surely came before he was an umpire and before a rule was put in place that forbade umpires to act as scouts or agents.

May 14—The Braves' scoreless streak reached 22 innings after they were shut out for the second straight game in a 6-0 loss to Rube Benton, Dave Davenport, and the Cincinnati Reds. Benton allowed only four hits in five innings before being tossed from the game by umpire Mal Eason to start the top of the sixth. Davenport entered and held Boston hitless over the final four frames. Little-known and -used outfielder Wilson Collins collected two of the Braves' four hits, while hurler Lefty Tyler dropped his fourth decision in five starts.

May 15—Boston dropped its sixth straight game and ran its winless streak to seven with a 4-2 loss to the Reds that put the Braves 10 1/2 games behind the first-place Pirates after only 19 games. And if not for a two-run rally in the top of the ninth, they would have extended their scoreless streak past 30 innings. Rabbit Maranville made four errors in the game, including three in the seventh inning, but only one of Cincinnati's runs was unearned. Paul Strand made his season debut in relief of Dick Crutcher and allowed an earned run in three innings.

May 16—Braves management released pitchers Frank Schmidt and Fred Herche to Montreal and Rochester of the International League, respectively, then watched their regulars get shut out for the third time in four games. Dick Rudolph continued to be on the short end of a brilliant performance as he allowed only one hit through seven innings before a single and triple in the eighth plated the only run of the game. The Braves mustered only three hits off Rube Benton and finished the day with only 50 runs in their first 19 games, by far the worst in baseball, including the Federal League.

May 18—In an article written by Giants manager John McGraw, the skipper called the Braves "disappointing" and lamented their inability to beat the Western clubs during their road trip, which had taken the Braves to Pittsburgh to take on the first-place Pirates. But McGraw spoke too soon as the Braves won their first game since May 4, beating the Pirates, 4-1. As usual, the Braves' hitters were stymied for most of the game, failing to score through seven innings, but consecutive two-run innings in the eighth and ninth secured the win for Bill James.

May 19—The Braves' success was short-lived as they fell to the Pirates, 7-5, in another game marred by an umpire's call, this time by Al Orth, who apparently lost track of the count during a critical at-bat by Pittsburgh outfielder Mike Mitchell. Mitchell eventually singled to drive in the winning run in the bottom of the eighth and the Pirates followed with an insurance run for good measure. Rabbit Maranville was Boston's hitting star, rapping out four hits, and Les Mann homered.

May 20—Another loss to the Pirates dropped Boston to 11 1/2 games out of first and 5 1/2 behind the seventh-place Cubs. Dolf Luque made his first start for the Braves and was solid through seven innings before weakening in the eighth and allowing the final two of Pittsburgh's four runs. The Braves managed only one tally off Wilbur Cooper, who had enemy batters pounding the ball into the ground all day. Maranville followed his great day at the plate with another terrible day in the field, committing four more errors, including two on the same play in the third.

May 21—Thanks to a two-run first inning highlighted by a Maranville run-scoring triple, and his excellent glove work, the Braves defeated the Cubs in Chicago, 3-1. Johnny Evers, returning to his old stamping grounds for the first time, received a rousing welcome from the fans during his first at-bat, then scored the first run when he walked and came home on Maranville's three-bagger. Lefty Tyler scattered seven hits over nine innings and got great support from his shortstop, who "covered seven acres of ground," according to Keene Gardiner of the *Chicago Tribune*.

May 22—It took almost six weeks but the Braves won back-to-back games for the first time all season with a 2-0 whitewash of the Cubs. Otto Hess, making his first appearance of the season, was brilliant, surrendering only four hits in the complete-game shutout. Maranville and Evers starred in the field, accepting 17 errorless chances between them, and at the plate, combining for two of the team's three hits and driving in the first run of the game.

May 23—In yet another light-hitting contest, the Braves fell to the Cubs, 2-1, when former Brave Bill Sweeney singled in the winning run in the bottom of the ninth. Maranville's schizophrenic play led to the winning run when he booted a grounder for an error to lead off the frame, his third miscue of the game. Despite pitching well yet again, Dick Rudolph suffered the loss and fell to 1-6. Dating back to May 7, Rudolph had pitched to a nifty 1.29 ERA and had only three losses and a tie to show for it.

May 24—The Braves took the fourth game of the four-game set, 3-2, and won their first series of the season. The team rapped out only six hits and no one had more than one, but timely hitting and a sacrifice fly in the fifth gave the Braves all the runs they needed for a victory. Bill James was less than masterful, allowing nine hits and six walks, but escaped with a win.

May 25—The *Boston Globe* printed updated stats and it wasn't pretty. Butch Schmidt led the team with a .270 average, and only Joe Connolly and Johnny Evers were hitting better than .250 among the rest. Through their first 26 games, the Braves had been outscored 109-66 and were hitting only .217 as a team. And despite the sometimes brilliant play of Rabbit Maranville, he had committed 20 errors and was fielding at an .871 clip through May 23. The list of pitching leaders was equally pathetic—Lefty Tyler topped Braves pitchers with a .400 winning percentage, followed by Dick Crutcher at .250, Dick Rudolph at .167, and Hub Perdue at .000.

The Braves went into St. Louis to face the Cardinals for the first time this season and pulled out another close 3-2 victory behind the hitting of Jack Martin and pitching of Lefty Tyler.

May 26—In a game that featured the hidden-ball trick and another Braves player being ejected by umpire Cy Rigler, Boston fell to St. Louis, 4-2. Johnny Evers lasted only three innings before his arguing over balls and strikes got him tossed from the contest. Then with the score 4-2 in the Cardinals' favor in the top of the seventh, Martin reached base and was "picked off" by the hidden-ball trick, which kept the Braves from getting closer.

May 27—For the second straight day Johnny Evers suffered the wrath of Cy Rigler, who threw him out of the game for remarks he made to the press box. Rigler also threw out Cardinals Lee Magee and Cozy Dolan for making a stink about his decisions. The Braves took advantage of a Miller Huggins error in the second and scored six runs, four of which came on a Rabbit

Maranville inside-the-park grand slam, and went on to win, 7-4. Ironically Rudolph had his worst game since May 4, allowing all four runs on 11 hits, but earned his first win in almost a month.

May 29—Bill James became another in a line of hard-luck losers when he allowed only three hits in a 3-1 loss to the Phillies. On the other hand, he issued six free passes, two of which came around to score, and was forced to groove a 3-2 fastball to Gavvy Cravath in the fifth rather than risk another walk and Cravath smashed it over the right-field wall for a homer. The Braves poled out nine hits, two each by Maranville, Joe Connolly, and Larry Gilbert, but left eight men on base.

May 30—The Braves split a doubleheader with the Phillies, losing the first game in 11 innings, 8-7, then winning the second game in ten innings by a count of 3-2. They should have had a sweep but Dick Rudolph and Lefty Tyler squandered a 7-0 lead in the morning game and allowed the Phils to tie the game with three runs in the bottom of the ninth. Another Cravath homer tied the second game in the eighth, but Evers drove in the winning run with a double in the top of the tenth to salvage a split.

June

June 1—STALLINGS' MEN TWICE OFF TO 2-TO-0 LEAD, BUT THERE THEY STOP. Indeed, the Braves jumped out to 2-0 leads against the Robins in both games of a doubleheader, but fell by scores of 6-2 and 4-2. Lefty Tyler was ineffective in the first game and lasted only 3⅓ innings before being yanked in favor of Dick Crutcher, but by then the game was out of hand. Game two was a tight 2-1 contest in Boston's favor until the sixth, when Brooklyn plated three to put the game on ice. The losses dropped the Braves to 10-24 on the year, 12 1/2 games out of first place.

Meanwhile John McGraw displayed a bit of prescience when he wrote, "Stallings' team is bound to come along, and it should pull itself together on this home stand."

June 2—A third straight doubleheader resulted in another split when the Braves took the first tilt over the Robins, 3-2, in 13 innings thanks to the performance of Bill James, who went all 13 frames and drove in the winning run. Cocreham lost the second game, 4-3, in a hard-fought contest that almost saw the Braves pull it out in the late innings. After the games, Stallings blamed his team's poor performance on his outfielders' inability to hit and the *Boston Globe* reported he was looking for at least two of them who could.

June 3—The Braves and Robins traded single runs in the first and remained tied until the fifth, when Brooklyn plated five runs on four hits, two of which were triples off the left-field scoreboard, a walk, and a throwing error. The Braves scored two in the eighth, but fell, 6-3.

June 4—The last game of the series against Brooklyn was rained out, enabling the Braves to catch an early train back to Boston where they'd begin a homestand against the Reds. Upon the team's arrival in Boston, George Stallings reminded the press about his dissatisfaction with his outfielders' inability to hit. "Time, time, and time again we have had the winning run on third base with only one out, and it so happened that we could not deliver the hit that would bring it home," Stallings said. He then mentioned that an outfielder had had four separate chances to bring in a run in a 1-0 loss to Cincinnati, but failed to do so. He didn't mention who the outfielder was but Tom Griffith was sent to Indianapolis of the American Association after hitting only .104 in 16 games.

Stallings also explained that Rabbit Maranville had been playing with a sprained wrist and tonsillitis, and felt that the extra batting practice his team would get at home would greatly improve their hitting. "Still, there is no use telling people what you intend to do. The proper way is to go out and do it."

June 5—Clearly Stallings knew what he was talking about as the Braves roughed up the Reds in the first game of a four-game set by a score of 7-2 in front of 3,000 fans who gave the team a warm welcome, much to the manager's surprise and delight. Among the Braves' nine hits were four doubles, two by Johnny Evers, and a Hank Gowdy home run. Hub Perdue scattered six hits to earn the victory.

June 6—The Braves took a 4-3 lead into the eighth inning, thanks in part to a bases-loaded walk to Maranville and a solo home run by Larry Gilbert in the fifth. But Lefty Tyler was victimized by bad luck in the top of the eighth when Buck Herzog hit a shot down the first-base line that looked foul but was called fair. With a runner ahead of him, that put runners on second and third with one out. Heinie Groh walked to load the bases. Tyler fanned the next batter to put him only one out away from escaping the jam. Alas, Dick Hoblitzel smashed a drive just past the outstretched glove of Gilbert and all three runners came home to give the Reds a 6-4 win.

June 8—Boston's hard luck continued with another late-inning heartbreaker when they blew a 2-1 lead in the ninth inning and lost to Cincinnati, 3-2. Bill James had been in complete control, holding the Reds to only one run on three hits through eight innings, but Bert Niehoff tied the game in the ninth with a homer, and his teammates followed with consecutive singles and an error by outfielder Jim Murray to complete the comeback.

June 9—LUCK TURNS BRAVES' WAY, FOR A CHANGE. In a tight contest that featured little offense, the Braves pushed the winning run across in the bottom of the fifth inning when Reds center fielder Fritz Von Kolnitz fell while trying to field a Johnny Evers liner. What should have been the third out of the inning became a run-scoring double, and Otto Hess made it stand up, allowing only five hits in the 3-2 victory.

June 10—For only the second time in 42 games, the Braves scored double-digit runs, beating the Pirates, 11-2, thanks in part to Rabbit Maranville's four hits and another homer by Larry Gilbert. Pittsburgh scored solo runs in the first and eighth, but it was all Braves otherwise. Dick Rudolph finally got run support in a game in which he pitched well and improved his record to 3-7.

June 11—With a 3-2 defeat of Pittsburgh, the Braves did something they hadn't done all year—win three games in a row. Once again Maranville was the star of the game, recording two more hits and fielding 12 chances flawlessly, prompting the *Boston Globe's* J.C. O'Leary to wax poetic about the Boston shortstop. "He had a greater number of chances than [Honus Wagner] and the way he handled them was a treat." Hub Perdue got the start but was yanked from the game sporting a 2-1 lead in the third because, according to O'Leary, he "did not appear to be extending himself." Bill James took over in the fourth and allowed only one run over the final six innings.

June 12—The Braves made it four wins in a row with a 5-3 win over the Pirates that featured yet another run-in with an umpire, this time Bill Klem, who accused Hub Perdue of discoloring the ball. Since Perdue had lasted only three innings in the previous game, Stallings gave him a chance to redeem himself and the veteran righty went the distance. But Klem tossed several balls out of play and insisted only new ones would be used while Perdue was on the mound. The teams were knotted at 3-3 until the bottom of the seventh when Gilbert blasted his third homer in six games to break the tie. Two batters later, Joe Connolly added a homer of his own for an insurance run the Braves didn't need.

June 13—Larry Gilbert belted another home run, his third of the series and fourth in seven games, to lead the Braves to a 4-3 win and a sweep over the Pirates. The winning run didn't come until the bottom of the eighth, when Les Mann and Hank Gowdy singled, then executed a successful double steal that pushed Mann across the plate. Rabbit Maranville contributed three more hits and Lefty Tyler earned the win.

In other news, George Stallings shipped a crate of eight baseballs that had been removed from Hub Perdue's appearance by Bill Klem to National League President John Tener with a letter of protest that insisted Perdue had done nothing illegal.

June 15—The Cubs made their first visit to Boston and broke the Braves' five-game winning streak with a 7-5 win against Otto Hess and Dick Rudolph. Hess lasted only 2⅓ innings before Rudolph took over, but the Cubs had already scored five runs to take a 5-3 lead, and added another in the third and one in the eighth to secure the victory. Maranville continued his stellar play, recording three more hits to give him a .667 average in his last five games, and after committing 22 errors in his first 30 games, he'd made only one miscue in his last 17.

Johnny Evers also maintained some consistency, although of the ignominious variety, when he was thrown out of the game in the seventh inning after arguing balls and strikes with umpire Al Orth. Maranville was equally unhappy with a called third strike in the same inning, but remained in the game. Regardless, both umpires required a police escort to their dressing room after the game.

A sterner look from Rabbit Maranville.

June 16—On a cool, blustery day that saw 4,200 fans come out to celebrate former Brave Bill Sweeney on Bill Sweeney Day, the Braves turned the tables on the Cubs and won, 7-5. Before the game, Sweeney was presented with gifts made of silver, including silverware, a tea serving set, a tray, and a percolator. The day also featured a concert and speeches, including one by Stallings. From there things got ugly, for none of the pitchers could navigate the wind and issued 17 walks as a result. Maranville went hitless in five at-bats but made another fine catch that saved two runs, and Gilbert tacked three more safeties to his total, giving him a modest six-game hitting streak during which he batted .524.

June 17—The Braves' hot streak continued with a doubleheader sweep over the Cubs, and neither game was close. The Boston Nationals celebrated Bunker Hill Day in front of 16,000 paying customers by thrashing Chicago, 8-3, in the first contest and 7-3 in the second. Lefty Tyler easily won the first game, earning his second straight victory and fifth of the year, and third baseman Charlie Deal doubled and tripled in four trips to the plate. Bill James had an even easier time in the afternoon tilt after his team handed him a 5-0 lead in the bottom of the first inning. Gilbert, Deal, and Les Mann had two hits apiece and Gilbert ran his hitting streak to eight games after going 3-for-9 in the twin bill.

June 18—In yet another game decided by poor umpiring, the Braves fell to the St. Louis Cardinals, 6-5, when the Cards plated two runs in the top of the ninth despite an obvious interference with Rabbit Maranville during what should have been a double play. With Chief Wilson on first and the Braves nursing a 5-4 lead, Art Butler accidentally blooped the ball toward the mound while he was dodging a Dick Crutcher pitch. Crutcher fielded the sphere and threw to Maranville, who was covering second. Rather than slide into the bag, Wilson went in standing up and, trying not to hurt the smaller Maranville, wrapped his arms around him so as not to knock him down, which not only pushed the shortstop off the base but kept him from throwing to first to retire Butler.

Umpire Bill Byron called both runners safe, which brought protest from the Braves' infielders, but to no avail. With two outs pinch-hitter Ivey Wingo singled to score Wilson, but Butler was held up by Charlie Deal, who blocked his path. In what appeared to be a makeup call, the umps called no interference on Deal despite howls of protest from the Cards. No matter, though, because Crutcher issued two free passes that forced the winning run across.

June 19—After an exciting 7-5 win over the Cardinals in which eight of the 12 runs were scored in the last two innings, the *Boston Globe's* J.C. O'Leary called the eighth inning "the liveliest session that has been seen here in a long time." Indeed. The Braves entered the frame with a 3-1 lead but the Cardinals' Cozy Dolan singled, then stole second, which incensed Johnny Evers, who produced spike wounds to his shoe and foot that proved his foot was between Dolan and second base when he tagged him. Umpire Mal Eason didn't appreciate Evers waving his shoe in front of the arbiter's face and ordered him off the field.

Dots Miller followed the argument with a homer into the center-field bleachers, and Chief Wilson followed with a homer into the right-field seats to give St. Louis a 5-3 lead. But the Braves rallied in the bottom of the inning and scored four runs to pull out the win.

June 20—In a pitchers' duel between Bill James and Pol Perritt that took only an hour and 44 minutes to complete, the Braves came out on top, 3-2, for their 11th win in their last 15 games. James held the Cardinals to only three hits, but walked five and hit three St. Louis batters. Perritt allowed only five hits and stopped Larry Gilbert's hitting streak at 10, but one of the hits off him was a solo homer by Otto Hess, playing first base in place of Butch Schmidt, who injured himself while sliding into second the day before.

June 22—The morning papers had Giants manager John McGraw calling the Braves "comers" and expecting them to finish atop the second division—"If [Stallings] isn't, he is liable to shoot three or four ball players, because he felt sure he was going to do better than he did last season before the race started." Then Lefty Tyler blew a late lead and fell to the Cards, 4-3. He didn't get any help from his defense, which committed five errors, including a crucial throwing error by catcher Bert Whaling that led to a three-run rally in the eighth from which the Braves couldn't recover.

June 24—With an 11-game deficit staring them in the face, the Braves had a golden opportunity to reduce it when the first-place Giants came to town, but they could manage only a split of a doubleheader to remain 11 games back. Dick Rudolph won the first game, 7-3, thanks to a 14-hit effort by his teammates, three of which came courtesy of Charlie Deal, who doubled and tripled, and two of which came from Joe Connolly, who homered for the third time this season. The second game belonged to Giants southpaw Rube Marquard, who held the Braves to only four singles in a 4-0 shutout.

June 25—The pitching of Paul Strand and seven runs from the offense pulled the Braves out of the cellar for the first time since May 7 when they edged the Giants, 7-6. After the Giants jumped out to a 4-2 lead against Bill James in only two innings, Strand almost beat the Giants by himself, throwing seven innings of two-run ball and going 2-for-4 with a double that knocked in the winning run in the bottom of the ninth. Gilbert, Connolly, and Hank Gowdy also had two hits each.

June 26—After only a day in seventh place, the Braves dropped a doubleheader to the Giants and fell to last place again, 12 games out of first. Although the Giants won handily in both games by scores of 8-4 and 10-4, Braves manager George Stallings insisted again that umpire Cy Rigler had it in for his team. In the fifth inning of the first game Rigler threw Lefty Tyler out of the game while he was at bat for arguing balls and strikes, then tossed Larry Gilbert, who was on deck and hadn't said a word. Of course, Johnny Evers stormed to Gilbert's defense and was also expelled.

J.C. O'Leary reported in the *Boston Globe* the next day, "Evers could tell better than Rigler whether any remark had been made by [Gilbert] and had a right to protect the latter, if he could, from arbitrary and unjust ruling. … The Boston team was not much good after this." The *New York Times* reported that Stallings and Braves president James Gaffney filed another protest against Rigler, who they insisted was "intentionally making decisions against the Boston team in order to handicap it," and that Boston "has been robbed of every game it has played with Rigler behind the plate." Even John McGraw stood behind the Braves, saying that Tyler, Gilbert, and Evers had been expelled from the contest for saying "nothing at all." Gaffney insisted that Rigler be banned from umpiring games involving the Braves for the rest of the season.

June 27—The Braves evened the series at three games apiece and exacted revenge on Rube Marquard, who had shut them out three days before, with a 4-2 win over the Giants. Dick Rudolph was both the pitching and hitting star, holding the Giants to five singles while going 2-for-4 at the plate.

June 28—Rabbit Maranville lent his voice to a benefit concert in the Brighton neighborhood of Boston in aid of the family of Inspector Thomas Norton, a Boston police officer who was shot and killed on June 19 during a gunfight with a man who was wanted for murder and robbery in Michigan. Maranville sang a solo and the benefit raised $75 for Norton's family.

June 29—With four doubleheaders on the horizon, J.C. O'Leary reported that the Braves had some injury concerns, most notably a charley horse that Charlie Deal had suffered before the season started and from which he still hadn't fully recovered. Butch Schmidt had finally recovered from a sprained ankle and was expected to return to the lineup in time for the June 30 twin bill, but Lefty Tyler had a sore shinbone and ankle that had affected his control.

On the bright side, statistics posted in the *Boston Globe* showed a team that had improved greatly since the month began. The squad as a whole was hitting .240, 15 points higher than on June 1, and fielding at a .968 clip, an improvement of seven points. Joe Connolly and Larry Gilbert were both hitting .301 and had combined to hit nine of the team's 17 home runs. And Maranville had boosted his fielding percentage 35 points, from .900 to .935.

June 30—O'Leary reported that pitcher Hub Perdue had been traded to the St. Louis Cardinals for outfielder Ted Cather and utility man George "Possum" Whitted. At the time of the deal Perdue was 2-5 with a 5.82 ERA in nine games and was suffering from tonsillitis that set him back even further. Cather was hitting .273 in 39 games and could play all three outfield positions, and though Whitted had hit only .129 in 20 games, he could play all over the diamond and give the regulars a day off when needed. O'Leary liked the deal, writing, "Both of these boys, under the direction of Stallings, may be developed into good players, and it is not thought that the Boston club got any the worst of it in the trade."

Later, in the first of two straight doubleheaders with the Phillies, the Braves split, losing the first game, 5-4, in 13 innings before taking the second contest, 4-2, in a game shortened by darkness. Boston lost a golden opportunity to sweep the doubleheader when it failed to capitalize on a rally against Grover Cleveland Alexander in the bottom of the 13th. Maranville singled off starter Eppa Rixey to begin the frame, prompting the latter's removal from the game. Stallings sent Connolly in to hit for Schmidt and Connolly responded with a run-scoring triple that just barely missed leaving the park for a game-tying homer.

With the tying run at third and no outs, Alexander broke the hearts of the hometown fans, who were "howling like a lot of Indians," and struck out Charlie Deal, Les Mann, and Bert Whaling to preserve the 5-4 win. The second game was a completely different story; after racking up 15 hits against Dick Crutcher and Paul Strand in the first tilt, the Phillies managed only four hits off Bill James in game two. Maranville's hot streak continued as he went 5-for-8 at the plate and made a fantastic leaping grab of a liner off the bat of Hans Lobert.

July

July 1—July began exactly as June had, with a doubleheader loss that dropped the Braves to 12 1/2 games out of first. Both games were ugly and nothing went the Braves' way. George "Iron" Davis made his 1914 debut in the first game and did little to impress the club, allowing seven runs in a 7-2 loss. Boston managed only six hits off Erskine Mayer and committed three errors, two by Mann. Then the Braves produced the exact same line against Alexander in a 5-0 shutout, and Mann committed two more errors.

Bill James warming up beside the stands.

Despite president Gaffney's appeal that Cy Rigler be restricted from umpiring Braves games, he was behind the plate for the second game and tossed Hank Gowdy from the contest after Gowdy argued about balls and strikes.

July 3—Gaffney made another trade, sending infielder Jack Martin to the Phillies for outfielder Josh Devore, and also announced that he'd signed Johnny Evers, Butch Schmidt, Rabbit Maranville, Dick Rudolph, and Hank Gowdy through the 1917 season, Paul Strand and Bill James through 1916, and Larry Gilbert through 1915.

Strand then "celebrated" his new deal by getting hammered by the Robins in the first of a five-game set. He allowed five runs on eight hits and three walks and fanned no one in four innings in the 6-5 loss. It also didn't help that the defense committed five errors in the game, including three before Brooklyn had sent three men to the plate.

July 4—The Braves reached a new low when they lost two more to the Robins and finished the day a season-worst 15 games behind the first-place Giants and five games out of seventh place. The first game was a back-and-forth affair that the Braves almost won in the bottom of the ninth when they plated three runs to tie the score at 4-4, but poor baserunning kept them from scoring the winning run and Brooklyn pushed three across in the 11th for a 7-5 victory. Bill James went the distance and allowed 17 hits. Boston rapped out 13 safeties, three by James.

The second game also went to the wire before Jake Daubert slid into home in the top of the ninth with what would turn out to be the winning run. With the score tied at 3-3, Daubert reached first on a fielder's choice, attempted to steal second, went to third when Hank Gowdy threw the ball into center field, and headed for home when Josh Devore bobbled the ball momentarily. Daubert and Devore's throw arrived at home at the same time and the runner knocked the ball loose from Gowdy's mitt. The play was almost costly for the Robins, however, for Daubert was knocked unconscious and had to be helped to the clubhouse. He wasn't badly hurt, though.

July 6—After getting 17 hits in one game on July 4, the Robins managed only 13 hits in a doubleheader loss to the Braves two days later, and managed only one run in 18 innings. Boston scored three in the third inning of game one and that's all it took to hand Brooklyn a 3-1 loss behind the fantastic pitching of Dick Rudolph. Dick Crutcher was even better in the second game, throwing a complete-game shutout for a 1-0 win.

The Braves had only four hits in the afternoon contest, but a run-scoring double by Les Mann that followed a walk to Possum Whitted sealed the game in the second frame. In fact it was the newest members of the team who had the most to do with the win. Whitted scored what turned out to be the winning run and Ted Cather made two outstanding grabs against the right-field wall that robbed Brooklyn of sure triples and kept them scoreless.

July 7—On their way to Chicago during their first road trip in more than a month, the Braves stopped in Buffalo to play an exhibition game against the Bisons of the International League and they were trounced, 10-2. Boston recorded only three hits and made three errors. Paul Strand and Gene Cocreham took turns on the mound for the Braves.

July 8—BRAVES TROUNCE O'DAYS MISFITS read the *Chicago Tribune* on the morning of July 9 after the Braves had defeated the Cubs 7-4 in 11 innings. It was actually a tight affair that Boston let get away when they blew a four-run second inning lead by allowing single runs to score in the third, fourth, sixth, and eighth. Another Johnny Evers banishment almost cost his team the game when his replacement, Oscar Dugey, made a wild throw that allowed the Cubs to tie the game in the eighth. But Boston scored three in the 11th to take a contest that saw 31 players take the field in what sportswriter James Crusinberry called a "farce."

July 9—Bill James recovered nicely from his previous 17-hit performance and held the Cubs to one run on only six hits in a 3-1 win, the Braves' fourth straight. And once again a brilliant defensive play kept an opponent at bay, this time by Les Mann. "Once when the two runs needed to tie were on the bags, Roger Bresnahan poled a terrific drive to left center that brought screams of delight from the eager fans," wrote Crusinberry. "But the joyous screams ended in a groan when outfielder Mann in some superhuman manner raced across the green and pulled down the ball."

July 10—In what turned out to be a terrible day for the club, the Braves lost their vice president, C. James Connelly, to a heart attack, then lost to the Cubs by an embarrassing score of 11-6. The 11 runs allowed matched a season worst and came on three doubles, three triples, and a home run off Otto Hess and Dick Crutcher. To add insult to injury or vice versa, Hank Gowdy suffered a dislocated finger on a foul tip in the fifth inning.

July 11—Thanks to Dick Rudolph's second straight gem, the Braves found themselves in the win column again with a 5-2 victory over the Cubs. Chicago scored its runs in the first and second innings, but Rudolph buckled down and held them without a run for the rest of the game. Boston tied the game at 2-2 in the third, scored two more in the fifth and one more in the ninth for good measure. The Braves rapped out ten hits and played error-free ball, while the Cubs managed only six hits and committed four miscues.

July 12—Boston sold outfielder Jimmy Murray to St. Paul of the American Association and outfielder Wilson Collins to Binghamton of the New York State League, then went out and put 12 runs on the Cardinals' scoreboard in St. Louis in a 12-5 win. Not only did the 12 runs mark a new season best but a lot of them came against former teammate Hub Perdue, who couldn't make it out of the fourth inning. Josh Devore and Bert Whaling led the 15-hit attack with three hits each, and five Braves scored two runs apiece. Since his debut with the Braves on July 4, Devore had hit .409 and scored seven runs in six games.

July 13—The Braves' offense continued to pour it on in the Mound City, rapping out another 17 hits in a thrilling 8-7 victory over the Cardinals in 12 innings, but it was another Rabbit Maranville defensive gem that sealed the win. After missing the previous game due to the death of his brother, Maranville came back in fine form, going 3-for-6 with three runs, and making so many great plays on defense that the *Boston Globe* claimed he'd "cut off as many runs for the Cards as the Boston team made."

But no play was more spectacular or timely than the one he made in the bottom of the ninth inning when he made a diving snare of a line drive by Chuck Miller. The catch preceded a Cozy Dolan homer that tied the game, whereas without Maranville's catch, the Cards would have won the game then and there. Instead, the homer tied the score at 6-6. The Braves pushed two across in the top of the 12th, then held off a rally for the win.

July 14—According to the *Hartford Courant*, Bill James was none too happy with a reporter who criticized him and James took matters into his own hands. "What happened could best be described by a pugilistic expert," wrote the paper. "This manner of resenting honest criticism went out of style long ago."

Hub Perdue exacted a bit of revenge by beating his old team, 3-2, despite allowing 12 hits and three walks. But the Braves left nine men on base and Lefty Tyler blew a 2-1 ninth-inning lead to earn his tenth loss of the year against only five wins. According to the *Boston Globe*, "Maranville's snug way of catching fly balls close into his stomach afforded the crowd vast amusement."

July 15—Otto Hess and Slim Sallee pitched to a 3-3 tie through eight innings in the final game of the four-game set before the latter settled the game with a two-run single in the bottom of the eighth that drove the Cards to a 5-3 win. Only three Braves recorded hits, including Hank Gowdy, who was playing his first game since dislocating his finger on July 10.

July 16—The game between the Braves and Reds in Cincinnati was called in the fourth inning after a storm drenched the field and made the skies so dark that outfielders were unable to see the ball. The score was 1-1 at the time.

July 17—"Nowadays a player of ability has only to play winning ball to show up those responsible for unjust criticism," said the *Hartford Courant* after Bill James resorted to fisticuffs to throttle a reporter who'd criticized him earlier in the month. Well, James responded with a four-hit shutout that netted him his ninth win of the season. Reds hurler Rube Benton was equally effective but singles by Johnny Evers, Maranville, and Butch Schmidt in the fourth brought in the game's only run. The three hits matched Boston's output in the other eight innings.

July 18—A 6-3 win over the Reds on the strength of triples by Johnny Evers, Les Mann, and Hank Gowdy gave the Braves a series win with one left to play in the three-game set. Evers and Joe Connolly combined for six of the team's 11 hits, and Dick Rudolph won his tenth game of the year.

July 19—Thanks to a rash of Cincinnati errors in the ninth inning, the Braves overcame a 2-0 deficit to win, 3-2, and leapfrog the Pittsburgh Pirates into seventh place, 10 1/2 games behind the first-place New York Giants. The Reds committed more errors (six) in the game than they had hits (five). According to Harold Kaese, author of *The Boston Braves, 1871-1953*, "As they left the field the [Braves] threw caps and bats into the air. They cheered like college boys. They almost smothered Stallings. 'Now we'll catch New York,' the manager told his men. We're playing thirty-per-cent better ball than any team in the league. They won't be able to stop us.'"

Tim Murnane of the *Boston Globe* gave credit for much of the team's recent success to Rabbit Maranville, whom he called a "natural infielder" who had "developed hitting strength" and who was "cool and shows to the best advantage at a time when extra fine ball playing is needed."

July 20—A 1-0 win over the Pirates coupled with a Brooklyn loss put the Braves in sixth place, their best showing since April 23. Neither team scored until the ninth when the Braves finally broke through against Wilbur Cooper. Lefty Tyler held the reeling Pirates to only four hits through eight innings, then Bill James slammed the door with a hitless ninth. Johnny Evers, who had gone into the game hitting .419 in his last 19 games, went hitless.

July 21—With a 6-0 win over the Pirates, the Braves suddenly found themselves in fourth place and five wins from a .500 mark. Dick Rudolph surrendered only three hits and earned his first shutout of the season, and Rabbit Maranville paced the offense with two hits, including a homer, his second of the season.

July 22—It seems Bill James should have beaten up more sportswriters. Since it was reported that he'd taken a writer to task for criticizing him, the big man allowed no runs in his next 22 innings, including a 1-0 shutout of the Pirates in the first game of a doubleheader this day that ran the Braves' winning streak to six games. It took 11 innings and errors by Honus Wagner and Max Carey, but Boston emerged victorious.

The second game was a different story, though. The Pirates broke Boston's winning streak when they scored six runs in the eighth inning for a come-from-behind 8-4 win. To that point Dick Crutcher had allowed only two runs and, according to the *Boston Globe*, "all was as peaceful as a country village, and the fans were leaving the park." But Crutcher couldn't hold the lead and the Braves fell to defeat.

July 23—For the second time in the five-game series, Lefty Tyler outdueled Wilbur Cooper and led the Braves to a 2-0 win. When all was said and done, the

Braves had four shutouts in five games and had held the Pirates scoreless in 43 of 46 innings.

July 24—Braves president James Gaffney arrived in Boston at 10:00 P.M. and told the press he was very pleased with the Braves' play of late. "Naturally I'm delighted with the showing the boys have made, and I hope they will be able to keep up their good work," he said. "In view of the poor start they got, which kept them in last place for quite a while, I think they have done wonderfully well to have worked into the first division."

July 25—The second-place Cubs went into Boston with an eight-game win streak and extended it to nine with a 5-4 win over the Braves. The game was witnessed by more than 16,000 fans, the most the Braves had drawn in years. Southpaw Hippo Vaughn went into the game with only four losses, and three of them were to the Braves, but this time he emerged victorious. As usual there was trouble with the umpiring, but this time a fan got involved and hit Bill Byron with a pop bottle after a double play killed the Braves in the bottom of the ninth. Byron had ruled earlier on a play that went against the Braves and the fan had had enough.

July 27—After Boston's blue laws kept the teams off the field for a day, the Braves broke the Cubs' streak with a 5-3 win behind the pitching of Dick Rudolph and the hitting of Johnny Evers and Hank Gowdy. Rudolph wasn't scheduled to pitch for at least one more day but Bill James had to leave in the second inning due to nausea and Rudolph was called upon to take over. He allowed only one earned run in seven innings and the Braves plated two in the bottom of the eight to break a 3-3 tie.

July 28—A steady drizzle postponed the third game between the Braves and Cubs, although some speculated that George Stallings had ulterior motives when he called the game off around 2:00 P.M., for Evers had a cold and couldn't play and Rabbit Maranville was suffering from a thumb injury. The game was rescheduled for September 26. It was also reported that Evers' children had been suffering from scarlet fever but had recovered, that James' attack of nausea had been temporary, and that Maranville's thumb injury might hamper his throwing but wouldn't keep him out of the lineup.

In other news, the Braves acquired left-handed pitcher Ensign Cottrell from Baltimore of the International League, which pleased Stallings. According to J.C. O'Leary, "Manager Stallings believes he will fit in nicely with the pitching staff and that he will be able to get a lot of good work out of him." Cottrell went 14-8 for the Orioles in 1913 and was said to have "plenty of smoke and a puzzling assortment of curves."

July 29—With Johnny Evers in bed with a cold, Possum Whitted stepped into his shoes and played well, rapping out two hits, including a triple, and "handling some nasty grounders as well as any second baseman in the business" to help lead the Braves to an easy 8-3 win over the Cubs. Boston scored five runs in the first three frames and never looked back as Bill James returned with an effective performance that saw him fan a season-high eight batters.

July 30—The Braves won their third game in a row and pulled to within two games of .500 with a lucky 2-1 victory over the visiting Cardinals. With the score tied 1-1 after three innings, hurlers Lefty Tyler and Dan "Rusty" Griner got down to business and put up goose eggs until the bottom of the ninth, when the Braves won the game thanks to two errors and a sacrifice. Griner allowed only one hit in the game, and both pitchers received fantastic defensive support at times, but St. Louis errors at crucial moments gave Boston the victory.

Outfielders Joe Connolly and Josh Devore threw out Cardinals on the bases, and Maranville, Whitted, and Butch Schmidt all made outstanding catches, the latter saving the win with a snare of a liner that would have plated the go-ahead runs in the ninth. For St. Louis, Lee Magee made two fantastic catches in center field, and Zinn Beck made a great stop at third to get Whitted before committing an error on Maranville's grounder that allowed the winning run to score.

July 31—With a 2-0 win over the Cardinals, the Braves reduced their deficit to single digits for the first time since May 18. Dick Rudolph continued to be brilliant, allowing only two hits to win his seventh straight game and run his record to 13-8. Former Braves hurler Hub Perdue went against his old pals again, and again Les Mann got the best of him, going 3-for-4 to lead Boston's six-hit attack.

August

August 1—In front of their largest crowd in franchise history, the Braves beat the Cardinals, 4-3, in ten innings to reach .500 for the first time all season. The game was played at Fenway Park and 20,000 fans came to watch what turned out to be a thriller. With St. Louis nursing a 1-0 lead through seven innings, the Braves plated three in the eighth and sent the crowd into a frenzy. But as many began filing out of the stadium certain of a win, the Cards scored two in the ninth to tie it at 3-3.

Boston rallied with two outs in the bottom of the tenth and scored the winning run on a double by Johnny Evers and a single by Possum Whitted. Bill James went the distance for the win.

August 3—The Braves returned to South End Grounds and won their sixth straight game, climbing to within 7 1/2 games of first place, the closest they'd been since May 1. Lefty Tyler took care of business both on the mound and at the plate, holding the Cards to no runs on only three hits and scoring the winning run in the bottom of the ninth for a nifty 1-0 win.

Red Sox president Joe Lannin sent word to Braves president Gaffney that the Braves could use Fenway Park for the remainder of the season free of charge. "As the Braves are doing wonderfully well, and the South End Grounds must be too small to accommodate their fans, I want to see Mr. Gaffney reap the profit of good luck," Lannin told the press.

August 4—Dick Rudolph followed up Tyler's performance with a shutout of his own, holding the Pittsburgh Pirates to only two singles in another 1-0 win. It was Rudolph's second straight two-hit shutout

Dick Rudolph demonstrating his grip on the ball.

and eighth consecutive victory. Rabbit Maranville made several fine plays behind Rudolph, handling eight chances "like the artist he is," according to O'Leary, and Evers "executed one of the greatest plays ever seen on the grounds" when he fielded a hard grounder behind second base and threw speedy Max Carey out at first by a stride. O'Leary gave the odds of stopping the ball at 100 to 1 and throwing out one of the fastest runners in the league at 1,000 to 1.

August 5—In an odd twist that saw all National League winners shut out their opponents, the Braves whitewashed the Pirates again, by a score of 4-0. Bill James joined the fun by tossing a four-hitter and allowed only one enemy runner to reach second base.

August 6—Although Lefty Tyler finally proved human, allowing two earned runs in five innings, the Braves earned their ninth straight win when Maranville belted a game-winning homer in the bottom of the tenth inning for a 5-4 victory. Despite suffering from a minor case of food poisoning, Maranville led the team with three hits, two steals, and six total bases, prompting his teammates to joke that whatever he ate to make him sick should be part of his regular diet. Putting a damper on the win, however, was news that Johnny Evers' daughter, Helen, was very ill with scarlet fever.

August 7—Saddened by news that Helen Evers had passed away earlier in the day, the Braves were flat and fell to the Pirates, 5-1, to break their nine-game winning streak. Recently acquired southpaw Ensign Cottrell earned his first start for the Braves but lasted only an inning, allowing two runs on two hits and three walks before being spelled by Dick Crutcher.

August 8—Amid reports that Johnny Evers insisted he wouldn't play again in 1914, the Braves defeated the Cincinnati Reds, 4-3, in ten innings after tying the game with a three-run ninth-inning rally. The game was played at Fenway Park for the second straight Saturday. Up until the ninth, the Reds had the game in hand behind the two-hit pitching of Shufflin' Phil Douglas, but the Braves tied the score on a walk, an error, two hits, and shoddy fielding, then won it when Josh Devore singled, moved to third on a bunt and groundout, and came around to score on a single by Maranville.

National League President John Tener didn't believe the rumors that Evers was through for the season, telling the press, "Evers is just now suffering the shock of a terrible affliction and is wrung with grief. Give him time to recover. He will play again, all right." In fact, George Stallings had received word from a friend of Evers, who said the second baseman would be back in Boston in time for Tuesday's game against the Reds, the last contest of the homestand. "The death of his little girl is a hard blow," said Stallings, "but Johnny Evers will bear up under it as he has under all his other trials; you may be sure of that."

It was also reported that the Braves had bought third baseman Red Smith from Brooklyn to "strengthen and fortify" the team. After two very good years with the Robins in 1912 and 1913, Smith had slumped in 1914 and was hitting only .245. But Charlie Deal was hitting only .217 at the time and third base was a weak spot.

August 10—A 3-1 Braves win over Cincinnati and losses by the Cubs and Cardinals, put the Braves in second place, just percentage points ahead of Chicago and St. Louis. Bill James continued his brilliant pitching and held the Reds to one run on six hits, earning his seventh straight victory, and pitching to a 0.89 ERA in his last 11 appearances. Not surprisingly the hitting star was Maranville, who rapped out three more hits, including a double, and scored two of the team's three runs.

Through Boston's first 97 games, Maranville was among the National League leaders in runs with 46 and stolen bases with 15, and Joe Connolly was fourth among all NL regulars in batting at .310. And Bill James, Dick Rudolph, and Paul Strand ranked third, sixth, and seventh in the league in winning percentage.

Lefty Tyler.

August 11—Lefty Tyler and Red Ames squared off in a fantastic duel that went 13 scoreless innings before being called due to darkness. The 0-0 tie coupled with St. Louis's win over the Giants dropped the Braves to third place, but they gained a half-game in the standings thanks to New York's loss. The Reds outhit the Braves 10-5 but the defense made several excellent plays to keep Cincinnati from scoring. Maranville had two of Boston's hits, giving him nine in his last five games. It would prove to be the last game ever played at the South Side Grounds, as the remaining games would be played at Fenway Park for the rest of the 1914 season and most of 1915 before Braves Field opened on August 18, 1915.

August 12—The *Washington Post* reported that "the general public throughout the major league territory is pulling for George Stallings and his Braves" because "Sporting sentiment usually favors the under dog." Because of the team's surge from last place to second the *Post* opined, "Should Stallings win a pennant he will have accomplished that which approaches the miraculous."

John McGraw, manager of the first-place Giants, didn't appear to be worried about the Braves, however. "I think the Braves have a better chance than the Cardinals [of ousting the Giants atop the standings], but even they cannot keep up their spurt for the simple reason that pitchers Rudolph, James and Tyler cannot stand it." Stallings had a few words of his own about their coming series with New York, though. "You may safely bet that the Giants are worrying more about the outcome of this series than we are," he said.

August 13— BRAVES SHOW GIANTS WHO'S WHO IN OLD LEAGUE read the headline in the *Boston Globe* after the Boston Nationals beat the Giants at the Polo Grounds, 5-3, to jump back into second place and cut New York's lead to 5 1/2 games. The Braves had 11 hits and were led by Ted Cather, who had three, and Dick Rudolph, who won for the 14th time in his last 15 decisions. Johnny Evers returned to the lineup and received a nice ovation from the New York crowd, then went 1-for-3. In fact, many in the throng were rooting for the Braves, especially the Bronx Lodge of Elks, who presented Rudolph with a diamond-studded watch charm prior to the game. And from fans at Fenway Park, who were watching the Red Sox play the Yankees, there were — according to the *Globe* — "spontaneous yells of delight whenever the score board man put up any runs for the Braves in the game in New York. Pres Joe Lannin of the Red Sox applauded most enthusiastically when the first run was recorded."

August 14— "BOSTON'S GAME FROM FIRST UP TO LAST OUT. Giants Again Shrivel to Pygmy Size Before Braves' Withering Fire," reported the *Boston Globe* on August 15. Boston jumped all over the Giants and had a 6-1 lead after five innings, which was more than enough for Bill James, who scattered six hits in a 7-3 victory that pulled the Braves to within 4 1/2 games of first place. Joe Connolly went 3-for-3 with a double, a homer, and a sacrifice fly that just missed leaving the park by a few feet.

Gowdy, Tyler, and Connolly at the batting cage.

August 15—John McGraw sent his old warhorse, the legendary Christy Mathewson, to the mound to salvage at least one game of the series, but Matty was bested by Lefty Tyler, who tossed his second straight extra-inning shutout to defeat the Giants, 2-0. Mathewson and Tyler exchanged goose eggs for the first nine innings before Boston plated two in the top of the tenth and sent 35,000 Giants fans home disappointed. It was the largest crowd ever to see a nonchampionship game at the Polo Grounds.

Hank Gowdy led the eight-hit attack with three safeties, including two triples, the second of which scored the go-ahead run. He then scored Boston's second run when Mathewson uncorked a wild pitch. The win brought the Braves to within 3 1/2 games of first place.

August 16—After going 28-6 with one tie in their last 35 games, the Braves were the talk of the baseball universe. The *Hartford Courant* called the team the "sensation" of the National League. J.C. O'Leary reported in the *Boston Globe* that the team was met in Cincinnati by telegrams from all over the country congratulating them for sweeping the Giants in New York, and were assured a warm welcome by fans on their return to Boston. The *Globe* reported that New Yorkers had dubbed George Stallings "The Miracle Man," even before the three-game series at the Polo Grounds.

McGraw called the Braves "dangerous," but wouldn't concede anything to them. "George Stallings thinks that he is going to win the championship, and most of his players also have the pennant bee buzzing in their heads," the Giants skipper wrote in his weekly review. "This notion is going to help crack them the nearer they get to the front."

August 17—Not only did the Braves not crack in their first two games against the Reds in Cincinnati, but they outscored Buck Herzog's boys, 16-4, in a doubleheader sweep that cut another half-game off New York's lead. Dick Rudolph, who went into the game with the league's fourth best winning percentage at .682, extended his winning streak to 11 games when Boston took the first game, 11-1. Bill James, who ranked second in winning percentage, earned his ninth straight victory and 16th of the season in a 5-3 win that wasn't as close as the score would indicate.

August 18—Dick Crutcher and Paul Strand contributed to Boston's pitching dominance, allowing the Reds only two hits, but two crucial errors and a lack of timely hitting led to the Braves' first loss since August 7. Newly acquired Red Smith, who'd made several spectacular plays since joining the team, stopped Pat Moran's hot shot to third and threw home in an effort to retire the potential go-ahead run, but the ball hit the runner in the leg and caromed all the way to the grandstand, allowing a second run to score. That was all the Reds would need to win, 3-1.

August 19—The Braves rebounded with a 3-2 win over Cincinnati and found themselves only two games out of first when the Pirates beat the Giants, 5-1. Lefty Tyler and Red Ames hooked up again after battling to a 0-0 draw in 13 innings on August 11, and this time Tyler emerged victorious. Boston spotted Tyler two runs in the first and he made it stand up with nine more frames of stellar work. In fact, had a couple of breaks gone his way, he could have extended his scoreless inning streak to 32, but the Reds scored a run in the bottom of the fifth and stopped his streak at 27.

August 20—With a 6-3 win over the Pirates, the Braves reduced the Giants' lead to only a game and a half. Dick Rudolph extended his winning streak to 12 and Joe Connolly led the team with two hits, but George Stallings wasn't about to get too excited about his team's play. "I have been in the game too long not to know how things are frequently upset and some one will come along and put three or four straight over on you."

August 21—While the idle Braves rested up for a Saturday doubleheader in Pittsburgh, the Giants fell to the Reds, 3-2, and saw their lead cut to one game. But the Braves weren't the only beneficiaries of the loss and had two other teams, the St. Louis Cardinals and Chicago Cubs, on their heels and within 3 1/2 games of first place.

August 22—The newspapers were teeming with news about the Braves and Giants; the *Chicago Tribune* compared John McGraw, "probably the hardest fighter in baseball," with George Stallings, "[one of] the greatest fighters the national game ever has known"; the *Washington Post* recounted how McGraw had cast off Dick Rudolph after two failed trials with the Giants, and how Boston was now benefiting from his pitching.

Only an extra-inning loss to the Pirates in the first game of the twin bill kept the Braves from tying the Giants for first place. Bill James fell behind early when he allowed two runs in the first three innings, but settled down and held the Pirates scoreless until the 12th, when they plated the winning run in a 3-2 loss. But the Braves rebounded in the second game, thanks to a positive contribution from an unexpected source, Otto Hess, who won only his third game of the season. Combined with a New York loss to Cincinnati, the Braves were within a half-game of first place.

August 23—Another Giants loss to the Reds had them tied for first place with the idle Braves with about 45 games left in the season. Since being a season-worst 15 games out of first place on July 4, the Braves had gone 33-8 to forge a tie for first place, and improved their winning percentage 157 points, from .394 to .551.

Joe Connolly's hot hitting had his average up to .328, only two points behind league leader Jack Dalton of the Robins. The *Boston Globe* reported that the Braves would look to fortify the club and was interested in adding another "winning" pitcher and a "good hitting" outfielder. In fact the team purchased veteran right fielder Herbie Moran from Cincinnati the same day the paper hit newsstands, but another pitcher was hard to come by because "any club that has winning pitchers needs them in their own business," according to J.C. O'Leary.

August 24—After only a day in first place, the Braves fell to second again when the Cubs drubbed them, 9-5, at the West Side Grounds. It was the most runs Boston had allowed since the Cubs scored 11 in a July 10 beating. Lefty Tyler got the start and lasted only two innings before Dick Rudolph took over. Chicago scored four times off Tyler and held a 4-2 lead until the fifth when the Braves jumped ahead, 5-4. Rudolph couldn't hold the lead, however, and his 12-game winning streak was snapped. Joe Connolly continued to hit the ball hard, smacking a double and homer in five at-bats.

The manager of the idle Giants, John McGraw, called the National League pennant race a "fine mess," but stood by his claim that his team would win the pennant. He also insisted that Stallings had gotten a "lucky break" when three of his pitchers "rounded into shape at the same time" and were "turning in victory after victory" for the Braves. McGraw credited Stallings with being one of the best handlers of pitchers in the country, but predicted Boston would be in trouble when a "reserve" hurler would be needed to pitch in a doubleheader.

August 25—A 4-1 win over the Cubs combined with a Giants day off put the Braves in a virtual tie for first again, although New York held a one-point edge in winning percentage. Bill James found himself in the win column for the 17th time thanks in part to heads up baserunning by his teammates and a great catch by Possum Whitted in the bottom of the ninth that kept the Cubs from mounting a rally.

James J. Montague printed a poem about the Braves in the *New York American*:

> They're not an "overpowering force"
> or "awe-inspiring sight,"
> They haven't any Zeppelins to scatter dynamite;
> They've got no field artillery to
> mow our forces down,
> They haven't any 10-inch guns to batter up the town.
> They even come from Boston,
> but the way they play the game
> Is making us uneasy, just the same.
>
> They haven't any famous stars, and Matty with a grin
> Explains with charts and records
> how they have no chance to win.
> They haven't got a leader with an iron fighting jaw
> To drive 'em to a victory like Mr. Jawn McGraw.
> They've never been a marker
> in the pennant race before.
> But just the same they're piling up the score.
>
> We aren't a bit afraid of them, for anyone can see
> That such a thing as walloping the Giants cannot be.
> We know we've clinched the pennant
> so it cannot get away,
> And that there's nothing left to do
> but join in the hurray.
> They haven't knocked us off our nerve,
> nor frightened us a bit.
> But just the same we sure do wish they'd quit!

August 26—Both the *Los Angeles Times* and *Washington Post* printed articles about George Stallings and his sharp tongue, the former claiming Stallings had driven the Braves to a "contending position for the pennant by sheer force of his invectives," and the latter stating that no manager in baseball had a better ability to "loosen some weird-sounding expletives" in times of stress than Stallings. "Stallings' words sting at first, but they have no ill after affect [sic]," wrote the *Post*.

The *Post* also reported that Rabbit Maranville had stolen one of Yankees outfielder Pete Daley's bats during the Braves' trip to New York in mid-August and that he had no intention of returning it. "When Daley gets back [to the Polo Grounds] tell him I've got his bat and I'm going to keep it," Maranville told the groundskeeper. "I'll pay him for it if he names the price, but he can't have the bat back. It's the best club I ever used..." Apparently Daley also had a fondness for that bat and was "preparing an ultimatum" at the time of the report.

On the field the Braves showed the fighting spirit that Stallings had instilled in them. Literally. After six scoreless innings, the Cubs finally broke through when Vic Saier homered in the bottom of the seventh to give Chicago a 1-0 lead. Heinie Zimmerman followed with a single that he tried to stretch into a double, but he was gunned down by Joe Connolly. Second baseman Johnny Evers went to tag his former teammate, who was coming into second head-first, and took exception to Zimmerman's attempt to knock the ball from his glove. Evers tagged Zim a second time, applying his glove to the runner's head, and Zimmerman went after Evers.

Zim was getting the best of the smaller man before Maranville and Butch Schmidt joined the fray. Maranville landed a punch and cut Zimmerman's lip before the fight was broken up and all four men were ordered off the field. As they left, Zimmerman threatened future retaliation, but Maranville stood his ground and the much larger man kept his cool. Saier's home run turned out to be the only run in Chicago's 1-0 win.

August 27—National League President John Tener fined Heinie Zimmerman and Johnny Evers $100 and Rabbit Maranvile $50 for their part in the fight the day before, then the Braves dropped to third place when they lost to the Cardinals, 3-2, in ten rainy and foggy innings that ended in controversy. According to the *Globe*'s J.C. O'Leary, the game shouldn't have been allowed to go into extra innings for it was so dark, foggy, and rainy that the outfielders couldn't see the ball. With the score tied at 2-2, Cozy Dolan skied a fly ball to left that Joe Connolly lost in the fog, and the winning run came home when the ball landed 75 feet behind him. With the win, the Cards leapfrogged the Braves into second place, only a game behind the Giants.

August 28—Rain postponed games in St. Louis and Chicago, leaving the league's top four teams with doubleheaders on the 29th. Despite holding slim leads over the Cardinals and Braves, John McGraw was convinced that the next week would propel his Giants toward another pennant. "Naturally they went a bit stale," he told the *New York Times*, "but with two clubs right on their heels and threatening to assume the lead, the men are going out to play ball as though they meant business."

August 29—A doubleheader sweep over St. Louis and a Giants' split with the Cubs put Boston back in second place, a half-game out of first. The Braves and Cards played in front of 30,000 fans, one of the largest to ever watch baseball in the Mound City, who were treated to a gem by Bill James in the first game and a late-inning comeback by the Braves in the second tilt. James shut the home team down in a four-hit 4-0 win, then Boston plated four in the top of the eighth of game two to erase a 4-2 deficit and win, 6-4.

August 30—Lefty Tyler capped off the month with another brilliant performance, surrendering only one hit to the Cardinals in a 2-0 victory that kept the Braves within a half-game of first place. Since July 1 the big three of Tyler, Dick Rudolph, and Bill James had gone 31-6 with one tie. J.C. O'Leary compared the Braves to a college team—"Each of them seems as well pleased when another does a particularly brilliant stunt as he would if he had performed the feat himself."

Three pitchers, 68 victories: Rudolph, Tyler, and James with manager Stallings.

August 31—With a .325 average Joe Connolly continued to trail only Brooklyn's Jack Dalton among National League regulars in batting. Hi Myers, also of the Robins, was batting .377 but in only 90 at-bats, and Eddie Grant of the Giants was hitting .340, but in only

144 at-bats. Dalton and Connolly had 340 and 280 at-bats, respectively.

September

September 1—Giants skipper John McGraw fired a salvo at the rest of the National League, claiming teams were conspiring against his team by throwing their poorer pitchers against the Braves' best.

September 2—BRAVES GAIN FIRST PLACE: Goal Long Striven For at Last Reached. With a doubleheader sweep over the Phillies and a Giants loss to Brooklyn, the Braves jumped into sole possession of first place for the first time all season. Dick Rudolph wasn't at his best, allowing five runs to the Phils, but he earned another win and fanned a season-high eight batters. Possum Whitted filled in at second base for an ill Johnny Evers and paced an 11-hit attack with two safeties, including a triple.

Bill James took the second game, 12-3, tossing a solid nine innings and leading the team with three hits in five at-bats. Boston tied a season-high with 12 runs, all of which came in the first three innings. James enjoyed leads of 5-0, 9-1, and 12-1 and cruised to his 19th win, tying Rudolph for the team lead.

Though Philadelphia Athletics manager Connie Mack wouldn't predict who would win the National League pennant, he called Stallings a "great baseball leader," and the Braves a team "to be reckoned with" if they faced his A's in the World Series.

September 3—Only a day after refusing to speculate about the NL, Connie Mack went on record in favor of a Braves pennant. "Nothing to it," Mack told the press. "The Braves will win all right. Any team that can do what they have done in the last six or seven weeks will grab the National League pennant."

Apparently the Braves didn't read the paper that morning; they fell to the Phillies, 7-4, while the Giants swept Brooklyn in a doubleheader to reclaim first place by a half-game. Lefty Tyler's magic finally ran out and he was hammered to the tune of four runs in only an inning of work, prompting Iron Davis to make a rare appearance that ate up five innings. Contrary to John McGraw's assertion that the Braves were facing their opponents' weaker pitchers, Phillies manager Red Dooin threw Grover Cleveland Alexander at them; he would go on to lead the NL with 27 wins.

September 4—The Braves showed their resiliency by overcoming a shaky outing by Bill James and two Philadelphia rallies to hold on for a 6-5 win and remain within a half-game of first place. The game went 12 innings and featured spectacular defense by Herbie Moran, who robbed Gavvy Cravath of a game-winning homer in the tenth and kept what could have been a home run from leaving the park only one batter later, and Pat Hilly, who returned the favor by robbing Moran of an extra-base hit in the 11th with a sensational catch.

Prior to Moran's drive, words were exchanged between Alexander and Johnny Evers after the hurler brushed Moran off the plate with a head-high pitch, then threatened to do the same to the Braves' captain. Evers took exception and headed toward the mound "to tell Alexander what would happen to him if he tried anything of the kind." Jostling and shoving ensued but order was restored. Evers got the better of Alexander when he doubled, but it wasn't until the 12th that the Braves were able to push across the winning run.

September 5—A rare start by Eugene Cocreham and extra-base hits by Evers, Rabbit Maranville, Joe Connolly, and Red Smith, who homered for the first time in a Braves uniform, resulted in a 7-1 win and a tie for first place. Not content to rest on their laurels, the Braves purchased the contract of right-hander "Salida Tom" Hughes, a major-league veteran who'd enjoyed limited success in the bigs, but who'd posted 149 career wins in the minors, including 17 for Rochester of the International League just prior to joining the Braves.

September 7—In John McGraw's weekly review of the National League he gave the pennant race edge to the team that took the upcoming series between the Giants and Braves in Boston, but also insisted his team had the advantage the rest of the way if it came down to pitching. "Each club faces doubleheaders to be played this month," he wrote, "and, as soon as Stallings is forced to work some other man besides one of his regular trio he weakens his club perceptibly."

With the NL pennant in the balance and only 35 games left in the season, tensions were high at Fenway Park, where the Braves and Giants played a morning-afternoon twin bill in front of 73,000 spectators, a record for Boston baseball. The afternoon game, a 10-1 drubbing by the Giants, almost erupted into a riot when Giants center fielder Fred Snodgrass responded to booing with a gesture toward the fans that brought flying pop bottles in retaliation.

Boston Mayor James Michael Curley jumped onto the field and demanded of a police lieutenant that Snodgrass be cited for inciting a riot, and of umpire Bob Emslie that the Giants outfielder be removed from the park. Both refused, but Bob Bescher took Snodgrass's place to end the ruckus. Lefty Tyler suffered his second straight poor outing and Boston batters could solve Jeff Tesreau for only four hits.

The morning game was more to the crowd's liking as the Braves plated two runs in the bottom of the ninth for a come-from-behind 5-4 victory over Christy Mathewson that gave Boston a short-lived one-game lead in the pennant race. With runners on second and third and no outs, Johnny Evers drove a shot to left that landed in front of George Burns and bounced over his head, allowing both runs to score. Dick Rudolph wasn't at his best but earned the win.

After Evers' game-winning drive, the crowd went nuts. "The crowd behind the ropes broke on the playing field and made a rush for the Boston players' dugout, yelling like a lot of wild men," wrote J.C. O'Leary in the *Boston Globe*. "The Boston players were jumping in the air like a lot of bucking bronchos.... (W)hen the crowd could cheer no more many of the overjoyed fans began throwing their straw hats in all directions and for a few minutes there was simply a cloud of headwear sailing around."

September 8—The Braves took the rubber match of their series with the Giants, 8-3, and jumped back into first place by a game. The contest was never in doubt; Boston held a 6-1 lead after only four innings and Bill James cruised to his 21st win, thanks in part to the hitting and fielding of Evers, who rapped out three hits and made a sensational catch of a popup behind second base, then doubled a runner off first with a quick throw that no one saw coming. "Evers had the play all figured out before he made the catch," wrote J.C. O'Leary.

The Boston crowd continued to ride Fred Snodgrass for his behavior of the previous day, but gave him a rousing ovation when he made a spectacular catch to rob Hank Gowdy of an extra-base hit. "Snodgrass, who had been 'booed' unmercifully previously to the play," wrote O'Leary, "was applauded all the way as he walked from the terrace, where he made the catch, to the bench." After acknowledging what O'Leary called a "clever performance," the fans went back to riding Snodgrass for the rest of the game.

September 9—Only two days after McGraw's declaration about the weakness of the tail end of Stallings' rotation, Iron Davis made the Giants skipper eat his words by tossing a no-hitter at the Phillies in the second game of a doubleheader that increased Boston's lead to a game and a half. According to Ed McGrath of the *Boston Post*, Stallings "played a trump card that he has had up his sleeve for over a month," when he started Davis. According to McGrath, Stallings was waiting for Davis to gain control of the "best breaking spitball he'd ever seen" before giving him another start.

On the other hand, Eugene Cocreham helped the second-tier pitchers' reputations not at all when he pitched to only five batters in the first game and left with the Phillies already up 1-0 and the bases loaded. Dick Crutcher allowed all three runners to score to close out Cocreham's line, then allowed six more runs over the next six innings in the 10-3 loss.

September 10—Stallings went back to his aces, Dick Rudolph and Bill James, and watched them handle the Phillies with ease in a doubleheader sweep that expanded their lead over the Giants to 2 1/2 games.

Rudolph followed Davis's no-hitter with a four-hit shutout in which he walked none and fanned six for a 3-0 victory, and James held the Quakers to only two runs on six hits in a 7-2 win.

All of Boston's batters got into the act at one point or another, and Rabbit Maranville displayed slick and steady glove work as usual, fielding 17 chances without an error, which prompted Tim Murnane to write, "Nothing could be smoother than the work of this wonderful natural ball player."

September 11—The Braves took their fourth straight game with Philadelphia, this time by a count of 6-5, when they scored two runs in the bottom of the ninth thanks to some sloppy play by the Phils. Stallings had to rely on his reserve pitchers and they weren't great, but did just enough to win. Four Braves had two hits apiece, including Butch Schmidt, who led the team with four total bases.

September 12—A late rally that saw the Robins score four runs in the eighth and ninth innings stopped the Braves' winning streak and kept them from extending their lead over the Giants to three games. Lefty Tyler had made quick work of Brooklyn through seven innings, but a Maranville error with two outs in the eighth followed by run-scoring hits tied the game and Tyler eventually fell to his third straight loss. The Giants split a doubleheader with the Phillies and were able to gain only a half-game on Boston.

September 13—The *Hartford Courant* reported that Maranville had started 38 double plays to that point in the season and was well on his way to breaking the record of 41 held by Art Fletcher. The paper also claimed that experts had pegged the Braves shortstop as the league's MVP and that he'd be receiving a Chalmers car at the end of the season.

September 14—Boston had to overcome seven errors, including three by Possum Whitted, filling in at second base for Johnny Evers, who was serving the last of a three-game suspension he incurred from his latest ejection, which Evers felt was unjustified. "I was swearing at the ball, not at [Umpire Mal] Eason," Evers explained. "He misunderstood me." Dick Rudolph came through in crucial moments and held Brooklyn to three runs in the 4-3 win. Joe Connolly went into the day leading the league in hitting at .328 and went 1-for-4.

September 15—A day after John McGraw told readers he expected the pennant race to be a fight to the finish, the Braves extended their cushion to 3 1/2 games when they put Brooklyn away, 7-5, and the Giants fell to the Phillies, 4-3. Brooklyn tallied five runs on 15 hits off Bill James, but Boston made even better use of their seven hits, scoring seven times in the second and third innings to take a lead they'd never relinquish.

September 16—"Evers Day" was bittersweet for the Boston second baseman, who'd learned that his home in Troy, New York, had been broken into and ransacked, and many pieces of silver he'd been given during his baseball career had been stolen.

Coincidentally enough, he was presented with more silver later that day before the Braves' game against the Cardinals. Then he and his team went out and beat St. Louis, 6-3, in a seesaw battle that featured a three-run eighth-inning rally highlighted by a Butch Schmidt two-run triple.

September 17—St. Louis scored the game's first run after only three batters, but Rudolph buckled down and held them without another tally for the rest of the Braves' 5-1 win. Red Smith paced Boston's offense with three hits, and Butch Schmidt added two hits and two runs to the cause.

September 18—The Giants were able to gain a half-game on the Braves when they beat the Reds while the Braves were battling the Cardinals to a 1-1 tie that was called after 12 innings on account of darkness. "Spittin' Bill" Doak allowed Boston only three hits in 35 at-bats, but Bill James was equally stingy with the runs, allowing only one on seven hits. Both teams lost runs at the plate thanks to poor calls by umpire Bill Hart, who called Evers out on a steal of home though he was clearly safe, and Miller Huggins out on a close play at the dish even though he was "palpably safe," according to J.C. O'Leary.

Wall Street betting commissioner Fred Shum offered odds of 10 to 6 on the Braves to win the National League pennant, odds of 2 to 1 on the Giants, and odds of 5 to 4 on the Philadelphia Athletics to win the World Series.

September 19—In his first start since tossing a no-hitter at the Phillies, Iron Davis went six innings before leaving in favor of a pinch-hitter, who helped the Braves wipe out a 3-1 deficit with a seven-run outburst in the bottom of the sixth. By the time Davis' turn came around, the Braves were up 4-3 and still had five runs to score. Hank Gowdy drove in four of the team's runs and Lefty Tyler held the Pirates scoreless over the final three frames to secure the win.

September 21—To John McGraw's credit, he continued to insist his Giants would eventually nose the Braves out at the end of the pennant race; all his club had to do was keep pace with Boston until September 30, when the teams would clash for six games at the Polo Grounds. That was easier said than done, as the Braves narrowly defeated the Pirates, 6-5, while the Giants were being shut out by the Cubs, giving Boston a four-game lead.

Rudolph was hardly at his best, but he battled for nine innings and came out on top thanks to a bases-clearing triple by Joe Connolly in the fourth that gave Boston the runs needed for victory.

September 22—Another Cubs shutout over the Giants and an 8-2 Braves win over Pittsburgh bumped Boston's lead to a season-high five games. The Pirates plated two in the top of the first off Lefty Tyler thanks to a botched rundown that should have resulted in the third out, but that was all they'd get for the rest of the day. Red Smith had three more hits, and Connolly again walloped a bases-loaded smash that scored three runs before he was nipped at third on what should have been another triple.

After the game, Harry Williams of the *Los Angeles Times* conceded the pennant to the Braves. "Five full games now separate the youthful Braves from the aged and tottering Giants, and the next step will be to bill the town of Boston for the world's series."

September 23—The Braves extended their winning streak to eight games with a 3-2 win over Cincinnati in game one of a doubleheader, before falling, 3-0, in the second tilt. Still, two New York losses at the hands of the Cardinals extended Boston's lead to six games, prompting Stanley Milliken of the *Washington Post* to declare that a Braves-Athletics World Series was all but certain. Bill James fanned a season-high nine batters and allowed only two unearned runs, but needed a "freak" home run by Red Smith in the bottom of the ninth to win, 3-2. Smith drove a shot to the center-field wall that took a hop into the outstretched hands of a young boy, who dropped it back onto the playing field. Umpire Ernie Quigley motioned Smith home from third base with the winning run.

Game two was uneventful as the teams combined for only eight hits, three by the Braves off 23-year-old rookie King Lear, who won his first major-league game and broke Cincinnati's 19-game losing streak.

September 24—The *Los Angeles Times* reported that the Braves were being "very cocky" by making applications for World Series tickets available with two weeks still to go in the season. But the *Chicago Tribune* reminded readers that the Braves merely had to win eight of their final 15 games to cop the pennant, even if the Giants won all of their remaining contests. And they'd

Dick Rudolph.

only have to go 5-10 to stay ahead of St. Louis if the Cardinals won their final 11 games.

Dick Rudolph made the Braves' road to a flag even easier when he shut the Reds down, 5-0, in the first game of a doubleheader, then Dick Crutcher battled to a 2-2 tie in a second tilt that was called after eight innings on account of darkness. Another Giants loss to St. Louis pushed them seven games off the pace. After the double dip, the Braves were treated to a "rousing reception" and dinner by the Filene Men's Club at the Filene Building.

September 25—George Stallings called upon Dick Rudolph for the second straight day and the Braves' horse tossed another shutout in a 2-0 win over Cincinnati. The keystone combo of Johnny Evers and Rabbit Maranville knocked out four of Boston's seven hits, and recorded six putouts and eight assists between them. They then took the second game of their third straight doubleheader, 4-3, behind the pitching of Bill James and batting of Red Smith, who rapped out two doubles and scored half of the team's runs. Even though the Giants finally won, they fell another half-game out of first.

September 26—The Braves hosted the Cubs for the last time in the 1914 campaign and, despite playing their fourth straight twin bill, thrashed the visitors by scores of 6-2 and 12-2. Lefty Tyler recorded his 16th and final win of the season in the first game, then Otto Hess made a rare start and gave the rest of the staff a breather in the easy game-two victory.

September 27—The *Washington Post* reported that Johnny Evers was on the verge of making more in one baseball season than any other player in history, estimating his potential take at $43,000. According to the *Post*, Evers signed a $10,000 contract, received a $25,000 signing bonus, would receive another $2,000 bonus if the Braves finished first, $1,500 if they won the World Series, and approximately $4,500 in extras from writing, advertisements, and other endorsements.

Meanwhile the *Boston Globe* reported that the Royal Rooters, Boston's band of rabid fans who turned out en masse for previous championship tilts, would be out in full force for the World Series, and applications, checks, and cash were being accepted to cover the cost of travel to Philadelphia, grandstand seats at Shibe Park, automobile transportation to and from the park, flags, pennants, and a 25-piece band.

September 28—Even though the Braves had yet to clinch the National League pennant, former major-league skipper Frank Chance weighed in on the coming World Series, predicting that the Braves would win two or three games but would fall to the Athletics. He insisted that winning the Series "would be too much to expect from a green and untried team lined up against a veteran that's still at the crest of its power, and has gone successfully through three different classic arguments."

On the field, the Braves moved one step closer to the fall classic, beating the Cubs, 7-6, for their sixth straight win.

September 29—After riding his big three—Dick Rudolph, Bill James, and Lefty Tyler—all season, Stallings tabbed newly-acquired Salida Tom Hughes to pitch the potential pennant-winning game, and he came through with an outstanding effort in which he allowed only one earned run on five hits and struck out eight in a 3-2 win over Chicago. The Braves managed only three hits, but drew 11 walks, one of which came around to score the winning run in the person of Evers, who was driven in by a Possum Whitted double in the bottom of the ninth.

After the game Cubs skipper Hank O'Day predicted that Stallings' men would be swept by the Athletics, that pitchers Eddie Plank and Chief Bender would be too hard for Boston to handle. But Stallings vehemently disagreed. "Any one who thinks the Athletics are not going to have a fight on their hands is laboring under a misapprehension," he told the press. "I think our chances of winning the coming series is just as good as theirs."

September 30—The much-anticipated series against the Giants at the Polo Grounds became a mere formality, but Stallings continued playing his regulars because, according to Mel Webb, "only hard every-day work will keep his club on its toes." Dick Rudolph and Joe Connolly starred in the first game, the former allowing only one run in a 7-1 win, and the latter going 4-for-5 with a triple and homer. Connolly rapped out three more hits, including a double, in the second tilt to lead a 13-hit attack, but Paul Strand couldn't hold a 6-0 lead and the game was called due to darkness with the score tied 7-7.

October

October 1—William Henry of the *Los Angeles Times* wondered why the Braves couldn't win the World Series, considering all of the other upsets that happened in baseball that year. "The Giants were doped to win the National League pennant by a mile," he wrote, "the Pirates were expected to finish a bang-up second and St. Louis and the Cubs were expected to battle for the basement. Look at 'em now. Take heed, then, before placing the family silverware in hock and placing the wherewithal derived there upon the Athletics."

BRAVES KEEP RIGHT ON BEATING GIANTS: "Play the Game For All You're Worth," Orders Stallings, and They Do. Iron Davis started the game with four hitless innings before barely holding on for a 7-6 win. Stallings' insistence that his regulars continue playing made it difficult for Hank Gowdy to recover from injuries to his hands caused by foul tips. The backstop committed two throwing errors that allowed the Giants to get back in the game, but J.C. O'Leary speculated that Gowdy would be healthy for the World Series.

October 2—Stallings finally gave some of his players a day off and it showed in an 11-5 loss to the Giants, their first loss since September 23. Oscar Dugey filled in for Johnny Evers and committed an error that led to a run; Possum Whitted spelled Butch Schmidt at first base and made a miscue that resulted in a couple of unearned runs; and Gene Cocreham threw five poor innings in which he allowed eight runs on six hits and four walks.

The loss didn't dampen the spirits of the Royal Rooters, however. Lawrence Sweeney reported in the *Boston Globe* that 200 members of the Rooters, including former Boston Mayor John "Honey Fitz" Fitzgerald, would be traveling to Philadelphia to support the Braves in the World Series.

In a bizarre twist, it was also reported that Braves president James Gaffney's interests in the team would be "disposed of or reduced to a minority interest" in 1915 because he was in the process of becoming owner and president of the New York Yankees. George Stallings was to be named manager of the Yanks.

October 3—The Braves played their sixth doubleheader in 11 days and split with the Giants, winning the first game, 4-1, and losing the second, 1-0, despite allowing only one hit. Bill James threw three hitless innings in a tuneup for the World Series, then Otto Hess took over and threw the final six to earn the win. Hess also led all batters with three hits. Dick Rudolph began the second game with three hitless innings in his final start of the season, then Dick Crutcher and Paul Strand combined to throw six innings of one-hit ball in relief. Unfortunately Crutcher walked the bases loaded in the fourth, then passed Eddie Grant to force in what turned out to be the winning run.

The *Hartford Courant* reported that odds favored the Athletics at 10 to 7, but that Christy Mathewson predicted the Braves would win the World Series, prompting the paper to write that they were "prepared to show the proper amount of surprise if Stallings brings his crew through the seven games with the laurel crown."

William Weart of the *Philadelphia Telegraph* predicted a decisive victory for the Athletics, insisting that Connie Mack's squad "outclassed" the Braves and had the "greatest money players" in the game. "Team for team, the Athletics outshine the Braves. They are better on the offense and the defense. They are better base runners. They have team play down to a science. They have veterans who have gone through the world's series fire and never have been found wanting. Against them will be a combination that has yet to prove its mettle in such a big event."

Hank Gowdy greeting Mayor Fitzgerald – grandfather of President John F. Kennedy.

October 4—Even though there were games still to be played, Braves second baseman and captain Johnny Evers and Philadelphia Athletics keystone man Eddie Collins were named their respective league's most valuable player and each was awarded a Chalmers automobile. Rabbit Maranville came in a close second to Evers, and though Evers' teammates were happy for their captain, the consensus among the team was that Maranville was more deserving.

Because it was Sunday and the Braves were in Brooklyn, they had the day off, so they held meetings as a team to discuss the World Series, then met with Pat Moran, former National League catcher with the Braves, Cubs, and Phillies, and future manager who would lead the Phillies to a pennant in 1915 and the Reds to a pennant and World Series title in 1919. Moran was said to know more about the Athletics than almost anyone and he was anxious to share his knowledge with the NL champs.

October 5—In a doubleheader tuneup in their final series of the season, the Braves pounded the Robins to the tune of 24 runs on 24 hits, including three homers, two triples, and three doubles. The first game was a 15-2 laugher in which the Braves scored multiple runs in five of the nine innings, including five in the fifth. Butch Schmidt and Ted Cather rapped out three hits apiece, and Possum Whitted homered. Dick Crutcher made his last start of the season and earned his fifth win.

The second game was closer but only because Brooklyn scored four runs in the bottom of the ninth to make the score a more respectable 9-5. Whitted and Les Mann homered for the Braves, and Tom Hughes earned his second win in as many starts.

After the twin bill, Giants legend Christy Mathewson met with the Braves in George Stallings' hotel room and spent an hour telling them what he knew about the Athletics and how to beat them.

October 6—The Braves split the final two games of the season, losing the first game, 3-2, and winning the second, 7-3, to finish the season with 94 wins, the most by the franchise since 1899. The afternoon game featured a "second string bunch" that Stallings called his "moss aggies," who were instructed "to show everybody what a scrub team could do if it wanted to."

The initial contest resulted in more than just a loss in the standings when third baseman Red Smith broke his ankle and ruptured ligaments while sliding into second base in the ninth inning, and was lost to the team for the rest of the year.

In his 60 games since being acquired from Brooklyn, Smith had been the Braves' second-best hitter behind Joe Connolly, hitting .314 with good power and a team-leading .401 on-base percentage. Charlie Deal, on the other hand, had been hitting only .210 when he was replaced in the lineup by Smith, and was expected to fill the void.

Stallings and Evers said all the right things afterward, endorsing Deal and insisting the infield wouldn't miss a beat without Smith, excepting his power at the plate. But betting odds favored the A's even more after Smith's injury was revealed, going from 10 to 7 to 10 to 4 1/2.

October 7—Two days before the World Series was to begin at Shibe Park in Philadelphia, Johnny Evers weighed in with his opinion about the Athletics. "The Boston club has a very good chance of beating the Athletics," Evers wrote. "Experts will be taking the players opposing one another on the two clubs, man for man, and drawing their conclusions in print from these comparisons. One team will be badly whipped as a result, and it will probably be Boston. These conclusions do not amount to anything to me. I have been through three world's series as a player … and I know averages do not win or lose them."

October 8—Detroit Tigers star Ty Cobb and former Boston Red Sox president John I. Taylor both picked Connie Mack's Athletics to take the World Series, although they had differing opinions about the Braves. Cobb gave the Braves an edge in pitching and claimed they had a fair chance to win; Taylor gave the Braves two wins at most, but felt the A's would win in a "walk" and that the Series would probably go only five games.

Former A's pitcher Rube Vickers gave some last-minute advice to Bill James, telling him to forget his fastball and go with a spitter instead. "They will all be taking their wallop at the first ball," Vickers told the young hurler. "Sink [your fastball] in your pocket and forget it, or they'll sink it in the concrete wall for you." Cobb agreed. "The Athletics will punish a fast ball," he wrote, "but they are weakest against a spitter or slow ball pitcher."

The night before the first game brought fireworks between the two managers, as Stallings threatened to punch Mack on sight after a dispute over the use of Shibe Park. Tim Murnane thought it was just for show, though, and that John McGraw had told Stallings the best way to beat the A's was to get Mack's "goat."

According to Harold Kaese, Stallings had planned the whole thing with Walter Hapgood of the *Boston Herald*, scripting a controversy to take place in front of a group of reporters that resulted in a contentious phone call with a bewildered Mack, who couldn't figure out why Stallings was angry about practice times only a day after the Boston skipper expressed no objection to the schedule.

A Stallings Anecdote

After the Braves had routed the Cubs twice in one afternoon and had increased their lead in the National League race to the point of all but certainty, George Stallings called his players about him for a heart-to-heart talk.

"I suppose," said the manager of the Braves, "that I have called you fellows a lot of hard names at various times during the season."

All the players nodded.

"I may," continued Stallings, "have said that you were fatheads, boneheads, ivory tops, feather brains and other things of that sort."

Again the players nodded.

"Well," said Stallings, "those names don't go. You're not any of the things I've called you. I'm not going to use any of those names again."

Then he paused and added, after due reflection, "At least not until the World's Series."

—*The Sporting News*, October 8, 1914, 4.

Another view of Hank Gowdy and Eddie Plank of the Philadelphia A's shaking hands before the 1914 Series.

The 1914 World Series

By Mark Sternman

Game One

Friday, October 9, 1914, at Shibe Park
Boston Braves 7, Philadelphia Athletics 1

The upstart Boston Braves surprised the defending World Series champion Philadelphia Athletics in Game One as postseason novice Dick Rudolph easily outpitched the seasoned veteran Chief Bender, 7-1. It was the first time in a Series game that Philadelphia manager Connie Mack—with four prior World Series under his belt—had to remove his starter for ineffectiveness rather than injury.[1] Rudolph's gem, delivered on a day when his wife gave birth to a girl, heralded a Series in which Braves pitching and dominating defense stopped Athletics hitting, showing that the unique pressures of the fall classic could not cool Boston manager George Stallings' hot squad.

One would have thought that the more experienced Philadelphia team would show more patience at the plate, defensive grace with its $100,000 infield, and moxie on the bases. In fact, the opposite transpired in all three categories, both in Game One and throughout the World Series. "The beating was perhaps the worst that has ever been handed to an opponent in the opening game of a postseason series between major league clubs," Tim Murnane wrote in the Boston Globe.[2]

The trio of Boston starters all used the aggressiveness of the Athletics against them. No one did so more effectively than Rudolph, who, after Game One, observed, "I found out what makes the Athletics such a hitting team. They're all what we call free swingers."[3]

One sportswriter gushed that Rudolph "pitched one of the most remarkable games in the history of the sport. ... He used a slow ball, a curve, his spitter, and not once during the game did the Athletics really threaten him."[4]

In addition to Rudolph's off-speed stuff, his "slow, deceptive delivery ... proved the Mackmen's undoing, for they are notoriously weak on this service, and Rudolph was at his best in this respect today."[5]

By failing to make Rudolph, who threw fewer than ten pitches in both the eighth and ninth innings, and the other Braves starters work, Philadelphia never forced Boston to turn to its questionable pitching depth, allowing Game Two starter Bill James to relieve Lefty Tyler in extra innings in Game Three and Rudolph to pitch Game Four on regular rest. With runners on the corners and none out in the second inning, for instance, "Barry helped Rudolph out immensely by fanning on a ball about a foot outside."[6]

With multiple baserunners in each of the first two frames, Game One began auspiciously for the Athletics. After Bender retired the Braves in order in the first, Eddie Murphy singled. Rube Oldring then bunted. Hank Gowdy "ran down to retrieve it and with little time to spare, shot it toward first base high in the air. By a wonderful jump, Schmidt speared the ball and got down on the bag in time to retire the sprinting Oldring."[7]

Rudolph then walked Collins to put runners on first and second for Frank Baker. Rather than take a strike following the free pass, Baker hit the first pitch toward

A's catcher Wally Schang stretches to retrieve a late throw after Gowdy scored from second on a Maranville single in the second inning of Game One.

"the right field grandstand seats, which Schmidt … mitted for the second out. Murphy tried to edge up to third … but Schmidt's bounding throw reached Deal in time … to tag out Eddie and end the promising inning in a cloud of gloom."[8]

"Schmidt's great throw and Deal's swift stab probably decided the game."[9]

The promising start fizzled with a single play that evinced several themes that would run throughout the Series: poor situational hitting and blundering baserunning by Philadelphia, and sharp pitching and sparkling defense by the Boston infield, including repeated fine plays by its unheralded corner players.

The Braves had timely hitting, too, especially from Gowdy, the surprising batting star of the 1914 World Series. Thanks to Gowdy, the Braves took a lead that they would not relinquish in the top of the second. Gowdy drove in Possum Whitted, who had walked, with a double, and Rabbit Maranville scored Gowdy with a single. The Athletics came back with a Stuffy McInnis walk and an Amos Strunk single. McInnis scored on an error by Herbie Moran in left, and Strunk went to third.

Philadelphia had the tying run on third with no out. But Jack Barry struck out, the first of eight K's for Rudolph, and Wally Schang hit to Johnny Evers, who "scooped up the ball and shot it to Gowdy, nailing Strunk at the plate by a very narrow margin."[10] Rudolph then sealed the squander by getting Bender to force Schang.

The Athletics ran into another out in the fourth inning, when Strunk tried to stretch a single, but "was cut down at second on Connolly's sharp relay into Maranville. Strunk probably would have made the midway sack had he not lost his stride in rounding first base."[11]

In his brief appearances in the 1914 Series, Strunk would struggle on the basepaths and in the field before giving way to injury. He made two hits in his first two trips to the plate, but failed in his final five opportunities. His successor, Jimmy Walsh, also fared poorly in center field and running the bases.

Boston got far better play from its key substitute. Over the next three games, the Braves, minus injured slugger Red Smith, who spent the Series in a Brooklyn hospital laid up with a broken leg, would barely exceed their run total from this first contest, but the fine fielding of Maranville remained constant throughout the quartet: "Barry smote a Texas Leaguer in the fifth inning. Connolly could not reach it, and Deal lacked the leg locomotion to get near it. Maranville almost dropped out of a cloud and with his back to the ball, he nailed it."[12]

The Braves broke open a 3-1 run game with a trio of runs in the sixth inning, when Bender was knocked from the box. With runners on first and second with one out, Whitted delivered the key blow, a two-run triple, when he "connected squarely with one of Bender's fast straight ones and it was going even faster and straighter toward the score-board in far centre field after Whitted had given it his special slugging treatment."[13]

Boston rooters at Shibe Park.

Eddie Collins receiving a new Chalmers automobile after winning the Chalmers Award for MVP in 1914.

Charlie Deal ended the four-run sixth inning by hitting into his third double play of the game. Forced into service because of the Smith mishap, the unheralded Deal made up for his lackluster bat with his glove in both the first and final frames of the game.[14] In the latter case, a Philadelphia paper noted, "No third baseman could have handled McInnis' solid crack in the ninth better than did Deal, who pulled the ball down with his bare hand."[15]

Deal later made the Series-clinching play on McInnis to end Game Four.

In a Series marred by runners giving up outs on the basepaths at inopportune times, the Braves had the opener's most daring baserunning play, too, when the slow-footed pair of Butch Schmidt and Hank Gowdy pulled off a double steal in the eighth to make the final score 7-1. "Collins caught Lapp's short throw, but in returning the ball Eddie threw high and Schmidt slid under Lapp."[16]

Stallings may have called the play to send a message that the Braves would not back down even up by a big score, or he may have simply wanted to avoid having Deal, in the box with Gowdy on first and Schmidt on third, hit into his fourth double play of the game.

With better starting pitching for Philadelphia, the runs would not come so easily for Boston for the rest of the Series, but the ultimate results would remain the same.

Notes

1. The Boston captain did point, however, to a physical affliction affecting Bender, writing that Chief "has had to have his arm treated with electricity after every game he pitched during the season and for several days afterwards to put life into it." John J. Evers, "Hank Gowdy and Rudolph Heroes," *Boston Post*, October 10, 1914, 11.

2. T.H. Murnane, "Game Is Braves' 7 to 1," *Boston Daily Globe*, October 10, 1914, 1.

3. "Dick Rudolph's a Modest Hero," *Philadelphia Bulletin*, October 10, 1914, 9.

4. Hugh S. Fullerton, "Connie's Machine Is Good As Ever, Says Fullerton," *[Philadelphia] Evening Ledger*, October 10, 1914, 2.

5. "Braves Win First Game, 7 to 1," *Boston Daily Advertiser*, October 10, 1914, 1.

6. Eddie Collins, "Eddie Collins Says Mackmen Have No Excuses," *[Philadelphia] Evening Ledger*, October 10, 1914, p. 2. After Game Four, Collins also complained, "We never attempted to find out anything about Rudolph. By this I mean whether it would be more to our advantage, say, to wait him out, or if bunting would upset him." Eddie Collins, "Pitchers Made Us 'Look Bad,' Says Collins," *[Philadelphia] Evening Ledger*, October 14, 1914, 2.

7. Paul H. Shannon, "No Excuses Left for Mack's Men," *Boston Post*, October 10, 1914, 11.

8. "Hank Gowdy Swung at a 100 P.C. Mark," *Philadelphia Inquirer*, October 10, 1914, 11.

9. R.E. McMillin, "Athletics Smashed by Braves 7 to 1," *Boston Journal*, October 10, 1914, 10.

10. "Two Important Plays in the Game," *Boston Post*, October 10, 1914, 13.

11. "Hank Gowdy Swung at a 100 P.C. Mark," *Philadelphia Inquirer*, October 10, 1914, 11.

12. "Mackmen's Defeat Decisive—But Remember They Came back in '11," *Philadelphia Bulletin*, October 10, 1914, 8.

13. Walter E. Hapgood, "Braves Win Opening Game of World Series," *Boston Herald*, October 10, 1914, 8.

14. "Tyler places great confidence in Deal. 'He is the dark horse,' the crack pitcher averred. 'I look for him to do great things. He's steady and calm and nervy, and while he is not as strong at the bat as Smith, he's no laggard with the stick,'" in "Smith's Loss Fails to Depress Braves," *Philadelphia Bulletin*, October 7, 1914, 17.

15. "Stallings' Braves Defeat Athletics; Knock out Bender," *Philadelphia Inquirer*, October 10, 1914, 1.

16. On the play, "Gowdy kept going for third and Lapp's throw beat him to the bag," in "Stallings' Braves Defeat Athletics; Knock out Bender," *Philadelphia Inquirer*, October 10, 1914, 11.

Game Two

Saturday, October 10, 1914 at Shibe Park
Boston Braves 1, Philadelphia Athletics 0

On an unusually warm October day in Philadelphia in front of more than 20,000 fortunate fans, the Boston Braves moved halfway toward winning the World Series for the first time with a dramatic 1-0 whitewashing of the Philadelphia Americans behind the brilliant two-hit pitching of Bill James, the unlikely ninth-inning offensive outburst of substitute third baseman Charlie Deal, and the defensive wizardry of Rabbit Maranville. The game represented a pitching duel for the ages featuring the veteran Eddie Plank and the youngster James.

By their actions and their inactions, both George Stallings and Connie Mack made the ninth inning a particularly memorable one. In fact, the World Series gamesmanship had begun even before the Series. Deal was replacing Charlie Smith, who had broken his ankle in the last game of the regular season. Mack commented that he regretted the injury to Smith "as he wanted the Athletics to meet the Braves at their best," words that would appear in a different light after Deal's heroics.[1]

The "bats of the Boston visitors, which had been so efficacious against the speed and curves of [Chief] Bender," had remained quiet as the scoreless game made its way to the final frame.[2] Ever superstitious, Boston manager Stallings sought to spark his team by turning to a human good-luck charm in reserve outfielder Josh Devore,[3] who replaced Game One winner Dick Rudolph on the first-base coaching lines in the ninth inning. By cause or by coincidence, Devore worked his magic quickly after Maranville grounded to Barry, his opposite number at short.

Deal lifted a fly to deep right-center field. "It was a long ball, but would not have been a difficult catch."[4] Amos Strunk, who "has always been classed with Tris Speaker for his ability in going back for balls,"[5] broke in but misjudged and/or lost the ball in the sun, which "shone brilliantly upon the soft greens of the in and outfields."[6] By the time Strunk had reversed direction and retrieved the smash, Deal had reached second safely with his first safety of the postseason (he would get just one more hit in the Series) and Boston's only extra-base hit of the game.

Wally Schang had Deal in trouble immediately, caught far off second base after a Plank pitch, but when Schang fired the ball to Jack Barry covering second, Deal daringly lit off for third and took the bag. "Barry did not throw to [Frank] Baker. He drew his arm back, but the throw never came. … Deal was directly in line with Baker and the throw might have hit the runner in the back and ended the chances of the Athletics right there."[7]

Now, with no score, one out, and Deal on third base, Stallings faced a decision on his pitcher, James. Stallings had had both James and Lefty Tyler warm up before

Philadelphia dugout, Shibe Park.

Game Two crowd in Philadelphia.

the game, but in a surprise to fans, who had expected to see Tyler perform,"[8] chose right-hander James to start Game Two. (Mack also had Plank take batting practice before Game One but had gone instead with Chief Bender, his usual opening-game hurler.) Should he dispatch a pinch-hitter to bat for James, and perhaps get the first run of the game across the plate? But James, who was "working a fast one and quick-breaker spitter on the Athletics" in pitching to the minimum 24 hitters through the first eight frames, so Stallings let Seattle Bill bat for himself against Gettysburg Eddie.[9] One can understand this decision given "the one game contributed by long Bill James was the most perfect piece of twirling skill seen in a world's series in many a day."[10]

To no avail. For the fourth straight time, Plank struck out his opposite number, which left Leslie Mann to face the southpaw with two down and Deal still on third in a game that had gone scoreless for its first 50 outs.

But Gettysburg Eddie faltered in the end. He forced Mann to go the other way, and the Bostonian "whacked a short safe one-shot that fleet, game Eddie Collins could not reach though he leaped four feet into the air and landed in a shapeless heap on the outfield turf."[11]

The single plated Deal with what turned out to be the only run of the ballgame.

Plank ended up hurling 129, 132, or 149 pitches in and out of trouble all day.[12] "Inning after inning the Braves got runners on the bases, and, just as they were about to strike their telling blow, gray-eyed Plank, still cunning and wily in the evening of his baseball career, suddenly would pull himself together and halt the Boston uprising."[13]

In his syndicated column, Ty Cobb credited Stallings' platoon system, one originally devised by Mack, for the run, writing, "(T)hat game was won by Stallings' shrewd shifts. He put Mann and Cather into his batting order in place of Moran and Connolly, to get two right-handed batters against a southpaw, and how well it worked the result showed."[14]

Having given the Athletics a pep talk before the game, Cobb hardly counted as an impartial observer but he still credited the Braves for heady play.

James, who had pitched unerringly after walking Eddie Murphy to start the game, struggled to hold the lead in the ninth, sandwiching walks to Jack Barry (on four pitches) and pinch-hitter Jimmy Walsh around a strike-out of Wally Schang. With the tying run on second and the winning run on first, James induced a hot shot through the box by Murphy that looked as if it would get through and tie the game.

But Johnny Evers had moved Maranville just to the right of the second-base bag, so Rabbit made three great plays in one by receiving the ball, brushing off the lumbering Walsh (Maranville "bounded away from Walsh like a rubber ball"[15]), and firing the pill to Butch Schmidt at first to turn a dazzling short-to-first double play, the game's only twin killing and the only double play Murphy hit into in all of 1914. It ended the game

Police in place before Game Two.

and the Shibe Park season. "Maranville's utterly impossible double play [saved] the whole show."¹⁶

Maranville had more than made up for dropping McInnis' foul fly for a one-out error in the eighth inning, a miscue that could have been a major one so late in a scoreless duel but that James mitigated by inducing Stuffy to sky to Deal at third.

In addition to the ninth-inning dramatics, each team threatened to score throughout the game although James did retire 15 Athletics in a row after walking Murphy in the bottom of the first.

Plank, by contrast, saw Bostonians reach base frequently, but pitched in a pinch by stranding Braves in scoring position in the first, second, fourth, and sixth. Schang ended the third by throwing out Johnny Evers trying to swipe second "by such a distance that the long chinned Trojan seemed to be standing still."¹⁷ Boston went down in order only in the seventh.

Deal's dash for third in the ninth capped off a game that featured audacious but often overly-aggressive baserunning. The other successful swipes included Deal stealing second in the top of the second with two outs,¹⁸ and Barry stealing second during Schang's ninth-inning fan.

In addition to Schang gunning down Evers, James picked off Murphy pitcher-to-first-to-shortstop in the first, Hank Gowdy threw out Schang trying to take third on a pitch of the dirt after Wally had broken up James's 15-in-a-row run with a sixth-inning two-bagger down the left-field line,¹⁹ and James picked off another batter—Collins this time—after Eddie had reached on an infield single to second with two outs in the seventh.

The final two baserunning mistakes for the Americans had similar outcomes but resulted in different reactions. Some, including Schang himself, thought Schang safe at third—postgame photographic evidence seemed to indicate that he had taken the bag—but umpire Bill

World Series scorebook.

Byron ruled otherwise.[20] The *Boston Evening American* credited Gowdy with "pegg[ing] him out, assisted somewhat by a perfectly splendid and stout-hearted tagging stunt by our old acquaintance, slight Charlie [Deal]."[21]

Byron's decision made Plank's grounder to short an inning-ender rather than an RBI that would have scored Schang and given the Philadelphians a critical 1-0 lead. In his column, Cobb implied that Byron, a National League umpire, might have exhibited bias in his call. No such controversy resulted from the Collins play, in which James caught Eddie napping as the latter hung his head after failing to retreat safely back to first.

Evers saw this as swift and divine retribution by the baseball gods. Having thought that his snap throw had in fact beaten Collins to first base, Evers after the safe call "threw his hands over his head, and everyone knew what he meant."[22]

Amazingly, Schang and Collins, the only two Athletics with base hits, both ended up making outs on the bases before a fellow Philadelphian could complete his turn at bat. Whether the Athletics took the Braves too lightly or failed to focus on the game with Federal League riches lingering in the minds of many ballplayers remains unclear; indisputably, however, in Game Two Boston played like a confident veteran bunch while the Mackmen made multiple mistakes, an odd state of affairs given that Philadelphia played Game Two, its fourth World Series in five years, in the friendly confines of Shibe Park.

The Braves did enjoy, however, a loyal and vocal fan base that made the trip from Boston to Philadelphia to cheer on the visitors and visit invective on the home team. The Royal Rooters, who had hassled Honus Wagner and his Pittsburgh comrades in 1903, stayed true to their city. Former Boston Mayor John Fitzgerald, known then as Honey Fitz and later as the grandfather of President John F. Kennedy, said "in the most courteous manner [that] Plank was one hundred years old, had a glass arm and was blind of one eye."[23]

Taking two in Philadelphia left the brash Bostonians feel that their miraculous run would continue. Stallings told his equipment manager to pack the road uniforms of the Braves and take them home rather than leave them at Shibe Park. Stallings said, "We won't be coming back. It'll be all over after the two games in Boston."[24]

Lest readers today accuse writers from yesteryear of spinning yarns in the afterglow of victory, Stallings' players made similar statements at the time. Gowdy hardly hedged: "We're out for four straight and it looks all the more and more that we were going to get them."

Herbie Moran, who did not even play in Game Two, predicted flatly: "The Braves will win four straight."[25]

Like the Chicago Cubs from 1906 to 1910, the only other team that then had reached the World Series with the same frequency as the Athletics, but had dropped off the pace due to age, the loss of Evers, and the lure of the Federal League, the end of this great Philadelphia squad seemed suddenly near.

Some of the rooters at Shibe Park during Game Two at Shibe Park.

Damon Runyon observed at the time, "The star of the American League seems to be slowly sinking."[26] Norman Macht wrote nearly a century after the game, "Nobody spoke in the home clubhouse after the game. Plank stood on a stool, head in his hands, while the others silently showered, dressed, and left."[27]

One could hardly fault Plank, at least, for his efforts in defeat.[28] He "pitched those nine exciting, thrilling innings just like the old master that he is. ... Hats off to Ancient Edward, like his rival, Matty, as great, or greater, in defeat as ever he was in victory."[29]

Newspaper reporters invoked Mathewson when summarizing the efforts of both the losing and winning hurlers. "James ... twirled a quality of baseball that would have been a credit to a Mathewson, a Johnson or a Rudolph."[30]

In his own newspaper article, Manager Stallings paid tribute to his winning pitcher, writing of James: "To him, almost alone, belongs the verdict."[31]

The last words belonged to the National League's Chalmers Award winner in 1914, Johnny Evers, who, after all, had a better view of the game than any sportswriter or historian. Though viewed today as a fierce partisan rather than a dispassionate observer, Evers astutely and evenly summed up the compelling contest, stating, "Bill James pitched wonderful ball, but he had little on that old veteran Plank."[32]

Notes

1. J.R. Cary, "Charles Deal, The Man Who Made Good in the Pinch-," *Baseball Magazine*, February 1915, 54. Massachusetts Governor David Walsh said after the game, "If I were Mr. Deal tonight I should not swap places with anybody on earth."
2. *Boston Evening Record*, October 11, 1914, 2.
3. Devore "considers himself a lucky fellow. Devore was turned over to Cincinnati by McGraw last year. Cincinnati sent him to the Phillies, and from here he went to Boston. ... He believes he is lucky because he was born on Friday the thirteenth." In "Punch Your Head' Stallings to Mack," *Philadelphia Bulletin*, October 8, 1914, 17.
4. John I. Taylor, *Boston Globe*, October 11, 1914, 9. Taylor was the former owner of the Red Sox.
5. "World's Series Echoes," *Sporting Life*, October 17, 1914, 3.
6. *Boston Evening Record*, October 11, 1914, 1. The sun had affected flies earlier in the game as well: "Baker flew to Whitted, who lost the ball in the sun, but finally spotted it again and made a fine catch after a long run." J.C. O'Leary, *Boston Globe*, October 10 (evening edition), 1914, 1. A little more than 15 years later, Chicago Cubs center fielder Hack Wilson would more famously lose a fly in the Shibe Park sun, a misplay that would help the Athletics win Game Four of their World Series 10-8 and eventually the Series in five games.
7. Damon Runyon, *Boston Evening American*, October 11, 1914, 3 of special World's Series section. In a newspaper column after the game, Barry himself wrote, "I didn't throw the ball because I couldn't. Schang's throw to me was perfect, but the ball slipped out of my hand and popped up on the top of my fingers and I couldn't throw it." Jack Barry, "Ball Slipped from Barry's Hand while Deal Was Stealing Third," *Philadelphia Bulletin*, October 12, 1914, 12.
8. *Boston Evening Record*, October 11, 1914, 1.
9. *Boston Evening Record*, October 11, 1914, 1.
10. John J. Ward, *Baseball Magazine*, February 1915, 33.
11. Nick Flatley, *Boston Evening American*, October 11, 1914, page 2 of a special World's Series section.
12. Newspaper accounts of the game use the higher figures; a history uses the lower one. T.H. Murnane in the *Boston Globe* had 149, and the *Philadelphia Inquirer* had 132. Norman L. Macht had 129 in *Connie Mack and the Early Years of Baseball*. Both papers agree that James threw just 92 pitches. The *Philadelphia Inquirer* had James at 76 pitches through eight innings, with innings three through eight at no more than ten pitches per frame. James threw 16 pitches in the pressure-packed ninth, 13 more than he had thrown in his most stressful inning to that point, the second.
13. *New York Times*, October 11, 1914.
14. *Boston Evening American*, October 11, 1914, page 1 of the special World's Series section.
15. *New York Times*, October 11, 1914.
16. William A. Phelon, *Baseball Magazine*, February 1915, 12.

17 Damon Runyon, *Boston Evening American*, October 11, 1914, page 3 of the special World's Series section.

18 "Happenings by three seem to follow that Deal boy. In the first game he walloped into three (double) plays, and yesterday he three times forces runners again before he landed that long fly that Strunk misjudged." "Braves Again Victors, Athletics' Falter in Field with Bats Silenced," *Philadelphia Inquirer*, October 11, 1914, sports section 3.

19 "Wally Schang suddenly broke the monotony of hitless Athletics' frames by driving a two-base hit past third, making second by sliding on his stomach and beating by a scant fraction of an inch a beautiful throw-in by Cather from deep left corner." Ed McGrath, *Boston Post*, October 11, 1914, 11.

20 "Photographs of the play also show Schang on the base with Deal still waiting for the ball." Hugh S. Fullerton, "Mack Keeps Men Secluded before Game in Boston," [*Philadelphia*] *Evening Ledger*, October 12, 1914, 2.

21 Nick Flatley, *Boston Evening American*, October 11, 1914, page 2, special World's Series section. "'It's all over and there's no use of complaining,' said Schang, 'but Deal hasn't touched me yet on that play. I made a hook slide and caught the outside of the bag with my foot. Deal's gloved hand swept around quickly but he never touched me. Byron called the play so quickly that he said I was out before the play was finished.'" "Mack and Braves Each Make a Tally Early in the Game," *Philadelphia Bulletin*, October 12, 1914, 2. According to Retrosheet, Lord Byron was umpiring first base, not third base, in Game Two.

22 John J. Hallahan, *Boston Herald*, October 11, 1914, 2.

23 F.J. McIsaac, *Boston Evening American*, October 11, 1914, page 4, special World's Series section.

24 Harold Kaese, *The Boston Braves, 1871-1953* (Boston: Northeastern University Press, 2004), 163.

25 Nick Flatley, *Boston Evening American*, October 11, 1914, page 4, special World's Series section.

26 Damon Runyon, *Boston Evening American*, October 11, 1914, page 3, special World's Series section.

27 Norman L. Macht, *Connie Mack and the Early Years of Baseball* (Lincoln: University of Nebraska Press, 2007), 642.

28 This was the last but hardly the first time when Plank lacked run support in the World Series: "Eddie Plank suffered his fourth shutout in world's series battles." "Braves Again Victors, Athletics' Falter in Field with Bats Silenced," *Philadelphia Inquirer*, October 11, 1914, sports section p. 1.

29 Nick Flatley, *Boston Evening American*, October 11, 1914, page 2, special World's Series section.

30 Walter E. Hapgood, *Boston Herald*, October 11, 1914, 1.

31 George Stallings, *Boston Evening American*, October 11, 1914, page 4, special World's Series section.

32 C.P. Stack, *Baseball Magazine*, February 1915, 73.

One of the higher-priced tickets to Game Two.

Shibe Park, Philadelphia.

Long Lines Waiting At Park Gates

At 1:30 yesterday afternoon a youth came over from East Boston with a sweater and a bundle of straw under his arm, and leaned up against the wall of Fenway Park as close to the $1 entrance for the world's series seats as he could get. His name was Jack Gordon, he said, and he intended to see the first of the big games in Boston.

Await Ticket Rush

That was the start of two lines for rush seats to the game that grew and grew, slowly at first in the afternoon, rapidly after dark closed down, and finally after midnight by leaps and bounds, as grown men with blankets and rugs came to line up behind the youthful early arrivals and make sure of the coveted seats.

At 2 a.m. today the vicinity of this part was the liveliest place in Boston with two lines of fully 500 each stretching away from the $1 and from the 50-cent entrances, and more coming every minute.

And all through it Gordon held his place. It was not for sale, he said, thought those of many early comers were, to the highest bidder.

Hot dog men and purveyors of more elaborate eatables reaped a harvest. A big squad of police was on hand, afoot and on horse, to see the game was played fair, but the crowd was a good-natured one and there was small trouble.

Sleeping on Straw

The patient waiters as evening came on devised a scheme of seats and benches to lie on out of loose boards found in the neighborhood. As this grew to an imposing structure, the police were compelled to order it removed, for fear it would interfere with the handling of the crowds when the ticket sale really started today.

Then, as if by magic, straw appeared, and the men and boys who were prepared to "stick" till the ticket windows should open at 9 o'clock this morning, squatted down to snooze the hours away.

One contingent in the 50-cent line had come in a crowd and started songs, which quickly spread till the night was made vociferous with somewhat questionable melody.

By midnight the lines had reached from the gates as far as the Fenway garage in one direction, and around the corner of the grandstand clear to the last grandstand seats in the other.

—*Boston Post*, October 12, 1914

Face In The Crowd

The man who three decades hence would manage the Manhattan Project caught World Series fever. General Leslie R. Groves, known as Dick, attended the first game in Boston. As noted by his biographer Robert S. Norris in *Racing for the Bomb: General Leslie R. Groves, The Manhattan Project's Indispensable Man*, "On the Columbus Day holiday Dick decided to go to the third game of the 1914 World Series. He got up at four in the morning and walked the mile and a half to Fenway Park. He was about twenty-fifth in line and stood there for five hours waiting to buy a ticket. At around nine o'clock a man offered Dick ten dollars for his place in line, but Dick refused…. Dick bought his ticket and went into the park, taking an excellent seat about twenty feet in back of first base, in the third or fourth row."

—Mark Sternman

Game Three

Monday, October 12, 1914 at Fenway Park
Boston Braves 5, Philadelphia Athletics 4
(12 innings)

In the second consecutive thrilling contest, Philadelphia played by far its best match in Game Three and even took a two-run lead into the bottom of the tenth inning thanks to some daring baserunning by Eddie Murphy and a shocking mental error by Johnny Evers, "the player who became famous for discovering that Merkle didn't touch second."[1]

But the booming bats of Hank Gowdy and a determined Evers brought Boston even in the tenth and, with darkness falling in the bottom of the 12th, the Braves bounced back to win on another Gowdy smash, a bunt, and a throwing error by hard-luck loser Bullet Joe Bush.

The dramatic finish seemed to clinch the Series for Boston and caused the press corps to reach for historic hyperbole: "Boston today threw down the statue of Hank Adams and set up that of Hank Gowdy, tossed the statue of Johnny Adams into the bay and set up one of Johnny Evers, and went wild. Nothing can persuade them that after triumphing [in Game Three] anything will stop them."[2]

Eerily, Game Three began as Game One had, with a double by Eddie Murphy, a sacrifice by Rube Oldring on which the Braves made a "masterly"[3] play, and a sacrifice fly by Eddie Collins. Unlike the opener, the Athletics took the lead this time, and for good measure Collins reached first on his fly ball when "Connolly, good dependable Joey, made a miserable error."[4]

Again, however, Philadelphia failed to capitalize more fully due to a baserunning blunder after Collins stole second base and Stuffy McInnis walked. Pitcher Lefty Tyler picked Collins off second. "Collins was playing too far away from second and Tyler's throw to Evers caught him sliding back to the bag," the *Philadelphia Bulletin* wrote.[5]

"This [was] the second time Collins has been caught in the series, a fault practically unknown to him in the American League campaign," said the *Philadelphia Inquirer*.[6]

World Series Game Three at Fenway Park.

Boston tied the score in the bottom of the second on a Gowdy double, the first of his three extra-base hits off of Bush, which plated Rabbit Maranville, who had singled and stolen second base thanks to "Schang's miserable throwing."[7]

Bush's own shortstop criticized the pitcher after the game for going after Gowdy in this key spot: "That hit by Gowdy's … was also a slip for Bush," said Jack Barry. "With Maranville on second, two out and the pitcher next up, the best play was for Bush to feed bad ones to Gowdy and take a chance on walking him."[8]

The Athletics regained the lead in the top of the fourth inning with a two-out rally ignited when McInnis doubled to left. Going the same way, Jimmy Walsh "hit a bounding single into left and Connolly, still shaken up [by hitting the stand on the McInnis double], juggled the ball long enough to let McInnis score."[9]

The Braves tied the score immediately although Boston would have taken the lead if Bush had not started the inning with a key defensive play, ironic given the way the game would conclude. Leading off, "Whitted hit a fierce low grounder … which Bush deflected just enough to allow Collins to make a wonderful stop and throw out at first."[10]

But a two-out single by Maranville that fell in front of A's center fielder Jimmy Walsh drove in Butch Schmidt, who had singled and gone to second on a grounder by Charlie Deal. Walsh was playing only because "Amos Strunk, crack centerfielder of the Athletics, is out … for the rest of the world's series with an abscess on his hand…. Strunk would have been waiting for Maranville's short fly which Walsh barely touched," the *Philadelphia Bulletin* wrote ruefully.[11]

The teams played scoreless ball until the tenth inning, thanks in part to defensive gems by Schmidt, Tyler, and Maranville.

Braves manager George Stallings, in his daily column, called out "Big Schmidt's play on Bush in the eighth inning when he led off with what looked like a sure two or three-base hit. Schmidt's wonderful stop and Tyler's lightening-like work in covering the base were the greatest plays of the game."[12]

As with his game-ending double play in the ninth inning of Game Two, "Maranville robbed Collins of a hit in the ninth when he raced over toward second, scooped up a low sizzler and nabbed the fleet Collins by inches at first."[13]

The Athletics appeared to have won the game in the top of the tenth inning when Home Run Baker singled to second with two outs and the bases full to score Wally Schang. Murphy, who was on second, also scored because "Evers forgot the bases were full … began patting himself on the chest, and kept it up so long that Murphy finally took a chance to steal home, and … he ran home without Evers even looking up at him or making an effort to throw the ball."[14]

Philadelphia still had two on with two out. In a World Series that featured little strong defensive outfield play, Possum Whitted made a key one on a fly ball by McInnis at a clutch time. Eddie Collins noted, "It looked like we would get a couple more when McInnis lined sharply to left centre, but Whitted made a good catch."[15]

But Boston did not concede defeat even when they were confronted by a disheartening deficit. Gowdy opened the bottom of the tenth with "one of those fine, long, low drives that delight the eye of the golfer,"[16] a "psychological swat that put the necessary courage into his teammates"[17] to complete the comeback. (It bounced in center field and went into the stands, a hit that counted for four bases in those days.) Herbie Moran walked with one out and Evers had his chance for redemption. He "drove a fierce low bounder right where Collins should have been playing for him with a curve being pitched."[18] A single, the hit sent Moran to third. Connolly's sacrifice fly knotted the game again, at 4-4.

Boston won the game in the bottom of the 12th inning. Gowdy doubled and Leslie Mann ran for him. Larry Gilbert, making his only appearance of the Series, batted for James and received an intentional walk to set up a force play. Herbie Moran bunted back to Bush, who "grabbed the ball as if it were a ball of fire, and hurled it into the darkness. It may have been within five feet of Baker; it may have been within ten feet of him, but it might have well been thrown into the grandstand for all the good that it did."[19]

Given their disparity in experience, Bush came under much more blame for his miscue than did Mack for leaving him in the game. According to a Philadelphia paper, Bush threw 140 pitches in nine innings and 181 overall in a herculean effort.[20] The Braves had clearly sought to drive up Bush's pitch count from the beginning of the game. In the bottom of the first, "Moran pulled a 'Roy Thomas' by fouling off four straight balls, all good ones, before lifting to Mack's second base guardian."[21]

With his deep bullpen and the darkness that would have prohibited additional play, Mack could have easily relieved Bush at different junctures[22] but chose not to do so and suffered again from his passivity, although the dimming light did make Bush's "speed more effective every minute."[23]

Boston proved faster than a speeding Bullet in taking Game Three and setting the stage for the possible first sweep in the history of the World Series.

Notes

1 "Bush's Wild Throw to Baker Cost Athletics Third Game," *Philadelphia Bulletin*, October 13, 1914, 10.

2 Hugh S. Fullerton, "Hub about Ready to Raise Statue to Hank Gowdy," *Boston Traveler*, October 13, 1914, 6.

3 "Notes of the Braves' Game," *Boston Traveler*, October 13, 1914, 7.

4 "Braves' Game Fight Wins 5-4 Victory after 12 Innings," *Boston Daily Advertiser*, October 13, 1914, 3.

5 "Detail of Each Ball in To-Day's Battle," *Philadelphia Bulletin*, October 12, 1914, 1.

6 "Gowdy the Rock Mack Tripped on," *Philadelphia Inquirer*, October 13, 1914, 10. Collins made no excuses in his column, writing, "I am deserving of severe criticism for getting pinched off second, as it helped the Braves' pitcher out of a tight hole." Eddie Collins, "Eddie Collins Says Mackmen 'in Last Ditch,'" *[Philadelphia] Evening Ledger*, October 13, 1914, 2.

7 T.H. Murnane, "Thrice in Lead, Athletics Lose Finally to Braves in 12th, 4-5," *Boston Daily Globe*, October 13, 1914, 6.

8 Jack Barry, "Inability to Hit in Pinches Caused Athletics' Defeat," *Philadelphia Bulletin*, October 13, 1914, 10. Connie Mack disagreed: "Our pitchers didn't pitch right to Gowdy. He isn't the hitter the World's Series statistics show. The pitchers were told what to pitch,

but didn't do it." "Silent Handful Greets Mackmen," *Philadelphia Bulletin*, October 14, 1914, 1.

9   R.E. McMillin, "Braves Victorious in Twelve Innings," *Boston Journal*, October 13, 1914, 8.

10 "Notes of the Braves' Game," *Boston Traveler*, October 13, 1914, 7.

11 "Strunk out of the Series," *Philadelphia Bulletin*, October 13, 1914, 10.

12 George T. Stallings, "Braves Gamest Club in History," *Boston Daily Advertiser*, October 13, 1914, 3.

13 "Notes of the Braves' Game," *Boston Traveler*, October 13, 1914, 7.

14 "Bush's Wild Throw to Baker Cost Athletics Third Game," *Philadelphia Bulletin*, October 13, 1914, 10. Of Evers's lapse, Maranville wrote later, "I yelled at Evers, who kept patting the ball in his glove. I yelled, 'Third, Johnny, third.'" This account just adds to the mystery of an odd play, as Maranville should have yelled home, where Murphy was going, rather than third, from where Murphy was coming. Walter "Rabbit" Maranville, *Run, Rabbit, Run* (Cleveland: Society for American Baseball Research, 1991), 33.

15 Eddie Collins, "Eddie Collins Says Mackmen 'in Last Ditch,'" *[Philadelphia] Evening Ledger*, October 13, 1914, 2.

16 "Braves' Game Fight Wins 5-4 Victory after 12 Innings," *Boston Daily Advertiser*, October 13, 1914, 1.

17 "Braves Capture White Elephants as Night Falls," *Philadelphia Inquirer*, October 13, 1914, 1. "Maranville was acting like a crazy man on the coaching lines." John J. Hallahan, "Detail Play of the Third Straight Game Captured by Braves," *Boston Herald*, October 13, 1914, 7.

18 Hugh S. Fullerton, "Bracing Ball Played by Both Teams" *[Philadelphia] Evening Ledger*, October 13, 1914, 2.

19 "Bush's Wild Throw to Baker Cost Athletics Third Game," *Philadelphia Bulletin*, October 13, 1914, 10. Barry, presumably close to the play from his shortstop position, said the throw "just grazed Baker's glove." Jack Barry, "Inability to Hit in Pinches Caused Athletics' Defeat," *Philadelphia Bulletin*, October 13, 1914, 10. A scout writing under a pseudonym claimed Bush "slipped and fell, throwing the ball into left field." "A's Chance to Win Is Slim One; Gowdy Is the Hero, Says 'X,'" *Boston Traveler*, October 13, 1914, 6.

20 Even a single outlet had disparate views of how well Bush had done. "Bush … acquitted himself so well that with a less aggressive and resourceful team than the Braves, he would have won." "Boston World Champions," *Sporting Life*, October 17, 1914, 2. "Bush was unequal to winning his own game; 'groove' balls to Gowdy, Evers and Connolly resulting in a homer, single and sacrifice fly which netted two runs and tied the game." Francis C. Richter, "The World's Series Sweep," *Sporting Life*, October 24, 1914, 2.

21 Bush threw 27 pitches to just four batters in the first inning, "the largest inning of the series for balls pitched." "Gowdy the Rock Mack Tripped on," *Philadelphia Inquirer*, October 13, 1914, 10.

22 In the third inning, "Pennock was warming up with great speed." John J. Hallahan, "Detail Play of the Third Straight Game Captured by Braves," *Boston Herald*, October 13, 1914, 7.

23 Jim Nasium, "Mackmen Buckle in Crucial Battle," *Philadelphia Inquirer*, October 13, 1914, 10.

Game Four

Tuesday, October 13, 1914 at Fenway Park
Boston Braves 3, Philadelphia Athletics 1

Backed by stout defense,[1] Dick Rudolph easily won his second game of the quartet, throwing just 94 pitches in a complete game as the Miracle Boston Braves shocked the baseball world by sweeping Connie Mack's Philadelphia Athletics, 3-1. Although Philadelphia finally cooled the scalding bat of Hank Gowdy, Boston captain Johnny Evers delivered a clutch two-out, two-run single in the bottom of the fifth that snapped a 1-1- deadlock, and sparked the Boston Nationals to their first 20th-century title in a postseason that no less a contemporary observer than Ty Cobb asserted "marks the crumbling of the great Mack machine."[2]

The Braves played superior defense, making notable plays in nearly every frame. The tone was set when the second batter of the game, Rube Oldring, "fouled to Gowdy. The high wind carried the ball back away from the plate, but Hank got under it and made a sterling catch."[3]

In the second inning, "(Charlie) Deal ran over in back of Rudolph, speared the ball with his gloved hand, shifted it to his left like lightning, and tossed out McInnis at first while still on the dead run."[4]

In the third inning Deal struck again with "a sensational stop over third base and retired Murphy by inches at first base. ..." The next batter, Oldring, singled, "tried to steal on the first throw to Collins and was retired, Gowdy to Maranville, by fully five yards."[5]

With the game still scoreless in the fourth inning after one out on "a remarkable stop of Collins' drive"[6] by Evers, Frank Baker singled and got to third thanks to a single by Stuffy McInnis, but on the play "Connolly returned the ball to Deal, who in a flash saw that Baker had it beaten, drove the ball to Evers and McInnis was caught trying to get to the base."[7]

Boston capitalized by taking the lead in the bottom of the fourth, which began with a walk to Evers. Unlike the Braves, the Philadelphians failed to make the key plays at the key times. Following Evers, "Connolly hit a sharp grounder to Collins, who had a double play in front of him. Eddie, however, foozled the ball, allowing Evers to reach second easily. ... Whitted [then] pushed a savage grounder at Collins, which hit Eddie on the foot and went for a base hit"[8] that moved Evers to third, from where he scored on a groundout by Butch Schmidt.

Philadelphia's starting pitcher, Bob Shawkey, quickly tied the score in the top of the fifth when he drove in Jack Barry with a double. But the Braves changed their tactics against Shawkey to retake the lead for good in the bottom of the same frame.[9] "The feature clout ... was contributed by Johnny Evers, who drove in both of Boston's runs ... on a fine young single to left field, Evers connecting when two were down with just a hit needed for Boston to break the tie and go into the lead."[10] Two runs scored on the blow, making the score 3-1 for the Braves, and that was the game's final tally.

With the Athletics needing baserunners to keep their season alive after Boston had taken the lead, "Maranville absolutely robbed Collins of a hit in the sixth inning, when he dashed back of second, grabbed Collins' liner with one hand and shot it to first."[11]

The Boston scorecard for the Series.

Fenway Park seating prior to the 1914 World Series.

The Athletics would not get another man on base until the seventh inning, when Jimmy Walsh, playing center field this day in the absence of the lamed Amos Strunk, walked and went to second on a wild pitch. With none out, Philadelphia merely needed to do what the Braves had done in the fourth inning, namely, move the runner around to score a run, which would have closed the gap to 3-2. But as in the second inning of Game One against Rudolph, Barry failed to advance the runner by striking out on a pitch that again "was off the plate";[12] even worse for the Athletics, "Evers grabbed Gowdy's throw down to second with one hand and slapped the ball on Walsh completing a sensational double play."[13]

As Ty Cobb harshly but justly observed in his postgame analysis, "There was no excuse for Walsh being caught at that stage. ... There was no reason for him to take chances."[14]

The play seemed to demoralize Philadelphia, as its last seven batters went down in order. "Even with the chances of the Athletics fading, Pennock [who had replaced Shawkey on the mound in the sixth] was sent up to bat"[15] to start the eighth and grounded out to second.

Mack's passivity and Pennock's impatience typified the slack Philadelphia attack throughout the World Series. Rudolph remarked, "I'd rather pitch against the Athletics than the worst teams in the National and American Leagues, and I know that my average would be far better. They swung at anything I sent up to them, whether low, high or wide. They did not show any batting judgment at all."[16]

Leadoff hitter Eddie Murphy followed Pennock in the eighth and skied to Mann, who "turned in a wonderful catch ... getting the ball out in left centre after a hard run. It was a regular Tris Speaker catch, and Spoke, who was in the press stand ... let out a mighty yell."[17]

The inning ended on still a third notable effort, when Evers made "a clever play on Oldring's short fly."[18]

The final frame started no better for the Athletics, who showed "evidence of the loss of heart" as "Eddie Collins ... led off in the ninth inning by striking out, the third strike being on a ball that almost hit the ground at his feet."[19]

Baker's groundout pushed the Athletics closer to their doom. Then, for a postseason that could have not looked better for the Braves, the game, Series, and season ended on a fittingly "pretty play":[20] "McInnis hit the first ball pitched. It went at Deal with great speed, but Charlie knocked it down and, after recovering, furnished the final play of the series with a fine throw to Schmidt."[21]

That substitute Charlie Deal closed the World Series made sense. Boston had an unheralded team, and a backup stepped up to backstop the miracle squad to a sweep few had foreseen. "Deal held up his end in startling style and his brilliancy was in evidence just at the time when it was most required. To him went the honor of making the final assist and all throughout he handled his position masterfully."[22]

With so many Braves playing masterfully, Boston captured the 1914 World Series in four convincing games.

After Game Four:

"Boston never knew a wilder baseball celebration than that which followed the fourth game. Thousands of fans swarmed around the Boston dugout, and Manager

Stallings had to make a speech. Rabbit Maranville was dragged from the showers, and, half-dressed, he too spoke to the crowd from the roof of the dugout. Then the crowd paraded with the band playing 'Tessie' and 'Along Came Ruth' around the park, through the Fens, down Huntington Avenue, and to Copley Square, where the beaten Athletics were serenaded in their hotel, the Copley Plaza. There were fully 5,000 fans in the human chain, and thrust to its head were all the Braves who came in sight, especially Maranville, who needed no thrusting."

—Harold Kaese, *The Boston Braves*, p. 166.

Notes

1. The *Boston Journal* called this "the third, and only the third, in the 145 that have been played for world's championships in which no errors were recorded in the score." The fact that Game Three ended on a throwing error made Game Four stand in even sharper contrast. *Boston Journal*, October 14, 1914, 8.
2. Ty Cobb, "Big Mack Machine Crumbled, Says Ty," *[Philadelphia] Evening Bulletin*, October 13, 1914, 10.
3. "Details of the Play," *[Philadelphia] Evening Ledger*, October 13, 1914, 1.
4. "Braves Win Title; Beat Athletics 3-1; 4th Straight Game," *Boston Daily Advertiser*, October 14, 1914, 8.
5. "Detail of Each Ball in To-Day's Battle," *[Philadelphia] Evening Bulletin*, October 13, 1914, 1.
6. T.H. Murnane, "World's Championship Comes Back to Boston," *Boston Daily Globe*, October 14, 1914, 6.
7. "Boston Braves Capture Title from Macks, 3-1," *Philadelphia Inquirer*, October 14, 1914, 12.
8. "Evers' Timely Sting to Centre Gave the Braves World's Title," *Philadelphia Inquirer*, October 14, 1914, 12.
9. "In the first part of the game, the Boston batters were waiting Shawkey out consistently, but suddenly in the fifth when they had him throwing over the first ball and not expecting them to swing at it, they switched and began to go after the first one that he was trying to sneak over. He had taken the Stallings bait. They had him work in the early innings. …Then they slugged him." Ty Cobb, "Overconfidence Beat the Athletics, Cobb Says of Record Rout," *Boston American*, October 14, 1914, 11.
10. Walter E. Hapgood, "Braves Now World's Baseball Champions," *Boston Herald*, October 14, 1914, 10.
11. Hal Sheridan, "Braves Win 3 to 1, Annexing Title as World Champions," *[Philadelphia] Evening Ledger*, October 13, 1914, 1.
12. Ty Cobb, "Overconfidence Beat the Athletics, Cobb Says of Record Rout," *Boston American*, October 14, 1914, 11.
13. "Evers' Timely Sting to Centre Gave the Braves World's Title," *Philadelphia Inquirer*, October 14, 1914, 12.
14. Ty Cobb, "Overconfidence Beat the Athletics, Cobb Says of Record Rout," *Boston American*, October 14, 1914, 11.
15. John J. Hallahan, "How the Braves Won the World's Baseball Championship of 1914," *Boston Herald*, October 14, 1914, 10.
16. "Braves' Victory Crowning Upset of Athletic Year," *[Philadelphia] Evening Ledger*, October 14, 1914, 12.
17. "Braves Win Title; Beat Athletics 3-1; 4th Straight Game," *Boston Daily Advertiser*, October 14, 1914, 8.
18. T.H. Murnane, "World's Championship Comes back to Boston," *Boston Daily Globe*, October 14, 1914, 6.
19. Paul H. Shannon, "Athletics Bow to Faster Team," *Boston Post*, October 14, 1914, 17.
20. Melville E. Webb, Jr., "Echoes of the Game," *Boston Daily Globe*, October 14, 1914, 8.
21. John J. Hallahan, "How the Braves Won the World's Baseball Championship of 1914," *Boston Herald*, October 14, 1914, 10.
22. Ed McGrath, "Braves Win Final 3 to 1 Now World Champions," *Boston Post*, October 14, 1914, 7.

The Miracle Braves.

"I Told You So"

My friends, meet Mr. Stallings' rotten crew,
Just now it's quite the proper thing to do;
Of course, they're just a bunch of nondescrips,
Too weak to e'en emit a kitten's mew.

"Just watch 'em crack," was said when they went fast;
"Such speed as that can never, never last";
They cracked the heads of all the teams about
And nailed that pennant ribbon to their mast.

"They'll get to Rudolph one of these bright days
And knock his benders forty diff'rent ways";
But Rudolph, James and Tyler went the route;
Now every one is helping sing their praise.

"They can not hit; they can not field, alas!
"The whole darn team is sorely lacking class";
But nearly always they brought home the meat,
From Connolly to Johnny Evers crass.

"Oh, yes, they're just a lot of lucky bums;
"They can't run and their fingers are all thumbs;
"Maranville is the whole show on the team –
"Oh, Evers, yes; the rest are mostly Rums."

All this before the season closed and more,
Until they batted down the pennant door;
Whereat the knockers picked the Elephants
And said there wouldn't really be a core.

Well, friends, the Braves have taken in the Macks,
And for the rest they're well prepared to fight;
McGillicuddy's tearing at his hair
And Boston money's plentiful as air.

And now we'll hear those funny cracks,
From those who claim a second guess,
"I told you so," you can't beat facts.

—O. R. C. in *St. Louis Globe-Democrat*

The Rest of 1914

October 13—Frederic Alfonso Pezet, Peruvian minister to the United States, announced that the Braves would make a tour of South America in 1915, and he hoped the trip "would be the means of furthering trade between the US and South American republics." The *Boston Globe* reported that Connie Mack and his A's departed for Philadelphia that evening, but before leaving, Mack called the Braves "the best team that has ever played baseball." Only Hank Gowdy greeted Mack before he left; Johnny Evers and George Stallings both insisted it was up to Mack to reach out to them and not the other way around.

October 14—Except for Red Smith, who was still in the hospital recovering from his injury, and Dick Rudolph, who rushed home to be with his new daughter, the Braves were honored at a banquet held by Boston Mayor James Michael Curley at the Copley Plaza. The *Boston Globe* reported that each Brave would receive $2,708.91 for winning the World Series, and each of the A's would receive $1,950.42.

October 16—D.J. Coffey of Winsted, Connecticut, won a coffin in a bet with C. Hugins of Collinsville, Connecticut, who chose the A's over the Braves. Hugins, an undertaker, put up a coffin in a wager with Coffey, a clothier, who wagered a new silk hat. The coffin ended up being the size of a baby, which was of little use to Coffey, who tipped the scales at 300 pounds.

October 17—Braves management refunded $7,095 to holders of Game Five tickets with an additional $14,347 to be distributed later.

Dick Rudolph was honored by the entire undergraduate body of Fordham University in New York, who escorted him from the institution's gym to its football field. Rudolph, a Fordham alumnus, was presented with a gold watch fob, then set the football up for kickoff. Fordham defeated Middlebury, 28-0.

Lefty Tyler parlayed his World Series share into a 422-acre farm in Nashua, New Hampshire. "The farm is not stocked now and I shall begin small, with cattle, and intend to raise stock," he told the *Boston Globe*. "I may produce milk and cream for market incidentally."

October 18—In Utica, New York, a team of Braves won an exhibition game, 6-2, behind the play of Johnny Evers and Rabbit Maranville, who homered in his last at-bat. Likewise, at the Lenox Oval in New York, a second team of Braves led by Dick Crutcher and Hank Gowdy beat a Newark squad, 4-2.

October 19—Hank Gowdy and Dick Rudolph made their vaudeville debut at Hammerstein's Victoria Theatre, showing the crowd the system of signals the Braves used against the Athletics, then demonstrating each pitch that Rudolph threw in the World Series.

But they weren't the only Braves who took to the stage. Word out of New York was that George Stallings would be the headliner at the Palace Theatre in the coming weeks, giving a monologue "full of the thrills, the humors and the melodrama of the diamond." And Rabbit Maranville signed a 17-week contract to perform on the Keith Circuit.

Meanwhile in Troy, New York, Johnny Evers was serenaded by a parade of ten bands, several drum corps, and more than 5,000 men. Afterward Evers was honored at a banquet at the State Armory, attended by about 500 people, including Stallings, James Gaffney, and John McGraw.

October 20—Putnam, Connecticut, scheduled a night and day for Joe Connolly, who made his professional baseball debut with Putnam in 1906. The Friday evening festivities were to include dinner at the Putnam Inn, entertainment at the Bradley Theater featuring a movie, songs, and vaudeville acts, and a banquet at Owl's Hall. Saturday afternoon was to feature a parade to the high-school baseball grounds, where an exhibition game would be played with Connolly and many of his former Putnam teammates in the batting order.

October 22—The *Hartford Courant* reported that Rabbit Maranville had accepted an invitation to be the guest of honor at a banquet to be held in Hartford on October 26. Among the expected attendees were Charles Hopkins Clark, editor of the *Courant*, Senator George M. Landers, and Judge Edward L. Smith.

October 23—The city of Columbus, Ohio, hometown of Hank Gowdy, announced it had completed plans for a reception honoring Gowdy that would include a parade of at least 10,000 people, a loving cup, and another gift "to which every citizen of Columbus will be permitted to contribute."

October 24—Larry Gilbert, a native of New Orleans, was to be honored with a Gilbert Day at Pelicans Park in New Orleans, where he'd be the recipient of several gifts from baseball enthusiasts and would play in an exhibition game despite Stallings' reluctance to allow him to play any more ball until the following spring.

In Putnam, Connecticut, Joe Connolly received a loving cup and $50, then pitched three innings in an exhibition game that his team lost, 6-4. Connolly, who made his professional debut as a star pitcher, launched a couple of balls over the houses beyond the right-field fence, prompting the opposing pitcher to walk him his last three times up.

October 25—Larry Gilbert led his team to victory in an exhibition game in New Orleans, driving in two runs in a 3-2 win. Prior to the game, Gilbert was honored with a parade and given a silver loving cup, a silver bat and ball, a gold watch, and a gold-headed umbrella.

Bill James was also successful, leading his All-Star Nationals to an 11-3 win over the All-Star Americans in Spokane, Washington. James surrendered three runs in the first inning, but, according to the *Boston Globe*, was "invincible" for the rest of the game.

October 26—George Stallings made his stage debut and needed encouragement from audience members to get him through his nervousness. "I have been in the center of action on the baseball field before 30,000 persons," Stallings told the crowd, "and have been as cool as ice. But I must confess I am enjoying at this moment all the delights of stage fright."

October 27—Columbus, Ohio, greeted Hank Gowdy like a conquering hero, meeting him at the train station with a procession of 100 automobiles that drove him to a parade of 8,000 people and seven brass bands. An estimated 20,000 people lined the streets to welcome him home, and his "coming was heralded" by a 21-gun salute at the State House rotunda. Gowdy was presented with a loving cup and a $300 diamond fob.

October 28—Les Mann was met by a parade upon his return to Lincoln, Nebraska, and was honored at a public reception. It was also reported that Joe Connolly, Oscar Dugey, and Herbie Moran had signed their 1915 contracts and that Lefty Tyler had inked a two-year deal.

October 30—Joe Connolly was honored again, this time in Manville, Rhode Island, where he received a gold loving cup. But he failed to make an All-Star team chosen by fans, writers, and other experts from around the country. Rabbit Maranville and Bill James were named to the team, however.

November

November 1—As if George Stallings needed more praise, the *Washington Post* speculated that other managers would adopt the skipper's strategy of platooning, especially in the outfield, and using a three-man rotation. According to the paper, managers scoffed at Stallings for setting up his outfield depending on the handedness of the opposing pitcher and felt that relying primarily on three pitchers rather than four would "wreck" the pitchers' arms.

The *Post* also felt that the success of diminutive players like Rabbit Maranville and Dick Rudolph would be a "great boon" to minor-league players of small stature. "In the future it is likely that fast infielders who have been passed up because of their tiny size will be given a big league trial."

In Los Angeles, Braves catcher Bert Whaling verified that Rube Vickers' advice to Bill James about not throwing fastballs to the A's paid off in spades. "James threw but one fast ball in that contest," he told Harry Williams of the *Los Angeles Times*, "and that was the one which Schang straightened out for a double. That convinced [James] that it wasn't exactly safe to provide speed for the Athletics to gaze upon. It was his spitter which had Mack's heavy hitters standing on one ear." Whaling also predicted the Braves would win another World Series title in 1915.

November 6—The *Boston Globe* reported that St. Joseph's Total Abstinence Society of the West End would present a performance called *The Frolic of the Braves,* a two-act, three-scene production that would serve as a chronological review of the Braves' season from spring training to the end of the World Series, and would include singing, dancing, and comedy.

November 8—Braves president James Gaffney conducted negotiations with Hot Springs, Arkansas, in an effort to secure a spring-training site, joining the Boston Red Sox and Pittsburgh Pirates, who already had permanent quarters there.

November 10—Ring Lardner recounted a story in which a reporter might have been one of the reasons the Braves won a championship. According to Lardner, the unnamed reporter wrote that Boston hurler Bill James had lost his nerve during an early-season game, inciting James to punch him in the nose. President Gaffney was prepared to trade James to St. Louis, suspend him for the rest of the season, or release him outright, but the reporter persuaded Gaffney to do none of the above, and the rest is history.

November 11—In Springfield, Massachusetts, Walter Maranville was married to Miss Elizabeth Shea. And in Boston, president Gaffney denied reports that the team had sold its grounds to the Sears-Roebuck Company, but admitted that the park was too small for the team but that he would sell the land only if a factory would be constructed to give more work to Bostonians. Gaffney wouldn't elaborate on potential sites for a new ballpark except to say he'd received many offers for sites and could "undoubtedly arrange to get the use of Fenway Park until the new park would be ready."

November 12—A's hurler Bullet Joe Bush outdueled Bill James in an exhibition game in Los Angeles that pitted American Leaguers vs. National Leaguers. The AL was represented by players from the A's, Red Sox, Indians, Yankees, Tigers, and Senators, while the NL was represented by players from the Cardinals, Giants, Phillies, and Braves. Red Sox first baseman Dick Hoblitzel starred for the AL with three hits and a triple; Giants shortstop Art Fletcher had two of the NL's five hits.

November 15—The *New York Times* reported that Dick Rudolph "will start off another world's championship event, when he fires the gun for the start of the twenty-second annual international six-day cycle race at Madison Square Garden." Due to the World War, the Paris and Berlin championship events had to be canceled and the race at the Garden was to be the only six-day event that year. Almost $40,000 was to be distributed among 18 teams, the largest group to compete to that point.

November 18—Braves ace Bill James told Harry Williams of the *Los Angeles Times* that George Stallings almost ruined him in 1913 by trying to get him to rely on a curveball instead of his fastball, spitball, changeup, and control. "I started off fairly well with the Braves in 1913," James told Williams, "but it was decided that my effectiveness could be increased if I was translated into a curve ball pitcher."

"I lost control, and a pitcher without control is about as reliable as a flying machine without a steering wheel. … I do not think it is a good idea to try and change the style of either a pitcher or a batter if they are naturally good in those departments."

November 25— Despite reports about Hot Springs, Arkansas, George Stallings announced that the Braves would train again in Macon, Georgia, in 1915, and that his players would report in the latter half of February.

November 26—The *Boston Globe* reported that Stallings had 1,000 bales of cotton to sell at his plantation in Haddock, Georgia, and that it would be a miracle if he was able to sell them. "Through the advice of New

York friends a scheme has been evolved to sell off his cotton at 10 cents a pound," wrote the *Globe*. Each person who purchased a bale would receive a receipt that included Stallings' picture and autograph.

November 27—Dick Rudolph was to write for the *Boston Globe* every Monday beginning on November 30. According to the paper, "His articles in the *Globe* will demonstrate what a youngster may achieve on the ball field by clean living and a scientific study of the great American game."

November 28—Johnny Evers spent the day in Boston, ate lunch with old friends at the Harvard Club, watched a high-school football game with Rabbit Maranville, then had dinner at the Maugus Club of Wellesley. The Braves' MVP gave a speech after dinner, as did T.H. Murnane, sportswriter and president of the New England League, and Herman Nickerson, the Braves' secretary.

November 29—In the first of a series of articles in the *Boston Globe* in which George Stallings was "to tell the Boston fans how he took hold of a 'misfit outfit' and developed world beaters in two seasons," he described how he first laid eyes on the Braves in 1912 in a series against the Giants at the Polo Grounds. "It is a baseball horror," he kept repeating to himself. "I have had considerable experience around ball teams," he wrote, "I have devoted 25 years of my life to baseball in one capacity or another, but I have never seen any club in the big leagues look quite so bad."

December

December 1—Braves president James Gaffney held the club's annual meeting to determine where they'd play their games in 1915, and elect the team's officers. Gaffney had previously announced that Herman Nickerson would remain the team's secretary, and Red Sox owner Joe Lannin had been given the AL's consent to make whatever deal he could for the Braves' use of Fenway Park if necessary.

During the meeting, Gaffney was re-elected president and treasurer; C.M Goodnow was elected vice president; F.R. Killeen was elected assistant treasurer; Nickerson was elected secretary; and Gaffney, Robert H. Davis, Stallings, Killeen, and F.W. Woodcock were named directors.

December 2—Former Brave Bris Lord, who last played in 1913 and had taken over as player-manager of the Southern Association's Memphis Chicks, was reportedly trying to convince George Stallings to schedule a three-game series for March 27-29, 1915. Stallings had yet to schedule any spring games, but was said to be "pleased" to schedule the games if he could.

December 5—Tim Murnane of the *Boston Globe* reported that grounds had been secured for a new ballpark that would be located on land once used for the Allston Golf Course. The land was 675 feet wide on Commonwealth Ave and went back 850 feet to the Boston & Albany Railroad. "While it will be impossible to have things in shape for the opening game," wrote Murnane, "[Gaffney] felt quite sure that Pres Lannin will allow him to use Fenway Park until such time as he is ready for the big opening."

December 7—The Braves dropped their lawsuit for conspiracy against the Federal League, the Baltimore Federal League Club, James Gilmore, Edward Hanlon, Otto Knabe, and pitcher Jack Quinn. "Counsel for the plaintiff stated in court that the Boston Club realized it would be difficult to collect damages for the loss of Quinn," reported the *New York Times*, "inasmuch as without him the team had won the greatest possible honors in the baseball world."

December 10—George Stallings discussed potential trades with Miller Huggins of the Cardinals at the National League meetings in New York, but admitted to being surprised that there was no market for the players he was shopping. The *Boston Globe* speculated that it was most likely because other managers realized they couldn't get the same performance out of said players than did the Georgia "Miracle Man."

Tim Murnane reported that nine of ten experts predicted the 1915 World Series would pit both Boston teams against each other. He also wrote of Johnny

Evers' illness, which had the Braves' captain confined to the Hotel Somerset with a 101-degree fever. According to Murnane, Evers arrived in New York with a bad cold on December 8 and was forced to bed the next day when it was discovered he had pneumonia.

December 11—Dr. John Herrity told reporters that Evers was in a "precarious condition" and it would take five days before the physician would be confident that Evers would pull through. His temperature had gone down, though, and Herrity gave the second baseman a "fighting chance." James Gaffney and George Stallings "called in expert medical advice" and were in "constant touch with the player's room at the hotel."

December 12—Evers again showed improvement and was expected to be able to go home to Troy in a couple of days, but the big news out of the New York meetings was the contract extension signed by Stallings that would keep him in Boston until 1918. "President James E. Gaffney would not tell what the financial terms were," wrote Tim Murnane, "but Stallings was more than pleased with the contract." Stallings and Gaffney also spent time discussing possible deals with Phillies manager Pat Moran, but no trades were made.

December 14—Although he was still holed up at the Hotel Somerset with pneumonia, it was reported that Johnny Evers' condition was "steadily improving."

December 16—James Gaffney arrived in Boston to meet with an architect to discuss details of the Braves' new ballpark in Allston.

December 17—According to Tim Murnane, the Braves' new park was to be the "last word in baseball plants," as James Gaffney had planned to use the best features from every other major-league stadium to build his new venue that was expected to seat 45,000 spectators. The grandstand was to be similar to the one at Detroit's Navin Field. The *Hartford Courant* reported that the park would be modeled after the New Yale Bowl and that the base of the stands would be placed 12 feet below street level, with an option to add a second deck and increase the capacity to approximately 60,000.

December 18—Murnane reported that Gaffney and Joe Lannin of the Red Sox reached an agreement for the Braves to use Fenway Park until their new facility was ready sometime in August. In an odd twist, though, Lannin signed scout Tommy McCarthy away from the Braves after McCarthy and Stallings were told that Gaffney wouldn't be considering the scout issue until late February. McCarthy called on Lannin and a deal with the Sox was quickly hammered out. To the Braves' credit, they were delighted that McCarthy was able to land a job with such a quality team.

It was also reported that Gaffney had signed 17 players to contracts that had the reserve clause omitted, contradicting an earlier report that Dick Rudolph's contract contained the clause and he was considering jumping the team because he felt the team had not "fulfilled its financial obligation to him." Gaffney explained he'd given Rudolph a $1,000 bonus at the end of the season and wasn't worried about his pitcher jumping ship.

In addition to signing many of his own players, Gaffney was trying to land third baseman Hans Lobert and utilityman Sherry Magee from the Phillies, even though Magee had his heart set on going to the Giants. Murnane opined that Magee going to New York would be a good thing for the league because it "depended on the Polo Grounds money for an existence." The 29-year-old was coming off a season in which he batted .314 with 15 homers and 103 RBIs, and paced the senior circuit in hits, doubles, RBIs, slugging, and total bases, and finished seventh in MVP voting.

December 20—In his syndicated column, Stallings wrote that he'd come up with the idea of platooning his outfield one night in June while lying in bed, and that it was similar to the way managers had used pinch-hitters in the past, but on a larger scale. The acquisition of Possum Whitted and Ted Cather from St. Louis in the deal that sent pitcher Hub Perdue to the Cards on June 28 gave Stallings the outfielders he needed to make his plan successful.

December 21—Dick Rudolph signed a new two-year deal with the Braves, quashing rumors that he'd jump the team and join the Federal League. The Braves also insured Rabbit Maranville's life for $25,000 and appointed the club as beneficiary.

December 24—Dick Crutcher's signed contract for 1915 was received at the club's offices, but the big news was the acquisition of Sherry Magee from the Phillies for two players to be named later (Oscar Dugey and Possum Whitted were eventually shipped to Philadelphia in February 1915). Magee had told Philadelphia management that he was through with the Phillies and held meetings with the Federal League's Baltimore club before agreeing to a trade to Boston, one of two cities he most wanted to play in. After the trade, Magee agreed to a two-year deal with the Braves.

December 27—In his weekly column, George Stallings said that he wanted to start Otto Hess in Game Four of the World Series but went with Rudolph instead to avoid criticism that the World Series was being prolonged for financial reasons. He cited the 1912 fall classic as an example, that Red Sox manager Jake Stahl received "ridiculous criticism" for starting Buck O'Brien in Game Five instead of Joe Wood, and that his choice "produced the material on which the knockers were glad to work."

The Braves skipper insisted Hess would have won Game Four, but he didn't feel right pitching him. "The baseball world knew that Rudolph had had sufficient rest to be sent back for the final game," Stallings wrote. "If Hess had started and had lost that contest, the pastime would have been done some very serious damage. ... I could not afford to risk that."

December 28—James Gaffney, F.R. Killeen, and R.H. Davis arrived in Boston to examine plans for the new ballpark, which called for 40,282 seats—948 box seats, 15,983 in the grandstand, 9,639 in the left pavilion, 8,376 in the right pavilion, and 5,336 in the center-field bleachers to be sold for 25 cents each.

"Pres Gaffney has been giving the pavilions and grandstand a great deal of thought," wrote Tim Murnane. "He also wants to see plenty of room for the outfielders, and this he has provided for in grand style, for there is room for home runs within the field, and the laying out of the diamond was done with proper regard for the players, who on many grounds are forced to play sun fields."

December 29—The *Christian Science Monitor* reported that Gaffney's lawyers had met with lawyers representing the owners of the Allston property where the Braves intended to build a new stadium, and that transfer of the property would be made later in the afternoon.

December 30—BOSTON BRAVES' DEALS SETTLED, GAFFNEY GOES, reported the *Christian Science Monitor* after the South End Grounds had been sold to the Mercantile Real Estate Trust Company and the Allston grounds transferred to the Braves magnate. With the deals finally complete, Gaffney was off to Haddock, Georgia, where he intended to spend ten days at George Stallings' plantation. Gaffney wasn't expected to be back in Boston until mid-February, and told reporters construction on the new park wouldn't begin until March.

December 31—Tim Murnane wrote in the *Boston Globe* that Gaffney "felt pretty well satisfied that he had still an excellent chance to secure third baseman [Hans] Lobert from the Philadelphia Nationals." Lobert was demanding a three-year deal at $10,000 per annum from the Federal League, who countered with a two-year deal worth $15,000. The Phillies weren't meeting his terms, either, so he was holding out. The New York Giants were willing to pay his asking price, but didn't have a third baseman to send back to Philadelphia.

Regardless, Lobert traveled to New York to meet with John McGraw and discuss the possibility of becoming a Giant in 1915. "No definite conclusion as to the proposed deal was reached tonight, however, although McGraw and others interested intimated that progress was being made." Lobert was traded to the Giants on January 4, 1915.

How An Exhibition Game Contributed To A Miracle

By Bob Brady

IN THE ESTIMATION of Rabbit Maranville, the fallout from an embarrassing midseason exhibition game loss proved to be the driving force behind the 1914 Braves' miraculous turnaround.

Like most teams of the era, the Braves would seek to pick up a few extra dollars by scheduling exhibition contests during open dates on their schedule. In addition to the revenue generated, these games also would serve as a break from the monotony of prolonged rail travel and help keep players' skills sharp.

On July 7, the Braves, Brooklyn Robins, Chicago Cubs, Cincinnati Reds, and Philadelphia Phillies each scheduled an exhibition game against a minor-league foe to fill a void in their respective schedules. The Braves were traveling from Brooklyn to Chicago to begin a western swing and decided to briefly stop in Buffalo for a contest against the International League Buffalo Bisons. The selection of the western New York state locale was far from random. Braves manager George Stallings skippered the Buffalo entry, then in the Eastern League, from 1902-06 and again in 1911. Stallings also led the club in 1912 when it joined the International League. He had directed the Bisons to first place finishes in 1904 and 1906. After his time in Boston, Stallings would return to the International League to manage the Rochester Colts/Tribe from 1921-27 and the Montreal Royals in 1928. A strong turnout was further guaranteed by the presence on the Braves roster of former Buffalo players Jim Murray and Hank Gowdy as well as past Eastern and International League adversary, Butch Schmidt.

At the time, the two clubs were headed in distinctly different directions. The Bisons were battling the Providence Grays and Rochester Hustlers for league supremacy while the Braves were in the National League cellar, 14 games behind the first-place New York Giants. The exhibition's outcome was reflective of the clubs' current levels of performance. The Braves were held to three hits by 25-year-old career minor-league hurler John Verbout and were handily defeated, 10-2. Much to the chagrin and disgust of Stallings, the Braves played sloppily and his pitchers issued six walks.

After the game, the Braves boarded their railcar and headed to Chicago. According to Maranville, Stallings addressed his team's poor performance as he strolled to his stateroom. "Big leaguers, Baa! You couldn't even beat a bunch of females." With that, the skipper slammed his stateroom door shut.

The players were in an angry mood after having been so excoriated by their manager. Maranville broke the silence by asking Johnny Evers a question: "Can you play better ball than you have been playing?" The second baseman responded, "Yes, I think I can." Maranville replied in a like manner and the two proceeded to pose the same question to each of their teammates. All responded positively. After this unofficial team gathering, the players adjourned to their berths to catch some sleep before their morning arrival in the Windy City.

The aftereffects of hitting rock bottom that summer's day in Buffalo appeared to have rejuvenated the Tribe. Maranville and company took three of the four games in Chicago and, from that point forward, went on a tear never before or since seen in baseball. Stallings' band of former misfits quickly became the talk of the baseball world as they rose from last to first over the second half of the season and claimed the World Championship in the fall.

Sources

Walter Maranville. *Run, Rabbit, Run* (Society for American Baseball Research, 2012).

Boston Globe, July 8, 1914

Rabbit with a more playful mien.

The National League Pennant Race of 1914

By Frank Vaccaro

In 1914 the Boston Braves held last place for 14 weeks before turning it around and winning the pennant. In more than 140 seasons of professional baseball, this rags-to-riches reversal has never been duplicated by another team.

National League contenders came in waves that season. It opened with Fred Clarke's Pirates winning 15 of 17, mostly on the road. This was followed by a spurt of Cincinnati's—great work by journeyman left-hander Earl Yingling here—that put the team in a games-ahead tie for first place on June 1. New York, the pre-season favorite and the three-time repeat champion, which had just toured the world in the offseason, broke away from Cincinnati two weeks later and claimed sole possession of first place for 85 days. Giants manager John McGraw was living high on the hog. On the morning of August 13, New York had a shiny 6 1/2-game lead. Pittsburgh and Cincinnati were both in the throes of remarkable collapses.

Raids by the upstart Federal League did rein in some players, bringing down the talent level of the established leagues. But Boston's three lost players—Hap Myers, Bill Rariden, and Fred Smith—really hadn't helped manager George Stallings the previous year. Add to that the fact that Boston's roster got a dream boost with the acquisition of Johnny Evers on February 11.[1] Evers, the major leagues' best second baseman, was to repeat as playing manager of the Cubs, but discovered that owner Charles Murphy had replaced him with Hank O'Day. The resulting Evers-Murphy conflagration was so bitter that Murphy, forgetting the Federals, released Evers on the spot. NL president John Tener intervened, ignored the release, and negotiated a swap of second basemen with Boston, sweetened by cash for Murphy. Boston was happy to pay.

Evers' winning attitude and junkyard-dog bark didn't inspire in April. In hindsight, Boston's 12-28 start may have revealed only a lack of confidence. A four-game sweep of Pittsburgh in the middle of June was the first glint that they could compete. The *Boston Globe* wrote that they were "generally looked upon … as having in them … the makings of a ball club."[2] Boston went on to bump Brooklyn into the cellar for a day, June 25, but slid back to 14 wins under .500 when Brooklyn swept the Fourth of July doubleheader. Fans laughed when a wild pitch lodged in the webbing of Braves catcher Hank Gowdy's mitt without his knowing it, and Gowdy spun around several times looking for the ball. The Braves looked like a last-place team, but manager Stallings held a clubhouse meeting and announced with ferocity: "The Braves would hold first place by September 1st!"[3]

It seemed cheap talk. Newspapers did not publish Stallings' prediction at the time, but June did become a turnaround month. A 3-2 loss on June 8 featured a Cincinnati score on a dribbler when no one covered home plate. In another loss, hosting the Cubs a week later, Dick Rudolph walked across the tying run and, with the bases still loaded, Charlie Deal botched an easy double-play ball. St. Louis won one game in the ninth inning when Chief Wilson "unavoidably" bear-hugged Maranville, who was trying to make a double-play pivot; then backup pitcher Dick Crutcher walked in the winning run.

The Braves closed the month 16-13 but opened July with five consecutive losses. In that aforementioned Fourth of July debacle, Boston was swept two games by seventh-place Brooklyn. In the morning game, Boston lost a ninth-inning rally when Bill James and Hank Gowdy both ended up on second base, and in the afternoon, the season bottomed out with a benches-clearing near-brawl after Lefty Tyler beaned Ollie O'Mara in the fifth inning.

"I don't see how the most optimistic can figure a finish in the first division," John McGraw said.[4] A week later, he said, "Stallings is liable to shoot three or four ball players."[5]

Even Boston's midseason wins were ugly. On June 19 the Braves were hosting St. Louis, and a fan leaned over the outfield wall and deflected a Dots Miller fly ball, which the umpires ruled a home run. In that same game, Johnny Evers argued a safe call by taking off his shoe and holding it up for ump Mal Eason to see just where the runner had spiked him, and not the base. Evers, who had once owned a shoe store, was ejected.[6] Pitcher Otto Hess, starting at first base because Butch Schmidt had a lame leg, hit a rare home run on June 20 to beat St. Louis, and untested Paul Strand accounted for a narrow victory over the Giants on June 25 with the game of his career: seven innings of great relief and two RBI hits, one a game-winning bottom-of-the-ninth double off Jeff Tesreau.

What happened next has defied analysis and sabermetric explanation ever since. The Braves went on to have the second-best second half in the history of pennant races. Their .782 winning percentage over their final 87 games is topped only by the 1906 Cubs. Their 60 wins in 75 games are also topped only by those same Cubs, and sustained play with an .800 winning percentage is exceeded by only five teams: the 1885 and 1906 Chicago Nationals, the 1944 Cardinals, and the 1998 Yankees. The Braves' comeback from 15 games out is the record: The 1978 Yankees were 14 games out. Other records that no other pennant winner has matched include overcoming a 13-game deficit for second place, being 16 wins under .500, and being in last place in the entire league as late as July 19.

In one 24-hour period ending July 21, Boston leapfrogged all four second-division teams: Pittsburgh, Brooklyn, Philadelphia, and Cincinnati. Then Boston reeled off 13 wins in 16 games to nab second place from Chicago and St. Louis on August 10. Stallings often relied on only three starting pitchers for long stretches in August, yet Boston finished the month 19-6. This included an eye-opening sweep of the first-place Giants that reduced their lead to 3 1/2 games. The superstitious Stallings shooed birds away from the Braves dugout and meticulously picked up any paper and garbage. He also never moved during the increasingly frequent Braves rallies, and one story had him bent over to tie his shoe for 27 minutes. His collection of good-luck charms grew out of control, and the team traveled with a chest for them: horseshoes, old gloves, old shoes, four-leaf clovers, pieces of tombstones, and sweatshirts. It was extra work for player-coach Oscar Dugey to move the chest from city to city.[7]

For the Giants, left-hander Rube Marquard lost 12 starts in a row, and Christy Mathewson and Al Demaree pitched inconsistently after July. Some suggested that they missed Wilbert Robinson's fatherly coaching. Robinson, at that time Brooklyn's manager, had been unceremoniously run off the Giants by McGraw over hurt feelings right after the 1913 World's Series.[8]

The highlight of the eye-opening sweep over New York was Hank Gowdy's tenth-inning RBI triple off Christy Mathewson on August 15, which broke a 0-0 tie. This devastating loss for New York sent the Giants reeling to a stretch that saw them win once in ten games, a stretch capped by a three-game sweep by the last-place Reds. On August 23 Cincinnati center fielder Herbie Moran capped that sweep by crushing an RBI double with two out in the bottom of the ninth. This put Boston into a tie for first place on an offday. Stallings so considered Moran a lucky charm that he immediately telegraphed the Reds and purchased his contract.

New York and Boston hammered it out through Labor Day weekend, when Boston took two of three hosting New York. The final game of this series, an 8-3 Boston showcase win on a Tuesday, gave the Braves sole possession of first place — and they never let go. New York hung tough for a few days but lost five in a row hosting Chicago and St. Louis. Boston clinched on September 29, when Possum Whitted's double in the ninth beat the Cubs, Tom Hughes throwing a five-hitter in his first NL start. Boston became, and remains (as of 2013), the only team to obtain a lead of ten games or more after entering September in second place.

Stallings, now the "Miracle Man," then made Boston the first team to sweep a World's Series.

Notes

1. *Boston Globe*, February 14, 1914.
2. *Boston Globe*, June 14, 1914.
3. *Boston Globe*, August 16, 1914.
4. *Boston Globe*, June 15, 1914.
5. *Boston Globe*, June 22, 1914.
6. The *Boston Herald* of May 4, 1909 had mentioned Evers' shoe store.
7. *San Francisco Chronicle, Sunday Magazine*, June 17, 1934.
8. *New York Times*, October 31, 1913.

The Press, The Fans, and the 1914 Boston Braves

By Donna L. Halper

It was late September 1914, and Herman Nickerson was perhaps the most popular man in Boston: It seemed thousands of people wanted his attention. There was a good reason for all the letters and telegrams: Nickerson was the secretary of the Boston Braves ballclub, a position he took in November 1912, after covering baseball for the *Boston Journal* for several years. Now that the Braves were going to the World's Series (and the majority of newspapers wrote it like that—World's Series), all requests for tickets came to his desk, resulting in large amounts of mail.[1] Also enjoying a similar surge in popularity was Ralph E. McMillin, who was currently covering baseball for the *Journal*. At a meeting in Philadelphia of the national baseball commission, McMillin was selected to handle press accommodations and decide which reporters would be given access; only those who were deemed "actual workers" would be eligible.[2] He not only had to sort out the real reporters from the pretenders; he was also tasked with setting up the press box so that the writers could effectively cover the games. He made special arrangements for 30 news wires, which gave the baseball writers and their telegraphers the connections they needed for sending the most up-to-date information to their respective newspapers.[3] And although many out-of-town newspapers could not spell his name right ("McMillan" was the most common misspelling), the local Boston baseball writers certainly knew who McMillin was: they selected him to be one of the three official scorers for the World's Series.[4] McMillin, who had come to the *Journal* from the *Boston Herald* in late 1913, already had a reputation for accuracy and fairness, so it was not surprising that his peers wanted to give him this recognition.

But the year 1914 did not start with thoughts of baseball. In fact, even the most loyal fans had other things on their mind. For many years the two most hotly discussed topics in Boston had been sports and politics, and as the old year ended, there was some unexpected, and very big, political news. In mid-December 1913, Mayor John F. "Honey Fitz" Fitzgerald suddenly announced he was withdrawing from the mayoral race because of poor health.[5] His decision not to seek re-election was welcomed by his two main challengers, City Council President Thomas J. Kenny and Congressman James Michael Curley; with the current mayor no longer a threat, and with two lesser-known candidates also dropping out, Curley and Kenny intensified their attacks against each other, making accusations of everything from corruption to incompetence to manipulation of the press. Curley even complained that local reporters were biased against him and wanted his opponent to win.[6] Thus, the New Year began amid an increasingly intense and bitter mayoral campaign; however, the city's political uncertainty did not stop Bostonians from participating in New Year celebrations. About 100,000 people gathered on the Common on New Year's Eve to listen to a band concert, sing songs, and watch fireworks; a number of local performers also entertained the large crowd, and Mayor Fitzgerald, his time in office winding down to only a few weeks, still greeted everyone and joined the festivities. The election took place in mid-January, and to the surprise of many people, Curley was victorious, winning by about 5,700 votes.[7] With a new mayor in place, it did not take long before fans began to think about spring training, and by mid-February, there was a big sports story to discuss: Johnny Evers might be traded from the Chicago Cubs to the Boston Braves.

First there were several days of rumors, as some writers expressed uncertainty about if and when the deal would get done.[8] Then, finally, the page-one headlines appeared in a number of Boston newspapers, announcing that the Boston Braves had in fact made this impressive addition to their roster.[9] The trade was very well-received locally; when Evers stepped off the train on February 18, he was warmly greeted by enthusiastic fans, and, as Ralph McMillin noted, the new player was treated like some kind of conquering hero. There was also a large contingent of reporters eagerly awaiting Evers' arrival:

Braves secretary Herman Nickerson promised them that they would have ample time for interviews and photographs.[10] The general consensus among the Boston press was that this was a winning move. *Boston Globe* reporter Jim O'Leary spoke for many when he praised the addition of Evers, saying he and Rabbit Maranville would make a "great pair" on the field.[11]

And what O'Leary or McMillin wrote really mattered to the fans. In 1914 baseball fans eagerly awaited their favorite daily newspaper; it provided essential information about the teams they followed and the players they liked. Many fans also had a favorite sportswriter, and they trusted him to keep them up-to-date on all aspects of baseball, from the latest trades and trade rumors to what the managers and players were saying. (In the past several decades, there had been a small number of women who reported on baseball, most notably Ina Eloise Young, a reporter from Trinidad, Colorado, who even covered the World's Series in 1908; but in 1914, the baseball writers were all men.)

And while today we have many ways to get the latest baseball news, in 1914 there was still no commercial radio to broadcast the games. There was, however, a growing interest in amateur (ham) radio. Ham-radio fans built their own stations, learned Morse code, and had fun sending and receiving messages; in an era before long-distance telephone service was common, hams especially enjoyed receiving messages from distant locations. One young ham-radio operator, Harold J. "Jimmy" Power, was about to graduate from Tufts College at Medford Hillside (as the area was then called). He would soon make his mark in Boston's broadcasting history, beginning in 1915, when he put an experimental station called 1XE on the air; he and his friends played music, took requests, and eventually gave some sports scores. But in 1914 there was no expectation of hearing anything on a ham station other than Morse code. If you wanted to know about your favorite baseball team and you couldn't get to the games, you could either go to Newspaper Row on Washington Street in downtown Boston and wait for the latest headlines to be posted on a chalkboard outside your favorite newspaper's office; or you could hope a reporter running into his newspaper to file a story would pause to give you some news; or more likely, you waited for the newsboys to appear with the newest edition of the paper, because you counted on the city's baseball writers to tell you everything you wanted to know.

In Boston there were a number of veteran sports reporters, the best-known of whom was the *Globe*'s Timothy H. (Tim) Murnane, considered the dean of the baseball writers. A former major-league player himself, Murnane had been covering Boston sports since the late 1880s, and he was still hard at work; these days, he tended to cover the Red Sox, but at times, especially when a big National League story broke, he would cover the Braves as well. However, it was usually Jim O'Leary who wrote about the Braves these days; he was also the *Globe*'s associate baseball editor, and another prominent sports reporter, Walter S. Barnes, Jr. (who sometimes wrote under the pen name of Sportsman), was the sporting editor. (While the word "sports" was in common use, the men who were in charge of the sports department were still referred to as the sporting editors.) Over at the *Boston Herald*, the best-known sportswriters included John H. (Johnny) Hallahan and Walter E. (Hap) Hapgood. Hallahan did not focus entirely on baseball; he also wrote about a variety of amateur and professional sports. But at certain times in 1914, especially during the World's Series, he was called upon to offer his analysis.[12] As for Hapgood, the Worcester native was now the *Herald*'s sporting editor, and it was he who generally reported on the Braves. The good relationship he developed with the team undoubtedly contributed to his being chosen as the Braves' new business manager in July 1915.[13]

At the *Boston American*, baseball was covered by Albert (A.H.C.) Mitchell and Nicholas J. Flatley; Mitchell, the paper's sporting editor, sometimes covered the Red Sox, and sometimes covered the Braves; he also had a column called "Sidelights on Sports." As the 1914 season progressed, it was Nick Flatley who wrote most of the articles about the Braves, assisted during the World's Series by Frederick (F.J.) McIsaac, later known in Boston as a drama critic. As the Braves began to contend, the *American*, like many of the newspapers, enhanced their coverage, with Flatley writing an additional column, "On the Firing Line with the Braves." It contained interesting tidbits about the players and about life in the big leagues. For example, Flatley noted the growing number of sportswriters suddenly following the team; he addressed a rumor that Hank Gowdy was soon to be married (Gowdy denied it); and he noted that the 11 P.M. curfew for players was being rigorously enforced.[14] The *American* also carried the baseball columns of syndicated writer Damon Runyon. As for the *Boston Post*, the sports page featured a column by former track and field star Arthur Duffey, who commented on the local sports scene and also answered questions from readers. The majority of the baseball coverage came from Paul H. (Herbie) Shannon and Edward C. (Ed) McGrath. Normally, Herbie covered the Red Sox and Ed handled the Braves, but as with several other newspapers, once it became clear that the Braves were going to win the pennant, all of the *Post*'s available sportswriters were called upon to provide extra coverage.

The *Boston Journal* had three experienced sports reporters, Francis Eaton, Peter F. Kelley, and the previously mentioned Ralph McMillin (often bylined as R.E. McMillin). Kelley, a veteran sportswriter who had left journalism in 1909 to be the secretary of the Boston Nationals (before they were called the Braves), returned to covering sports in 1913. But in early 1914 he was the subject of an interesting rumor; several newspapers reported that he would once again leave journalism, this time to become the secretary of the Chicago Cubs.[15] Kelley soon denied it; he said he was happy working at the *Journal* and had no intention of leaving. Whether he had actually planned to leave and the deal fell through, or whether someone had disseminated some inaccurate information was never explained; there was evidence that Kelley had been offered the position with the Cubs, but as for why he turned it down, at least one sporting editor was skeptical that Kelley refused it out of a love for sports reporting. There had to be more to it, but Kelley did not say anything further.[16] As for his loyal readers, all they knew was that Kelley was going to stay at the *Journal*, where he continued to write about the Boston sports scene, including an occasional story about the Braves.

Francis Eaton and Ralph McMillin were versatile baseball writers, and each was able to report on either of the Boston teams; but McMillin had something about him that was unique: he was not only a reporter but also a poet. He would often write humorous verses about the human condition, in a column he called "The Pilaster"; and sometimes he would bring his rhyming skills to his baseball column. A good example was this verse about how everyone expected him to have an answer when the Sox or the Braves were in a losing streak:

> No rest is mine—my neighbors ride me,
> With hoarse guffaw sit down beside me,
> Inquire in tones that split the air for blocks,
> "Hey, what's the matter with the Sox?"
> Or if, perchance, said Sox are climbing,
> And I, at peace, sit down to quiet rhyming,
> Lo and behold, the self-same conclave raves,
> "Hey, what's the matter with the Braves?"
> I shun the crowd, and hate the yell of it,
> For I don't know, and that's the helluvit.[17]

By 1914 more and more Boston newspapers were allowing star sportswriters to have their own byline, but one of the few papers to resist that trend was the *Boston Daily Advertiser*. Even when it covered the Series, and placed the stories about the Braves on page one, no reporter's name was mentioned. The same was true at the *Boston Evening Record*: the Braves were the subject of a number of articles, but all of them lacked a byline.

And then there was the *Boston Evening Transcript*, the newspaper preferred by the city's upper-class elites. Evidently the editors had decided that baseball was lower class (an unfortunate myth—a number of Boston's movers and shakers enjoyed attending a baseball game); even when the Braves won the pennant and went on to the Series, the *Transcript* did not cover it. There was a sports page, but it was filled with news about yachting, college athletics (especially the elite colleges, like Harvard or Yale), and even fox hunting. The *Transcript* did carry the baseball standings, but that was all. The policy of ignoring major-league baseball entirely was one that was also followed, although for different reasons, by some of the suburban and out-of-town newspapers. Newspapers like the *Quincy Daily Ledger* seemed to believe that people who wanted to read about Boston sports teams would buy the Boston papers, so the focus at the *Ledger* was hyper-local. The athletic coverage was entirely about Quincy's high-school and amateur sports teams. When the Boston papers were giving up-to-the-minute reports on the Braves' exciting pennant chase, the *Ledger* reported on the local bowling league. But on the other hand, if you lived in Lowell or Worcester, the newspapers there tried to maintain a balance: They covered local sports, but they also covered the Red Sox and Braves.

In Worcester, for example, there had been extensive coverage of the Red Sox pennant fight in 1912, reported by James H. Power of the *Evening Gazette*. In 1914 Power was still there, but the *Gazette* seemed more focused on covering the city's minor-league franchise, the Worcester Busters, who were about to finish in second place in the New England League. Perhaps attendance was suffering, because the *Gazette* was hyping a free ticket giveaway with "no strings attached."[18] As soon as the Busters' season ended, the *Gazette*'s attention shifted to the Braves, although most of the stories seemed to come from wire-service reporters. The same was true at the *Worcester Evening Post*, where one bylined reporter, Phil Carney, provided the latest gossip about local and national sports in his "Sportalk" column; much of the rest of the coverage came from syndicated columnists and wire-service reports. In September the *Post* made the Braves' pennant chase a major focus of its sports page, with a big box headlined in bold "**IF.**" Inside the box were the current standings and the coming games being played by the Braves and the Giants. The *Post* then calculated the various possible scenarios: If the Braves won a certain number of games that week and the Giants lost a certain number, what affect this would have on the Braves' chance of winning the pennant. At the *Worcester Telegram*, they too got caught up in the Braves' pennant chase, although they were yet another newspaper that rarely allowed their reporters a byline. There was one especially interesting aspect of the *Telegram*'s coverage: The paper carried a series of sports cartoons entitled "Stars by Stallings." If the name sounded familiar to Braves fans, it should have—it was manager George Stallings' 19-year-old son, George Stallings, Jr.; he had become a syndicated sports cartoonist, and his sketches were carried by a number of newspapers.[19]

In Fitchburg and Lowell, the major newspapers (including the *Fitchburg Sentinel* and the *Lowell Sun*) maintained the custom of keeping their reporters anonymous; for example, the *Sun* referred to the person covering baseball as the "*Sun*'s baseball writer." And like the Worcester newspapers, the publications in Fitchburg and Lowell found the Braves' run for the pennant worth covering. During the regular season, Boston sports news was usually placed on an inside page, but when it became obvious that the Braves were serious pennant contenders, the coverage intensified, and by September there were often front-page stories.

But in the midst of the Braves' exciting season, there was also another baseball story preoccupying the fans of that region, and legendary Boston baseball writer Tim Murnane was in the middle of it. As most fans knew, in addition to writing for the *Globe*, Murnane was the longtime president of the New England League, which not only had a minor-league franchise in Worcester, but also fielded teams in cities like Lowell and Lawrence. In 1914 the year began with a franchise in Fitchburg, but in late July the team was suddenly moved to Manchester, New Hampshire, causing Fitchburg's fans much consternation. One reporter took Murnane to task in the pages of the *Lowell Courier-Citizen* and in the *Fitchburg Sentinel*, which reprinted it; he said the league was putting a poor product on the field, nearly all the teams were losing money, and the Fitchburg franchise was never given a chance to succeed.[20] But on the other hand, the *Sentinel* was quick to praise the Boston Braves: Although local fans were frustrated by the loss of their team, thanks to the Braves' "wonderful fight" for the pennant, local fans remained interested in baseball, rather than turning their attention to other sports.[21]

Baseball fans in other cities were also interested in the Braves, and nowhere more so than in Springfield, home to Walter "Rabbit" Maranville. The Springfield papers followed him as much as they followed the Braves, taking great pride in noting that he was a local boy who made good.[22] As with many of the out-of-town newspapers that covered Boston sports, the stories were generally on an inside page, but given the local tie to one of the Braves' star players, the Springfield newspapers were quick to move Braves coverage to page one in September, especially whenever Maranville's play led to a victory.[23] As further proof of his popularity, when he married Elizabeth Shea in November, the Springfield papers treated it like a news story. To his many fans, it probably did seem worthy of attention: Much as modern fans obsess about their favorite players, fans back then also wanted to know as many details as the press could provide. So reporters obliged, taking their readers to the Maranville-Shea wedding and providing information on everything from the ceremony to the food to the guests who attended.[24]

Several major international news events occurred during 1914. Catholics worldwide were saddened to learn that Pope Pius X had died in late August; his successor, Pope Benedict XV, became pope on September 3. And an even bigger story began in late July, when the World War broke out in Europe. (It was not called World War I by the press, because nobody in 1914 could imagine that there would someday be a second such war.) And while the newspapers all gave the conflict front-page coverage (some papers even began printing a "War Extra" edition), the story did not seem to evoke as much emotion as it would three years later, when America finally entered the war. In fact, as the fighting intensified in September 1914, right in the midst of the Braves' pennant drive, several Boston newspaper columnists remarked on how sports fans were so preoccupied with baseball that the war in Europe seemed utterly inconsequential to them. A *Boston Journal* editorial remarked, semi-facetiously, that if the warring countries of Europe could only have settled their differences on the baseball diamond, the world would be a much better place.[25] The war remained an ongoing story throughout the rest of the year, nearly always on page one. But given how important baseball was to the fans of Boston, it should come as no surprise that when the Braves clinched the pennant in late September, that story was as much front-page news as the reports of the war. One typical example was found on the front page of the *Boston Herald* on Wednesday morning, September 30: On the right side of the page, there was a big, bold headline that stated, **"Report German Right Wing Broken and in Full Rout; Allies Pursue in Motors."** And on the left side, in only slightly smaller typeface, the headline read, **"Braves Clinch the National League Flag."**

If you loved sports and you lived anywhere near Boston, the chances are you gathered with other fans on Newspaper Row whenever you could. However, it was not just sports fans who made their way to Lower Washington Street. People from all walks of life often stood in front of the offices of the various newspapers, awaiting breaking news headlines; they soon became familiar with the young men who posted the headlines on the chalkboards. For example, at the *Boston Globe*, that duty fell to Benjamin "Brownie" Gelb. Brownie was part of an interesting game, because the newspapers on Newspaper Row not only competed for scoops for their print edition; they also competed to see who would be first to get the latest news from the telegraphers inside to the readers gathered on the street. And the people who stood there, awaiting the latest headlines, were not always passive about the wait, nor were they shy about expressing their opinion of a story. Sometimes debates, or even arguments, would break out after a certain news item was posted to a newspaper's bulletin board. While sports sometimes brought out people's emotions, the *Boston Journal* noted that when the war in Europe began, it inspired much passionate discussion from people who had relatives overseas. Many were so impatient to get the news that police had to tell them to calm down.[26] And as you might expect, each of the newspapers claimed that its bulletin board was the most reliable, or that it had the biggest crowds, or the most accurate information.

In addition to reporters, telegraphers, and staff members who wrote the bulletins, the newspapers also relied upon hundreds of newsboys, who would spread out all over the area to hawk the latest print edition or hurry out with an "extra" when something major took place. No matter where you lived, you undoubtedly saw newsboys every morning and every evening, standing at the entrance to the subway or train stations, or near the shopping district, or wherever else they saw a crowd of potential readers. Most Boston papers cost between 1 and 2 cents (the *Boston Evening Transcript* cost 3 cents, and the *Boston Sunday Herald* cost 5 cents), and while you could buy the daily papers at your local newsstand, many people got accustomed to buying them from a newsboy. (Contrary to their name, they were not all "boys"—some were grown men.)

Customers often came to regard their newsboy as a friend, since they saw him nearly every day. An example of this affection was seen in early May, when a newsboy named Louis Gold was killed. Gold was a 26-year-old Russian immigrant, a popular young man with a winning personality, whose family had come to the US when he was a boy. At the age of 13, he had lost his left leg to a severe infection, but he never let his disability stop him. His goal was to one day be a newspaper illustrator, and he often made sketches for people to enjoy; but for now, the "one-legged newsboy," as he was often called, sold papers 16 hours a day, usually in front of the Haymarket Square subway station.[27] It was there, late one night, where he was accidentally shot by a woman who was aiming a gun at a man she was having a quarrel with; she missed and the bullet struck Louis Gold, who died the next day. What happened after his funeral was unprecedented: Newspaper Row went silent in his memory; newsboys temporarily stopped hawking their papers, and more than 1,500 members of the Newsboys' Union marched in a procession in his honor. Even motor-cars driving in traffic near Lower Washington Street remained quiet, not honking their horns, but simply waiting for the procession to pass. As the flags on all of the newspaper buildings flew at half-staff, crowds gathered along Newspaper Row to watch the solemn procession. People from all walks of life paused to show their respect to Louis Gold, as the funeral cortege passed through the streets where he had sold his papers and made his sketches.[28] Several weeks later, a benefit concert was held at the Majestic Theatre, attended by members of the public as well as Mayor Curley and other dignitaries. Featuring performances by well-known local musicians, actors, and actresses, it raised more than $1,000 for Louis Gold's family.[29]

When October came along and Braves were in playing for the world's championship, many fans made the pilgrimage to Newspaper Row, where they stood in front of their favorite newspaper and discussed the news as it was posted on the bulletin boards, or discussed what the megaphone man had just announced. Others who lived far away from downtown Boston relied on their local newspaper: The *Lowell Sun* was one of many that provided the story of the game by megaphone, as the *Sun* announced to its readers on page one on October 9: "The Sun will cover the world's series in every particular for the local fans; a megaphone account of the game, play by play, being given from the second floor of the *Sun* building." Braves fans also gathered in other cities, in front of other newspapers; and for those papers that did not provide the megaphoned play-by-play, many opted for a number of extra editions, with the box score on page one and game accounts that were updated every couple of hours. Also, some fans took advantage of another option. A number of theaters had provided the scores by leased wire in 1912, but now, there was an additional piece of technology—an "electric score board."

As it was described in an advertisement in the *Fitchburg Sentinel* (Shea's Theater on Day Street was leasing it for the Series), the electric scoreboard was "[t]he most wonderful invention of the day." Fans could purchase their tickets and then sit in the comfort of the theater and "watch" the game.[30] The device was actually a diamond-shaped board, which made use of flashing lights and other special effects to illustrate the plays as they were taking place. On each side of the scoreboard, the batting order for each team was listed. There were lights to represent the runners on base, other lights to represent various plays—an error was indicated as a flickering light, for example. There were even some sound effects: When there was a hit, the sound of an electric bell was heard, so the fans would know someone had just gotten on base. And in case you were confused by all the names and sounds and flashing lights, a board operator at the theater announced each play verbally after receiving the information from a Western Union telegrapher at the game. The operator of the scoreboard told the *Sentinel* that each play was flashed upon the scoreboard within five to ten seconds after it was made at the ballpark. And while all of this may sound like a strange way to experience a game, in 1914, it was greeted very positively. Sellout crowds gathered at Shea's Theater to cheer on the Braves; they reacted enthusiastically as news of each run was posted to the scoreboard.[31] A similar device was on display in Boston at the Grand Opera House on Washington Street evidently presupposing a male audience, the proprietor of the Grand Opera House announced in his advertisement that after the game had concluded, there would be a performance of burlesque.[32] And for those who had no desire to watch burlesque, there was also an electric scoreboard at the Tremont Temple (which was not a synagogue, but a Baptist Church).

There was one other aspect of World Series coverage that the fans seemed to enjoy. Some newspapers invited big-name major leaguers to write guest columns and offer their perspectives on the games. Unfortunately, as Washington sportswriter Bill Peet had pointed out in 1913 (in a story that was very much underreported in Boston, but widely reprinted in newspapers in Denver, Salt Lake City, Springfield (Illinois), and a number of other cities that did not have a major-league team), the big-name players were really not writing the stories. Rather, they were paid for the use of their name and a local sportswriter did the actual writing. Supposedly this practice was going to stop, but as Peet noted with disappointment, it still seemed to be going on.[33] He offered a list, both in 1912 and again in 1913, of which reporters were doing the ghostwriting, and they included some well-known New York and Boston beat writers: to cite a few examples, John N. "Jack" Wheeler of the *New York Herald,* and later the *Telegram,* was the ghostwriter for Christy Mathewson; the *Boston Globe*'s Tim Murnane wrote on behalf of Tris Speaker; and when Walter Johnson offered his opinion, it was really Ralph McMillin of the *Boston Journal* doing the opining.[34] It is not clear whether fans knew they were reading the work of ghostwriters, but the practice of claiming that a famous player was going to report on the Series continued in 1914, with banner headlines in the *Boston American, Boston Post,* and several other newspapers, announcing which "players" would be writing their thoughts about the games.

In 1914, whether you lived in Boston or as far away as North Adams in western Massachusetts, it seemed everyone had become a Braves fan (the *North Adams Transcript,* hometown newspaper of the McMillin family back when Ralph was growing up, made sure coverage of the Series was on page one; so did many other newspapers big and small, all over the state, including some that rarely covered Boston sports at all). And whether it was a theater with a leased wire, a venue with an electric scoreboard, a newspaper with a bulletin board and a megaphone, or the annual World's Series gathering on Newspaper Row, the fans couldn't get enough information, and the baseball writers and telegraphers did their best to keep up with the demand. There may have been a war going on in Europe, but for the local baseball fans, all that mattered was the Braves, who not only won the pennant but then went on to sweep the Athletics, something few out-of-town reporters ever expected they would do. In fact, many nationally known baseball writers said the Braves didn't stand a chance—among them was Henry P. Edwards of the *Cleveland Plain Dealer,* whose World's Series predictions were generally quite accurate, but not this time;[35] veteran syndicated columnist Hugh S. Fullerton also missed the mark, predicting a long series, and saying the Athletics would win in the end because they knew the Braves' weaknesses.[36]

To be honest, not many local reporters had predicted that the Braves would be so dominant over the Athletics. But there was at least one person who predicted the Braves would not only win but make it a sweep: Wild

Bill Donovan, the former Detroit pitcher who was now manager of the Providence Grays. He had been hired to write his World's Series commentary for the *New York Tribune*, and he said the Braves were a cinch to win the World's Series. But as it turned out, he never said it; rather, his ghostwriter (Bill MacBeth of the *Tribune*) was responsible for the quote.[37] It would not be until 1934, when Jack Wheeler wrote a syndicated column about his own career as a ghostwriter that there was an explanation of how the quote came to be: Donovan's ghostwriter could not find him (not even in the taverns where he was alleged to hang out). Desperately needing a quote before his newspaper went to press, the reporter made one up. Donovan was supposedly furious when he read it, as he felt it put him in an awkward position. But once the Braves won the first two games, Wheeler said, Donovan decided to embrace the quote and accept the plaudits of Braves fans who said he was a genius.[38] But this story is problematic: Wheeler himself admitted in his 1934 recollections that he *thought* it was Donovan; however, the only Donovan quotes I was able to find about the World's Series said quite the opposite. In the *Springfield Daily Republican* on October 8, 1914, Donovan was quoted as saying the Athletics (not the Braves) were the better team, because of their hitting. "The Athletics are a sure-fire bet in the series," Donovan said.[39] Or perhaps that was just the work of a different ghostwriter. We may never know. But what we do know is that even the negative quotes did not dissuade their loyal fans from rooting for the Braves; in fact, they ignored the writers who predicted doom for the team. Eventually the national press had to admit the obvious fact: The Braves won the Series because they "play[ed] a better game, a nervier game, a harder game, displaying more sticktoitiveness, more pluck, [and] more ability to play the game for all they were worth...."[40] And in Boston, as crowds rejoiced on Newspaper Row, once again, it was a great time to be a fan.

Notes

1. "Begins Preparing for World's Series," *Springfield* (Massachusetts) *Union*, September 25, 1914, 20.
2. "Press Box Arrangements," *Springfield* (Massachusetts) *Republican*, October 1, 1914, 10.
3. "Champion Endurance Contest in Series Sale," *Springfield* (Massachusetts) *Daily News*, October 7, 1914, 1.
4. "Official Scorers for World's Series Named," *Muskegon* (Michigan) *Chronicle*, October 2, 1914, 12.
5. "Mayor Is Out of the Race," *Boston Globe*, December 18, 1913, 1.
6. "Stay Late to Hear Curley," *Boston Globe*, January 4, 1914, 1, 14.
7. "A Review of 1914," *Boston Globe*, December 27, 1914, 43.
8. T.H. Murnane, "Gaffney Tries Hard," *Boston Globe*, February 12, 1914, 7.
9. For example, T.H. Murnane, "Evers Now Full-Fledged Brave," *Boston Globe*, February 14, 1914, 1; and Francis Eaton, "Baseball Shaken by Evers Affair," *Boston Journal*, February 14, 1914, 1.
10. R.E. McMillin, "Welcome To Our City, Johnny!," *Boston Journal*, February 19, 1914, 1.
11. Jim O'Leary, "Johnny Evers Joins Braves," *Boston Globe*, March 5, 1914, 7.
12. John J. Hallahan, "How the Braves Won the World's Baseball Championship of 1914," *Boston Herald*, October 14, 1914, 10.
13. "Braves to Have Business Manager," *Boston Herald*, July 30, 1915, 4.
14. Nick Flatley, "On the Firing Line With the Braves," *Boston American*, October 7, 1914, 8.
15. "Kelley Worked Under Six Leaders," *Boston Herald*, February 1, 1914, 16.
16. Nolly J. Sams, "Sporting Gossip," *Charleston* (South Carolina) *Sunday News*, February 15, 1914, 15.
17. R.E. McMillin, "Braves Finish in Bargain Session," *Boston Journal*, July 6, 1914, 10.
18. "Free Tickets for Gazette Baseball Fans," *Worcester Evening Gazette*, September 7, 1914, 9.
19. "Pictures of the Braves," *Boston Traveler*, March 21, 1916, 5.
20. "League Season Was Very Poor," *Fitchburg* (Massachusetts) *Sentinel*, September 15, 1914, 6.
21. "General Sporting News," *Fitchburg Sentinel*, September 15, 1914, 6.
22. "Springfield Boy Shows 'Em All How," *Springfield Union*, April 11, 1913, 20; also "Rabbit Is Club Backbone," *Springfield Daily News*, October 5, 1914, 8.
23. "He Starts Scoring and Also Ends It," *Springfield Union*, September 12, 1914, 1.
24. "Maranville Is Now Benedict," *Springfield Daily News*, November 11, 1914, 2.

25 "War and Baseball," *Boston Journal*, September 8, 1914, 6.

26 "Wordy Wars in Newspaper Row," *Boston Journal*, August 28, 1914, 3.

27 "Louis Gold, Newsboy," *Boston Journal*, May 8, 1914, 6.

28 "Newsboys in Procession," *Boston Globe*, May 8, 1914, 10.

29 "Theatre Stars Aid Louis Gold Family Benefit," *Boston Herald*, May 18, 1914, 7.

30 "Shea's Theater," *Fitchburg Sentinel*, October 10, 1914, 7.

31 "Electric Score Board at Shea's Theater," *Fitchburg Sentinel*, October 8, 1914, 5.

32 "Grand Opera House," advertisement, *Boston Herald*, October 11, 1914, 37.

33 "Play Ball Only, Orders Johnson," *Oklahoma City Daily Oklahoman*, March 7, 1913, 8

34 William Peet, "Do You Know Who Writes the Dope You Read?" *Denver Post*, February 28, 1913, 13.

35 "H.P. Edwards Ends 26 Years on Staff," *Cleveland Plain Dealer*, January 12, 1928, 1, 26.

36 Hugh S. Fullerton, "Hugh Fullerton Refuses to Admit Best Team Won First World's Series Game," *Trenton* (New Jersey) *Evening Times*, October 10, 1914, 13.

37 John Wheeler, "Second Guesser," *Spokane* (Washington) *Spokesman-Review*, February 21, 1952, 4.

38 John Wheeler, "Honest Ghost in Baseball Closet," *Cleveland Plain Dealer*, October 7, 1934, 4.

39 "Baseball Briefs," *Springfield Daily Republican*, October 8, 1914, 10.

40 "Braves Win Title, Beat Athletics 3-1; 4th Straight Game," *Boston Daily Advertiser*, October 14, 1914, 1.

Return of the Miracle Braves

by Bob Brady

SPECIAL EVENTS WERE scheduled throughout the Senior Circuit in 1951 to celebrate the league's "Diamond Jubilee" 75th anniversary. In conjunction with the milestone, the National League produced an official history in the form of a hardcover book, *75th Anniversary of the National League*, that contained league and individual team narratives along with vintage photographs.

National League ballclubs celebrated this historic event during the season with a variety of ceremonies at their ballparks. The Boston Braves chose to bring back surviving members of the 1914 Miracle Braves championship team as part of the Tribe's jubilee commemoration. Three years earlier, several of the former South End Grounds stars had returned to the Hub as guests of the Tribe to attend the Braves-Indians World Series. This time, a three-day affair was put together by Braves owner Lou Perini, culminating in pregame festivities at Braves Field before the Saturday, June 2, match-up with the visiting Cubs. Fittingly, Boston and Chicago were the only National League clubs to have operated continuously since the circuit's formation in 1876.

Time had taken its toll in the 37 years that had elapsed since the Braves' last (and final) world championship. Eleven of the 34 ballplayers on the Tribe roster over the course of the '14 campaign were deceased. The first to depart the scene was pitcher Otto Hess in 1926, followed in 1929 by manager George Stallings. The last survivor of this historic ball club would be Jack Martin, a utility infielder. Martin played in 33 games before being swapped to the Phillies in midseason for outfielder Josh Devore. Martin closed this chapter of the Miracle Braves' history upon his death on July 4, 1980. He was 93. On a bit of an ironic note, pitcher George "Lefty" Tyler died of a heart attack on September 29, 1953, 39 years from the date the Braves clinched the Miracle National League pennant.

The honorees who had arrived in the Hub on May 31 were ushered to the studios of WNAC-TV to take part in the Braves' weekly television program, *Baseball in Your Living Room*. Interviews on local radio also were scheduled. Perini treated the '14 veterans to a well-attended luncheon the following day at the Hotel Somerset. Waiters served the meal attired in replica 1876 uniforms. The Miracle Braves entourage was formally introduced to area representatives of the press at the gathering. Also in the ballroom were National League president Ford Frick and old-time ballplayers Fred Tenney, Tom Corcoran, and Alex Ferguson. Tenney and Corcoran were the oldest surviving former National Leaguers. Tenney's time with the Braves went all the way back to 1894 and he twice skippered the club (1905-07 and 1911). Corcoran's big-league career ranged from 1890 to 1907, primarily as a shortstop with five ballclubs. Ferguson broke into the majors in 1918 and spent time pitching for the Red Sox during his ten-year career.

President Perini presented each of the honored Miracle team guests with commemorative tie clasps and personal copies of the National League anniversary book and the *Baseball Encyclopedia*. Wives who accompanied the honorees received orchid corsages. Perini continued

Ticket stub from the 1951 reunion on the Braves' 75th anniversary.

his largess before the Braves-Cubs game the following day when he bestowed an engraved gold watch upon Hugh Duffy, who had batted a lofty .440 for the 1894 Boston Nationals. (For many years Duffy's average was listed as .438, but it gained two points when SABR researchers found an extra hit that Duffy had not been credited with.)

Prior to the start of Friday night's game, the celebrants of the next day's events met in the hotel lobby and reminisced with reporters. When queried as to the ingredient that led them on their triumphant march to the pennant, they cited team spirit. Manager George Stallings' deft leadership was duly noted. Pitcher Bill James stated, "We belonged in eighth place when we were there and without Stallings we belonged there at the end of the season." Catcher Hank Gowdy seconded James' opinion: "George made us a great team."

Even in 1951, the old-timers grumbled about baseball's changing salary structure. Staff ace and 1914 26-game winner James remarked that his largest contract was for $2,600 or about what he figured to be a week's paycheck for Red Sox star Ted Williams. The familiar and often heard refrain of being born too early echoed among the group. Gowdy expressed his dismay at the emerging practice of signing untested talent to huge bonuses. Cleveland's recent inking of pitching prospect Billy Joe Davidson for a reported $150,000 was mentioned as a case in point. The old backstop's judgment in this regard proved to be on target. The Indians' investment in the southpaw failed to yield a return as Davidson never performed on a big-league mound.

Gowdy, however, was sympathetic to the plight of modern-day pitchers. "Don't be rough on the pitchers today," the old catcher remarked. "It is much tougher pitching in the present game with the present hyped-up ball than it was 30 years ago." Gowdy reflected on conditions when he was still active: "Remember in the old days, they didn't throw balls out of a game like they do now. You could really do things with a curve using a roughed-up ball. Today, if there is just a little spot on a ball, it is thrown out. That's rough on a pitcher." Former coach Fred Mitchell agreed with the aged backstop:

"Let those batters today hit at the old ball we did in 1914 and there wouldn't be as many men in the .300 class."

First sacker Butch Schmidt entertained the group with an anecdote of his own. He proclaimed that the Braves could have acquired Babe Ruth in 1914 from the International League Baltimore Orioles. Schmidt had played in Baltimore from 1908-12 and was an acquaintance of club majority owner Jack Dunn. "I scouted Ruth myself when he was pitching for St. Mary's Industrial School [and] recommended him to (team owner Jim) Gaffney when the Baltimore Orioles were breaking up," he revealed. Dunn was under significant financial stress brought about by competition with the upstart Federal League Baltimore Terrapins who forced him to relocate his club to Richmond in 1915. Schmidt claimed that for $10,000, Gaffney could have picked up not only the Babe but also pitcher Ernie Shore and catcher Ben Egan. However, Gaffney said, "$10,000 was too much to pay for ballplayers." Instead, the neighboring Red Sox jumped at the deal. Schmidt's tale indicates that the "Curse of the Bambino" might have been cast upon not one, but both of Boston's baseball franchises!

Gaffney's reluctance to invest in talent was the subject of another tale offered by Fred Mitchell. Manager Stallings had sent him to Terre Haute, Indiana, in 1915 to scout southpaw Art Nehf, then pitching for his hometown Highlanders of the Central League. Nehf led the league in strikeouts (218) and ERA (1.38) and recorded 19 victories. Recognizing the potential of the 22-year-old hurler, Mitchell agreed to the purchase of his contract for $3,500, with $1,500 due immediately and the balance a year later. When Stallings informed Gaffney of the acquisition, he drew a strong rebuke from the owner. "I've 25 ballplayers now and some of them are for sale. I'm not buying any more." Stallings and Mitchell were forced to reach into their own pockets for the down payment. On August 21, 1915, Nehf proved his value in his first big-league start, witnessed by Gaffney and an audience of nearly 30,000 at Braves Field. He shut out the Pirates, 2-0, and struck out six to ensure a Braves doubleheader sweep. The rookie out-dueled the Bucs' 21-game-winning ace, Al Mamaux,

Flyer promoting the anniversary.

in the process. In addition, Nehf drove in both runs. During the game, Mitchell intentionally threw his glove out in front of Gaffney's seat so that the owner would be forced to see him at the end of the contest. While retrieving his glove, Mitchell heard Gaffney yell, "Hey, Mitchell, when is the second payment due?" The first-base coach was relieved to know that he and Stallings were no longer on the hook for the purchase.

Red Smith, an August pickup from Brooklyn who took over hot-corner chores for the '14 Tribe, recalled that he had earlier helped deliver the Braves to the National League basement with a timely extra-inning hit. While with the Robins, Smith tripled in the 11th inning of the initial game of a July 4 doubleheader in Boston, securing the first of two victories for the visitors. Smith was sold to the Braves just about the time that the club shifted its home games from the South End Grounds to Fenway Park. "I shall never forget how glad I was to have our team move over to Fenway Park and get a crack at that neighborly left field wall...." His batting average reflected favorably on the change in scenery (.314 for the Braves versus .245 for Brooklyn) but his good fortune ran out when he broke his leg sliding into second base shortly before the start of postseason play.

A number of members of the '14 club elected to travel to Braves Field the day before the scheduled celebration to take in a game. On the opening night of a two-week home stand against "western" clubs, they witnessed Johnny Sain gain his third victory of the season in a 3-2 defeat of Chicago. Pinch-hitter Sam Jethroe drove in the winning run in the seventh after walks to Sibby Sisti and Buddy Kerr and a wild throw to third by 43-year-old Cubbies knuckleballing relief pitcher Dutch Leonard. Among those in the stands were Rabbit Maranville, Hank Gowdy, Bill James, and George "Lefty" Tyler. With the exception of Maranville and Gowdy, who preferred seating close to the field, the heroes of '14 viewed the contest from the roof-top Sky View seats that had been constructed prior to the 1948 season. The old-timers weren't the only guests of the Braves that night. The Braves also entertained 15 girl gymnasts from Stockholm, Sweden, who were on tour in the United States and were provided with their first look at a baseball game courtesy of the Tribe.

Festivities kicked off on June 2 with a parade down Commonwealth Avenue to Braves Field. The old-timers assembled at the Hotel Somerset at noon for the trek to the Wigwam. Lou Perini and Ford Frick headed up the delegation that was transported to the field in antique automobiles provided by Brookline's Larz Anderson Museum. The procession commenced at 12:45 under the escort of the police and a detachment of United States Marines. Bowdoin College's a cappella choral group, the Meddiebempsters, named after the Maine town of Meddybemps (derived from a Native American term for "plenty of fish") also rode in the parade. The octet donned 1876 baseball uniforms for the occasion and later performed a Gay Nineties medley at the Wigwam.

When the parade reached the Commonwealth Armory, it was joined by the almost 100-piece Harvard University band. As Harvard and Bowdoin students were in the midst of their final exams, special steps had to be taken to assure their participation. The bandsmen wore their uniforms to their exams and then were given box lunches and hustled onto a bus that was driven to the Allston destination with the way cleared by members of the Cambridge police. A couple of the Meddiebempsters took morning tests at their Brunswick, Maine, campus and then hopped on an airplane to make the celebration.

Inside the armory, nearly 3,000 Little Leaguers from Massachusetts, Maine, New Hampshire, and Rhode Island had assembled in uniform waiting to join the procession. Units from the Army and Navy added to the throng that entered the ballpark for the 1:15 kickoff of festivities. The Mutual Broadcasting Company was on hand to air the day's special events and the ballgame to over 352 of its affiliates and to the armed forces overseas.

The Diamond Jubilee Celebration preceded the day's Braves-Cubs contest at the Wigwam. Fans cheered as the parade of old-time automobiles circled the playing field, passing before the visiting and home dugouts. In each of the ancient jitneys was a member of the Marine Corps, holding a sign that identified the honored guests in the respective buggy. Paraded before the crowd in addition to Gowdy, Mitchell, James, Smith, Schmidt, and Tyler were outfielder Herb Moran, catcher Bert Whaling, outfielder Les Mann, third baseman Charlie Deal, pitchers Dick Crutcher and Paul Strand, as well as batboy Willie Conners and George Stallings, Jr., substituting for his father. Instead of donning replicas of their '14 togs, the guests appeared in current Tribe tomahawk-style uniforms. Posed group portraits of Schmidt, Whaling, Stallings Jr., Mann, Smith, Crutcher, Tyler, Moran, Deal, Strand, Mitchell, Gowdy, and James on the front step of the home dugout were snapped by press photographers and sent to papers across the country for publication in the next day's editions.

Each of the old-timers was called out onto the field by Ford Frick to assume his former position. Mitchell and Stallings Jr. reported to the first and third base coaching boxes, respectively. Gowdy and Whaling, catcher's mitts in hand, stood behind home plate. James, Tyler, and Crutcher took to the mound while Schmidt and Smith ambled to first and third base. Deal subbed for the late Johnny Evers at second base while Messrs. Mann, Strand, and Moran walked to their outfield positions. The placement of pitcher Strand in the outfield was not entirely out of place as an accommodation to the dearth of reunion representatives at that position. In 1915, he appeared in five games in the outfield for the Braves in addition to performing his normal mound duties. Strand later converted full time to the outfield and re-emerged there in 1924 with the Philadelphia Athletics. As would be expected, batboy Willie Connors was situated on the sidelines.

Fan favorite Rabbit Maranville drew the day's greatest ovation as he was introduced and jogged to his position at shortstop. The diminutive infielder had missed the parade as he had had to make a quick trip to New York to fulfill a commitment to a sandlot baseball group. Flying back to Boston on Lou Perini's private aircraft, he rushed from the airport in time to dress and just make it to the Wigwam for the introductions. Maranville "warmed up" by taking a few groundballs, flipping one behind his back to Deal at second. When announcer Les Smith informed that crowd that the irrepressible Rabbit would perform his legendary "vest pocket" catch, a roar came from the stands. Hank Gowdy threw a ball high in the air toward the peppery shortstop and Maranville gingerly backed up toward left field, cupped his hands and caught the ball at belt level to the delight of all. Rabbit then twisted his cap sideways on his head as he had done throughout his playing days. He expressed his regret that time constraints prevented further "infield practice."

The Harvard Band and the Meddiebempsters provided their entertaining musical interludes during the event. After performing, they took seats in the front section of the right-field pavilion. Immediately prior to the start of the game, a large reproduction of the National League's 75th-anniversary logo was unveiled on the Braves Field mound. On a somber note, NL President Frick asked the crowd to remember the deceased members of the 1914 squad, "Captain Johnny Evers, [Joe] Connolly and others…" "And let's not forget that other great ballplayer who died just ten years ago today—Lou Gehrig," Frick concluded.

Watching the day's events and the game from the stands was 91-year-old C.A. Brown, who claimed to have been present at Boston's first National League game on May 30, 1876. Unfortunately, he and the other 15,127 in attendance witnessed the Braves go down to defeat, 7-5, despite some ninth-inning last-minute attempted heroics. Tribe starter Warren Spahn had one of his infrequent poor outings, lasting less than two innings, yielding four runs on six hits and two walks. Earl Torgeson provided some excitement, blasting an eighth-inning two-run homer, five rows into the Jury Box. Cubs "senior citizen" reliever Dutch Leonard squelched the bottom of the ninth inning rally, retiring the side after coming in with no outs and two Braves on base.

Seated behind home plate during the game, the "Miracle Men" couldn't help but contrast "Stallings' baseball" against the current version. At one point when the Braves filled the bases and the next batter swung at the first pitch and hit into a double play, Bill James reflected, "Under Stallings, the batter wouldn't swing at the first pitch. Maybe the pitcher would have walked the next man up and forced in a run." James remarked that Stallings always said, "Let the pitcher lick himself, if possible." Les Mann and Red Smith both observed, "We won the pennant in 1914 by bunting. It's a different game today." The old-timers got caught up in the excitement of the last-inning rally and later expressed their appreciation to the present-day Braves for trying pull out a win for them.

Despite all of the hoopla surrounding the celebration, the turnstile figures were disheartening, especially when one considers that the grand total was a bit "padded." Passes were handed out to the 2,985 Little Leaguers, 157 servicemen, and 2,001 Knothole Gang members, leaving just 9,984 paying guests. The lukewarm reception drew an editorial rebuke in the June 13 issue of *The Sporting News*. Baseball's "Bible" expressed disappointment toward the fans' "So what?" reaction to the jubilee commemoration and honoring of the game's pioneers. As the *TSN* editorialist opined, "The game owes a great deal to these old-time heroes, whose achievements helped the majors over a period of struggle and made possible the sport's present solid place in American life."

Miracle Teams:
A Comparison of the 1914 Miracle Braves and 1969 Miracle Mets

By Tom Nahigian

ONE OF MY favorite things about baseball is watching a really bad team get its act together and in short order achieve the ultimate: a World Series championship. Two of the most memorable teams to do this are the 1914 Miracle Braves and the 1969 Miracle Mets. Both teams showcased baseball in its purest form, with great pitching, airtight defense, and timely hitting.

Before The Miracle

Before their respective world championship seasons, both the 1914 Braves and the 1969 Mets were truly terrible. The Boston Braves of 1909-1912 were the worst team in baseball, with records of 45-108 in 1909, 53-100 in 1910, 44-107 in 1911, and 52-101 in 1912. They finished last each season and in all four seasons were more than 50 games out of first place.

The early New York Mets were a joke. They earned the title of "Amazing"—derisive in this case—because of their amazingly poor play. In their maiden season, 1962, they won 40 and lost 120. They finished last for their first four seasons, jumped up to ninth place in 1966, then dropped back down to last place in 1967, going 61-101.

The Managers

Neither the Braves nor the Mets would have been miracle teams without the strong leadership of their managers, George Stallings and Gil Hodges. Both were highly skillful managers. According to the *Bill James Guide to Baseball Managers*, Stallings ranked 26th all-time as a manager with a rating of plus 30 wins over expected wins. Hodges ranked 27th, with a rating of plus 28.

In the season just before their miracle years, each team hired their new manager and had a stabilizing season, moving from bad to almost respectable. The Braves hired Stallings for the 1913 season and jumped to 69-82, a losing mark but their most victories since 1902 (when they played as the Beaneaters). Stallings had previously managed the Phillies, Tigers, and Yankees. He improved the Yankees by 24 1/2 games in his first season and improved them another 11 games his second season. Stallings was a bright man, graduating from the Virginia Military Institute in 1886 at age 17. He was an intense manager and, according to writer Tom Meany "could fly into a schizophrenic rage at the drop of a pop fly." Tom Daly, a former coach with the Red Sox, once said, "Stallings knew baseball as Einstein knows algebra. It was a privilege just to sit and listen to him talk baseball." Stallings had a cup of coffee as a player, getting into seven games and was primarily a catcher.

Hodges had a long and successful career, playing 18 years for the Brooklyn and Los Angeles Dodgers and the Mets, primarily at first base and doing some catching in his first two seasons. Hodges learned firsthand the superior instruction taught by the Dodgers farm system, masterminded by Branch Rickey. Hodges was also a college man, having attended St. Joseph's College in Rensselaer, Indiana. He was tough, too, but in a quieter way, and his players loved him. He led by action more than by words. He managed the Washington Senators for five years and although they never won a pennant, they showed steady improvement each year, moving up to 76 wins in his final season with them in 1967 (seventh place, at 76-85). The Mets hired Hodges for the 1968 season and improved to 73-89, their best record up to that point. Hodges started rebuilding the Mets immediately, recommending Tommie Agee and Al Weis, whom he had seen play in the American League. Both played key roles in the championship season.

Team Strengths

Both teams had many things in common: Each was youthful, had great pitching, won the pennant by a comfortable margin, defeated a far superior team in the World Series, and enjoyed short-lived success.

The Braves were led by their three pitching aces: Dick Rudolph (27 years old) 27-10, 2.36 ERA; Bill James (22) 26-7, 1.90; and Lefty Tyler (24) 16-14, 2.09. The Mets were also led by their aces: Tom Seaver (24) 25-7, 2.21 ERA; and Jerry Koosman (26) 17-9, 2.28.

Both teams featured strong defense up the middle. The Braves featured stalwart catcher Hank Gowdy, an outstanding double-play combination of Johnny Evers and Rabbit Maranville, and Possum Whitted and others in center field. The Mets had defensive wizard Jerry Grote behind the plate, Bud Harrelson at shortstop, a platoon combination of Ken Boswell (mediocre glove, good bat) and Al Weis (solid glove, weak bat) at second base and Tommie Agee in center field.

Both teams platooned heavily. Stallings in 1914 was the first to platoon at more than one position over a long period of time and the first to do so as a positive strategy. He juggled 11 outfielders and only first baseman Butch Schmidt, second baseman Evers, and shortstop Maranville had more than 400 at-bats. The Mets platooned at first, second, third, and right field. Tommie Agee and Cleon Jones were the only Mets with more than 500 plate appearances.

Key Moments and Hot Finishes

Both teams played reasonably well through the midpoint of the season, reached a galvanizing moment, then got red-hot and cruised right through to a world championship. The 1914 Braves were in last place on July 4 with a record of 26-40, 15 games behind the front-running New York Giants. "We not only were in last place on the Fourth of July," Johnny Evers used to stay, "but just after the holiday we lost an exhibition game to a soap-company team. That's how bad we were." The Braves started their hot streak soon after. They reached fourth place on July 21 and second place on August 12, and passed the Giants for keeps on September 8. They closed with a drive of 34 wins in 44 games and ended up winning the pennant by 10 1/2 games over the Giants, going 94-59, a 25-game improvement over the previous season.

The Mets stayed on the heels of the first-place Chicago Cubs for much of the season. In a showdown with the Cubs in mid-July, the Mets proved they belonged, taking two out of three in New York and then in Chicago. On July 30 the Mets were in the midst of getting thumped by their expansion cousin Houston Astros, dropping a double header, 16-3 and 11-5. During the second game, Hodges walked out slowly to the pitcher's mound, then continued out to left field to have a chat with Cleon Jones. The manager walked back to the dugout with a contrite Jones walking about ten steps behind. Hodges felt Jones had not hustled on a ball.

The Mets trailed the Cubs by 9 1/2 games on August 14, then got red-hot, winning 38 out of 49 games. They ended with a record of 100-62, eight games ahead of the Cubs, and a 27-game improvement from the previous season. It was the first time the Mets had achieved a winning record. The Mets continued their winning ways in the National League playoffs, sweeping the Atlanta Braves in three games, showing offensive muscle (9-5, 11-6, and 7-4 were the scores) rather than great pitching.

The 1914 Braves scored 657 runs (second in an eight-team league) and allowed 548 runs (third in the league). The Braves led the league in complete games with 104 and finished second in shutouts with 19. The Mets scored 632 runs (ninth in a 12-team league) and allowed 541 runs (second fewest in the National League). The Mets finished fifth in complete games and led the league in shutouts with 28. The Mets allowed the fewest earned runs in the league.

The World Series

In the 1914 World Series the Boston Braves were matched up with Connie Mack's Philadelphia Athletics.

The A's were a dynasty at that time, having won the World Series in 1910, 1911, and 1913. The series opened in Philadelphia with Rudolph beating Chief Bender, 7-1. In Game Two James outdueled Eddie Plank, 1-0. The Braves borrowed Fenway Park from the Red Sox to host Game Three, and edged the A's 5-4 in a 12-inning thriller. The game was tied entering the bottom of the 12th when catcher Gowdy led off with a double. A pinch-runner came in. After an intentional pass, the winning run scored when the Athletics' pitcher, Bullet Joe Bush, threw away a bunt attempt trying to get the lead runner at third. This was almost exactly the same way the Mets won Game Four of their showdown with the Orioles. The Braves continued their sweep of the Series, taking Game Four, 3-1, with Dick Rudolph defeating Bob Shawkey.

The Braves outscored the A's 16-6 and held them to a .172 batting average. The Braves pitchers fashioned a 1.15 ERA in the 1914 World Series.

In the 1969 World Series, the Mets were matched up with an outstanding Baltimore Orioles team, winner of 109 games. The Orioles were beginning their dynasty, the following season winning 108 games, the pennant, and the World Series, and winning the American League pennant for a third consecutive season in 1971 with a team boasting four 20-game winners.

It looked promising for the Orioles in Game One when Don Buford homered off Tom Seaver in the first at-bat of the first inning. Mike Cuellar shut down the Mets and beat Seaver in Game One, 4-1. The Mets evened the series, taking Game Two by a 2-1 score, Jerry Koosman outdueling Dave McNally and getting last-out relief help from Ron Taylor, who retired Brooks Robinson with the winning runs on base. The teams traveled to New York for the next three games. Getting sterling pitching from Gary Gentry (6⅔ innings) and Nolan Ryan, home runs by Tommie Agee and Ed Kranepool, and two circus catches by Agee, the Mets took Game Three, 5-0. In Game Four, Tom Seaver took a 1-0 lead into the top of the ninth. The Orioles tied the score, then the Mets won the game in the bottom of the tenth. In an ending similar to Game Three of the Braves-A's matchup, catcher Grote led off with a double, was replaced with a pinch-runner, an intentional walk followed, and the winning run scored when the pitcher threw away a sacrifice bunt attempt (this time to first base).

The Mets took Game Five and the Series in come-from-behind fashion. Trailing 3-0 in the bottom of the sixth, they got a break when Hodges convinced home-plate umpire Shag Crawford that Jones had been hit by a pitch, producing a ball smudged with shoe polish as evidence. Jones was given first base (reminiscent of Nippy Jones for the Milwaukee Braves in the 1957 World Series). Donn Clendenon immediately followed with a two-run homer. Weak-hitting Al Weis tied the game in the seventh with an unlikely homer. The Mets plated two more in the eighth on a couple of doubles and an Oriole error. The Mets won 5-3, capping off their miracle season with a world championship as the Braves had done 55 years earlier. The Mets defeated the Orioles in a sweep of sorts, dropping the opening game but then winning the next four.

The Mets outscored the Orioles 15-9. Mets pitchers held the Orioles to a .146 batting average and posted an ERA of 1.80.

After The Miracle

Neither team could repeat their miracle season. The Braves finished second in 1915 and then slowly drifted out of pennant contention. They would not return to the World Series until 1948. The Mets stayed in contention in 1970, finishing third, six games out, then drifted toward .500 and won an unlikely pennant in 1973 with a mediocre record of 82-79.

Sources

Research materials that were helpful in preparing this article were four books by Bill James: *The Baseball Book* 1990 and 1992 (which inspired this report), the *Historical Baseball Abstract,* and the *Bill James Guide to Baseball Managers*; two books by Neft and Cohen: *The Sports Encyclopedia: Baseball* and *The World Series*; the 1970 *Sporting News Baseball Guide*; *The Year the Mets Lost Last Place* by Paul Zimmerman and Dick Schaap; *The Milwaukee Braves* by Harold Kaese and R.G. Lynch; Fred Lieb's *The Story of the World Series*, *Total Baseball* (fourth edition) edited by John Thorn and Peter Palmer; and *The Ultimate Baseball Book* by Daniel Okrent and Harris Lewine.

Bob Brady adds: The 1969 Mets had a remote link to the Boston Braves. Third baseman Ed Charles was signed by them in 1952. The 19-year-old started out his pro career with Boston's Provincial League Quebec Braves affiliate.

An Unexpected Farewell:
The South End Grounds, August 1914

by Bob Ruzzo

The End of the Beginning

When the Boston Braves left the field at the South End Grounds on Tuesday, August 11, 1914, the glorious opening chapter of professional baseball in Boston passed into history without notice. After a frustrating 13-inning, 0-0 tie with the Cincinnati Reds, all that mattered that day was that the Braves had fallen a half-game behind the second-place St. Louis Cardinals in their quest to track down John McGraw's league-leading New York Giants.[1]

There would always be another game tomorrow, although the forecast for the next day's contest seemed somewhat dubious for Boston cranks contemplating a trip via the Tremont Street streetcar to the city's South End. Fans of the franchise had been making a similar journey for decades, first by horse-drawn car, then by electric streetcar.[2]

For the South End Grounds, the third iteration of a ballpark on the same city block, however, tomorrow never came. Major-league baseball was never again played on the 4 1/2 acre site.[3]

With Wednesday's game postponed because of rain, the Braves left town the next day on an extended road trip, never to return to the location that served as their home for longer than any other facility in the more than 140-year history of the franchise. Upon their return to Boston in September, Fenway Park, less than two years old and still sparkling, beckoned. After the Braves started the following season in Fenway with the permission of their American League cousins, in August 1915, Braves Field would become the team's new home.

Over the course of the South End Grounds' more than 43 years of service, baseball, the nation, and the city of Boston had all changed dramatically. At the South End Grounds, these forces of change were marked both on the field and in the stands.

Today, many aspects of the first National Association of Base Ball Players game at the site on May 16, 1871, between the Boston Red Stockings and the Troy (New York) Haymakers would seem bewildering, if not downright amusing.[4] The pitcher stood in a box some 45 feet from home and delivered the ball by means of a straight-armed submarine style motion to a batter who could both call for his preferred pitch height and, if he didn't like them, foul pitches with impunity. His catcher had no mask and typically stood several feet behind home, hoping to "[catch] the ball on its first bounce." The pitcher wore no glove; neither did any of his fielders.[5] This was baseball as the game was played by the first of its "major" professional leagues in a largely agrarian nation six years removed from a debilitating Civil War.

Over the next four decades the sport transformed itself, reflecting the fluidity of a country entering a dynamic new age of industrialization. Despite many detours along the way, by August 1914 the game had taken on nearly all of its fundamental character, as the flickering celluloid images of that era primitively attest.

At the same time, the city of Boston was growing exponentially, swelling its ranks from 250,526 (seventh largest in the country) to 670,585 (fifth) in 1910.[6] Immigrants of every stripe filled its streets, particularly the baseball-mad Irish, who during this time transformed City Hall from a bastion of Yankeedom into a virtual Irish colony.

During this era of chaotic change, Boston's baseball franchise was a source of stability and success. Indeed, for most of this period, baseball had one constant. Boston was its king.

And the South End Grounds were figuratively, and for six sweet years literally, its palace.

In this early photograph taken at the Grounds, Philadelphia's Kitty Bransfield is tagged by Boston third baseman Bill Sweeney.

The South End Grounds: Home of the Braves (and the Red Stockings, Red Caps, Rustlers, Beaneaters, and, while we're at it, even the Doves)

Having seen their various amateur baseball squads suffer ignominious defeats at the hands of the professional Cincinnati Red Stockings in 1870, Boston baseball enthusiasts sprang into action after the Red Stockings disbanded once their 87-game winning streak was snapped by the Brooklyn Atlantics. In January 1871 a corporation known as the Boston Red Stockings Club was capitalized to the tune of $15,000. Ivers W. Adams was selected president, but more importantly, George and Harry Wright were recruited to put the team together, a task that they (Harry in particular) accomplished with ultimately alarming success. Harry persuaded a number of former Cincinnati teammates to join him in Boston, but his true ten-strike was signing pitcher Al Spalding from the Forest Citys.[7]

The grounds for this new team were located along the border between Boston's South End and the newly annexed town of Roxbury, which had become part of the city of Boston in 1868.[8] The site was rectangular in shape, bounded on the east by Berlin Street (which was later incorporated into Columbus Avenue), and by the tracks of the New York, New Haven, and Hartford Railroad (Providence Division) to the west.[9] The railroad proved to be a harsh neighbor. "Passing trains could be counted on to periodically rain smoke and cinders down on the third base patrons and on the field itself," a baseball historian has written. "If the wind was right and the traffic was heavy, games were halted in order to allow the haze generated by the trains to clear."[10]

A Providence and Boston Railroad roundhouse was situated to the north of the playing field, and Camden Street lay beyond that. The southern perimeter was marked by a narrow passage known as Walpole Street, giving rise to the frequently used alternative appellation for the park: The Walpole Street Grounds. "Although a concession stand was in evidence from the beginning, rest rooms were not."[11] The park was also known as the Union Baseball Grounds, Boston National League Base Ball Park, or the Boston Base Ball Grounds.

Whatever name was used, the playing grounds were unusual in shape. Left field (250 feet) and right field (255 feet) were extremely close to home plate, and a compensatingly huge center field (450 feet) gave the park many of the characteristics of the bathtub-shaped Polo Grounds. It was said the park was "like a bowling alley. It only had one field: center."[12]

The grounds were at first leased from the railroad and its associated structures were quite simple. "The pavilion looked like a big volunteer fireman's carnival booth."[13] This covered seating area "was of simple design and resembled many of the parks of the era. The main grand stand was quite boxy, containing approximately twenty five rows of seats under the cover of the overhanging roof. The roof was held up by six supports."[14] "Four rows of primitive box seats and a smaller wooden bleacher section sat in front of the grand stand behind a three foot wooden fence."[15] Fifty cents brought admission to the grandstand, while a quarter was all that was required to sit in the uncovered "bleaching seats" that paralleled the basepaths. Standing room was plentiful, particularly in the generous confines of center field. At first the park was surrounded by a 12-foot-high wooden fence. Two ticket booths stood guard on Walpole Street, directly across the street from the groundskeeper's house.[16]

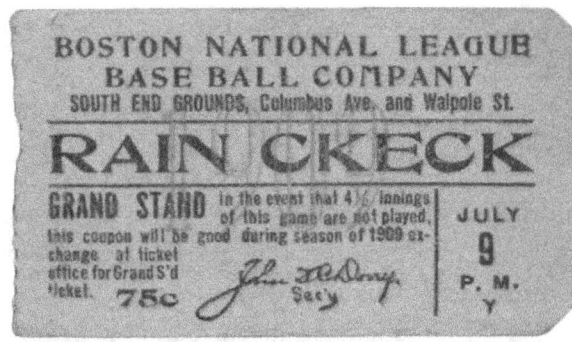
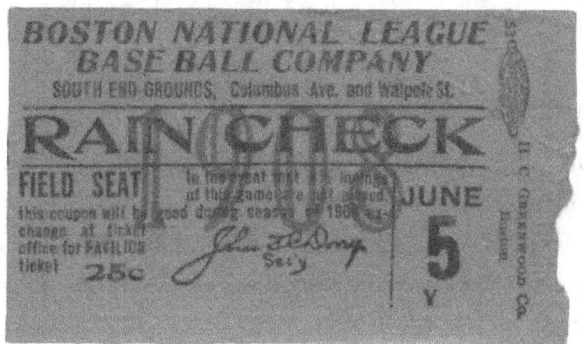

South End Grounds ticket stubs from the period when the club was known as the "Doves," reflecting its ownership by the Dovey brothers.

In these rather modest surroundings, the Red Stockings successfully began their professional odyssey in a match against a picked nine on April 6, 1871, before a packed house. "[A] full five thousand persons … the largest number ever assembled before in these grounds" were on hand, with some standing on top of the fence and others watching from rooftops.[17] With Spalding pitching, the professionals defeated the opposition 41-10, thereby establishing two long-term local institutions: on-field success and inventive attempts to avoid paying the entrance fee.

With Spalding leading the way, the Bostons swept to four consecutive National Association titles between 1872 and 1875. In his signature season of 1875, Spalding posted a record of 54 wins and only five losses. Boston's one-sided dominance of the National Association was a major factor in its eventual collapse. William A. Hulbert of Chicago became the driving force behind the newly formed National League.[18]

A Shift in the Balance of Power

At its core, this change represented a massive shift in power from players (in the National Association of Base Ball Players) to clubs and their owners (in the National League of Base Ball Clubs). Hulbert was also the driving force in luring Spalding along with three other Boston star players to Chicago: second baseman Ross Barnes, former catcher turned outfielder/first baseman Cal McVey, and catcher Deacon Jim White. When these "Four Seceders" came to Boston on May 30 for their first game in Chicago White Stocking uniforms, the *Boston Globe* reported that there had "never been so great a crowd at any base ball match ever played in this country, certainly not in this city."[19] The crowd of between 10,000 and 12,000 spectators, which the *Globe* described as "almost appalling," literally tore down the fences at the South End Grounds, according to one account.[20] The Four Seceders won that day, 5-1, and their defection led to a pennant for Chicago and a frustrating fourth-place Boston finish (a mere eight games over .500, landing the team in the middle of the eight-team field) in the National League's inaugural season.

The consequences of the passage of power to the owners were reflected quite clearly at the South End Grounds. By 1876 the presidency of the Boston club was vested in the hands of Nathaniel Taylor Apollonio, who was not shy about endorsing an exciting new method of protecting the security of the gate. In a postcard ad for the Washburn & Moen Manufacturing Co. of Worcester, Massachusetts, the Red Stockings president sang the praises of that company's barbed-wire fence. Installing it atop the wooden fencing "increased the size of [the] gate from $400 to $500" on the first day it was utilized.[21] Interestingly, the postcard ad also features opaque screening strung along the first-base side above the perimeter fencing in an apparent effort to thwart non-paying spectators watching from "wildcat bleachers" on neighboring rooftops. The battle against these so-called "dead heads" was well and truly under way. It would escalate to near epic proportions in the years to come.

Three Cheers for the Triumvirs?

On-field success in the form of a pennant returned with impeccable timing to Boston in 1877, coinciding as it did with the rise of the so-called triumvirate (typically shortened to Triumvirs) of Arthur H. Soden, James B. Billings, and William H. Conant to power. According to franchise historian Harold Kaese, "Boston's threesome wielded fully as much power in the National League as their predecessors did in the Roman League and they survived to live considerably longer and happier lives."[22] At first, Boston's fans could also not have been happier, as the Triumvirs brought immediate successive pennants with them to power and secured, during the span of their collective careers, a total of eight championships.

The Triumvirs, however, had a schizophrenic quality about them. They were innovative and, upon occasion, more than willing to open their collective wallets in pursuit of glory. A prime example was the acquisition of slugger and speedster Michael "King" Kelly from Chicago in 1887 for the astounding sum of $10,000. The following season Kelly was joined by pitcher John Clarkson, a fellow refugee from Chicago. This so-called "$20,000 battery" was showcased in the magnificent brand-new grandstand built by the Triumvirs.[23]

Although team president Soden is forever remembered as the originator of the hated reserve clause, his game-changing, free-spending approach to the practice of buying big player contracts is virtually forgotten. Truth be told, this is due to the fact that the Triumvirs were notorious penny-pinchers. "Complimentary tickets were virtually unknown," and "players were encouraged to enter the stands and wrestle fans for foul balls."[24] On one occasion Soden "ripped out the press box to make room for more paying customers. Players' wives had to buy tickets to get in."[25]

Even worse, when it came to public relations, the Triumvirs were profoundly inept. For example, when team profits declined from $120,000 in 1897 to $90,000 in 1898, team treasurer Billings lamented: "We lost thirty thousand dollars last year." In 1905 president Soden told manager Fred Tenney: "We don't care where you finish so long as you don't lose money with the team."[26] Ironically, when other teams in the League did lose money, Soden frequently provided the cash to keep other teams (and the league) afloat.[27]

Nonetheless, the relationship between fans and ownership soured over time, resulting in a "sorry exit" when the team was sold in 1906.[28] Before that occurred, the South End Grounds and its surrounding environs experienced a roller-coaster ride of highs and lows.

Sullivan's Tower

Despite, or perhaps because of, their team's successes on the field, the Triumvirs were in an almost constant battle against outlaw "dead head" spectators attempting to avoid the price of admission. The rooftops of the adjoining city streets presented an economic opportunity for enterprising individuals who were amenable to hosting large groups of visitors. At the forefront of this band of hardy entrepreneurs was one Michael Sullivan, who lived behind right field on Berlin Street, near Burke Street. His "roost," more commonly known as Sullivan's Tower, was constructed level by level over time in lockstep with the efforts of the Triumvirs to block the view. Sullivan's Tower was "an architectural monstrosity"[29] that grew over time into a Boston landmark.[30] In the view of many, "Sullivan's Roost was as much a feature of a National League game in Boston as the contest itself."[31] In its day, Sullivan's Tower was as prominent and well known as the CITGO sign in modern-day Boston; in fact, one lyrically inclined fan penned a poem in tribute to the tower that was published in the *Boston Globe*.[32]

The tower had originally been built "upon the roof of a stable, but [was later] strengthened and braced and made a separate structure."[33] The passage by the state legislature of Chapter 374 of the Acts of 1885 gave new teeth to the authority of building officials to address issues of public safety in structures of all types. Thus empowered, local officials visited or "raided" (in Sullivan's view) the edifice. Efforts to declare it unsafe under the new law failed, however, and a subsidiary effort to challenge the lack of a permit for its construction met

Upper right corner of the photo shows "dead head" spectators with their nonpaying rooftop viewing access into the Grounds.

with a similar lack of success.[34] Ironically, at one point, the *Boston Globe* reported that Soden's rather poorly constructed fence "was either blown down or helped down," and that same morning a satisfied Sullivan was observed perched on his grandstand smoking a pipe.[35] Soden quickly rebuilt.

In 1887 an adventurous *Globe* reporter paid over his 15 cents and made the trek up Sullivan's Tower. The story unfolds: "At first it was an obscure staging, modestly peeping over Mr. Soden's fence. Mr. Soden's fence was raised a few feet one day, and the next day another story had been added to Mr. Sullivan's staging." And so, on (and up) it went.

At 80 feet in height, the roost was more than double the height of the surrounding buildings. The staging was "honestly built of good timber enough of which has been employed in its construction to amply satisfy the most exacting of building inspectors," and thus compared favorably to Mr. Soden's rebuilt fence, which, incredibly, was nearly as high as Mr. Sullivan's Tower, and not nearly as well constructed. "If both were let alone the roost would be standing a dozen years after the pickets of the fence had been blown to the four winds by the blasts of springtime."[36]

As time went on, and levels were added, the viewing platform of Sullivan's Tower diminished in size. Nonetheless, it is difficult to credit accounts that "as many as 500 fans climbed [Sullivan's Tower] to see a game."[37] By 1887 the most recent "addition" to the roost, while adding eight feet of height, cut the viewing platform in half from its earlier 30 feet square. About 30 spectators were present for the late-season game attended by the *Globe* reporter, in a year in which the Bostons finished fifth.

South End Grounds II: The Grand Pavilion

The end of the 1887 season brought the curtain down on the first iteration of the South End Grounds. In September the Triumvirs announced plans to build a new facility on the site at Walpole Street.[38] The initial cost estimate was reported as $25,000.[39]

The decision was long overdue. The old familiar grounds were the only site "unchanged since the beginnings of the National Association"[40] and Soden had promised to rebuild the "shoddy grounds" as far back as the conclusion of the 1883 season, when a surprising pennant run had set new attendance records.[41]

It was worth the wait. Designed by Philadelphia architect John Jerome Deery, the new grounds consisted of an elaborate two-tiered, curving grandstand, complete with a series of towers featuring conical "witches caps."[42] The Grand Pavilion, as it came to be called, "resembled a medieval castle or fairground."[43] The *Boston Herald* proclaimed it a "grand stand unequaled for beauty and convenience in the country."[44]

The grandstand was almost never built as originally conceived. Although architect Deery assured the Triumvirs during their negotiations that the cost "would not exceed $35,000," hard cost estimates were considerably higher and, upon opening, "the actual cost [was] reported at [$]70,000." Nonetheless, the *Herald* reported that "the idea of abandoning the plan of having a new stand was not entertained for a moment." The question was whether to forge ahead or to build a less elaborate and less expensive structure instead. Not surprisingly, the *Herald* claimed it had influenced the outcome directly by pressuring the Triumvirs through the publication in mid-September 1887 of an elaborate description of Deery's master plan, complete with three drawings.[45] Just days prior, the *Globe* had publicized its estimate that the Triumvirs had made $100,000 during the 1887 season alone.[46]

Pressured or not, the Triumvirs went ahead despite the enormous costs. Optimism for the coming campaign abounded. In early April the *Boston Globe* published a cartoon entitled "Winning Cards" featuring a poker hand containing Clarkson, Kelly, and the new grandstand as three of the cards, predicting: "With this combination, the Boston Nine should be able to win a pennant and make a small fortune for the Triumvirs."[47]

The semicircular grandstand seated 2,800 persons. The lower tier accommodated 2,072 in nine sections labeled "A" (third base) through "I" (first base). Ample provision was made for "reporters and telegraphers" behind home plate. The home clubrooms were located on the first-base side, while the visitors were perched on the third-base side.

The balcony sat an additional 772 in seven sections.[48] Approximately 2,000 seats were also available in each of the two bleacher sections in left field and right field.[49] A *Boston Herald* account indicated that restaurants were located "on the extreme ends of the pavilion." "Toilet rooms were provided for the ladies with all the modern improvements." A concerted effort was made to keep the patrons of the grandstand separate from those sitting in the bleachers. The restaurants were configured so that both grandstand and bleacher patrons could be served "without in any way interfering with each other and neither can any patron of the outside seats obtain, by any subterfuge, admission to the pavilion through the restaurants."[50]

The ballpark was visually imposing. The "witches caps" sat upon four tulip-shaped columns, two at each end of the curving grandstand.[51] From Walpole Street, the full majesty of the edifice was evident. At either end sat large square brick towers with bays on the corners of their upper reaches. In between rose the central 82-foot brick and terra-cotta tower. The lower 40 feet of the tower were brick, while the upper reaches were made of terra cotta. Ticket offices were located on either side of the central tower. The Triumvirs also completed efforts to widen Walpole Street in order to improve access which provided "a good comfortable entrance" to the ballpark.[52] "While the park was complimented on its architecture ... [it was] criticized for its lack of comfort and poor sight lines."[53]

After a lengthy season-opening road trip, Opening Day festivities on May 25, 1888, were a noteworthy affair, notwithstanding the 4-1 loss to Philadelphia. "Boston's upper crust, a big slice of the lower crust and a mighty congregation of the intermediate" were on hand.[54] Dignitaries in attendance included former Governor Ames, who thought the game was "more amusing than a session of the Legislature," and the mayors of both Boston and Cambridge, numerous other elected officials, and the spouses of the famed members of the "$20,000 battery." Nearly 15,000 fans were in attendance, more than doubling the new park's 6,800-person seating capacity. The chill east wind made some spectators miserable, "but still it was a great game — for the management."[55] The season held true to this form, with the Beaneaters finishing fourth but drawing more than an estimated 300,000 paying customers to the new grandstand, bringing smiles to the faces of the Triumvirs.[56]

Those smiles truly blossomed in 1891 when second-year manager Frank Selee of Melrose, Massachusetts, and his talented roster, including Clarkson, Kelly, and pitching star Kid Nichols, took the first pennant in eight seasons home to Boston. It was the first of three consecutive pennants for the Bostons. Attendance, which had slipped as low as 147,539 in 1890, had climbed back to 193,300 by 1894.[57] While their success on the field could not be imitated, the short-lived (one year) Boston franchise of the upstart Players League had, in 1890, taken a cue from the Grand Pavilion. The club "spared no expense in planning for the new pavilion for their Congress Street Grounds" since any "baseball park [was] now incomplete without a grand pavilion," in the view of the *Boston Globe*.[58]

As 1894 dawned the Triumvirs were indeed baseball's kings, ruling from their grand castle. What could possibly go wrong?

The Great Roxbury Fire of 1894

As visually striking as the Grand Pavilion was (despite its poor sightlines and uncomfortable seats), its tenure as Boston's home grounds was brief and its end spectacular. Constructed of wood, it is unsurprising that its end came by fire. Indeed, 1894 saw a series of fires at ballparks in Baltimore, Chicago, and Philadelphia as well as Boston. Some believed that "the fires were being set deliberately, and some went so far as to hint that Sabbatarians" were to blame, seeing in the fires a conspiracy to stop Sunday baseball, which the National League had sanctioned in 1892.[59]

No such conspiracy was at work in the South End, although the precise cause of the fire on May 15, 1894, was (and perhaps remains) a matter of some dispute. The *New York Times* believed the fire was caused by "some small Roxbury boys" who had "set themselves up as rivals to Mrs. O'Leary's cow."[60] The *Boston Herald* concurred in this probability.[61] The more widely accepted account, appearing in the *Boston Globe*, told of a carelessly disposed match falling upon sawdust and timbers beneath the stands.[62]

A rotting portion of the center-field bleachers had been removed during the offseason and workers had left sawdust and debris behind, under the right-field seats.[63] Curiously, the detailed description of the careless smoker was provided by 14-year-old James Laskey who had, in the two nights following the fire, not returned home. He had been "bunking out … just to see how it would seem."[64] Just as remarkably, the *Boston Herald* noted that the "bleachers were boarded underneath and there was no interstices, so that it would be an impossibility for a person to drop a match or cigar to the ground."[65] Despite the somewhat questionable veracity of this youthful witness, Laskey's account was embraced by most. As a result, "all theories and suspicions of incendiarism [were] wiped from the minds" of property owners and city officials.[66]

The fire began during a league match between Boston and Baltimore, in the third inning. Noticing the flames, Boston right fielder Jimmy Bannon tried to stomp out the fire with his feet. He was unsuccessful. The wind apparently shifted and "the fire roared to life."[67] The game was halted. The fire would dictate that day's winners and losers.

Within an hour, 12 acres were destroyed, 1,900 people were made homeless and the grandstand, "the handsomest in the country" in the opinion of *Sporting Life*, had been forever lost in the second worst fire in the history of the city of Boston.[68] The Triumvirs chided the Boston fire department (and police) for a slow response to the danger. Indeed, the *Boston Herald* concluded that there was one reason for such an extensive loss: "Somebody Blundered."[69] John Haggerty, the groundskeeper, tried valiantly to sound the alarm and appeared to be "the only man who acted with any sense," perhaps befitting a man whose home lay across Walpole Street from the burning grounds.[70]

The franchise faced a crisis on two fronts. The immediate need to find a place to continue the still-young season was solved starting the next day by the use of the Congress Street Grounds. Located near a pier in South Boston, these were the former home grounds of the city's Players League and American Association teams.[71]

The second problem was more complicated. The Grand Pavilion and its associated facilities were worth $75,000, according to Triumvir Conant, but according to a list of insurance claims published two days later, the facilities were insured for only $45,000.[72] The Triumvirs were severely criticized for underinsuring the Grand Pavilion and for the consequences that this underinsurance portended for the rebuilt ballpark.

In point of fact, the Triumvirs were hardly unique in their plight. Initial estimates (subsequently revised upward) pegged total losses from the fire at $300,000, only half of which was insured. The city of Boston lost both a school and a fire department "hose house" in the blaze. Neither the school nor the hose house was insured. According to one H.R. Turner of the Niagara Insurance Company, the fire, while "deplorable from a humanitarian standpoint," would "hardly be felt by the insurance companies," due to small tenement houses in the area. Very few "of these occupants carr[ied] any insurance." Then, in a statement callous enough to have come from one of the Triumvirs, he concluded: "The fire could not have happened in a locality more advantageous for insurance interests."[73]

One thing was certain. The long-running competition between the Triumvirs' fence and Sullivan's roost was over. "[T]he fire played no favorites. It leveled them both."[74]

While the criticism of Triumvir penny-pinching with insurance colors the subsequent discussion of the disappointing results of their rebuilding effort, a plausible case for caution could be made. In 1894 the country was in the midst of a severe recession following the Panic of 1893; indeed, employment would not return to 1891 levels until 1900. As a result of "the disruption in the financial system, some nonfinancial businesses found it difficult to obtain the funds they needed to meet payrolls and were forced to suspend operations."[75]

Thus, the Triumvirs—who after all had been willing to spend the money to construct the Grand Pavilion despite horrendous cost overruns—may have pulled back on their reconstruction efforts due to their lack of faith in the ability of *other* enterprises to keep paying (and employing) potential fans.

A more pointed—and irrefutable—criticism of ownership appeared in *Sporting Life*. The weekly chastised the Triumvirs for failing to properly police up the months-old debris in the area, and for even more egregiously failing to provide for a fire hydrant or a fire hose to be maintained on site. This "'pennywise and pound foolish' method of management" left the club unprepared for the preventable tragedy that unfolded.[76]

To capture such action at home plate at the Grounds during this era, the photographer had to position himself close-by on the playing field.

Internal view taken from the Grounds' Walpole Street side.

South End Grounds III: Is It Better to Burn Out Than to Fade Away?

The combination of a lack of insurance proceeds and a lack of confidence in the overall economy produced a rebuilt ballpark on a smaller scale than its majestic predecessor. What was impressive was that it was built at a breakneck pace. The Bostons defeated New York in the rebuilt grounds before 5,206 fans on July 20, barely two months after the fire.[77]

The new grandstand was a modest, single deck structure with "twin spires … suggestive of the Churchill Downs racetrack"[78] and a seating capacity of 900. The number of bleacher seats was increased to compensate for this shortcoming. "[T]he only stands in the outfield were a small set of bleachers in [right field] called the pie bleachers because they were triangular shaped, like a piece of pie."[79] "Although not as impressive as the old building, the new park had more comfortable seating and better sightlines."[80] Its seating capacity was approximately 5,000.[81]

Within a year the inadequacy of the rebuilt grounds had become apparent and the push to upgrade the facility began. In 1895 two iron wings were added, bringing the grandstand's seating capacity to 2,300.[82]

The addition was timely; the Beaneaters rebounded to win consecutive pennants in 1897 and 1898, ending the three-year dominance of the Baltimore Orioles.[83] Thereafter, the team's fortunes receded and in 1906 the Triumvirs sold the team to George and John Dovey, who had partnered with a "theatrical man named John Harris."[84] It was a poor investment decision for the new owners. The Beaneaters finished last for the first time in franchise history in 1906, the South End Grounds were in disrepair—"an ugly little wart" in the words of one description—and there was a new team in town.[85]

Five years earlier, the American League's Boston team [as of the 1908 season, known as the Red Sox] had, through the maneuverings of Connie Mack, among others, taken up residence literally on the other side of the tracks. The Huntington Avenue Grounds, built in 1901, were bordered by the New York, New Haven, and Hartford Railroad on the east, a mirror image to the South End Grounds' western boundary. The American League "park was new, neat, and larger than the South End Grounds, of which the public had grown weary."[86] The price of admission was half that at the National League park. Little wonder, then, that on the date of the upstart league's inaugural home opener, they outdrew the Nationals substantially. With the benefit of at least 70 "jumpers" from the National League, by 1902 the American League was outdrawing the National League by some 300,000 fans.[87] Among the fans attracted to the new Boston team was saloonkeeper Michael "Nuf Ced" McGreevey. McGreevey (and his Royal Rooters) had originally been supporters of the Beaneaters, and a version of the slogan for his Third Base Saloon had adorned the left-field wall at the South End Grounds.[88]

The Dovey brothers' major contribution to the physical facility at Walpole Street was the construction of new outfield bleachers for the 1908 season, although they had also supplied a new scoreboard the year before.[89] A 40-foot-wide strip across the outfield was dedicated to the new seating, with an open space retained in the vicinity of the flagpole in center field. Overall seating capacity grew to 11,000.[90] When George Dovey died suddenly, his brother John ultimately took his stead, but soon the team was sold to a syndicate headed by William H. Russell. In less than a year Russell, too, was dead and the "Doves" who had briefly become the "Rustlers" were again in search of new ownership.

In December 1911 the team was sold to a new troika of leaders, headed this time by Tammany Hall hard-charger James E. Gaffney, the club's treasurer. The franchise soon acquired a new nickname — derived from the term "Sachem," which was used to describe the leader of Tammany Hall — the Braves.

Gaffney immediately set out to improve the tired South End plant.[91] Based on the recommendations of co-owner John Montgomery Ward, a series of changes to the configuration of the South End Grounds were put through. Given the permanence of its urban boundaries, the grounds had always retained its rectangular configuration. *Green Cathedrals* reports its dimensions at LF 250 (1894), LC 445, Deepest LC 450, CF 440, Right Center 440, RF 255.[92] The addition of outfield bleachers in 1908 decreased the straightaway left-field, left-center-field and center-field dimensions by between 38 and 43 feet.[93]

Ward's changes involved removing the left-field bleachers, adding another section to the grandstand and shifting the diamond toward right field to bring "the foul line over the left-field fence at a distance of 350 feet or more than 100 feet farther down the field than at [the] present time."[94] However, the 1912-1914 left-field dimension is reported in other reputable sources as 275 feet. The 350-foot distance description quoted above was provided by Tim Murnane of the *Boston Globe*, himself a former ballplayer, and has the ring of authenticity. The contemporary accounts of the *Boston Post* and the *Boston Herald* confirm that this indeed was the plan.[95]

The record nonetheless is not perfectly clear. *Sporting Life* first reported in February that "the task of changing around the old South End Ground is greater than was at first supposed" and then in March reported "that the fielding space is increased about 15 feet."[96] Murnane tells a different story. His Opening Day 1912 account reported that all 10,000-plus spectators "enjoyed the many changes made at the park, the transformation giving about 25 percent more room for hitting."[97] Finally, Harold Kaese, author of the seminal history of the franchise in Boston, also reports a 350-foot left-field distance in 1912.[98]

In right field, what was happening was indisputable. The firm of Waitt and Bond, manufacturer of the well-known Blackstone cigar, erected a modern cigar factory (reputed to be the world's largest) at 716 Columbus Avenue.[99] The factory building, which still stood in 2013, loomed over the grounds from the opposite side of the street. Kaese wrote that Jay Kirke, a powerful left-handed hitter whose fielding was less than graceful, often launched fly balls in that direction, frequently followed by the sound of tinkling broken glass. Eventually the factory was closed and a new facility opened in New Jersey.[100]

Gaffney also made numerous cosmetic improvements to the Grounds, painting the entire plant "green with crimson trimmings" so that the facility "altogether present[ed] a very attractive appearance."[101] "The walks to the field seats on either side of the field [were] relaid in blue stones" improving the park's appearance so much that "[o]ld time patrons of the park [would] not know the place. ... More money [was] spent on decorations than the Triumvirs ever spent in their lives on such things."[102]

Gaffney was in a state of perpetual motion. In the fall of 1913, he acquired a parcel at Columbus Avenue and Walpole Street that would allow for the existing grandstand to be demolished, the playing field to be enlarged, and a new modern grandstand erected.[103] In mid-January of 1914, Gaffney was reported to be returning to Boston the next week to review bids for a new concrete grandstand.[104] He also installed a new scoreboard in deep center field at the start of the 1914 season.[105]

Standing on the threshold of a major financial commitment to the four-decades-old location, Gaffney hesitated. The fateful, wonderful miracle season of 1914 began.

The End of Days

It was success that ultimately spelled the end of the South End Grounds. The maniacal climb of the Miracle Braves flooded the facility beyond its capacity. By early August 1914, Red Sox president Joseph Lannin, who had only just previously acquired a small stake in the Braves franchise, put Fenway Park at the disposal of the Braves without charge.[106] Gaffney, ever the cagey politician, initially accepted only for Saturday and holiday game days.[107] Upon their return from the road, the Braves played a Labor Day morning-afternoon doubleheader against the Giants in Fenway. Nearly 75,000 attended the two games, and the Braves never returned to the South End.[108] For the 1914 season, the combination of access to Fenway and a baseball miracle for the ages lifted Braves attendance to 382,913, first in the National League.[109]

Gaffney never looked back. Frustrated by an undersized facility plagued by "clouds of smoke from the locomotives [that] interfered with the play and the comfort of the spectators,"[110] he scoured the Boston area for sites that would accommodate his vision of a playing field unencumbered by urban boundaries. He found just such a location on the site of a former golf course, bounded ironically by the same harsh neighbor—the railroad—that he had fled the South End to avoid.

When Gaffney's Braves moved from the Walpole Street facility, they were obliged to sell the grounds subject to an "iron bound agreement" that the land could not be used for baseball, an effort to block the grounds from falling into the hands of the Federal League.[111] And so the Braves left the familiar confines of the South End, despite the fact that to that time "[m]ore championships [had] been won on those old grounds than on any other in the world."[112]

Taking the grass from their infield with them, the Braves moved on. Moving to the expanse of Braves Field, however, "was like moving from a modern three bedroom apartment into a nineteenth century mansion."[113] The franchise was never the same, appearing in only one World Series in nearly four decades in Allston.

Today the site of the old South End Grounds barely countenances a memory of its storied past. The railroad is still there, in the form of the Southwest Corridor, and Columbus Avenue and the old cigar factory both have tales that they could tell. Now owned by Northeastern University, most of the field is occupied by surface parking and a garage. But if one goes just north beyond the garage, in the area where the old railroad roundhouse once stood south of Camden Street, there lies a trio of modest playing fields. Two of the fields are framed by small wooden stands and a larger array of concrete and aluminum seating sits there quietly as well, providing at least a distant echo to the cheers from the bleaching boards of the late 19th century.

Notes

1. J.C. O'Leary, "13 Zeros Apiece," *Boston Globe*, August 12, 1914, 7.
2. In 1896, Chickering Station on Camden Street was closed. Prior to that time, the station was also heavily trafficked by baseball fans.
3. Ronald M. Selter, *Ballparks of the Deadball Era* (Jefferson, North Carolina: McFarland & Company, 2008), 20.

4 This was the date of the first National Association match. The first match between the Red Stockings and a picked nine took place on April 6 of that year and is described below.

5 Harvey Frommer, *Primitive Baseball* (New York: Atheneum, 1998), 61-68 (describing changes in the game from the mid-1870s to the new century).

6 census.gov/www/through_the_decades/fast_facts (retrieved June 15, 2013).

7 Harold Kaese, *The Boston Braves 1871-1953* (Boston: Northeastern University Press, 2004), 5, 7.

8 Sam Bass Warner, Jr., *Streetcar Suburbs, The Process of Growth in Boston (1870-1890)* (Cambridge: Harvard University Press, 1962), 41.

9 Alan E. Foulds, *Boston's Ballparks and Arenas* (Lebanon, New Hampshire: Northeastern University Press, published by the University Press of New England, 2005), 8. (The New York, New Haven, and Hartford Railroad leased the Old Colony Railroad in 1893, which by that time included the Boston and Providence Railroad.)

10 Bill Felber, *A Game of Brawl* (Lincoln: University of Nebraska Press, 2007), 60.

11 Foulds, *Boston's Ballparks and Arenas*, 8-9.

12 Michael Benson, *Ballparks of North America* (Jefferson, North Carolina: McFarland & Company, 1985), 39.

13 Benson, *Ballparks of North America*, 39.

14 Foulds, *Boston's Ballparks and Arenas*, 8-9.

15 Benson, *Ballparks of North America*, 39.

16 Foulds, *Boston's Ballparks and Arenas*, 8-9.

17 Kaese, *The Boston Braves*, 9.

18 Hulbert's bold maneuvering to establish the National League is described in detail in Michael Haupert's fine SABR biography, at sabr.org/bioproj/person/d1d420b3.

19 *Boston Globe*, May 31, 1876, 1.

20 Kaese, *The Boston Braves*, 19.

21 Michael Gershman, *Diamonds: The Evolution of the Ballpark* (Boston: Houghton Mifflin Company, 1993), 29.

22 Kaese, *The Boston Braves*, 22. The First Triumvirate of Rome was a political alliance between Gaius Julius Caesar, Marcus Licinius Crassus and Gnaeus Pompeius Magnus (Pompey the Great). Crassus died in battle approximately seven years into the alliance, whereupon Caesar and Pompey fought a civil war. The survivor, Caesar, ultimately was assassinated on the Senate floor.

23 *Sporting Life*, April 11, 1888, 1.

24 Kaese, *The Boston Braves*, 47, 23-24.

25 Benson, *Ballparks of North America*, 39.

26 Kaese, *The Boston Braves*, 113, 111.

27 Brian McKenna's SABR biography of Soden makes for entertaining reading on the extraordinary life of this Triumvir. sabr.org/bioproj/person/a1b2e0d0.

28 Besides their own miserliness and constant financial clashing with the team's human capital [the players], the Triumvirs' demise was hastened by poor on-field performance and the introduction of competition in the form of the American League in 1901.

29 Kaese, *The Boston Braves*, 68.

30 Peter Morris, *A Game of Inches: The Stories Behind the Innovations that Shaped Baseball: The Game Behind the Scenes* (Chicago: Ivan R. Dee, 2006), 429.

31 *Lewiston* (Maine) *Evening Journal*, July 29, 1914, 9.

32 *Boston Globe*, July 10, 1889, 5.

33 *Boston Globe*, August 1, 1885, 3.

34 *Boston Globe*, August 20, 1885, 4.

35 *Boston Globe*, August 19, 1887, 8.

36 *Boston Globe*, September 5, 1887, 4.

37 Donald Hubbard, *The Heavenly Twins of Boston Baseball* (Jefferson, North Carolina: McFarland & Company, 2008), 109.

38 *Boston Herald*, September 16, 1887, 5.

39 *Boston Globe*, August 19, 1887, 8.

40 Foulds, *Boston's Ballparks and Arenas*, 13.

41 Kaese, *The Boston Braves*, 37.

42 Unlike Fenway Park, which has evolved into a double-deck structure, the Grand Pavilion was designed and built as a two-tier facility, the only such structure in Boston baseball history.

43 Foulds, *Boston's Ballparks and Arenas*, 15.

44 *Boston Herald*, May 25, 1888, 5.

45 *Boston Herald*, May 25, 1888, 5.

46 *Boston Globe*, September 12, 1887, 8.

47 *Boston Globe*, April 8, 1888, 1.

48 *Boston Globe*, May 25, 1888, 5.

49 Lowry, *Green Cathedrals*, 108.

50 *Boston Herald*, May 25, 1888, 5; for a fascinating discussion with Tom Shieber of the Baseball Hall of Fame describing the Classic Ballpark Tours interactive exhibit featuring the South End Grounds, see: Paul Ferrante, "Travel Back in Time to Boston's South End Grounds," August 20, 2012, sportscollectordigest.com. Retrieved June 24, 2013.

51 Lowry, *Green Cathedrals*, 43.

52 *Boston Globe*, May 14, 1888, 8.

53 Foulds, *Boston's Ballparks and Arenas*, 15.

54 *Boston Post*, May 26, 1888, 2.

55 *Boston Globe*, May 26, 1888, 4.

56 Tim Murnane, "Hub Happenings," *Sporting Life*, October 3, 1888, 7.

57 Baseballalmanac.com/teamstats/roster. Retrieved July 15, 2013.
58 *Boston Globe*, February 23, 1890, 22. For an excellent history of the Congress Street Grounds, readers are directed to Charlie Bevis's ballpark biography of that facility, at SABR.org/bioproj/park/33169c79.
59 Gershman, *Diamonds: The Evolution of the Ballpark*, 53. Sunday baseball in Boston would remain controversial for decades.
60 *New York Times*, May 16, 1894, 1.
61 *Boston Herald*, May 16, 1914, 1.
62 "Was a Match," *Boston Globe*, May 18, 1894, 1.
63 Foulds, *Boston's Ballparks and Arenas*, 19.
64 *Boston Globe*, May 18, 1894, 1.
65 *Boston Herald*, May 17, 1894, 3.
66 *Boston Globe*, May 18, 1894, 1.
67 Paul Ferrante, "The Most Beautiful Ballpark Ever?" August 9, 2012, sportscollectordigest.com. Retrieved June 24, 2013.
68 *Sporting Life*, May 26, 1894, 3.
69 *Boston Herald*, May 16, 1894, 1.
70 *Boston Post*, May 16, 1894, 3.
71 Philip J. Lowry, *Green Cathedrals* (New York: Addison-Wesley, 1992), 108.
72 *Boston Globe*, May 18, 1894, 4.
73 *Boston Globe*, May 16, 1894, 5.
74 Kaese, *The Boston Braves*, 68.
75 Mark Carlson, "Causes of Bank Suspensions in the Panic of 1893," Federal Reserve Board (2002), federalreserve.gov/pubs/feds2002/200211pap.pdf. Retrieved June 11, 2013.
76 *Sporting Life*, May 26, 1894, 5; *Sporting Life*, June 2, 1894, 1.
77 Foulds, *Boston's Ballparks and Arenas*, 19.
78 Felber, *A Game of Brawl*, 60.
79 Selter, *Ballparks of the Deadball Era*, 18.
80 Foulds, *Boston's Ballparks and Arenas*, 19.
81 Selter, *Ballparks of the Deadball Era*, 18.
82 Tim Murnane, "Building Iron Wings," *Boston Globe*, January 13, 1895, 16.
83 Frommer, *Old Time Baseball*, 107.
84 Kaese, *The Boston Braves*, 115.
85 Kaese, *The Boston Braves*, 101, 113.
86 Kaese, *The Boston Braves*, 101.
87 Frommer, *Old Time Baseball*, 60.
88 Gershman, *Diamonds: The Evolution of the Ballpark*, 75.
89 Kaese, *The Boston Braves*, 115.
90 Tim Murnane, "Bleachers in Center Field," *Boston Globe*, January 7, 1908, 5.
91 Gaffney also once and for all provided the team with an enduring nickname. He chose the name Braves in deference to the Sachem, the symbol of his Tammany Hall. Previously, the franchise had been known as the Red Stockings, Red Caps, Rustlers, Beaneaters, and the Doves, as well as simply the Boston Nationals.
92 Lowry, *Green Cathedrals*, 109.
93 Selter, *Ballparks of the Deadball Era*, 20.
94 Tim Murnane, "Ward's Field Changes to Be Put Through," *Boston Globe*, January 20, 1912, 7. By the end of July 1912, John Montgomery Ward had sold his stake in the team, resigning as its president. Gaffney became the new president of the franchise.
95 *Boston Post*, January 20, 1912, 13; John J. Hallahan, "To Make Over South End Park," *Boston Herald*, January 20, 1912, 6.
96 *Sporting Life*, February 12, 1912, 7; March 30, 1912, 3.
97 Tim Murnane, "Boston Braves Play to 10,264," *Boston Globe*, April 12, 1912, 1.
98 Kaese, *The Boston Braves*, 129.
99 *Moody's Manual of Railroads and Corporation Securities: Volume 2* (New York: Poor's Publishing Company, 1921), 728.
100 Kaese, *The Boston Braves*, 125-6.
101 *Boston Globe*, March 26, 1912, 6.
102 *Sporting Life*, April 6, 1912, 7.
103 *Sporting Life*, October 18, 1913, 2.
104 *Sporting Life*, January 17, 1914, 14.
105 *Sporting Life*, April 25, 1914, 7.
106 *Sporting Life*, November 29, 1913, 3.
107 *Sporting Life*, August 8, 1914, 3.
108 *Sporting Life*, September 26, 1914, 8.
109 baseball-reference.com. Retrieved June 5, 2013.
110 A.H.C. Mitchell, "The World's Champions," *Sporting Life*, December 26, 1914, 3.
111 Tim Murnane, "Baseball Exit for South End Grounds," *Boston Globe*, December 20, 1914, 15.
112 *Sporting Life*, December 26, 1914, 3.
113 Kaese, *The Boston Braves*, 173.

The Time(s) the Braves Played Home Games at Fenway Park

By Bill Nowlin

Playing Game Three and Game Four of the 1914 World Series at the larger-capacity Fenway Park was not the first time the Boston Braves had played a home game at Fenway and it wouldn't be the last. In all, the team played 87 regular-season games at Fenway, as well as the two World Series games.

The days of the war between the two leagues were nearly a decade in the past and both the Braves and Red Sox had new ownership that hadn't been through those battles. As the 1914 World Series approached, president Joseph J. Lannin of the Red Sox extended the courtesy of an invitation to his counterpart, Braves president James E. Gaffney, offering the use of the larger park on occasion. He was well aware that brand-new Fenway Park (the home of the Red Sox, which had opened in 1912) had an initial seated capacity of 24,400 whereas the Braves ballpark, known as the South End Grounds, had expanded since its own birth in 1894 but could nonetheless accommodate only about 11,000 paying customers.[1]

The first regular-season games the Braves played at Fenway Park preceded Lannin by a little more than a year. After the 1913 schedule had been set, president Gaffney approached Red Sox president James McAleer and vice president John I. Taylor to ask if the Braves could (while the Red Sox were on the road) play a pair of two-admission doubleheaders at Fenway during 1913 because of its larger capacity. Consent was promptly and graciously granted.[2]

The first of the 1913 doubleheader was on April 19, a morning/afternoon Patriots Day twin bill hosting the New York Giants. The Braves had held their home

Fenway Park in 1914.

opener on April 17, a 3-2 loss to the Giants, and then lost 14-3 on the 18th. Ownership was expecting a big turnout and therefore, with the Red Sox' consent in hand, the Braves scheduled two games at Fenway Park, bracketing the running of the Boston Marathon—a morning game at 10:30 and an afternoon game to begin at 3:30.

Under threatening skies, the morning crowd of 6,500 saw the Giants take the third game in a row from the Braves (7-2) while in the afternoon 16,700 saw the Braves drop a fourth, 10-3. The first of the games lasted two hours and the second one lasted two hours and one minute.

The Braves had also anticipated a large crowd for the May 30 Memorial Day doubleheader against the visiting Brooklyn Superbas and took advantage of Fenway once more. Separate admissions were in order once more, a morning game and an afternoon game, and the weather was perfect. The attendance was similar—6,000 and 16,000. The Braves lost a tight one to Brooklyn in the morning, giving up two runs in the top of the ninth and going down, 2-1, but they won the afternoon game, 7-6. As it happens, there was another twin bill on May 31, this one at the South End Grounds, and they drew the largest crowd there in years, upwards of 12,000. Boston lost the first game of the single-admission doubleheader, 2-0, and Boston and Brooklyn battled to a 3-3 ten-inning tie in the second game before it was called due to darkness.

In 1914, during the regular season, the Braves played a number of games at Fenway. Though the Red Sox franchise was now owned by Joseph J. Lannin, the team was very willing to allow the Braves the use of Fenway when the Sox were out of town (and by this time with outright hostilities ended between the two leagues, schedulers had coordinated team travel in the two-team cities so that the Braves would be in Boston when the Red Sox were out of town, and vice versa.)

The first time in 1914 that the Braves used Fenway was on August 1. The Braves had been in last place, 11 1/2 games behind, on July 15. But then they had won 11 out of 13 games and had climbed to fourth place, though they were still nine games out of first. They were playing a 3:00 P.M. game against the third-place St. Louis Cardinals, and August 1 was a Saturday. Looking for a larger gate, they scheduled the game at Fenway Park. It was "Springfield Day" and the weather barely cooperated, though had it not been a little ominous, it was thought that as many as another 4,000 might have come. Nonetheless, the *Boston Globe* termed the 20,000 fans who turned out "the largest crowd that ever attended a National League game in Boston." It was a "corking game"—St. Louis scored once in the first and held that thinnest of leads until Boston scored three runs in the bottom of the eighth. The Cards tied it with two in the ninth, and the Braves prevailed when Possum Whitted drove in the winning run with two out in the bottom of the tenth.

The homestand continued, and Red Sox owner Lannin could see that the Braves were beginning to draw larger crowds than the South End Grounds could hold. He telegraphed president Gaffney on the evening of August 3 that the Braves were welcome to use Fenway Park for the rest of the season, completely free of charge:

J. E. Gaffney, President, Boston N.L. B.B.C.—If it would be any advantage to your club to play at Fenway park for all of this season, you are welcome to use the same free of all charge. Congratulations to you and Manager Stallings on the fine showing of your club. J. J. Lannin.

The Red Sox were 7 1/2 games behind the Philadelphia Athletics, in second place.

Gaffney telegraphed Lannin back on the morning of August 4:

J. J. Lannin, President, Boston A.L. B.B.C., St. Louis, Mo.—Please accept my thanks for your most generous offer. It was the thought of a true sportsman and is appreciated not only by myself, but the public of New England. Braves look like contenders, so may take advantage of your offer on Saturdays and holiday. Permit me to congratulate you upon the fine progress the Red Sox have made under your ownership. Boston needs two pennants, let us go after them. J. E. Gaffney.

The Braves lost on August 7 at the South End Grounds, but it was their only loss of the week. They had won 16 of 19 and, though still in fourth place, they were just 7 1/2 games out of first—and only two games out of second place. So with another Saturday game on the schedule—August 8 against Cincinnati—president Gaffney accepted Red Sox president Lannin's offer yet again. It wasn't the biggest of crowds—but it exceeded 14,000 (more than the capacity of the South End Grounds) and those who stuck it out to the end left elated. The Reds took an early 3-0 lead, and the Braves failed to score at all until the bottom of the ninth. The story is told in more detail elsewhere, but with one out in the bottom of the ninth, and after an error and a freak hop on another batted ball, manager Stallings began to work what he called (in the words of the *Boston Globe*'s Jim O'Leary), the "finesse in his system" and they tied it, 3-3. Rabbit Maranville drove in the winning run in the tenth.

The team didn't lose again until the 18th of August, by which time they were on a long road trip from August 13 through September 5. They returned home in time for a Labor Day doubleheader on September 7. After the games on September 5, the Braves were in a tie for first place with the Giants, both teams at 67-52. And it was the Giants they'd face on Labor Day. Thanks to the schedulers, the Red Sox were conveniently out of town for the rest of the month, until October 1—so, Fenway Park it was.

All the reserved seats were sold out a couple of days in advance. The park was mobbed. There were a reported 35,000 fans at the 10:30 game in the morning, and 38,000 at the 3:00 P.M. game. The *Globe* reported that for both games there were 5,000 to 6,000 outside clamoring for admission even after ticket sales were cut off and the gates closed, and a large photograph in the September 8 edition showed some of that crowd milling outside. "Nothing like these figures has ever been approached before," the next day's *Globe* commented. With total attendance for the day at 73,000, the paper observed, "The Boston club has had years when the attendance for the entire season has not been greater than that of yesterday." One did have to go back

Boston newspaper advertisement for tickets to September 10 Braves game at Fenway.

a ways, but between 1871 and 1887 the largest turnout for a season at the original incarnation of the South End Grounds had been 55,240.[3]

On September 7 those who took in the morning game were pleased to see a come-from-behind 5-4 victory, with the Braves scoring twice in the bottom of the ninth to win. The excitement of the crowd was compared to that of the deciding game of the 1912 World Series, when the Red Sox beat the same Giants. The masses behind the ropes in the outfield broke through and flooded the field. Cheering continued until voices gave out and there followed a scene where hundreds—perhaps thousands—of straw hats were all flung in the air, "simply a cloud of headwear sailing around." Some of those leaving after the game got right back in line for the afternoon affair. That game was scoreless through three, but the Giants began to pile up runs and the final was a lopsided 10-1 loss for Boston. The two teams were back in a tie. A day later, president Gaffney announced the precise total of paid admissions: 74,163. Or 74,162—accounts differ, by one fan.

In 1914 the largest crowd the Braves could hope to draw in their own park might have been a thousand more than the capacity 11,000—thus, the two games netted something like 50,000 paid admissions they might otherwise have been unable to bank, more than tripling their revenue.

From this point on, the Braves took full advantage of Lannin's offer, and not just on Saturdays or holidays, playing 25 more games at Fenway Park—right through the final home game of the year, September 29. By this point, the team was a full eight games up on the second-place Giants and there were, including the September 29 game, 11 games to play. But it was the last time local fans could see them at home. On September 30 they played the first two of six games against the Giants in New York, and then wound up the season with four games in Brooklyn.

In 1913, the team had drawn total paid attendance of 208,200 but with the pennant race and the larger-capacity Fenway Park available to it during the end of the season, the Braves drew 382,913 in 1914. They'd been playing at the South End Grounds since 1894. It seemed time for a new park, one with larger capacity.[4]

It was only on December 1, 1914, that president Gaffney announced the team would leave its home grounds on Walpole Street and play in a new facility. They hadn't yet fully decided on the new site, but hoped to secure one and begin construction in March 1915, so they could be ready to play games in their new home park by July. President Lannin had assured Gaffney that the Braves could continue to play their home games at Fenway until the new field was ready.

On December 4 Gaffney announced the decision to move to a site on Commonwealth Avenue between Babcock and Pleasant Streets, about a mile farther out from downtown Boston than was Fenway Park. The site had previously served as the Allston Golf Club. The planned seating was for 40,282—much larger than Fenway, leapfrogging it for total capacity.

With the time it took for construction to be complete, the Braves played most of their 1915 home season at Fenway Park. The first game they played in their new Braves Field facility was on August 18, 1915, when they beat the St. Louis Cardinals, 3-1, and drew an overflow crowd of 46,000 fans with another 6,000 reportedly turned away.

Flipping things around, not quite two months later, the Red Sox played their first game with Braves Field as their temporary home park—Game Three of the 1915 World Series on October 11.

Mirroring the Braves' borrowing of Fenway for the 1914 Series, president Gaffney had telegraphed the Red Sox on September 22 offering the Red Sox the use of Braves Field because it was now the larger-capacity park; the offer was accepted at once, and the Sox held their first workout there on September 28 to become more familiar with playing in the new facility.

The Red Sox played their home games of both the 1915 and 1916 World Series at Braves Field, two games in 1915 and three in 1916. As with the two games the Braves had played at Fenway in 1914, all five Red Sox games at Braves Field ended in victories. Every one of the seven games one team played in the other's ballpark was a World Series win.

There came a time later when, for several years, the Red Sox played their Sunday home games at Braves Field, before local law permitted them to play at Fenway Park, but that's another story.

Schedule of the home games the Braves played at Fenway Park

1913: April 19 (2 games) and May 30 (2 games) — total of 4 games

1914: August 1 and 8; September 7 (2 games), and then September 8, 9 (2 games), 10 (2 games), 11, 12, 14, 15, 16, 17, 18, 19, 21, 22, 23 (2 games), 24 (2 games), 25 (2 games), 26 (2 games), 28, and 29 — total of 29 games

And also the two 1914 World Series games.

1915: April 14, 15, 17, 19 (2 games), 20, 21; May 6, 7, 8, 10, 11, 12, 14, 15, 18, 19, 20, 21, 22, 24, 25, 27, 28 (2 games), 29, 31 (2 games); June 1, 2, 3, 22, 23, 24; July 9, 10 (2 games), 12 (2 games), 13 (2 games), 15, 16, 17 (2 games), 19, 20, 21, 22, 23, 24, and 26 — total of 52 games

1946: April 28 (2 games) — total of two games

All in all, that totals 87 regular-season games and two World Series games. Interested in won-loss totals? The years broke down as follows for the regular-season games:

1913: 1-3
1914: 23-4-2
1915: 31-20-1
1946: 2-0

Overall totals: 57-27-3 (plus the two wins in the World Series games)

The games the Braves played at Fenway in 1946 were because of an unfortunate incident in preparing Braves Field for play in the preseason. The April 17 home game at the Wigwam was one of the most colorful openers in major-league history; the fresh coat of green paint on the seats hadn't fully dried in some places and "hundreds" left the park with a little extra green on their "stylish new Easter topcoats, fancy, expensive fur jobs worn by feminine fans on the brittle afternoon; a variety of gabardine and tweeds…" (*Boston Globe*). The next day, with a smaller crowd expected, some 6,000 seats were roped off and inaccessible, but come April 28 — with the atmospheric conditions still not conducive to a proper drying of the paint, and anticipating a larger turnout for the doubleheader against the Dodgers, the Braves requested and were granted the temporary use of Fenway Park.

Of the team's home games in 1914, their record was 51-25-3. Two of the tie games were at Fenway Park (September 18 and the second game on September 24), one was at the South End Grounds on August 11. They also played tie games at Forbes Field in Pittsburgh (May 11) and the Polo Grounds in New York (the second game on September 30). Of their 79 home games, the records in the two parks were:

South End Grounds   28-21-1
Fenway Park   23-4-2

Games the Braves Have Played At Fenway Which Were Not Home Games

The Braves also played another 40 games at Fenway, but not as the home team — these were exhibition games over the years which pitted the visiting Braves against the home-team Red Sox. The two teams often squared off in preseason City Series games. The first of these was in 1926, on April 9 and the last in 1952.

The first time the two teams played each other in Boston was at Braves Field, on April 11, 1925. The first time they both played at Fenway Park was on April 9, 1926. The last time the Boston Braves played the Red Sox at Fenway was on April 12 and 13, 1952. The following year, the Braves moved to Milwaukee. Just a few weeks earlier, with the announcement of the franchise move not yet made, the Boston Braves played the Red Sox in Sarasota on March 14 and in Bradenton on March 16. The following year, the Braves moved to Milwaukee — so it was the Milwaukee Braves who played at Fenway for two preseason games in 1953, on April 11 and April 12.

The teams occasionally also played each other during spring training at such unlikely locales as Bluefield, West Virginia, in 1954.

From 1931 through 1934, the two teams had played each other in exhibition games during the season, but all four of those had been played at Braves Field. It wasn't until July 10, 1945, that the two played an in-season exhibition game at Fenway Park.[5] They also played a Community Fund benefit game at Fenway on July 11, 1949.

The Milwaukee Braves played benefits for the Jimmy Fund at Fenway Park on July 22, 1957, July 20, 1959, August 21, 1961, and June 3, 1963. The franchise's third geographically-based Braves team, the Atlanta Braves, played a Jimmy Fund benefit at Fenway on June 6, 1966.

Boston and Milwaukee had also played each other at Cooperstown in 1955, and did so again in 1963.

Once interleague play was initiated in 1997, the Atlanta Braves and Boston Red Sox were deemed "natural rivals" (a bit of a reach as it was recalling an era more than 40 years in the past when the two teams had played in the same city) and the Braves played regular-season games at Fenway Park—sweeping a three-game series—from August 29-31. They next played in Boston on June 4-6, 1999, and subsequent years, recording a total of 24 interleague games prior to the 2012 season, winning 15 and losing 9.

Exhibition games between the Red Sox and Braves played at Fenway Park

Preseason:

April 9, 1926: Red Sox 6, Braves 1
April 8, 1927: Red Sox 13, Braves 2
April 9, 1927: Braves 6, Red Sox 5[6]
April 12, 1930: Braves 4, Red Sox 3
April 11, 1931: Red Sox 7, Braves 2
April 9, 1932: Braves 2, Red Sox 1
April 8, 1933: Red Sox 7, Braves 0
April 14, 1934: Red Sox 8, Braves 2
April 14, 1935: Braves 3, Red Sox 2[7]
April 12, 1936: Bees 8, Red Sox 4
April 18, 1937: Red Sox 10, Bees 8
April 16, 1938: Bees 6, Red Sox 2
April 16, 1939: Red Sox 1, Bees 0[8]
April 14, 1940: Bees 7, Red Sox 3
April 13, 1941: Braves 10, Red Sox 3
April 12, 1942: Braves 7, Red Sox 5
April 18, 1943: Red Sox 5, Braves 3
April 19, 1943: Braves 6, Red Sox 1
April 15, 1944: Red Sox 3, Braves 2
April 15, 1945: Red Sox 6, Braves 5
April 12, 1946: Red Sox 11, Braves 5
April 13, 1946: Braves 7, Red Sox 3
April 14, 1946: Red Sox 19, Braves 5
April 13, 1947: Red Sox 7, Braves 7 (tie, 16 innings)
April 17, 1948: Red Sox 2, Braves 1
April 18, 1948: Braves 3, Red Sox 2
April 16, 1949: Red Sox 5, Braves 2
April 17, 1949: Red Sox 4, Braves 3
April 18, 1949: Red Sox 6, Braves 2
April 16, 1950: Red Sox 3, Braves 1[9]
April 15, 1951: Red Sox 6, Braves 3
April 12, 1952: Red Sox 12, Braves 7
April 13, 1952: Red Sox 2, Braves 1
April 11, 1953: Red Sox 4, Braves 1
April 12, 1953: Braves 4, Red Sox 1

As noted above, it was the Milwaukee Braves who played the Red Sox at Fenway in two 1953 preseason games, the last two times any Braves team played preseason games in Boston. Total: 35 games. Note that from 1936 through 1940 the Braves were known as the Boston Bees.

In-season exhibition games between the Braves and Red Sox at Fenway Park:

July 10, 1945: Red Sox 8, Boston Braves 1
July 11, 1949: Red Sox 6, Boston Braves 2
July 22, 1957: Milwaukee Braves 13, Red Sox 4
July 20, 1959: Milwaukee Braves 7, Red Sox 3
August 21, 1961: Milwaukee Braves 4, Red Sox 1
June 3, 1963: Red Sox 5, Milwaukee Braves 2
June 6, 1966: Red Sox 5, Atlanta Braves 3

Interleague games with the Braves at Fenway:

1997: August 29 (Braves 9, Red Sox 1); August 30 (Braves 15, Red Sox 2); August 31 (Braves 7, Red Sox 3)

1999: July 9 (Red Sox 5, Braves 4); July 10 (Braves 2, Red Sox 1 in 11 innings); July 11 (Braves 8, Red Sox 1)

2000: July 7 (Braves 5, Red Sox 3); July 8 (Braves 5, Red Sox 1); July 9 (Red Sox 7, Braves 2)

2001: July 6 (Braves 6, Red Sox 5 in 10 innings); July 7 (Red Sox 3, Braves 1); July 8 (Braves 8, Red Sox 0)

2002: June 28 (Braves 4, Red Sox 2); June 29 (Braves 2, Red Sox 1); June 30 (Braves 7, Red Sox 3 in 10 innings)

2005: May 20 (Red Sox 4, Braves 3); May 21 (Braves 7, Red Sox 5); May 22 (Red Sox 5, Braves 2)

2007: May 19 (Braves 13, Red Sox 3 and Red Sox 14, Braves 0); May 20 (Red Sox 6, Braves 3)

2009: June 19 (Braves 8, Red Sox 2); June 20 (Red Sox 3, Braves 0); June 21 (Red Sox 6, Braves 5)

2012: June 22 (Braves 4, Red Sox 1); June 23 (Red Sox 8, Braves 4); June 24 (Red Sox 9, Braves 4)

More than once, the Braves thought about moving permanently to Fenway

Bob Brady of the Boston Braves Historical Association explains: "Fenway Park had appeal to the Braves' ownership over the years because of a number of factors. The club's anemic attendance was a mismatch in the larger-capacity stadium; the field's spacious Deadball Era design, despite frequent modifications, proved unappealing to current fandom; and the economically struggling ballclub was faced with the additional expense of having to rent its ballpark from the estate of the park's original builder, James E. Gaffney."

The Braves owner from 1923-35, Judge Emil Fuchs, was perpetually battling to stay afloat, and at one point sought to modify Braves Field to capitalize on the legalization of dog racing in Massachusetts. The Gaffney Estate, in turn, was rumored to be considering ousting the Braves and leasing the park to the Boston Kennel Club. For either scheme to work, the Tribe would need to utilize Fenway Park for home baseball games. The kibosh was put on such plans when Tom Yawkey's reaction was reported along the lines of "Over my dead body."

Post-mortems conducted by Boston's sports scribes after the departure of the Braves to Milwaukee revealed further attempts by the National League franchise to access Fenway Park. The *Boston Globe*'s Clif Keane contended that there had been four substantive approaches over the years: by Judge Fuchs in 1934, by Bob Quinn in the late 1930s, by Quinn's son John in 1947, and by Lou Perini the following season. John Quinn's encounter seemed to sum up Yawkey's philosophy toward sharing Fenway Park with his senior circuit neighbor. Quinn quoted the Sox owner's explanation of his rejection of the request: "I'm a funny person. What's mine is mine and I don't let anybody else have any part of it." Perini met with Yawkey the following season and received a firm turndown. As a result, Perini went on to purchase Braves Field from the Gaffney Estate in 1950.

In direct contrast to Keane, Gerry Hern of the *Boston Post* headed a column, "Why Did Perini Refuse Fenway." Hern previously had achieved a bit of baseball writing immortality when he penned the so called "Spahn and Sain and Pray for Rain" ode in a September 14, 1948, *Post* piece. Hern's contention was that Yawkey had made a "kind offer" to Lou Perini to allow the Braves

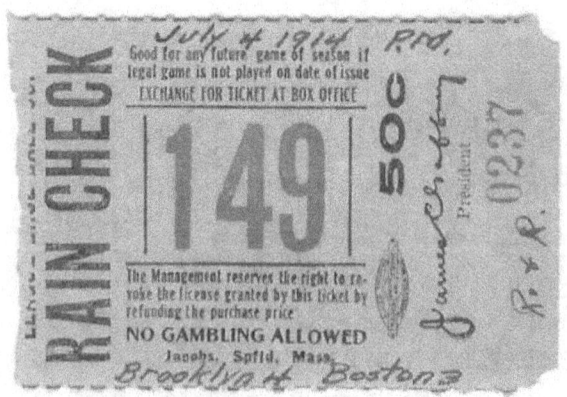

Stub to July 4 Braves games, at Fenway. The Braves lost both games and remained in last place, 15 games out of first.

to use Fenway Park in 1953 and that Perini had turned it down.

One has to wonder whether the alleged gesture was anything more than a publicity move after the inevitable forces leading to the franchise shift had been unleashed. Yawkey and his fellow owners wanted to thwart Bill Veeck's attempts to move his Browns and to force the maverick owner out of the national pastime. Political forces, especially emanating from Wisconsin, posed a potential threat to the antitrust exemption enjoyed by the Lords of Baseball.

In addition, the Braves had had African Americans on their roster since 1950, when Sam Jethroe integrated baseball in Boston. The "Jet," along with Jackie Robinson and Marvin Williams, had been unceremoniously ushered from Fenway Park after a questionable "tryout" by the Red Sox in 1945; they never heard back from the Sox. Bill Bruton and Jim Pendleton had made the Braves team in '53 and other minorities (such as Hank Aaron, Wes Covington, and Felix Mantilla) were quickly advancing in the minors. To allow the Braves onto Fenway's turf might have led to added and unwanted pressure on the Red Sox owner from local politicians and the public to follow suit.

Bob Brady continues: "Considering a 'what if' the Braves had received and accepted the offer reported by Hern and played at Fenway, I suspect that the tenancy would have been relatively short. The success of the Braves would have proven an embarrassment to Yawkey, who was dealing with a ballclub in decline despite the presence of an aging Ted Williams. Had the Braves bought themselves a little more time in Boston, Perini, with his successful construction contracting business, may very well have sought to follow the country's postwar population shift from the cities to the suburbs and sought a site just outside of Boston with sufficient room to build a modern stadium with adequate parking. Yawkey, who had grumbled about his aging facility in the past, might have been forced into a similar move or become a tenant of the Braves!

Notes

1. Glenn Stout breaks down Fenway's seated capacity as 11,400 grandstand seats, 8,000 in the pavilion, and 5,000 in the center-field bleachers. Standing room could accommodate another 2,500 patrons and more. Glenn Stout, *Fenway 1912* (Boston: Houghton Mifflin, 2011), 95, 96. Fans were sometimes packed in the outfield itself, restrained by heavy ropes.
2. *Boston Globe*, February 25, 1913.
3. http://www.baseball-almanac.com/teams/bravatte.shtml
4. A pennant race makes a huge difference, however; it wasn't until 1930 that the Braves topped their 1914 home attendance.
5. The July 10, 1945, game was a replacement for the All-Star Game, which was canceled that year because of World War II travel restrictions. Instead, some teams (including the Braves and Red Sox) played exhibition games with nearby teams.
6. For some reason, the Braves batted last in this game, and thus did not need to bat in the bottom of the ninth.
7. This game marked Babe Ruth's return to Boston in a Boston uniform. The Babe was now playing for the Boston Braves.
8. This was Ted Williams's first appearance in a game at Fenway Park.
9. Braves rookie Sam Jethroe played in the game, the first time he had played on the Fenway field since the 1946 tryout with Jackie Robinson and Marvin Williams, widely considered a sham, to become the first African American player on the Red Sox. Ted Williams' eighth-inning three-run homer won the game; Jethroe was 0-for-4. At the end of the season he was named National League Rookie of the Year.

Photograph of 1914 World Series at Fenway.

The Kisselkar Sign

THE ADVERTISEMENT APPEARED in a 1914 Boston Braves World Series program which was reproduced in 1979. Bob Brady of the Boston Braves Historical Association notes that it documents a Braves player's unique accomplishment during one of the games the team played at Fenway Park in 1914. He says, "The Kisselkar sign and offer would seem to be the granddaddy of Ebbets Field's famous Abe Stark 'Hit Sign, Win Suit' outfield wall adornment and Jordan's Furniture's recent 'Monster Hit' promotions at Fenway."

Bob further informs us that the Kissel Motor Company was based in Hartford, Wisconsin and operated by founder Louis Kissel and his sons George and William from 1906-31. The company had a reputation for manufacturing finely crafted vehicles, and both actor Fatty Arbuckle and aviatrix Amelia Earhart were among those who owned Kissel Kars. The company reorganized in 1931 and went on to produce outboard motors. Today, 940 Commonwealth Avenue is home to Boston University's Center for Psychiatric Rehabilitation and across the street from the Agganis Arena.

Twenty-five dollars was a fair amount of money relative to ballplayer salaries in 1914. Per capita income in the United States that year was $377.

Ballplayer salaries seemed paltry by comparison to today's, but a major-league ballplayer (and many in other leagues, including some of the industrial leagues and more popular semipro leagues) were often above the average. The highest salary that year was purported to be Tris Speaker's $18,000. He'd made $9,000 the year before. Very few players had reached five figures before the launch of the Federal League in 1914, there was greater competition to sign or retain the better ballplayers and salaries peaked in 1914 and 1915. Most players in 1914 made a lot less, with the average perhaps just under $2,500. This was still well above the $377 national average per capita income — but $25 was still a considerable sum.

Ford reduced the prices of their 1914 touring cars to $490 in August 1914. Kissel Kars cost considerably more, priced at $1,850. But $25 was not a trivial sum, and boosting the offer to $50 was obviously better. One

"RED" SMITH
Boston's Third Baseman

$50.00 TO ANY PLAYER HITTING THE KISSELKAR SIGN IN LEFT FIELD

"Red" Smith got $25.00 for hitting the sign Sept. 22nd before we changed the offer from $25.00 to $50.00.

THE KISSELKAR—NEW ENGLAND BRANCH
GEORGE H. LAWRENCE   F. B. HOLMES
940 COMMONWEALTH AVENUE

"EVERY INCH A CAR"

COME UP AND SEE THESE WONDERFUL CARS

would think that a player hitting the sign would have attracted some attention in the press. Of the four major Boston newspapers, only one mentioned it in its game story—the *Boston Journal*. The *Globe*, the *Herald*, and the *Post* all noted that Smith's ball had struck the wall, that he'd made a double on the hit and driven in the eighth and final run in the 8-2 win over Pittsburg. It was a six-hitter for Lefty Tyler. Smith's hit came off Pittsburg reliever Erv Kantlehner. It was quite a drive. The *Herald* said, "Red Smith was the afternoon's chief swatsman, getting two singles, topped off with a double that hit [the] left field fence fully 20 feet from the ground, and hit it so hard that 'twas a wonder the ball didn't go right through the boards." The *Globe* explained that Smith's well-struck ball went "crashing into the advertising boards in left."

But only the *Journal*'s R. E. McMillin noted the extra significance of Smith's seventh-inning smash. McMillin wrote, "Whitted walked and Schmidt sacrificed. Smith thereupon hit a left field sign offer [sic] $25 for a bang that nicked that particular spot and took two bases on the money wallop."

The Red Sox were on the road, in Detroit, and Ray Collins pitched two complete games against the Tigers, winning 5-3 and 3-0.

The Trail Blazers In Indian File

By R. E. M.

No. 1—J. Carlisle (Red) Smith

You may talk of golden sunsets
    In the wild uncharted West,
Where the far horizon flashes
    Like a turkey's crimson crest.
You may talk of nights that follow,
    Black as charcoal, grim and weird –
That's the way it is in Brooklyn
    Since J. Carlisle disappeared.

There's the sunset, Titian scarlet,
    Peeping out beneath his hat;
But there's also pennant sunshine
    In the flashing of his bat.
And when night fell over Brooklyn
    And the Robins roosted low,
Boston heard his morning bugle
    Screaming out a two-base blow.

You may boost your brunette beauties,
    Rave about some other blondes;
Here's a bloke whose bashful cudgel
    To a pennant cry responds,
And to carve in magic symbols
    Up and down Fame's monolith,
Sterling deeds and diamond virtues
    Of a red-haired guy named Smith.

    —*Boston Journal*, September 11, 1914.

No. 2—Harry [sic] (Hank) Gowdy

When Bill James shoots a fast one, or Rudolph bends a hook,
Or Tyler shows us something that was never in the book;
The Iron Duke, accoutred in armor and all that,
Grabs up whatever remnants may trickle by the bat;
His strong arms grip the willow and bust the crashing blow,
His name's a family by-word clear out to Buffalo.
We read of old Columbus. To him we tip the cap,
But here's the bloke who really put Columbus on the map.

    —*Boston Journal*, September 12, 1914.

No. 3—Josh Devore

He lernt his diamond law down there with Jawn McGraw,
His name's Joshuway alwaysthere Devore.
He knows a thing'er two, yes, ye bet yer life he do,
Jawn knows, too, what he didn't know before.
    Yes, we swan he must be getting' on.
    Smoke up, Napoleon, and see who's here.
    Not young Josh, ain't nobody else, b' gosh,
    Jus' come to tell you that it ain't yer year.
Jown sent Joshuway down to Philadelphiay.
Josh had lernt to be a howlin' swell.
Wandered round a little bit, Stallings needed him a bit.
Kinda likes the boy cause he fights like—well.
    Now, we swan, McGraw must be getting' on,
    Smoke up, Napoleon, and look whos' here.
    Not young Josh, little guy you canned, b'gosh,
    Over here to tell ya that it ain't yer year.

    —*Boston Journal*, September 14, 1914.

No. 4—Joe Connolly

Not to boost, nor yet to knock it,
There's a place they call Woonsocket
    (If they let it off as easy when they speak of it at all).
It was there some years ago, we
Discovered littly Joey,
    In his little bib and rompers hard at work at playing ball.
Now Woonsocket's in Rhode Island,
State of sandy beach and highland,
    Where the trains have time to whistle, when they through the landscape pass.
East to west it's just a single,

North to south a two-base bingle –
    Little Joey's hits broke windows in the town of Brockton, Mass.
When they found they couldn't hold him
In the State, they up and told him
    That he'd have to take and beat it where there was more room to play;
So he started up the ladder,
Making big league pitchers sadder,
    But he hasn't found the lot yet where his crashing hits will stay.

    — *Boston Journal*, September 15, 1914.

No. 5 — Johnny Evers

Above the schooroom's stifled hum
    The hist'ry teacher's voice arises;
In steady flow the questions come,
    To meet each pupil's vague surmises –
Who founded Rome? Who built the Sphinx?
    Who slammed the Persians in the gizzard?
In vain the class just sits and thinks,
    And wracks its brains from A to Izzard.

At last upon each girl and boy
    The teacher frowns exasperation;
And shouts, "How did the Greeks beat Troy?"
    Behold their utter consternation.
A moment blank. A frightened pause.
    A voice breaks through its fear-embargo:
Please, miss, the Trojans lost because
    They traded Evers to Chicago!"

Inventor of the keystone pad,
    No man's a greater fan than I am.
I take my hat off to the lad
    Who links your greater fame with Priam.
Methinks I, too, can hear him call,
    When Troy was full of base deceivers –
"My kingdom for some inside ball,
    Odds bodkins, wherethehell is Evers?"

    — *Boston Journal*, September 16, 1914.

No. 6 — Larry Gilbert

The clams that roam the bounding sea,
    And all our conversations parry,
Are noisy, boist'rous as can be,
    Compared to Larry.

His loudest song's a two-base slam,
    His game is tight and scrappy;
He holds the secret, why a clam
    Is always happy.

Which is, not bland and solemn sleep
    As is advanced by science filberts –
But just because his game is deep –
    And so is Gilbert's.

    — *Boston Journal*, September 17, 1914.

No. 7 — Bill James

Ed Walsh, Apollo Belvidere,
    Adonis — devil with the dames –
Take off your crowns, for see who's here
    Who else but Curveless William James.
Curveless? Well, so we once had read,
    And speak now rather by the book;
Although we mind that it is said
    That Bill has gone and got the hook.

But whether with a hook or not,
    He spins the onion at the foe,
His stuff can surely hit the spot,
    Cut off the run and smear the blow.
Apollo and Adonis may
    Have had the edge for classic curve –
It's thirty-five to one that they
    Weren't one, two, three with Bill for nerve.

    — *Boston Journal*, September 18, 1914.

No. 8 — Leslie Mann

Swifter than Cobb in his uttermost striving.
    Bursting like shrapnel upon the deep plan,
Here is the base of our leaders' contriving,
    The speed and the nerve and the prowess of mann.

Bucking the line, the first wall of the Giants,
    Steadfastly plugging he plows through the ruck;
Casting aside all the dope and the science,
    Trusting to Mann and his old-fashioned luck.

    — *Boston Journal*, September 19, 1914.

No. 9 — George Tyler

The starboard stars are shining bright –
    Big Bill and Fordham Dick –
And in the glory of their light,
    We lamp above the teeming fight
A broad sure pathway to the right –
    A pennant on our Stick.

But brighter still, it seems to me,
    Our port start rides the swell
With steady motion swift and free,
    The cross-fire hook across the knee,
The smoky shoot that tells us he –
    Is THERE and "All Is Well."

    — *Boston Journal*, September 21, 1914.

No. 10 — Little Dick Crutcher

He doesn't tower above the jam,
    Like Falkenberg or Splinters Sallee.
He is not Big Bill James to stand
    Like young Adonis up an alley.
But when a foreign batter squints
    Along the line to find this Crutcher –
If ever he has been in Dutch –
    Then he's in dutcher.

An iron arm and steely heart
    And just enough to sort of mold them
Together into one small frame;
    To tie them up and sort of hold them –
But when the umpire heralds forth
This stately, magic name of Crutcher,
Forget the stuff of greater stars –
    This guy is mucher.

    — *Boston Journal*, pg. 8, September 22, 1914.

No. 11 — Herbert Moran

When you talk to Johnny Evers, to be sure, it's Captain John –
    Cap — Cap — Captain of the leaders of the race –
When you write to Mister Stallings you just tack his titles on,
    And you always call him boss up to his face;
But when the Boston wrecking crew starts out to slam a guy,
Picks up its nimble Louisvilles with murder in the eye,
Starts out to massacre the stuff some hurler whizzes by,
    Then, behold, another leader takes his place.

Oh, his bat lies on his shoulder like a steeple upside down –
    Bat, bat, bat that looks bigger than the man –
And the visor of his helmet's at an angle from the crown
    As he's squinting up the alley from his post beside the pan;
He isn't any Lashaway in stature pose or size,
He isn't built like Tyrus Cobb, though he has Tyrus' eyes,
And when he pipes that fast one he just nails it on the rise,
And the wrecking crew just follows up Moran.

    — *Boston Journal*, September 23, 1914.

No. 12 — George Whitted

One-half of Hubbard Squash Perdue
As we recall it went for you –
That's why the Squash with swelling chest
Goes round and lays it on the rest;
And why the folks in Gallatin
When winter once in truth sets in
Are bound to hear an oft told tale
Of how old Hub is sure a whale.
"Hey, look at me," we hear him say
At almost any time of day.
"Feel of my arm, size up my eye,
Forget that yarn that I've gone by
Or Stallings thought I was a dub.

He swapped me for a whole league club
For Whitted with his glove and bat
Is sure about exactly that."
Which we contend ourselves is true
For if you're half of Hub Perdue
To this plain fact we are committed
That Hub is surely not half Whitted.

— *Boston Journal*, September 24, 1914.

No. 13 — George Davis

We look away across the years –
Long, sorry years of fallen hopes –
To where another flag appears,
Gay tugging at its South End ropes,
Beneath the towering flagpole tall,
Close clustered stands a happy throng –
Kid Nichols, Tenney, Duffy, Stahl,
Old Bobby Lowe and Herman Long,
Among them, too, there stands at rest
A high-brow youth of well knit frame,
Who sports the "Boston" on a chest
That once set forth a fairer name;
A lad who earned another crown
On fields of academic thrills,
And brought his skill and prowess down
Resplendent from the Berkshire Hills.

For Lewis, in the olden days,
We sang our songs and cheered our cheers.
We twined him with the victor's bays
And dinned our praises in this ears,
Of doughty heart, the Dartmouth grad,
Old Harvard breeds the classic dome,
And yet it takes a Williams lad
To go and bring the bacon home.

— *Boston Journal*, September 25, 1914.

No. 14 — Teddy Cather

Who made the countryside resound
In thunderings from shore to shore?
Who slipped from mouth to mouth
The classic name of Theodore?
Who wiped the sward up with his foes
And towered above with sweeping slather?
Who made the Big Stick's fame secure?
T. Roosevelt?
  No.
    T. Cather.

— *Boston Journal*, September 26, 1914.

No. 15 — Richard (Dick) Rudolph

Since when the world was in the rough
    A prophet's been a bum at home;
His neighbors couldn't see his stuff,
    They twined no laurels on his dome,
But dished him out the icy stare
Until he went away from there.

So there beside the Hudson's flow,
    Young Richard rudolph bent his slants
When all the world was young, you know,
    And e'er he'd grown to adult pants;
He had the smoke, but in the Bronix
His folks gave him the heart of onyx.

A turn-down here, a turn-down there
    They couldn't see him not at all.
The good McGraw with indly air
    Declared the kid was too small;
The neighbors put him on the hummer,
"That boy," they said, "should be a plumber."

But now upon Manhattan's streets
    The rooters swing the merry sledge
They tell of their young Richard's feats
    That gave the Braves the bulging edge,
"McGraw?" they cry! "Say, spill some more.
I think I've heard that name before."

"An erring boss, a boob, a hisk,"
    They rave, but in their heart declare,

"The boy for us is Fordham Dick,
   "I always knew that Kid was there.
"He always was a pitcher; sure
"I was his friend when he was poor."

Which goes to show, no matter where or what the frame,
New York claims always high, low, jack and game.

— *Boston Journal*, pg. 8, September 28, 1914.

No. 16 — Walter J. (Rabbit) Maranville

When David slung his sling-shot three times around his head,
Then let it go with all his might he knocked Goliath dead.
Behind crouched his people, stiff in mortal dread and terror,
But when he rung the bell they cried "He never makes an error.
   We'll keep our optics on that guy,
   He'll be a wonder, by and by."

When little Jack went down the pike and slew the ogre grim,
His mother waited at the gate for further news of him.
At last he came. She cried for joy, for she had feared the worst.
Said Jack, quite modest, "'T was a cinch. I offered at the first."
   Whereat his mother said, "I'll bet
   That kid will hit four hundred, yet."

So runs the tale of little guys in story, song and science.
The runts that take their nerve in hand and put it onto Giants.
Small wonder, too, that from the past the fans acquire the habit
Of looking forward years ahead whene'er they see the Rabbit,
   And passing 'round the sapient word –
   "When he grows up he'll be a bird."

— *Boston Journal*, September 29, 1914.

No. 17 — Gene Cocreham

Behind the far-flung skirmish line
The rescue warriors wait and hope,
Warm up their hook and spitters fine
And study uup the autumn dope.
Unless some star may get the gate,
Their daily task is warming benches,
And yet they also serve who wait
With rifles loaded in the trenches,
And burst with eager zest upon the scene
Ato stop a rally — same as Gene.

— *Boston Journal*, September 30, 1914.

No. 18 — "Chuck" Deal

The charley horse of Charley Deal
Might be the subject of this spiel,
A painful subject without doubt
To weave a tuneful lay about –
   You know just how we feel.

Much better then it were, we wot
To tell how on the corner hot
This wounded soldier risked his neck –
The deal lay upon the burning deck –
   Like Johnny on the Spot.

Moreover, too, it seems to us,
That as we lamp the season's fuss,
For once without a hint of frame
Here is a Deal that's also game –
   A deuced plucky cuss.

— *Boston Journal*, October 1, 1914.

No. 19 — Paul Strand Of Spokane

Here is no foreign Strand –
   Nor yet a Red Sox Shore –
But one whose native land
   Awaits the daily score.
No toll of battles grim,
   But yield of willow staves –
The great Northwesst cries, "What of him,
   OUR hero of the Braves!"

— *Boston Journal*, pg. 11, October 2, 1914.

No. 19 — Bert Whaling

Here is a guy that you'd naturally think
Would be out on the ocean, the blue bounding drink –
For if ever a name had a salt sailor twang
As well as a hint of sperm hunter's gang –
    It's Whaling.

But this is just where your dope is skewgee;
This bloke, notwithstanding, is never at sea,
And the handle you think has a strong saline tang
Is merely the echo of some crashing bang –
    He's whaling.

For whaling on sea and whaling on land
Is something quite different, as you'll understand
If you ever stand by when he hammers the spud
And send it to left with a dull sickening thud –
    Some whaling.

    — *Boston Journal*, pg. 11, October 3, 1914.[1]

No. 20 — Oscar Dugey

Down on the plains of Texas, where the Lone Star banner waves,
The Rangers put their guns in hock to wager on the Braves;
And up along the Rio Grande across the sun-baked plain
A hundred thousand throats send forth this old war-time refrain
    What will Dugey do to them?
    He will not do a thing to them.
    Does Dugey fear the Mackmen?
        NO!
    He ain't afraid of h---l!

    — *Boston Journal*, October 5, 1914.

No. 21 — Otto Hess

When Noah built the blooming ark and set it on the tide
He saw that all the pasengers were snug and taut inside;
Then straightway pushed the yachtlet off into the raging stream,
When little Ham and Japhet set up an awful scream:
"Oh, farther dear, don't hasten yet upon the briny mess.
What will our happy fam'ly be without old Otto Hess?"
Old Noah liked to please the kids. He poled the bark to shore,
Old Otto climbed the for'ard deck. The boat was launched once more.
And out it hove upon the deep, across the bounding waves,
And saved, so we have often heard, our Otto for the Braves.

    — *Boston Journal*, October 6, 1914.

No. 22 — Charlie Schmidt

If you ever saw a walrus that could do ten seconds flat,
Or an elephant that threw a half a mile;
If you met a hippopotamus that pegged them like a gat,
It's a lead pipe cinch you'd have to crack a smile,
And while your merry laughter was ripping off a gale
Why then we'd show you Charlie Schmidt
You watch him run and hurl and hidt
And then you cry — we'll bet on idt –
Take all the rest away, this guy's a whale.

    — *Boston Journal*, October 7, 1914.

Der Landsturm

When the King's Own shot to pieces
When the King's Own's shot pieces
And the Royal Guard is smashed
And the first line of defenses
Shows where foemen's lead has crashed
Then behold the Landsturm standing
Ready there to do or die
But they'll never beat the Mackmen
We won't need their help — that's why.

    — *Boston Journal*, October 8, 1914.

Notes

1   Note: the *Journal* itself ran two No. 19s.

The Story of the 1914 Braves

by George Stallings

NOTE: His son George Stallings Jr. did some of the illustrations.

From late November 1914 and through January 31, 1915, Braves manager George Stallings wrote for yet a third newspaper—a series of ten columns which recounted the season and the World Series with a bit more perspective.

It's rare to be able to read such detailed comments from a major-league manager so quickly after a World Series win. Although the series was obviously written by a sportswriter collaborating with Stallings, and although the manager was never going to give away any true secrets, it does give us a detailed look at the 1914 season nominally from the winning skipper's point of view.

How much of this was truly written by Stallings himself is difficult to know. It was common enough at the time for people actually involved in the games to have bylined articles in the newspapers. During the Series itself, Johnny Evers had a column going and so did Christy Mathewson. Oddly, Stallings also had a daily column during the games—more than one of them! The *Boston Post* featured a daily column by Stallings during the World Series, and so did the *Boston Herald*! A different bylined account in each paper. You'd have to wonder about the questions of exclusivity, and how much time Stallings would have had left to prepare for the games if he were writing columns for two different daily (and competing) newspapers in Boston.

Of some additional interest, the *Boston Traveler* had a daily column written by "X." The explanation? "The articles are written by a veteran big league player and scout, whose intimate connection with the game makes it advisable to sign the articles 'By X.'"

These articles by George Stallings ran in the *Boston Globe*, beginning on November 28, 1914—a little over a month after the World Series had ended. The same series ran in the *New York Tribune*, and perhaps other newspapers as well.

Part One—November 29, 1914

STALLINGS' OWN STORY OF HOW HE MADE WORLD'S CHAMPIONS OUT OF THE BRAVES

Famous "Miracle Man" in a Series of Articles, to Tell the Boston Fans How He Took Hold of a "Misfit outfit" and Developed World Beaters in Two Seasons

Evolution of a "Baseball Horror" Into a Powerful Machine Through the Genius of a Great Manager

By GEORGE T. STALLINGS
Manager of the Boston Braves

The first look I had at the Boston club after I knew that I was to manage it was late in the season of 1912, when the team was playing a series with the Giants at the Polo Grounds in New York under the leadership of John Kling, the old Cub catcher.

I came down from Buffalo after the close of the International League season to get an idea of the team I was to manage. As I sat in the grandstand with James E. Gaffney, the owner of the club, and sized it up, I could think only of one expression which fitted the team.

"It is a baseball horror," I kept repeating over and over to myself. In the meantime, of course, Mr. Gaffney was not aware of my thoughts or the impression that his club was making on me.

"What do you think of this team?" he suddenly asked me. "Well," I replied, "I guess we will have to make some changes."

"You are the absolute boss of the playing end of the club," he answered. "Run it as if the club were your own and as if your own money were at stake."

That sounded good to me, and it was the first flash of sunshine that I had discovered in connection with my new job. I might add right here that Mr. Gaffney has made good on his promise not to interfere, that I have had an absolutely free rein in managing the playing end of the club.

As an indication of how all-embracing was the task of rebuilding the team, I want to point that, of the men who came under my charge when the club was turned over to me immediately after the close of the 1912 season, Tyler and Hess, both pitchers, are the only two who remain.

It has always been my misfortune, if you care to look at it that way, to have completely down-and-out teams wished on me to manage. I have ever displayed a marvelous aptitude for getting hold of baseball wrecks. But when I looked over the Boston team on that to me memorable September afternoon at the Polo Grounds I knew that I had reached the limit.

Never Saw Anything Look Quite So Bad

I have had considerable experience around ball teams; l I have devoted 25 years of my life to baseball in one capacity or another, but I have never seen any club in the big leagues look quite so bad. The players were slow, ambitionless, careless and incapable. The thing which impressed me most was the absolute lack of spirit, the team taking the breaks in the game as they came along without any effort to crowd its opponents when openings presented themselves or to rally and stave off defeat when pushed.

Any baseball man in my position would have realized at once that the team must be revolutionized completely, so to that end, as soon as the season closed and I took over the management, I began to purchase, dicker and swap. Understand, I am not complaining over my lot. To me there is a certain fascination in taking a decrepit hope and making it a winner, the fascination of solving a puzzle. But I have run a little ahead of my story, which, I suppose, should begin at the beginning.

In 1912 James E. Gaffney and John M. Ward had taken over the Boston club, and John Kling was the manager. With the fortunes of the team falling as the season progressed, Mr. Ward desired to sell out his stock, and Mr. Gaffney agreed to purchase it if he could be assured of securing me to manage the club, To this end he made two trips to Buffalo, where I was managing the International League team in that city, to talk over his proposition with the owners of the Buffalo club and me. These visits occurred in August.

Naturally, I was eager to get back into the big league, for the overwhelming ambition of my life ever since I have been connected with baseball has been to win a world's championship, and it is impossible to win a world's championship in a minor league. In all my experience as manager I have had only two contracts, one with the New York American League team, the other with the Boston club. In every other instance I have served without a scrap of paper between the club owners and me. However, I have owned stock in several minor league teams. Therefore, it would have been easy for me to have blown out of Buffalo without a word if I had wanted to do it that way. But I didn't, and the owners of the club were very fine in giving me my opportunity to leave and not attempting to stand in my way. The deal for me to go to Boston was fixed up in August, but no contract was signed by Mr. Gaffney and me until after the close of the 1912 season. Both of us felt that it would not be fair to John Kling, then the Boston manager, for the announcement to be made that another would take his place while he was still the active boss, and would have to remain in charge of the club, aware that he was slated to go.

Different Ideas From Some

I think I have a little different ideas from some of the other managers on how a ball club should be conducted and I started to apply these as soon as I took hold in Boston. Of course, I could not begin to build up the spirit of the team until I actually had the players together in their uniforms at Spring practice, and I deem the spirit of a club to be one of its most important aspects. Spirit did a good deal toward beating the Athletics in the World's Series.

I have always contended that the secret of building a ball club is in making a team out of what you have in hand and then trading and purchasing and drafting to strengthen the flaws when the opportunities bob up. Many managers believe that as soon as they take charge of a club they must go out and buy ball players who have good records right and left. I don't believe that a baseball machine which will eventually be successful can be purchased in these days. It must be carefully constructed, piece by piece.

Gowdy and Mitchell

My first two acts after I took hold of the Boston club were to send Gowdy to Buffalo for a year, which was one of the agreements made when the owners of Buffalo gave me permission to go to Boston, and to sign Fred Mitchell.

The sending of Gowdy to Buffalo proved to be a very lucky move for me, because it gave the tall catcher a chance to work every day under the watchful and keen eye of Clymer, the manager who succeeded me in Buffalo and who did a lot toward developing Hank. He was returned to me a much improved man.

I picked up Mitchell, the veteran catcher, who had been with me with the Yankees and in Buffalo, because I thought that I might as well begin to build at the bottom and get some brains on the club. Mitchell is the greatest man in his line, to my way of thinking, at developing young pitchers. There is not a better one in the country for teaching a youngster the "balk motion," which is very valuable, in fact, almost essential, to the successful boxman.

Perhaps all of my readers may not fully comprehend what I mean by the "balk motion," so I will devote a little space to explanation. When a base runner steals second or third you will frequently hear the fans in the stands roasting the catcher for permitting the steal. As often as not it is the pitcher's fault for not watching the runner and holding him up. If a runner gets the jump — by which I mean a good start — the most perfect throw in the world from a catcher will not nail

Manager, and author, George Stallings.

him at second. Once a pitcher begins his motion toward the batter, the base runner has the right to start. If a pitcher begins his motion, sees out of the tail of his eye that the runner is starting, and then throws to first base, the runner is given the base anyway, as a penalty on the pitcher for balking.

Difficult Move to Acquire

A good "balk motion" means that the pitcher makes the runner believe that he is starting his motion to the batter in order to bait the runner off the bag, but the pitcher does not go far enough with it so that the umpire can call a balk. In other words, the boxman comes as near making a balk as he can without actually committing one. It is a difficult move to acquire and needs much patience and practice to learn.

If a pitcher gets a reputation for having a good move toward first base, the runners will hang close to that bag and few bases will be stolen. Without the jump, it is almost impossible to steal a base, and a runner on second in a close game is very much more dangerous than one on first. It takes more than a single to score him from first. Usually, a one-base blow will do it from second.

Eddie Plank is one of the few starts who has not a good move toward first, but his natural position in the box—he is a left-hander and so directly faces the runner on first—offsets this to a great extent.

Therefore, I signed Mitchell for his ability to handle the pitchers and teach them the "balk motion" and other tricks of the trade. Mitch has a world of patience in training young pitchers, and they all love him. Any time a youngster says, "Come on. Let's warm up a little," Mitchell slips on the big glove and takes the pitcher off to a corner of the lot where they can be alone and none can overhear his comments. Then he talks to the man quietly about his faults, never getting after him roughly and discouraging him. He leaves that "rough stuff" to me. Mitchell makes Job look irascible when it comes to patience. To him I give the credit for the present Boston pitching staff, because of his careful handling and advising. I think I have not gone too far when I have called Mitch my right eye. No ball club can have much success without a good pitching staff. Mitchell made wonders out of Rudolph, James, and Tyler. He did more with Tyler than any one of the three.

A Year to Get James Right

Understand that I am not trying to detract from what these pitchers have done themselves, for they are all great workers in their art, but nearly every twirler requires proper handling to be developed. The usual run of pitcher is pretty raw when he first comes up to the big league. It took a year of fussing to get James right. He had worlds of "stuff" when he first came to me from the Seattle club, but he needed a lot of polishing. He was only a kid when I first got hold of him in the spring of 1913. He is but 22 years old now.

In all my experience, I have never seen a pitcher more anxious to make good than this young six-foot specimen. I almost had to take his uniform away from him to stop him pitching at the close of practice and trying what Mitchell and I had told him. He never wanted to quit working. As soon as I saw the spirit of this young giant I knew that he was bound to make good for me, because a player with this great determination and ambition is sure to produce.

"James is going to be a wonder some day," declared Mitchell to me after morning practice early in the season of 1913. Mitchell and James had had a long session that day, each working hard.

"He's going to be as sensational as Johnson when he is ripe," I predicted.

I consider James as valuable a pitcher as Walter Johnson today, and my statement is backed up by the fact that he led the National League pitchers last season and did some wonderful twirling in the World's Series when a young pitcher would be expected to lose his nerve. His feat of shutting out the veteran Eddie Plank with the hard-hitting Athletics behind Plank is something that requires nerves and the goods. James has both these in abundance.

But once more I am running ahead of my yarn.

The First Real Gem

During the Winter of 1912-13, before I ever had charge of the team in uniform, I signed Rudolph, and he was the first gem that I added to the roster of the Boston club of whose value I was aware. James I knew nothing of then. I knew of Rudolph's ability from having seen him perform with the Toronto team of the International League the preceding season. I realized then that Rudolph was sure to impress. He had been sent to Toronto by John McGraw after a brief tryout with the Giants late one Fall when he was in no condition to show his best stuff.

McGraw never cared much for small twirlers, although I have always contended that a smart man can pitch

Evers and Stallings on the Braves bench.

whether he is tall or short. However, when McGraw turned Rudolph over to his friend Joe Kelley, the manager of the Toronto club, he kept a string on him. He was not to be sold to any other Big League team except the Giants, but Rudolph was ambitious and declared to Kelley after the season of 1912 that he would quit the game unless he could get a chance in the Big League.

"I can make good," announced Rudolph. "If I can't get any higher than a minor league, then I am going to try some other profession." This stand on his part made a hit with me. I wanted a man with that ambition in him.

It was a case of losing Rudolph any way he looked at it, so Kelley put it up to McGraw. The Giants' manager was well supplied with pitchers at that time, and he agreed to let me have Rudolph. McGraw and I have always been very good friends, and he was glad to help me out in any way he could in my new job, which, I guess, he considered to be pretty hopeless at best. Thus did Rudolph come to me in that first Winter. Now I consider him in a class with Mathewson for possessing pitching brains, a high compliment.

James, Rudolph, and Tyler

With James, Rudolph, and Tyler, I knew that I had the nucleus of a pitching staff, even though I could see a good deal of work ahead before I would begin to realize on the investment. Half of successful managing is patience.

No one can expect sensational results over night, because baseball clubs are not built in that hurried way. Lack of patience is responsible for the bad showing of half the teams, and the man who usually shows it is the club owner. When you find a club owner changing managers year after year, you can be sure that he is short on patience and that he will go a long route before he will have a winning team.

Frequent changes in leadership upset the players and mean that the system and style of play are changed season after season. No team can get anywhere on this uncertain basis. Mr. Gaffney was keeping his word with me all this time and leaving me strictly alone. His patience with me has been a big factor in the successful building up of the club.

Heart to Heart Talks

When I first faced the members of the Boston team in Macon, Ga. in the Spring of 1913, I had before me a misfit outfit, but some material with which to build and which could be developed, I felt sure. As I always do, I have the players a little talk on the first day.

"You have probably heard more or less about me from members of other clubs I have handled," I told the men assembled in that room in the Macon hotel. "Now I want you to forget all that. Your informers may have 'knocked' or 'boosted.' It makes no difference to me. I want you all to found your opinions of me on what you see of me from now on.

"First, I wish to tell you that I am a strict disciplinarian, but that I won't fine any of you men. I have never taken a nickel of a player's money since I have been in baseball.

"We are all here for work and not for play. We are here to begin training for a season of hard work in which no ball game is going to be considered lost by this club until the last man is out. Everybody must bear that in mind, because it is important. And we will have a session in what I call the schoolroom every morning to go over plays."

Two of the wise players were inclined to smirk at this. I noticed this at work, because I was looking for it.

"I've had players tell me before that they have come up to the big league to play baseball and not to go to school," I continued, talking at the smirkers. "Any man who misses these morning sessions had better pack his trunk." The two smirkers, I might add, are no longer with the club.

In this fashion, in the Spring of 1913, I began being the pulmometer of the Boston club. I wouldn't know how to act if I should ever have a real ball club wished on me. And I realized that day as I never had before that I had some job on my hands.

Part Two—December 6, 1914

STALLINGS STUDIED HIS MEN FROM ALL ANGLES

"Miracle Man" Describes His System Which Made World's Champions.

Tests to Which the Material Was Subjected.

How He Proved Gameness.

Methods That Gained Confidence of Players.

"Frame Up" Which Made 'Rabbit' Maranville the Great Player He Now Is.

To me the Spring practice period is one of the busiest and most critical of the year for a ball club, for it is then that a manager must begin to get acquainted with the new men, make his selections from his flock of recruits, and start to build his team. The Spring of 1913 will always be regarded by me as the most important in my baseball career, since it was then that I faced for the first time the Boston club with which I was destined in two years' time to win a World's Championship. I would never have thought it possible at the time.

Observation will do more in the first week of Spring practice than all the instructions ever compiled. Long ago I discovered a very satisfactory process by which I could test out the steel of a recruit in the Spring. Nearly every youngster comes to a training camp full of ambition and he looks for attention from the manager.

Some of them will lose their ambition and pepper after a week or two if I ignore them entirely. Then I know that this sort of a man lacks the stuff to make a real big leaguer. But if I don't say anything to a recruit for a week or two, and he keeps fighting all the harder to make good, I know that he is the real thing and I start to work with him. He has shown he has the courage to plug away and force me to recognize him.

A young fellow came to me in that Spring of 1913 who had made a big record in the minor leagues as a pitcher, and I looked for him to be a wonder. I left him alone during the first week of the Spring training, and he seemed to sulk and that looked bad to me.

He had so much "stuff" when he got the Winter kinks out of his arm, however, that I began to coddle him a little, and I thought I might have been wrong in my preliminary diagnosis. With a little petting, he came along through Spring practice in good shape and I thought I had a find to help out my scanty collection of pitching talent. It must be borne in mind that at this time Rudolph had little or no big league experience, and Bill James was absolutely raw.

Well, this young fellow worked along and started the season with my club. Two months after the championship race had begun I let him go because he was such a temptation to me.

Perhaps that sounds like a strange reason to the ordinary follower of baseball but it is the true one. The young fellow just lacked gameness. My test, that of ignoring him in the Spring camp, had revealed this, but I had refused to be convinced and had carried him along.

Had Most Everything, But Wasn't Game

He had most everything that a successful pitcher needs. He fielded his position smoothly and possessed a good balk motion toward first base so that runners would not get any lead on him. He would warm up fine and look like a million dollars in practice, but he always weakened in the pinch.

When one pitched ball might win or lose, he would shoot it up in the "groove" and a game would be "blowed" for me. This boy would have been a Mathewson except for the one big weakness—he wasn't game. So this "temptation" of mine went back to the minors. The reason I call him a temptation is because I could not let him warm up without starting him, and, when I did put him in the box I knew he was going to blow the game unless the team stuck a lot of runs under him at the getaway. This young pitcher is dead now, but if he had lived to 1,000,000 years old he would never have been anything but a busher. So I sure saw one bright-looking prospect fade into the minors that year of 1913.

[Clearly, Stallings is describing pitcher Buster Brown.]

But I must get back to the Spring practice. At the first meeting of the players I always make it a rule to take my seat in the middle of the group and talk to them. I lay down and explain the regulations which will govern the club during the season and tell them about hotel arrangements, the conditions under which they will work, etc.

Study of Mental Capabilities

In Spring practice, one of the first things I begin to study is the mental capabilities of the players, because a smart ball player is a real gem. Nine times out of ten, I have a man's intelligence number by the end of the first week of Spring practice. During this first week there is no baseball actually played, but a good deal is talked in the "schoolroom" in front of the blackboards. The first afternoon on the field is a romp for the players to work out the Winter kinks from their muscles a little.

The club I faced that first Spring did not encourage me much, and, as I gathered the players around me, I knew it would be up to me to turn a lot of them back to the minors. Most of them were not big leaguers, and they had learned a lot of slovenly habits with the Boston team of the past.

But I had no intention of making a wholesale raid on the so-called veterans, until I could see some material in sight to take their places.

This is the mistake made by many managers when they first take hold of a tail-end club. They rip the whole team apart immediately. It is my idea to put in a man here and another there when the opportunity comes along to grab the desirable player, and to go ahead with what I have until it is possible to collect the kind of club I like. I am not a believer in stars, and I don't think a good machine can be built up by buying men with big reputations right and left. Stars, as a rule, are temperamental and hard to manage. I have made my experience with them.

As I say, when I first faced that Boston club, I knew that many of the players would have to go but it was not such a difficult task as the one which confronted me when I took charge of the Yankees and gathered such starts as Keeler, Kleinow, Elberfeld, Chesbro, and the rest of them around me and then realized that these men were fading.

It would be up to me, a manager fresh from the "bushes," to let them all out and to stand the outcry and criticism which the move was bound to arouse, since each one of these stars had a big following and was popular with the newspapers.

Fans and newspapers do not realize that a player is failing to cover as much ground as he used to as quickly as a manager does. Many old stars are very clever at hiding their weaknesses, as they begin to realize them quickly. For instance, a third baseman will shift slightly toward the bag in covering his position and give the shortstop more ground to take care of, so that the hits will not go between him and the cushion.

After Willie Keeler had gone with the Toronto team of the International League, Joe Kelley's club was playing my Buffalo outfit on Memorial Day and it so happened to the weather was warm and sultry. Willie had one of his old days, pulling down a couple off the fence, picking a line drive off his shoe laces, and covering acres of ground in the outfield. He showed up at the bat with a couple of hits which he pushed over third base, he pulled one to right field, and wound up by dropping down a bunt and beating it out. Keeler had never looked better.

"We'll win the flag sure," declared Kelley that night. "Willie Keeler had come back and is as good as he ever was."

But the weather turned cold and damp the next day, and Willie was all drawn up in a knot. Not long after that he quit the game for good, and I think the Toronto team finished seventh that season.

The Case of "Hap" Myers

After sorting out the recruits in the Spring of 1913, I came back North with a club with which I knew I could give several teams in the big league a battle and make trouble generally. For pitchers I had Hess, Buster Brown, Tyler, and Perdue. Besides, I had some youngsters, of which James and Rudolph looked best. Each needed seasoning, but James required the most. I knew that Rudolph would be able to show something for me that year.

Hap Myers was on first base, and he delivered a very good season for me. When I parted with Hap I received more criticism for the move than for any one I have made since I took hold of the club. To the public Myers had looked good, and he had helped me out that first season. But Myers would let ground balls go over that base for two-baggers that were baseball crimes.

Butch Schmidt came to the team in the Fall of 1913, and he showed me enough in that short period to warrant my parting with Myers. It was this that brought the storm of criticism upon me, but I had been looking for something better and knew that I had it after the brief glance at Schmidt in the Fall.

One reason for the knocking over this move, most of which came the following Spring, was because Schmidt is the sort of player who takes on weight in the Winter, and it is hard for him to get into condition. Last Winter he let himself get stout, but he will take care to keep his weight down this year, as I warned him about this after the World's Series, and I expect that he will be good in the Spring when we start the new campaign.

Schmidt is the surest man on a thrown ball that I have ever seen on the bag. He did not drop one last season. This steadies up an infield more than can be told on paper, for an infielder is going to let that ball go from any angle, knowing that if it reaches anywhere near first Schmidt will get it.

A little advice about his footwork around the bag and covering for different batters developed Schmidt into one of the best first basemen in the league before last season ended. Myers was sold to Rochester at the conclusion of the 1913 race and went from there to the Federal League.

Sweeney was on second base that first year, and there was never any question of Maranville winning the position of shortstop. He had shown me what he could do in the first few weeks.

What Made the "Rabbit"

I will close this installment by relating an incident which proved to be the making of Maranville.

When he started with the club as a regular in the Spring of 1913 he was a bashful kid. So Sweeney, then the captain of the team, Fred Mitchell, the veteran coach, and I framed one up on Maranville to give him a little self-confidence. It was agreed that in the "skull" practice, which is what our opponents call the morning sessions when we talk over plays in our schoolroom, Mitchell would sit next to Maranville and I should take the wrong end on a play under discussion. When, according to the arrangement, I kept insisting that the play should be made the wrong way, Maranville had nothing to say until Mitchell nudged him.

"It's your play," prompted Mitchell. "Don't let him get away with that stuff. He's wrong. Tell him so."

Maranville spoke up rather bashfully.

"I don't think that's right, Chief," he said. "It ought to be made the other way."

I stormed back and Mitch nudged him again.

"Go after him," urged the coach. "You are right. Show him up."

So Maranville replied again, a little bashfully. We argued the thing for a long time that morning and did not come to any decision. The next day we went at it again and, under Mitchell's coaching, Maranville took the other side with a little more firmness.

The play was the double steal with runners on first and third bases. The dispute was over which man, the second baseman or the shortstop, should take the short throw.

One player has to cut in for the short throw, and it is not natural for the second baseman to do it, since he can keep his eye on the runner on third and shoot the ball to the catcher of that man makes a break for the plate. If he sticks to the bag, then the ball is passed along to stop the runner going to second.

Sweeney had a bad hand that Spring and his arm was none too strong, so that he had not gotten the runner going home once. This had naturally been tipped off around the league and was losing us a lot of games. The Rabbit argued that he should cut in, since he could get the ball away quick and his speed and agility made it possible for him to take a flash at third base to see whether the runner had started.

"Well, it hasn't worked once the other way," argued Maranville, "so I don't see where you are going to lose anything by letting me take the throw."

Finally, I weakened. "Kid, I believe you are right. Try it that way if it comes up today," I told him.

As luck would have it, the play came up twice that afternoon, and both times it went through on each occasion and saved two runs. Afterward, in the clubhouse, I slapped him on the back and said, "Well, boy, you're there. I never knew before that you were a real Big Leaguer."

"I Showed Stallings Something"

This happened on Saturday. When the club is in Boston, Connolly and Maranville both leave town over Sunday to spend the holiday at their homes, and they make part of the journey together. The following Monday morning I was overseeing some outfield work when Connolly came up to me and said, "We had a lot of fun on the train Saturday night, the Rabbit and I."

"How's that, Joe?" I asked him.

"You should have heard the Rabbit."

"What did he say?" I asked.

"He said, 'Gee, I guess I didn't show that Stallings something this afternoon. I made him admit he was wrong on that play at second!'"

This incident made Maranville a different player. It was nearly the end of the season before he knew it was all a frameup, and then there was no chance of ruining him, for he was a National League sensation. The day he won the argument from me in the clubhouse and made me surrender before all the other players, he got confidence. With the confidence came his wonderful game spirit which had always been lying dormant. Today I consider Maranville the greatest players to come into the game since Cobb cracked his way into the ranks of the big leaguers.

Part Three—December 13, 1914

WORK ALL SIDE OF A PLAY FOR "PERCENTAGE"

Stallings Makes This the Clubhouse Slogan And the Practice on the Field.

Give Me a "Kid" Team If the Owners Have "Patience," Says the "Miracle Man."

How He Developed Such Material as He Had.

Athletics Did Not Discover Deal's Weakness Because It Had Been Corrected.

The team with which I opened the season of 1913 was made up largely of kids, with aging veterans scattered through it here and there. Sweeney, at second base, and Devlin, at third, were the men with big league experience in the infield, while Perdue, Tyler, and Buster Brown were the pitchers who came to me marked "seasoned." My outfield at that time was a movable feast, practically an unknown quantity from day to day.

Give me a "kid" team if the owners of a club will extend the manager a little time. I had James and Rudolph to develop as pitchers, and I knew each one would make a star if I had the opportunity to bring out the best in them. This required patience on the part of the owners. Maranville, I felt sure, would be another star, and my ideas of Rudolph, James, and Maranville were borne out by the performances of these three in the recent World's Series, as I think the members of the Athletics will testify.

As soon as I take hold of a ball club I am always with it. Where the Braves team is, there you will find Stallings. I didn't turn my morning practice over to the coach of the pitchers; I am on hand myself to talk to the players in the clubhouse at the "skull" rehearsal and to direct the plays on the field. Every player is in uniform, too, unless he can show good cause why he should not be. I do not flee away from the hotel with friends as soon as I arrive in a town, but I am around the joint with my team.

How I Would Handle "Zim"

A practice that I have always followed with fair success is to associate more with the "kids" on the club than with the veterans. Therefore, if any follower of baseball should happen to see me around our hotel when the club is on the road he will find me eating and fanning with the young fellows. I can feed a lot of baseball into them at these times when they are discussing plays and problems. I can also obtain a good line on their characters and figure the best way to handle them to get out all the baseball there is in them.

That is the real secret of success—obtaining the maximum of efficiency there is in a man—or yourself. There are many ball players on other big league clubs that I could get a lot more work out of than they show under their present arrangements. I do not say this boastfully. Some men should be "ridden," others coaxed and a few salved. They must be treated as individuals, not as a class.

For an example, take Heinie Zimmerman. Heinie, to my way of thinking, is one of the greatest natural players ever to put on a big league uniform, if not the greatest, yet he had not reached the place he should hold among start because of one weakness—his temper.

My little club could get Zim up in the air so far in two innings last Summer that he would not know whether he was afoot or a-horseback the rest of the afternoon.

If Zimmerman were on my team, one of the first things I would do would be to have the home bench back of third base, instead of having it back of first. Then the visiting team would not be in a position to keep after Zim from the bench, at least not while the club was at home. Heinie would have only friends on his side of the diamond in that case.

To show how Zim's bat follows the ball, I recall an incident in connection with a game that we were playing against the Cubs last season.

Zimmerman tried to dodge a pitched ball and cracked it over first base for a double with his head turned away. Some followers of the game would call that luck, but

I think it just goes to show how his stick follows that ball as it comes to the plate up to that last moment.

"Couldn't Close His Mouth"

Zim tells this story on himself: He became involved in an argument with Henry O'Day when the latter was umpiring the season before last, and O'Day tried to cut Zim off with this blast:

"If you say another word, I'll set you down for three days and fine you 50."

"I knew he would do it," declared Heinie, in telling me about it, "and my mouth was open when he said it. I tried to close it, but I just could not stop myself from saying: 'You old squarehead. You must be crazy.'

"I really wasn't to blame, because I tried hard not to make any crack which would get me in bad, but I just couldn't stop myself. O'Day made good and fined me the 50, and put me down for three days."

Zimmerman got back at me once last season when the race was hanging between the Giants and my club.

I am particularly superstitious, and I encourage my whole ball team to be, because I think it helps to make it a winner.

The Cubs were playing my team one afternoon late in August, and Zim knew that I always like to keep the space in front of our bench clean of any stray bits of paper. I consider it bad luck to have paper there. So he kept tearing up little bits of newspaper and scattering it over the lawn, and I had my substitutes constantly cleaning them up. They certainly had an active afternoon.

"I'm a ball player and not a ground keeper," protested Josh Devore, when I asked him to clean up the littler

"Why don't you show me, then?" I asked him.

I don't know where Zim got all the newspapers from unless he was borrowing them from friends in the stand. Take it from me, Zimmerman is a great ballplayer, and I would like to have him to handle.

Getting the Percentage

This digression on Zimmerman was the result of a remark I made that much depends on how the individual players are handled. What I try to drill into the "kids"—and the veterans, too, for that matter, although you cannot do such an awful lot with a veteran after he has become "set"

In his ways and the old ambition has begun to ooze as the result of a too long association with a tailender—is that the "percentage" is what we are all looking for.

In the vernacular of the profession, "getting the percentage" means playing everything so as to have a little something in your favor. In other words, it means that the whole game should be figured out beforehand as carefully as possible.

"Get the percentage" is our clubhouse slogan. I impress upon the men that no matter what the play is they should see that our club gets the best "percentage."

For instance, if there is a runner on first base, the batter should try to hit to right field because there is less chance of doubling the man at second, and his prospects of getting two bases on the blow if the ball should happen to fall safe are greatly improved. Another play we made very often last season and which led several managers to allege that I was crazy, was to sacrifice with a runner on first base and one out. This meant that it put a runner on second with two out and that nothing except a base hit would score him. But the move won four or five games for us last season, and four or five count for a lot if you are coming down the stretch in a tight race.

Well, when I started out that first season with the Boston club, I tried to drill into the men the necessity for getting the "percentage" as often as possible, and of how important it was to show everybody we were game. Playing tight baseball, and making every chance count, soon shakes the confidence of your opponents, and it was not long before the other managers in the league began saying. "That Boston bunch is a tough one to beat."

As soon as this report got around and back to me — as everything will do quickly through the susceptible routes of big league gossip — I knew that we were making progress. That was a sure sign.

Always Trying to Add Strength

All this time I was looking to strengthen my team, for I was naturally far from satisfied, but there was no use in blasting away the whole club, for I must try to make good with what I had at first and pick up men to fill holes as the opportunities came along.

No manager is ever satisfied with his club, even after he has won the World's Championship, and he keeps a sensitive finger constantly on its pulse. As soon as I saw a man who looked likely and who was available I would grab him and fill him in.

I got Joe Connolly after waivers had been asked on him, and he turned out to be one of the best outfielders in the league and a wicked hitter. He had the baseball in him, but no one else had gotten it out. He needed some developing and fussing with.

In 1913 the race had not progressed very far until I had my men figuring on both ends of a play before they made it.

Some managers maintain that our morning "skull" practice is foolish and that nothing can be learned in baseball except as it comes out on the field. Perhaps a few of them will have changed their minds by next year — possibly one or two are convinced that it has some slight value now. But I maintain that no play can be effectively organized unless both ends are worked out, so that the men who are to take part in it may know what their jobs are. This method has brought some success to us, anyway, and we are going to stick to it.

It was toward the latter end of my first season with the club that I drafted Deal from Providence. He had been with the Detroit team and had been turned back to the minors. He joined us during the last series of the 1913 season in Philadelphia.

Here is a man who showed his wonderful gameness when he stepped into the berth at third base for the World's Series after Red Smith had been hurt. He had been out of the game from the middle of the season when he had been injured, which led me to get Red Smith from Brooklyn, and, with Deal's recovery, he found his place too well filled for me to risk breaking up the combination by restoring him to his job with Smith tearing the cover off the ball.

Deal Stood the Test

Deal did not sulk and complain, but went to work for the team, warming up pitchers and doing the thousand and one odd jobs around a ball club which contribute so much to its success but which do not put the man's name in the box score or the newspaper headlines.

Neither did he "knock" Smith, but, on the contrary, boosted him. So when Red was hurt just before the World's Series, I did not worry, in company with the newspapers and the clubs friends over his loss. I knew what Deal could do, and that he would show his gameness. It is unnecessary for me to add that he did.

Ty Cobb has long been a good friend of mine, since we both live in Georgia and spend a part of each Winter hunting together. Notwithstanding this, Ty is very loyal to the American League. He came to see me on the morning of the first game of the World's Series in Philadelphia at my hotel.

"Are you going to play Deal at third, George?" he asked.

"I think I will," I told him.

"I know him," answered Cobb, "and he has a weakness at the bat, so that, if a pitcher pitches to him right, he will never hit the ball. I am going to tell the Athletics all I know about him, which I gathered while he was with our club. I owe it to the American League."

"Go to it," I replied.

I hardly think the Athletics' pitchers found this weakness because it doesn't exist now. Deal overcame it.

With the coming of Deal, I was read to let out Devlin, the old Giant third baseman, who in his day was one of the grandest performers at the hot corner every to field a ball. I always like to try to take care of them men who have been faithful and age on my hands, as does John McGraw, so I got Devlin a job managing the Oakland club.

As I have said, I obtained Connolly by refusing to waive, and Mann, the fast outfielder, was traded to me by the Buffalo club of the International League. By this time I was working on my outfield which I had neglected until I could get my infield whipped into some sort of shape.

A manager cannot build up all departments at once, and he is foolish to try to, since concentration is necessary to success.

Many leaders make the mistake of trying to revive a club.

After trading, buying, and selling, the Boston team finished the first season under my management in fifth place, much to the surprise of baseball men all over the country. Rariden, the catcher, Tyler, Hess, Perdue, and Sweeney were the only players who had been with the club when I took hold a year previous and who were still with the team at the end of my first year. Tyler and Hess are the sole survivors.

Johnny Evers hit .438 (7 for 16) in the World Series.

Said He Would Win Pennant

It would be foolish for me to say that I was not encouraged by the progress made during the first season. I was, and Mr. Gaffney appeared to be, too. He had kept stanchly to this promise all this time and had left me alone in handling the players. This was a big help.

During the Winter, I made a statement which was to come back to me often during the first part of the fight of last season as a shaft of ridicule. Talking with several newspaper men in the Waldorf Hotel in New York at the time of the annual league meeting, I declared myself.

"Where will you finish next season, George?" asked one. "Are you going to win the pennant?"

"I don't know about winning the pennant," I replied. "but I am going to finish higher next year than I did last, which means the first division."

Later Mr. Gaffney purchased Johnny Evers, and then I saw my newspaper friends gain. "We'll win the champion ship, now that we have Evers," I told them.

From the day the deal for Evers was made I was never shaken in my belief that we would finally come through, because then I knew I had a balanced ball club.

The Federals did not do us much harm, because there were few players on my club a year ago with big names, and they were playing for stars who could be used as advertising bait. The development of the Federals was a good thing for the Boston team in a way, because they weakened other clubs in the league.

But we would have won anyway, for the Feds did not hurt the Giants and the Athletics. I guess they would be glad to try for some of our players now, but they would have to offer very big salaries to get anyone loose. In fact, I don't believe that a single man on the payroll would leave the Boston club now under any condition. He would be very crazy if he did, not fit for a "foolish" farm.

However, Rariden, the catcher, and Jack Quinn, the pitcher, went with the outlaws last Spring. I wonder how often each one has regretted his move since. I saw

Quinn, whom I have known for a long time, as he was with the Yankees and also in the International just after we had won the World's Championship.

"I made a big mistake, George," he admitted. "I wish I had stuck with you. Bill Rariden does, too."

"Why didn't you ask me about it before you made up your mind, and I would have steered you right," I told him.

"I wish I had," he replied ruefully.

I guess Rariden was even more grieved to miss that World Series sugar, since his bankbooks are his favorite reading.

Poor Start in 1914

But the first part of the season of 1914 was not to be such easy sailing for me. I brought the club back from the South in tip-top shape and ready to make a battle from the start. We ran into some of the sort of weather for which Boston is famous, or infamous, and it certainly cut into the condition of the players, who had just left the Sunny South with its warmth and the climate for putting the men in shape. We got those cold, damp, wet Spring days that will stiffen up a team.

There is one game I am satisfied to lose each year, and that is the first one of the season. The "dope" will show that clubs which have taken the opener never carry much luck through the season. When Brooklyn beat us on that first day last year, I felt we would have some luck and were in for a good season. But the series of calamities which followed rapidly in the first two months and a half began to shake my faith in the superstition. However, it proved to be all right.

Part Four—December 20, 1914

WHEN THE MIRACLE BEGAN TO DEVELOP

Idea Came to Stallings After He Had Gone to Bed

His Manipulation of Outfielders an Elaboration of the "Pinch Hitter" Scheme.

Big Spurt Which Landed World's Championship Started in July.

Strong Talk to Perdue That Made "Hub" Want to Whip the Manager.

In the articles that I have been writing so far, I have been dwelling mostly on the dark side of the situation I faced when I took charge of the Boston team, a tailender. From this point along I will have more to say about the silver lining to the cloud.

However, last season did not open very brightly for the Braves. As I said in the article last week, we did not parade this tough luck to the public, or we tried not to.

Evers could not do himself justice until June because he had a badly sprained back and Rabbit Maranville caught tonsillitis. Deal developed a bad case of "charleyhorse," and nothing will cure this disability of a ball player except complete rest. I could not rest Deal because there was no one else for his place, and he played along gamely, practically on one leg.

The team hung in last place and the newspaper began to "kid" us and our supporters were inclined to desert.

Besides the team being torn to pieces with injuries and sickness the pitchers were away off form on account of the cold, raw weather, and my outfield was not hitting. It looked like a bad ball club during those first two months and a half, and even Mr. Gaffney was a little discouraged at times, although he was out at the grounds every day that we played at home, rooting like a mad "bug."

Those first weeks of the season were some of the toughest times that I have ever put in with a ball team, and often I had to set my teeth to keep off the gloom.

Change Came In June

Along in June, Evers began to get back into condition with the warmer weather, and the pitchers started to show more, so that I was encouraged, but my outfield still worried me.

I knew if I had some hitting outfielders, we could start to climb, but where to get hitting outfielders in mid-season is a problem to stump any manager.

On a trip to New York in May, I met a friend of mine. My friends, by the way, were not so numerous in those days as they have been since the World's Series.

"What's the matter with your club, George?" he asked me.

"It would be all right if we had some hitting in the outfield," I answered. "The rest of the boys are coming along all right."

He did not believe me and just smiled, because he thought I was pulling a bad alibi. I told the same thing to Mr. Gaffney.

"Well, I wish we could get that hitting," he replied.

Then the idea came to me in bed one night just before I fell asleep, and I got up and wrote it down on paper to be sure to have it by morning. That is an old habit of mine—to write down ideas which come to me in the night, since I have found that in years past, if I did not take this precaution, they have evaporated by the next day- some of my best plans hit me at night after I am in bed.

The scheme which I had was really only an enlargement of a practice that many managers had carried on in a desultory sort of way for several seasons. In the past, leaders had selected a pinch hitter according to the style of pitching. They would send a right hander up to bat against a southpaw or reverse it.

Working on this notion, the idea struck me that I would shift my whole outfield, according to whether a right hander or left hander was working against us. But I did not have sufficient material at the time to try it, so I decided to pick it up quietly. The scheme was intended to supply the missing batting punch in the outfield.

Made the Deal for Devore

Devore has always been a lucky player for me. I developed him in Newark before he went to the Giants, and the team had luck all the time he was along. I made a deal for him to come to Boston.

Connolly was a left-handed batter who could sting the cover off the ball against right-handers, but who had not hit much against southpaws. I had another good left-hand swinger in him. It was this weakness of his against southpaws, however, that made me believe in the man. He was the one man on my club who batted over .300 last season, and I believe my shift which, through most of the season, brought him into the game strictly against right-handers, was responsible for this good record.

Let us see what were going to be the advantages of the club aside from the more added batting strength which, of course, was the principal factor in causing me to adopt the course.

When a left-handed pitcher goes into a game and see right-hander after right-hander come up against him, it begins to wear on his nerves, especially if it is a tight battle. It means that he is not facing and "spots" in the batting order. They are all tough to "set down."

The strain will usually tell, and I believe that this weakening of several southpaw pitchers won many contests for us at first. As a rule, left-handed twirlers are not the most reliable citizens of the world anyway, and I figured this shift would begin to worry them from the start so they would count us around the circuit as a hard bunch to beat with a southpaw working against us. It worked out this way.

Most of the other managers did not approve of my scheme of shifting men, and some of the newspapers began to "kid" the club by saying nobody could determine the regular lineup from say to say. Said one writer, "The Boston club is not a team, but just a collection of players. Nobody can tell from day to day who will be where."

But I have a notion that some of the other managers will pay attention to the shift next year because it's a great way to beat a left-hander, one of the best, when he sees almost an entire team marching up to the plate and facing him from the right side of the pan. Even some of the managers who hinted that George Stallings was crazy when I first pulled it may do some experimenting with it.

Get Right-Handed Hitters

I was short of right-handed hitters, however, and so I started out to get a couple. "Hub" Perdue is a pitcher, and an excellent entertainer as well, for he is a good story-teller, but the raw climate of Boston did not do his arm since he is getting into the "old soupbone."

The weather just settled in it last spring. Therefore, I fixed up a trade with Miller Huggins of St. Louis, which brought Whitted and Cather to Boston and which sent Perdue to St. Louis.

Let me state baldly right here and without any reservations that I never regretted the trade. Perdue pitched good ball with the Cardinals, and I am glad of it. The weather suited his arm better in St. Louis than it did in Boston, and he had a good year. I talked with Perdue on the last trip the St. Louis club made east, and he was feeling pretty sore about being out of the World's Series, as it looked sure then that we would be the next champions of the National League, but he "kidded" about his misfortune as he does about everything.

"I'm glad I've still got my home, George," he declared. "That is something to be thankful for, anyway. You must have known you were going to get into the big series when you eased me off the club. I always cut into the tough luck for my share."

While we are discussing "Hub" I want to relate a little story about him.

I have a regular system of working pitchers that I always stick to. I pick two pitchers for every game and call them No. 1 and No. 2. One day early last season I picked James for the first pitcher and Perdue for the second.

As soon as the contest starts No. 2 pitcher is supposed to hike out to the warm-up pen and take just enough work to be ready to go into the box in case the man working cracks. In this way I am not caught without a warm pitcher, and many a ball game is saved. Its purpose is expressed in our club slogan, "Always get the percentage."

Strong Talk to Perdue

"You're No. 1 pitcher today, Bill," I said to James, "and, Hub, you're No. 2."

We were playing on the road and so, being the visitors, we went to bat first. We tore in and made four or five runs in the first inning, which was an unusual thing for the team in those days.

James went to work and got away bad. He could not throw the ball near enough to the plate for the batter to reach it with a pole, and they filled up the bases on him. I was getting pretty anxious when I happened to look around and saw Hub comfortably slouched down on the other end of the bench. My temper cracked under the strain.

"Why, you big, lazy, lumbering chump," I said, and then I went on from there and called him a lot of names. "Didn't you hear me tell you that you were the No. 2 pitcher today? Do you think that assignment entitles you to a ringside seat here on the bench? Get out there and warm up or get out of the park and never come back."

The lacing I gave Hub was a pretty strong one, even for me, and it curled him up like salt on a snail. James steadied up right afterward, and Perdue did not need to pitch. The incident slipped out of my mind until after the game, when I found Hub sitting in the clubhouse looking very sore.

"What's the matter, Hub?" I asked him.

"I was just trying to make up my mind whether to try to lick you for what you said this afternoon and then blow the club, or whether to take it. "I can't afford to blow the club, I guess."

"Listen, Hub," I told him. "You ought to have seen enough of me by this time to know that what I say in the heat of a game don't go. Now, forget it. I didn't mean anything except I wanted to impress on you that when I tell you that you are No. 2 pitcher, you are to be in shape to step into that box at a second's notice. Many a ball game has been lost because the manager was caught with all his pitchers cold."

Condition Came All at Once

Until June 1 there was nothing to do but grit our teeth and wait. The return of the club to condition came all at once in the latter part of June and the team began to improve and play real good ball from that date. The players held up their heads and the pitchers got right.

From July 6, when we started our big spurt, which took us to the World's Championship and which made all the baseball world gasp, the club improved every day that the players put on their uniforms. The Evers deal was the big thing for the club. He helped the team very materially all the way. As we continued to win, the players gained confidence and the club went ahead, day after day.

Deal was still playing on one leg, however, on account of his "charley horse," and I began to search for a fit man to fill that hole. The Brooklyn club was having trouble with Red Smith, and he was making threats about jumping to the Federals. I arranged a deal that would bring him to Boston.

"Don't do it," warned a pretty wise baseball man and a friend of mine. "You'll never be able to do anything with him. That fellow is a baseball anarchist."

But, notwithstanding this tip, after completing the deal with Brooklyn, I wired Smith to come to Boston, and agreed to terms in one talk. Mr. Gaffney was at the conference, and, as Red was leaving the office, he remarked to Mr. Gaffney: "Well, I'll see you at the park tomorrow afternoon."

"Tomorrow morning," corrected the boss.

"What for?" asked Smith, surprised.

"Morning practice" was the answer.

"What? Do you fellows still hold morning practice up here? We haven't had any in Brooklyn for a month."

"We all like it," I told Smith.

He went away wondering whether he would or not, but apparently in doubt. I guess he thought it would cut into his mornings, but he showed up the next day, and it wasn't long before he was enjoying it—or, at least, he said he was.

Let me point out right here that the club engaged in morning practice every day we were at home or when we had the opportunity for it right up to the end of the season, and even during the World's Series under circumstances that I will relate in a subsequent article.

Never Had to Urge Evers

This morning practice was not a "stall" either, as some managers make it, but each player put on his uniform and actually got out on the field, unless he could show some very good reason why he shouldn't.

Near the end of the season Johnny Evers laid off because he was down in his weight and I wanted him to build up. It is not necessary to urge any work on a man with Evers' temperament. You are more likely to be forced to ask him to take it easy.

Smith proved to be the real man to fill the hole at third at that time, and he added to the team just what he needed most, hitting strength. He could pole them with any sticker on the club. I never, in all my baseball experience, have seen a player come to a club in mid-season and fit into the team play better. I don't recall his missing one sign after he joined us and went to work.

The trade was a big thing for the team, because it rounded out the infield, giving me a chance to rest Deal, and added hitting strength. In fact, I was very lucky in all the trades that I made during the season, since the players I obtained fitted into our machine just as I wanted them to.

I don't claim that I outjockeyed anyone in deals through shrewdness, since some of the men I gave up I figured to be just as valuable as those I obtained in exchange, but the players I passed along did not fit into my plans as well. Managers should think of this in making swaps. It is not necessary for either man to get the best or worst of it in a trade. One club may need pitchers and the other outfielders. The man with a lot of pitchers can afford to trade one for some outfield talent and neither will be stuck.

The Whitted and Cather trade about this time rounded out the club nearly to my satisfaction and we started to travel in only one direction—ahead.

Whitted was lazy when he first came with the team, but, like other men who came to me supposed to have certain bad habits, he soon got over this and was full of ambition and pepper. It is easy to take a bad habit out of a man if you know how to treat him and study him carefully beforehand.

In another article I will have something to say on how I act on the bench and how I treat the different men. Much has been written about me, as I am on the bench, so much in fact that I feel now as if I would like to have something to say myself.

Most fans were surprised when I plated Whitted in the outfield, but it all fitted into my plans.

Now I have reached the stage in my story where the team was ready to begin its plunging journey to the world's championship. I intend to tell in the other articles how we fought along, shoulder to shoulder, until our dream was realized and we had won the world's championship. Some of the most interesting phases of the development of the team lie in this part of the story, I think.

Part Five—December 27, 1914

STALLINGS KNEW HE HAD RESERVE STRENGTH

Used Only Three Pitchers in Series—Could Have Shown Others

Might Have Won Fourth Game From Athletics With Hess, He Thinks

Did Not Wish to Invite Criticism in Case of Defeat

Cry Might Have Gone Up That Rudolph Was Kept Out to Prolong Series

When the Boston club started its sensational winning streak, our opponents, and the Giants especially, declared it was due solely to the pitching of Rudolph, James, and Tyler. The manager of one of the teams, which was far higher in the standing of the clubs in August than were the Braves at that time, declared to me: "Just as soon as one of your pitchers cracks, the club will sink back again."

"I have others under cover," was my reply. And this manager laughed at me. September came along, however, and our pitchers had not cracked, and we were up with the Giants about Labor Day. It was then that the followers of the New York club figured my pitching staff would surely go, for the Braves finally took the lead and had to make the pace, always one of the biggest strains of the game. But I had spent much time studying my men, and I knew them. One night about this time I was talking to several New York newspaper reporters, and one said: "Do you think your three pitchers will hold on now, George?"

"If they don't," I replied, "I have others to put in the box. There is one young fellow I have been nursing along carefully for some time, and I am just about ready to take the blanket off him now. I think he will show you something in another week."

"Well, I come from away out in Missouri," answered this newspaperman. "I want to be shown."

Davis Was Then Trotted Out

It wasn't a week afterward that George Davis shut out the Philadelphia National League club without a hit, and if there is one thing the Phillies can do it is paste that ball. Davis is a youngster who came to me with some little experience but who was still very rough. I turned him over to "my right eye," Fred Mitchell, and he had been working with Davis all Summer before I finally started him. I wanted conditions to be right for him.

Next season this boy is going to be primed for a great year, and I think he will be a sensational surprise to the fans. He has in stock all the necessities of a great pitcher—speed, curves, a spitter, and fair control. This latter quality has and will improve. He is strong, so that he can stand lots of work. He won the strength test at his college a few years ago.

It did not take me long to show my newspaper friends that I had other pitchers under cover who could go the distance. As a matter of fact, I would have pitched Hess in the last game of the World's Series if it had not been for the danger of criticism from fans. Hess was never nearer right in his life, and he would have won that game, but I was up against a delicate situation. I thought it all over carefully and decided to come back with Rudolph for this reason: The baseball world knew that Rudolph had had sufficient rest to be sent back for the final game. If Hess had started and had lost that contest, the pastime might have been done some very serious damage, because the cry would inevitably gone up that the series was being prolonged intentionally so that the contending clubs would make more money. I could not afford to risk that.

When the Red Sox beat the Giants in 1912 there was some ridiculous criticism in Boston of how Stahl worked his pitchers.

Second guessers asserted that he should have used "Joe" Wood in the Monday game, when the Sox had won three and lost only one. Instead, he started "Buck" O'Brien, which choice produced the material on which the knockers were glad to work.

Taking this incident into consideration, I decided that there was nothing for me to do except to come back with Rudolph, although I know now as things broke, that Hess would have come through for me.

Had Other Pitchers

I simply relate these incidents to show my readers that the Boston club was not forced to reply on three pitchers only through the stress of that National League campaign, and, if one of them had cracked, another man almost as good, if not quite as good, would have taken his turn. But so long as the trio was winning for me, I would have been foolish to change my luck by working another man. That is strictly my business—to win ball games.

The idea that my club could not hit was exploded toward the end of the race, too, because it was nothing for us to get five and six runs to the game, and the pitchers had pretty easy sailing after the end of August.

The reason that the batting averages of some of the players look so bad is because the team did not make a good start, and the men were not in condition during the first part of the race. This is the period during which their averages were hurt. But I guess the club proved conclusively in the World Series that it could hit.

In spite of all the talk of the Boston team "cracking" after we began our winning streak, it never worried me until we had actually headed the Giants and got out in front. Then I knew we had a young club, and that the strain might begin to tear at the heart-string of some of the players. All my energies were bent at that time to keeping every man with a stiff upper lip, and I resorted to some pretty vigorous methods.

One of my players I chased right out of the park during a double-header because he missed a chance in the field that should have been easy for him. The strain was telling on him. I knew, and something drastic had to be done. I figured that the best tonic was to make him mad, and I sized the situation right, as events proved, although I was taking a chance, not only on those two games which were important to us, but also on breaking the player's heart.

The incident occurred during the stress of the closing months of the campaign. This player had been one of the few on the club who had shown any of the effects of the struggle. When he missed that ball which he should have caught in his trousers pocket, I immediately made up my mind what I should do, although I had been debating and uncertain over the problem for days before.

As he came into the bench, I said: "Beat it out of the park and don't come back for the second game. I don't want a hound like you around."

The player went, and he was so mad that he would not speak to me for several days, although, of course, he showed up the next day. He got back to his old style and played great ball. His anger cured him of the nervousness, as it will often do in such case. However, such treatment would have broken the spirit of a ball player of another type. A manager must study his men carefully before resorting to such tactics.

Evers a Great Help

All through the battle to the pennant, Johnny Evers proved to be a big help to me.

Hank Gowdy hit .545 in the Series. In Game Three homered in the bottom of the 10th to keep the Braves in the game, then doubled to lead off the 12th and scored the winning run.

On every successful ball club there is generally a sort of lieutenant who stands close to the players and who can slip them valuable advice. Matty holds this position on the Giants, although he has no official title or designation All ball players, even those on other teams, look up to the big pitcher because they know that he is fair, and a word of advice from him carries a great deal of weight. Matty settles all arguments among the Giants, and the players generally abide by his decision without a murmur.

When Gowdy first came to the Braves, he had not been used to playing every day, since he was only a substitute in New York, and regular catching irked him. McGraw passed him along, and his general reputation, when he came to Boston, was that he was lazy.

They tell a story about Hank while he was with the Giants which can be taken for what it is worth. Gowdy was anxious to get away from the club and go home for two or three days, and he asked for McGraw's permission.

Why should I let you go?" asked Mac. "Nobody else gets vacations."

Gowdy was catching in batting practice the next afternoon, and he had an idea. The pitcher shot up a fast one, and Gowdy stuck a finger right into it. It split open his hand, and he had to quit catching.

"Can I go away, Mac, until it gets well?" asked Gowdy. "I suppose so," replied McGraw reluctantly.

The relating of this incident is no criticism of Gowdy. When a young fellow is only a substitute on a team, with three or four catchers ahead of him any time it comes to selecting one to work, he cannot see much in the future, and it is liable to take the ambition out of him.

As I have said, one of the best things that I ever did was sending Gowdy to Buffalo for one season, where he had a lot of experience. Still, when he first returned to the Braves, he had a notion that he should not work every day. I overheard a conversation between Gowdy and Evers down at the other end of the bench one day last season.

Said Gowdy: "Well, I am working every day. I don't see why I should. Rariden only catches once in a while."

"I play every day, don't I? answered Evers. "and Maranville and Schmidt, and the rest of us except the pitchers. Why shouldn't you work every day? What are you, one of those twice-a-week guys?"

Gowdy had no answer for that. And it was not long afterward before he would get sore if I did not tell him to catch every day.

"Why don't you let me work today, George?" he would say, if I thought to lay him off.

How Gowdy Was Developed

I relate these anecdotes, which come to my mind, to show how different men must be handled to get the most out of them. Gowdy was developed through driving and urging—and abusing a little. Evers helped a lot in this, and today I consider Hank one of the greatest catchers in the game.

Before the World's Series I prophesied to a newspaperman: "I'll bet you right now that Gowdy outhits, outcatches and outthrows Schang in the series."

At that time Schang was rated as the greatest catcher in the game, but he played with me a year in Buffalo once and I knew something about him. He is a fine, clean young fellow, but I could not let this fact stand in the way of what I had discovered—that he could not hit a slow ball with a fish net.

Before the World's Series between the Giants and the Athletics in 1913, I sent McGraw a wire from Bsoton, saying that I would drop off in New York on the way to my plantation in Georgia, as I had some information for him. I was not able to stay for the series, but as I was eager to see the National League entry win, I thought I would tip McGraw off to what I knew.

I met him accordingly in New York and went over the Athletics with him.

"Whatever you do, John," I warned him, "don't let any of your pitchers give Schang a fast ball. If you do he will break up your ball game for you. I know."

I guess Mac was not so sure that I knew, but he took my advice and warned him pitchers. Marquard got into a hole with two or three on the bases and Schang at the bat in the first game. Rube stuck the fast one over and Schang pickled it for three bases. Away went the ball game.

I had said to McGraw: "Throw the ball to him underhand, if necessary, but don't give him a fast one."

Many pitchers, however, figure that they know more than anybody else, and this fact accounts for most of the hits in the pinches. Matty lobbed the ball to Schang in that series, and he could not do anything with it. But that wise old boy figures every batter all the time. Some pitchers get in the hole, and they forget everything you tell them.

I warned my pitchers before the series that they must work Schang, and work him right. They did. He got only one fast ball during the series at which he had a chance to hit, and he knocked that over third base for a double. James was trying to sneak a fast one over on him and outguess him after he had been slow balled to death.

What the Substitutes Did

McGraw claims that he is responsible for Gowdy.

"How do you figure that, Mac?" I asked him.

"He came to me as a first baseman," answered McGraw, "and I hit on the idea of putting a mask on him. I first stuck him behind the bat."

When McGraw put Gowdy behind the bat, he began the career of one of the greatest catchers the game is yet to know, I think. The big fellow has a wonderful arm, good speed, fine batting ability, splendid courage, and a level head with which to run a team and handle pitchers.

In concluding this article, I want to touch on the substitutes and what they had to do with our march to victory. Our opponents contended all along that injuries or illness to one of the regulars would ruin the club, since I did not have any secondary strength. This belief was held by the same group which believed that my pitching staff would not hold up.

But when Johnny Evers was out of the game two or three times toward the end of the season, the team did not fall off in its winning gait, although Evers' absence from the batting order for any great length of time would naturally be a serious blow. He is, of course, one of the brainiest and best players to ever put on a glove.

After Red Smith broke his leg, just before the World's Series, it was generally supposed that what little chance the Boston club had of beating the Athletics was gone, but Deal filled the hole and filled it full. Of course, after getting Devore, Cather, and Whitted, I had plenty of outfielders.

However, the substitutes on the Boston club deserve credit for something else — their spirit — and this spirit had much to do with our ultimate success, I believe. On many ball clubs the extra men are jealous of the regulars. Frequently, I have heard a man say:

"What you do think of that big stiff working regularly, and me on the bench? The boss is just tipping himself off to how little he knows. He must be blind."

But that jealous spirit was missing on the Boston club. Every man on the bench during every game was pulling his heart out for the team to win and encouraging the players on the field. They were also after our opponents constantly.

Among the substitutes you will usually find the key to the spirit of a ball club, and when you get a lot of extra men who are sore and sullen there is not much spirit on that ball club. After Red Smith replaced Deal in his job last Summer Deal did not complain or whine, but he warmed up extra pitchers to make himself useful.

When Evers made the one "bone" play of his career and led his head drop in the third game of the World's Series every man on that bench thought that the mistake would be fatal, but each one made it a point to slap John on the back after the inning and say: "Never mind, John, old boy. We have three more in which to beat them!"

The men on the bench were fighting all the way just as hard as the men on the field, and I believe much of the credit for our final success should go to the men on the bench.

Part Six: January 3, 1915

HE KEPT UP THE DRIVE AFTER CLINCHING PENNANT

Stallings Did Not Let Braves Relax After They Won One Race

"Eased Off" for One Night Only, and Then Sent Them on the Jump Again

His Plan of Campaign Against the Athletics

"I Don't Order Every Play, and Make a Machine Of a Player," Says "Miracle Man."

Up to the point when the Boston club clinched the National League championship, the strain was bad enough, but the real test was after we were sure of the flag. I made up my mind that we could beat the Athletics, and that, to this end, I would ride our "luck" to a World's Championship. I say "luck," because that is what the newspapers called it, but they didn't call it "tough luck" when we were losing. They never do. We were just a rotten ball club then. Baseball "luck" amounts to getting a team in a winning stride and then keeping it in the winning stride. Personally, I don't call that luck.

The night that the club finally clinched the championship we were scheduled to leave Boston for a series with the Giants at the Polo Grounds. There was a good deal of difference between this series and our previous one with the New York club. In the one preceding, we had played three games, and fans all over the country declared just before it began that the Braves were traveling at a fast gait, far ahead of their real speed.

This late August series was the important one of the season from the point of view of our club. If we lost it, the spirit of the players might droop. If we won it, it was certain you could not be able to convince them that any team in the world could beat them. We won three straight games.

Had Been Figuring on Athletics

There was naturally a good deal of rejoicing among the boys on the train going over to New York from Boston for the last series of the season with the Giants the night we were sure of the championship. Most of them had not begun to look ahead to the World's Series at that time. But I had. I was figuring on the Athletics even then.

From my American League experience as a manager, I felt that I knew more about the Athletics than any other leader in the National League, and more than a good many in the American. I do not intend this for a boast. I had absorbed much information about the other teams in the league during the period that I served as manager of the Yankees. Just before the train got in New York—it was due to arrive at 10 o'clock—I called the players around me and said:

"Well, boys, you've won the championship, and I'm proud of you. You can all ease off a little tonight if you want to, and I am going to be blind. Never mind what time you get in. Do just as you please tonight, but I want to see you all in my room for a talk at noon tomorrow."

I couldn't tell you just what time any of those players got in that night, and I didn't care. However, I never left the hotel myself, for I was already figuring on the World's Series. My big problem was how to work the team back on edge after the snap of the strain following the winning of the National League pennant. I was afraid to let the players rest too much for fear that they would go stale. Johnny Evers came up to my room about midnight and found me marking a lot of figures on a pad.

"I guess it's up to you to do the worrying, George," he said. "I'm going to bed. I used to be the official worrier for any ball club I was on, but I've cut it out."

There Was No Letup

Finally, I decided on the plan that I followed successfully, except for one thing—and that happened in the final game of the season. I would work my regular team, as I had worked it through the last weeks of the race, as if we were not sure of anything, and I would "ride" the men harder, if possible, to keep them on edge through the nerve-racking period. The next day the players reported to my room at 12 o'clock. Some of them looked as if they had forgotten how to tell time the night before.

"Boys," I began, "you have had your little celebration. Now I want you all to forget that you have won the pennant and go on and play ball in this series with the Giants, and the one to follow with Brooklyn, as if each team were neck and neck in the race with you. If I catch anybody 'dogging' it, I am going to be rough with him sure."

In spite of the tough night, my club went out and beat Tesreau that afternoon, and beat him badly. We would have beaten him just the same if we hadn't had the flag sure, and if winning it had depended on that series. I told a newspaper man over in Boston before we had won the pennant that my club would beat McGraw's best bet, Tesreau, the next time he started against us, and we did.

"I've found out enough about him now to beat him sure," I said. "We'll beat his spitter, and we'll beat his fast one. Watch us."

By way of a digression, I want to say that the clinching of the pennant by the Boston Club before the final Giant series was a fine and perfect proof of the honesty of baseball, for if I had brought my club to the Polo Grounds neck and neck with the Giants that series would have meant a grand gate in a tough season. The winning of the World's Series in four games was another bit of evidence which should serve to convince the "croakers" of the honesty of the game.

Devore Had His Day

Nobody had so much fun in that final series with the Giants as Josh Devore. He had been cast aside by the New York club, and had come back as a member of the team that had put the Giants out of the race.

"Aren't you afraid of them 'kidding' you out there today, Josh?" I asked him before the first game of the series.

"Let me play, George," he replied. "They've got a great chance to 'kid' me. I'll show you. Let me play as a favor to me."

I put Josh in, and he just "rode" that Giant team to death.

"It's a wonder some of you 'bushers' wouldn't join out with a good 'big league' club," he would say.

"What are you, the mascot?" came the chorus from the New York bench.

"I would rather be the mascot with the winner than a bench warmer with a loser," replied "Josh."

He made up for everything in that series. In a way I was glad, for Devore is a good little ball player and had always brought me luck. He was with my Newark club when it was a winner.

During those trying days between the time when we cinched the championship until we went into the World's Series, the Boston club showed its grand spirit. Every man was playing right up to his limit and working his heart out. Evers would drop into my room each night before he went to bed.

"What are you worrying about tonight, George?" he would ask. "I know you are always worrying. You've got to. It's your job."

Every day at noon we would have a meeting in my room at the hotel for "skull" practice, going over the plays and signs. Although we had a set of signals that I don't think any ball club in this world would have gotten on to we heard rumors that the Athletics had been tipped off to them. We framed up an entire new set, and a coacher or base runner could have looked square into the catcher's glove and never have gotten these. Mack's men failed to get a sign of ours in the series so far as I know.

I want to say that my club was prepared more thoroughly for the World's Series than any team ever was before. We went after the weaknesses of the Athletics as I have learned them when in the American League, and we figured at the daily "skull" practice how to cover up our own, for every team has weaknesses and we recognized ours. I can't tell what they are naturally. We made it a point to ask everybody that we thought might have some accurate information about the Athletics for pointers, and the warning that he had fired at us time after time was "Don't let them get your signs."

Rehearsing the Signals

We were told this so often that the young fellows on the club got to dreaming about it and the result of this was the series of signals that I mentioned above. We rehearsed these over and over. One night, while the team was at its hotel in New York, I heard somebody mumbling in a room near mine. I knew that all the rooms in that part of the hotel were occupied by my ball players, so I walked down the hall and found the door of the room on a crack. I looked in.

Rudolph was standing at one end and Gowdy was crouched at the other, giving signs in an imaginary glove. As he switched from one code to another Rudolph would call them.

"Curve ball, inside," said Dick.

"Fast one, outside. Spitter," mumbled Rudolph.

I tiptoed away without either one knowing that I had seen the rehearsal. Spirit of that sort wins victories, and Rudolph displayed his wonderful gameness in doing that in his room just as much as he did under actual fire in the series when he pitched grand ball. This was the spirit which won for us. To show how hard my team worked, not a man missed a sign during that World's Series.

Just to give an idea of what a tight organization we had, I will relate an incident that occurred during the final series of the season in Brooklyn. I was sitting in a field box with a friend, and Mitchell was running the club on the bench. Whitted was at the bat, with a man on first base and none out. Tyler was coaching at third base. He glanced at me in the box and I have him the sign for Whitted to hit. Tyler flashed the sign to Whitted, and the latter busted a curve ball for a couple of bases. Tyler, on the field, had caught this sign from me out of all the crowd.

It would have been the same if I had been sitting upstairs in the last row of the grandstand. It was a tight ball club, and the organization of it counted in both the National League race and the World's Series.

"I Don't Order Every Play"

Yet I do not run a ball club so tight that I kill a man's individuality. I rave on the bench, it is true, and I did up to the last game of the National League race, because I figured this would keep up the pepper during the World's Series that won for us on the season.

It did, too, I guess. But I don't order every play, and make a machine of a ball player.

If you think for a man whenever you can, you will blot out his individuality, and quick thinking is one of a player's greatest assets.

So many plays come up when a manager does not have time or the opportunity to think for a ball player that it is best to let him think for himself most of the time. I insist on quick thinking on both ends of a play, however, for fast brain work on one end does no good. If the base runner is going to pull off some play, the batter must know about it, and be ready to join in. We worked hard on all these ends in our preparation for the World's Series. And it all paid.

The team went along smoothly enough getting ready for the big battle until the last day we were scheduled to play a National League game. There was a double-header in Brooklyn. I started most of my regulars, and resulted in a stroke of bad luck that many of our followers thought had killed what little chance we were supposed to have in the post season series.

It occurred in the ninth inning of the first game, when Red Smith, the hard-hitting third baseman, made a false slide for second and his leg doubled under him and under the bag. He didn't stand on it again until long after the series, when he got up off a hospital bed, for his leg was broken. Strangely enough, Johnny Evers was one of the first to rush to Red, and Johnny looked back at me on the bench and barely whispered the news.

Realized the Damage

"Red's out," he said, under his breath. But I heard and understood. If he had said nothing, I would have known by his looks. I had realized it when I saw Red go down.

It was before the series between the Athletics and the Cubs in 1910 that Evers himself had broken his leg in almost the same way when he started to slide for the plate in a game with Cincinnati, after the Cubs had the championship clinched. Clarke, catching for the Reds, drew the slide with a bluff to catch a ball that was never thrown, and Evers had started to hit the dirt and then held up. Clarke has not yet given up regretting that he made the move which kept Evers out of the series.

"I'll never make another bluff," he said to Evers time and time again since.

"I was my fault," answers Johnny, "for not going through with the slide when I once started it. You weren't to blame, Tommy."

Between the games, I went to the clubhouse and called all the players together except Smith, who was on the way to the hospital. The whole club was naturally heartbroken.

"Rabbit, you're out of the game," I said to Maranville, "and you, Evers, and Connolly, and the rest of you regulars."

I wasn't going to take any more chances with my veterans. I had had my lesson as a result of leaving them in the game in an effort to keep them on a fine edge. Then I turned to the second team.

"Now, you moss agates, who have been whining around all season for a chance," I said to the substitutes, "you're going to get it. I want you to show me that a team of substitutes can win. This game means a lot to the spirit of the ball club. Now, go out and get this next and last game of the season."

Never Missed A Sign

It was a terrible looking team. Pitchers were in the outfield and extra catchers were freely scattered through the lineup. Tyler's brother was catching, but those boys, all out of their regular positions, went out there with jaws set, and they beat the life out of the regular Brooklyn club. They never missed a sign and played like champions. I believe they would have defeated the World's Champions that afternoon with that spirit. It did my downcast regulars a lot of good, because it showed them that a second team could win.

That is the way I prepared all along. After we had cinched the pennant, I would pick one particular game and say: "Now let's get this one." The team would hustle and fight for it. My idea was to show them that they could win when they wanted to.

There is no use in saying that we were not downcast the night Smith was hurt. We were. The players met in my room, and I gave them a talk.

"All we've got to do," I told them, "is to bite off more and chew harder."

After the accident to Smith, I got all sorts of advice from well wishers suggesting different shifts to strengthen the supposedly weak third base position. But I knew I was going to play Deal, for he was right and ready to go in after his long rest. His work in the series vindicated my judgment.

As I reviewed the day, just before I went to bed that night, it seems like the most disastrous of my career, and I could think of only one stroke of good luck I had had.

Some time before I had told Alexander, the Philadelphia pitcher, he could charge a suit of clothes to me if he beat the Giants in a critical series. He did, and I got the bill that night. It was only $20. He might of stuck me $100. This made me smile, and I turned in.

Part Seven: January 10, 1915

STALLINGS' STRATEGY IN THE GREAT BATTLE WITH MACK

Details of the Skirmishing Which Preceded Memorable Series of 1914.

Regrets "Big Blow Up" With Connie, But It Aroused Fighting Spirit of the Braves.

How the Athletics Were "Crossed" on Signals.

Chief Benders Little Byplay to Get Evers' Goat Failed—Johnny Too Old a Bird

Our real preparation for the World's Series began after the last contest of the National League schedule had been played, and I took my club to Philadelphia two days before the opening game. Of course, from the time that we knew we had the championship cinched we had been preparing our signs and studying the Philadelphia team and going over the weaknesses of the Athletics together, and figuring how we could get the "percentage," which, as I have said, is our clubhouse slogan.

The Athletics were also making some preparations and did not hold our club so lightly just before the series as some of the fans seemed to think. A few of the Philadelphia players made some byplays which were ineffective, but which showed that they had been doing some thinking. Most of the Boston players went out to Shibe Park on the day of the last game of the American League schedule, when the Athletics were playing the Yankees.

Connie Mack knew that the Boston club was present, looking his team over, and so he pulled something which was meant to have a two-fold effect. The Yankees had nothing to gain or lose by winning or losing that last game, but they had a chance to help the American League in the World's Series. Therefore, the New York pitchers went into the box and just laid the ball over the plate in the "groove" with nothing on it, and the Philadelphia hitters busted it all over the lot.

Sure Way to Cure a Batting Slump

Mack figured that this would give his players confidence, since the surest way to cure a batting slump is to have a twirler go in the box during hitting practice and believe that they can bat any sort of pitching, and often they can. This is the old remedy for the batting slump. Therefore, Mack probably thought this hard hitting in the last game of the season would give his men confidence.

But, more important, he probably figured it would scare us. The manager of the Athletics thought that if some of our young pitchers in the stand saw the reputed heavy artillery of the Athletics smearing the delivery they faced all over the field, their confidence would be shaken when they stepped into the box.

But I had been training their confidence for just this ordeal. I told the whole club to show up in my room at the hotel right after dinner that night. In the meantime, I had carefully collected all the box scores of the Athletics for the previous month, thanks to a newspaper friend of mine.

"You boys saw the Athletics batting that ball pretty hard out there today," I told my men. "So I have brought along the box scores of their last games of the season to show that they can't hit hard when the pitcher is putting something on the pill. Of course, when a twirler stands up there and just throws them over, as the pitchers did today, a blind man could bust them. Even old Fred Mitchell here could have made a couple of home runs on that stuff."

Athletics in a Slump

As a matter of fact, the Athletics has been in a batting slump, and a pretty bad one, for some time just before the series, although the pitching they faced would have made any club look like it was in a slump. But on the night of this meeting my players made a careful study of the box scores that I had collected, and they saw that the hitting of the Athletics had not been terrific at all.

Especially did my pitchers study these box scores, and their confidence was not shaken a bit by them, but strengthened a little if anything.

I was bending every energy to win that series, for this was the big chance of my career, and I knew it. I did little sleeping the last two or three nights before the first game. Neither did I sleep for several nights after the last game, although I knew we had the thing I wanted most won, and they could not take it away from us. The strain had been great. If the series had run a game or two longer I think I would be in an asylum now.

On the same day that the Athletics played the Yankees in the final game of the American League season, Chief Bender did a peculiar thing, which may or may not have been framed up beforehand. Johnny Evers was sitting in the last row of the grandstand all by himself, watching the contest, when Bender came stalking along behind the seats. He tapped Evers on the shoulder, and Johnny looked around.

"Oh," said Bender, apparently surprised. "I thought you were a gambler that I was looking for. There he is down there. I see him now."

The Chief strolled along over to the man he said he was seeking, but this fellow was a big, stout party, so Evers told me, with no more resemblance to Johnny than a billboard has to a calling card. Evers thought the Chief was trying to show him the confidence he had in the team's ultimate success by hinting that he was going to bet a little of his own money, although I don't believe he did.

"But what did the Indian pull it on me for?" asked Evers. "Why didn't he pick some of the younger fellows that he might perhaps have scared?" They were sitting all around the stand. He shouldn't have tried it on an old bird like me."

Wordy Battle With Mack

Then came the big blowup, which I regret now, but which, I figure, was a big help to my team then, though we would have won without it.

I had been trying to hit upon a scheme that would send my club into the series fighting mad, with a real grouch over something definite. The sun in the outfield at Shibe Park is bad for a ball player who is not used to the grenade, and so I asked Connie Mack if he minded if we took a little practice in his park on the day before the first contest while his club was not using it.

When it begins to get along toward the late afternoon on those grounds, the outfield is one of the toughest in the country to play because the sun slants right into the fielders' eyes.

Of course, Mack and his club were used to the grounds where the contests in Boston were to take place, because it was the American League park, and the Athletics had been playing ball there all summer. Therefore, I thought it only fair that our outfielders should get a couple of hours in Shibe Park to accustom them to the conditions.

There was a bunch of newspapermen standing by the telephone booth, and they could hear what I said to Mack through the glass door, and the whole business got into the papers. The reporters knew I was talking to Connie. I suppose we were both excited and worked up from the strain of the series.

"Well, what do you think of that?" I said to my players, who had been attending "skull" practice when I went out to the telephone. "Connie must be a little more worried over this team than he pretends to be. He won't let us use his park to practice in. He bawled me out over the telephone, and we had quite a row."

I then went on and told my players more of the details, and they all got mad, just what I wanted. They had their grouch, and it was a swell one. I knew from that moment that they would go out there and "ride" the Philadelphia team to death, and I also knew that any club which would "ride" the Athletics would beat them.

The old Detroit team used to win from "Connie" Mack's club right along in this way. My row with "Connie" Mack was worth more to me than a week's practice in his park, because it put the players in just the frame of mind in which I desired to have them meet the enemy.

To See That Men Get Rest

The big final problem that I faced was to see that my men got the proper rest on the night before the opening game and during the series, and this is the problem which every manager faces before a World's Series, and especially the man who is leading a club into it for its first time.

The great trouble with the Giants in the three World's Series that they have played recently was that they couldn't get good rest; that they worried over the job ahead of them.

Marquard pitched the opening game of the series against the Athletics in 1912, and I know for a fact that he didn't sleep a wink the night before, and there were others on the club nearly as bad.

Rube wasn't himself at all, and he didn't pitch as he had been told to pitch. He should have been good against the Athletics because they have so many left-handed hitters in their batting order, and Mac probably figured it this way in picking him. Of course, a pitcher like Matty isn't worried, and he gets his rest as usual and works his game. But he is one in a lifetime.

Matty was sitting in the lobby of the Majestic Hotel in Philadelphia the night before the game he pitched in the series of 1913 when he beat Plank in that wonderful battle. Clark Griffith came along, as the story goes, and started to chat with Matty. In spite of the fact that Griff is a good talker, he suddenly found himself talking to a man who had dozed off in his chair. Griff shook him and said: "You'd better get up in the hay, Matty."

"I guess I had," replied the big pitcher, getting up and yawning and stretching. "I expect to work tomorrow, and I must have my rest." That's how much the prospect bothered "Big Six." Matty probably slept as soundly that night as he did any night of his life. But for the rest of the Giants, they didn't get their rest.

"If only I could have made them forget baseball and take their regular rest," McGraw has complained to me since in discussing the series.

Giants Didn't Show True Form

The Giants did not show their real game in any one of the three series in which the club has taken part lately. From their wild swinging at the bat and from their uncertain work in the field, it was evident that they were worried.

It is a "chop" hitting team ordinarily. In the World's Series it turned into a free swinging club, nearly every man taking a "Moriarty" at the ball.

The New York players also read all the newspapers, and the criticism and comment worried them. Chief Myers was all upset during the series of 1912 by some articles in the newspapers which criticised him for not catching a foul fly in the first game.

Therefore, all my efforts in those final two or three days were bent on keeping my players from worrying. I stopped them reading newspapers as much as I could. Then I began to figure on a way to handle the pitcher I intended to work so that he would get this full rest before his game.

My choice for the opening contest, which is always the toughest, was Rudolph, who has a heart of iron, but I wanted to be sure he didn't fret. Much of the worry falls on the pitcher in that first game. A man is naturally afraid that he may be forced to quit under fire when all the world is looking to him to show his best.

It is the same way with any man in other jobs when he comes to the supreme test in his career, as a World's Series is the supreme test for a ball player. He is bound to fret and worry and generally is not at his best.

The night before the game I called Rudolph aside and said to him: "Dick, I don't expect to work you tomorrow, because I think we can get away with the game without starting you. But you had better get your regular rest now, because it might be necessary for you to step into the box there and pitch a little if things break that way and we have to take some one out. I just want you to be ready."

The result was that Rudolph went to bed that night with no anxiety of his mind. He did not think he would pitch the next day, so he had nothing to worry over, and he slept sound and came to the job fresh and clear-eyed. That afternoon, just a little while before game time, I told Rudolph to warm up, and I warmed up Tyler and James, too, so that Dick would still believe he was not going to start. When it was time for me to name my pitcher, I said to him: "Well, Dick, you have warmed up so good I have changed my mind and decided to start you after all."

Rudolph went out and pitched the game of his life. He worked those Athletic hitters better than they had ever been worked before to my knowledge.

"If I don't pitch them a strike all afternoon I am not going to give them a 'groove' ball to hit at," he told me as he started for the field. He didn't.

"Cold Turkey" Hitters

Some of the men on that Philadelphia club are what we call in baseball parlance "cold turkey" hitters. That is, they want to know where the ball is coming, and whether it is going to be a fast one or a curve before they swing at it. But we knew this, and I don't believe that a batter got tipped off once in the series to what was going to be pitched. They weren't sure until after the ball left the twirler's hand. Our plans were too carefully made to permit any sign stealing. For this reason, Rudolph made Oldring, McInnis, and some of those other "cold turkey" hitters look pretty bad, for he was "crossing them up" all the way. He pitched a wonderful game.

A lot had been printed in the papers before the series about me carrying batters along with a set of signs from the bench and telling a man just what to do when he was at the plate. It is true that I had carried along some of them all season, but I knew that Connie and his lieutenants would be looking for this, so I framed it to "cross" them here also.

I had another man on the bench give the signs to the hitter, and the Athletics were all watching me right through the series. I told this other man how to handle the batter, and we stopped them again there. I gave nothing but "phoney" signs, which meant nothing, to worry them.

I could not figure for sure whether Mack would start Bender or Plank in that first game. Of course, I thought it would be Bender, for Mack had once said that the Chief was the best single-game pitcher in the world if there as just one battle to be won. I guess Connie has changed his views now.

But I was not leaving anything to chance in that series which I could figure out beforehand. No ball player on my club ever eats much lunch, because I think a hearty meal in the middle of the day makes a man logey and heavy and not fit for work in the afternoon. Many a player has eaten his way right out of the big league by stuffing at lunch when he has accepted a chance at that old table d'hote bill-o-fare and did not want to see the club stuck because the players did not eat what the management was paying for.

For the two games of the series which were played in Philadelphia, my club dressed at the National League Park, which is only a few blocks from Shibe Field, and then they went from one park to the other in taxicabs in their uniforms.

Preparing Till Last Minute

On the morning of that first game I had my men out at the Phillies' field at 11 o'clock taking a workout. I had a left-handed pitcher throwing to the right-handed batters and a right-handed pitcher throwing to the left-handed swingers in the other corner. They busted that ball unmercifully for a couple of hours before the team ever went near Shibe Park.

Hank Gowdy pickled the first one pitched to him in practice, and I believe that wallop gave him the confidence which made him the batting hero of the series. Also, this arrangement made me sure that no one was stuffing himself with lunch.

We went to Shibe Field with a little edge on the Athletics after our two hours' practice, and the fruits of this "percentage" were shown along about 3:30 in that first afternoon, when Bender retired from the box. We had also carried the Athletics off their feet with our rush. But I am running a little ahead of my story.

The result, however, must have been somewhat of a surprise to the Chief, who, when the Athletics' manager asked him what he thought of the Braves, replied, "Why should I go over to New York to watch them 'bushers' play? I can beat them with one hand tied."

Connie had told Bender to go to New York to look over our club in that final series with the Giants at the Polo Grounds, and the Chief did not think it necessary. I agree with him. I don't believe it would have helped him any.

The Athletics took the field for the first inning of that opening game as if they were bored by the fact that they had to waste their time playing the series; as if they wanted to get it over with as quickly as possible, as languidly as they would have gone to work if it had been a series with the Clevelands in midseason.

Bender got thoroughly warmed up and then "kidded" with the crowd by throwing the ball underhand. My club went out there with jaws set and full of spirit. We had the edge on our opponents, and I knew it then and was surer than ever that we would win.

I hope I haven't written any of this installment boastfully. I have merely wanted to tell the reader what happened and to say that we went to work in that first game ready to the minute.

Part Eight: January 17, 1915

STALLINGS AND SOME PET SUPERSTITIONS

Playing Hunches and Avoiding Jinxes Part of the Game

Men Play Better if They Think Luck Is With Them

That Canceled Sleeping Car Reservation

Talking Through the Game Criticized, But 'Most Everybody Does It

From the minute that my ball club went out for that first World's Series game in Philadelphia until the last man was thrown out in the final contest in Boston I was on edge. My nerves were fringed with nervous prostration, but never for a minute did I believe we were willing to lose that series.

Just before the first game started a New York newspaper man, Bill Hanna, came down to our bench and talked to Johnny Evers. Johnny was all worked up over Connie Mack's refusal to let us have the park for practice.

"We are going to beat then," said Johnny to Hanna, "and we are going to give them the worst showing up any club ever got in a World's Series. Watch us go after them from the jump."

"You seem to be really sore about it, John," said Hanna. "Do you think you are going to win? I don't see on what you base your opinion."

"I am sure," answered Johnny, "and I think we are going to win because we are a better ball club and because we have more fight in us than they have."

That was the spirit with which our team went to work in the first contest of the series and in every one that followed. It wasn't long before I guess that Bender began to wish that he had spent the time to make a study of the team of "bushers," as he had termed our club beforehand, but, at that, I hated to see the Indian forced to quit under fire. He was a great pitcher in his day and has a lot left in him yet.

American Leaguers have told me that the Indian did not pitch his game that day, but I believe we would have beaten him, no matter how well he had pitched. By the way he worked I judge that he held our hitters too lightly until he found he was beaten. Then it was too late, and he was too far spent to make a switch.

Waiting for the Fast Ones

"All through the season," said Clark Griffith to me afterwards, "Bender was pitching more with his head than his arm. He knew he did not have the speed and the break to his curve ball that he used to carry, so he was crossing American League hitters and pitching at their weaknesses."

Bender could not "cross" our hitters because he did not know their "grooves," but he was trying to get by on his speed, which surprised me.

He would get the count two strikes and two balls on a batter, or two strikes and three balls, and then he would come with his fast one, which the hitter would naturally be looking for. That is the one my hitters were "busting."

In the American League they tell me that Bender has been curving that one when he had two and two or three and two on a hitter. But we didn't have to look at many curves. The Chief must have thought he could get away with it by burning that fast one through as he used to when he had all his speed, but he found he couldn't.

However, he did not change his style of pitching, and we finally drove him out of the box. As I say, I think he held our club too lightly at first, and when he found we could hit that fast one it was too late.

The Athletics were surprised by the way our players went after them in the first game, because I guess they expected us to take it for granted that we would be beaten when we started.

Every hitter who went up to the plate had something to say to Bender, and so did the players on the bench.

I don't believe that the talk actually worried the Indian very much, because he is too old a stager to be fretted by conversation, but, when he found us hitting him, the verbal roasting didn't do him any good.

It might have been observed by a close witness that he did not wear his customary smile long. In the case of a veteran pitcher conversation does not harm him much if he has the stuff, but it showed the other members of the club how we felt and that we weren't worried by Bender or the rest of them.

Knew He Didn't Have It

I recall a story that Christy Mathewson told me in this connection when he won that extra-inning game which caused so much talk from Plank in the 1913 series.

"A lot of the younger fellows on our club were after Plank from the bench that day," said Matty. "The southpaw just ate that up.

" 'What right does a Civil War veteran like you got in there?' they were hollering at him.

" 'Don't bother that guy,' I told him. 'Save your wind until Connie starts one of his youngsters.'

"When a veteran like Plank is right there is no use trying to worry him by taunting him with jibes. If he has the stuff and knows it he is going to pitch his game anyway."

But Bender did not have the stuff and he knew that, too, so our broadside of conversation probably got under his skin to some extent. He acted as if it did, anyway, for he came back at two or three of the hitters, which is a sure sign. Usually, when right, he says nothing, only smiles.

My players also went after the other members of the club, leaving only Jack Barry and Eddie Murphy alone. Especially did they "ride" Oldring and Collins.

Rube did not show up very well in the series as a result of the roasting he received, and I don't know where some of those fighters on my club got all the dope from on the different members of Mack's team, but they certainly had it right and got results.

I wouldn't have let them use it except that Connie had stirred us up before the series by his refusal of the park for practice. The Braves were on to all the little personal weaknesses of the Athletics.

One man was "ridden" because somebody on the Boston team had heard indirectly that he had thrown down a pal over a matter of $50. They never let up on him for this.

Another they kept telling that he couldn't remember his own name when he came to bat, and I don't believe he could have told you if you had asked him right quick, he was so worried.

The members of Mack's team tried to come back at us, but in only a half-hearted sort of way. They were surprised by the rush with which we went at them.

Everybody's Doing It

Perhaps some of my readers do not think it fair to indulge in conversational tactics of this sort, but the practice is as old as the hills and the game of base ball itself. All the great teams have done it with the possible exception of the Athletics.

Members of both the Cubs and Giants have told me that Mack's team went through their World's Series with their clubs without a peep out of them, and I think that this lack of combativeness has hurt their drawing powers during the regular season. They do nothing but play baseball when they are on the field. Otherwise, they are colorless.

Even in football the varsity players keep talking to each other and trying to take away the nerve of their opponents, and that is supposed to be a gentleman's pastime.

I know of one college baseball game in which a team started the ninth six runs behind and won out by calling the opposing pitchers worse names than a National League umpire told me he had ever heard in major circles.

This umpire was calling them behind the bat in the contest. They drove that pitcher clear through the sky, and there was a high "sky" that day, too. And college boys don't play baseball for a living, or for a stake of several thousand dollars, as the men in a World's Series do.

The Braves were only following the examples of such great teams as the Baltimore Orioles, Cubs, and Giants. The Cubs under Chance were always snarling and talking. The Giants do it, too, while in the American League the Detroit Tigers in their palmy days used to beat the Athletics right along by "riding" them.

Superstition to the Limit

Ty Cobb has told me some stories of how the Tigers, headed by Jennings, would keep after Mack's quiet players until they had them off their balance.

Germany Schaefer, Jim O'Leary, Delahanty, and some more made life very miserable for the Athletics. They were a tough bunch, that old Detroit team, and finally a permanent feud grew up between the two clubs following that 17-inning tie in Philadelphia in 1907, I think it was, which really beat the Athletics out of the pennant.

Mack has long been very bitter against Jennings and even accused him of tipping McGraw off to some of the weaknesses of the Athletics before the 1911 series with the Giants. The feud still lives.

Year before last the Washington team could beat the Athletics right along by "riding" them, and now there is a feud between the Senators and Mack's club, can you blame me for letting my team go in there after the Athletics when I knew all this and just had to win that series?

Another thing which I did was to play superstition up to the limit in that series. Always, since I have been in baseball, even in the minors, I have been very superstitious and afraid of jinxes and have played hunches.

If I should put on my shirt or a sock wrong side out by mistake, I would never change it. It is not good if you do it on purpose.

I have encouraged superstition among my players because there is a lot of psychology in it. If the players enter a game believing the signs are set for them to win, it stands to reason that they are going to play better baseball than if they believe luck is against them.

Men in every profession agree that there are some days when they can perform their tasks better, feel more like doing them than on others. I have all sorts about this.

Superstition makes ball players feel as if they were winners oftener than they would be otherwise, and feeling like a winner when you start is more than half of the battle in baseball or any other business, for that matter.

A Horror of 13s

I don't see why the baseball public should be interested in my superstitions particularly, but I have received so many letters asking me about these that I intend to expose a few of them.

In the first place, I don't like $2 bills, and I never taken them if I can get ones instead. I have had a lot of my touch luck when I have been carrying $2 bills and I never laid a hand of one during the World's Series.

Throughout the season, of course, I have to come in contact with some of these, but I would fold them over and tear the corners off just as soon as I got hold of one to kill the jinx. If any of the readers of this story come across a $2 bill with the corners trimmed off they will know that $2 bill had circulated somewhere in the Boston club.

All my players got to doing it last season, and our luck changed as soon as we began to play this $2 bill jinx off the map. It was at about the same time that we started winning ball games regularly.

When I was manager of the Buffalo team in the International League, my chauffeur brought me back a license for my automobile which had three combinations of "13" in it.

You could add up two of the numbers to make 13. Add up two more and subtract one of the other figures and you had 13 again, and there was one straight away "13" in the whole number of five figures. When he showed it to me, I thought I was jinxed for life.

"Take that back where you got it," I told him, "and tell the Secretary of State that I want to license number with no combination of '13' in it. If he can't give you that, then sell the car, and you lose your job. I wouldn't ride in a machine with a license like that on it. I would be killed the first day sure."

The chauffeur took the objectionable pad back and brought me one with nothing on it, out of which 13 could be made. He knows better now than to bring around a license with the jinx number on it.

Even Matty worked around the 13 thing by getting the license number 83 for his car, applying early on purpose. Some of my ball players, having experienced the prosperity of the World's Series now have automobiles, but you can bet there isn't anything that looks like 13 among those licenses.

Jinxed by a Fallen Towel

When my club is winning I always try to do everything just the same way every day. I go to the ball park by the same route I took when things began to break for us, and I leave my automobile in exactly the same spot.

Unfortunately there was a crowd going to the grounds the first day we were at home after things began to come our way last year, and I got out of my car a couple of blocks from the park because I could walk through the crowd faster than a machine could be driven.

We won that day, and I have to get out at the same place and walk to the park from there for the rest of the season. Some folks thought I was crazy when there was plenty of room in the road to ride, but I didn't care what they thought so long as we won. When a ball player is going well he will always try to do everything each day just as he did when things started to break for him, even to putting on his uniform in the same order of garments and hanging his towel just as he did on the lucky day.

Readers may laugh at this, but I have known a big league player to go like a house afire for weeks and follow out religiously a certain clubhouse formula each afternoon.

Then one day somebody knocks down his towel and it is hung up on another hook. He finds it there, believes he is jinxed and he goes out and plays rotten ball. Nothing like that could happen in our carefully ordered clubhouse. I watch out for these little things. Can you blame a manager for falling for superstition?

After we won that first game in the World's Series we were very careful to repeat every act just as we had performed it on that first day. We dressed at the Phillies' park at the same hour and had batting practice before going to Shibe Park for the Saturday game exactly as we had done on the victorious Friday.

We were sure that Plank would oppose us on that second day, so I worked my hitters, especially the right-handers, against the best left-handed pitching we had outside of our first-string man, Tyler.

In fact, we have morning batting practice before each of the games in Boston, too. We never took any chances in that series we could help. We were playing everything to get the "percentage" right up to the limit.

The Most Important Play

Perhaps some of the fans would like to know what I consider to be the most important play of the first game of the World's Series. In my judgment, it was when Schmidt caught that foul fly and turned, all off his balance, shooting the ball to third base and nailing the runner by the combination of his good throw and the nervy work of Deal, who was looked upon as a substitute and a weak spot in our lineup.

I did not look on him in that way, for I knew him, but our opponents and a lot of the fans did.

When the Athletics were met with that play they knew that they were up against a ball club and that they could not beat us by getting us to throwing the ball around. They had beaten other clubs that way, and they thought they might us.

Their whole attitude toward our club changed after that play, and they realized there they would have to work hard to win. I honestly believe this was the turning point in the series.

Beaten Before They Started

Now, to mention the last bit of superstition that I played in connection with that series. We won three games and the fourth was scheduled to take place on our home grounds in Boston.

If we lost that, according to the rules for playing the series laid down by the National Commission, the whole works had to jump back to Philadelphia for the fifth game the next day.

The players were at their morning "skull" practice on the day of the last game, when the secretary of the club came into the clubhouse, where we were meeting.

"Well, George," he said. "I've made a reservation on the train to Philly tonight in case we need to go back for another game, which I hope we won't."

"Cancel it," I told him, before all my players. "Cancel it right away. It is bad luck, and I don't want any reservation on that train, even if we have to go over there in day coaches, or Mr. Gaffney has to hire a special. I haven't even packed a bag, and I don't intend to, either, because I won't need it."

The ball players all heard me say this, and it had the desired effect. The secretary of the club canceled the reservation as I told him to do, and I didn't even have my bag packed.

If we had lost that game, we would have had no time to pack bags or to prepare the uniforms, bats, and other luggage and paraphernalia, for we would have had to hustle even to make the train. Therefore, the players knew that they just had to win it, and they did, and the series with it.

The knowledge that I was confident we would win helped them, I believe, although the Athletics were a beaten team before they even started that last contest. I don't think that they would have won a game from our club if the two teams had been playing yet.

I don't know what it was, but we had "something" on them, and Connie Mack admitted it when he started to break his great machine up this Winter. A beaten team, like a beaten fighter, seldom comes back.

Part Nine—January 24, 1915

STALLINGS' TRIBUTE TO SOME OF HIS MEN

Every Man Working for Victory, Even Those on the Bench

Connie Mack Alone Did Not Come to Shake Hands

Substitutes Who Played Like Regulars

Few Defeats When Stars Were Absent From The Game

Much has been written and said about the "breaks" of ball games, and I want to go on record as saying that most ball games are won by a manager taking advantage of the "break"; but never was a contest played in which a team worked harder to get the "percentage" of than my club did in the third battle of the World's Series.

The hardest run ever scored was the one that the Braves made in the 10th inning of the third contest, which tied it up.

As I had said in all these articles, our spirit swept the Athletics off their feet, and, from the first, my little ball club showed Mack's champions that we were not afraid of them, their batting averages, or their record.

But the inning which absolutely broke our opponent's heart and made our club sure of victory was that 10th. I don't believe it had ever been duplicated. After we had finally won that contest, I went into the clubhouse and found my players shouting: "Hurrah for the next world's champion!" They knew that the series was theirs.

Since then, I have been told by a certain American League ball player who visited the clubhouse of the Athletics after their defeat that they as plainly showed that they realize they were beaten as my boys did that they had won. Among themselves, they were grumbling and their heads were hanging.

In their half of the 10th inning, the Athletics made two runs, and it looked to every one on the field as though Mack's team was finally to hang up a victory — that is, to every one except the members of our little ball club.

The Philadelphia team earned one of those runs. The other slipped across the plate when Evers let his head drop after losing a chance to cut the run off because the ball took a bad bound, could not be fielded, and hit him on the chest. Another run slipped over then, and Mack's club had a lead of two.

When Johnny came to the bench, every man on the Boston team walked over and spoke to him.

"Never mind," they said one after another. "We've got three more games to win it in. You've done enough for this ball club to afford to kick one way once in a while."

No One Admitted Defeat

But not a man on the team conceded defeat. The substitutes, who had not taken any active part in the actual playing, started to show what they were worth to the club by tearing up and down the bench and shouting their lungs out. Every one was moving on that bench. We intended to make it just as hard as we could for the Athletics to hold that lead.

Then Hank Gowdy, the castoff of the Giants, came up to the plate and busted one for a home run. That was just a plain slam, but it took some of the wind out of the Athletics. They then realized that the two run lead was not a safe one.

The tieing run was at the plate, as we express it in baseball. It means that the man who would tie the score if he got around the bases was at the bat. This was the hardest one ever pushed around.

Every man on our club was working for it, working his heart out, whether he was in the coaching box, at the bat, or on the bench.

Any one who saw that game will never forget the spirit. Rabbit Maranville was on the coaching line at first base, running wild. Every man on the bench was waving a sweater or a mackinaw and saying something except me. I just sat tight.

It was the typical "break" of a ball game, only bigger. It is useless to recite here just how that run was made, since it has been told so often.

I am only glad that Evers' hit was one of the big factors in getting it. But we worked for every foot that runner moved around the bases, and each move was carefully thought out. When we finally got it, we knew that the game and the championship would be ours. The winning run was only a matter of time.

That is why I found my players singing in the clubhouse afterwards and speaking of themselves as the next world's champions. We all knew it then, and so did the Athletics.

Gowdy Not Married Yet

Perhaps in these concluding articles of this story it would do no harm to speak of individuals. With the superb pitching Gowdy's catching stands out. It was the big feature of the series, although I expected it of Hank, for I knew better than any one what he could do.

Before the series, in fact, on the day after we had clinched the National League pennant, I got to talking to Christy Mathewson out at the Polo Grounds where we were playing out farewell series with the Giants.

"What is Gowdy going to do for you, George?" Matty asked me.

"I'll make you a bet right now," I replied, "that he out-hits, out-catches, and out-throws Schang in the series."

Matty did not make the bet, but he would have lost it if he had. You see, I knew something of Schang, for he had worked on my club when I had been the manager in Buffalo.

Personally, he is one of the finest fellows that ever put on the chest protector and mask. But, as I have implied before in this story, he cannot hit a slow ball with a fish net. The only fast one he got within reach in the series he busted over third for two bags. That was one that Bill James threw him.

When a man is not hitting as he should it always hurts the rest of his game, and Schang did not catch as well as he was expected to. We played on every weakness we knew. We showed him spirit from the first, and nothing but spirit made that tough run in the 10th inning possible.

During the series, while we are talking of Gowdy, it was reported that some young woman had promised to marry Hank if our club won. Gowdy has asked me to deny this.

"Why, it got me in bad," he complained to me after the third game. "Every young woman I know expects me to marry her now if we win."

"That's no reason for your taking it easy," I told him.

This report was started by some one who thought it was a good story. Hank is not married at this writing, and we certainly won the series.

The fourth game was easy, and, as I have said, I did not need to work Rudolph in it. We could have won with almost any one else pitching. But I came back with the great star to avoid any criticism.

After the last out in the final game, the whole Philadelphia team came over to our bench and shook hands with us, except Connie Mack. Connie had been used to somebody congratulating him, and so Ira Thomas, the captain of the Athletics, carried his message.

"Connie said the crowd was so bad he didn't think he could get across the field," Thomas told me as he shook hands, "so he sent his congratulations by me."

The Despised Second String

I'm sorry that Connie did not come himself, for I was anxious to forget whatever little difficulties we have before the series. I could afford to do that and I have done it.

The other members of the Athletics, however, were very sincere in their congratulations. Johnny Evers had rushed to get off the field, and Eddie Collins followed him clear back through the bench, where we got out under the grandstand to our clubhouse to shake hands.

"You did great work," said Collins to Evers. "And you deserved to win."

A year before McGraw had been shaking this boy by the hand and telling him that he was the greatest ballplayer in the world. Collins was as game when defeated as he had been when his club had won.

And so we won the series.

If the reader will stand for a little analyzing, I want to say that I believe our victory was due to the great spirit of the men on the Boston club, combined with the organization and preparation.

I have already said that not a man missed a sign during the four games. The team had been drilled through the plays like soldiers. We left nothing to chance which we could figure out beforehand. The Athletics were meeting a machine with a hair trigger and as sensitive as a rifle equipped with one and as deadly.

Critics had said during the regular season that I had no second string payers. I want to call attention to a few facts.

Evers was out of 24 games last season and yet of this number we won 22. It is a great thing when a club can lose a wonderful player like John and still keep on winning. Rabbit Maranville was out of two, and the team won both games. The reason for Maranville's absence was the death of his brother.

Schmidt was out of nine games because of a bad ankle, and we won all nine. Smith was hurt for four games, and we did not lose one while he was out.

When men like Evers, Maranville, Schmidt, and Red Smith are out of a batting order and a club keeps on winning, what is the answer? It is all the psychology of winning. Once a ball club gets doing right, there is no stopping it. My second string beat the life out of Brooklyn in the last game of the season.

It is the spirit of victory, and we certainly had it in a highly aggravated form during the World's Series. I guess that these facts and statistics I have quoted prove that we could win with stars out of the lineup. I don't say that we could right along for several weeks, but this makes it plan that injuries did not stop us.

Rare Praise From Griffith

My players took their victory calmly. They did not tear around Boston that night, and every man reported at the ball park at 10 o'clock the next morning as usual.

The Athletics took their defeat very bitterly, even Connie Mack, they had all been so sure of winning. I felt most sorry for John Coombs, because the great pitcher of the past had quite a large sum of money bet on his team, as I heard it.

It was a heavy loss, and he was destined to be turned out of the club shortly afterwards. I got this gossip from members of my team who saw the player on the Athletics in their hotel after the game.

All was not harmonious on the way back to Philadelphia on the train following their defeat, I am told. Several players on the Athletics tried to place the blame, and the result was much argument. It was at this time, as I hear it, that Mack decided to break up his team, and he has stuck to his resolution.

Outside of Gowdy, to whom I have already given honorable mention, every man on my team and the bench deserves praise. Especially is this true of the pitchers. They all showed great ball when it was put up to them to deliver.

Dick Rudolph came out of the pitching end with the best record, but I don't doubt that any of the other regular twirlers would have won two games if they have been given the chance. No pitcher ever used his head better than Rudolph did in the series. Clark Griffith, who was an old pitcher himself, said to me after it was all over: "I have never seen such pitching as you got. I doubt if my staff could have done better."

This is rare praise from Griff, for when he speaks of his staff he means Walter Johnson. Secretly, I believe that the Washington manager was pulling for us because he carries no great love for the Athletics or Connie Mack. There has long been a feud between the two clubs, but Griff never admitted to me that he favored any one except the American League entry.

The smile he wore after the last game, however, did not impress me as being one of sympathy for Mack and his men. After the first game Rudolph said to me: "I don't mind pitching to this 'Home Run' Baker. He hits something like Zimmerman, only left-handed. I don't think he will bust many balls over the fence for me. He won't hit a ball to left field."

Rudolph had this player figured right.

While Schmidt, our first baseman, did not show up any too flashy in the series to the ordinary spectator, nevertheless the players and I realized what he meant to the team. There is a first baseman who did not drop a thrown ball throughout the season.

Every time an infielder grabbed the pill he did not pause a minute to shoot it to Shmidty, because he knew that Schmidt was going to pick it off if it was within possible reach. Give me a ball player's opinion of another every time, especially when it is a boost.

Molded Into One Machine

Of course, Evers and Maranville need no praise. Both played wonderful ball. Charlie Deal went into the lineup a substitute with the eyes of all the spectators and the members of the Athletics on him, expecting him to weaken and prove the fatal flaw in the club. He showed great baseball, and his play with Schmidt in getting a runner at third base on a long throw in the opening game was the very first "break" which turned the series our way, in my opinion.

After Red Smith was hurt I received thousands of letters from fans urging me to play Whitted at third base, but I knew what Deal could do, and he didn't disappoint me. If he had, by any chance, I don't suppose that these second guessers would ever have let me alone.

The outfielders did their part, and my shift worked, so that the club hit as hard against left-handers as right. It was a great ball club, with no trace of a yellow streak in it. The team was a conglomeration of material when we started, but we all worked to mold it into a machine.

One man was patted on the back and another abused. I will develop any player except one with a "yellow" streak in him, and that is the first thing I test out and seek in a recruit. If he has any trace of it I don't want him in the lineup, because the team has not a chance to come through as my club did in the World's Series.

Managers must learn their men and they must have an aptitude to study character and mold it. Otherwise they will never make a ball club. We played everything to the limit in the series because we all knew that there was a game ball club to carry it out, with every member tested.

As an example, with a man on second base and the play planned, Barry went after a low curve, which he did not have a chance to hit, with the count three and two on him. The runner on second base at this stage was naturally pulled off with Barry's swing, and Gowdy's throw to Evers put him out and finished the inning.

It got out us of an ugly hole, since there were men on first and second and only one out at that time. Plays like that will change a whole ball game and series.

Well, we have it now for a year and they can't take it away from us.

Part Ten—January 31, 1915

EXPECTS THE BRAVES TO REPEAT IN 1915

Stallings Says He Cannot See How The Club Can Be Beaten

Perhaps, before concluding this story on the Braves club, it would not be altogether out of the way for me to take a look at the prospects for next year as I see them. Let me say baldly and without any apologies for the statement that I expect my club to win the National League championship again next season, and later the World's Series. I don't see how they can beat us.

One big reason for this expression of confidence on my part is the addition to the Boston team of Sherwood Magee, formerly of the Phillies, a man that I consider to be one of the best and hardest hitters in the big league. The records for last season show what his value to a club is, for he drove in more runs than any other batter on our circuit, a total of 101, if I remember rightly. That is the hitting in a pinch which counts and brings returns.

With Red Smith and Magee in that batting order next Summer an opposing pitcher is going to face a couple of sluggers who are liable to break up the ball game for him any time. Even though Magee has been more or less dissatisfied in Philadelphia for the past season or two and even threatened to jump to the Federals, he has made a remarkable record with the Phillies. I predict that he will play more baseball with our club than he has ever shown in his life before. I have lately received word from Red Smith that the leg he broke just before the World's Series is as good as ever. He closes his letter: "Take it from me, George, I am going to be in the next series."

As to the Coming Season

Maybe it is a little premature to begin to indulge in predictions for next season, but since I have no regrets to express for the record of last, I don't see why I shouldn't. I may never have such a good chance again.

My club next year is going into the race with better prospects than have been carried by any I have ever handled. If anything, it is stronger than the team which finished the race last Summer and won the world's championship. I have several recruits who went through a season on the bench, and who will be able to deliver, if necessary, next Summer. In passing, I want to mention one young player from whom I expect great things—Strand, the pitcher. He will be a wonder next Summer, and, along with young Davis, should compose the greatest pair of recruit pitchers ever to be uncovered in a single season. I expect to take the blanket off both of them and work them regularly, so that I can give my regular trio a little more rest between games. These three are all at the height of their careers, however, so that I should have few pitching worries next Summer.

Many followers of baseball have asked me, personally, and many others have written to ask, how I get a line on minor leaguers. Some apparently think that I depend entirely on scouts. Of course, I have some trusted veterans to look over prospects for me, but I don't depend as much on scouts as most managers.

When I was a young fellow I started to go to medical school in Baltimore, but I never took my degree, for baseball kept me from being a physician. I was deeply interested in medicine, and especially surgery at the time, however, and used to make copious notes on the lectures for reference purposes. I still have those notes and, indeed, frequently administer first aid whenever any of the negroes employed on my plantation are injured or seriously ill and need quick treatment.

Takes Notes and Keeps a Diary

At this time my father was a contractor, and was building the Customhouse at Jacksonville, Florida. Capt Ed Andrews, the old centerfielder of the Philadelphia club gave me a chance to play after I met him on a trip down to Florida to see my father. It was 25 years ago.

That was the end of the medicine, but I never gave up the habit of keeping notes which I had acquired at medical school, and right now I have a trunk full of diaries, half finished stories on baseball, theories, and data on bush league talent. This data has proved invaluable to me, as have my diaries. I have kept a diary ever since I have been in baseball, writing it up religiously each night before going to bed, and some day I may permit parts of it to be published if any one cares to use it, but that time will be after I am through with the game actively, which day I hope, will never come, for I certainly love the sports, its problems, and its fights.

After the season of 1912 several friends of mine, including Capt Huston who, with Col Jacob Ruppert, recently bought the New York Yankees, and Ed Barrow, the president of the International League, were at my place in Georgia hunting. In the party was a well-known cartoonist.

"How do you know all about those young players?" the artist asked me.

I went to my trunk and dug out several handfuls of data and showed the figures to him. He has never quit kidding me about them since.

"Say," he will remark, "can you tell me, George, what year measles broken into the Big League?"

But with this data I can pretty near tell what any bush leaguer has been doing when he is recommended to me, and I send a scout out to look at him to make sure he isn't tied up into 17 knots with the "charley-horse" or something else before I buy or put in a draft for him. But I don't have to send scouts all over the country, wasting time and railroad fares on wild-goose chases. I can generally tell pretty accurately from my data whether a busher is worth looking at or not.

Fake "Holdups" Put on the Run

A lot of fans may be interested in an incident which occurred in connection with the hunting party I just referred to but which has no bearing on baseball.

However, it has some connection with the surgical profession, or came very near having. Every member of the party was on the place except the cartoonist, who was a day or two late getting down, this being a general habit of cartoonists, I have found. Many visitors believe that the part of Georgia in which I live is very wild, and, to induce this notion, we frequently speak pointedly and in loud tones of expeditions "to kill So-and-So, if he don't quit shooting my plantation hands."

We all decided to frame it up on the cartoonist, who was making his first visit, and we arranged for a phony holdup, putting masks on some of the negroes who were to be led by a squad of my visitors, It is quite a drive from the railroad station to my place through heavy Georgia mud.

Ed Barrow was selected to go to the railroad station to meet the guest and make sure that he did not carry a gun which was loaded, as such a factor often proves embarrassing as a property in a phony holdup. Barrow was to relieve the visitor of his weapon, if he carried any, in order to protect the life insurance companies from being forced to redeem any of the policies held by the embryo agents. When Barrow met the cartoonist, he said: "Listen! You know this is a pretty bad country, down here? Have you got a gun with you?"

"Sure, I have," promptly answered the cartoonist, producing a very long, blue weapon that Barrow has said since looked like one of those 42 centimeter affairs of German parentage.

"You had better let me carry it," urged Barrow. "I know how to handle it down here better than you do."

"Not on your life," responded the cartoonist. "I came down here to shoot something."

"Is it loaded?" asked Barrow.

"You bet it is," readily responded the visitor, whirling the chambers and exhibiting the noses of the bullets.

Barrow felt that there was only one thing for him to do—give up.

"Listen," he began, "They have planned a fake holdup down the road here a piece, to scare you. Don't shoot any one."

"Leave it to me," answered the visitor.

So, when the "highwaymen" sprang out of the bushes, the cartoonist cut loose with his cannon, and there has never been such a scramble in the history of Georgia since Gen. Sherman made this march to the sea. Those pseudo highwaymen tore their clothes and scratched themselves on brambles and loose stones in an effort to get away, while the negro driver, who did not know about it all, fell backwards off his seat, and the team ran away.

Of course, the cartoonist was firing over everybody's head.

Will Continue the Old Policy

I will continue next season handling my club along the same general lines that I followed last year. All teams require constant building up. No manager is ever entirely satisfied. When the Athletics were at the top of their great strength and winning stride, I'll bet Connie Mack spent many sleepless nights worrying over some weakness, of which the general public had no knowledge. The same applies to several of the great players of the different clubs who have physical ailments and weaknesses that they frequently conceal from everybody, including their manager.

I have always made it a rule to put my team up at the best hotels, much to the disgust of many owners, but not Mr. Gaffney. Let me say here that since I have been connected with the Boston club, even when it was away down in the going and a posing proposition, had he made a single murmur about expanses. Good hotel accommodations keep the players in a better frame of mind, and they can deliver better ball. This is important in the extreme.

When a team is losing a manager is forced to keep fighting against stagnation all the time. As soon as many pitcher stagger and the club gets in a tight place, that old feeling of "Well, what's the use?" comes over the men, and they lose all ambition for everything except the "first and 15th of the month," which are the paydays in the big leagues.

These are some of the cares to which a manager falls heir when he starts building a ball club, and none should be in a better position that I. I have often said that if I go the wrong way after they finally call me out in this world's game, my worst punishment would be to manage an indifferent ball club, with a wild pitcher and a boneheaded catcher.

Hardest Job in Baseball

It is all right to speak of inspiring a fighting spirit in a team, but this is one of the hardest and most delicate jobs in baseball. Once the spirit begins to show, that club will begin to climb, and the other teams will be forced to reckon with it as a factor in the race.

It is the most valuable asset of a baseball team. In some players this fighting spirit lies dormant, and only has to be aroused. Into some you can drive the spirit, while others can be shamed into it, and a few are just plain "yellow," and never will be game.

In trying to build up the various ball clubs of which I have had charge at different times, I have usually begun with the catcher, for on him the club's defense is focused, as he is the only man in a position where every play is in front of him. A good, smart catcher is the first ingredient of a strong defense, and once you have one, with a good "whip," working right, a manager is over the first big hurdle of reconstruction.

When I took charge of the Yankees we had Blair and Sweeney, both young. Of the two, one was inclined to be indifferent, and failed to be the great man we expected. The other gradually got the fighting spirit, and became during the second year of my term in charge of the team one of the stars of the game.

I shall keep after my club this year so that the players will fight as hard as they did last year. I won't let them ease off for a minute because they have won one world's championship. Some of my best men condition slowly in the Spring, so that the fans must not be surprised if we do not get away with a big burst of speed from the jump. As I have said in a previous installment, I am superstitious about winning the first game, so don't be alarmed if we drop it. Then, you can never tell about baseball luck.

Plantation Hands "Loyal"

Several years ago the Yankees were training down in Georgia, and we were scheduled to play an exhibition game with the Newark club of the then Eastern league near my place. All my negroes came over to watch the contest, and showed their confidence in me by betting mules, farming implements, etc. that the Yankees would win.

Fortunately, they could not wager very extensively, since there were few takers, and, of course, I did not know anything about it.

It was a warm day, and old Joe McGinnity was working for the minor leaguers. He was never better, and he made that young team of mine look bad, giving us a good trimming. After the defeat I found several things on the place, such as mules, plows, etc. missing, and discovered that my hands, through their loyalty to me, had lost them in betting. It was not exactly baseball luck, for McGinnity was right that day, but it was tough luck for me, because it took me some time to get my implements and livestock out of "hock."

Steadily, next season, I will be trying to build. Sherwood Magee is a big step in this direction. In spite of the fact that I publicly picked my entire club as the All-American team following the World's Series, I may make some changes. But just cut out this prediction and paste it inside your hat:

When next October rolls around, we will be there, or thereabouts.

END

This series was copyright 1914 by the Wheeler Syndicate, Inc. and it ran in newspapers across the country. In Boston, it was the *Boston Globe* which ran the series of articles beginning on November 29, 1914 and running through January 31, 1915. In New York, it was the *New York Tribune*.

In preparing the Stallings pieces for publication in this volume, we have not changed a single word but have corrected misspellings of proper names in the text and very occasionally modified the original punctuation. Stallings' practice of putting almost every nickname into quotation marks is one we decided to dispense with.

Thanks to Steve Steinberg.

This section was prepared by Bill Nowlin.

Braves rooters heading to Fenway to see the World Series.

Mr. Warmth

Braves' manager George Stallings had a reputation for being sarcastic, profane, and even sadistic towards his players. His legendary temperament would reveal itself on a number of occasions.

A rookie once entered a dugout where Stallings was seated. Detecting a foul odor, the freshman presumptuously chided his skipper that the place smelled like a sewer. Stallings tartly responded, "That's my breath. By this time tomorrow, you'll be too far away to smell anything."

One afternoon, Stallings gave a start to his third-string catcher. Immediately the move proved disastrous. In the very first inning, the back-up backstop cleanly fielded a bunt but then proceeded to hit the runner on the back of the head while attempting to throw to first base. The baseball bounced into right field, enabling the runner to advance all the way to third base. Irate, Stallings not only yanked the catcher but also informed him that he was being demoted to the minors. The flabbergasted fellow questioned the severity of the penalty for just one bad throw. Stallings rebutted his receiver's conclusion. "I'm not firing you because you hit the runner on the head. I'm canning you because he was able to reach third. Any time a catcher of mine can't kill a man with a peg on the head, he's through."

Stallings' personality often revealed a distinct lack of sympathy for a struggling player. One of his pitchers had a tendency to yield an above-average number of walks. During a windy afternoon contest, the hurler gave up eight consecutive free passes. Caught up in a hopeless situation, the pitcher forlornly looked towards the dugout, anticipating a call to the showers from his manager. Instead, he heard Stallings bellow, "Stay out there and throw, you ape! Maybe the wind will blow a strike across the plate for you."

Flashback to a Braves Miracle ... 1914. Boston Braves Historical Association, 2001. Drawn from contemporary 1914 *Boston Herald* accounts.

Very Superstitious

Included among the complex traits of Braves manager George Stallings was his fear of jinxes and hoodoos. These idiosyncrasies transcended standard superstitions. For example, birds that landed on the playing field had to be shooed away as quickly as possible. Stallings believed that if one should land on a bat, extreme bad luck quickly would follow.

Maintaining good luck, Stallings held, demanded that he not make changes to his appearance or in his conduct. When the Braves embarked upon a winning streak, as they often did in 1914, he would don the same suit, regardless of condition, every day until the club eventually suffered a loss.

This pattern of behavior also included his diet. Once Stallings enjoyed a pre-game piece of pie at a nearby restaurant before reporting to the ballpark. The lemon meringue dessert had been so delicious that day that he treated himself to a second slice. The snack coincided with the onset of a Braves winning streak and for the next nine days the dutiful manager dined on that same menu selection in the same quantity so as not to break the beneficial spell. In his mind, the prospect of acquiring ulcers was a small price to pay for his club's continued success on the diamond. History is devoid of the fact as to whether Stallings would ever again possess the desire to dine on lemon meringue pie once the string of victories had concluded.

This account largely relies upon Herman L. Masin's book *Curve Ball Laughs*.

By The Numbers

By Dan Fields

Boston Braves in 1914:

0

Hits by the Philadelphia Phillies against George "Iron" Davis on September 9—the first-ever no-hitter at Fenway Park. Davis walked five batters and struck out four as the Braves won 7-0 in the second game of a doubleheader. This was the only shutout in the hurler's career.

1-2-3

Order in which Johnny Evers, Rabbit Maranville, and Bill James finished in voting for the Chalmers Award (National League) for most valuable player. They were the first trio of teammates to accomplish this feat in MVP voting. (The other teams with 1-2-3 finishers were the 1941 Brooklyn Dodgers, 1959 Chicago White Sox, and 1966 Baltimore Orioles.) Evers is one of only five players ever to win the NL MVP award without a .300 batting average, 30 home runs, or 100 RBIs that season (excluding pitchers).

4

Runs batted in by Rabbit Maranville on an inside-the-park grand slam on September 26—the first-ever grand slam at Fenway Park. The slam, off Hippo Vaughn, sparked a 6-2 victory over the Chicago Cubs in the first game of a doubleheader.

4-0

Record of the Braves against the heavily favored Philadelphia Athletics in the World Series. It was the first-ever four-game sweep of the Series. Manager George Stallings never returned to the World Series, but he is one of only five managers with a perfect record in the World Series.

4-18

Record to start the regular season, including six shutout losses.

8th

Place (out of eight National League teams) of the Braves on July 18, their latest date in last place. With 35 wins and 43 losses, the Braves trailed the first-place New York Giants by 11 games. The Braves then won 59 games and lost only 16 over the remainder of the season and won the pennant by 10 1/2 games over the Giants.

9

League-leading number of times that Johnny Evers was ejected from a game.

15

Most games behind first place by 1914 Braves. On July 4 the Braves lost both games of a doubleheader against the Brooklyn Robins. Their record of 26 wins and 40 losses put them 15 games behind the New York Giants. The Braves are the only team, under the old eight-team league format, to win a pennant after being in last place on the Fourth of July.

16

Most games under .500 by 1914 Braves. On June 8 the Braves had only 12 wins against 28 losses.

19

Shutouts by Braves pitchers, including 18 in a span of only 75 games between July 6 (second game of doubleheader) and September 25 (first game of doubleheader).

26 + 2

Wins each by Bill James and Dick Rudolph during the regular season and the World Series.

143

League-leading number of double plays by Braves fielders.

407

League-leading number of putouts as shortstop by Rabbit Maranville. Only three other shortstops have had more putouts in a season, but Maranville didn't even lead the majors that year—Donie Bush of the Detroit Tigers led the American League with 425 putouts and still holds the single-season record.

.545

Batting average by Hank Gowdy in the World Series. The catcher had six hits (including five extra-base hits) in 11 at-bats, becoming the first player with at least 10 at-bats to hit over .500 in a World Series.

574

League-leading number of assists as shortstop by Rabbit Maranville. This was a major-league record until 1920.

.788

League-leading winning percentage of Bill James, with a record of 26 wins and 7 losses.

.976

League-leading fielding percentage as second baseman by Johnny Evers.

Around the majors in 1914:

0.96

Earned-run average of Dutch Leonard. The Red Sox hurler allowed only 24 earned runs in 224⅔ innings. This is still the major-league record for lowest ERA in a season.

2

Unassisted double plays by Boston Red Sox outfielder Tris Speaker in 1914 (on April 21 and August 8). Speaker also had two unassisted double plays in 1918 while playing for the Cleveland Indians. Only three other outfielders in major-league history have accomplished the feat twice in one season.

3

No-hitters in the major leagues in 1914. In addition to the gem pitched by George "Iron" Davis of the Braves, Joe Benz of the Chicago White Sox no-hit the Cleveland Naps on May 31, and Ed Lafitte of the Brooklyn Tip-Tops threw the first no-hitter in Federal League history on September 19 against the Kansas City Packers.

3

Detroit Tigers baserunners thrown out by New York Yankees catcher Les Nunamaker attempting to steal in the seventh inning on August 3. No other catcher has matched this feat in one inning.

4

Errors committed by Cleveland Naps shortstop Ray Chapman in the fifth inning of a 7-1 loss to the New York Yankees on June 20. Five other players in major-league history (all playing at short or third base) have had four errors in one inning.

6

Sacrifice bunts by Brooklyn Robins first baseman Jake Daubert during a doubleheader against the Philadelphia Phillies on August 15. Hobbled by an ankle injury, Daubert laid down two sac bunts in the first game and four more in the second game.

7

Innings pitched by 19-year-old Babe Ruth in his major-league debut, on July 11. The strong outing helped lead the Boston Red Sox over the Cleveland Naps, 4-3.

7

Batters hit by pitches in a game between the Detroit Tigers and Washington Senators on August 24. This American League record was not matched until 1971.

9-1

Score by which the Chicago Chi-Feds beat the Kansas City Packers in a Federal League game on April 23. This was the first major-league game at Weeghman Park, which became home to the Chicago Cubs in 1916 and was dubbed Wrigley Field in 1926.

18

Players already under contract with the National League or American League who switched to the Federal League. During its two-year existence (1914 and 1915), 81 former or current major leaguers and 140 former or current minor leaguers joined the upstart league. Its efforts to attract star players from the rival leagues caused salaries to skyrocket.

19

Home runs by Philadelphia Phillies outfielder Gavvy Cravath (all hit at home) to lead the National League.

21

Innings in a game between the New York Giants and Pittsburgh Pirates on July 17. Both starting pitchers (Rube Marquard and Babe Adams, respectively) went the distance, with the Giants winning, 3-1. After making the final out, New York outfielder Red Murray was knocked unconscious by a bolt of lightning. Murray recovered and played the next day, but Marquard suffered from a fatigued arm and lost his remaining ten decisions of the season.

22

Games that Detroit Tigers center fielder Ty Cobb missed because of a broken thumb suffered in a fight at a butcher's shop. Cobb also missed several weeks earlier in the season after a pitch fractured a rib. Despite playing in only 98 games during the season, Cobb led the American League with a .368 batting average (under current rules, Cobb would not have enough at-bats to be eligible for the crown).

23

Age of New York Yankees shortstop Roger Peckinpaugh when he was named interim manager of the team after Frank Chance resigned in early September. The youngest-ever manager guided the Yankees to 10 wins and 10 losses.

28

Wins by Washington Senators pitcher Walter Johnson, most in the American League. He won at least 20 games every year from 1910 through 1919, racking up 265 victories during the decade.

122

League-leading number of runs scored by Eddie Collins, who won the Chalmers Award (American League) for most valuable player. The Philadelphia Athletics second baseman finished second in batting average, stolen bases, and bases on balls. On December 8 Collins was sold to the Chicago White Sox for a reported $50,000.

3,000

Career hits by Honus Wagner on June 9 and Nap Lajoie on September 27. Before 1914, only Cap Anson had reached 3,000 hits.

Sources

Gary Caruso, *The Braves Encyclopedia* (Philadelphia: Temple University Press, 1995).

Bill James, *The New Bill James Historical Baseball Abstract* (New York: The Free Press, 2001).

Society for American Baseball Research, *The SABR Baseball List and Record Book* (New York: Scribner, 2007).

Burt Randolph Sugar, ed., *The Baseball Maniac's Almanac,* third edition (New York: Skyhorse Publishing, 2012).

atlanta.braves.mlb.com

baseball-almanac.com

baseball-reference.com

retrosheet.org

sabr.org/bioproject

thisgreatgame.com/1914.html

Career stats for Rabbit Maranville:

5

Teams for which Maranville played (Boston Braves, Pittsburgh Pirates, Chicago Cubs, Brooklyn Robins, and St. Louis Cardinals).

5

Years in top ten in MVP voting.

20

Age at first game on September 10, 1912, for the Boston Braves.

43

Age at final game on September 29, 1935, for the Boston Braves.

177

Triples, tied for 19th most in major-league history.

.258

Batting average, the third lowest among Hall of Fame players (not including pitchers).

300

Sacrifice hits, 11th most in major-league history.

672

At-bats in 1922 (for the Pittsburgh Pirates) without a home run, a major-league record. That year Maranville had 198 hits and scored 115 runs—both career bests.

1928

Only other year in which Maranville won a pennant (with the St. Louis Cardinals). The Cards were swept by the New York Yankees in four games in the World Series.

2,153

Games as shortstop, ninth most in major-league history.

2,605

Hits, the most in major-league history by a player born in Massachusetts.

5,139

Putouts as shortstop, most in major-league history.

7,354

Assists as shortstop, fifth most in major-league history.

8,967

Assists (any position), most in major-league history.

10,078

At-bats, 25th most in major-league history. Maranville is one of only five players with 10,000 at-bats and fewer than 3,000 hits.

Sources

Society for American Baseball Research, *The SABR Baseball List and Record Book* (New York: Scribner, 2007).

Burt Randolph Sugar, ed., *The Baseball Maniac's Almanac*, third edition (New York: Skyhorse Publishing, 2012).

baseball-reference.com

Creature Feature

By Dan Fields

Two players on the Miracle Braves were best known by their animal-inspired nicknames –Walter "Rabbit" Maranville and George "Possum" Whitted— and another player, the combative Johnny Evers, was called "The Human Crab." Evers and Maranville are among the dozens of Hall of Famers with animal monikers. The others include:

Ernie "Mr. Cub" Banks
Jake "Eagle Eye" Beckley
Wade "Chicken Man" Boggs
Jesse "The Crab" Burkett
Orlando "Baby Bull" Cepeda
Andre "The Hawk" Dawson
William "Buck" Ewing
Jimmie "The Beast" Foxx
Lou "The Iron Horse" Gehrig
Leon "Goose" Goslin
Rich "Goose" Gossage
Clark "The Old Fox" Griffith
Charles "Chick" Hafey
Harry "Slug" Heilmann
Miller "Mighty Mite" Huggins
Jim "Catfish" Hunter
Al "Mr. Tiger" Kaline
Walter "Buck" Leonard
Joe "Ducky" Medwick
Johnny "The Big Cat" Mize
Charlie "Old Hoss" Radbourn
Ryne "Ryno" Sandberg
Duke "The Silver Fox" Snider
Tris "The Grey Eagle" Speaker
Norman "Turkey" Stearnes
George "Mule" Suttles

Contributors

Dennis Auger grew up in New Hampshire and now resides in Massachusetts with his wife Elaine. Besides being a lifelong Yankees fan and a SABR member, he is a clinical supervisor at an outpatient substance abuse facility. He has written several articles covering baseball during the 1893-1919 era.

Thomas Ayers is a lifelong Blue Jays fan who was born and raised in Toronto. He is a labour lawyer who has earned degrees from the University of Toronto, the London School of Economics and Queen's University. He has contributed five other biographies to the SABR Baseball Biography Project.

Peter C. Bjarkman is a Cuban baseball specialist and the senior writer for www.BaseballdeCuba.com. In the words of Latin American sports historian Joseph Arbena, "Peter Bjarkman is doing for Cuban baseball what Ry Cooder has done for Cuban music."

Maurice Bouchard, a SABR member since 1999, spends more time in front of his computer trying to find the maiden names of obscure players' mothers than he should admit. He has worked as an author, editor, or fact-checker on nine SABR team books, starting in 2005 with *'75: The Red Sox Team that Saved Baseball*. An academic cicada, Bouchard recently completed a second masters degree (this one from Simmons College Graduate School of Library and Information Science) 14 years after his first one, which in turn was 14 years after his undergraduate degree. The discipline for the 2025 degree is anyone's guess. At the time of publication, Bouchard and his painfully beautiful wife Kim are living with their two pooches in Westford, New York, just ten minutes' drive from 25 Main Street, Cooperstown.

Bob Brady joined SABR in 1991. He is the current president of the Boston Braves Historical Association and has edited its quarterly newsletter since 1992. Bob has contributed biographies and supporting pieces to a number of SABR publications as well as occasionally lending a hand in the editing process.

Frank Ceresi is an attorney, professional appraiser, writer, and baseball historian (see http://www.fcassociates.com). He is also the Curator of TheNationalPastimeMuseum.com, a virtual baseball museum which launched on Opening Day of 2013. Frank and his wife Barbara live in Arlington, Virginia.

Clem Comly is a 30-year SABR member and co-chair of its Statistical Analysis Committee. Clem is vice president and treasurer of Retrosheet and a volunteer from its beginnings. Clem is Retrosheet's Cy Young of play-by-play translation and computer input. If Clem never did another game a new volunteer would have to code and enter each play from every game from 1932 through 1944 to beat Clem's record. Clem was a fact checker for all of the bios in this book.

Rory Costello was drawn to participate in this project for two reasons. First, as a Williams College alumnus, he was very interested to learn more about George Davis. Second, his interest in the nefarious doings of Tammany Hall made Big Jim Gaffney a most enjoyable topic. Rory lives in Brooklyn, New York with his wife Noriko and five-year-old son Kai.

Jerrod Cotosman is a CPA who oversees the State of Colorado's Medicaid accounting. He became a Red Sox fan at age 7 in the summer of 1978 after reading a book about Fred Lynn. He has written a novel and an anthology of short stories and lives in Denver with his wife and daughter.

Peter Cottrell lives with his wife in Gaithersburg, Maryland and is the Information Technology Director for that city. He became a Washington Senators fan in 1968, switched to the Baltimore Orioles in 1972, and gratefully accepted the Washington Nationals as his favorite team in 2005. A member of the Bob Davids Chapter of SABR, this is his first biography for BioProject; to his knowledge, he is no relation to the subject of his story.

Jon Dunkle lives in Lancaster County, Pennsylvania and is a fan of the minor leagues.

As a lifelong Phillies fan, **James Elfers** is enjoying the team's current golden age. He is also the author of *The Tour to End All Tours: The Story of Major League*

Baseball's 1913-1914 World Tour (University of Nebraska Press), which tells the story of the Giants-White Sox world tour of a century ago. He is currently at work on a history of how the National Football League barely survived World War II.

Greg Erion is retired from the railroad industry and currently teaches history part time at Skyline Community College in San Bruno, California. He has written several biographies for SABR's BioProject and is currently working on a book about the 1959 season. He and his wife Barbara live in South San Francisco, California.

Charles F. Faber is a retired university professor and administrator, living in Lexington, Kentucky. He had been a baseball fan since 1936, rooting for several teams over the years, but always against the Yankees. A longtime SABR member, he has written biographies for the SABR BioProject and contributed to books edited by other SABR members. Currently he is co-editing a book with Joseph Wancho on the 1934 St. Louis Cardinals. McFarland had published eight of his books so far. Number nine, *Major League Prodigies: Best Seasons by Players Under 21*, is scheduled for publication in the fall of 2013. He has also published college textbooks on educational administration and school law and written extensively on education, country music, and the American presidency.

Dan Fields is a manuscript editor at the *New England Journal of Medicine*. He loves baseball trivia, and he regularly attends Boston Red Sox and Pawtucket (RI) Red Sox games with his teenage son. Dan lives in Framingham, Massachusetts, and can be reached at dfields820@gmail.com.

Peter M. Gordon is a writer and content expert living in Orlando, FL. He first joined SABR in 1984 and has contributed several articles and biographies to SABR publications and websites. His company, PMGordon Communications, creates and distributes content for clients across all media platforms. Peter blogs about content development at www.myprogramidea.blogspot.com, and is a published poet whose first collection. *Two Car Garage*, was published in 2012. Peter teaches in the Film Production MFA program at Full Sail University.

Chip Greene has been a SABR member since 2006. The grandson of former major leaguer Nelson Greene, Chip, a management consultant, is a regular contributor to the BioProject, having written many player bios for the website, as well as several of the recent book projects. Currently he is editing an upcoming BioProject book about the three-time champion Oakland A's. An avid and lifelong Orioles fan, Chip lives in Waynesboro, PA, with his wife, Elaine; daughters, Anna and Haley, and their diabetic dog, Karl.

Donna L. Halper is an Associate Professor of Communication at Lesley University, Cambridge MA. A media historian who specializes in the history of broadcasting, Dr. Halper is the author of five books and many articles. She is also a former broadcaster and print journalist.

Craig Hardee is a native of North Carolina whose baseball rooting interests include the Dodgers and more recently the Rays. He enjoys researching North Carolina natives who played major league baseball and has a fledgling website covering North Carolina native major leaguers at http://www.ncmajorleaguers.com. Craig is married with three children and two grandchildren.

Gary R. Hess is a retired history professor who lives in Bowling Green, Ohio, with his wife Rose. Both are natives of Pittsburgh and lifelong Pirates fans. His biographical sketch of Otto Hess (no relation) is his first venture into baseball history.

Joanne Hulbert, co-chair of the Boston Chapter and SABR's Baseball Arts Committee, spends long hours obsessively gathering baseball poetry when not at Fenway Park. A resident of Mudville, a village of Holliston, MA she occasionally leaves her poetic pursuit to indulge in something completely different. She has found that there's always something poetic about the life of an obscure and often forgotten player who has a story just as important and valuable to baseball history as any hall of fame inductee.

Bob Joel is a diehard Chicago Cubs fan who is accepting that any team can have a bad century. He is an avid baseball card and memorabilia collector, whose collection dates back to 1887. While not watching, discussing, or writing about baseball, Bob is a Certified Financial Planner and principal of a wealth management firm. Bob holds a degree in history from Florida State University and lives with his lovely wife and two beautiful daughters in Jacksonville, Florida.

David Jones was editor of SABR's book *Deadball Stars of the American League*, a 2006 publication which was one of the first of SABR's collaborative efforts assembling baseball biographies.

Martin Kohout, a native of San Francisco, received a bachelor's degree in English literature from Williams College and a master's degree in American studies from the University of Texas at Austin. He worked for many years as a writer and editor for the Texas State Historical Association and then for Humanities Texas, the state affiliate of the National Endowment for the Humanities. He is the author of *Hal Chase: The Defiant Life and Turbulent Times of Baseball's Biggest Crook* (2001), which won SABR's first annual Larry Ritter Award. He is currently the minister of propaganda for Madroño Ranch: A Center for Writing, Art, and the Environment.

Len Levin, a member of SABR since 1977, is a retired newspaper editor who spends a lot of time editing for SABR publications. On non-baseball days he edits the written decisions of the Rhode Island Supreme Court. He is the chairman of SABR's Southern New England Chapter.

An artist, fly fisherman, and organic gardener who resides in South Hero, Vermont, **Dick Leyden** has contributed articles to the path-breaking book *Green Mountain Boys of Summer* and to SABR's *Deadball Stars of the National League*. Among his favorites is his article "The Vermont Baseball Confederacy," which appeared in *The Northern Game…and Beyond*. He has collected nearly all of the baseball cards of the 34 Vermonters in the major leagues and has painted portraits of all these "Green Mountain Boys of Summer." The portraits appears in a set of 36 baseball cards published by the Vermont Historical Society. He is currently working on a book about the Northern League.

A native of Massachusetts and the founder of Seamheads.com, **Michael T. Lynch, Jr.** lives in Portland, Oregon and has been a member of SABR since 2004. His first book, *Harry Frazee, Ban Johnson and the Feud That Nearly Destroyed the American League*, was published by McFarland Publishing in 2008 and was named a finalist for the 2009 Larry Ritter Award in addition to being nominated for the Seymour Medal. His second book, *It Ain't So: A Might-Have-Been History of the White Sox in 1919 and Beyond*, was released by McFarland in December 2009. His work also appeared in *Opening Fenway Park in Style: The 1912 Boston Red Sox*.

Wayne McElreavy is a lifelong Red Sox fan who lives in Claremont, New Hampshire, and specializes in research on players and team from New Hampshire and Vermont.

Carol McMains is a lifelong fan of the national pastime. She and her husband Les live in Pleasantville, Iowa with their all-time favorite third baseman, son Brady.

Jack Morris, a lifelong Phillies fan, is a corporate librarian living in East Coventry, Pennsylvania with his wife and two daughters. His baseball biographies have also appeared in the books *The Team That Forever Changed Baseball and America* (1947 Brooklyn Dodgers) and *Bridging Two Dynasties* (1947 New York Yankees). He is not the Jack Morris of World Series fame but, every once in a while, wishes he was.

Tom Nahigian grew up in the Boston area and remains a fan of the Red Sox, Celtics and Bruins. A SABR member since 1983, Tom enjoys the baseball writings of Bill James and Roger Angell. He and his wife make their home in Pasadena, CA. He enjoys playing Strat-O-Matic Baseball and reads as many baseball books as he can. Tom wrote the profiles of Fred Lynn and Dean Chance for the SABR Biographical website.

Bill Nowlin has been vice president of SABR since 2004, another sort of miracle year for a baseball team from Boston. Most of his 40-plus books have been Red Sox-related, though he's also written about musical and political history. He was a co-founder of Rounder Records and lives not all that far from Fenway Park, where the Boston Braves played home games in the 1914 World Series.

Bob Ruzzo is an attorney with the Boston office of Holland & Knight, specializing in land use and affordable housing. He has been happily married to the enemy (a Yankees fan) for 12 years (2004 and 2007 were particularly happy years). He has authored SABR articles on the history of Braves Field and the role of fate in the demise of the Federal League. Based upon the lifetime records of Mel Ott and Eddie Mathews, he is convinced that Tony Conigliaro would have hit over 500 career home runs had he not been hit by a Jack Hamilton pitch on August 18, 1967.

John Shannahan is Captain of the Mudville Base Ball Club, a vintage base ball team based in Holliston, Massachusetts, dedicated to the preservation of the Massachusetts Rules of 1858 as well as to the notion that our fine town sufficiently influenced Ernest Lawrence Thayer so as to inspire the writing of his famous Casey at the Bat poem. Shannahan also plays as "Orator" Jim O'Rourke for The Boston Red Stockings Vintage Base Ball Club, where much like the recent Hall of Fame inductee, he has been known to expound on the game, often far beyond the reasonable listening ability of his audience.

David Shiner has written a large number of articles, interviews, book reviews, and stories about baseball for sports magazines, research journals, and literary publications. He was selected to present original work at the Babe Ruth Conference at Hofstra University (1995) and the Jackie Robinson at Long Island University (1997), and was the keynote speaker at the United Kingdom's annual meeting of the Society of American Baseball Research in 2000. He is also the author of *Baseball's Greatest Players: The Saga Continues*, a sequel to Tom Meany's *Baseball Greatest Players*. Dr. Shiner has been a member of the faculty at Shimer College in Illinois since the mid-1970s.

John A. Simpson has written five scholarly books on Civil War memory and Southern baseball history and biography, as well as many encyclopedia entries, journal articles and biographical selections. A member of SABR since 1996 and a lifelong Phillies fan, Simpson coached high school baseball for 15 years. He lives with his wife, Shirley, in Kelso, Washington.

Mark S. Sternman has previously profiled three Boston Nationals: Jack Burdock and Sam Wise in *Baseball's First Stars*, and Fred Tenney in *Deadball Stars of the National League*. Director of Marketing & Communications for MassDevelopment, Sternman lives in Cambridge with his wife Kate and stepdaughter Ella.

Frank Vaccaro was born in Rome, Italy and is a Teamsters Local 812 shop steward for Pepsi Cola workers and distributors for Northern Queens, NY. He lives in Long Island City with his Czechoslovak-born wife Maria.

A lifelong Phillies fan who also follows the San Francisco Giants, **Charlie Weatherby** is a Wilmington, Delaware, native who is a social work supervisor at the Independent Adoption Center, a domestic open adoption program. He is also a softball fanatic and manages the Marin Joe's Giants Over-40 club, has a pitching record of 931-465, and counts 80 championships during the last 40 years. A periodic contributor to SABR's BioProject, he now lives in Novato, California, with his wife, Sara Duggin, and their cat, Panther.

SABR BioProject Books

In 2002, the Society for American Baseball Research launched an effort to write and publish biographies of every player, manager, and individual who has made a contribution to baseball. Over the past decade, the BioProject Committee has produced over 2,200 biographical articles. Many have been part of efforts to create theme- or team-oriented books, spearheaded by chapters or other committees of SABR.

THE YEAR OF BLUE SNOW:
THE 1964 PHILADELPHIA PHILLIES
Catcher Gus Triandos dubbed the Philadelphia Phillies' 1964 season "the year of the blue snow," a rare thing that happens once in a great while. This book sheds light on lingering questions about the 1964 season—but any book about a team is really about the players. This work offers life stories of all the players and others (managers, coaches, owners, and broadcasters) associated with this star-crossed team, as well as essays of analysis and history.
Edited by Mel Marmer and Bill Nowlin
$19.95 paperback (ISBN 978-1-933599-51-9)
$9.99 ebook (ISBN 978-1-933599-52-6)
8.5"X11", 356 PAGES, over 70 photos

DETROIT TIGERS 1984:
WHAT A START! WHAT A FINISH!
The 1984 Detroit tigers roared out of the gate, winning their first nine games of the season and compiling an eye-popping 35-5 record after the campaign's first 40 games—still the best start ever for any team in major league history. This book brings together biographical profiles of every Tiger from that magical season, plus those of field management, top executives, the broadcasters—even venerable Tiger Stadium and the city itself.
Mark Pattison and David Raglin, editors
$19.95 paperback (ISBN 978-1-933599-44-1)
$9.99 ebook (ISBN 978-1-933599-45-8)
8.5"x11", 250 pages (Over 230,000 words!)

SWEET '60: THE 1960 PITTSBURGH PIRATES
A portrait of the 1960 team which pulled off one of the biggest upsets of the last 60 years. When Bill Mazeroski's home run left the park to win in Game Seven of the World Series, beating the New York Yankees, David had toppled Goliath. It was a blow that awakened a generation, one that millions of people saw on television, one of TV's first iconic World Series moments.
Edited by Clifton Blue Parker and Bill Nowlin
$19.95 paperback (ISBN 978-1-933599-48-9)
$9.99 ebook (ISBN 978-1-933599-49-6)
8.5"X11", 340 pages, 75 photos

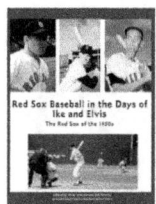

RED SOX BASEBALL IN THE DAYS OF IKE AND ELVIS: THE RED SOX OF THE 1950S
Although the Red Sox spent most of the 1950s far out of contention, the team was filled fascinating players that captured the heart of their fanbase. In *Red Sox Baseball*, members of SABR present 46 biographies on players such as Ted Williams and Pumpsie Green as well as season-by-season recaps.
Edited by Mark Armour and Bill Nowlin
$19.95 paperback (ISBN 978-1-933599-24-3)
$9.99 ebook (ISBN 978-1-933599-34-2)
8.5"X11", 372 PAGES, over 100 photos

The SABR Digital Library

The Society for American Baseball Research, the top baseball research organization in the world, disseminates some of the best in baseball history, analysis, and biography through our publishing programs. The SABR Digital Library contains a mix of books old and new, and focuses on a tandem program of paperback and ebook publication, making these materials widely available for both on digital devices and as traditional printed books.

MEMORIES OF A BALLPLAYER
by Bill Werber and C. Paul Rogers III
Bill Werber's claim to fame is unique: he was the last living person to have a direct connection to the 1927 Yankees, "Murderers' Row," a team hailed by many as the best of all time. Rich in anecdotes and humor, Memories of a Ballplayer is a clear-eyed memoir of the world of big-league baseball in the 1930s. Werber played with or against some of the most productive hitters of all time, including Babe Ruth, Ted Williams, Lou Gehrig, and Joe DiMaggio.
$14.95 paperback (ISNB 978-0-910137-84-3)
$6.99 ebook (ISBN 978-1-933599-47-2)
250 PAGES, 6"X9"

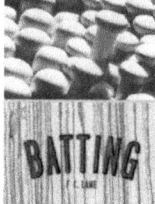

BATTING by F. C. Lane
First published in 1925, *Batting* collects the wisdom and insights of over 250 hitters and baseball figures. Lane interviewed extensively and compiled tips and advice on everything from batting stances to beanballs. Legendary baseball figures such as Ty Cobb, Casey Stengel, Cy Young, Walter Johnson, Rogers Hornsby, and Babe Ruth reveal the secrets of such integral and interesting parts of the game as how to choose a bat, the ways to beat a slump, and how to outguess the pitcher.
$14.95 paperback (ISBN 978-0-910137-86-7)
$7.99 ebook (ISBN 978-1-933599-46-5)
240 PAGES, 5"X7"

NINETEENTH CENTURY STARS: 2012 EDITION
First published in 1989, *Nineteenth Century Stars* was SABR's initial attempt to capture the stories of baseball players from before 1900. With a collection of 136 fascinating biographies, SABR has re-released *Nineteenth Century Stars* for 2012 with revised statistics and new form. The 2012 version also includes a preface by John Thorn.
Edited by Robert L. Tiemann and Mark Rucker
$19.95 paperback (ISBN 978-1-933599-28-1)
$9.99 ebook (ISBN 978-1-933599-29-8)
300 PAGES, 6"X9"

GREAT HITTING PITCHERS
Published in 1979, *Great Hitting Pitchers* was one of SABR's early publications. Edited by SABR founder Bob Davids, the book compiles stories and records about pitchers excelling in the batter's box. Newly updated in 2012 by Mike Cook, *Great Hitting Pitchers* contain tables including data from 1979-2011, corrections to reflect recent records, and a new chapter on recent new members in the club of "great hitting pitchers" like Tom Glavine and Mike Hampton.
Edited by L. Robert Davids
$9.95 paperback (ISBN 978-1-933599-30-4)
$5.99 ebook (ISBN 978-1-933599-31-1)
102 PAGES, 5.5"x8.5"

SABR Members can purchase each book at a significant discount (often 50% off) and receive the ebook edtions free as a member benefit. Each book is available in a trade paperback edition as well as ebooks suitable for reading on a home computer or Nook, Kindle, or iPad/tablet.

Join SABR today!

If you're interested in baseball—writing about it, reading about it, talking about it—there's a place for you in the Society for American Baseball Research.

SABR was formed in 1971 in Cooperstown, New York, with the mission of fostering the research and dissemination of the history and record of the game. Our members include everyone from academics to professional sportswriters to amateur historians and statisticians to students and casual fans who merely enjoy reading about baseball history and occasionally gathering with other members to talk baseball.

SABR members have a variety of interests, and this is reflected in the diversity of its research committees. There are more than two dozen groups devoted to the study of a specific area related to the game—from Baseball and the Arts to Statistical Analysis to the Deadball Era to Women in Baseball. In addition, many SABR members meet formally and informally in regional chapters throughout the year and hundreds come together for the annual national convention, the organization's premier event. These meetings often include panel discussions with former major league players and research presentations by members. Most of all, SABR members love talking baseball with like-minded friends. What unites them all is an interest in the game and joy in learning more about it.

Why join SABR? Here are some benefits of membership:

- Two issues annually of the *Baseball Research Journal*, which includes articles on history, biography, statistics, personalities, book reviews, and other aspects of the game.
- One issue annually of *The National Pastime*, which focuses on baseball in the region where that year's national convention is held (in 2013, it's Philadelphia)
- Regional chapter meetings, which can include guest speakers, presentations and trips to ballgames
- "This Week in SABR" e-newsletters every Friday, with the latest news in SABR and highlighting SABR research
- Online access to back issues of *The Sporting News* and other periodicals through *Paper of Record*
- Access to SABR's lending library and other research resources
- Online member directory to connect you with an international network of passionate baseball experts and fans
- Discount on registration for our annual conferences
- Access to SABR-L, an e-mail discussion list of baseball questions and answers that many feel is worth the cost of membership itself
- The opportunity to be part of a passionate international community of baseball fans

SABR membership is on a "rolling" calendar system; that means your membership lasts 365 days no matter when you sign up! Enjoy all the benefits of SABR membership by signing up today at SABR.org/join or by clipping out the form below and mailing it to: SABR, 4455 E. Camelback Rd., Ste. D-140, Phoenix, AZ 85018.

SABR 2013 MEMBERSHIP FORM
2013 dues payable by check, money order, Visa, MasterCard or Discover Card;
online at: http://store.sabr.org; or by phone at (602) 343-6455

	Annual	3-year	Senior	3-yr Sr.	Under 30
US	❏ $65	❏ $175	❏ $45	❏ $129	❏ $45
Canada/Mexico	❏ $75	❏ $205	❏ $55	❏ $159	❏ $55
Overseas	❏ $84	❏ $232	❏ $64	❏ $186	❏ $55

Add a Family Member: $15 each family member at same address (list on back)
Senior: 65 or older before 12/31/2013
All dues amounts in US dollars or equivalent

Participate in Our Donor Program!
I'd like to desginate my gift to be used toward:
❏ General Fund ❏ Endowment Fund ❏ Research Resources ❏ _____
❏ I want to maximize the impact of my gift; do not send any donor premiums
❏ I would like this gift to remain anonymous.

Note: Any donation not designated will be placed in the General Fund. SABR is a 501(c)(3) not-for-profit organization & donations are tax-deductible to the extent allowed by law.

NAME _____
ADDRESS _____
CITY _____ STATE ____ ZIP _____
HOME PHONE _____ BIRTHDAY _____
E-MAIL: _____
(Your e-mail address on file ensures you will receive the most recent SABR news.)

Dues $ _____
Donation $ _____
Amount Enclosed $ _____

Do you work for a matching grant corporation? Call (602) 343-6455 for details.
❏ check/money order enclosed   ❏ VISA, Master Card, Discover Card
CARD # _____
EXP DATE _____ SIGNATURE _____

Mail to: SABR, 4455 E. Camelback Rd., Ste. D-140, Phoenix, AZ 85018

www.ingramcontent.com/pod-product-compliance
Lightning Source LLC
Chambersburg PA
CBHW051359070526
44584CB00023B/3214